Client-Centered and Experiential Psychotherapy in the 21st Century:

Advances in theory, research and practice

Edited by
Jeanne C. Watson,
Rhonda N. Goldman
and Margaret S. Warner

PCCS BOOKS
Ross-on-Wye

First published in 2002

PCCS BOOKS
Llangarron
Ross-on-Wye
Herefordshire
HR9 6PT
United Kingdom
Tel (01989) 77 07 07
website www.pccs-books.co.uk
email contact@pccs-books.co.uk

**Client-Centered and Experiential Psychotherapy in the 21st Century:
Advances in theory, research and practice**

ISBN 1 898059 43 8 (paperback)
ISBN 1 898059 49 7 (hardback)

Cover design by Denis Postle
Printed by Bookcraft, Midsomer Norton, Somerset, United Kingdom

Contents

RESEARCH

PRACTICE

Preface

This book grew out of the Fifth International Conference on Client-Centered and Experiential Psychotherapy, held in Chicago, Illinois from June 24–29, 2000; a meeting which brought together more than two hundred practitioners, researchers and theorists from around the world. Over the last decade there has been foment and excitement in client-centered and experiential circles as we have struggled with issues of identity, philosophy and future direction of this broadly humanistic approach to psychotherapy. The Chicago conference marked not only a return to the birthplace of client-centered theory and practice but was important in facilitating reflection on our past, grappling with the conflicts and similarities of the present, and determining a vision for the future. This process has been distilled in the collection of papers that make up this volume. The papers represent unique voices under the client-centered and experiential umbrella, each helping to define and challenge us as we move into the twenty-first century.

We have grouped these papers into three sections: theory, research and practice. The first contains an exciting collection of papers that challenge us to think about our underlying assumptions and suggests new conceptualizations that can enrich our future development. The section opens with a paper from Lietaer that offers a unitary vision for both client-centered and experiential psychotherapy based on their common assumptions and history. Ellingham's paper begins to expand the theoretical foundations of client-centered therapy based on the formative tendency. Schmid's paper continues the debate about the similarities and differences inherent in experiential and client-centered approaches and argues for the recognition and acceptance of each of them. The papers by Stumm, Kahn and Raskin revisit the topic of empathy to re-examine the similarities and differences between Rogers, Firenzci and Kohut; contributing their own unique understandings of these three very important theorists and the role and function of empathy in psychotherapy. Hendricks articulates the important contribution of Gendlin's approach to client-centered theory and practice. This topic is explored further in Purton's paper on the practice and philosophy of focusing. Hayashi and Kara suggest the important contribution that a Taoist understanding of the self can add to client-centered and experiential practice. The important role of the organismic valuing process and ethics in client-centered theory is explored by Hawtin, while Proctor examines the nature of power in the client-centered relationship. Finally van Kalmthout reflects on the challenge of client-centered theory and practice in a postmodern world.

The theory section is followed by ten chapters that highlight new areas of research that are essential to maintain our place in the academy and as a viable and growing alternative to other approaches. Behr and Becker present data on their new measure of emotional experiencing, which emphasises the important role that Rogers' view of emotional functioning can play in the current literature on emotional intelligence. Brodley's chapter enhances our understanding of Rogers' practice of empathic understanding, while Greenberg and Rushanski-Rosenberg's chapter presents data from a qualitative study that provides insight into the inner processes in which therapists engage when trying to be empathic with their clients. There are a number of qualitative research studies presented in this volume; some would argue that the methodology of qualitative research is most congruent with client-centered theory and practice. Krycka and Lambo present a new approach to qualitative inquiry based on Gendlin's focusing technique as they examine gay and lesbian experience. A qualitative study of the role and function of congruence in client-centered practice is provided by Grafanaki, and Wilkins and Mitchell-Williams examine the theory and experience of engaging in person-centered research. A number of authors intent on facilitating more research are working on measures to operationalize a number of core client-centered and experiential processes. Iberg presents data on his measures of focusing and Watson and Prosser present data on their measure of expressed empathy. Finally the chapters by Bozarth and Bohart present cogently argued critiques of the move towards empirically supported treatments.

The practice section presents work with diverse populations and conditions. Baljon discusses the use of focusing as a technique for supervision, to encourage congruence in supervisees. Ways of integrating a client-centered perspective into graduate teaching are presented by Hannon and Eckersell. Coffeng and Warner demonstrate the use of client-centered and experiential techniques with severely distressed clients. Coffeng provides a model of his work with dissociated clients and Warner a way of understanding client-centered work with clients suffering from schizophrenia. Van der Moolen elaborates her work with clients suffering from psychosomatic conditions, while Pörtner describes its relevance to working with people with special needs. Missiaen discusses the practice of client-centered group psychotherapy, while the papers by Gaylin and Sikkema emphasise the importance of fundamental aspects of client-centered and experiential psychotherapy, the relationship and unconditionality respectively. The chapters by Stiles and Glick, Stinckens, Lietaer and Leijssen, and Goldman explore the use of experiential and client-centered techniques with different aspects of the client's personality. Goldman presents a model of working with unfinished business, Stinckens et al. provide models of working with the inner critic and Stiles' paper discusses the use of empathy with multi-voiced clients. Rogers and Jaison show how client-centered and experiential theory and practice can be integrated into alternative approaches, in the former case expressive art therapy and in the latter solution-focused. Finally, Lovering's paper provides us with timely insight into working with Hispanic populations.

We hope that this volume will excite and challenge you to validate your commitment to client-centered and experiential ways of working as well as open up new avenues of thought and practice.

Jeanne Watson, Rhonda Goldman and Margaret Warner
May 2002

Germain Lietaer
Katholieke Universitiet Leuven, Belgium

The Client-Centered/Experiential Paradigm in Psychotherapy: Development and identity

1. INTRODUCTION: THE POST-SCHOOL PHASE OF CLIENT-CENTERED PSYCHOTHERAPY

What Barrett-Lennard (1998, p. 58) calls the 'post-school phase' of client-centered psychotherapy began around 1965. With the end of the Wisconsin project (Rogers, Gendlin, Kiesler and Truax, 1967a), the earlier unity surrounding Rogers as a central figure fell away and a more diversified landscape of centers and personalities gradually appeared, not only in North America but also on other continents. Our psychotherapeutic orientation has developed considerably over the last 35 years (see Lietaer, 1990). The consequence of this is that we are now confronted with a number of sub-orientations that demonstrate many aspects in common yet at various points clearly show their own points of emphasis. One might briefly sketch the situation of client-centered/experiential psychotherapy as follows. First and foremost there is client-centered psychotherapy, with its emphasis on the basic attitudes of the therapist and on the empathic deepening of the inner frame of reference of the client (Barrett-Lennard, 1998). In the course of time there arose from this source two experiential approaches: the focusing-oriented approach of Gendlin (1996) and the process-experiential perspective of Greenberg, Rice and Elliott (1993). A greater process directedness, and with it a more differential approach to specific processes and problems, are typical of these two experiential sub-orientations. Alongside this there is the influence of interpersonal psychotherapy — with figures such as Yalom (1995) and Kiesler (1996) who take the here-and-now relationship with the therapist as both focus and medium for corrective interpersonal experiences. Another sphere of influence is existential psychotherapy (Yalom 1980; Swildens 1997; van Deurzen-Smith, 1996), which underlines the confrontation with the 'givens of life': death and decay, freedom and responsibility, a core sense of being alone and the necessity of oneself creating meaning in life. Finally, there are a number of 'non-verbal or action-oriented aids' that have a place within many approaches, but have also been employed by several client-centered/experiential therapists as powerful forms of experiential unfolding: psychodrama (Wilkins, 1999; Verhofstadt-Denève, 1999), Gestalt chair work, body-oriented procedures, creative expression (Silverstone, 1997), and so on.

In a nutshell, these are the sub-orientations that one encounters within the broader paradigm. They are often employed as distinct approaches. But one can increasingly find training centers where several of these 'wings' are combined. This is the case with the training center at the University of Leuven, among others, and we have therefore broadened the name of our program to 'Client-centered/experiential'. We see the different sub-orientations as distinct 'voices within a polyphonic whole'; we do not hold them to be conflicting perspectives but rather as the 'united colors' of one and the same paradigm. This does not mean that all of our faculty and associates have achieved the same sort of integration. Some feel themselves to be more 'classically Rogerian', others more focusing-oriented; some like to work with the two-chairs technique, while others prefer to focus on the here-and-now interaction between client and therapist. But all have been influenced by the different sub-orientations and remain open to various approaches. Our trainees highly appreciate this plurality; they find it intrinsically enriching and it provides them with the freedom to sort out their own style.

When in 1988 we organized the first international congress, it was 'natural' for us, given our integrative orientation, to have focused on the broader paradigm of 'client-centered *and* experiential' psychotherapy. We were rather shocked — during and following the conference — at the ambivalent feelings and tensions such a 'marriage of sub-orientations' evoked in some of the participants (e.g. Brodley 1990). Later as well, at the foundation of the World Association of Person-centered and Experiential Psychotherapy and Counseling (WAPCEPC), this broader fusion of perspectives constituted one of the factors that raised considerable resistance in certain circles.

It is within the framework of this controversy that I would like to reflect, in this chapter, on the question: Has the client-centered/experiential paradigm its own identity? Does it possess sufficient coherence or is it just a smorgasbord of perspectives that in many aspects differ 'too much' from each other in crucial ways? In responding to this question I will first outline a proposal of a renewed fundamental theoretical framework in which all 'wings' may find their place. Thereafter I will run through the different dimensions of our therapeutic system with an eye to identifying common ingredients.

2. BROADENING ROGERS' PROCESS EQUATION

In a number of significant publications between 1957 and 1961, Rogers formulated his fully matured vision of the therapeutic process that has become known as the 'necessary and sufficient conditions' (1957) or as the 'process equation' (1961c). This process equation reads as follows: 'The more the client perceives the therapist as real or genuine, as empathic, as having an unconditional regard for him, the more the client will move away from a static, unfeeling, fixed, impersonal type of functioning, and the more he will move toward a way of functioning which is marked by a fluid, changing, acceptant experiencing of differentiated personal feelings' (1961c, p. 42). However significant this Rogerian basic framework has been, and in my opinion still is, it demonstrates a number of 'one-sided' observations. The contribution of the therapist is described only in relational terms; the therapeutic relationship is conceived almost exclusively as safe context; alongside this the change process in the client is held to be one single and central process without differentiation. If we are to do justice to the evolution that has taken place over the last forty years within our discipline, then we must give this fundamental structure of our therapy theory — which Rogers, himself, described as 'crude and tentative' — a facelift. In what follows, and with the help of Figure 1, I will attempt to do this.

2.1. The contribution of the therapist: being and doing

Rogers gradually abandoned a technical approach to therapeutic responding and began to formulate the contribution of the therapist in terms of experiencing and communicating a triad of relational attitudes: acceptance, empathy and authenticity. In this way the therapist's 'manner of being' was given far more emphasis than his or her 'manner of doing'; too much so, in my view. The communication of these attitudes always demands response implementation, whereby the required technical competence cannot be set aside. It requires considerable training in order to be able to echo the significant messages of our clients in an accurate way, to communicate acceptance and still set boundaries when necessary, or to reveal something of our selves without imposing it on the client. For Rogers, this response implementation had become so 'spontaneous' that he no longer experienced it as 'competence' but simply as the offer of a relational climate; 'spontaneous' becomes in fact 'that which is over-learned'. It appears to me a more balanced view to divide up the role of the therapist into a relational and a task-oriented component. These two components must of course be fundamentally bound up with each other, as in osmosis, in order to avoid the danger of falling into 'wooden techniques'.

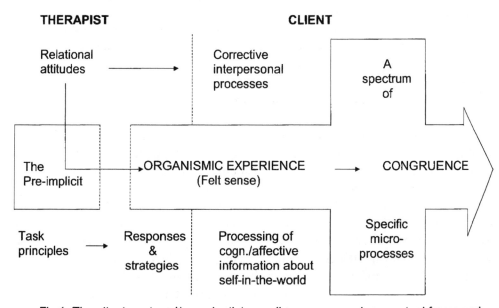

Fig 1. The client-centered/experiential paradigm: a renewed conceptual framework

Insofar as the relational component is concerned, we point to the basic Rogerian attitudes mentioned earlier that are crucial in the formation and maintenance of a good working alliance. On the task-oriented side, the main objective of the therapist can be defined as follows: the facilitation of an optimal experiential process of self-exploration (in contrast to a purely conceptual exploration process). This task-oriented principle — one that can further be differentiated (see Greenberg, Rice and Elliott, 1993, pp. 112–17) — becomes concrete in specific responses, strategies (or broader intentions) and procedures. That the relational and the task-oriented components within the contribution of the therapist are not to be separated can be observed in the impact our responses and interventions have on the client process. Here also we can always distinguish an interpersonal and a task-oriented or information-processing dimension. I will illustrate this with the aid of empathic responses, but the same could be done for interactional responses such as feedback, confrontation and self-disclosure.

As Vanaerschot (1993) described them, empathic responses have a relational impact. They minimize alienation, confirm the client in his or her 'being', promote clients' capacity for self-empathy and encourage the client to trust his or her own experience as a compass for life. Following Vanaerschot, however, the same responses also strongly enhance the quality of the self-exploration process that in fact can be described as a processing of affective and cognitive information concerning 'oneself-in-the-world'. First and foremost, empathic responses deepen the process of experiencing itself: they help the client to be more attuned to the experiential source from which he or she speaks, and through evocative reflection (Rice, 1974) new facets are brought to the surface. Further, empathic reflections encourage the cognitive (re)structuring of information: the client's attention is directed to aspects that he or she might too easily overlook; through differentiated and integrated reflection (Wexler, 1974; Toukmanian, 1990) this information can be better organized. The therapist thus functions not only as a companion, but at the same time as an auxiliary information-processor.

Highlighting this 'dual-track' with regard to the contribution of the therapist helps us to combat the impression that client-centered/experiential therapy is concerned with nothing more than offering a 'good relation'. It provides us a distinct and equally valuable window through which we can highlight task-oriented principles, forms of responding and procedures as essential elements of our work.

2.2. The relationship: context and medium

When the central role of the relationship in client-centered therapy is pointed out, reference is usually made, first and foremost, to the Rogerian basic attitudes, which are meant to provide a safe *context* for in-depth self-exploration. Indeed, these 'therapist conditions' form the first part of Rogers' process equation. We see this contextual influence as comprising three layers. First, as crucial ingredients of the relational bond, the Rogerian basic attitudes exercise an appreciable influence on what the client can let seep through in his pre-explicit experiencing. Thus a client after many hours of therapy might say: 'What I talked about until now is actually not the crux of my problem; what really matters is . . .' Secondly, they offer the client the support and safety needed to communicate and explore openly what is present at a felt-sense level. Thirdly, the therapist conditions and the responses that spring from them guarantee a constructive run of the client's exploration process. It is perhaps this three-way influence that causes the working alliance to be the most powerful predictor of therapeutic success in all orientations (Horvath and Greenberg, 1994; Gelso and Carter, 1994; Orlinsky , Grawe, and Parks, 1994).

Apart from that, the therapeutic relationship not only functions as a context or a condition for other task-oriented therapeutic processes, but also serves as *medium* for corrective interpersonal processes, as a place for 'further living', as Gendlin (1967) puts it. The client lives in the here-and-now relationship with the therapist, something that breaks through previously established interpersonal patterns (see, e.g., Yalom, 1980). Contrary to their past experience, clients may feel that the therapist really believes in their capacities, that their experience is taken quite seriously, that they are not rejected when expressing aggressive feelings, that their therapists remain stable when they express feelings of despair, that their limits are respected and so on. Rogers repeatedly refers to this process in his therapy comments. He describes as a crucial therapeutic moment the time when Jim Brown is able to allow the therapist's warm concern:

> In this relationship there was a moment of real, and I believe irreversible, change. Jim Brown, who sees himself as stubborn, bitter, mistreated, worthless, useless, hopeless, unloved, unlovable, *experiences* my caring. In that moment his defensive shell cracks wide open, and can never again be quite the same. When someone *cares* for him, and when he feels and experiences this caring, he becomes a softer person whose years of stored up hurt come pouring out in anguished sobs. He is not the shell of hardness and bitterness, the stranger to tenderness. He is a person hurt beyond words, and aching for the love and caring which alone can make him human. (1967, p. 411; emphases in original)

Together with this kind of corrective interpersonal experience, a process of internalization of the therapist attitudes takes place. In this vein Rogers describes the consequences of an empathic climate as follows. 'Thus, the persons have become, in their attitudes toward themselves, more caring and acceptant, more empathic and understanding, more real and congruent. But these three elements are the very ones that both experience and research indicate are the attitudes of an effective therapist' (1975, p. 9). We believe this to be a very essential form of personality change, albeit mostly a 'silent' one, i.e. one which is not explicitly talked about in the verbal interaction.

Besides functioning as the context and as the silent medium for corrective interpersonal experiences, the client-therapist relationship can also function as an open arena in which to explore explicitly the client's interactional style. This process — characterized by metacommunication about the here and now relationship — occupies a central position primarily within the interpersonal wing of psychodynamic psychotherapy; but it has gradually come to be seen as an important process by our orientation as well (see van Kessel and Lietaer, 1998). This form of differentiation in our conceptual framework demonstrates in a more nuanced way the full scope of our approach regarding the lines along which the therapeutic relation exercises an influence on the client's change process.

2.3. The change process of the client: a spectrum of specific microprocesses

In his *A Process Conception of Psychotherapy* (1961b) Rogers brilliantly dealt with the 'nucleus' of the change process. This implies a development from a rigid structuring to a processual functioning in which the self-schemes become flexible and allow themselves to be influenced by whatever becomes sensed in experience, with as a consequence the client becoming more congruent. This nuclear process however can further be differentiated in a spectrum of specific microprocesses; these can be of an interpersonal as well as of an intrapsychical nature and often are a mixture of both. Over the last twenty years, we have in fact left the anti-diagnostic position behind, and have developed, within the various subdisciplines, a whole series of 'process-diagnostic lenses'. These have allowed us to observe in a more nuanced way and therefore have helped us to discover the means to break through specific experiential process-blocks. We need only think of our body of knowledge of the different phases of therapy with their diverse process tasks, of levels of experience, existential themes, dream work, clients' styles of information processing, types of unsolved conflicts, specific micro-processes of focusing, and so on. We also think of the steadily increasing number of publications on working with specific client problems (Lietaer, Van Balen and Rombauts, 1990; Greenberg, Rice and Elliott, 1993; Finke, 1994; Lietaer and Van Kalmthout, 1995; Sachse, 1996, 1997; Eckert, Höger, and Linster, 1997; Greenberg, Watson, and Lietaer, 1998). This appears to me to be not only a promising evolution but a necessity as well if we are to carve out a more significant position in the world of clinical psychology and psychiatry.

This broadened conceptual framework appears to me to be more balanced and attractive than Roger's process equation because it explicitly leaves room for 'ways of being' as well as 'ways of doing' on the part of the therapist. It recognizes diverse sub-processes of relational impact, and the role of a process-diagnostic approach to identify specific processes and problems. Moreover, with this model one explicitly chooses for an osmosis — or at least an open dialog — between a variety of sources of inspiration from the experiential-humanistic tradition (as was described in the introduction to this chapter). All of this has a positive effect on our image-building, for it places recent developments in relief. Such a broader paradigm is for that matter quite necessary if our discipline is to survive at the university; special courses for separate sub-orientations are in fact never offered. This is equally the case for the psychodynamic, cognitive-behavior and systemic paradigm. The same is also true of research: bringing together all outcome and process studies out of the broader paradigm makes a more significant impression on the professional and academic world than a separate presentation of each sub-orientation, as can be seen from the recent survey by Cain and Seeman (2002). And I do not wish to emphasize only the political — strength from unity — aspect here. I am equally convinced that an intensive dialog between related sub-orientations — with an eye to their deeper integration — is intrinsically enriching and mutually fruitful.

3. ASPECTS OF IDENTITY

The question that must be answered is this: does such a broader paradigm exhibit sufficient coherence? Is there a common identity and nucleus that binds the diverse subdisciplines together?

In order to formulate an answer — personal and tentative — to this question, I propose investigating the paradigm from three perspectives: its view of the human being, its focus on experience and person-centeredness, and its working alliance. In doing so I will reflect on the identifying features, and on the possible divergence between sub-orientations.

3.1. Image of the human being

All of the above-mentioned sub-orientations belong to the so-called 'third force', the humanistic approach in psychology. One important dimension in which humanistic psychology — with key figures such as Rogers and Maslow — differed from behaviorism and psychoanalysis was its image of the human being. In this regard we find the following aspects frequently mentioned in the literature:

• The person is not a solely reactive but a *proactive* being, driven by a tendency toward actualization. This tendency has been described by Rogers as follows: 'By this I mean the directional trend which is evident in all organic and human life — the urge to expand, extend, develop, mature — the tendency to express and activate all the capacities of the organism, or the self. This tendency may become deeply buried under layer after layer of encrusted psychological defenses. It may be hidden behind elaborate façades which deny its existence; it is my belief however, based on my experience, that it exists in every individual, and awaits only the proper conditions to be released and expressed' (1961a, p. 351). This description assumes that humans are not only directed to homeostasis and tension reduction, but actively seek new stimulation that can further their growth. It also means that the client in therapy is seen as an active agent and self-healer (Bohart and Tallman, 1999; Brodley, 1999; Rennie, 1998). The task of the therapist is then not to treat the client in a directive way but to create as much room as possible for his or her tendency toward actualization. This means that providing a secure climate in which the client feels 'fully received' (Rogers, 1961b) is crucial.

• The human being is not completely determined, but to a certain extent an architect of him-or herself. Within the boundaries of one's fate there is still *a margin of freedom*. In essence, it is the objective of psychotherapy to increase this freedom, to facilitate self-determination, self-responsibility and freedom of choice. This position stands in sharp contrast to how the goal of psychology is often described from a positivistic vantage point, namely as the 'prediction and control' of human behavior.

• Human beings are *pro-social*: their longing for contact and attachment belongs as much to the core of their being as their more self-centered tendencies. Brodley (1999) describes the innate pro-social potentialities of the human being as follows: 'They include the capacity for identification leading to feelings of sympathy for other persons, capacity for empathy, affiliative tendencies, tendencies toward attachment, communication, social cooperation, and collaboration, capacities for forming moral or ethical rules, and tendencies to engage in struggles to live according to moral or ethical rules' (p. 111). As a corollary of this vision one may posit that human nature — under optimal growth conditions — is trustworthy. Rogers' conviction on this point is very clear. 'When we are able to free the individual from defensiveness, so that he is open to the wide range of his own needs, as well as the wide range of environmental and social demands, his reactions may be trusted to be positive, forward-moving, constructive. We do not need to ask who will socialize him, for one of his own deepest needs is for affiliation and communication with others' (1961a, p. 194).

• The person lives in a field of tension between *autonomy and belonging*. One of the key objectives of our existence entails finding the balance between these two poles. Whenever this effort is unsuccessful one slides either into fusion or into isolation. Although this thematic has been developed particularly within the interpersonal-psychodynamic school embracing significant authors such as Rank, Sullivan, Winnicott, M. Mahrer, Yalom, Kohut, Stern and Benjamin, it links exceptionally well with the theory building of Rogers (1959) and a number of young authors of our orientation. Thus Schmid, from a philosophical and anthropological perspective, defines the person as follows:

> The attempt to grasp man as a person thus means that he has to be understood equally as a
> distinctive independent being (the individualistic aspect of the conception of the person) and
> as a being who originated and originates from a loving encounter (the relational aspect). His

nature can neither be understood only through his being-from-himself and his being-for-himself, nor merely through the being-from-relationship and the being-in-relationship. The sovereignty — and therefore freedom, respect and dignity of the person, his non-transferability and indivisibility, his corporeality and uniqueness, his capacity for self-reflection and self-experience, as well as commitment — and therefore his orientation towards relationships, his dependence on others, his fundamental concentration on community, his capacity for dialogue, partnership and I-thou relationship, his striving for transcendence — are intrinsically part of what it means to speak of a human being as a person. Neither conception of the person excludes the other as long as neither of them is defined as absolute. Essential elements of the person are independence *and* dependence on relationships, sovereignty *and* commitment, autonomy *and* solidarity. (1998a, p. 45)

Biermann-Ratjen (1998), from a developmental psychology perspective, also enjoins this theoretical heritage, while van Kalmthout (1995) describes the fundamental conflict between autonomy and belonging as an exceptionally fruitful framework for a person-centered interpretation of human problems.

These four aspects of a humanistic conception of the human being — that moreover share a close relationship with each other — are, in my opinion, in large measure shared by representatives of the diverse sub-orientations. There are of course differences of 'gradation' both within and between sub-orientations. For some, for example, the belief in the power of the actualization tendency is the cornerstone of their vision of therapy, a vision that therefore comprises the assumption that non-directivity forms the nucleus of their working method. Others, in contrast, who equally insist on the self-agency of the client, more strongly emphasize that the actualization tendency can be seriously damaged, that such damage is sometimes irreparable, and that 'self-maintenance' (and not 'self-actualization') can sometimes be the only realistic objective. Moreover, it is held, more directive forms of intervention are sometimes necessary in order to restore the process of self-actualization.

Insofar as the 'pro-social' character of humans is concerned, here again we uncover clear differences of opinion. One need only recall the open letter from Rollo May to Carl Rogers in which May accuses Rogers of situating the cause of evil too far outside the human person (May, 1982). In general, the presupposition of the social grounding of human nature (in contradistinction to the classic Freudian view, in which the dangerous impulses of the Id must be controlled) is accepted by the diverse wings of our paradigm. But the confidence that a fully functioning person arrives at social-constructive choices 'spontaneously' as it were, is not shared to the same extent by everyone. Some see this as a typically human task that demands much courage, and by virtue of which the individual is sometimes faced with a wrenching conflict between choices. Insofar as the dialectic between autonomy and belonging is concerned, it is typical of all forms of humanistic psychotherapy that initially the emphasis has been placed on the pole of autonomy. During the last two decades however considerable criticism has arisen in this regard, among others from the feministic camp (Jordan, Kaplan, Miller, et al., 1991), and as a result greater attention is being given to the dimension of interconnectedness. This development has been echoed in the 'charter' of the WAPCEPC. The organization intends to function as a forum for professionals 'who have a commitment to an understanding of both clients and therapists as persons, who are at the same time individuals and in relationship with others and their diverse environments and cultures' (see the website www.pce-world.org).

3.2. Person-centered and experiential

The name of our World Organization contains two terms: 'person-centered' and 'experiential', elements that indeed belong to the nucleus of our identity. But what precisely do these terms denote? And is it not precisely in their regard that we encounter a divergence of vision between the sub-orientations?

3.2.1. Person-centered

In the evolution of client-centered psychotherapy the term 'client-centered' has more and more come to be replaced by 'person-centered' (Rogers, 1987). At the outset one wished to point to the greater breadth of the field addressed in the 'person-centered approach': education, peace work, community building, organizational development, training of non-professionals, and human relations in general. More and more however the term 'person-centered' is also being preferred in the field of psychotherapy and counseling. What is then the precise meaning of 'person-centered'? In my opinion the term has much to do with the objectives of therapy. On the one hand there are types of therapy that are 'disorder driven'; they are more closely related to the medical model, strongly underline the use of specific techniques to address specific problems, and limit themselves more to symptom reduction as the primary aim. On the other hand one finds open-exploratory types of therapy that have a broader objective: the person as a process of becoming. In this perspective the symptom is viewed as only the top of the iceberg, as a 'concentrated carrier of meaning' (van Kalmthout, 1995, p. 40) that provides, both for client and therapist, the entry point for a deeper exploration of how the client relates to him- or herself and to others. Bohart, O'Hara and Leitner (1998) describe this process as follows:

> The goal is to provide a relationship as an optimal context within which an active, agentic client can reflect upon the patterns of his or her life. The therapist interacts with the client and through that interaction provides the client with an opportunity to experientially explore, examine, reflect, have a creative, co-constructive interactive experience with the therapist, and through all this, reevaluate whatever life choices the person has made/is making, and revise if necessary. This may be motivated by the client's experience of distress, and one goal of the therapy may ultimately be to help the client alleviate the distress. But the focus of the therapy is not the distress, as if the distress were a 'pathogen' to be removed, or a 'condition' to be diagnosed and 'treated.' Rather, distress is seen as secondary to the individual's pursuing a more satisfying, meaningful life, and that is the primary focus of the therapy. (1998, p. 144)

The holistic outlook is typical of the person-centered approach: the client's complaints are never treated in isolation but in relation to the broader functioning of the whole person. Alongside this element, attention is directed not only to eliminating the pathological element but equally to addressing the healthy resources in the person and the growth potential that is so often snowed under (van Kalmthout, 1995).

3.2.2. Experiential

The focus on the phenomenological world of the client is typical of all the sub-orientations within the client-centered/experiential paradigm. The 'inner experiencing person' stands central to its dynamic. Although, diverse terms (such as 'inner frame of reference', 'organismic experience' or 'bodily felt sense') are employed by the different subapproaches, and the experiential process is studied in the light of diverse theories (such as the information processing and emotion theories), the subjective experiential world of the client, as privileged avenue for therapeutic work, remains the most typical characteristic of the experiential-humanistic therapies. In this, they clearly distinguish themselves from behavioral therapy (where the accent is laid on separate behavioral reactions as targets), from systems therapy (where the interaction itself is placed to the fore), and from psychoanalytic therapy (where the unconscious and the relation between Id, Ego and Superego form the center of attention).

Within the experiential-humanistic family in the course of time an enormous body of knowledge has been built up about the experiencing process and how it develops into personality change (Rogers, 1959, 1961b; Gendlin, 1964; Wexler, 1974; Greenberg and Paivio, 1997; Greenberg and Van Balen, 1998). Together with a number of aspects belonging to the working alliance (see below), the focus on the experiencing process to my mind constitutes the deepest core of our paradigm. The experiencing process is seen as the substratum of psychological life and it comprises affective, cognitive and volitional aspects. As Barrett-Lennard writes: 'Personal experience is usually imbued simultaneously with feeling and with meaning: feelings help to inform meaning and meanings contribute to what is felt' (1998, p. 91). One can distinguish different levels of consciousness — from preconceptual body sensing to reflective consciousness — and the symbolization of what is implicitly felt leads to unfolding and steps of change. Typical for experiential therapies is a profound trust in the 'wisdom' of the body: the organismic valuing process is seen as the 'compass' of the actualizing tendency, the 'voice' of our adaptive emotional system; it contains a future-oriented growth direction and action tendencies. Self-exploration then is seen as most fruitful when it is experiential and not merely conceptual, when there is a zig-zag movement between conscious symbolization and felt sense. The overall outcome of this kind of self-exploration is an increase in process quality of functioning, the self-concept or self-schemes becoming more flexible in the sense that they let themselves be influenced and changed by new information.

Looking at these two cornerstones of our paradigm, we are confronted with a strange situation: I think that all experiential therapists agree that they are person-centered; yet not all person-centered therapists agree that they are experiential. The hesitation of some of us to label ourselves as experiential has little to do with the focus as such. I really think that *all* client-centered/experiential therapists see the experiential/phenomenological world of the client as the central avenue of their work — but it has to do with *how* as a therapist one tries to facilitate experiential self-exploration. There are — as Warner calls it — 'levels of interventiveness', which she defines as 'the degree to which a therapist brings in material from outside the client's frame of reference, and the degree to which this is done from a stance of authority or expertise' (2000, p. 31). It is indeed the case that, concerning levels of intervention, we find big differences among person-centered therapists of different sub-orientations (and even within sub-orientations): from almost exclusively empathic following to responding more from one's own frame of reference, giving process directives or proposing some specific procedures. It is my conviction however — as I will discuss under the next point — that within certain limits a more process-directive style can be implemented in a way that does not interfere with the self-agency of the client.

3.3. The working alliance

Rogers will likely be remembered in the history of psychotherapy for his vision of the relational basic attitudes of the therapist and his insistence on their importance for the therapeutic change process. But what is the essence of the working alliance for the client-centered/experiential therapist? First and foremost I believe that there are several relational ingredients that in our theoretical construction are more strongly emphasized than in other orientations, yet in practice are not our 'privilege'. And here I refer to: congruence, a nonjudgmental stance of acceptance, (general) understanding, dedication, a confirming attitude, non-possessive warmth, respect and non-manipulation. Research has demonstrated that these 'ingredients' (sometimes put in other terms) can be found in *all* good therapies, whatever their orientation (Orlinsky, Parks and Grawe, 1994). Alongside these, I detect a number of aspects that undoubtedly give our method its own color:

• *Moment-by-moment empathy* as a continuous endeavor throughout the therapy process. Every therapist, of course, tries to understand his or her client, but the step-by-step attunement to what the client is experiencing and the communicative checking of it as a continuous foreground activity, is typical for our orientation. Also, in the more process directive sub-orientations, this constant following or coming back to the experiential track of the client is emphasized as a concomitant baseline activity of whatever the therapist does (Bohart and Greenberg, 1997).

• *A high degree of personal presence.* More than in other paradigms the client-therapist relationship is defined as encounter (Schmid, 1998b). This has been emphasized most strongly in existential and interpersonal psychotherapy. But also in client-centered therapy there has been a shift 'from alter ego to I-thou' (Lietaer, 1993), in which a freer 'use of self' (Rogers et al., 1967b) became prominent. I want to stress, however, that the personal presence of the client-centered/experiential therapist is not fostered by more self-disclosure, and explicit here-and-now metacommunication only. The whole stance of full attention, of active listening in a warm and acceptant climate, of communicating one's understanding with personal flavor, are equally if not more important. In this sense I agree with Schmid not to look at personal presence as a fourth core condition, but as a 'gestalt characteristic' of Rogers' triad of conditions: 'it comprehensively describes the basic attitudes of authenticity, unconditional positive regard and empathy, in an existential way and on a deeper, dialogical-personal level' (1998b, p. 85).

• *An egalitarian, dialogical stance.* It has been the merit of Carl Rogers to 'democratize' the helping relationship (Gendlin, 1988). The lesson he learned was that in order to provide actual help, the therapist has to be in touch with the problem as the client experiences it, and follow the client within his or her own frame of reference. Not the therapist, but the client, knows best! This basic principle remains important, also in sub-orientations where process directivity is more explicitly part of their working method. It is on purpose that I do not use here the term 'non-directive' because I think it is a confusing and inaccurate one (Lietaer, 1998). Psychotherapy is always a process of co-construction and hence directive in nature. What is important is that the process remains in the hands of the client, that client and therapist collaborate on an equal basis, each with their own expertise and resources (the client more on content, the therapist more on process). With Warner (2000) I am convinced that different levels of interventiveness are acceptable and possible within a dialogical and non-imposing working alliance. We can look at ourselves as 'midwives' who by following and steering in a balanced and gentle way, facilitate the unfolding of the self-directed process of our clients. Using diagnostic knowledge or proposing certain procedures can be part of our working differentially with clients, as long as we stay in touch with their experiential track, as long as we use these procedures or knowledge only as tools: only as 'fishing lines, not fish' (Gendlin, 1974, p. 243). I know there are sharp differences in opinion on this issue among us; yet we all strongly value — and more so than in other paradigms — a working alliance with an egalitarian basis.

• *Cruciality of the Rogerian therapist conditions.* As I already mentioned, several ingredients of the Rogerian triad of therapist conditions are widely accepted by other orientations as important 'bonding aspects'. Yet, what remains typical for our paradigm is the belief that these conditions are 'crucial', that all in all they are more important than the technical aspects of our work. However also here we are confronted with differences. For some these conditions are 'necessary and sufficient', for others they are 'necessary but not sufficient' and should be supplemented with other procedures. I think we will never be able to find the answer to the sufficiency issue, since therapist conditions are never maximally implemented and no studies are available in which all clients are cured. We should realize however that we agree that the Rogerian therapist conditions are *crucial*.

4. CONCLUSION: FIRST AND SECOND ORDER ASPECTS OF IDENTITY

It should be evident from my overview that, in my opinion, the various approaches within the client-centered/experiential paradigm do indeed share a common core of identity. With an eye to providing a nuanced synthesis, I make a distinction between first order and second order identity aspects. In Figure 2 I indicate where I situate each of the aspects mentioned. First order aspects are elements that I see as specific for our paradigm; they belong to the deepest core of our identity. Second order aspects are explicitly emphasized in our therapy theory, yet they are also characteristic of some other paradigms or of some sub-approaches in them.

Figure 2. First and second order identity aspects of the client-centered/experiential paradigm

First order:
- focus on the experiencing self
- moment-by-moment empathy
- a high level of personal presence
- an egalitarian, dialogical stance
- a belief that the Rogerian therapist conditions are *crucial*

Second order:
- holistic person-centeredness
- emphasis on self-agency and self-actualizing process
- self-determination and free choice as human possibilities
- pro-social nature of the human being
- autonomy and solidarity as existential tasks

As shown in Figure 2, experience-centeredness falls under the first order aspects, whereas person-centeredness comes under the second order aspects. This is because most other open exploratory forms of psychotherapy are equally not symptom-driven but person-centered. As to the characteristics of the image of the human being, I include them under the second order aspects. Again because they are not unique to our paradigm: self-agency, for example, is certainly implied in many other approaches, and the pro-social nature of the human being is also acknowledged in the object-relational and self psychology wing of the psychodynamic paradigm.

To me the unique gestalt of first and second order identity aspects gives to the different branches a sound basis of commonality, more than enough to feel as a close family, as 'one nation, many tribes' (Warner, 2000). Of course there are differences too among the tribes, but more of degree than essence, in my opinion. But these differences are certainly not greater than in other paradigms. More importantly, we should learn to tolerate some ambiguity and welcome the diversity: it's a sign of being alive and an occasion for debate, further reflection and cross-fertilization.

REFERENCES

Barrett-Lennard, G. T. (1998). *Carl Rogers' Helping System. Journey and substance.* London: Sage.

Biermann-Ratjen, E.-M. (1998). On the development of the person in relationships. In B. Thorne and E. Lambers (Eds.) *Person-centred Therapy. A European perspective.* London: Sage, pp. 106–118.

Bohart, A. C. and Greenberg, L. S. (Eds.) (1997). *Empathy reconsidered. New directions in psychotherapy.* Washington, DC: APA Books.

Bohart, A. C., O'Hara, M. and Leitner, L. M. (1998). Empirically violated treatments: Disenfranchisement of humanistic and other psychotherapies. *Psychotherapy Research, 8, (2),* 141–57.

Bohart, A. C. and Tallman, K. (1999). *How Clients Make Therapy Work.* Washington, DC: APA Books.

Brodley, B. T. (1990). Client-centered and experiential: Two different therapies. In G. Lietaer, J. Rombauts and R. Van Balen (Eds.) *Client-centered and Experiential Psychotherapy in the Nineties.* Leuven: Leuven University Press, pp. 87–107.

Brodley, B. T. (1999). The actualizing tendency concept in client-centered theory. *The Person-centered Journal, 6*(2), 108–20.

Cain, D. and Seeman, J. (2002). *Humanistic Psychotherapies: Handbook of research and practice.* Washington: APA Books.

Eckert, J., Höger, D. and Linster, H. W. (Eds.) (1997). *Praxis der Gesprächspsychotherapie. Störungsbezogene Falldarstellungen.* Stuttgart: Kohlhammer.

Finke, J. (1994). *Empathie und Interaktion. Methodik und Praxis der Gesprächspsychotherapie.* Stuttgart: Thieme.

Gelso, C. J. and Carter, J. A. (1974). Components of the psychotherapy relationship: Their interaction and unfolding during treatment. *Journal of Counseling Psychology, 41,* 296–306.

Gendlin, E. T. (1964). A theory of personality change. In P. Worchel and D. Byrne (Eds.) *Personality change.* New York: Wiley.

Gendlin, E. T. (1967). Therapeutic procedures in dealing with schizophrenics. In C. R. Rogers (Ed.) *The Therapeutic Relationship and its Impact: A study of psychotherapy with schizophrenics.* Madison: University of Wisconscin Press, pp. 369–400.

Gendlin, E. T. (1974). Client-centered and experiential psychotherapy. In D. A. Wexler and L. N.

Rice (Eds.) *Innovations in Client-centered Therapy.* New York: Wiley, pp. 211–46.

Gendlin, E. T. (1988). Carl Rogers (1902–87). *American Psychologist, 43*(2), 127–8.

Gendlin, E. T. (1996). *Focusing-oriented Psychotherapy. A manual of the experiential method.* New York: Guilford Press.

Greenberg, L. S. and Paivio, S. C. (1997). *Working with Emotions in Psychotherapy.* New York: Guilford Press.

Greenberg, L. S. and Van Balen, R. (1998). The theory of experience-centered therapies. In L. S. Greenberg, J. C. Watson, and G. Lietaer (Eds.) *Handbook of Experiential Psychotherapy.* New York: Guilford Press, pp. 28–57.

Greenberg, L. S., Rice, L. N. and Elliott, R.. (1993). *Facilitating Emotional Change. The moment-by-moment process.* New York: Guilford Press.

Greenberg, L. S., Watson, J. C. and Lietaer, G. (Eds.) (1998). *Handbook of Experiential Psychotherapy.* New York: Guilford Press.

Horvath, A., and Greenberg, L. S. (Eds.) (1994). *The Working Alliance: Theory, research and practice.* New York: Wiley.

Jordan, J. V., Kaplan, A. G., Miller, J. B., Stiver, I. P. and Surrey, J. L. (1991). *Women's Growth in Connection: Writings from the Stone Center.* New York: Guilford Press.

Kiesler, D. J. (1996). *Contemporary Interpersonal Theory and Research. Personality, psychopathology and psychotherapy.* New York: Wiley.

Lietaer, G. (1990). The client-centered approach after the Wisconsin-project: A personal view on its evolution. In G. Lietaer, J. Rombauts and R. Van Balen (Eds.) *Client-centered and Experiential Psychotherapy in the Nineties.* Leuven: Leuven University Press, pp. 19–45.

Lietaer, G. (1993). Authenticity, congruence and transparency. In D. Brazier (Ed.) *Beyond Carl Rogers: Towards a psychotherapy for the 21st century.* London: Constable, pp. 17–46.

Lietaer, G. (1998). From non-directive to experiential: A paradigm unfolding. In B. Thorne and E. Lambers (Eds.) *Person-centred therapy. A European perspective.* London: Sage, pp. 62–73.

Lietaer, G. and Van Kalmthout, M. (Eds.) (1995). *Praktijkboek gesprekstherapie. Psychopathologie en experiëntiële procesbevordering.* Leusden: De Tijdstroom.

Lietaer, G., Rombauts, J. and Van Balen, R. (Eds.) (1990). *Client-centered and Experiential Psychotherapy in the Nineties.* Leuven: Leuven University Press.

May, R. (1982). The problem of evil: an open letter to Carl Rogers. *Journal of Humanistic Psychology, 22*(3), 10–21 (with comments by Rogers, Bakan and Friedman in Nr. 4).

Orlinsky, D. E., Grawe, K. and Parks, B. K. (1994). Process and outcome in psychotherapy: Noch einmal. In A. E. Bergin and S. L. Garfield (Eds.) *Handbook of Psychoptherapy and Behavior Change.* New York: Wiley, pp. 270–376.

Rennie, D. L. (1998). *Person-centred Counselling. An experiential approach.* London: Sage.

Rice, L. N. (1974). The evocative function of the therapist. In D. A. Wexler and L. N. Rice (Eds.) *Innovations in Client-centered Therapy.* New York: Wiley, pp. 289–311.

Rogers, C. R. (1957). The necessary and sufficient conditions of therapeutic change. *Journal of Consulting Psychology, 21,* 97–103.

Rogers, C. R. (1959). A theory of therapy, personality and interpersonal relationships as developed in the client-centered framework. In S. Koch (Ed.) *Psychology: A study of science, Vol. 3.* New York: Mc Graw Hill, pp. 184–256.

Rogers, C. R. (1961a). *On Becoming a Person.* Boston: Houghton Mifflin.

Rogers, C. R. (1961b). A process conception of psychotherapy. In *On Becoming a Person.* Boston: Houghton Mifflin, pp. 125–59.

Rogers, C. R. (1961c). A process equation of psychotherapy. *American Journal of Psychotherapy, 15,* 27–65.

Rogers, C. R. (1967). A silent young man. In C. R. Rogers, E. T. Gendlin, D. J. Kiesler and C. B.

Truax (Eds.) *The Therapeutic Relationship and its Impact: A study of psychotherapy with schizophrenics.* Madison: University of Wisconsin Press, pp. 401–16.

Rogers, C. R. (1975). Empathic: An unappreciated way of being. *The Counseling Psychologist, 5*(2), 2–10.

Rogers, C. R. (1987). Client-centered? Person-centered? *Person-centered Review, 2,* 11–13.

Rogers, C. R. et al. (Eds.) (1967a). *The Therapeutic Relationship and its Impact. A study of psychotherapy with schizophrenics.* Madison: University of Wisconsin Press.

Rogers, C. R. et al. (Eds.) (1967b). A dialogue between therapists. In *The Therapeutic Relationship and its Impact. A study of psychotherapy with schizophrenics.* Madison: University of Wisconsin Press, pp. 507–20.

Sachse, R. (1996). *Praxis der Zielorientierten Gesprächspsychotherapie.* Göttingen, Germany: Hogrefe.

Sachse, R. (1997). *Personlichkeitsstörungen. Psychotherapie dysfuntionaler Interaktionsstile.* Göttingen, Germany: Hogrefe.

Schmid, P. F. (1998a). On becoming a person-centred approach: A person-centred understanding of the person. In B. Thorne and E. Lambers (Eds.) *Person-centred Therapy. A European perspective.* London: Sage, pp. 38–52.

Schmid, P. F. (1998b). The art of encounter. In B. Thorne and E. Lambers (Eds.) *Person-centred Therapy. A European perspective.* London: Sage, pp. 74–90.

Silverstone, L. (1997). *Art Therapy. The person-centred way* (2nd edn.). London: Jessica Kingsley Publishers.

Swildens, J. (1997). *Procesgerichte gesprekstherapie.* (Rev. edn.). Leusden: De Tijdstroom.

Toukmanian, S. G. (1990). A schema-based information processing perspective on client change in experiential psychotherapy. In G. Lietaer, J. Rombauts and R. Van Balen (Eds.), *Client-centered and experiential psychotherapy in the nineties* (pp. 309–27). Leuven: Leuven University Press.

van Deurzen-Smith, E. (1996). *Everyday Mysteries. Existential dimensions of psychotherapy.* London: Routledge.

van Kalmthout, M. (1997). *Persoonsgerichte psychotherapie.* Leusden: De Tijdstroom.

van Kessel, W. and Lietaer, G. (1998). Interpersonal processes. In L. S. Greenberg, J. C. Watson, and G. Lietaer (Eds.) *Handbook of Experiential Psychotherapy.* New York: Guilford Press, pp. 155–77.

Vanaerschot, G. (1993). Empathy as releasing several micro-processes in the client. In D. Brazier (Ed.), *Beyond Carl Rogers: Towards a psychotherapy for the twenty-first century.* London: Constable, pp. 47–72.

Verhofstadt-Denève, L. (1999). *Theory and Practice of Action and Drama Techniques. Developmental psychotherapy from an existential-dialectical viewpoint.* London: Jessica Kingsley Publishers.

Warner, M. S. (2000). Person-centered psychotherapy: One nation, many tribes. *The Person-centered Journal, 7*(1), 28–39.

Wexler, D. A. (1974). A cognitive theory of experiencing, self actualization and therapeutic process. In D. A. Wexler and L. N. Rice (Eds.) *Innovations in Client-centered Therapy.* New York: Wiley, pp. 49–116.

Wilkins, P. (1999). *Psychodrama.* London: Sage.

Yalom, I. D. (1980). Existential isolation and psychotherapy. In *Existential Psychotherapy.* New York: Basic Books, pp. 392–415.

Yalom, I. D. (1995). Interpersonal learning. In *The Theory and Practice of Group Psychotherapy.* New York: Basic Books, pp. 17–46.

Ivan Ellingham
Hertfordshire Partnership NHS Trust

Foundation for a Person-Centred Humanistic Psychology and Beyond: The nature and logic of Carl Rogers' 'Formative Tendency'

Jacob set out from Beersheba and went on his way to Harran. He came to a certain place and stopped there for the night, because the sun had set; and, taking one of the stones there, he made it a pillow for his head and lay down to sleep. He dreamt he saw a ladder, which rested on the ground with its top reaching to heaven, and angels of God were going up and down on it. (Genesis, 28: 11–12)

What will it take to generate a bona fide science of psychology?

The view I hold is that such a science will come about only through the construction of a unitary pattern of ideas — a 'paradigm,' to use Thomas Kuhn's term; a 'metanarrative' to employ postmodernist discourse — whereby we will be able to integrate into a seamless web the empirical findings and theoretical contributions of contemporary psychology's smorgasbord of rival and competing conceptual approaches. 'What we need for a science of mind,' as Susanne Langer (1967) has written, 'is not so much a definitive concept of mind, as a conceptual frame in which to lodge our observations of mental phenomena' (p. 17).

Postmodernists, with their renowned 'incredulity towards metanarratives' (Lyotard, 1984, p. xxiv), would undoubtedly view any attempt to forge such a frame as a pointless exercise. Postmodernist pessimism notwithstanding, my aim in the present paper is to point the way towards the fabrication of a framework of ideas capable of serving as the foundation block for a genuine science of psychology. The specific task I take on is that of characterising the nature and logic of a concept that I believe to be capable of serving as the central pivot around which such an ideational scheme can be constructed.

My rationale for adopting such a strategy derives from analysis of paradigmatic schemes in well-established sciences. What we find at the core of these ideational vehicles are one or two highly abstract concepts which are not only defined in a rigorous and precise manner, but which possess great power in applying to a wide range of events. On Langer's (1962) testimony, 'Newton's concept of gravity as a property of matter was such a concept; so was the concept of evolution which Darwin's *Origin of Species* sprang upon the world' (p. 13). It is concepts like these, says Langer, that facilitate 'the reconception of facts under a new abstractive principle, in a new intellectual projection'. 'The sciences are really born,' she avers, 'when their key concepts reach a degree of abstraction and precision which makes them adequate to the demands of exact, powerful, and microscopically analytic thinking.'

What then is the concept around which a unitary ideational frame for a science of psychology can be constructed?

It is none other, I propose, than that concept that Carl Rogers (1980) hypothesised 'could be a base upon which we could begin to build a theory for humanistic psychology'; the concept which 'definitely forms a base for the person-centered approach'; that concept which he himself formulated and named the 'formative tendency' (p. 133).

Broad as Rogers' own claims are, however, what I am claiming is broader still. I am not just claiming that Rogers' notion of the formative tendency 'forms a base for the person-centered approach'; not just that it 'could be a base upon which we could begin to build a theory for humanistic psychology'; but that it constitutes a base upon which we can build a theory for psychology as a whole, i.e. a genuine scientific paradigm. In brief, that Rogers' concept of the formative tendency possesses the potential to serve as the central concept for an ideational scheme by which psychology can become a bona fide science, a science which is not just humanistic and person-centred, but which embraces the entire range of theoretical approaches within the discipline — viz., the neuro-biological, the behavioural, cognitive-developmental, cognitive-behavioural, psychoanalytic, and transpersonal.

For the paradigmatic potential of the formative tendency to be so realised, it is necessary, as I see things, to go beyond Rogers in terms of the rigour and precision that he himself employed in defining this crucial concept, both with respect to its general nature and to its intrinsic logic. I base the present attempt to generate an enhanced definition of the formative tendency upon the premise that person-centred theory as a whole (inclusive of the formative tendency) is a particular expression of an emerging scientific paradigm, one that has been variously labelled *holistic*, *organismic*, and *process* ('HOP,' for short, cf. Capra, 1996) — other expressions of this paradigm being *field theory*, *general systems theory*, and *eco-psychology*. It is this HOP paradigm, as Fritjof Capra attests (Capra, 1982), that is currently in the process of supplanting its predecessor: the mechanistic paradigm grounded upon the views of Descartes and Newton. Person-centred theory, in general, and the concept of the formative tendency, in particular, I argue, can be further elaborated and refined through harmonic synthesis with the formulations of thinkers who, though outside the fold of the person-centred approach, nevertheless espouse the common HOP worldview upon which it is based (see Ellingham, 2001).

Such then is the operational premise that lies behind the present paper. In it I make use of ideas formulated by a number of HOP thinkers in pursuit of my aim of defining the formative tendency with greater rigour and precision. Thinkers whose ideas I draw upon in this way are Arthur Koestler, Susanne Langer, Michael Polanyi, Alfred North Whitehead, and last, but most importantly, Lancelot Whyte. For not only was Rogers profoundly indebted to Whyte in his formulation of the formative tendency, but other aspects of Whyte's thought provide us with the means of augmenting Rogers' formulation, both in their own right and through indicating conceptual links with the other thinkers mentioned.

To begin with, given that my intention is to set Rogers' concept of the formative tendency on a par with such scientific concepts as Newton's concept of gravity and Darwin's concept of evolution, I look to shed light upon the nature of scientific concepts per se. I base my exposition almost exclusively upon that of Susanne Langer, as set within her discussion of the notion of 'logical form' and the nature of logic.

LOGIC AND SCIENTIFIC CONCEPTS

According to Whitehead (1938/1968), it was logician Henry Sheffer who 'emphasised the notion of pattern, as fundamental to logic' (p. 52). For Sheffer, and for Susanne Langer, Sheffer's and Whitehead's student, logic as an intellectual pursuit thus represents 'a science of pure forms', 'a science of order', where 'anything may be said to have form that follows a pattern of any sort, exhibits order, internal connection' (Langer, 1953a, pp. 40, 24). 'Form' as the logician defines it, i.e. 'logical form' is therefore manifested in a wide range of different mediums, or 'contents,' and doesn't just refer to the commonplace notion of physical shape.

Just how wide ranging the notion of logical form is, relates Langer (1953a), is indicated by the many synonyms we employ to refer to 'form' in this very general sense. 'We speak,' she highlights, 'of physical, grammatical, social *forms*; of psychological *types*; *norms* of conduct, of beauty, of intelligence; *fashions* in clothing, speech, behaviour; new *designs* of automobiles or motor boats; architectural *plans*, or the *plans* for a festival; *pattern, standard, mode* and many other words [here we might add *Gestalt, whole, paradigm, configuration, scheme, structure, system, template*] all signify essentially the same thing in specialised usage or subtle variations of meaning' (p. 24).

Such synonyms give us some inkling of the way in which 'the content of a logical form may be psychical, musical, temporal, or in some other way non-physical, just as well as physical' (p. 42). Not only, then, does logical form have relevance for the realm of the spiritual, for instance, but to 'contents' that are dynamic as well as static. It thus becomes clear how Langer can claim that 'logic applies to everything in the world' (p. 41), and how Whitehead is able to prophesy that 'Symbolic Logic, that is to say the symbolic examination of pattern with the use of real variables, will become the foundation of aesthetics,' from whence, he asserts, 'it will proceed to conquer ethics and theology' (Whitehead, quoted in Mays, 1959, p. 98).

As to the relevance of the notion of logical form to science and scientific understanding, the generation of scientific concepts like Newton's concept of gravity or Darwin's concept of evolution is based, says Langer, upon our ability to apprehend the same form or pattern in diverse contents — that is, on our ability to discern relationships of analogy between different phenomena. So, for example, 'the swing of a pendulum, the swaying of a skyscraper, the vibration of a violin string over which the bow is passing . . . the shaking of Grandpa's palsied hands . . . the quiver of a tuning fork . . . the vibration of a parked automobile with the engine running' are all identified as exhibiting the common pattern (i.e. logical form) of 'rhythmic motion to and fro' (Langer, 1953a, pp. 35, 36).

Now it may be, as Langer suggests, that different people generate individually different 'mental pictures' of the pattern in question. However,

> when we consider the common form of various things or various events, and call it by a name
> that does not suggest any particular thing or event, or commit ourselves to any mental picture
> — for instance, when we consider this common form of various movements, and call it by a
> name such as 'oscillation' — we are consciously, deliberately abstracting the form from all
> things which have it. Such an abstracted form is called a *concept*. From our concrete experiences
> we form the *concept of oscillation*. (Langer, 1953a, p. 36)

What facilitates such conjuring of concepts is the employment of easily manipulated representational devices (whether pictorial image, verbal proposition or mathematical formula), devices that themselves manifest and express the abstract form in question. Such devices are what we call symbols, 'formal analogy, or congruence,' being 'the prime requisite for the relation between a symbol and whatever it is to mean' (Langer, 1953b, p. 27).

'The fact,' Langer elucidates, 'that so many things in nature exemplify the same forms makes it possible for us to collect our enormously variegated experiences of nature under relatively few concepts' (p. 36), and, we might add, represent them symbolically. 'If this were not the case,' she goes on to explain,

> we could have no science. If there were not fundamental concepts such as oscillation, gravitation, radiation, etc., exemplified in nature over and over again, we could have no formulae of physics and discover no laws of nature. Scientists proceed by abstracting more and more fundamental forms (often seeing similarities among the abstracted forms, or concepts, themselves and thus gathering several concepts into one); and by finding more and more things that fall under certain concepts, i.e. that exhibit certain general forms. (1953a, p. 36)

In his concept of gravity, Newton symbolised in mathematical terms a common order or pattern to events on earth and in the heavens. Verbally expressed and pictorially represented, Darwin's concept of evolution identified a common order or pattern that governs and unites all living things. Rogers' formative tendency, as we shall see, is of *metaphysical* proportions (see O'Hara, 1999, p. 64), claiming to identify a single order or pattern to every level of the universe; to be, that is, a conceptual stitch uniting all aspects of the universe in a seamless whole.

It is to consideration of Rogers' formulation of this all-embracing concept that I now turn, particularly to the matter of its close connection with the views of Lancelot Whyte.

CONGRUENCE BETWEEN ROGERS AND WHYTE: THE FORMATIVE, MORPHIC OVERLAP

Rogers officially unveiled his concept of the formative tendency in a short paper delivered in 1975, but not published until 1978 (see Rogers, 1978). Five years later, Rogers presented a more elaborate characterisation of the same concept set within an extended version of this earlier paper (see Rogers, 1980). As Rogers defines the formative tendency there is a clear concordance between his ideas and views of Lancelot Whyte set out in Whyte's 1974 book *The Universe of Experience*. This concordance is hardly surprising, given that Rogers acknowledges that his formulation of the formative tendency owes 'a special indebtedness' to this work of Whyte, and also explicitly equates Whyte's concept of a 'morphic tendency' with his own 'formative tendency' — an equation reinforced by Whyte's actual deployment of the term 'formative tendency' as a synonym for 'morphic tendency' (Whyte, 1974, p. 58).

Let us look, then, at the equivalent manner in which the two authors define their respective concepts. Consider first how each states his fundamental thesis.

'My main thesis,' declares Rogers, 'is this: there appears to be a formative tendency in the universe, which can be observed at every level' (1978, pp. 23–4; 1980, p. 124). 'I hypothesise,' he amplifies,

> that there is a formative directional tendency in the universe, which can be traced and observed in stellar space, in crystals, in micro-organisms, in more complex organic life, and in human beings. This is an evolutionary tendency toward greater order, greater complexity, greater

interrelatedness. In humankind, this tendency exhibits itself as the individual moves from a single-cell origin to complex organic functioning, to knowing and sensing below the level of consciousness, to conscious awareness of the organism and the external world, to a transcendent awareness of the harmony and unity of the cosmic system, including humankind. (1980, p. 133)

By comparison, Whyte (1974) states his fundamental 'world view' in the following manner: 'There is present on many levels in nature a tendency toward, order, form, and symmetry; hence in living systems toward organic coordination; and in man [*sic*] toward personal coordination' (p. 20).

A second point of equivalence has to do with the two authors' descriptions of the workings of the formative tendency in living systems. In this context, both consider the formative/morphic tendency to be responsible not only for *creation* but for *preservation*, for *maintaining* new forms as well as *spawning* them. In Rogers' case, such discussion occurs with reference to that 'part of' the formative tendency that he terms 'the actualising tendency,' the part 'in living systems' (Rogers, 1980, p. 134). The actualising/formative tendency is therefore for Rogers 'a tendency toward fulfillment, toward actualisation, involving not only maintenance but also the enhancement of the organism' (p. 123).

Similarly, it is in the context of a discussion of the nature of living organisms that Whyte (1974) refers to a 'vital surplus' being associated with the morphic tendency (p. 82). 'The presence of this vital surplus,' contends Whyte, 'implies that the total processes in organisms are not merely life-preserving, but life-enhancing, not merely adaptive but formative and sometimes creative' (p. 83).

A third equivalency between Rogers and Whyte, one of primary importance for our present discussion, is that both authors identify the same logical pattern as exemplary of the workings of the formative tendency. For his part, Rogers (1980) speaks of the 'evolutionary tendency toward greater order, greater complexity, greater interrelatedness' exhibiting a pattern wherein 'every form that we see or know emerged from a simpler, less complex form' (pp. 125, 133). While in a similar vein, Whyte (1974) asserts that 'every finite thing that man [*sic*] can observe ipso facto has form, and was, we find that we must assume, formed sometime from something less formed, and the term 'morphic' is no more than a convenient term to cover all these particular cases and countless others' (p. 44). Such an assertion is not something entirely new, according to Whyte, since 'the principle that well-formed terminal states can arise from less-formed initial ones has long been recognised' (p. 43).

Following this brief examination of the close equivalence between Rogers' and Whyte's formulations apropos the formative tendency, I move on now to highlight and further develop features of Whyte's (1974) thought that are neglected by Rogers. This further development entails both pointing up connections with, and making use of, ideas formulated by yet other HOP thinkers.

THE FURTHER DEVELOPMENT OF FEATURES OF WHYTE'S THOUGHT NEGLECTED BY ROGERS

There are, in my view, at least three important aspects of Whyte's thought that are neglected by Rogers. The first concerns the hierarchical structure of the universe that is expressive of the workings of the formative tendency; the second, the presence of qualitatively different morphic processes at each level of this hierarchical structure; the third, the notion that the qualitatively different levels of morphic processes give rise to qualitatively different modes of consciousness.

(1) A hierarchical structure to reality

To my mind, the most prominent feature of Whyte's thought that is neglected by Rogers is the ramification that when the formative tendency is defined as an ubiquitous tendency that, on the one hand, works to maintain existing forms and, on the other, creates new forms more complex than their predecessor, then of necessity the universe as a whole, and all aspects of it, will exhibit a hierarchical structure, a hierarchical logic.

'The universal morphic process,' declares Whyte (1974), 'generates the coordinating tendency of organisms and the order-seeking tendency in the human mind and in all of these the morphic tendency operates on levels forming a hierarchy' (p. 61).

Whyte is very clear, therefore, that intrinsic to the 'world view' he is positing is the presumption that 'the known universe as a whole, and every organism, including man [*sic*], contains a graded sequence of units in each of which a formative tendency has been, or still is, present' (p. 58). It is a scheme of things, attests Whyte, in which

> the universe is arranged in a series of discrete 'levels,' which for precision we call a hierarchy of wholes and parts. The first fact about the universe is its organisation as a system of systems from larger to smaller, and so also is every individual organism. (p. 43)

Whyte links such a conception with that of Arthur Koestler, who, Whyte recounts, 'has introduced the useful term *holon* for any unit which (a) contains parts, and (b) is also a part of a larger unit, that is for all units in hierarchies, *excluding any largest and smallest units*' (pp. 135–6).

Given that Whyte identifies a connection between his thought and that of Koestler, I find it surprising that Whyte does not go on to point up what for me in this context is an even more important concordance: that between his (Whyte's) ideas and those of Michael Polanyi, another organismic thinker — my surprise derives from Whyte's definite familiarity with Polanyi's ideas (see Whyte, 1974, p. 88). For, with regard to such a hierarchical perspective on reality, what carries special significance for me is Polanyi's delineation of 'the structure of tacit knowing' (Polanyi, 1968, p. 88), a hierarchical structure brought about when a complex form emerges from a less complex forebear — i.e. due to the operation of the formative tendency, or 'orderly innovating tendency,' as Polanyi terms it (1964, p. 386). Thus, whereas Whyte refers in a general fashion to 'nature and mind showing us their common form' (1974, p. 61), it is Polanyi, through his characterisation of the abstract form of the structure of tacit knowing, who spells out more explicitly the character and logic of the common form intrinsic to all 'levels' of reality, to the creative activity of the ubiquitous formative tendency.

Consider, then, Polanyi's explication of this abstract or logical form intrinsic to the workings of the formative tendency.

To make his meaning plain, Polanyi employs an example from human visual perception. Building upon the Gestalt psychologists' principle that the whole is greater than the sum of the parts, Polanyi invites us to think of a pair of stereoscopic photographs, viewed in the proper way, one eye looking at one, the other eye looking at the other. The objects shown in the two pictures appear in their joint image as distributed in depth, and tangible. This is what we see at the focus of our eyes; but it involves the sight of the two component pictures: cover these up and we see nothing at all. But we do not see these two pictures in themselves. In a way, we look through them or from them, at their joint image. So I shall class our awareness of them as subsidiary and observe that the way we look at them integrates their sights into a spatially deepened image to which they contribute. Thanks to our integration, the two flat pictures effectively function as clues to a spacial image. (Polanyi, 1968, p. 86)

What Polanyi presents us with here is an example of a more complex form (the 'spatially deepened image') being created from a simpler form (that of a flat picture): an integrative, creative transformation occurring by way of a 'gestalt switch' from the focal flat picture to the focal spacial image: a formative process in which what was once focal, the flat picture, becomes subsidiary to, a constituent element within, a more complex focal form. When we speak of the more complex form being on a higher level than its simpler forebear, then over time what we have are two levels of a hierarchy, a hierarchy which in the abstract can be thought of as made up of additional levels, 'above' and 'below'. The flat pictures, for instance, can be thought of as made up of the simpler forms of straight and curved lines.

This formative process of a 3D image being created by integrating the two flat pictures can be represented in the following way:

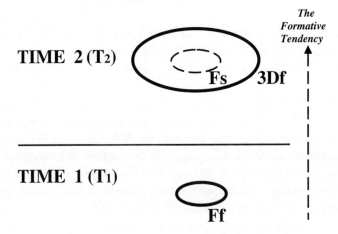

Figure 1

Figure 1 represents the working of the formative tendency from an initial time T1 to a later time T2, a time in which focal form Ff (of the flat picture) is creatively transformed into focal form 3Df (the spatially deep image) wherein F continues to be present in a subsidiary way as Fs. 3Df is therefore logically congruent with Ff insofar as form F is manifested by both focal forms.

In Figure 2, the structure of tacit knowing — the logical pattern expressive of the formative tendency — is represented even more abstractly and an additional level of development is imagined to have taken place.

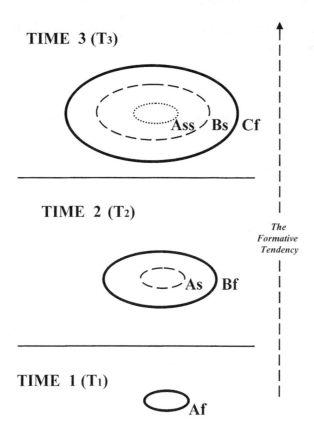

TIME 3 (T₃)

TIME 2 (T₂)

The Formative Tendency

TIME 1 (T₁)

Figure 2

Figure 2 is intended to represent the completely general case where two more complex forms, forms B and C, have emerged over time from an initially existing form, form A. This diagram, it may be noted, is similar to others produced by such individuals as Ken Wilber (1995, p. 115) and Rupert Sheldrake (1988, p. 95), and accords with the notion of a 'nested hierarchy', a notion popular with evolutionary theorists, in general, and evolutionary psychologists, in particular. It also bears comparison with hierarchical formulations of the nature of reality developed by such proponents of *general systems theory* as Ludwig von Bertalanffy (see Seeman, (2002)).

Special features intrinsic to the abstract pattern depicted by figure 2 are:
- the existence of a congruent relationship between levels defined in terms of possession of a common logical form.
- the necessary continued operation of the organisational principles of lower-level forms when the lower-level form has a subsidiary presence in a higher form. Or, as Polanyi puts it, 'The higher-level principles rely quite generally on the laws governing the lower levels' (1969, p. 218).
- a situation in which the character and nature of a higher-level form cannot be predicted beforehand from the character and nature of a lower-level predecessor. In other words, an act of creation is represented in which the emergence of the higher-level form from a lower-level form represents the formation of something new.

• the universal application of the depicted abstract pattern to all levels of existence, especially to human consciousness.

As Polanyi sees things, therefore, interpretation of the above logical template provides us 'with a picture of the universe filled with strata of realities joined together meaningfully in pairs of higher and lower strata . . . which tend to link up into a series forming a hierarchy' (1966, p. 35), a picture in which 'living beings consist in a hierarchy of levels, each level having its own structural and organismic principles' (1965, pp. 219, 218). This 'stratified structure to living things,' claims Polanyi, 'will include the structure of consciousness in higher animals' (p. 211), a contention which accords with Whyte's view that 'until we can interpret mental processes as organised in a hierarchy of levels, each marked by its function, we shall achieve no clarification of this puzzling issue: the status of consciousness in the universe,' (1974, p. 35). I shall say more about the nature of consciousness shortly.

Before I do so, it is also worth noting how a diagram like figure 2 can be used to represent not only the creation of new forms, but also deterioration or disintegration; and how, beyond this, one can portray the process referred to by Kazimierz Dabrowski (1964) as 'positive disintegration' and by Arthur Koestler (1980) as 'regress to progress', a sequence of events which Koestler sees as intrinsic to 'the creation of novelty in mental evolution . . . [and] biological evolution' (p. 349).

Consider, therefore, the following diagram.

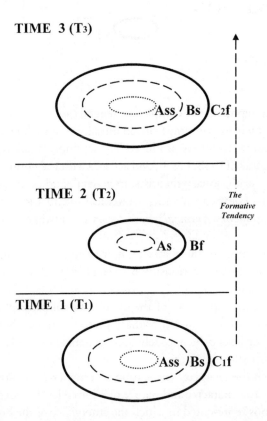

Figure 3

What figure 3 represents is first the disintegration of focal form C1 such that (at Time 2) form B once again becomes focal, while higher-level form C1 disintegrates and no longer exercises an entraining influence over form B. Thereafter, (at Time 3) form C2 comes into being, a form which accommodates forms A and B in a more adequate and comprehensive fashion than form C1.

In later discussion I have more to say on interpretative uses of the above diagram, particularly in relation to psychotherapy. For the moment, though, I return to consider two other features of Whyte's thought that are neglected by Rogers: the notion of qualitatively different morphic processes at each hierarchical level, and of different modalities of consciousness being associated with these individual levels.

(2) Qualitatively different patterns of process at each hierarchical level

In expounding his 'world view,' Whyte points up that while overall there is a common abstract form expressive of the workings of the formative tendency, at individual levels the concrete character and modality of its expression is different. In this regard, Whyte speaks of a 'hierarchy of morphic . . . [or] formative processes,' and of the importance of trying '*to discover the hierarchy of morphic rules relating all levels in all relevant processes*' (1974, pp. 78, 52). Such a depiction accords with Polanyi (1965) who refers to 'each level having its own structural and organismic principles' or 'organising field' (p. 218), and with Sheldrake (1988) who speaks of 'morphogenic' or 'morphic fields' that 'contain other morphic fields within them in a nested hierarchy or holarchy' (p. 317). Interestingly, both Polanyi and Sheldrake base their conception of such formative fields or principles on the ideas of C. H. Waddington, the evolutionary theorist who coined the term 'chreod' meaning 'necessary path' to characterise the formative influence of such fields or principles (see Waddington, 1977, pp. 106ff). Waddington envisaged the influence of chreods or canalised pathways as akin to grooves or valleys on snow-covered mountain slopes. The path of development is thus like the path in the snow a skier is constrained to follow in skiing down a mountain. When more and more skiers follow a particular path its groove becomes deeper and more strongly influences later skiers to follow that path.

As with Waddington, the morphic rules or organising fields that are of special interest to Whyte are those governing living processes and organisms. In this instance, Whyte's formulations closely accord with the views of Langer and Whitehead, particularly where he identifies the pattern of pulsation, of 'down and up motions' (1974, p. 78), as the pattern intrinsic to morphic processes at this level. In a living organism, declares Whyte, 'pulsations underlie every function,' leading to 'endless cycles at each level' (p. 79).

In my view, therefore, it is highly significant that it is just such an interpretation that Langer presents in her magnum opus, *Mind: An Essay on Human Feeling* (1967, 1972 and 1982). For in this work she gives a detailed exposition of the evolution of life and mind explained on the basis of the cyclical repetition of pulsatory activity — of 'acts', as she calls them. By seeing 'acts' as special kinds of 'events', Langer thus builds upon the views of her mentor Whitehead, who in his 'process philosophy' or 'philosophy of organism' takes 'events', units of patterned activity of a 'vibratory' or 'throbbing' nature, to be fundamental to a process conception of reality. For Whitehead, therefore, 'the reality is the process,' and 'the event is the unit of things real,' such that we best think of ourselves 'as process immersed in process beyond ourselves' (1925/1967, pp. 72, 152; 1938/1968, p. 8). Linking with what has just been said about morphic fields, that which Whitehead refers to as 'process beyond ourselves' may be equated with such fields.

Whitehead's notions, in particular, are extremely abstract and not easy to grasp, so allow me to elaborate upon them further. To maintain, as Whitehead does, that 'the reality is the process' is to assert a position radically at odds with the Cartesian-Newtonian view that the world is ultimately made up of two kinds of irreducible and unchanging stuffs or substances, namely matter and mind. Factors that led Whitehead and other process theorists to turn away from the Cartesian-Newtonian towards a process paradigm include:

(i) The impossibility of satisfactorily resolving the notorious 'mind-body problem' in Cartesian-Newtonian terms. If, as in this paradigm, one defines the person as made up of matter and mind, one can only achieve a unitary conception of the person in terms of (a) matter, the approach of materialism; or (b) mind, the approach of idealism; or (c) a more abstract concept than that of substance in terms of which mind and matter and their interrelation can be conceived. In this last case, though, by ceasing to treat the substances of matter and mind as fundamental, one is in effect abandoning the bedrock notions of the Cartesian-Newtonian paradigm, and thereby the paradigm itself. When Whitehead and others take the concept of process as primary and seek to construe both matter and mind in terms of this concept, it is such a course of action that is being pursued.

(ii) Thanks to Darwin, the notion that unchanging matter is the essential constituent of all aspects of reality has received a body blow in that if matter had indeed been unchanging, the evolution of all things from matter, ourselves included, could not have occurred. In addition, thanks to Einstein and other modern physicists, we now know that a more precise and fundamental way of conceiving the physical realm is in terms of patterned activity, process, set within a field of such activity, as waves are set in the sea — each individual 'wave' being what Whitehead terms an 'event'. So construed, what we take to be physically unchanging is a relative affair since 'enduring things are the outcome of a temporal process' (Whitehead, 1925/1967, p. 108). On the one hand, the repetition of the same pattern in event after event will, like the same picture on successive frames of a movie film, be apprehended as an unchanging form; on the other, if our experiencing of change were to be spread over a far greater time scale, what we presently take as unchanging, the form of a huge mountain, for instance, could be seen to exhibit a pattern of movement — akin say, to the way in which the filming of the budding and growth of a plant carried out by slow-action cameras produces a film in which the process is so speeded up that we are able to perceive the pattern of change.

The insight that the developments in modern physics imply a paradigmatic re-visioning of our perspective on reality; the notion that biological organisms are more complex wholes of patterned activity that have evolved from simple wholes of patterned activity such as atoms — such developments as these led to the generalising of the process view to all aspects of reality, in particular to our understanding of the human being. We, too, like other enduring 'things', are complex wholes of patterned activity, 'organisms' like the atom and plant; each one of us 'like nature . . . a system of processes' (Whyte, 1974,) governed by the general evolutionary principle of 'the evolution of complex organisms from antecedent states of less complex organisms' (Whitehead, 1925/1967, p. 107). Such is the basis on which a process paradigm seeks to comprehend the person in a unitary fashion, to construe as a single system of processes the various aspects of the person that our ordinary language-laden sense-making finds it hard to interrelate, viz., our 'physical', 'psychological', and 'spiritual' being. Whether one is focusing upon the molecules in our bodies, the ideas in our minds, or our mystical visions, the process paradigm aims to interpret such features as expressions of particular patterns of activity — the trick being to determine the pattern behind the common sense appearance.

For his part, Rogers can be said to be very much in tune with such a process perspective. Not only did Rogers conceive 'nature as process' (1963, p. 19), but he endorsed the view, relates Harry Van Belle, that the person be described 'first of all as a tendency, a process, an activity or functioning rather than an entity which then does this *actualising*,' since to see the person as an actualising entity 'would imply that he [*sic*] could be described as (also) being something *other than* this activity, as a substance that is itself to itself, regardless of how it functions' (Van Belle, 1980, p. 71). Further, in formulating the concept of the formative tendency beyond that of the actualising tendency, Rogers would seem to have advanced beyond conceiving physical nature and 'life' alone in process terms and to have moved towards conceiving all aspects of reality in such a manner, i.e. to have adopted the position of Whitehead. A proviso here, however, is that in Whitehead (unlike Rogers but in accord with Whyte) there is an explicit link between the view of reality as process and its having a hierarchical structure. Intrinsic to Whitehead's process thought is the view that reality is made up of different levels of pulsating activity of comparative complexity, such pulsations being rhythmically joined together and interrelated. Reality, that is to say, is to be thought of as made up of 'gradations of rhythms' wherein 'the more perfect rhythm is built upon component rhythms' and where 'every great rhythm presupposes lesser rhythms without which it could not be' (Whitehead, quoted in Emmet, 1966, p. 229).

(3) Qualitatively different modalities of consciousness associated with different hierarchical levels

Mention of hierarchically gradated rhythms brings us to the third facet of Whyte's thought overlooked by Rogers: the place of consciousness and human awareness in such a multi-level scheme. It is Whyte's (1974) contention that psychology awaits 'the formulation of a theory of the characteristics of subjective experience, of the qualities of human awareness' and that such a lack can be remedied 'by treating the hierarchy of morphic processes as primary' (p. 67). By adopting such an approach, says Whyte, 'each type of awareness can be determined by the character of a changing pattern, as in music for example' (p. 67). In other words, just as differing patterns of pulsating activity of a guitar string give rise to different musical notes, so differing patterns of pulsating organismic activity give rise to different modalities of consciousness.

To conceptualise consciousness in this fashion is to do so in a way that is very similar to Langer and Whitehead — both of whom deploy the term 'feeling' as a generic term for all aspects of consciousness, i.e. 'all mental experience — sensation, emotion, imagination, recollection, and reasoning, to mention only the main categories' (Langer, 1962, p. 18). In Whitehead's words, consciousness both 'flickers' and is 'the way of feeling . . . [a] particular nexus', or interconnection of events (1929/1969, pp. 312, 305). Whereas, for Langer, consciousness is said to arise when 'an organism feels something, i.e. something is felt' when 'some activities (especially nervous ones) above a certain limen of intensity, enter into a 'psychical phase' (1967, pp. 21, 22). 'What is felt,' Langer posits, 'is a process, perhaps a large complex of processes, within the organism' (p. 21). Thereby, the evolution of consciousness is to be interpreted as the evolution of feeling as a function of the evolutionary development of more and more complex patterns of process. Given, though, that the universe so evolved constitutes a hierarchy of morphic processes, it is fitting to refer, as Whitehead does, to 'a hierarchy of categories of feeling' (1929/1969, p. 192); or to speak, as Whyte himself, of 'a hierarchy of mental processes' (1974, p. 106).

Langer herself in her magnum opus *Mind: An Essay on Human Feeling, Vols. 1, 2 and 3* provides a detailed exposition of the evolutionary development of non-organic, organic and cultural events (i.e. units of process) that has resulted in the emergence of the human organism. In tandem with this exposition she provides a masterful account of the development of consciousness, particularly in its realisation in animals and early humans. Overall Langer is concerned to depict such development as a differentiation from modes of awareness of a vague, global and emotively charged character to those that are highly differentiated and specific and less emotively charged. In so doing she links her theorising with that of Ernst Cassirer, in particular his account of mythic consciousness, that mode of human awareness that preceded that of modern reasoning.

The conception of human awareness of Langer, Whitehead and Whyte is not necessarily at odds with the views of Rogers or person-centred thought in general. Rogers himself, for instance, drew upon the image of a fountain to represent the character of human awareness in the context of evolution. In so doing he depicted it as both a feature of the processes that comprise the human organism, and most particularly of those processes operative at the highest organismic level at any moment in time. As he put it,

> the ability to focus attention seems to be one of the latest evolutionary developments in our species. This ability can be described as a tiny peak of awareness, of symbolising capacity, topping a vast pyramid of nonconscious organismic functioning. Perhaps a better analogy, more indicative of the continual change going on, is to think of the pyramid as a large fountain of the same shape. The very tip of the fountain is intermittently illuminated with the flickering light of consciousness, but the constant flow of life goes on in the darkness as well, in nonconscious as well as conscious ways. (Rogers, 1980, p. 127)

Related, too, is Rogers' early depiction of the workings of the actualising/formative tendency 'in the direction of greater differentiation of organs and of function' (Rogers, 1951, p. 488). But in lacking a more specific account of the nature of such development, Rogers' presents an essentially two-level or dualistic model as he focuses on the psychotherapeutic transition from 'gut level' experiencing, or an 'unverbalised visceral flow', to symbolised or verbalised, accurately labelled awareness (Rogers, 1980, p. 158). In this respect, Rogers' theorising is very much linked with that of Eugene Gendlin and Gendlin's portrayal of psychotherapy involving an implicit 'bodily felt sense' being symbolised or 'carried forward' from the 'edge of awareness' to explicit awareness (Gendlin, 1996).

As we have seen, though, Rogers does envisage a further level in the development of consciousness in characterising 'a transcendent awareness of the harmony and unity of the cosmic system, including humankind' (Rogers, 1980, p. 133). But whether such awareness is indeed a further development from ordinary language-laden consciousness is a moot point.

Overall, then, the hierarchical conception of human consciousness developed from Whyte, Langer and Whitehead is at odds with Rogers' views in (a) characterising two or more levels/modalities of consciousness prior to the development of our everyday awareness; (b) identifying an analogous relationship between these levels and our evolutionary past — the premise being that of Polanyi: that 'we can see at a glance all the levels of evolution at a glance in the human being' (1966, p. 36).

Rogers might better have followed Whyte more closely in his use of the metaphor of the fountain, for it seems he borrowed this image from an earlier work of Whyte, *The Next Development in Man* (1948). In this work Whyte does more than make a comparison with a single fountain. Rather he states than 'an organic system is like a fountain balanced upon a pyramid of fountains' (Whyte, 1948, p. 49). Instead of the tip of just one fountain being 'intermittently illuminated', what is envisaged is the illumination of the tips of these other fountains also. These, too, can generate focal awareness.

INTERPRETATIONS

What I have presented so far has been of a quite abstract nature. To support my overall thesis that the formative tendency can serve as the conceptual linchpin for a paradigm of psychology, I round off by focusing on more concrete issues. First, on how the preceding characterisation of the formative tendency might be deployed to integrate the major non-humanistic approaches within psychology. Second, on how light can be shed on that mental phenomenon of crucial interest to advocates of the person-centred approach, the phenomenon of psychotherapeutic change. Summarising the premises on which such interpretations will be based, these are:

   (i) that the human being is a complex whole made up of increasingly complex levels of functional activity/process, an 'organism' that is part of the 'supra-organism' of the universe as a whole;

   (ii) that the hierarchical scheme depicted above represents the logical relationship which exists between the different levels in the human being;

   (iii) that the increasing complexity of the levels of functional activity intrinsic to the human being is itself a function of an evolutionary history in which higher level 'morphic' fields and their inherent organisational principles have successively 'jump[ed] into being' (Sheldrake, 1988, p. 173). Each person is thus a living epitaph of this evolutionary process insofar as 'we can see all the levels of evolution at a glance in the human being';

   (iv) that consciousness arises as a function of the intensity of activity at the various levels, with human consciousness arising in relation to the upper levels;

   (v) that the development of consciousness involves differentiation from a global, vague and emotively charged form to a more specifically delineated and less emotively charged form;

   (vi) that where the various theoretical approaches within psychology differ is in terms of their primary interest lying with different levels of the functional activity constitutive of the human being.

1. Integration of theoretical approaches

(i) The neuro-biological approach

In terms of the above premises, the neuro-biological approach is construed as principally concerned to study those processes intrinsic to the human being that are of an early evolutionary pedigree, those exhibited by the brain and nervous system especially. Processes are fundamental and anatomical structure comes into being as a kind of 'sedimentation' of past processes, thereby assuming an organisational form that accommodates and consolidates the ongoing multi-level activity characteristic of the respective morphic fields. In Whyte's words, 'the presence of structure furthers the repetition of the process by which it was formed' with the result that 'every structure provides evidence of the form of the process by which it was formed' (1948, p. 33). Such a conception fits with that of Paul MacLean (1973) who identifies a three-level 'phylogenetic hierarchy' to the 'anatomical organisation and chemistry' of the human brain. It accords, too, with Sheldrake's assertion that

> the morphic fields that organise behaviour are not confined to the brain, or even to the body, but extend beyond it into the environment, linking body to the surroundings in which it acts. They co-ordinate sensation and action, bridge the sensory and motor regions of the brain, and co-ordinate a nested hierarchy of morphic fields, right down to those that organise the activity of particular nerve and muscle cells. (1988, p. 198)

One may also see a link here with Eugene Gendlin's conception of 'the body', 'a term Gendlin uses comprehensively to mean the total brain-mind environment as we sense it' (Ferguson, 1980, p. ix).

(ii) The behaviourist approach

In employing the present hierarchical scheme as an interpretative frame for the contributions of behaviourists, what needs to be borne in mind, in my view, is how many of these contributions are based on research with non-human animals. Langer's account of animal mentality, of animal behaviour being governed by immediate feeling, thus springs to mind as an extremely fruitful way of interpreting behaviourist contributions in hierarchical process terms. Here one relevant connection vis-à-vis person-centred theory is Langer's characterisation of 'subception' (discrimination without awareness in humans) as a subsidiary form of a mode of awareness that in animals is focal in nature (Langer, 1972, p. 116). The relevance of this connection lies in Rogers' (1959) use of the notion of subception to provide a theoretical explanation of individuals finding situations anxiety-arousing, without knowing what it is that is making them anxious.

(iii) The cognitive-developmental approach

Apropos the cognitive-developmental approach in psychology, an immediate affinity of thought can be discerned between the present hierarchical scheme of things and the theorising of Jean Piaget — certainly with respect to the logic intrinsic to Piaget's developmental scheme of higher-level cognitive operations being built upon and emerging from lower-level ones. And where the cognitive operations of scientific thought are concerned, the highest level on Piaget's cognitive hierarchy, the ability of the human mind to intuit a common pattern to the world of events and particular number schemes can be interpreted in relation to the hierarchical logic of the formative tendency, a logic capable of being represented by, for instance, the ordinal number series, of first, second, third, etc.

(iv) The cognitive-behavioural approach

I have already mentioned above how behaviourist explanations might be supplanted by interpretations based on Langer's account of animal mentality. Insofar as behaviourist thought has been combined with information-processing models to form cognitive-behaviourism, it is noteworthy that such an amalgamation has led to the development of a number of hierarchical models of human mental functioning (see Williams, Watts, McLeod and Mathews, 1997). There would thus seem to be scope for interpreting such models in terms of the present hierarchical model based on the formative tendency.

(v) The psychoanalytic approach

With respect to the interpretation of psychoanalytic thought in hierarchical process terms, significant inroads can be made, in my view, on the basis of the following interconnections. For a start, the notion of a developmental hierarchy is intrinsic to Freud's theorising and that of many of his followers. In particular, the emphasis on developmental process by object relations theorists — W. R. Fairbairn, for instance, was much influenced by Whitehead — could see a reinterpretation in terms of the nature and logic of the formative tendency and a building up of a person-centred theory of personal development. And then, as far as Freud's key concept of the unconscious is concerned, reinterpretation of this notion can be achieved, as I see it, on the basis of Langer's explication of a mode of human consciousness, non-discursive awareness, having emerged subsequent to animal mentality and prior to rational, discursive awareness. Langer's account of non-discursive awareness is based on Cassirer's portrayal of mythic consciousness, where both she and others have seen an equivalence between Casssirer's depiction and Freud's characterisation of those 'primary processes' that represent the defining characteristics of the psychoanalytic unconscious (see Langer, 1949). As Alfred Lorenzer comments: 'It is remarkable that Cassirer arrives at a description of mythic thought that corresponds exactly to Freud's presentation of 'processes affected by a primary process' (quoted in Krois, 1987, pp. 83–4).

(vi) The transpersonal approach

On the matter of employing the present conception of the nature and logic of the formative tendency to scientifically make sense of the contributions of transpersonal psychology and the realm of the 'spiritual', it is perhaps worth reiterating that logic deals with any and every realm of human experience. 'Spiritual' reality is in consequence just as substantial from such a point of view as 'material' reality. When, therefore, Langer draws attention to our calling 'a certain series of successively 'higher' spiritual experiences 'the ladder of faith' (1953, pp. 28–9), she can be seen to be alluding to a scheme expressive of the hierarchical logic of the formative tendency. It is in the writings of Ken Wilber, though, the main proponent of transpersonal psychology, that we find the most detailed and substantive endorsement of the relevance of such a hierarchical scheme for interpreting the domain of the mystical and spiritual (see in particular Wilber, 1995, chap. 2).

2. The phenomenon of psychotherapeutic change

Earlier I employed figure 3 to represent that feature of the workings of the formative tendency dubbed 'positive disintegration' by Dabrowski and 'regress to progress' by Koestler, the 'pattern of *reculer pour mieux sauter*, of a temporary regression followed by a forward leap' (Koestler, 1980, p. 439). Koestler sees this pattern as intrinsic not only to mental evolution in general, but to psychotherapeutic change in particular. 'Psychotherapy, ancient and modern,' he declares,

> from shamanism down to contemporary forms of analytical or abreaction techniques, has always relied on that variety of undoing-redoing procedure which Ernst Kris, an eminent practitioner, has called 'regression in the service of the ego'. The neurotic, with his compulsions, phobias, and elaborate defence-mechanisms, is a victim of rigid, maladaptive specialisation — a koala bear hanging on for dear life to a barren telegraph pole. The therapist's aim is to induce temporary regression in the patient; to make him retrace his steps to the point where they went wrong, and to come up again, metamorphosed, reborn. (pp. 438–9)

The person-centred therapist's aim is simply to create a psychological climate facilitative of client psychotherapeutic change, and so person-centred practitioners would dispute Koestler's claim that the therapist's conscious intent is to *make* the client regress. But such a point aside, how valid is it from a person-centred point of view to interpret the pattern of psychotherapeutic change so facilitated as 'regress to progress', i.e. in terms of figure 3?

Certainly Godfrey Barrett-Lennard (1980) believes that such a 'regressive' interpretation of the nature of psychotherapeutic change is not in accord with person-centred theory. 'Intensive, personal therapy,' asserts Barrett-Lennard,

> in keeping with other potently formative experiences, has some of the elements and qualities of birthing. In the case of client-centred therapy, this does not imply regression to redo an earlier stage of development but does connote emergent shifts in awareness and ways of processing experience, broadly in the direction of a more self-transcending way of being. (p. 118)

According to Barrett-Lennard, therefore, the person-centred theoretical interpretation of psychotherapeutic change is that of a straightforward gestalt switch, as depicted by figure 3 of an instantaneous shift from C1f to C2f.

At first sight, Barrett-Lennard's position would also seem to be that of Rogers himself, who in his 1959 theory statement identifies the positive transformation of the 'gestalt' of the person's self-concept as the core feature of psychotherapeutic change. Defining the self-concept as 'a gestalt which is available to awareness', Rogers compares the change from old to new self-concept to 'the favorite text book illustration' of a gestalt switch, that involving 'the double picture of the old hag and the young woman' (1959, pp. 203, 201). In other words, psychotherapeutic change consists in an instantaneous pattern shift.

But that this is not the whole picture is made plain in a more detailed account of such a gestalt switch given by Rogers in *Client-Centered Therapy* (1951). There Rogers relates that when in client-centred therapy the client experiences an

> atmosphere of safety, protection, and acceptance, the firm boundaries of self-organisation relax. There is no longer the firm, tight gestalt which is characteristic of every organisation under threat, but a looser, more uncertain configuration. (1951, p. 193)

Under the auspices of this looser, 'sufficiently relaxed' self-configuration the client 'discovers experiences of which he has never been aware, which are deeply contradictory to the perception he has had of himself, and this is threatening indeed' (p. 193). The person, says Rogers, may retreat 'temporarily to the former comfortable gestalt, but then cautiously moves out to assimilate this contradictory experience into a new and revised pattern . . . It involves more accurate symbolisation of a much wider range of sensory and visceral experiences' (p. 193).

'Essentially,' Rogers declares, 'this is a process of disorganisation and reorganisation' (p. 193). Which said, might it not be more accurate to term it a process of organisation, disorganisation and reorganisation. That is, of regress to progress as depicted by figure 3?

Is, then, the pattern of psychotherapeutic change in the client one of a straightforward gestalt switch from less to more comprehensive, or is there an intervening stage of regression?

Logic would appear to dictate that there is at least some form of disorganisation or loosening of an existing pattern (gestalt) in order for new more primitive components to be incorporated into a more comprehensive pattern. Perhaps whether we designate the disorganisational phase a regression or not may depend on how extensive is the disintegration or loosening of the existing higher-level form. So, for instance, John Perry, claims that psychosis can represent a condition of regression prior to progression to greater personal integration. In line with person-centred theory, Perry relates how the provision of a psychotherapeutic environment can transform an early intense psychotic episode into 'a disintegrative phase of what may be regarded as a developmental process' (Perry, 1999, p. 3).

Further light is shed on this issue, in my view, by Erich Fromm (1982) in his account of the nature of 'regression' in the context of psychoanalytic psychotherapy. 'If the analysand during the analytic hour becomes a child altogether,' declares Fromm, 'he [*sic*] might as well be dreaming' (1982, p. 43). According to Fromm, regression in therapy is not that of the client's total self, but of a part of it. The person doesn't literally become a child again, but exhibits an 'oscillating' awareness of their adult self on the one hand, while focusing upon infantile self-experiencing on the other, i.e. upon self-experiencing of an evolutionary earlier and less complex nature.

Seen in this light, figure 3 could be taken as specifically referring to a particular part of the self that has to be dismantled into its lower-level constituents in order that a more comprehensive higher-level integration can be achieved. A metaphor for the psychotherapeutic process might thus be that of building a brick house and then realising that not only are there some bricks left over, but that instead of a porch at the front of the house there is simply a brick wall. In other words, bricks earmarked on the house-plan for constructing a porch had either been unused or used to fill in the hole in the wall intended as the entranceway inside the porch. To remedy this state of affairs, the part of the wall filling in the hole would first have to be dismantled into its constituent bricks. These bricks could then be combined with those left over in order to create the more comprehensive gestalt of the porch and entranceway. In other words, just a part of the house would have to be dismantled.

Such a conception of psychotherapeutic change as involving the essential retention of the higher level pattern of the self, while bringing into focus lower-level elements that either do not fit or have yet to be employed, accords with both the views of Rogers and Gendlin. Both refer to psychotherapeutic change as the focusing upon and incorporation into the self of 'gut-level', 'unverbalised visceral' 'experiencing', at 'the edge' of awareness (Rogers, 1980, p. 158; Gendlin, 1996, p. 17).

It is in the light of this notion of incorporating such lower-level process into a person's self-gestalt that Dave Mearns and Brian Thorne (2000) propose reconfiguring 'Rogers' concept of Self' to include 'subceived' . . . 'edge of awareness' material' (p. 175). Such a proposal merits consideration, but does seem reminiscent of Rogers' essential two-level theorising. If it is indeed intended to mean defining the self in terms of merely two levels of organismic activity, this would differ from the present hierarchical scheme which points to the definition of self on a more-than-two, multi-level basis.

CONCLUDING REMARKS

There are advocates of the person-centred approach who consider Rogers' formulation of the formative tendency to be a step away from science, a product of his 'loopy' later years, a symptom of the 'Californication of Carl Rogers'. Mearns and Thorne (2000), for instance, 'suggest that Rogers' development of theory was not advanced during his 'California' period' (p. 89). I would like to think, though, that the preceding discussion might prompt those who hold such views to think again. Indeed, that it might encourage all who have an interest in the further development of person-centred theory to take Rogers' concept of the formative tendency extremely seriously — notwithstanding that he conceived it while 'taking it easy' in California. My hope is that the formative tendency will eventually be judged to have been a very fruitful notion, not only for the scientific development of psychology as a whole, but, in particular, for our scientific understanding of psychotherapy. Perhaps today, 'we have to ask ourselves whether nature does not contain within itself a tendency to be in tune, an Eros urging toward perfection' (Whitehead, 1933/67, p. 251). Perhaps tomorrow, the existence of such an 'erotic' tendency will be blindingly obvious — as it was, it seems, for Carl Rogers; and, on one occasion, for me (see Ellingham, 1984).

REFERENCES

Barrett-Lennard, G. T. (1998). *Carl Rogers' Helping System.* London: Sage.

Capra, F. (1982). *The Turning Point.* New York: Simon and Schuster.

Capra, F. (1996). *The Web of Life.* New York: Harper Collins.

Dabrowski, K. (1964). *Positive Disintegration.* London: Little, Brown.

Ellingham, I. H. (1984) Towards a science of mind: Schizophrenia, mysticism, artistic creativity, scientific discovery, psychedelic experience and extrasensory perception as functions of a symbo-organismic scheme of human mental functioning. *Ann Arbor: University Microfilms International, No. DE084-09767.*

Ellingham, I. H. (2001). Carl Rogers' 'congruence' as an organismic not a Freudian concept. In G. Wyatt (Ed.) *Congruence.* Ross-on-Wye: PCCS Books.

Emmett, M. (1966). *Whitehead's Philosophy of Organism* (2nd ed.), New York: St. Martin's Press.

Ferguson, M. (1980). Introduction. In E. T. Gendlin, *Focusing.* New York: Bantam Press.

Fromm, E. (1980). *Greatness and Limitations of Freud's Thought.* London: Abacus.

Gendlin, E. T. (1996). *Focusing-oriented Psychotherapy.* New York: Guilford Press.

Koestler, A. (1980). *Bricks to Babel.* London: Pan Books.

Krois, J. M. (1987). *Cassirer: Symbolic Forms and History.* New Haven: Yale University Press.

Langer, S. K. (1949). On Cassirer's theory of language and myth. In P. Schilpp (Ed.) *The Philosophy of Ernst Cassirer*. La Salle: Open Court.

Langer, S. K. (1953a). *An Introduction to Symbolic Logic* (2nd ed.). New York: Dover Press.

Langer, S. K. (1953b). *Feeling and Form*. New York: Scribners.

Langer, S. K. (1962). *Philosophical Sketches*. Baltimore: Johns Hopkins University Press.

Langer, S. K. (1967, 1972, 1982). *Mind: An essay on human feeling, Vols. 1, 2 and 3*. Baltimore: Johns Hopkins University Press.

Lyotard, J-F. (1984). *The Postmodern Condition*. Manchester: Manchester University Press.

MacLean, P. D. (1973). *A Triune Concept of the Brain and Behavior*. Toronto: University of Toronto Press.

Mays, W. (1959). *The Philosophy of Whitehead*. London: George Allen and Unwin.

Mearns, D. and Thorne, B. (2000). *Person-centred Therapy Today*. London: Sage.

O'Hara, M. (1999). Moments of eternity. In I. Fairhurst (Ed.) *Women Writing in the Person-Centred Approach*. Ross-on-Wye: PCCS Books.

Perry, J. W. (1999). *Trials of the Visionary Mind: Spiritual emergency and the renewal process*. Albany: State University of New York Press.

Polanyi, M. (1964). *Personal Knowledge*. Chicago: University of Chicago Press.

Polanyi, M. (1965). The structure of consciousness. In M. Grene (Ed.) *Knowing and Being*. Chicago: University of Chicago Press, 1969.

Polanyi, M. (1966). *The Tacit Dimension*. Garden City: Doubleday.

Polanyi, M. (1968). The body-mind relation. In W. R. Coulson and C. R. Rogers (Eds.) *Man and the Science of Man*. Columbus, Ohio: Merrill.

Rogers, C. R. (1951). *Client-centered Therapy*. Boston: Houghton Mifflin.

Rogers, C. R. (1959). A theory of therapy, personality and interpersonal relationships, as developed in the client-centered framework. In S. Koch (Ed.) *A Study of a Science: Vol. 3. Formulations of the person and the social context*. New York: McGraw-Hill.

Rogers, C. R. (1963). The actualising tendency in relation to 'motives' and to consciousness. In M. R. Jones (Ed.) *Nebraska Symposium on Motivation, Vol. 11*. Lincoln: University of Nebraska Press.

Rogers, C. R. (1978). The formative tendency. *J. Humanistic Psychology, 18*(1): 23–26.

Rogers, C. R. (1980). *A Way of Being*. Boston: Houghton Mifflin.

Seeman, J. (2001). On congruence: A human system paradigm. In G. Wyatt (Ed.) *Congruence*. Ross-on-Wye: PCCS Books.

Sheldrake, R. (1988). *The Presence of the Past*. London: Fontana.

Van Belle, H. (1980). *Basic Intent and Therapeutic Approach of Carl R. Rogers*. Toronto: Wedge Publishing Foundation.

Wilber, K. (1995). *Sex, Ecology, Spirituality: The spirit of evolution*. Boston: Shambhala.

Waddington, C. H. (1977). *Tools for Thought*. London: Jonathan Cape.

Whitehead, A. N. (1967). *Science and the Modern World*. New York: Free Press. (Original work published 1925)

Whitehead, A. N. (1967). *Adventures of Ideas*. New York: Free Press. (Original work published 1933)

Whitehead, A. N. (1968). *Modes of Thought*. New York: Free Press (Original work published 1938)

Whitehead, A. N. (1969). *Process and Reality*. New York: Free Press. (Original work published 1929)

Whyte, L. L. (1948). *The Next Development in Man*. New York: Henry Holt.

Whyte, L. L. (1974). *The Universe of Experience*. New York: Harper and Row.

Williams, J. M. G., Watts, F. N., MacLeod, C. and Mathews, A. (1997). *Cognitive Psychology and Emotional Disorders*. Chichester: Wiley.

Peter F. Schmid

University of Graz and Institute for Person-Centered Studies, Vienna, Austria

'The Necessary and Sufficient Conditions of Being Person-Centered': On identity, integrity, integration and differentiation of the paradigm

Abstract. A wide variety of persons, associations and methods call themselves person- or client-centered. Is it possible to define what it really means to be person-centered? Or is it a ('postmodern') question of what you like and what you believe? Where are the limits? Is it possible to indicate a core? And if so, what is it? Is everybody person-centered who claims to be or is the title only appropriate to those who repeat what Carl Rogers already said? Is the experiential approach developing the paradigm or is it an aberration? Is it possible to combine orientations, to integrate methods and add techniques? Is there actually a 'Beyond Carl Rogers'? Or is an exegesis of his 'holy scriptures' what it is all about? What are the prospects of the development and influence of what once was regarded a radical paradigm? And, last but not least: Is a person-centered world association endangering the integrity and genuineness of the approach? A clear stance is argued that it is indeed possible to name the necessary and sufficient conditions of being person-centered. The subject is discussed from an anthropological, epistemological, technical and political perspective. Furthermore, naming the 'core conditions' of a person-centered point of view has tremendous practical consequences. And the question of being person-centered ultimately turns out to be an ethical one.

A variety of persons, institutes, associations and methods or even techniques call and consider themselves to be person-centered. Thus the question arises: Is it possible to define what person-centered really means? Or is it a question of personal belief and of what you like? Are there any limits? Is it possible to name central and crucial points? And if so, what are they?

Is everybody person-centered who claims to be? Or is the title appropriate only to those who repeat what Carl Rogers already voiced? Are the various directions which evolved, e.g. focusing or experiential psychotherapy, a development of the approach or a deviation? Are they suborientations of a general paradigm or are they betraying the original intention and indicating a radical paradigm shift? Can one combine orientations, integrate methods and add techniques? Is there something like a 'Beyond Carl Rogers?' Or is an exegesis of his 'holy scriptures' what it is all about?

Is it inadmissible orthodoxy or even fundamentalism to look for the 'core conditions of the approach'? Or even worse: Is raising the question evidence enough to prove one's rigidity? Does one have to reckon with being accused of offending the principles of openness, individuality, democracy, development, etc. if such questions are raised? And on the other hand: Is it pure eclecticism and a lack of a clear point of view, violating the integrity of the therapeutic relationship offered and incompatible with the image of the human being to integrate ideas and methods from other schools? Isn't it even necessary for example, to supplement systemic ideas in order to keep the approach up to date?

These and many more questions are often raised and heavily discussed. Some of the so-called 'Carl sayers' (people who were on familiar terms with Rogers) are accused of playing the role of moral guards, others are blamed for destroying the original power of the approach in order to increase their reputation or income or recognition by health insurance companies or even worse: the zeitgeist.

Some of these questions also came up in the course of the building of the World Association: How broad should it be? Who should be invited for membership? Is such an association endangering the integrity and genuineness of the approach? Is the idea of an association person-centered at all? Is it finally the grave for the paradigm because it would mix up too many different approaches? Will it serve as a means to those who want to use the name 'person-centered' in order to promote their own ideas? Or will it be a necessary way to give more public relations and public interest to a paradigm, which no longer is as strong and influential as it used to be?

I am aware that it is of high risk to deal with these issues and that it is not very likely that I will make a lot of friends by doing so. But I am convinced that it may be worse to avoid a clear discussion and to ignore the essentials.

Thus I will try, from my personal point of view, to name some ideas relating to these questions. I will do so not from a pragmatic or a superficial point of view, but from a fundamental point of view. I will show that the foundation of person-centered therapy and of the person-centered approach in general is rooted in ethics[1] and will discuss the consequences of this as far as the possibility and meaningfulness of cooperation in a worldwide person-centered association. I hope this chapter will stimulate exchange and I am looking forward to hearing other opinions on the matter and to enter into dialogue.

I. THE FOUNDATIONS: PSYCHOTHERAPY AS AN ETHICAL DISCIPLINE AND PROFESSION

Obviously Carl Rogers was fully aware of what he was claiming in stating the hypotheses of the 'necessary and sufficient conditions of therapeutic personality change' in 1957. This is the impression the reader gets, when he or she takes a look at the carefully written article in which each word is weighed precisely.

Today almost nobody doubts that these conditions, especially the so called core conditions, are *necessary*. But the whole point — and after half a century still the revolutionary crux of the matter — is the statement that they are *sufficient*. Rogers emphasized this from the very beginning and kept the conviction, which he himself called 'rigorous' (1959) for his whole lifetime (Rogers, Heppner, Rogers and Lee, 1984).

The 'formula', although emphasizing that its assertions are a meta-theory applying to psychotherapy in general and not to client-centered therapy only, is the fundament for everything which may justly call itself person-centered, historically as well as theoretically and systematically. In its nucleus this statement comprises everything which is essential for person-centered theory, at least implicitly.

[1.] Ethics here is understood as the foundation and not as a consequence of anthropology or practice. Ethics must not be misunderstood in a moralistic or casuistic way; it denotes — from a phenomenological and anthropological point of view — the philosophy of the challenge of living in terms of how to live responsibly.

The article also expresses the ideas, which do not fit into the theory. In his provocative statement Carl Rogers (1957) specifies a number of ideas and practices which on the basis of the hypothesis formulated prove not to be necessary for psychotherapy. The 'significant omissions' he notes, for example client typologies. Rogers did not think it necessary to offer different conditions to different groups of clients. Nor did he see psychological diagnosis as a precondition for therapy. He did not see psychotherapy as essentially different from personal relationships in everyday life or therapy training as something especially related to intellectual qualities instead of experience.

Many implications of this theory were only later elaborated by Rogers and others. And as a parallel to explicating more and more precisely the anthropological foundations (e.g. Schmid, 1991; 1994; 1996) the practice of the theory was also developed further (Farber, Brink and Raskin, 1996).

This is no coincidence. It is conspicuous that in Rogers' basic statement almost nothing is said about the practical therapeutic procedure and the behavior of the therapist. Rogers did not formulate instructions of how to act. Of course, there is the principle of nondirectivity in this claim; of course, there is an underlying image of the human being that includes some and excludes other ways of acting; but on the whole the statement is a set of principles formulated on quite an abstract level. Concrete actions that derive from it and the resulting theory of action are left open.

To give an example: The conditions do not say anything about how communication between therapist and client should take place. Verbal communication is not preferred to other ways of interacting, e.g. with the body or by playing or by artistic means. Later Rogers (1975; 1970) stated that a variety of personal techniques are compatible with the basic attitudes. Thus there is a lot of room for genuine person-centered work. But this does not mean that whatever someone does is person-centered as long as he or she calls it 'person-centered' or as long as he or she is convinced of being person-centered.

Being asked to respond and response-ability: The foundations of person-centered acting establish an ethical position

Rogers elaborated his approach out of his experiences in relationships. His theory is drawn out of phenomenology and is formulated close to experience. Also in later refinements it stays near to experience. What Rogers observed in therapies and from whence he drew his hypotheses were not indifferent data but 'facts' out of experience, out of being touched and moved personally. This means that they imply a distinct value judgment.

The same applies to psychotherapy overall. By doing psychotherapy and by reflecting this theoretically, a decision is made to respond to the misery, to the grief, to the life of another person, to share their joys and sorrows. It derives from being addressed by the other, from being touched, from being asked, being called, from being appealed to, from a demand. This means that the need of the other is there first and that psychotherapy is responding, is answering to a demand.[2] Thus all psychotherapy takes its origin at the Other. It sees him or her as a call and a provocation.

---

[2] In German: Psychotherapeutisches Handeln entsteht aus dem Angesprochen–Werden, und gründet daher in einem An–Spruch.

From an encounter philosophical point of view the other is an Other on principle. This means that he or she is somebody, who is strange to me, who surprises me and whom I have to meet with respect and an attitude of not-knowing. The fellow being is the one to whom I am opposed, face to face, and whom I have to face — neither monopolizing nor rejecting him or her. Since the presence of the Other always 'comes first' and is seen as a call for a response I cannot escape because nobody can respond in my place. We are obliged and responsible to the Other and owe him or her an answer. This causes the Other to become a 'priority'.

What happens in psychotherapy, if it is understood as an encounter relationship, is that the client is opening up and revealing him- or herself. The task of the therapist then is not to try to get knowledge about the client but to acknowledge the person who is showing him- or herself (see below). From this view of relationships in general, psychotherapy in particular, also follows a new — non-individualistic — understanding of self-realization as realization in and out of the relations in which the individual lives. Self-realization is never possible without the realization of the Other. In therapy this applies to both, client and therapist.

The point is: *Especially starting from a phenomenological consideration, as Carl Rogers did — and not out of morals! — psychotherapy must be regarded as an ethical phenomenon.*

Taking a closer look at the core of person-centered theory, as expressed in Rogers' 1957 statement, one finds that the ethical foundation is already included here: Psychotherapy means responding to incongruence, to a vulnerable or anxious person. Even more: If these six conditions are necessary and sufficient for a constructive development of the person by means of psychotherapy, then it is an obligation for the therapist to take them into account (contact, client's incongruence, communication of therapist's attitudes) or to offer them respectively (congruence, unconditional positive regard, empathy).[3]

The therapist is seen as somebody responding to the needs of another person and therefore responsible in the communication. (In German: Der Therapeut ist ein auf die Not Antwortender und daher Ver-Antwort-licher.) In a word: Psychotherapy is ethically founded.

This should not be misunderstood in a moralistic way. Ethics denotes moral philosophy, not casuistry or moralizing. The philosophical basis for this understanding of psychotherapy can among others be found, very well developed, in the thinking of the Lithuanian encounter philosopher Emmanuel Levinas (1905–1995), that I have pointed out and described in detail earlier (Schmid, 1994; 1998a; 1998b; 1998c). Even more radical than Buber, Levinas (1978; 1980; 1983) describes the interconnectedness of the person, because his thinking really begins with the Other. The starting point of his anthropology is the absolute being different, the otherness of the Other: According to Levinas the fundament of self-consciousness is not the reflection (of the I through the Thou) but the experience of relationship, which — think of developmental psychology, e.g., of the child, 'conceived' and born into relations! — always comes first and has its origin in the Other. This marks a shift from the 'I-Thou'-relationship to a 'Thou-I'-relationship (and thus managing to get closer to the verge of the 'We'). The Other is here beforehand. Thus a fellow being is no longer degraded as an alter ego but truly

---

[3.] A closer examination of Rogers' 'necessary and sufficient conditions' from an encounter philosophical (dialogical) and ethical perspective can be found in the English language in the series on Rogers' therapeutic conditions. 'Evolution, theory and practice': Schmid 2001c (authenticity/congruence), 2001d (comprehension/empathy), 2001e (acknowledgment/unconditional positive regard), 2002 (presence/contact and perception).

respected as an other one, an absolute different person, an enigma: 'Encountering a human being means being kept awake by an enigma' states Levinas (1959, 120). For the Other he uses the metaphor of 'visage' which reminds us of the origin of the term person (coming from the Greek 'prosopon' and meaning 'face'). This face addresses us, speaks to us, even demands and challenges us. Thus response-abilty is the basic category of being a person: Out of encounter arises the obligation to respond.

Accordingly, psychotherapy means engaged and solidary service to the fellow person. The suffering person demands this involvement. This corresponds with the duty of response-ability. The commitment towards the Other means a responsibility that originates in the basic dependency of the human being on his fellow beings. Here I want to point to the commitment-concept of Ute and Johannes Binder (1981, 179–274), which deserves more attention and appreciation.

Levinas, professor at the Sorbonne in Paris who lost his whole family in the holocaust, a thinker of tremendous importance who has hardly been discovered by the person-centered approach yet, again and again points out that all of occidental philosophy (and this also applies to psychology as its 'daughter' and psychotherapy as its 'grand-daughter') including its so-called humanistic orientation in the 20th century has remained 'egology'. And, indeed, this fixation on the I is clearly predominant in the terminology of the numerous self-terms in Humanistic Psychology and despite all positioning against an objectification and instrumentalization finally indicates a reduction of the Other, of what the Other means to me. In this connection even a well-known sentence by Martin Buber (1923, 18) like 'I become through the Thou' all of a sudden sounds quite differently: even here, as is to be suspected, everything is still focused on me. This, however, presents the ideals of the humanistic movement as such in a new light. And according to Levinas the following applies: 'What once seemed to be a distinctive human quality, the absolute desire to determine and realize oneself, 'self-determination' and 'self-realization', has proved the reason for violence against the other human being. Not the enforcement of the ego's objectives must become the basis of the 'humanism of the other human being', but the perception of the other. This is an ethical relation.' (Waldschütz, 1993)

In this perspective psychotherapy (and all psychosocial, pedagogical, political, pastoral etc. acting) receives *a socio-ethical dimension* leading from the categories 'response' and 'responsibility' to a new understanding of self-realization which can only become reality in what Levinas called 'diakonia [diakony]' — a term with the same meaning as 'therapy', i.e. 'service'. In the interpersonal encounter, which we call therapy, addressed and asked to respond, we assume a deep responsibility, an obligation in which our fellow man expects us to render the service we owe to each other. By responding we only fulfil our duty. What we owe each other is nothing else but love. Thus, encounter in dialogue turns out to be a condition for self-consciousness, a common transcendence of the (totalitarian) status quo, it is infinity — 'Totalité et infini' is the title of Levinas' major work. Encounter is a start without return: Abraham, who starts his journey to an unknown country without return, and not Ulysses, who at the end returns to his starting point, is, according to Levinas, to be seen as the symbolic character.

While Buber starts to explore the question of what man is by understanding him as the dialogical nature of being-two and thus relatively contained, Levinas pushes on: from the Other to the Others. I and the Other, my fellow human beings, are not an isolated entity;

there is also 'the Third One', who himself is a fellow-man; there are the Others. Therefore how to act is no longer obvious, and among others the question of justice and the necessity of judgement arise. A new understanding of We emerges: not any more the We of the two of us, but rather of the three of us — where two — lovingly — include a third one in their community (as Richard of St. Victor's term 'condilectio' indicates). In such a way instead of duality, the pair, I and Thou, now the tri-unity turns out to be the foundation of interpersonality. Therefore duality does not exclude, but rather includes the Third One, because it is predisposed to transcend itself towards the group.

The person-centered approach implies a number of ethical implications that definitely prepare for getting beyond 'egology'. In doing so ethics cannot be deduced from anthropology but we have to realize that person-centered anthropology has always been ethics first. Traditional ethics orients acting by principles that are deduced from philosophical ideas. However, a philosophy orienting itself by experience, as corresponds to the person-centered approach, realizes ethics as the first philosophy. It does so from the experience in the encounter, which is taken seriously down to the roots. Especially out of the personal experience of encounter — being addressed and thus encouraged by the Other — a legitimate claim to an answer and to acting in the kairos (see below) is derived — and this is what person-centered ethics as dialogical ethics is about.

There is no doubt that the paradigm shift of Levinas and Rogers — an understanding of the human being quite fundamentally focusing on the other's view — is to be seen as a parallel: the principal precedence of the Other corresponds with the *client*-centeredness of psychotherapy.

Above all it requires us to understand psychotherapy from an ethical point of view. Therapy is responding to a suffering human being's cry for help, a response-ability rooted in fundamental ethics.

The human being as a person: from knowledge to acknowledgment in psychotherapy

Rogers' article, published in 1957, implies two essential dimensions of an image of the human being. The first condition already deals with the interpersonal relation — Rogers himself said that he originally wanted to use the term 'relation' instead of 'psychological contact', but was afraid of academic recognition — and the five others define the characteristics of such a relation. All of them include the belief that the human being has the possibility and tendency to develop in a constructive way on the basis of his or her resources, if a certain form of relationship is provided. In other words, the six conditions presuppose that a human being develops constructively on his or her own, if he or she finds him- or herself in a facilitative relationship. Without hypothesizing an actualizing tendency, which rests on both, the individual resources and the ability of relating, the conditions two to six would make no sense.

With that, exactly those two dialectic dimensions of being human are denoted for which in the occidental history of theology and philosophy the term 'person' was coined: Autonomy and interconnectedness (or relationality), independence and interdependence, self-reliance and commitment, sovereignty and solidarity. Whatever other motives might have been important to introduce the term 'person-centered' — it is obvious and clear that this was done consciously and on purpose to denote an anthropology central for the 'person'-centered approach.[4]

Thus the fundamental hypothesis of the actualizing tendency which Rogers consistently indicates to be the only axiom must be seen in the dialectical tension of these two dimensions (Schmid, 1999a; 2001b). Seen from an historical perspective the focal point was on the individual aspect — this can be understood as necessary for historical reasons, especially in rejecting the psychiatric, psychoanalytic and behavioristic model, and quite often led to the reproach of an individualistic approach, as being 'typical US-American'. But the relational dimension was formulated from the very beginning (see the first condition in the 1957 statement about the principle of contact) and it was taken for granted in acting in a non-directive, client-centered way, even if its theoretical conceptualization as encounter and its practical differentiation in multiple forms of acting was elaborated only in later periods of the development of the paradigm.

In his precise description of person-centered psychotherapy, Rogers (1980) explicitly puts these two dimensions at the beginning of his article.

In short: *Person-centered psychotherapy is the practice of an image of the human being which understands the human being as a person and thus encounters him or her personally acknowledging him or her as the Other* (in Rogers' terms: with unconditional positive regard and empathy out of a congruent attitude or: in authentic presence out of a way of being with him or her) *instead of objectifying him or her by trying to know him or her, to get knowledge over him or her.*

The relation person to person as encounter: From diagnosis and abstinence to im-media-te presence

This also means that an essential trust in the experiential world of the client and its centrality for psychotherapy is unrenounceable for a truly *person*-centered approach.

Such an approach quite fundamentally rules out any conception of oneself in the role of the therapist or helper or teacher or social worker or pastoral worker etc. as an expert on the problems or on the person of the partner in counseling, therapy, education, supervision or any other helpful relation whatsoever. Such an approach also rules out an abstinent attitude of the therapist instead of a relationship person to person. And it rules out that the therapist considers himself as an expert in the correct usage of methods and means, and even excludes any preconceived use of methods and techniques, a use which is not rooted in the immediate experience of the relationship. The only 'means' or 'instrument' employed is the person of the therapist him- or herself. And only where an 'any means has fallen apart' encounter takes

---

[4] Only recently I was given a manuscript by Rogers from 1955 (!), in which Rogers already gives a process definition to the question he asked himself 'What is a person?': A 'fluid process, potentiality, a continually changing constellation, configuration, matrix, of feelings, thoughts, sensations, behaviors. The structure of the process seems configurational, not additive. [...] Another way of stating this is that a person is a human process of becoming'; (Rogers, 1955, 1). He goes on — in the following sequence: 'The person as process seems to me most deeply revealed in a relationship of the most ultimate and complete acceptance; a real I–Thou relationship' (ibid. 2) and 'In my experience, the deepest contacts I have with persons reveal them, without exception, to be directional in process, and my experience of that direction is contained in such terms as positive, constructive, creative, toward autonomy, toward maturity, toward socialization, in the direction of growth, toward greater richness or differentiation.' (Ibid.) Already here relationality and individuality can be found as the two characteristics of the person. (More material can be found in Schmid, 1994, 107).

place, as Martin Buber (1923, 19) stated unsurpassably and precisely also grasping the process of such a relationship.

Therefore the person-centered approach differs radically from all other approaches that in the meantime have all more or less found their way to the core conditions. However, these approaches consider Rogers' conditions, attitudes and definitions only as preparatory work meant to establish a certain climate or rapport, as obviously-human preconditions so to speak, upon which the actual therapeutic work still has to be constructed. From a person-centered stance the basic attitudes need no supplementation by specific methods reserved for the expert. 'Expertism', if it has to be described, lies exactly in the ability to resist the temptation of behaving like a traditional expert (even against the client's wishes) — that means, solving problems with the help of techniques rather than facing them as persons.

In Carl Rogers' words: To work as a person-centered therapist is not only 'a way of being', but 'a way of being with' — in German, according to Ludwig Binswanger (1942) e.g., the term 'Miteinandersein' (not only 'Mitsein') is accurate to describe this philosophy of life.

The existential and *im-media-te* ('without means') presence as understood by encounter philosophy, the personal being-with which leads to a togetherness denotes that, in his or her psychophysical presence, the person who offers a person-centered relation opens up to his partner(s) the possibility to concentrate on the fertile instant and thus on oneself and his or her relations. The very instant is called 'kairos' according to the Greek god of 'the favorable opportunity', who had to be seized by his mop of hair in front, when hurrying past because in the back he was close-cropped. In the kairos it is important to take advantage of fallow potential and to seize the opportunity. A person-centered 'way of being with' is applied kairology.

In spite of all inflation the term 'encounter' in general and in the person-centered approach in particular has undergone, it has to be stated that the essential element of encounter consists in the fact that the human being meets a reality which moves him or her deeply, which is counter to him or her. En-counter is not simply an experience, it is an 'experience *counter*' which opposes the affected one. Encounter is an essentially different experience from what an idealistic and subjectivistic understanding of (solely intrinsic) development presupposes. In contrast to an understanding that development or fulfillment is coming completely from itself, encounter means that it is an alien, an Other, another reality, another person, which or who en-counters my reality, which or who encounters me. This makes up the existential dimension and unavoidability of an encounter.

Thus the person-centered relationship is to be regarded as a process providing room, valuing spontaneity and creativity. As to psychotherapy it is a process in which both client(s) and therapist(s) develop towards a personal encounter. Where the person of the therapist or/and of the client exposes himself or herself to the given Other, he or she can enter into a dialogue — even more so, he or she is called to do so.

To sum it up: Ethics out of phenomenology and the anthropology and epistemology (see below) which evolve from it form a unity — a way of encountering the Other.

II. THE CORE: THE NECESSARY AND SUFFICIENT CONDITIONS OF BEING PERSON-CENTERED

On this basis now it is possible to formulate what I consider to be the essential points for being person-centered in psychotherapy (in individual as well as group psychotherapy). One can easily translate this for other professional work.

Ethics

It is unrenounceable that ethics is grounded in the experience of encounter. This means being asked to respond to another person in need, i.e. responding out of response-ability and solidarity — as stated above. This characterizes person-centered acting, psychotherapy included, as a political action, not only a private or individual way of acting.

Anthropology

It is indisputable that the image of the human being underlying the understanding of him or her in psychotherapy is based on the view of men and women as persons, denoting the dialectics of autonomy and interconnectedness — as also stated above. This implies the centrality of the trust in the actualizing tendency as *the* motivational force which constructively can 'work' in facilitative relationships. And it implies that the necessary and sufficient conditions for such relationships in psychotherapy described by Carl Rogers are crucial for this endeavor and that they are in no way to be understood as techniques or methods but as a way of being with the client by the *person* of the therapist — a way of being which can truly be called an encounter person to person. (Unless one takes the original Greek notion of the term 'method' ['meta hodos'], which incidentally means: 'to be on the way with somebody, to follow somebody', or the original meaning of 'technique' ['techne' which means 'art']). In his or her presence the therapist takes the person as a whole as he or she is in his or her moment-by-moment process (including the becoming in the past and the possibilities of further developing in the future) without a specific intention or goal for the other. (By the way this implies also to conceptualize that persons are men and women and are not neutral and therefore are different — an important fact for overcoming a one-sided male perspective, not only on specific gender issues but in general in philosophy and psychotherapy.) To take the person as a whole also means not to concentrate solely on feelings or on verbal interaction but also to allow and pay attention to the body and the spirit, to cognitions and ideas.

Epistemology

It is indisputable that epistemology is based on empowerment. Heterogeneity, enduring contradictions and partial views are what are required. Therapy is a co-construction of acknowledgment. Thus power has to be shared or even more: the power of the person has to be acknowledged. State of the art is to view oneself as a therapist in the position to be empowered by the client.

The person-centered approach is committed to an epistemology based on phenomenology, is constructivistic (there are a variety of possibilities to understand), pluralistic (there are a variety of possibilities to approach) and personal (the person is seen as a whole), and therefore is oriented to dialogical, empathic and hermeneutic communication ('hermeneutic' in the broader sense of understanding the meaning of personal communications, not in the meaning of interpreting them by an expert, pretending to know better what the author of a statement meant than the author himself — as the term 'hermeneutic empathy' is used by some authors (e.g. Keil, 1996).

Theory of personality and developmental psychology

Psychotherapy is considered to be a special form of personality development and interpersonal relationship. Thus consequences can be drawn for other forms of relationship and fields of life. This corresponds to an approach which is oriented more on the process of the development of a so called 'healthy' person and not on a personality theory arising from a theory of disease. The basic principles apply to all persons, independently of categories like 'neurotics', 'psychotics', 'borderlines' or 'normals'. Instead of a theory of diseases or illness in the sense that this is commonly used in psychotherapy, only a theory of the suffering persons is consistent with the essentials, since the approach is person- and not problem- or goal- or solution-oriented. (This does not at all rule out the precise study of different processes!)

Personality development brings about an increasing capability to fully live in the moment and to more and more be able to perceive both phenomena and changes less distortedly or selectively and to live relationships more realistically. (Person-centered theory is much more interested in processes than in structures.) This coincides with more self-determination and self-responsibility.

The same applies to psychotherapy training. Learning how to do person-centered therapy is a matter of personality development, not of acquisition of techniques. A genuine 'training', or better: education of psychotherapists,[5] consistent with the approach, is oriented on the development of the personality of the trainee and not on the training and practicing of skills.[6]

Theory and practice of therapy

The therapist focuses on the inner world of the person of the client as it appears to the client and as it is experienced, understood and evaluated by him or her and follows him or her in this inner world, wherever the client moves. In this sense it is an experiential and phenomenological approach. The therapist is available for the client as a living person and not only in his or her function as a therapist. It is crucial for the development of both, client and therapist that they both direct their attention as free of judgments and interpretations as possible to the immediate present experiencing in the relationship. The attitudes of authenticity, unconditional acceptance and sensitive empathic understanding play a decisive role in this process. This implies a radical counterposition to expert-oriented approaches (in terms of the contents as well as the process), emphasizing that the person as such and not

---

[5.] The German word 'Aus-bildung' is more exact, because it denotes the process of becoming.

[6.] Needless to say that 'skills' in the sense of personal capacities or task-oriented abilities are necessary to do therapy or counseling and thus need to be learned and practiced. But in a person-centered understanding they are a consequence of personality development. Accordingly the Network of the European Associations for Person-Centred and Experiential Psychotherapy and Counselling stated that 'person-centred . . . training and further training in psychotherapy and counselling' is to be 'understood as the facilitation of personalisation, i.e. the development of the personality, of the trainee by a person-centred . . . relationship and encounter between the trainers and the trainees aiming at the personal and professional abilities required to offer, establish, maintain and develop person-centred . . . relationships with clients' (NEAPCEPC 2001).

techniques, methods or skills are the changing factor. The therapist offers a way of being with the client making possible a process of communication and encounter which *moves towards* mutuality and dialogue.

Naming the 'core conditions' of a person-centered point of view has tremendous practical consequences: On the basis of the stated convictions the concrete design, arrangement and setting of the therapy orientates and adjusts to the needs and possibilities of the client and the possibilities of the therapist. The therapeutic relationship can express itself in multiple ways, verbally, bodily, with the help of creative or artistic 'means' and the like.

Research and development of theory

Philosophical reflections arising from therapeutic work are an important part of the development of psychotherapy, in the single case as well as in terms of psychotherapy as a whole. Continued research, including empirical studies, is necessary in order to improve the quality of and to further develop psychotherapy. Concerning the theory of science, an adequate and thus independent understanding of science and research is needed and still has to be developed. It must include the persons engaged in the process and replace the traditional paradigms of medicine, natural science and research. Theory has continuously to be revised according to experience and research (and not the other way round).

Practitioners, theoreticians and researchers are invited, even urged to find their own and independent ways on the basis of these convictions and attitudes which represent a philosophy of life, to experiment in a responsible way and to support each other. This points to a world-wide psychological, social, cultural, political and — first of all — ethical challenge which gives neither room to orthodoxy or fundamentalism, nor to an unreflected eclecticism or an attitude of 'do what you like as long as you do it congruently'. The person-centered approach, beyond psychotherapy, is an attitude, a way of being in many fields of life and interpersonal work, which stands counter to many streams of the zeitgeist, e.g. those of efficiency which think only in categories of how to eliminate problems as quickly, inexpensively and painlessly as possible.[7]

---

[7] In short, person–centered therapy can be described as follows: It is a way of relating to other persons, be it one on one, be it in groups, which fosters personality development through personal encounter. It assumes that each person is given the capability and tendency to make use of his or her immense resources in a constructive way. A human being is able to live his or her own life and live together with others in a satisfying way by trying to understand him– or herself more and more accurately and is able to open to the continuous flow of his or her experiencing with less and less defence. This tendency towards the actualisation of one's own possibilities is encouraged and facilitated by an encounter person to person — a relationship whose quality is characterized by a respect for each client in his or her individuality. The therapist is present to him or her in an authentic, congruent way, experiencing unconditional positive regard in a deeply empathic and nonjudgmental way and both client and therapist develop their personalities together in this relationship (cf. Schmid, 1999b).

The World Association requires a commitment to the following principles:
• the primary importance of the relationship between client and therapist in psychotherapy and counseling
• to hold as central to the therapeutic endeavor the client's actualizing process and phenomenological world
• to embody in one's work those conditions and attitudes conducive to therapeutic movement first postulated by Carl Rogers
• to have a commitment to an understanding of both clients and therapists as persons, who are at one and the same time individuals and in relationship with others and their diverse environments and cultures
• to have an openness to the development and elaboration of person-centered and experiential theory in light of current and future practice and research.

III. THE CONSEQUENCES: DIFFERENTIATION AND COOPERATION

On consistency, compatibility and congruence

It is obvious: There *is not one way* of acting in a person-centered manner. Rogers himself acted differently in the span of his lifetime and he encouraged others explicitly to find their own ways in therapy and practice (e.g. Rogers, 1959, 16). There is a wide range from Virginia Axline's play therapy to the therapeutic implications in the work of Carl Rogers and his colleagues with large groups and to their intercultural activities towards the end of his life, from the early case studies to the late demonstration interviews, from counseling students to the clinical work with hospitalized, so called psychotic clients. And there is a wide range from Rogers' work to the various theories and ways of doing practice today.

On the other hand not everything can be called person-centered, if the term is to mean anything. It is not sufficient for someone to call himself or herself a person-centered therapist: it relies on the consistency of the image of the human being with which he or she practices the person-centered approach and their compatibility with person-centered principles. If the convictions or actions of somebody do not stand comparison with these principles, it is only fair to name them differently. This does not say anything about being better or worse. It just calls different things by another name.

The image of the human being underlying person-centered acting can be clearly conceptualized. Thus a person-centered way of relating cannot be combined with other orientations in any way whatever. It has distinct anthropological, epistemological, developmental psychological positions including a theory of motivation of personality and relationship and a theory of the suffering person and his or her therapy. It coincides with certain views of theories of science and methodologies of research and does not coincide with others. But foremost, as I tried to show, it is an ethical position (Schmid, 1998d; 1999a).

There is no proof that the theory and practice initiated by Rogers and others is right. There are other assumptions and they also have good arguments. The difference lies in the different ethical and philosophical basis and therefore leads to different consequences. It is of no use to have an argument about the image of the human being that is always a matter of belief, of 'basic beliefs'. Thus it makes no sense to judge other approaches out of the person-centered theory set or to quarrel about who is right. But it is useful to enter into dialogue and to question one's own convictions (cf. Schmid, 1998a, 115f; Slunecko, 1996).

This position is not orthodox, rigid, dogmatic or exclusive but an attempt to clarify and achieve mutual understanding. To distinguish is simply a matter of reason and honesty. To adhere to a position does not judge the efficiency, the correctness or the quality of the work of others. Respectfully and critically dealing with differences helps each approach to develop its own theory and practice.

Thus integrating other positions, adding methods, developing new points, combining approaches, etc. is always a matter of compatibility with the basic beliefs — especially for ethical reasons, since the client has a right to be offered a responsible and consistent relationship.

- Approaches that are convinced that Rogers' conditions are not sufficient, have to be complemented or modified, orientations which think there is evidence that the therapist should have a more or less guiding function, stimulating experience, influencing the process in a certain way or direction, making interventions in order to instruct the client, focus on certain aspects, levels, feelings, subjects or ways of proceeding, have intentions for the client;

• training programs that predominantly aim at teaching skills, giving tools to the trainee, those who aim at providing a set of preconceived techniques to make use of, instruments to diagnose the other (instead of a common diagnostic process out of the relationship);

• differentiations of so called sub-orientations to be used with different clients or applied on groups of diseases, orientations which prefer one condition to the others, attitudes which stress either the substantial or the relational aspect of being and becoming a person more than the other, which prefer either the intra- or the interpersonal dimension of therapy

— all these positions may have good arguments but they are different from the approach which Carl Rogers and others called 'person-centered'. (From a person-centered point of view they often may appear to be a reduction to an aspect, that Garry Prouty (1999, 4) calls a 'phenomenological reduction', the reduction of the person to a part of it, the process, or the instrumentalization of the relationship, the intentional use of empathy or selective listening to certain aspects fostering them instead of the person as a whole. But, as stated above, it does not make sense to judge another point of view with other foundations.)

Naming the differences AND working together

But they — or most of them at least — are closer to the 'original' or 'genuine' person-centered understanding than many others. Germain Lietaer (personal communication, June 19, 2000) is right: On a broader level it makes sense to distinguish between psychodynamic, cognitive-behavioral, systemic orientations and our orientation which in this view can be summarized as 'person-centered and experiential' and may include some other humanistic approaches. Their roots are in the theory of Carl Rogers and they derive from him.

I am convinced that it is necessary both to work together and to clearly be aware and name the differences. Therefore, no doubt, common conferences (like the ICCCEP, now PCE Conference) are of use. In terms of the World Association this seems to be crucial. An ongoing dialogue makes more sense than splitting up; it enriches instead of fostering ideas of excommunication and fantasies of purity and — not the least — it makes us stronger at a time when the approaches deserve co-operation in order to be influential in therapy, philosophy and health politics.

Person-oriented or goal-oriented — the ethical decision of the therapist

The decision for a certain therapy or a certain therapeutic acting is an ethical one, as is the decision for psychotherapy as such. After all it will not come as a surprise if I state that therapy understood as personal encounter is the realization of an ethical stance which holds the conviction of the kairotical empowerment of the client instead of the egological power of the therapist.

Carl Rogers gave such a decisive impulse and left us such a rich legacy that a concrete realization of a number of consequences is yet to come. The fundamental positions of Rogers are not at all outdated — on the contrary they are not yet sounded out by far, in their radicalism, their profound humanism, and their critical potential. (Schmid 2001a)

The approach, claiming to be an overall philosophy of culture, challenges us to an increasing understanding of the conditio humana and to what it means to be a human.[8]

Obviously a paradigm shift *within* the approach announces itself in all that. The person-centered approach may well face a turning-point in its self-understanding. If ethics and the underlying image of the human being are taken seriously it becomes obvious that the approach needs further development. Such a development goes in the direction of becoming a truly dialogical and social approach, a creative, flexible and kairotical approach. (For psychotherapy this for example would mean that relational and social factors are given much more weight and that, in the long run, psychotherapy and sociotherapy interplay.)

In respect to an ethically founded anthropology — the step from the individual to the person, from relation to encounter will be made as a step from the view of the person-centered relationship as an I-Thou-relationship to a view as a We-relationship as well and therefore finally towards a social therapy as well. Then the I will not only be found as a response to a Thou, but the I will also be a response to a We.

Then the approach will consequently be seen as a social approach. Sociotherapy besides psychotherapy will be ranked highly in the frame of an overall therapeutic point of view implying the communities people live in. Thus the political significance becomes obvious.

A dialogical understanding of therapy and group work, really carrying out the paradigm shift from treatment, caretaking and counseling to encounter, transcends models which concentrate on the individualistic self as well as models which exclusively concentrate on a simply systemic-oriented approach. As soon as this step is truly taken schools are not the issue any more, but the issue is to really understand and practice therapy and group work as dialogue. Or expressed in a more provoking way: the person-centered approach must intend and aim at making itself superfluous, just as a good therapist has to do.

In order to reach that goal a lot still has to be done.

If the approach is taken seriously as an 'approach' and not as a ready-made doctrine, 'not as a 'school' or dogma but as a set of tentative principles', to quote Carl Rogers and John Wood (1974), then it still is the emancipatory approach par excellence.

Almost half a century after Rogers' revolutionary statement in 1957, at a time when goal- and method-oriented approaches of psychotherapy are booming, a genuine *person*-oriented conviction might be even more necessary. Even if in various orientations, e.g. in newer psychoanalytic or systemic schools, personal concepts and the real relationship in therapy gain a growing influence — undoubtedly an impact of person-centered therapy — the approach radically and solely centered on the person remains not caught up with.

To oppose the temptation of *becoming more and more technical and one-sidedly oriented towards efficiency*, a characteristic of our days, is an ethical challenge as well — one that might be more acute than ever.

[8.] Thus it needs to deal with ecological questions as well.

REFERENCES

Binder, U. and Binder, H-J. (1981), *Klientenzentrierte Psychotherapie bei schweren psychischen Störungen*, Frankfurt am Main (Fachbuchhandlung für Psychologie) 1981; *Klientenzentrierte Psychotherapie bei schweren psychischen Störungen. Neue Handlungs- und Therapiekonzepte zur Veränderung*, 3rd compl. rev. edn. 1994.

Binswanger, L. (1942). *Grundformen und Erkenntnis menschlichen Daseins*. München: Reinhardt, 1942; 5th edn. 1963.

Buber, M. (1923). *Ich und Du*. Heidelberg: Lambert Schneider, 8th edn. 1974.

Farber, B A., Brink, D. C. and Raskin, P. M. (1996). (Eds.). *The Psychotherapy of Carl Rogers: Cases and commentary*. New York: Guilford Press.

Keil, W. W. (1996). Hermeneutic empathy in client-centered therapy. In U. Esser, H. Pabst and G.-W. Speierer (Eds.) *The Power of the Person-Centered Approach. New challenges, perspectives, answers*. Cologne: GwG, pp. 65–80.

Levinas, E. (1959). Der Untergang der Vorstellung. In Levinas, E. (1983), pp. 120–39. Orig. In Husserl 1859–1959. Recueil commémoratif publié à l'occasion du centenaire du philosophe, *(Phaenomenologica VI)*. Den Haag: Nijhoff.

Levinas, E. (1978). *Autrement qu'être ou au delà de l'essence*. Den Haag: Nijhoff, 1974; 2nd ed. 1978.

Levinas, E. (1980). Totalité et infini. Essai sur l'extériorité, Den Haag: Nijhoff, 1961; 17th ed. 1980.

Levinas, E. (1983). *Die Spur des Anderen. Untersuchungen zur Phänomenologie und Sozialphilosophie*. Freiburg: Alber, 3rd edn. 1992.

NEAPCEPC (2001). Principles for person-centred and experiential training and further training, http://www.pce-europe.org

Prouty, G. (1994). *Theoretical Evolutions in Person-centered/Experiential Therapy. Applications to schizophrenic and retarded psychoses*. Westport, CT: Praeger.

Rogers, C. R. (1955). Some personal formulations, (manuscript).

Rogers, C. R. (1957). The necessary and sufficient conditions of therapeutic personality change. *Journal of Consulting Psychology, 21*, 2, 95–103

Rogers, C. R. (1959). A theory of therapy, personality, and interpersonal relationships, as developed in the client-centered framework. In S. Koch, (Ed.) *Psychology, the Study of a Science. Vol. III: Formulations of the person and the social context*. New York: McGraw Hill, pp. 184–256.

Rogers, C. R. (1970). *On Encounter Groups*. New York: Harper and Row.

Rogers, C. R. (1975). Client-centered therapy. Cassette recording. In *Psychology Today*. Brooklyn, NJ.

Rogers, C. R. (1980). Client-centered psychotherapy. In H. I. Kaplan, B. J. Sadock and A. M. Freedman, (Eds.) *Comprehensive Textbook of Psychiatry, III*. Baltimore, MD: Williams and Wilkins, pp. 2153–68.

Rogers, C. R., Heppner, P. P., Rogers, M. E. and Lee, L. A. (1994). Carl Rogers: Reflections on his life. In *Journal of Counseling and Development, 63*, 14–20.

Rogers, C. R. and Wood, J. K. (1974). The changing theory of client-centered therapy. In A. Burton, (Ed.) *Operational Theories of Personality*. New York: Brunner/Mazel, pp. 211–58.

Schmid, P. F. (1991). Souveränität und Engagement. Zu einem personzentrierten Verständnis von 'Person'. In C. R. Rogers and P. F. Schmid, (Eds.) *Person-zentriert. Grundlagen von Theorie und Praxis*. Mainz: Grünewald, pp. 15–164; 4th ed. 2000.

Schmid, P. F. (1994). *Personzentrierte Gruppenpsychotherapie. Ein Handbuch. Vol. I: Solidarität und Autonomie*. Cologne: Edition Humanistische Psychologie.

Schmid, P. F. (1996). *Personzentrierte Gruppenpsychotherapie in der Praxis. Ein Handbuch. Vol. II: Die Kunst der Begegnung*. Paderborn: Junfermann.

Schmid, P. F. (1998a). *Im Anfang ist Gemeinschaft. Personzentrierte Gruppenarbeit in Seelsorge und Praktischer Theologie. Vol. III: Beitrag zu einer Theologie der Gruppe*. Stuttgart: Kohlhammer.

Schmid, P. F. (1998b). Face to face. The art of encounter. In B. Thorne and E. Lambers, *Person-centred Therapy: A European perspective.* London: Sage, pp. 74–90.

Schmid, P. F. (1998c). On becoming a person-centered approach: A person-centred understanding of the person. In B. Thorne and E. Lambers, *Person-cenered Therapy: A European Perspective.* London: Sage, pp. 38–52.

Schmid, P. F. (1998d). State of the Art: personzentrierten Handelns als Vermächtnis und Herausforderung. In *Person, 1,* 15–23.

Schmid, P. F. (1999a). Personzentrierte Psychotherapie. In G. Sonneck and T. Slunecko, T. (Eds.) *Einführung in die Psychotherapie.* Stuttgart: UTB für Wissenschaft—Facultas, pp. 168–211.

Schmid, P. F. (1999b). Person-centered essentials — Wesentliches und Unterscheidendes. Zur Identität personzentrierter Ansätze in der Psychotherapie. In *Person, 2,* 139–41.

Schmid, P. F. (2001a) Encountering a human being means being kept alive by an enigma (E. Levinas). Prospects on further developments in the Person-Centered Approach. In J. Marques-Texeira, and S. Autunes, (Eds.) *Client-Centered and Experiential Psychotherapy.* Lisbon: Universita Católica Portuguesa.

Schmid, P. F. (2001b). Personzentrierte Persönlichkeits- und Beziehungstheorie. In P. Frenzel, W. Keil, P. F. Schmid and N. Stölzl, (Eds.) *Person-Klientenzentrierte Psychotherapie. Kontexte, Konzepte, Konkretisierungen.* Vienna: WUV.

Schmid, P. F. (2001c). Authenticity: The person as his or her own author. Dialogical and ethical perspectives on therapy as an encounter relationship. And beyond. In G. Wyatt, (Ed.). *Congruence.* Ross-on-Wye: PCCS Books, pp. 217–32.

Schmid, P. F. (2001d). Comprehension: the art of not-knowing. Dialogical and ethical perspectives on empathy as dialogue facing the unexpected in personal and person-centred relationships. In S. Haugh and T. Merry, (Eds.) *Empathy.* Ross-on-Wye: PCCS Books.

Schmid, P. F. (2001e). Acknowledgement: the art of responding. Dialogical and ethical perspectives on the challenge of unconditional personal relationships in therapy and beyond. In Bozarth, J. and Wilkins, P. (Eds.). *Unconditional positive regard.* Ross-on-Wye: PCCS Books.

Schmid, P. F. (2002). Presence: Immediate co-experiencing. In G. Wyatt and P. Sanders, (Eds.) *Contact and Perception.* Ross-on-Wye: PCCS Books.

Slunecko, T. (1996). *Wissenschaftstheorie und Psychotherapie. Ein konstruktiv-realistischer Dialog.* Wien: WUV.

Thorne, B. and Lambers, E. (1988) (Eds.). *Person-Centred Therapy. A European perspective.* London: Sage.

Waldschütz, E. (1993). Was ist 'Personalismus'? In *Die Presse, Spectrum,* December 24, p. 12.

Marion N. Hendricks PhD

Director, The Focusing Institute, Spring Valley, NY, USA

What Difference does Philosophy Make?
Crossing Gendlin and Rogers

What difference does philosophy make to us as psychologists or as ordinary people? Is it important that Gendlin as a philosopher, teamed up with Rogers? Rogers eliminated diagnosis, and the imposition of any content on clients' experiencing. He thereby opened a space which Gendlin articulated philosophically. Rogers pointed out the richness of this crossing and how fundamentally it shaped client-centered psychotherapy. 'I would like to mention my special indebtedness to Eugene Gendlin, William Kirtner and Fred Zimring, whose demonstrated ability to think in new ways about these matters has been particularly helpful and from whom I have borrowed heavily' (Rogers 1961, p. 128). Currently, a new epistemology is being called for in the human sciences. We have it in our own tradition.

Client-centered/Experiential psychotherapy is about people becoming free from internal oppression, from externally imposed role structures and definitions, or from ideologies. This therapy asserts the beingness of any particular person. The freeing process involves the ability to say, in relation to any situation, 'Wait.' Such a bodily felt gesture, putting out your hand and saying, 'Just a minute . . . ' breaks up the immediate interaction/demand and brings about a pause. The pause creates an internal space in which the person becomes able to ask, 'How is this for me? What is my sense of this whole thing?' We focus on our own sense of the situation. Such a pause can also be created in a relationship that feels safe. This is a quietly revolutionary power in relation to any kind of imposed structure.

The point of philosophy has always been to free people. It enables us to examine the assumptions implicit in our language. We become able to see what model is built into our concepts and words. The kind of concept we use to think about ourselves and others makes a difference in how we interact or treat ourselves. If our concepts assume separated objects seen from the outside by an observer, they 'close' experience, because from an external point of view actual experiencing is left out. The external picture takes its place. This is a kind of oppression. In practice, client-centered psychotherapy frees people from this kind of oppression by entering into the client's frame of reference. However, our original theoretical concepts assumed an external point of view and made it difficult to articulate the freeing power of our practice further. Gendlin's Philosophy of the Implicit built concepts that open experience. If we understand this kind of concept, we can further articulate our tradition in a way that reveals a highly developed and radical philosophical base.

We are used to concepts which assume that everything consists of separated entities in the beginning. Then it is difficult to account for how the separated entities come to be in interaction. For instance, 'How does a baby know how to nurse?' Our concepts assume, 'Here's a baby and over there is a mother.' Then it is a puzzle how they get together. We assume two separated bodies, each in its own skin envelope. It is another way to think if we assume that mothers and babies are one single interaction process to begin with. As long as the baby was in the womb, there was only one mother-baby system. When the baby comes out it makes sucking motions with its mouth. We can see that the baby is still in one system with the mother's body, her milk, hugs, warmth, and care. We can express this by saying that the baby's sucking 'implies' the mother's breast. It is just as true that the mother with milk in her breast implies a baby. In a sense a baby is a mother-implying. Without a mothering person, the baby literally dies. This is an example of a kind of concept we can call 'interaction first'. Instead of two entities, we begin with one process.

Here is another example: Rather than first thinking about lungs and then thinking about air and wondering how they 'got together', we can think first about the process of breathing. Lungs are an ongoing process. In breathing, the lungs imply the air. In a sense, the lungs are air. The structure is a product of process. The minute breathing stops, the lungs as a separate entity begin to disintegrate. If we grasp this fundamental move of putting process first, we might first say, 'There is a running,' and only secondarily say, 'There is a boy running,' This changes the way we think.

THE PUZZLE OF CONGRUENCE: HOW CAN SOMETHING BE THERE AND NOT BE THERE?

This assumption of separated entities first is in our client-centered terms. Rogers' defined congruence as the 'extent to which words match feelings' or a 'more or less accurate representation in awareness of what we're feeling'. Incongruence is, for example, 'experiencing annoyance, but being unaware of it'. These definitions give rise to problems:

- They require an outside observer who judges that the client is feeling something, which is not there from within the client's experience.
- Where is the missing experience? How can words or 'representations' 'match' an experience which isn't there? And even if the experience is present, how can words 'match' it?
- Congruence cannot be well measured or researched

I will discuss these problems:

(1) If I have feelings which I don't feel, then I cannot judge whether I am congruent. I cannot know that I am unaware of something that I am unaware of. This leaves it for the therapist, to say, 'You're feeling annoyed, but you are not aware of it.' This puts therapists in the position of making an externally judged determination of congruence, which undercuts the basic client-centered position and which we would not do in practice.

(2) There is a problem about experiencing that is not there. Where is it? Is there really another experiencing process going on under what the person is feeling? Who is feeling that one? We all know there can be something 'unaware' or 'unconscious', but it cannot be the same kind of thing which conscious experience would be if it were there. This is the client-centered version of the old problem that denying the unconscious is superficial, but thinking of it as an unconscious duplicate of conscious experiencing cannot be right.

Matching words to experience that is not there is part of this problem. How can we compare our representations to something that we are not aware of? Even if we could somehow compare our words against 'hidden' feelings, how can words be the 'same' as feelings? Our concepts assume two initially separated entities: feelings and words. We judge whether the words accurately match the feelings. In this comparing activity, what can 'sameness' or 'match' mean? The two things we are comparing are assumed to have no inherent relation.

(3) Rogers understood that the definitions in use could not lead to measurable variables for the research he wanted: ' . . . most urgently needed of all is a method whereby we might give operational definition to the construct experience in our theory, so that discrepancies between awareness and experience, might be measured. This would permit the testing of some of the most crucial hypotheses of the theoretical system' (Rogers 1959).

One early attempt to measure and research congruence defined the low end of it on a scale as: 'The first person's verbalizations are clearly unrelated to what he is feeling at the moment, or his only genuine responses are negative . . . ' (Truax, 1967). This gives us no criterion for judging what 'clearly unrelated' means, and it confuses incongruence with negative feelings. Not falling into this pitfall, Brodley (personal communication, 2000) says, 'I am at a loss to imagine how congruence could be measured, given that integrated states include awareness of conflicted or disturbed feelings, as long as the person has accurate symbolizations.'

Let's start with a process first

I will show that when people refer to experience in a certain way they may find something where the missing experience is supposed to be, but is not. They don't find the missing experience, but they do find a vague sense that they cannot at first define. They discover if they pay attention to that vague sense for a while, they can speak from it. As they speak from it, it comes into focus. What comes was not already known in advance. It comes with an easing in the body. Just these words say exactly what that vague sense turns out to have been. We say, 'Oh, that is what that was.' Other words we tried did not bring this easing. This is a *process* of allowing a body sense of some situation to form, paying attention to it, asking into it, waiting and allowing something to come from it.

We have a capacity to speak from an actual present process, rather than comparing two entities, one of which is missing. If we use this kind of process concept, we can solve the problems of external judgment and the seeming impossibility of measurement. I will give you several examples of this odd kind of sensing and 'carrying forward'.

I forgot something, but I don't know what

You are on the way to the airport. Suddenly, you realize that you have forgotten something, but you are not sure what. There is a persistent, nagging feeling that will not let you alone. You poke and poke at it. 'What is it?' You try out 'Is it this?' No response in your body. This 'sense' is very concrete, but it doesn't have any content. It's right there. You can almost 'touch' it. It isn't exactly a body sensation, but it is 'right there', usually felt in the solar plexus area of the body. Finally, after a while, 'it' opens! There is a big breath, and an 'Oh, that is what it is!' When you remember, you know that you remember. You don't just think so. There is a whole body response. And even if it is bad news, like you forgot your other notes for your talk, there is still a body sense of relief. That nagging feeling that won't let you alone, but does not yet have words, is a felt sense. The experience of words emerging that change what was implied is a carrying forward.

I forgot what I was going to say

Another example is when you are trying to make a point. You don't already have your point in words, but you have a sense of it. Where is this sense of your point? Where do you experience that? It is bodily, but not like a cramped muscle. But it is palpable. If I lose my sense of the point I'm about to make, I can't say anything. In ordinary language we say, ' I forgot what I was about to say.' Again, you can try out various guesses or ideas, but they don't do anything. Then there is the moment when you get back your sense. You say, 'Oh, there it is!' and you have to be a bit careful, because it is still not in words. If you stay next to it, then you get the sense back strongly enough so fresh words form and you go on to make your point.

We all have these experiences. They show the kind of paying attention in your body that lets us get a 'felt sense' of any particular situation. By paying attention to that felt sense in a certain way, words or images or gestures emerge that 'carry it forward'.

A felt sense is what forms at the there-and-not-there juncture

We could use the old concepts and say of both examples that we are feeling something, but are not aware of what we are feeling. But this now has a new meaning.

Once we refer and a felt sense comes, we are no longer just blankly incongruent, trying to match words to something not there. We have something directly there, but we don't yet know what it is. What I forgot is 'not there' in the sense that there is no explicit content. It 'is there' in being concretely, bodily felt as a disturbing sense of something forgotten. The paradox of something there and not there resolves. *When words carry forward a felt sense it is not because they match, but rather we feel the effect of the words in our bodies.* We can feel that we must remember the dentist, buy a present, make a phone call, but these are not what we forgot. When we 'remember' what we forgot, this has a powerful effect in which our bodily restlessness 'opens' and we know what we forgot. We don't just have a 'word' or 'representation' of the missing notes, but we get a whole complexity about why they were important, what differences it will make in my presentation not to have them, all the work that went into preparing them that I won't be able to use and so on. A felt sense is very different from anything that an external judge would infer. It is complex, not yet cognitively defined, and when the person speaks from it the facets that emerge are always more specific, colorful and alive than any ideas an external judge could invent.

Rather than referring to feelings or to words as content entities, we are referring to a process that includes implicit meaning. 'Two deficiencies of [Rogers'] theoretical statements . . . cause misunderstanding: (1) experience is identified with conceptual contents; (2) aware feeling is not precisely understood to contain implicit meaning' (Gendlin, 1962, p. 253). The process of felt-sense-symbolizing has an original continuity, before feelings and words are separated entities. Process terms are the kind of terms we are using to solve our puzzle about congruence.

INSTANCES OF CONGRUENCE AND INCONGRUENCE

When we see the trouble the old language leads to, we are likely to say, 'But that isn't what we mean by congruence!' We don't mean comparing words to experience that is not there. Of course we do not literally mean 'matching', but the point here is that the concepts we are using bring unexamined assumptions which then prevent us from saying what we do mean.

Let's look at some instances of congruence and incongruence. If we use our new kind of process terms, rather than the language of matching entities, we can solve the problem of the external judge, as well as create research measures.

Example 1. I get a sense of . . . it's this kind of . . .

> That's almost exactly what the feeling is — it was like I was living so much of my life . . . in terms of being scared of something . . . I get a sense of — it's this kind of pleading little boy. It's this gesture of begging. 'Won't you do this for me? Who, me? Beg? . . . That's an emotion I've never felt clearly at all — something I've never been . . . (Pause) I've got such a confusing feeling. One is, it's such a wondrous feeling to have these new things come out of me. It amazes me so much and there's being scared that I've so much of this. (Tears) . . . I just don't know myself. Here's suddenly something I never realized, hadn't any inkling of — that it was some thing or way I wanted to be. (Rogers, 1961, p. 149)

Rogers comments on this example as showing a *process*, (experiencing incongruence as it disappears), but he is still hampered by concepts that require measuring the 'discrepancy' or 'match' between two already separated entities — 'experiencing' and 'self-concept' or 'awareness':

> Here we see a complete experiencing of his pleadingness, and a vivid recognition of the discrepancy between this experiencing and his concept of himself. Yet this experience of discrepancy exits in the moment of its disappearance. From now on he is a person who feels pleading, as well as many other feelings . . . The incongruence between experience and awareness is vividly experienced as it disappears into congruence. (Rogers, 1961, p. 148–9)

Our new kind of terms let us lay out this process exactly. The client now feels pleading, a feeling of which he 'hadn't any inkling'. So we again have the paradox of 'there but not there'. But we can say exactly the sense in which the missing begging was and was not there, and how it comes to be here now.

Begging was not there
Clearly, begging gestures or begging words were not there before this interaction. This is a person who never begged, 'Who me? Beg? Never.' His whole astonishment testifies to the sense in which this begging was *not there* until now.

The as-yet-unknown feeling is there
Using our concepts, we can say the begging was there in the sense that the 'certain unknown feeling' (Rogers, 1961, p. 148)[1] the client was paying attention to implied begging. But until the gesture now emerges, he does not know what it was that was implied. The begging

---

[1] Rogers' use of the phrase 'certain unknown feeling' points at this new kind of concept. If a feeling is 'unknown' how can it be a certain feeling? As soon as it is a certain feeling, then it is known in some sense. Gendlin names this a 'bodily felt sense'.

gesture is not sitting already *formed* in the implying. *Implying is a different kind of concept.* There is no hidden picture of what the unknown feeling will become when it is explicated. 'Implying is not the same as what will occur. It doesn't look the same. Implying in this sense is non-ikonic, non-representational' (Gendlin, 1997, p. 9). The client's 'feeling' implied an interaction in which it was safe to beg. The begging that was implied could not happen before because the needed interaction with the environment did not occur. In that sense it was not there. But in another sense, it is carried in the body by whatever processes are on-going. And so in a sense, it is always there.

Focusing on the felt sense lets us know what 'was' there

By attending to what is ongoing, rather than making up ideas about what is not there, we are able to reconstitute the interaction so that what is implied can now take place. How does the client do this? He pays attention to something directly sensed, that does not yet have any words, symbols, gestures, but is nonetheless tangibly felt. He remains next to his felt sense and allows it to open into words and gestures. He pauses, gropes, generates a metaphor, 'It's this kind of . . . it's this kind of pleading little boy. It's this gesture of begging . . . ' The symbols emerge out of the felt sense, rather than as deductive schema imposed by us or by himself. The begging gesture and words emerge from this implying and carry it forward. The client pleads. This 'change' is a whole body movement, with tears and 'a wondrous feeling to have these new things come out of me'.

Carrying forward is a better concept than matching

What is the relationship of the begging words, 'Won't you do this for me?' to a feeling he cannot yet define? Carrying forward is a better term for this relation than matching, which is judged by sameness. The current begging is not 'matching' some time when the client was begging unconsciously. His point is that he was not begging before and is shocked to find himself doing so now. We can't get the feeling accurately unless it opens into what it needs to be: 'Oh, that's what it was.' Carrying forward is our new kind of process concept, rather than matching two entities for sameness. 'Won't you do this?' emerges from the felt sense, making a kind of change that yet is continuous with the feeling. 'Continuity is not just bits pressed close or continuous, but the functioning of each in the last and the next' (Gendlin, 1997a). This kind of change is experienced in the body as a felt shift. Rather than sameness, we have 'wondrous new things'.

Example 2. I didn't know their inability to speak was so painful

Here is a second example of this incongruent-congruent process:

> 'Oh that's what that is . . . (Crying) . . . I didn't know that their inability to speak from their experience was so painful to me then. It was really a terrible thing for me that shaped much of the rest of my life.'

Again here is this odd structure that the client is *now* sensing a pain that she felt, *then*, but didn't know then. She only now can say what she felt then. Something odd is happening here to time. We need a concept for a time relation that lets what 'was' there be changed by the present interaction.

If we start with the assumption of the past and present as two separate entities along a time line, then we are at a standstill. If the client's pain from then is sitting back there in time, we have again the problem of how something that was not there can be there. If what is sitting there in the photographed past is the painfulness-not-felt, how can she come to now feel what was there but not as felt? The kind of concepts that begin with separated entities in space and time do not let us say what we mean.

The freshly-gone-on-in-past is capable of much more than the fixed-photograph-past

The client is in a process which retroactively changes the past! Unlike in her family of origin she is now in an interaction in which she and her therapist do speak from experience. The current interaction is carrying forward what was implied in her felt sense — the need to be with others who can speak from their experience. As this carrying forward takes place, she experiences now how the lack of such speaking from experience then harmed her. It is only as the current interaction reconstitutes the person's experience that she can know how she carried that stoppage in her body then. This harmed 'back there' is derived from this *present* experiencing.

> The past functions not as itself, but is already changed by what it functions in. One has lived past the stoppage which the problem literally was. Now, from the changed relevance, in this changed whole context, one formulates what the problem was in a new way. One formulates the problem in a world in which the problem is solved, in a context changed by that solving. (Gendlin, 1997, p. 233)

We have much more to think with now that we have this new kind of process concept, than when we had definitions with the old assumptions.

REDEFINING TERMS

The old definitions make separated entities in space and time: feelings are in one location and 'representations' in some other location. Awareness takes more or less accurate pictures of these 'feelings'. Feelings sit inside us already formed, but in the dark. Awareness has nothing to do with what they are. This has been called the flashlight model. We shine the light of awareness on the feelings. The light does not affect what they are. It just lets us see them, more or less accurately. Using this kind of concept, we are forced to pretend to compare things in two spatial locations to see how much the same they are. We judge congruence by a comparing activity. Congruence is a 'match', a sameness.

It is the power of philosophy to show us how our concepts don't allow us to say what we mean. These definitions 'close' the experience we mean to point to.

Feelings are an implying of what needs to occur

From seeing how our new concepts work in the above examples, we can go on further and ask: what is a feeling? It is no longer a separated entity, but more like hunger in the baby for milk. We can't know what a feeling 'was' until it opens into what it implies or needs to be. This changes our definition of 'feelings'. We do not assume that feelings are things that sit somewhere, already explicitly formed, either 'in' or 'out' of awareness. Rather feelings are an implying of that which needs to occur. We can pay attention to this bodily implying, rather than looking for feeling contents that are not there except by someone else's judgment.

Congruence is carrying forward

The paradoxes 'there and not there' and 'only incongruent at the moment I am congruent' helped us hold in place something that we could not yet say in the public meanings of words. Paradoxes protect a 'moreness' or 'richness' that has not yet carried forward into words. Forming paradoxical sentences is one step in this method of thinking — Thinking at the Edge — (Gendlin, 2002) which makes concepts which have felt experience built into them.

Now we can redefine congruence using our new kind of terms. Congruence is not a matter of accuracy, match or comparison in terms of similarity. We could say our definition is the opposite of 'match'. *It is exactly when there is change that we are congruent.* Let's say congruence is the experience of wondrous new experiencing coming out of me! Congruence is when our words emerge from our felt sense and carry it forward.

Similarly, we have translated incongruence into a manner of process. It is not a question of inaccurate matching, but rather of not referring to our ongoing felt sense in the interaction. We might say that incongruence is when one treats oneself as if from an external perspective and guesses or attacks oneself with contents of which one is unaware!

CONCLUSIONS: WHAT DIFFERENCE DOES THIS NEW KIND OF CONCEPT MAKE?

Where have we come? What are some of the differences this new kind of concept makes?

A first-person process

We redefined congruence as a carrying forward of experience. Carrying forward is a symbolizing that changes us such that what was implied is carried forward and no longer implied. When I am congruent my words emerge from my own bodily felt sense. This is a *first-person process* marked by a whole body response — tears, a deep breath, laughter and a deep sense of: 'Oh, that is what that is.' *Because it is a first-person process, I can say whether I'm congruent, because the carrying forward is an experience I have.* This solves the first problem we had. What I can find, I don't need an 'expert' to tell me.

We have also solved the confusion about the content of feelings defining congruence. Neither forgetting my notes for my talk nor 'begging' are happy contents. What is experienced as 'wondrous' is not positive contents or emotions, but the process of carrying forward.

We might say that incongruence only exists retroactively. A person cannot be incongruent to themselves except in the mode of being congruent, meaning already having gone on past what was blocked or stopped. As client-centered therapists we know this so deeply — that all living creatures makes perfect sense if we can enter their world. This is the cornerstone of our unflagging respect for our clients.

Practice: now we can find what is there and not there

Our process-first definition of congruence furthers our practice. We specify a process that lets us and our clients find that which is 'there, but not there'. We have a term other than explicit or unaware. What is there is not feelings sitting hidden under a blanket. What is there is something from which a felt sense can form. Instead of assuming what isn't there, we find what is there. We attend to a body sense of our situations — 'it's kind of like . . . ' We discover an experiential version of 'the unconscious' that we can actually go to and change occurs. There is much elaborate work on helping someone find this level of process when they don't know it (Cornell, 1996; Gendlin, 1996; Leijssen, 1998).

When therapists do not respond to the felt sense, their clients may become less Congruent.

C1: And yet I feel . . . *there's something underneath it all but I don't know what* . . . (felt sense) and if I kind of knew what it was . . . I might feel differently, I don't know. But it's *vague right now.*

T1: Okay. If things could be a little more *definite*. If you were really able to *identify the cause* . . . you really think that you'd be able to *cope* with it then. But right now you can't seem to put your finger on what the *real problem* is.

C2: Yuh . . . and . . . that . . . like when you say that . . . that makes me mad because I feel . . . you know like I'm . . . intelligent. I can figure things out. And yet . . . right now I don't know what the hell's going on with me.

The client's felt sense — 'There's something underneath it all, but I don't know what' — is the rich, intricate, directly sensed, but not-yet-known place from which movement would come. The client has given a clear prescription that if she can just sense more into this unclear place, something would move: 'If I knew what it was . . . I might feel differently . . .' Not knowing this carrying forward of the implicit process, the therapist, while verbally understanding the client's content, uses cognitive, closed, defined words ('definite', 'identity', 'cope', 'real problem') that cannot point to or invite her felt sense to open. The client is left self-critical and, probably, rightfully, angry at the therapist. The therapist could have pointed to the felt sense, 'You can sense something right there underneath . . .' which would have helped the client stay next to her felt sense so that it might open. This can now be taught in therapist training programs.

Research: As a first-person-process we can measure congruence

Rogers was a researcher. He wanted to measure that clients get more congruent over the course of therapy. He also wanted to test his hypothesis that if therapists were congruent, clients would become more so. The old definitions of congruence did not lead to good measures. Measuring the discrepancy between one's ideal and actual self on Q-Sorts was not a good method. By incongruence we don't mean a recognized failure to live up to our goals about how we would like to be. This requires two content entities — ideal self-concepts and actual self-concepts — which we then compare for sameness. Our definition lets us specify the characteristics of a congruent process such that it can be operationalized and measured. This carrying forward (focusing) manner of process, defines the higher stages of the Process/ Experiencing scale. The begging example was used by Rogers to illustrate Stage Six on the

Process Scale (Rogers, 1961, p. 148). We already have a reliable measure of congruence and it has been found to predict or correlate with successful outcome in psychotherapy (Hendricks, 2001).

We also know from research that therapists, as in the example above, who do not respond to a client's felt sense depress the client's congruence. And therapists who themselves attend to their felt sense tend to have clients who also do so (Sachse, 1990).

PHILOSOPHY OF THE IMPLICIT: THE NEW EPISTEMOLOGY

Gendlin came to the collaboration with Rogers in 1952 as a philosopher. He was formulating a Process Model, part of his Philosophy of the Implicit. Honoured in the field of psychotherapy with awards from three divisions of the American Psychological Association, his work in psychology is one application of his philosophy. He developed, not just more concepts, but a fundamentally different kind of concept, which puts process or activity first and then derives separated entities, empty space and linear time from process.

To think about human beings, the most developed *human process* was taken as a starting point, rather than an entity model. The philosophical inquiry began with the carrying forward relationship between words and experiencing . 'We know carrying forward is possible. We're here and we have this experience, so we know it's possible. We can ask, 'What would a person have to be, such that this experience is possible?' 'What is a body, such that it can do this?' 'What is behavior, such that this can happen?' This felt-sense explicating process was crossed with every aspect of human process and development. Therefore, all of the terms have already in them this interrelatedness between symbols and experiencing. This move humanizes the definition of behavior, gesturing, symbolizing, culture, language. We can think about each of these dimensions of bodily lived experience with concepts that have lived experience built into them.

It is beyond the scope of this paper, but we can go on from here very much further. We can ask how it is that the body felt sense has language already implicit in it. How does the body 'know' about our situations so that it opens into words that change how we are in our situations? A series of steps exactly lays out how there is a symbolic relation in the body's own nature. There are exact concepts for how it is that we can only know our incongruence in the moment of being congruent. This has to do with the way in which a bodily felt sense (a direct referent) is very different from our culturally slotted emotions.

In this new space something can happen which was implied, whereas in the old space . . . of our actual situation it couldn't. The direct referent forms from a sequence of (in a way) fulfilling what was required.

There is therefore a great physical relief when a direct referent forms. Many processes in the body return to their more usual way, no longer carrying the stoppage. The interaction in the situation is still implied, still awaiting being done . . . but the body has lived on and the stoppage has been resumed by a new object, the referent.

When the direct referent comes . . . it is from a sequence of 'perfect feedback', each bit being what the previous bit focally implied . . . The referent is therefore not only a sense of the difficulty, but a new object made by a solving of the difficulty . . .

One has lived past the stoppage which the problem literally was. Now, from the changed relevance, in this changed whole context, one formulates what the problem was in a new way. One formulates the problem in a world in which the problem is solved, in a context changed by that solving. (Gendlin, 1997, p. 233)

The body finds itself in this kind of concept

Many readers of this book know the carrying-forward relationship between symbols and experiencing, and teach about the implicit in training programs. I've included examples not from psychotherapy, because I am interested in a philosophical point. I am trying to show a different kind of concept with which we can think better about any human process. Isadora Duncan talks about going to her dance studio, where she would stand in the middle of the room and wait, with her hands over her solar plexus. She would stand for as long as it took for movements to come from her felt sense of what she wanted to create. Then her dancing, gesturing, body movements carry forward her felt sense. The dance arises out of the felt sense, rather than being imposed on her body. Einstein is quoted as saying, 'I knew the answer to relativity for 15 years before I had it.' In what sense did he know the answer and in what sense did that knowing guide his search? What Duncan and Einstein pay attention to is an implicit knowing which 'implies' an occurrence that changes it, just like your sense of what you want to say implies words that will carry it forward and thereby change what is implied.

The old concepts are able to generate our technological world, but they can oppress human experience, because they require the perspective of an external observer. They drop out bodily lived experience.

> Expression always involves being carried forward. We cannot call something 'expression' from an external point of view only. Beautiful ice patterns are expressive to us, who are carried forward by patterns, but not to the ice. (Gendlin, 1997, p. 133)

There is no way to grasp this new kind of concept without it carrying you further. 'Going on further' is already in each term. So, anything you speak about goes on further. One understands this kind of concept by having it function. Because this is a language of human bodily derived concepts, your body 'recognizes' itself in them. We are thinking about human beings with concepts modeled on a first-person human process instead of on inanimate physical objects or separated units. We badly need this kind of concept in all of our human sciences. Client-centered therapy is often accused of being theoretically simplistic. Let us further use this new epistemology to reveal the sophisticated philosophical base that already underlies, and is formative in, our client-centered practice.

REFERENCES

Cornell, A. W. (1996). *The Power of Focusing.* Oakland, CA: New Harbinger Publications.
Gendlin, E. T. (1981). *Focusing.* New York: Bantam.
Gendlin, E. T. (1996). *Focusing-oriented Psychotherapy.* New York: Guilford Press.
Gendlin, E. T. (1997). *A Process Model.* New York: The Focusing Institute: www.focusing.org
Gendlin, E. T. (1997a). *Experiencing and the Creation of Meaning: A philosophical and psychological*

approach to the subjective. Evanston, IL: Northwestern University Press.

Gendlin, E. T. (2002). *Introduction to Thinking at the Edge.* New York: The Focusing Institute: www.focusing.org

Hendricks, M. (2001). Focusing-oriented/Experiential Psychotherapy . In D. Cain and J. Seeman, (Eds.) *Humanistic Psychotherapies: Handbook of research and practice* . Washington, DC: American Psychological Association.

Leijssen, M. (1998). Focusing Microprocesses. In L. S. Greenberg, J. C. Watson and G. Lietaer (Eds.) *Handbook of Experiential Psychotherapy.* New York: Guilford Press, pp. 121–54.

Rogers, C. (1959). A tentative scale for the measurement of process in psychotherapy. In E. A. Rubinstein and M. B. Parloff, (Eds.) *Research in Psychotherapy.* Washington, DC.: American Psychological Association, pp. 96–107.

Rogers, C. R. (1959). A theory of therapy, personality and interpersonal relationships as developed in client-centered framework. In S. Koch, (Ed.) *Psychology: A study of a science, Vol. 3.* New York: McGraw-Hill.

Rogers, C. R. (1961). A process conception of psychotherapy. In *On Becoming a Person.* Boston: Houghton Mifflin.

Sachse, R. (1990). The influence of therapist processing proposals on the explication process of the client. *Person-Centered Review, 5(3),* 321–47.

Truax, C. B. and Carkhuff, R. R. (1967). *Toward Effective Counseling and Psychotherapy.* Chicago: Aldine Press.

Sarah Hawtin

University of East Anglia, Norwich, UK

The Organismic Valuing Process and Ethics
in Person-Centred Theory

The exploration for this paper began as a predominantly philosophical endeavour; an attempt to understand the extent to which client-centred, and subsequently person-centred theory, as originally formulated by Carl Rogers, is a statement with dual meaning. It clearly offers a view of human psychological functioning, but my initial question was to what extent it also proposes a theory of the good life from an ethical perspective. In short, does person-centred theory tell us not only how we live, but also how we ought to live?

The question has arisen through contemplating the extent to which the experiential quality of my individual existence can offer meaning and coherence to life. Rogers writes of therapeutic process that:

> . . . this process . . . appears to be a movement away from the pole of defensiveness toward the pole of openness to experience. The individual is becoming more able to listen to himself, to experience what is going on within himself . . . He is free to live his feelings subjectively, as they exist in him, and also free to be aware of these feelings. He is more able fully to live the experiences of his organism. (Rogers, 1961a, pp. 187–8)

Through therapy I can become more attuned to the process quality of my experiencing (Rogers, 1961a), but this alone does not straightforwardly seem to offer a justification for action. Alongside this I have become fascinated with the dilemmas clients bring to our work which have an unmistakable moral or ethical dimension. The question for them is not just 'What is good for me?' but simply 'What is good?' and this inevitably seems to demand reference to people and things outside the experiential realm of the individual.

I am concerned too with the danger of finding person-centred theory to be a form of emotivism. As a philosophical view, emotivism asserts that the meaning of ethical statements is reducible to expressions of emotion, in particular expressions of likes and dislikes. Linked to this is the focus of person-centred theory on the subjective experience of the individual and its reliance on the potential of the individual phenomenological world as a trustworthy source of values (Rogers, 1964). This view opens up the potential criticism that the value of individual feeling is over inflated and a form of narcissistic self-promotion encouraged. In this respect, emotivism feels profoundly unsatisfactory, suggesting as it does that our emotions are the beginning and end of ethical truth. In addition, differences in relationships become characterised as the clash of competing feelings. It therefore seems necessary to find an ethical understanding that acknowledges, yet also transcends, the individual.

It is through moving backwards and forwards between, on the one hand, my thoughts on what constitutes ethics and morality and, on the other, person-centred theory that this paper has evolved. Others have written interestingly and informatively on the way values and in particular ethical values inform therapeutic practice (Tjeltveit, 1999; Gordon, 1999), but I have chosen not to begin with precise definitions. As a result, in the discussion that follows I realise that I attempt to draw out a definition of ethics in parallel with trying to examine person-centred theory.

THE ORGANISMIC VALUING PROCESS AND THE INDIVIDUAL

To begin my discussion, I want to start by looking briefly at the conceptualisation of the organismic valuing process and its relationship to the actualising tendency. There are two reasons for this. Firstly, as a concept, the organismic valuing process centres on our capacity for choice and decision making. Secondly, the actualising tendency is an important referent by which we exercise that choice.

Rogers wrote about the organismic valuing process as follows:

This concept describes an on going process in which values are never fixed or rigid, but experiences are being accurately symbolised and continually and freshly valued in terms of the satisfactions organismically experienced; the organism experiences satisfaction in those stimuli or behaviours which maintain and enhance the organism and the self, both in the immediate present and in the long range. The actualising tendency is thus the criterion. (1959, p. 210)

More recently Goff Barrett-Lennard has written:

In infancy, and *through healthy child- and adulthood, human beings engage in an organismic valuing process.* Experiences tending to maintain or enhance the organism are valued positively, and the converse, negatively. Under certain conditions . . . the organism develops strong inhibitory tendencies and 'defensive' patterns that block the flow of some classes of experiential data, impair and restrict the organismic valuing process, and imply a lowering of integration. (Barrett-Lennard, 1998, pp. 75–6)

These statements contain several key assumptions with regard to the organismic valuing process:

1. It is present from birth, as an essential part of any organic entity;
2. It has the capacity to determine both long- and short-term satisfactions;
3. Smooth functioning of the organismic valuing process is dependent upon uninhibited experiential processing;
4. It is a process;
5. It is *not* part of the self-structure, but according to the Rogers' definition, it will work to maintain and enhance the self-structure, raising the possibility that the actualising tendency is not the only referent to which the organismic valuing process defers.

When discussing the organismic valuing process, Rogers used a classic example of an infant who eats when he feels hungry, but then rejects food when full; the same object being selectively valued, depending on the feeling need of the baby. In '*Toward a Modern Approach to Value: The Valuing Process in the Mature Person*' (Rogers, 1964), he also gives a more complex example of a young man who finds himself failing chemistry, a vital component of his medical degree.

In therapy it emerges that he has introjected the values of his parents, through picking up subtle signals that they valued him more when thinking of medicine as a career, than when he thought of himself as an artist. This second example illustrates how we can lose touch with our organism, and, in the case of this student, 'how out of touch he is with his *own* valuing process' (my emphasis, Rogers 1964, p. 173).

Also highlighted is the relationship of the organismic valuing process to the actualising tendency. It is by reference to the actualising tendency that the organismic valuing process determines whether a particular event or experience is to be valued positively or negatively, that is to say the extent to which it is taken to be genuinely enhancing. This conceptual relationship means that it is impossible to examine the organismic valuing process without at the same time examining the actualising tendency. The language here can be confusing. Stating that the organismic valuing process derives its capacity for discrimination from the actualising tendency starts to give a feeling of internal overpopulation. For this reason it feels important not to give the organismic valuing process some form of ontologically independent status; rather the organismic valuing process is a *functional discriminative capacity*.

Although the organismic valuing process is discussed very little, without it person-centred theory would seem like an attempt to describe a ship without a compass. Drive and desire might be present, but no capacity to differentiate in relation to experience. Put this way, the organismic valuing process also seems to appeal to a common-sense notion of how we go about things. It fits with the idea that we weigh up the pros and cons of various things, that we can feel immediate attraction and absolute revulsion. It seems to make sense of the fact that we have different tastes and interests. It lends credence to the struggles of clients to determine what they really want in difficult situations.

THE ORGANISMIC VALUING PROCESS AND ETHICAL CHOICE

Simply viewing the organismic valuing process as a discriminative capacity does not seem to move us beyond the sort of emotivism described earlier. One way to do so is to focus in more detail on ethical or moral choices, for one very particular reason: ethical and moral choices are a form of choices particular to human beings and do not seem to occupy any other organic or inorganic form.

This can be taken in at least two ways:
1. Ethical choice is a distinct form of choice exercised by human beings
2. Ethical choice is essential for our understanding of how we are constituted as human.

Ethical choice as a distinct form of choice exercised by human beings

Viewed this way, humanity is logically constituted prior to notions of ethics or morality: we have a conception of what it is to be human which is not dependent on notions of ethics. Drawing on the work of Morris, Rogers distinguished between different types of values and the definitions he outlined lend support to the idea that as human beings we face distinct value decisions. Three classes of values were outlined; after Morris, Rogers refers to these as 'operative', 'conceived' and 'objective' values (Rogers 1964, pp. 170–1).

Operative values

The first of these is perhaps relatively unproblematic. 'Operative' values centre on choices relating to the physical functioning of the organism. Here the example of the infant accepting and rejecting food clearly applies and we can understand this as also being relevant to any organism.

Conceived values

'Conceived values' bring us much more clearly into the realm of choices distinct to human beings. It is in this realm that I think the example of the young medical student sits and I believe it is in this realm that moral choice, as distinct from purely individual likes and dislikes, begins to come to the fore. With conceived values, our understanding does not emerge as freestanding and independent. It is carried in language and our interactions with others: it is as much part of our social context as it is part of our individual experience. For example, I can't understand the notion of 'doctor' or 'artist' without drawing on a wider social understanding of these roles (Hawtin and Moore, 1998). Person-centred theory has always placed a greater emphasis on phenomenological subjective experience as the pathway to a more universal truth; however there is an increasing body of constructivist and post-modern thought described by Maureen O'Hara as 'reveal[ing] psychological reality to be uniquely personal . . . but at the same time coextensive with the cultural contexts in which any individual develops consciousness' (O'Hara, 1997, p. 12).

In itself, this suggests that many of the choices we face are already rooted in more than our individual experience and this may provide hope in moving us away from emotivism. Yet there are ways of negating this potential. One such relates to the nature of social constructionism and the difficulty of understanding 'truth' in such a post-modern view. Whilst it seems that the idea that much of my apprehension of the world and myself in the world is shaped and formed through the conceptual systems we create, ethics and morality fall into a category where many would argue for something more universal or transcendent to support them. This is not a yearning for a modernist correspondence theory of truth, but rather a desire to feel that such choices express something deeper than an individual or collective wish. This comes back to the client who wants to know what is the good thing to do, not just what is good for them or even good in societal terms.

Objective values

Lastly Rogers spoke of 'objective' values; values where truth is logically independent of people desiring them. Rogers simply stated, 'People use the word in this way when they wish to speak of what is objectively preferable, whether or not it is in fact sensed or conceived of as desirable. What I have to say involves this last definition scarcely at all' (ibid, pp. 170–1).

Ethical choice as essential for our understanding of what constitutes us as human

The alternative to ethical choice as distinctive to human beings is ethical choice as essential to our understanding of how we are constituted as human. I think this takes us further in considering the organismic valuing process. Many philosophers have examined moral choice from this perspective. For instance, the existential tradition lays a heavy emphasis on the imperative to be: authentic action originating within us is what characterises us as subject, rather than object, and existential therapy aims to bring out the fullest implications of this (Yalom, 1980). The influence of existential thinking in Rogers' writings is well known, with Kierkegaard and Buber being two key figures.

Authenticity is one strand of existential thought: the character of relationship is another. Peter Schmid has explored the implications of personhood emerging through relationship in '*On Becoming a Person-Centred Approach: A Person-centred Understanding of the Person*' (Schmid, 1998). We are born into relationship, dialogue and encounter. As such, the existence of the other demands a response. As Schmid puts it 'This is why . . . responsibility is the fundamental category of being a person: from the encounter arises the obligation to respond' (Schmid, 1998, p. 43). Interestingly Schmid goes on to discuss how we are neither wholly preconstituted individuals, nor formed entirely through relationship. He states: 'Only in the dialectic of both interpretations, which for a long time were considered to be and apparently were incompatible. . . does the mystery of the person become accessible' (Schmid, 1998, p. 45).

From the relational perspective, we have little choice but to take account of others and the external world and this is necessarily an ethical perspective. We have to look beyond ourselves if we are to understand ourselves as human, but in contrast to social-constructionist theories, the relational perspective indicates a path which can perhaps take us beyond self- or collective interest. Relating this to person-centred theory, and in particular the relationship between the organismic valuing process and the actualising tendency, there is a challenge to be faced if we want to take this path. As a directional tendency, and as the referent of the organismic valuing process, there must be a way of understanding the actualising tendency that encompasses this ethical directedness. If we are to understand our humanity as residing in our capacity to be moral, then the actualising tendency must entail this.

THE ACTUALISING TENDENCY AND THE SEARCH FOR TRUTH

In terms which feel very familiar to person-centred theorists and practitioners, Vaclav Havel in his essay 'The Power of the Powerless' writes about what he feels are self-evident facts about human nature. He states: '[L]ife, in its essence, moves towards plurality, diversity, independent self-constitution and self-organisation' (Havel, 1985, p. 29). He adds, 'The essential aims of life are present naturally in every person. In every one there is some longing for humanity's rightful dignity, for moral integrity, for free expression of being and sense of transcendence over the world of existences' (Havel, 1985, p. 38). Alongside this he acknowledges another key factor in our existence and what he perceives to be the resultant implications:

> In everyone there is some willingness to merge with the anonymous crowd and to flow comfortably along with it down the river of pseudo-life. This is much more than a simple conflict between two identities. It is something far worse: it is a challenge to the very notion of identity itself. (Havel, 1985, p. 38)

Havel is showing how we are vulnerable through our natural desire for peace, security, freedom and dignity and it is this that makes us complicit in our own oppression, fostering and furthering the ways of being which secure acceptability and recognition. This seems to parallel almost exactly the person-centred view of the need for positive regard and also Rogers' understanding of the organismic valuing process as functioning to maintain and actualise the self-concept as well as the organism.

It was Rogers own assertion that the majority of us are compelled by introjected values. He stated: 'I believe that this picture of the individual, with values mostly introjected, held as fixed concepts, rarely examined or tested, is the picture of most of us. By taking over the conceptions of others as our own, we lose contact with the potential wisdom of our own functioning, and lose confidence in ourselves' (Rogers, 1964 p. 176). There is perhaps a slightly difference balance between Rogers and Havel here. Havel seems to suggest that our core struggle is exactly that, in essence a fundamental choice we can exercise. By contrast, Rogers gives the impression of an accidental and pervasive involvement in losing touch with our wisdom. This disconcerts me, as if others are the source of power and we are seduced, saved from complicity by our naïveté and our longing for love. We become prisoners in a form of intra-physic trap for which we are not responsible. A corollary of this is that therapy then becomes a form of liberation from oppression, the more or less conscious quest for freedom from internal constraints in order to contact the flow of life more fully. The understanding I find more compelling is that our desire for security, peace and dignity as part of the actualising tendency itself — given certain contexts — subverts itself, transposing basic human wishes into the negation of the very dignity we seek. We never lose touch with our longing, but its expression becomes a parody of itself. As such, this happening is an expression of our nature, not its concealment.

Another question arises here: if there is a fundamental ethical desire and it is not the desire for freedom from oppression, what might it be? Havel offers a strong alternative conception: that the moral aspect of the actualising tendency, and therefore the referential touchstone of the organismic valuing process, is the desire for truth. This is not a truth that is restricted to individual phenomenological experience; it is not just about intra-psychic congruence or indeed expression of that subjective truth. It is also about an unwillingness to live within the lie (as termed by Havel) and to perpetuate those actions and rituals that we accept through the desire for security or through believing ourselves powerless to make a difference. Havel outlines the way he believes that in Czechoslovakia individual acts of 'living within the truth' gradually coalesced to create a visible force capable of challenging the status quo. For the individual involved such a stand becomes *necessary of itself*, rather than a means to an end, because socially and politically the individual does not necessarily have the power to effect change. Although being subject to the oppression of ideology in Havel's terms or conditions of worth in person-centred terms is an expression of our nature, Havel insists the individual does have the capacity to rise above such a way of being. The crisis of identity at stake he sees clearly as a moral crisis. Allowing ourselves to merge into the social and political context of our existence, and allowing our own security and social advancement to be the bedrock of our existence, is to live as what Havel terms a 'demoralised' person. Our full humanity no longer exists because the capacity to act in a self-determined way has been abrogated. Havel is clear: we have no place to hide, no sphere in which our ethical responsibilities are set down: 'This means our responsibility is ours, that we must accept it and grasp it *here, now*, in this place in time and space where the Lord has set us down' (Havel,

1985, pp. 80–1). He also offers a sobering warning. Havel is certain that the dire nature of the Czech situation allowed a flourishing of moral sensibility in a way that the more materially comfortable social system of consumerism and technological advancement may not.

Where I believe this view bridges the individual/universal gap is that the desire for truth reaches beyond the individual and may indeed mean our demise through the denial of social approbation and even death. Havel argues not for the liberation of the true nature of the individual, but for the liberation of truth. It is not even necessarily a conscious act of sedition, but simply an assertion of the wish for truth in the face of lies, an embodied ethical imperative which takes us beyond the self through the desire for a broad authenticity, rather than the desire for freedom. This offers an understanding of truth that is beyond the individual and also recognises our social constraints and the inherent vulnerability of our nature in the face of those constraints.

THE EXPERIENCE OF KNOWLEDGE AND CHOICES

There is a further aspect of this discussion without which the rest is rather pointless. It is an epistemological consideration. Put bluntly, how do we *know* when we are making good choices?

It would seem that the source of our truth, however universal or non-dependent on our individuality, needs to lie in some form in the finite and limited context of our existence. Most obviously it is our body that offers this grounding. In this respect our body is not a vehicle in which we travel through life, it is more of a lightning conductor, the route through which our energies take form and expression. Viewed at a purely physical level we are a part of a wider system, responsive to and in many ways at the mercy of the physical context we inhabit.

This systemic conception of our existence is part of the underpinning of process conceptions of psychotherapy and, using Eugene Gendlin's understanding of the valuing process, I want to briefly discuss the body as a value source. Early in his exploration of experiential processes, Gendlin discussed the correlation between felt-sensing and values (Gendlin, 1967). He laid out the process nature of arriving at 'value-conclusions' (e.g. choices or goals), asserting that, as therapists, the way we have confidence in our clients' choices is not related to them settling upon goals or beliefs we approve of or believe to be true. Rather we are confident if the decision-making process gives full weight to the felt-senses involved. This he terms a process which has 'experiential clarity' (Gendlin, 1967, p. 181).

This process is potentially ever changing. As we attend to the immediate felt-sense and accurately symbolise it, an inner shift or resolution is experienced, which at the same time leaves space for further (possibly contradictory) experiencing to arise. In this way, the process moves forward from felt-sense to felt-sense. This Gendlin expressed as: 'This two-sidedness, this fact that an aspect of the process can be "complete", and yet is also open to further interaction involving further needs for resolution, is an aspect of the basic relationship between experiencing and symbols' (Gendlin, 1967, p. 186). Hence Gendlin isolates both a directional tendency in our experiencing and also identifies the relationship of symbols or concepts to feeling as being one in which the felt-sense can inform our thinking, but not the other way round, despite the fact that finding symbolic expression for our experiential awareness facilitates its flow and change. Knowledge of good fit between symbols and the felt-sense comes with an unmistakable and irreducible physical experience of rightness, the 'A-ha' moment or the sudden relaxation of tension that comes with knowing 'that's just it'.

This turns up a way of looking at decision making which places the experience of the person as prior to any conceptual system. Again referring to Gendlin, he states, 'The process is *not determined by any value-conclusions* that are *aimed at*, but by its own experiential, felt data to which the individual inwardly refers' and 'It is true that often the client does hold certain value-conclusions and strongly wishes to remain loyal to them. As value-conclusions, these are quite helpless to affect the experiential process' (Gendlin, 1967, p. 184). We may have deeply cherished beliefs, but our bodies may register and communicate quite different truths. In this way we are part of a wider system, which belief alone cannot determine.

It would seem that Gendlin offers us a much fuller account of the practicalities of the organismic valuing process than Rogers. He locates the source of knowledge in the body and additionally attempts to explain how such an organismic valuing process relates to our symbolic, conceptual and therefore social lives. This takes us close to the territory of emotivism, but with a distinct difference, I think. Without doubt, Gendlin is saying it is our bodily felt-sense that can guide us; it is individual experiencing that provides wisdom. However, he clearly locates the individual within a wider physical system and as a result of this states, 'It will therefore not be surprising if there are definable general values at which any human body and person will arrive when an experiential process of differentiation as outlined above occurs. It would mean that all human bodies and persons are organised in certain ways' (Gendlin, 1967, p. 188). At the very least, this seems to suggest it is not 'my' feelings that are the source of ethical truth, but that there is a more transcendent wisdom to which the body can give expression, but which cannot be determined by the individual, nor by collective beliefs. It is not without complications, but this seems to offer at least the beginnings of a potential understanding, whereby the felt-sense can be seen as a source of ethical wisdom.

CONCLUSION

By seeking to move beyond emotivism, whilst still staying true to person-centred theory, it seems necessary to see our humanity as having an ethical dimension. This effects the understanding of the actualising tendency and its relationship to the organismic valuing process. Alongside this, experiential theories may begin to offer a fuller understanding of the functioning of the organismic valuing process. In this way, person-centred theory seems to inevitably encompass ethical considerations. It cannot tell us the answer to specific moral dilemmas, but leaves little doubt that ethics are written into our existence in a way that is inescapable.

REFERENCES

Barrett-Lennard, G. T. (1998). *Carl Rogers' Helping System: Journey and substance*. London: Sage.

Gendlin, E. T. (1967). Values and the process of experiencing. In A. Mahrer (Ed.) *The Goals of Psychotherapy*. New York: Appleton-Century-Crofts.

Gordon, P. (1999). *Face to Face: Therapy as ethics*. London: Constable.

Hawtin, S. amd Moore, J. (1998) Empowerment or collusion? The social context of person-centred therapy. In B. Thorne and E. Lambers, *Person-centred Therapy: A European perspective*. London: Sage

Havel, V. (1985). *The Power of the Powerless*. London: Hutchinson.

O'Hara, M. (1997). Emancipatory therapeutic practice in a turbulent transmodern era: A work of retrieval. *Journal of Humanistic Psychology, 37*(3).

Rogers, C. R. (1959). A theory of therapy, personality, and interpersonal relationships, as developed in the client-centred framework. In S. Koch (Ed.*) Psychology: A study of service Vol. 3, Formulations of the person and the social contract*. New York: McGraw-Hill.

Rogers, C. R. (1961a). A therapist's view of the good life: The fully functioning person. In *On Becoming a Person*. London: Constable, pp. 183–96.

Rogers, C. R. (1961b). 'A Process Conception of Psychotherapy' in *On Becoming a Person*, (pp. 125–59). London: Constable.

Rogers, C. R. (1964). Toward a modern approach to values: The valuing process in the mature person. In H. Kirschenbaum and V. Henderson (Eds.) *The Carl Rogers Reader* (1990). London: Constable.

Schmid, P. F. (1998). On becoming a *Person*-Centred Approach: A person-centred understanding of the person. In B. Thorne and E. Lambers (Eds.) *Person-Centred Therapy: A European perspective*. London: Sage.

Tjeltveit, A. C. (1999). *Ethics and Values in Psychotherapy*. London: Routledge.

Van Kalmthout, M. (1998). Person-centred theory as a system of meaning. In B. Thorne and E. Lambers (Eds.) *Person-Centred Therapy: A European perspective*. London: Sage.

Yalom, I. D. (1980). *Existential Psychotherapy*. Basic Books.

Sachiko Hayashi and Atsushi Kara
University of Aizu, Fukushima, Japan

Understanding Self Through Taoist Emptiness

1. INTRODUCTION

No one is free of cultural, historical, and social value systems. An important issue is that within each individual there are several and, sometimes, contradictory value systems. Both within oneself and in relationships with others, conflicts are experienced both among such values and between the feelings/thoughts of must and must-not associated with these values. Many voices seem to be arguing inside an individual. Some speak loudly, whereas others barely whisper or are not even acknowledged. This causes discomfort and a need to resume a stable self. One function of counseling is to provide a safe space in which clients can freely listen to as many internal voices as possible and let the voices listen to each other (Mearns, 1994). A counselor cooperates with the client in reconciling disorganized or contradictory stories spoken by different selves.

The ancient philosophy of Chuang Tzu (China, circa 4th Century BC) represents an extreme in accommodating multiple values. He advocated an attitude of regarding *all things as equal* and free from all values. For him, any value system represented a bias and by detaching from it, pure awareness of the world could be achieved. Such a pure state of mind plays an important role in understanding and reorganizing the self toward integration.

2. SELF IN COUNSELING

According to Fujio Tomoda, one of the first advocates of PCA in Japan, the contents revealed by a client in counseling sessions undergo transition in the following manner: from symptoms to self, from environment to self, and from other people to self (Tomoda, 1969). As Tomoda himself described, this was only a simplification of the actual process of counseling. However, it is often the case that, as the counseling process develops, the stories the client narrates become increasingly centered on the self. This voluntary description of the self is a result of the safe and free counseling space given to the client and often reveals a deep sense of values.

As described by other authors (such as Enomoto, 1998), the concept of self differentiates into contextual selves, each of which is loaded with (or freed from) values acquired in relation to various social roles. This hypothetical organization of a person made up of multiple contextual selves is a view we endorse in this paper. Our main interest is in studying the dynamics involved in coordinating multiple selves, which leads to a congruent understanding, harmony and sometimes a structural change of a multi-value system. Our single focus in this article is to learn from Taoist philosopher Chuang Tzu's work how we can achieve a balanced view of ourselves by regarding all value conflicts as part of, or events of, the perfect whole.

3. USE OF THE USELESS

Chuang Tzu is one of the principal figures of Taoism. The 33 chapters of the book of Chuang Tzu were compiled over a long period over more than two thousand years ago, and it is not certain which parts are his original writings. We start from the concept of *the use of the useless,* which is a representative theme he mentions repeatedly to emphasize the incomplete and narrow-scoped nature of human value systems. Recognizing the utility of seemingly useless things is the first step toward a value-free understanding of the self. The following passage is one of Chuang Tzu's typical expressions on the use of the useless:

> The mountain trees do themselves harm; the grease in the torch burns itself up. The cinnamon can be eaten and so it gets cut down; the lacquer tree can be used and so it gets hacked apart. All men know the use of the useful, but nobody knows the use of the useless! In the World of Men, Chuang Tzu, (Watson, 1968, pp. 66–7)

Useful things get destroyed. Useless things remain safe. At a superficial level, the idea is just a maxim on the art of self-protection: that is, talent may be accompanied by danger, therefore, pretend to be incompetent and be careful to hide talent from others. However, Chuang Tzu's attitude to life was more sophisticated. He even stresses the positive use of the useless:

> The earth is certainly vast and broad, though a man uses no more of it than the area he puts his feet on. If, however, you were to dig away all the earth from around his feet until you reached the Yellow Spring, then would the man still be able to make use of it? . . . It is obvious, then, said Chuang Tzu, that the useless has its use. External Things (Watson, 1968, p. 299)

(Note: The Yellow Spring is a place underground where people are destined to go after their death.) The use of the useless is a philosophy that removes the boundary between the useful and the useless. The useful does not have a high value, nor does the useless have a low value. Chuang Tzu tried to see no boundary at all between poverty and wealth, criticism and honor, youth and senility, etc. His central idea was to *regard all things as equal.* Even life and death are equal:

> I received life because the time had come; I will lose it because the order of things passes on. Be content with this time and dwell in this order and then neither sorrow nor joy can touch you. In ancient times this was called the 'freeing of the bound.' There are those who cannot free themselves, because they are bound by things. But nothing can ever win against Heaven — that's the way it's always been. What would I have to resent? The Great and Venerable Teacher (Watson, 1968, p. 84)

However, Chuang Tzu did not praise death and did not reject the world. Instead, he enlarged it to include the whole universe. The goal is to become one with all things and to coexist with Heaven and Earth (Chan, 1963, p. 186). *The use of the useless* was a rhetoric that tried to free the mind from conventional values. A simple-minded judgment cannot be made on the value of anything, including the value of oneself. 'His goal was absolute spiritual emancipation and peace, to be achieved through knowing the capacity and limitations of one's own nature, by nourishing it and adapting it to the universal process of transformation.' (Chan, 1963, p. 177).

All functions of the self are nothing but a tiny part of the universal process of transformation. We often plant a specific dominant image of self firmly into our minds and take it as if it comprises the whole self. Spiritual emancipation gives equal *raison d'etre to* all aspects of one's inner dispositions. Therefore, we cannot simply say that some parts of us are true or right and other parts are not true or wrong. The real problem lies in the attitude of regarding oneself from within a narrow viewpoint. We do not have to classify and evaluate any feelings and thoughts inside us as good or bad, right or wrong, central or peripheral, etc. In this extreme philosophy of leaving all values, a new objective way of looking at the reality of self emerges as described in the story of Chaos below.

4. CHAOS

Chaos is a Taoist metaphor used to denote the initial state of the universe where nothing is differentiated. Chuang Tzu described Chaos as the ideal state of nature and all artificial human acts against Chaos must be denied. The following allegory is one of the best-known passages of Chang Tzu that enigmatically laughs at the stupidity of the acts of humans:

> The emperor of the South Sea was called Shu [Brief], the emperor of the North Sea was called Hu [Sudden], and the emperor of the central region was called Hun-tun [Chaos]. Shu and Hu from time to time came together for a meeting in the territory of Hun-tun, and Hun-tun treated them very generously. Shu and Hu discussed how they could repay his kindness. 'All men,' they said, 'have seven openings so they can see, hear, eat, and breathe. But Hun-tun alone doesn't have any, Let's try boring him some!' Every day they bored another hole and on the seventh day Hun-tun died. Fit For Emperors and Kings (Watson, 1968, p. 97)

The death of Hun-tun symbolizes the loss of a pure and innocent mind. If you force such a mind to cast itself into a form, however natural and proper the form seemed to be, it would die. The reality or pure experience that is not yet carved into human language is also symbolized by Hun-tun. For Chuang Tzu, language and analytical thinking were destined to fall into error:

> Chickens squawk, dogs bark — this is something men understand. But no matter how great their understanding, they cannot explain in words how the chicken and the dog have come to be what they are, nor can they imagine in their minds what they will become in the future. You may pick apart and analyze till you have reached what is so minute that it is without form, what is so large that it cannot be encompassed. But whether you say that 'nothing does it' or that 'something makes it like this,' you have not escaped from the realm of 'thing,' and so in the end you fall into error. Tse-Yang (Watson, 1968, p. 292)

By cherishing Chaos and abandoning analytical thinking, we can perceive reality with absolutely no bias. Although a chicken is a chicken and a dog is a dog if we call them so, the chicken and dog we saw before we hadn't even learned the words chicken and dog were the true chicken and dog. When we look at them with an empty mind and apart from language, what we are looking at will exhibit the unexpected variations of reality. We interpret the Taoist Emptiness in our counseling context as regarding the diverse events and processes inside us as Chaos in this sense.

5. MIRROR

Looking into self with an empty mind is a way to understand diverse needs and value systems inside us. The needs and values are not necessarily sorted out and the conflicts between them may cause harm if the person sides with only one of them. Chuang Tzu gives a prescription for 'being empty' together with other classical Taoist philosophers:

> Be empty, that is all. The Perfect Man uses his mind like a mirror — going after nothing, welcoming nothing, responding but not storing. Therefore he can win out over things and not hurt himself. Fit for Emperors and Kings (Watson, 1968, p. 97)

Self eludes understanding if it is analyzed into many individual pieces of meanings. Self is Chaos that needs to be understood as a whole. The mirror symbolizes such a holistic understanding through a pure mind. 'Being empty' is the only way of seeing the chaotic variations of reality in an unbiased manner. *The fasting of mind* is another famous passage from Chuang Tzu, introduced to the PCA literature in Japan by Tomoda (Hayashi, Kuno, Osawa, Shimizu, and Suetake, 1998, 2000; Ito, 1995; Morotomi, 1994; Tomoda, 1968, 1994).

> Make your will one! Don't listen with your ears, Listen with your mind. No, don't listen with your mind, but listen with your spirit. Listening stops with the ears, the mind stops with recognition, but spirit is empty and waits on all things. *The Way gathers in emptiness alone. Emptiness is the fasting of the mind.* In the World of Men (Watson, 1968, pp. 57–8)

When you listen to your self with your ears, you will hear nothing. When you try to understand your self with your mind, you will encounter misunderstandings and conflicts. Only when empty, can you experience the self as a whole.

6. CHANGING THE SELF

Each aspect of a personality has its own identity that sometimes manifests collision with each other. Still, the personality as a whole tries to remain as a persistent system and protests against any threat of change. The inconsistency of self-concept is regarded as a great threat to the existence of the human being, as described by D. Mearns (Mearns, 1994, p. 89).

> Self-concept is an attitude just like any other: each of the specific opinions, beliefs, feelings and evaluations about our self might well be changeable if and only if we could get it in isolation, but we cannot. These elements are all bound up together and they support each other against the threat of change. Our client may not like his self-concept, but still that self-concept will seek to preserve itself by maintaining its internal consistency, because inconsistency is a greater existential threat to the human being than simple negativity: we can cope with feeling bad about oneself more easily than we can cope with existential confusion.

Understanding Chuang Tzu's ideas on 'regarding all things as equal' and 'being empty' provides one with free and unbiased eyes and enables one to look at the inconsistent reality of selves. Carl Rogers' core conditions called the immediate attention of early Japanese PCA scholars in terms of their correspondence with Chuang Tzu's way of pure experience. The present authors' thesis is that this Taoistic pure perception of self, with all conflicts of internal values as they are, is the critical precondition to the next step: reorganizing the self. This precondition is a peaceful but powerful way to alleviate the existential threat of inconsistency, not only for a single client but also for a group.

7. CHANGING A GROUP: CORPORATE DYNAMICS AND PCA

Taoist philosophy finds readers in contemporary business sectors. Lao Tzu's philosophy is popular among corporate managers worldwide (e.g. Ruggenthaler, 1994). In a corporate environment, a great variety of different and often-conflicting value systems exist. The description of D. Mearns cited above applies equally to corporate group dynamics, when the term 'self' was replaced by the term, 'group.' Despite the conflicts of opinions and beliefs among group members, the group as a whole often resists change. In a goal-oriented group like a product development team, it is an important task for the manager to constantly expose the team to the market requirements and to continuously improve product design, quality-assurance and trouble-shooting skills. Sometimes the manager needs to change the overall development process. However such attempts to change groups very often fail when imposed in a top-down manner.

The process of changing a group is analogous to that of counseling. The attitude of the manager in delivering respect to all of the opinions and beliefs in the group helps the members to listen to different views within the group. The group then will extend the way of viewing multiple values to the surrounding outer world. This means that the group will be more objectively aware of their functional position in the organizational mission and in the marketplace. This awareness provides the sole motivation for the group to change.

In this analogy of corporate group dynamics to counseling process, the highest hurdle is for the manager to initiate and maintain the value-free attitude toward the entirety of the feelings, opinions, and beliefs held by the group. This is almost certainly a suicidal act from a power-dynamics viewpoint. Yet, this seems to be the only way for a group to experience the complexity of its existence and to understand the need for change. Moorman's nice Haiku describes such a process of change with conciseness:

> When my story
> is heard by another
> it becomes a new story

> From Person-Centered Haiku (Moorman, 2000)

When someone listens to the story told by each of our selves, whether the selves are personality aspects within a single person or members of a group, we will have taken the first step towards self-alteration.

REFERENCES

Chan, W. T. (1963). *A Source Book in Chinese Philosophy.* Princeton: Princeton University Press (pp. 177, 186).

Enomoto, H. (1998). *Jiko no Shinrigaku* (Psychology of Self). Tokyo: Science Inc.

Hayashi, S., Kuno, T., Morotomi, Y., Osawa, M., Shimizu, M. and Suetake, Y. (1998). Client-centered therapy in Japan, *Journal of Humanistic Psychology, 38*(2), 103–24.

Hayashi, S., Kuno, T., Morotomi, Y., Osawa, M., Shimizu, M. and Suetake, Y. (2000). Japanese poetry and the Client-Centered Approach. *The Person-Centered Journal, 7*(1), 4–17.

Ito, H. (1995). *Counseling, The 4th Edition.* Tokyo: Seishin Shobo.

Ruggenthaler, P. T. (Translation) (1994), *Lao Tse, Das Tao Der Staerke*, Verlag Orac im Verlag Kremyr and Scheriau, Vienna.

Mearns, D. (1994). *Developing Person-centered Therapy.* London: Sage.

Mooreman, J. (2000). Person-centered haiku, *The Person-Centered Journal, 7*(1), 18–20.

Morotomi, Y. (1994). Shinku ni okeru Jinkaku Henka (Personality change in vacuum), *Counseling Kenkyu, 13,* 7 and 62–71, Tokyo: Nihon Counseling Center.

Tomoda, F. (1968). Rogers to Roso (Rogers and Lao-Chuang philosophy), in *The Complete Works of C. R. Rogers, Vol. 18,* Tokyo: Iwasaki Gakujyutsu Shuppansha, p. 299.

Tomoda, F. (1969). *Jiko no Kozo* (The Structure of Self). Tokyo: Nihon Counseling Center.

Tomoda, F. (1994). Kyo wa Shinsai nari (The Fasting of Mind), *Counseling Kenkyu, 13,* 7, and 71–2, Tokyo: Nihon Counseling Center.

Watson, B. (Translation), (1968). *The Complete Works of Chuang Tzu.* New York: Columbia University Press.

Gillian Proctor
Leeds Community Mental Health Trust, Leeds, UK

Power in Person-Centred Therapy[1]

INTRODUCTION

In this paper, I will explore three aspects of power I have identified in the therapy relationship. I will examine how Rogers' theory of person-centred therapy addresses these aspects of power, present critiques of these attempts and finally suggest resolutions of these critiques. I contend that Rogers' person-centred theory can responsibly consider ethics of power in therapy, subject to certain conditions.

I have identified three aspects to the power imbalance in the therapy relationship from the literature on power in therapy (following DeVaris, 1994, see Proctor 2002). These are: the power imbalance inherent in roles of 'therapist' and 'client', the personal history of the therapist and particularly the client with respect to the experience of power and powerlessness, and the power distribution with respect to the social structural positions of the client and therapist. All these aspects combine to create the subjective experience for each person of power or powerlessness and the material reality of individuals with respect to their ability to have control or power over their own lives.

I will also consider three types of power, following Starhawk (1987), and how these are theorised within person-centred therapy. Starhawk (1987) distinguishes three types of power: 'power-over', 'power-from-within' and 'power-with'. 'Power-over' refers to domination. 'Power-from-within' comes from the root of the word power, meaning to be able, and she describes this as an inner strength from a sense of mastery at one's own ability and innate value. This strength also arises from the sense of connection or bond with other humans and the environment. 'Power-with' is the power of individuals within a group of equals, to suggest and be listened to. She emphasises the danger that this can become authority and that 'power-with' is only possible among those who are equal and who *recognise* they are equal.

THE ROLES OF THE THERAPIST AND CLIENT

Rogers (1978a) explains the implications of the philosophy and values behind person-centred therapy; that clients are to be trusted to find their own way and all clients know the best way for them, as opposed to the therapist knowing best, or having expert knowledge:

[1.] This is a condensed version of Chapter 6 in *The Dynamics of Power in Counselling and Psychoherapy*, Ross-on-Wye: PCCS Books, 2002, pp. 84–103.

The politics of the person-centred approach is a conscious renunciation and avoidance by the therapist of all control over, or decision-making for, the client. It is the facilitation of self-ownership by the client and the strategies by which this can be achieved; the placing of the locus of decision-making and the responsibility for the effects of these decisions. It is politically centred in the client. (p. 14)

The non-directive attitude and the actualising tendency

The nondirective attitude is a way for the therapist to express their commitment to avoid client disempowerment (Brodley, 1997). Rogers (1978a) pointed out the implications of this principle of nondirectivity on the part of the therapist by discussing the threat to counsellors of his views (p. 7): 'I was making it clear that if they agreed with me, it would mean the complete disruption and reversal of their personal control in their counselling relationship.' Rogers (1978a) contends that the premise of the actualising tendency challenges the need to control people, challenges (p. 8) 'the view that the nature of the individual is such that he cannot be trusted — that he must be guided, instructed, rewarded, punished, and controlled by those that are higher in status.'

Demystification of therapy

Another way in which Rogers addressed the imbalance of power in the therapy relationship was to make person-centred therapy transparent and explicit, to demystify therapy. He did this by explaining exactly what the therapist does in therapy and by providing much tape-recorded and video-recorded material for public use. He placed great importance on the clarity of the process and content of therapy and the accountability of the therapist to be able to demonstrate the extent to which he/she fulfilled the core conditions. He also demystified the therapist as a person by stressing the concept of congruence.

The facilitative conditions

Rogers (1978a) examines the core conditions of congruence, unconditional positive regard and empathy with respect to their political implications and the power imbalance between client and therapist. He points out (p. 10) that congruence 'gives a maximum space to be — for the client and the therapist. The therapist is saying, in effect "Here I am, as I am." There is no hint of any kind of control over the client's response to her way of being. To the contrary, finding that the therapist is permitting herself to be as she is, the client tends to discover that same freedom.' He then discusses the implications of unconditional positive regard and concludes (p. 11) that 'It is a powerful factor, but it is in no way manipulative or controlling in the relationship. There is no judgment or evaluation involved. Power over her own life is left completely in the hands of the client. It provides a nurturant atmosphere but not a forcing one.' With regard to empathic understanding, Rogers (1978a) argues that it assists the client to gain a clearer understanding of and hence a greater control over her own life; i.e. it aims directly to increase the client's subjective feeling of personal power.

Rogers (1978a) describes person-centred therapy as 'revolutionary' with respect to the political stance and philosophy it upholds. He defines politics (Rogers, 1978b; p. 1) by saying 'politics involves the question of where power is located, who makes the choices and decisions, who carries out or enforces those decisions, and who has the knowledge or data regarding the consequences of those decisions. It involves the strategies involved in the taking of power, the distribution of power, the holding of power, and the sharing or relinquishing of power.' He asserts that opposition to person-centred therapy sprang up (p. 16) 'primarily because it struck such an outrageous blow to the therapist's power.' He challenges the notion of expert knowledge which gives power, and believes in the power of congruence. Rogers (1978a; p. 250) explains 'In such an individual, functioning in a unified way, we have the best possible base for wise action. It is a process base, not a static authority base. It is a trustworthiness that does not rest on static "scientific" knowledge.' Here, Rogers appeals to inner knowledge and experience, not the rationality of science.

Personal histories

The self-concept can be understood as the internalisation of power of others over the client. Rogers (1978a) theorised that psychological distress is the result of a split between the organismic self and the self-concept. He has found that as a client experiences the facilitative conditions of person-centred therapy, in reciprocity with the conditions provided by the therapist, the client begins to listen more acceptantly to her/himself, (s)he begins to prize her/himself more as the therapist as prized her/him, and (s)he is able to more openly be her/his experiencing within. Thus, trust in the organismic self increases, and as this happens, the client's history of powerlessness decreases in potency and the client's subjective feeling of power or control over his/her own life increases. Rogers describes this process (1978a; p. 12): 'By listening to the feelings within, the client reduces the power others have had in inculcating guilts and fears and inhibitions, and is slowly extending the understanding of, and control over, self.' Gradually, the trust of the organismic self increases and the client's personal history of powerlessness (internalised in the self-concept) becomes a less powerful mechanism of disempowerment.

SOCIAL STRUCTURAL POWER

In the later part of his life, Rogers began to specifically address concerns about the social context of society and power. His main contention is that the Person-Centred Approach is a revolutionary way to understand and change oppression, particularly by facilitating communication between those who are oppressed and oppressors in large groups. Rogers (1978a) argues that the Person-Centred Approach can be used to help people who are members of oppressed groups. He gives an example of a facilitated meeting between 'health consumers', who were poor, mainly black people in America, and 'health providers'. He argues that the process of facilitating each person to be heard enabled much greater understanding to be established between both groups. This process meant that all views were heard; there was no necessity for members of the oppressed group to speak with a unified voice to be heard. He claims that as they were heard, members of the oppressed group grew in confidence to speak and initiate change and that the group moved towards revolutionary but realistic steps to change the situation, steps which were later carried out, and real material change in conditions did happen. Here, Rogers seems to be referring to Starhawk's concept of 'power-with', the positive power gained from collectivity.

This explains something about why Rogers believed his approach to be so revolutionary. It does not only attempt to improve conditions for people in oppressed groups, but also works towards changing the whole social system, based on hierarchy, power and oppression, to one where each individual is listened to and considered, and change is considered from every perspective.

CRITIQUES OF ROGERS

Power in the roles: transparency

Lowe (1999) critiques Rogers' idea of transparency of therapy and of the therapist, by pointing out that however transparent, therapy is still institutionalised within a particular mode of practice. Fish (1999) cites Foucault who also argued against the possibility of 'transparency' in therapy, and claimed that this aim derives from the concept of power as necessarily negative and avoidable. (For more details of Foucault's approach to power, see Proctor, 2002.) Fish (1999; p. 67) quotes Foucault (1980; p. 298) who states about power relations in therapy: 'The problem, then, is not to try and dissolve them in the utopia of completely transparent communication but to acquire the rules of law, the management techniques, and also the morality, the ethos, the practices of the self, that will allow us to play these games of power with as little domination as possible.'

As Lowe (1999) notes, claims to make therapy transparent do not remove the inherent power inequality in the roles of therapist and client. However much a therapist does not behave like an expert, the role of the therapist is still there, and the client could always be aware that at any point the therapist *could* choose to use the power in this role. The therapist could of course use the power for the client's benefit; but this notwithstanding, there is still a clear inequality in the positions of therapist and client which is not removed by any kind of therapist egalitarian behaviour or attitude.

However, Bozarth (1998) considers this argument and cites a discussion between Rogers and Buber where Buber makes the claim that the therapist-client situation is always unequal. In reply, Rogers argues that this unequal relationship does not accurately describe the therapy relationship. Bozarth (1998; p. 21) quotes Rogers saying 'This is something immediate, equal, a meeting of two persons on an equal basis, even though, in the world of I-It, it could be seen as a very unequal relationship.' Bozarth suggests that this disagreement is due to the different definitions of power used by Rogers and Buber. He suggests that the person-centred position with regard to power is derived from the view of power from the Latin etymology, 'portiere', that essentially means to be all you are capable of being. He suggests that the counter-position seems to focus on the definition of power as 'possession of control, authority, influence over others'. Here Bozarth seems to be making the distinction between Starhawk's (1987) concepts of 'power-from-within' and 'power-over'. The person-centred concept of power focuses on power as positive, strength within oneself, and a respect for others and their 'power-from-within'. At other times (particularly when talking about groups), this power is seen to be further enhanced by coming together with others for mutual benefit, where all are seen as equal in terms of respecting each individual's 'power-from-within'. This refers to

Starhawk's (1987) concept of 'power-with'.

Bozarth (1998; p. 21) suggests that the equality in the person-centred therapy relationship is 'in the attitude of the therapist's willingness to trust the client to go in his or her direction, way and pace. It is the equality of two individuals in relationship.' It is clear that the theoretical and ethical position of the person-centred therapist not to dominate, control or direct the client is paramount in the claims to equality in person-centred theory. Larner (1999) similarly echoes the person-centred view of the revolutionary power of the person-to-person therapy relationship. He claims (p. 46) 'This stance of being-with-the-other *is* politically empowering, as a human situation where a dialogue of meaning and sharing takes place.' Brink (1987) suggests that the objectively real inequality in the therapist-client relationship can be transcended by a felt sense of equality that comes spontaneously when they meet as persons with common humanity.

Burstow (1987) explores in detail the ways in which there is both equality and inequality in the person-centred therapy relationship. She suggests that the therapist and client are equal as humans and in worth and are equally capable of realising their own unique potential. However she stresses that they are necessarily unequal in their roles; that the therapist is the helper and the client the helpee. She quotes Buber (1970; p. 179), saying 'there are . . . many I-you relationships which by their very nature may never unfold into complete mutuality if they are to remain faithful to their nature.' Burstow emphasises that this role of being the helpee necessarily makes the client more vulnerable, although she also stresses the strength which may arise from this vulnerability. She suggests that the danger of asserting equality where it does not exist can be that the vulnerability of the client is missed.

In focusing on these aspects of the therapist's behaviour as just another person, there is a danger that the power inherent in the role of therapist is missed. It may be that what is understood to be therapeutic in person-centred therapy is the relationship between two people; but one of them is still there in the role of the client, and the other in the role of the therapist. There are different powers in society attached to each of these roles and this inequality is established in the institution of therapy. Person-centred theory emphasises the agency of individuals at the expense of missing the effect of structures of power on individuals. The potential implications for a person-centred therapist of ignoring structural power are that they could miss opportunities to help clients from their own position, and they could underestimate or misunderstand the effects on clients' lives of any structures of power. As Larner (1999; p. 49) also emphasises, 'Professional authority, power and social hierarchy in the therapeutic institution are *real* enough.'

Critique of nondirectivity

Pilgrim and Treacher (1992; p. 164) also warn about the dangers of nondirective approaches avoiding issues of power. They assert: 'The new client-centred discourse is to be characterised by one party having more formal knowledge than the other. As psychotherapists have known for years, an approach to professional work which actually minimises authoritative directiveness, is itself, an extremely effective way of having power over clients. Non-directiveness and contrived neutrality are themselves evidence of professional power and choice.'

Grant (1990) argues that psychotherapy is a moral enterprise and we need to examine the morality of the practices of therapy. He claims that the principle of non-directivity in person-centred therapy can be justified either instrumentally (it helps the client) or morally (for respect for the client). He emphasises (p. 82) that 'The liberation that can come from client-centred therapy is accomplished by respecting clients as autonomous beings, not by making them autonomous beings.' He points to the importance of principled non-directivity as being a moral choice to respect the client, and contends that: 'It is, within this framework, always right to be nondirective and always wrong not to be.'

Grant (1990) explains further the concept of principled non-directiveness and how this is a moral choice out of respect for the client; an attitude, not a behaviour, an absence of intention (p. 78). 'The therapist does not attempt or intend to make anything happen — growth, insight, self-acceptance — in the client, but rather provides the therapeutic conditions in the belief that they are expressions of respect and with the hope that the client will make use of them.' He further clarifies that non-directiveness is not a choice that withholds other ways of being from the client.

> Principled nondirectiveness is an attitude, not a set of behaviours. Having the attitude does not mean a stock or a 'hands off' approach to relating to clients, although the most common expression of it is empathic understanding responses. Living the attitude means being open and responsive to clients' requests and indications for other types of response . . . Principled nondirectiveness is an expression of an absence of the *intention* to make anything in particular happen, and of an openness to following the client's direction. (p. 81–2, original emphasis)

He compares principled nondirectiveness with instrumental nondirectiveness, where the therapist chooses to be nondirective when (s)he believes this is in the best interests of the client. This concept of instrumental nondirectiveness (which Grant argues is more relevant to humanistic therapies in general, whereas principled nondirectiveness characterises Rogerian person-centred therapy) is criticised by Pilgrim and Treacher (1992) with respect to the therapist using their power to be nondirective. However, principled nondirectivity, which characterises person-centred therapy, is in contrast non-withholding and does not represent the power of the therapist in making a choice for the patient, but instead, facilitating the client to make their own choice.

Inequality in personal histories

The insistence in person-centred theory on an equal relationship in therapy also misses another aspect of power in the therapy relationship: the power in the personal history of the client and therapist with respect to the experience of power and powerlessness. Psychological distress in the client results from the experience of conditions of worth which cause the self-concept to be separated from the organismic self, leaving the client in a state of incongruence. One of Rogers' (1957) core conditions is that the client is in a state of incongruence; another that the therapist is in a state of congruence. In addition, Rogers' (1957) sixth condition emphasises the importance of the client's perception of the therapist. The way that the client experiences the therapist will not be determined just by how the therapist acts but also by how the client has experienced others in the past. Whilst Rogers hypothesises that the provision of the core conditions will provide a corrective experience for the conditions of worth previously experienced by the client, it is likely there will be a period of time before the client experiences these conditions as genuine and something to be trusted. At least until the point where the client perceives the conditions experienced by the therapist, this discrepancy in states of (in)congruence provides another aspect to the inequality in the therapy relationship which can be obscured by claims to equality.

Burstow (1987) similarly points out that there are areas in which the therapist and client are not necessarily equal or unequal, but the likelihood is that the therapist will have more power. These areas are in their level of coping skills and their comfort with life; areas in which she suggests there is likely to be inequality. The inequalities in these areas could be seen as a result of personal histories. She also gives examples of a client's vulnerability being missed by a belief in an equal relationship. However, it is just as likely that a client's coping skills may be much greater than those of the therapist as they may have encountered much more difficult circumstances. Either way, there will be an inequality of power arising from personal histories, which is likely to become apparent in the difference between the client's and the therapist's perception of their own 'power' from-within'. Here, a client's personal history of powerlessness may mean it is difficult for a client to feel their own 'power-from-within' in the therapy situation, however much a therapist does not use 'power-over'.

Larner (1999), instead of emphasising the possibility of therapy being a relationship between equals (two people), stresses the ethical challenge to work within a relationship of unequals. He claims that integral to the ethics needed are a position of humility and using non-power by the therapist. He proposes a deconstructing therapy which he claims (p. 41) 'is obliged to be both powerful and non-powerful . . . That therapists can be powerful, but sacrifice themselves for the sake of the other, allows the power of the other to emerge.' This concept of being 'non-powerful' seems to refer to the attitude of the person-centred therapist. Larner (1999; p. 47) further explains 'Deconstructing psychotherapy is involved in the process of ethical engagement in "I-thou" relations. Therapeutic power is balanced by the ethical stance towards the other, putting the other first before self, recognising others as subjects in their own right.' Here he refers to Buber's concept of 'I-thou' relations which was also used by Rogers to explain the person-to-person relationship in person-centred therapy. Larner (1999; p. 48) further concurs with person-centred theory saying, 'The therapist does not relate to the client in terms of a theory of the other, but as *strangely* other.' Here he emphasises the respect for the other as a separate being and the basis of phenomenology, which is core to the Person-Centred Approach. Larner (1999; p. 48) further seems to be commenting on the core conditions in the Person-Centred Approach when he suggests 'The conscious movement of the therapist towards the other as an ethical stance allows true dialogue of unequals, in which both therapist and client are powerful *and* non-powerful.' This confirms the commitment of the person-centred therapist to not use 'power-over' the client and to affirm both the therapist's and the client's sense of 'power-from-within'.

Power in social structures

Pilgrim (1983) examines the potential liberation inherent in models of psychotherapy as opposed to the medical model. He asserts that the more a model takes account and 'defers to' the social context, the greater the possibility of liberation from the social control of the medical model. He accuses humanistic models of being reductionist (or individualising) and 'psychologizing politics'. However, he does seem to account for individual practitioners also deferring to the social context when he suggests that (p. 127) 'Psychoanalysis and humanistic therapies have often functioned conservatively by being hijacked by individualism, so that social change is judged irrelevant, dangerous or a substitute for a more valuable change of heart.' Thus, he acknowledges the possibility of practitioners functioning in a less conservative, more socially aware way. Nevertheless, he criticises the Rogerian idea of the revolutionary impact of groups understanding each other. He claims (p. 129): 'The material realities of ownership and control do not disappear because the representatives of labour and capital take off their ties, roll up their sleeves, and struggle to communicate honestly with each other. The search for inner harmony and the struggle for political justice are twin tasks facing humanity. One cannot substitute for the other, no matter how hard the evangelists of either cause persuade us otherwise. However, by keeping in mind their social context, a synthesis rather than a mutual substitution is possible in theory and practice.'

Waterhouse (1993) compares feminist therapies with person-centred therapy in a feminist critique of person-centred therapy. She points to similarities between the two types of therapy with respect to the importance of equalising counsellor-client relationships and eradicating dualistic thinking. However, she accuses that (p. 58) 'In his concept of the person, Rogers consequently neglects to problematise gender, race and class.' She contrasts the two approaches, commenting (p. 61):

> In contrast to Rogers' harmonic view of human relationships, feminists point to the many examples of gender inequality which create profound conflicts of interest between women and men . . . Personal issues, emotional distress and individual breakdown are consequently viewed as political issues . . . Person-centred approaches stress the uniqueness of each person's experience whereas feminist approaches stress the commonality of women's experiences.

Waterhouse (1993) claims that by not recognising the political in the personal, the person-centred therapist is in danger of giving unwarranted weight to the individual's power to effect change in their everyday lives irrespective of material or socio-political constraints, and possibly colluding with blaming the individual for not being able to change. She further seems to imply that a person-centred therapist withholds help or care by the stress on self-reliance which I would suggest is a misunderstanding of principled nondirectivity in person-centred therapy. Despite acknowledging Rogers' awareness of socio-political contexts in his later work, she then discusses his later contributions no further and thus misses the potential for understanding person-centred therapy in a social context.

However, Waterhouse (1993) makes an important point with respect to the necessity for person-centred therapists to address issues of oppression in training with respect to self-exploration. She explains that (p. 62), 'Without such training the person-centred counsellor is left at best with a vague, and at worst a naïve view of what it means to be a "person."' She does seem to recognise that there is potential for a person-centred therapist understanding of the 'self' to mean 'self-in-social-context', (both in relation to others and social structures), but criticises Rogers for the lack of this emphasis saying (p. 66): 'He fails to acknowledge the extent to which our capacity to be empathic is affected by our experience as subjects in a social structure.' Similarly, Kearney (1996) addresses what needs to be done to keep the radical sociological and political nature of person-centred therapy, saying (p. 86): 'I believe that if we regularly fail to challenge our own and our clients' internalised ideologies we lose the radical dimensions of person-centredness and turn it into a much less powerful force for change than it should be.'

Kearney (1996) considers class, and the relation of this to the power imbalance in the therapy relationship. She explains the importance of class in therapy, saying (p. 77): 'Political factors such as class enter into counselling through the power imbalances between client and counsellor, in the language client and counsellor use, in the different class-based meaning structures through which we speak and hear; in the different vocabularies and codes we use and in the different class-based experiences we may have.' She points to the danger of reinforcing the inequality in power in therapy by ignoring class influences. She criticises Waterhouse's (1993) critique of Rogers, suggesting (p. 82):

> I do not believe that the person-centred focus on the individual necessarily excludes awareness of the social constraints of people's lives in principle, though I believe that it may, and often does, in practice . . . It is, I suggest, perfectly possible to focus on the 'self-actualising tendency of the socially positioned individual' . . . If we hold onto this awareness, I believe it becomes much less likely that we will practice counselling in a way that disregards the oppressive external structures which form the restrictive scaffolding of people's lives.

Kearney (1996) further suggests that Rogers himself saw the political radicalness of his approach, and theorised internalising oppression through conditions of worth. She contends that person-centred theory is directly concerned with identifying external oppressions. This is also corroborated by Rogers' theory of the actualising tendency, a tendency towards constructive growth both for the individual and others in relationship with the individual (See Brodley, 1999 for more detailed discussion on the pro-social nature of the actualising tendency in humans.) This is further emphasised by Rogers' descriptions of the process of growth and the healthy functioning person (Rogers, 1961).

If person-centred therapists can focus on understanding a unique individual in their social context with awareness of the social structures which affect and construct the lives of individuals, there is a real chance a balance of understanding of structures and individual agency can be maintained. Therapists can aim for an understanding of the context but without assuming the impact of the context on any one individual.

CONCLUSION

From a post-structuralist perspective, power is ubiquitous. (For more details on a post-structuralist perspective on power, see Proctor, 2002.) We cannot avoid power in relationships, but can be aware of power dynamics and try and negotiate them with the least domination possible. At times, person-centred theory and therapy is in danger of obscuring power in the therapy relationship by the focus on the equality of the person-to-person relationship. However, person-centred therapists can responsibly consider ethics of power if:

1) We do not forget the structures of power involved in the roles of therapist and client.
2) We do not obscure inequalities in the relationship with respect to states of (in)congruence and the effect of personal histories.
3) We aim to understand the socially-positioned individual.
4) We look at our own positions as therapists regarding power and our potential for oppression.

(Ways to consider these issues are explored in more detail in Proctor, 2002.)

To take these issues seriously, and really try to aim for the least domination in therapy relationships, there are implications for both training and supervision of person-centred therapists. Within both these areas, therapists need to be encouraged to become aware of structures of power in society, within therapy and the effect of their own history of power and powerlessness. Person-centred therapists need to constantly consider their own and their clients' positions with respect to power.

REFERENCES

Arendt, H. (1963). *On Revolution.* London: Penguin.

Bozarth, J. (1998). *Person-Centred Therapy: A revolutionary paradigm.* Ross-on-Wye: PCCS Books.

Brink, D. (1987). The issues of equality and control in the client- or person-centred approach. *The Journal of Humanistic Psychotherapy, 27,* 27–38.

Brodley, B. T. (1997). The nondirective attitude in client-centered therapy. *The Person-Centered Journal, 4* (1), 27–38.

Brodley, B. T. (1999). The actualizing tendency concept in client-centered theory. *The Person-Centered Journal, 6* (2), 108–20.

Buber, M. (1970). *I and thou.* (W. Kaufman trans.) New York: Scribner.

Burstow, B. (1987). Humanistic psychotherapy and the issue of equality. *The Journal of Humanistic Psychotherapy, 27,* 9–25.

DeVaris, J. (1994). The dynamics of power in psychotherapy. *Psychotherapy, 31,* 588–93.

Fish, V. (1999). Clementis's Hat: Foucault and the politics of psychotherapy. In I. Parker (Ed.) *Deconstructing Psychotherapy.* London: Sage, pp. 54–70.

Foucault, M. (1980). *Power/Knowledge: Selected interviews and other writings 1972–77.* Brighton: Harvester Press.

Grant, B. (1990). Principled and instrumental non-directiveness in person-centred and client-centred therapy. *Person-centred Review, 5,* 77–88.

Kearney, A. (1996). Rogerian counselling and politics. In A. Kearney, *Counselling, Class and Politics: Undeclared influences in therapy.* Manchester: PCCS Books, pp. 77–86.

Larner, G. (1999). Derrida and the deconstruction of power as context and topic in therapy. In I. Parker (Ed.) *Deconstructing Psychotherapy.* London: Sage, pp. 39–53.

Lowe, R. (1999). Between the 'No Loner' and the 'Not Yet': Postmodernism as a context for critical therapeutic work. In I. Parker (Ed.) *Deconstructing Psychotherapy.* London: Sage, pp. 71–85.

Pilgrim, D. (1983). Politics, Psychology and Psychiatry. In D. Pilgrim (Ed.) *Psychology and Psychotherapy: Current trends and issues.* London: Routledge and Kegan Paul, pp. 121–38.

Pilgrim, D. and Treacher, A. (1992). *Clinical Psychology Observed.* London: Routledge.

Proctor, G. (2002). *The Dynamics of Power in Counselling and Psychotherapy: Ethics, politics and practice.* Ross-on-Wye: PCCS Books.

Rogers, C. R. (1957). The necessary and sufficient conditions for therapeutic personality change. *Journal of Consulting Psychology, 21,* 95–103.

Rogers, C. R. (1961). *On Becoming a Person: A therapist's view of psychotherapy.* London: Constable.

Rogers, C. R. (1978a). *Carl Rogers on Personal Power.* London: Constable.

Rogers, C. R. (1978b). *My Political View.* El Escorial workshop: Unpublished paper.

Starhawk. (1987). *Truth or Dare: Encounters with power, authority, and mystery.* San Francisco: Harper and Row.

Waterhouse, R. (1993). 'Wild women don't have the blues': A feminist critique of 'person-centred' counselling and therapy. *Feminism and Psychology, 3,* 55–71.

Campbell Purton
University of East Anglia, Norwich, UK

Focusing on Focusing: The practice and the philosophy

In this paper I explore some philosophical issues in the background of focusing, and then make some suggestions about how the philosophy has implications for some current discussions about the practice of focusing. In particular I think that what I have to say about the philosophy has something to contribute to (a) the question of how important it is to emphasise the distinctiveness of the felt sense as contrasted with other kinds of experiencing, (b) the question of the importance of clearing a space and (c) the issue of whether it is helpful in focusing to speak in terms of 'parts' of a person.

THE INTRICACY

As I understand it, what is central to the theory of focusing is the relation between experiencing and symbolic forms, such as words, images and gestures. Our experiencing is rich and intricate beyond anything that our symbols can render, but it is also very specific, in the sense that only certain specific symbolic formations will render it. I will use the word 'render' here to convey the central relationship or process with which focusing works. This word — like all words — has itself a richness and intricacy of the sort which interests us. The word 'render' has uses which include *causing to become* as when something renders us helpless. Then there is the sense of *translation* (rendering something into English). There is the sense of *performing a version of* a play, or a piece of music. And, seemingly very different, there is the rendering of a wall with a coat of plaster.

The use of the word 'render' is itself an example of what Gendlin calls the intricacy of our language and of our experiencing. The different uses of the word 'render' pull out different aspects of the relationship between experiencing and its symbolisation. Thus our symbols can be seen as rendering our experience first in the sense that they *cause our experience to become* more explicit, more focused, and more communicable. Then there is a sense in which they *translate* our private experiencing into a public language. Our symbols *present a version of* our experiencing, rather as a particular performance of a play presents that play (there could be other versions). And then they are a presentation of our complex bumpy experiencing to public view, as the rendering of a wall presents a smooth, finished appearance to the wall. As Wittgenstein noted, words do not work in a simple representational or conceptual way. It is not that there is a single sort of process in the world to which we attach the label 'rendering', and that this sort of process goes on wherever the word 'rendering' applies. Wittgenstein's (1963, I, 66) famous remark about how we should approach how words work was 'Don't think, but look!' And when we look at different examples of renderings, what we find is not something single and simple, but that which Gendlin calls the 'intricacy'. In therapy it is the same: someone is angry, but the term 'anger' can conceal the intricacy of that particular person's situation in all its specificity. There is an anger of hurt, an anger of indignation, an anger of revenge, but each of these has its possible subdivisions, which in the end can only be rendered by telling the stories of the situations involved.

Symbols, then, render the intricacy of our experiencing, and they do this in several different ways. Gendlin (1962/1997) discussed this in his first book *Experiencing and the Creation of Meaning*. For example, there is the rendering of what we are experiencing by phrases such as 'that feeling' or 'all that business'. In this case there is minimum conceptual content. The words are working in a purely referential way. Then there is the rendering of experience by familiar words already in the language as when we say, 'This funny feeling is actually resentment, you know.' Different again is the rendering through metaphor: 'The feeling is . . . hmmm . . . it is the feeling that my life has become an empty box.'

THE FELT SENSE

The rendering of experience in symbols requires attention to the experiencing. We have to stay with the feel of 'all that', we have to sense it as a whole. Then we can refer to 'all that thing', or to the feeling that comes to be experienced as resentment, or the feeling that gets rendered as an empty box. These feelings of something are what Gendlin initially called the 'direct referent', and later the 'felt sense'. They are what we refer to or sense in ourselves when we give some sustained attention to our experiencing of a situation. Such direct referents or felt senses are not usually already there when we turn our attention to our experiencing. It is rather that they form in the context in which we are trying to render the experiencing. The felt sense is right at the interface between the experiencing and the symbol, and it has to form or emerge from that interface.

All this is not specifically related to therapy. This rendering of experience into new symbolic forms is needed and present in any area of life outside of formal argumentation in disciplines such as logic and mathematics. In science it has long been apparent that there is no purely logical process of deriving new theories either from the old ones, or from the results of observation and experiment. This has led some philosophers of science to deny that there is any procedure for creating new and better theories. It is held by such thinkers that the invention or discovery of scientific theories must be a matter of sheer inspiration or conjecture; the logic of scientific discovery is to be found solely in the procedures for testing the conjectures (Popper 1959). However this account hardly seems to square with the historical facts. It is true that scientists don't deduce their theories from the experimental data, but nor do they just dream them up out of the blue. A scientist typically wrestles with his data and with the current theories, trying to see how the two can be reconciled. He becomes aware of places where something is wrong, where something doesn't fit. He holds on to this sense of the problem, coming back to it again and again. It is out of this staying with the problem that a new way of looking at it may emerge, a way that subtly takes account of all the ins and outs of the situation which the scientist has been wrestling with. (This is true, incidentally, not only of scientific discovery but also of discovery in such fields as logic and mathematics (Hadamard, 1954). The same does not apply when we are working with axiomatised formal systems, but as my philosophy of science tutor Heinz Post used to say, 'An axiomatised theory is a dead theory.')

The general theory of the rendering of experience into symbols applies not only in scientific and mathematical discovery, but in any creative field. Because this is so it has been possible to apply the ideas of focusing to, for example, creative writing (Perl, 1994) and painting (Goldfarb 1992). Gendlin himself has developed a version of focusing (called 'Thinking at the Edge') which works with thought rather than feeling, and which can be applied in any area where one needs to develop new concepts. But this does not exhaust the areas of application for focusing. The writing of a poem, the composing of a piece of music, the expression of feeling in dance and song, these all typically involve the focusing process of staying with a vague yet precise feel of something and then finding ways to bring it forth, to render it in symbolic form. Indeed, apart from the routine practicalities of human life, almost everything which goes on in human culture — art, ritual, music, storytelling — has at its heart the rendering of experience in symbols. I am inclined to think that the essence of focusing lies close to the essence of what it is to be human; but this is no surprise if we think of the human world as characteristically a symbolic world. I will return to this point about what characterises the human world shortly, but first need to say something about another aspect of focusing which is prominent in its therapeutic application.

'CLEARING A SPACE' AND 'DISIDENTIFICATION'

In Gendlin's (1981) classical account of therapeutic focusing there is a stage which comes before the seeking for the felt sense. This is called 'clearing a space' or 'putting things down'. In later writings, Gendlin (1984) has said that this preliminary practice is itself very therapeutic, and that without it the rest of the focusing procedure is unlikely to work well. But this practice of 'putting things down' does not seem to be necessary in the non-therapeutic applications of focusing. In the nine steps of the 'Thinking at the Edge' procedure there is nothing that corresponds with 'putting things down', and it is hard to see any parallel for this process in other forms of creative activity. 'Putting things down' is distinctive of therapeutic focusing.

To see why this is so we need to look at what is involved in the notion of 'putting down'. Clearly it is a metaphorical phrase, and one that can sometimes lead to trouble. When it is suggested to a focuser that they might like to put something down, they may feel that this is wrong for them. They may want instead to hold, or relate to, or say hello to the ' something'. Some focusing teachers use the terminology of 'disidentifying' here. To put a feeling down is to disidentify from it. I don't think that this is quite right, but I will use the term for the moment since it is a familiar one. The use of imagery is often helpful in disidentifying: one can visualise 'all that awful business' as being over on the other side of the room, or across the river, or however far away it needs to be for the focuser to feel relaxed about it. But as Gendlin (1984) emphasises, this visualisation is not itself the disidentifying. If when the awful business is pictured as being on the other side of the river there is no shift in one's bodily feeling, then disidentification has not taken place.

But what exactly is 'disidentification' ? It may help first to ask what we are disidentifying from. There has been some discussion recently about this. Ann Weiser Cornell (1995) writes of getting a distance from the felt sense; Elfie Hinterkopf (1998) challenges this, saying that what we get a distance from is the problem or situation with which we are working. But neither of these ways of putting it seems quite right to me. It can hardly be the felt sense we step back from, since the felt sense is what is connecting us with the problem or situation: the felt sense is the sense of that whole thing. But what does it mean to 'get a distance from a problem'? And why don't we need to do this in the non-therapeutic applications of focusing?

I think the answer to the second question is that in the non-therapeutic applications the problem-situation is not *our* situation; we are not tangled up in it. Because it is not our situation we already have a distance from it: it is just a situation which we happen to be trying to render more effectively in symbols. When Einstein in developing his general relativity theory was struggling with all that business about light and gravity, trying to render what he could sense in mathematical form, he was himself involved only as the one who questions, probes, listens, senses. But when we focus on a personal difficulty *that which we focus on* is also us. The situation is not just *a* situation, it is *our* situation. In focusing on a personal issue we are not just refining our consciousness of something, but refining our consciousness of ourself. Focusing on a personal problem involves not just consciousness but self-consciousness. To be able to look at ourself we need to take up a position in respect to ourself which is analogous to the position which other people take in relation to us. Other people can look at our personal situation in just the way in which Einstein looked at light and gravity. But we can't do this if we are immersed in the situation. When we are immersed in or overwhelmed by a problem, we are living it, expressing it in our behaviour and our speech. Often when someone says 'I'm angry' these words constitute angry behaviour as much as shouting or stomping around. We are behaving here, not reflecting on our behaviour. In the case of other people we can't live or express their anger; we can only be aware of it, note it, respond to it, reflect on it. So if we imagine ourself as another person faced with our anger we necessarily move ourself into a position of being aware of the anger rather than behaving it.

This, I suggest, is what disidentification amounts to. We imaginatively look at ourselves in our situation as if we were looking at it from another person's point of view. This sort of move can of course be helpful in therapy generally — 'Suppose it were someone else in this situation. What would you think they should do?' Such a move gives us a perspective on ourself, and this metaphor of a perspective goes with the metaphor of a space in which we have that perspective, and a position in that space from which we can see ourself.

What we are doing when we 'put something at a distance' is imaginatively stepping back from ourself, and seeing ourself as though from outside, from the sort of distance a kind friend might see us. We are not stepping back from the problem exactly (I am not sure how to understand that), but from ourself. We are in a sense imagining the personal problem to be over there, but a personal problem can't exist without the person who has the problem, so really we are imaging *ourself*, as being over there. This incidentally leads to a variation on the putting down imagery which I have been trying out myself: Having identified each problem-situation which is currently active in us, we picture a little theatre in which that situation is being played out. There we are, in that situation, having those relationships with those people. Nearby is another little theatre where our next problem is being played. Let's see what is going on there . . . and so on. However the imagery is not our main concern here. What we are interested in is an account of disidentification itself, irrespective of how it is imaged.

I have been saying that in disidentifying we look at ourself as if from the point of view of another person. I now want to elaborate on this and link it with my earlier suggestion that there is something about focusing which is close to the heart of what it is to be human.

TWO LEVELS OF DESIRE AND AVERSION

In an important philosophical paper Harry Frankfurt (1971) distinguishes between two different kinds of desires or aversions which we may have. The first kind includes all those things which we happen to like or dislike. We all have as it were a profile of our preferences, the sorts of things we go for and the sorts of things we don't go for. This also seems to be true of many animals. However in the case of human beings there is a second level to our desires and aversions, in which we have preferences about which desires and aversions it is good to have. For example, someone may be frightened of spiders but want not to be. Or we can want to eat lots of chocolate but also wish we didn't have that desire. Phobias and addictions are only the extreme ends of a spectrum whose middle range includes all those situations where we find ourselves wanting things we really would prefer not to want, or avoiding things which we really don't want to be avoiding. In short, we often want to be a bit different from the way we are. Because of this second level of desires and aversions human beings are open to two different kinds of conflict. The first kind is a conflict which takes place between two desires on the first level, for example the conflict between wanting to go swimming and wanting to lie in the sun. Such conflicts are usually resolvable without very much reflection. We do what we most want to do, though reflection may help us to get both the things we want: if I lie in the sun now I can still go swimming later, whereas if I go swimming now it will be too cool to lie in the sun later, so I'd better lie in the sun now. The second sort of conflict is not between two first-level desires but between a first-level and a second-level desire. For example, I'm always wanting just to lie around these days, but I wish I wasn't like that. I want to be the sort of person I used to be, who was active and creative. This sort of conflict has a different kind of structure from the first. The ideal solution here is not to have it both ways. The ideal solution is that the first-level desire should fade out so that I no longer want just to lie around. Similarly, the person who is afraid of spiders wants to be free of that fear, and the addict wants not to have the cravings which they do have.

On the first level our desires and aversions are just what they are, and what we do will be the resultant of the various forces which are acting. The natural image here is that of homeostasis, where the interplay of the different forces results in an overall maintained state of the organism. Where we think of the organism as conscious we can think of the balance as one of maximising pleasure or minimising pain, but the general organic principle involved does not require there to be consciousness.

THE PERSONAL VS THE ORGANIC

The conceptualisation of human beings in terms of the organic principle runs through much psychotherapeutic thought; versions of it are clearly there in the theories of Freud, of Jung, of Rogers. But it is equally clear that the organic pattern leaves out just what is most characteristic of human beings. As human beings we don't simply act on our strongest desire or fear, or take the homeostatic resultant of all the forces that are acting on us. We also reflect on and make efforts to modify our desires and fears. For a human being desires and fears are not simple 'givens': they are open to assessment, to evaluation. Some of them we wish to cultivate, others we wish to weed out. I think that Nietzsche says somewhere that the human soul is like a garden. To create a garden the gardener has to take into consideration the natural propensities of various plants, the lie of the land, the climatic conditions and so on. Creating a garden cannot be a forced, mechanical business. You can't grow just anything anywhere. The organic aspect is crucial. But the gardener does not just let things grow as they will — that would produce something, but it would not create a garden. It would not *create* anything. Creation requires familiarity with the natural forms and forces at play in a situation, but also a vision that will transform the situation. Creativity brings something new to the forms that are already there, so that these forms themselves are changed. A garden is not just a re-arrangement of what was already there; even with the introduction of no new plants it is a different kind of entity from the purely organic system which preceded it.

What makes the garden different from a merely organic system is the vision of the gardener. If we apply this to human life in general, we see that what makes us different from the animals is our capacity to reflect on our desires and aversions and to make efforts to transform them in the light of what we see as good or valuable. Yet something still needs to be said about how this distinction between us and the animals, between the personal and the organic, comes about. How is it that there can exist such a fundamental distinction, when from another point of view we are simply highly complex animals?

I believe that the answer to this lies in the way in which human beings come into the world. Studies of infant development in the last twenty years or so strongly suggest that the infant's world is an interpersonal world from the start. The infant responds primarily not to its physical surroundings as such but to its mother or caregiver. The human infant is adapted to a life of interpersonal relationships, and its developing awareness of its physical environment is mediated through the more basic interpersonal context. For example, an infant at around one year of age encounters something which is unusual and potentially frightening. Rather than simply withdrawing or becoming upset the infant glances at his or her mother as if checking on mother's response to the situation. If the mother smiles encouragingly the infant proceeds to investigate the unusual thing, but if mother looks alarmed or discouraging the infant withdraws or becomes upset (Stern, 1985). A natural way of describing this situation is that the infant is not sure about what he or she is experiencing. Is this something frightening or not? Whether the thing is frightening is not settled simply through the infant's own bodily experiencing. Whether it is frightening or not depends on what has been called a 'social reference', a reference to how it is for someone else. It goes without saying that whether the thing is frightening does not depend *only* on how mother sees the situation; the infant's own bodily reactions equally come into the picture. The point is that whether this thing is frightening is something that is, as it were, negotiated between infant and mother. It seems plausible that the infant is wired up to respond to the world in this sort of way; other people come into the infant's world not as one sort of entity among all the others but as part of the framework of the infant's experiencing. Well before language develops, the child's world is a shared world, with input to experience both from his or her own body and from significant others. Once language does develop, the point applies with even more force: whether a situation is one to which the English word 'frightening' applies is clearly not something which the child can settle simply through consulting its own experience.

The interpersonal nature of human experiencing makes that experiencing something very different from the experiencing of a non-social animal. (I leave aside the question of borderline cases amongst social animals. Dogs, for instance, sometimes seem to stand very close to the borderline. Unlike cats, dogs will sometimes look to their owner as if to see how to take a situation.) A non-social animal simply has the experiences it has, whether perceptual or emotional. The animal simply sees something red, or is afraid, for example. But for a human being there are always, as it were, questions around one's experiencing. For instance, I'm experiencing commiseration with you over your misfortune, yet is that quite right? Isn't there a touch of glee in this? I seem to be feeling anxious, but is it really what you'd call anxiety? Isn't it actually a sort of excitement? Even with something as seemingly clear-cut as colour perception the same querying can arise: I really like these magenta curtains, but I may start having doubts about their colour when someone else says firmly that they are not magenta but mauve. Such situations can be unsettling, but I think that our response should not be to say that in the end I have to go by my own subjective experiencing. For I am trying to see how things are, and the human form of experiencing is such that other people always have some input into how things are.

We got into this discussion of the difference between human and animal experiencing, through asking what is involved in disidentification. What we can say now is that the capacity for disidentification is rooted in what it is to be a person. A person is precisely that sort of being which can look at itself as if from outside. People have this capacity because the human form of experiencing necessarily involves the bringing of alternative perspectives. For a person, how anything is, is how it might be for an 'us'; there *is no* simple 'how it is just for me' which is unconnected with how others might see it. The human world in general is a world in which there are alternative perspectives. This is manifest most basically in the way in which we see objects from perspectives or points of view in a three-dimensional space. My perspective is only one possible perspective, and it can sometimes be demolished by my realisation of how the same object looks from other perspectives. From my perspective this is a pool of water, but I have to let go of this perspective when you, who are close up to it, report that there is no water there. Then I have to change how I see it from 'pool' to 'mirage'.

But this general capacity to see things from different perspectives gets a new twist when we realise that it applies not just to the way things are, and the way other people are, but also to the way we are ourselves. Just as it is not simply 'given' that this is a pool of water, so it is not simply given that I am, say, feeling guilty. Rather, I may come to see, it is shame or embarrassment that I feel (Purton, 2000a). To come to see this I need to stand back and look at the whole situation, at my feelings certainly, but also at how other people are seeing it, the whole context, the alternative views that are possible. I need to get a sense of that whole business, and then to render that felt sense in symbolic form.

This completes my philosophical discussion. I want now to consider briefly its implications for practice.

IMPLICATIONS FOR PRACTICE

(a) The importance of the felt sense

One implication is that the notion of the felt sense is central to focusing, where 'felt sense' means that vague yet precise sense of 'all that' from which steps of symbolic change arise. For this reason I think that Ann Weiser Cornell's (1996) way of introducing the felt sense can be misleading. She writes (p. 29):

> Take time to notice how you are feeling in your body. You might notice sensations, emotions, or a kind of overall mood or atmosphere . . . There's no need to be to particular about what you are looking for; you're interested in anything that feels like *something* . . . what you notice might be unclear, slight, subtle or vague, or it might be very strong and definite. Sense anything: an emotion like 'sad' or 'scared', a sensation like 'tight' or 'jittery', an image like 'a knot' or 'a rock' — anything at all. Don't worry about whether what you are feeling is a felt sense. Just keep on sensing . . . Each felt sense is unique.

Her reason for introducing the felt sense in this way is that clients may otherwise ignore the feelings they do have in a search for the elusive felt sense. (Cornell 1998). This is no doubt true, but it does not justify blurring the distinction between the felt sense and other experiences. All kinds of experiences may lead into a felt sense, but until the felt sense is experienced the change steps of the focusing process cannot occur.

(b) The importance of clearing a space

A second area of discussion amongst focusing teachers centres around the question of the importance of clearing a space or putting things down. Gendlin himself has increasingly emphasised the importance of this in therapeutic focusing. He writes:

> Focusing is divided into six specific 'movements'. In a difficult situation it was natural to attempt only the very first one, which we always considered merely preliminary, called 'clearing a space'; it is now far more than preliminary. This preliminary movement already had become important in its own right a few years ago, when we found, over and over again, that it very often leads to a very large space which is often experienced with a spiritual quality. Next we learned . . . that focusing can be taught successfully in a weekend . . . if about one third of the time available is spent just learning this first movement exactly. (1984, p. 266)

Ann Weiser Cornell (1996, p. 65) at first sight seems to play down the importance of clearing a space. She does not refer to it at all in her basic focusing instructions. It only appears about two-thirds of the way through her book, in the 'troubleshooting' section, where it is presented as a useful procedure in the following kind of situation: 'There may be many things that want your attention today. It is as if you have walked into a room and everyone is shouting for your attention. If it feels like chaos when you bring your awareness into your body you may want to do a Focusing process called "clearing a space"'.

However, in her version of focusing there is something else which in effect plays the role of clearing a space, i.e. the procedure of 'saying hello'. That is, instead of putting a problem down somewhere one says 'hello' to it. This sounds very different, but the difference is mainly in the imagery. From a philosophical point of view the two procedures come to the same thing. 'Saying hello' is a picturesque way of acknowledging the problem, of saying 'that's there'. What is important is the acknowledging, the awareness of that whole thing, which one can only have from a disidentified position. But I suspect that 'saying hello' can easily lead away from rather than towards a felt sense. 'Saying hello' tends to fix the form of that to which we are saying hello. It becomes a part of us, an inner entity which can be dialogued with, and we then move away from focusing and into those varieties of therapy which work with parts or subpersonalities. These procedures are valuable, but they are not focusing.

(c) The question of 'parts'

This leads to my third and last point. I think that my discussion has implications for the way in which some focusing teachers talk in terms of 'parts' — e.g. 'You are noticing a part of you which is upset.' Such talk of 'parts' is of course a very old way of conceptualising human personality. In Plato's Republic the soul is divided into the desiring, spirited and rational parts; Freud has his ego, id and superego; Jung his complexes and archetypes; Transactional Analysis its Parent, Adult, Child. In the person-centred tradition such generalised talk of parts has been looked at with some suspicion (Mearns 1999), but there still seems room for 'parts' which are idiosyncratic to the individual person, e.g. 'the bit of me that always gets upset when people shout'. It seems to me that focusing-oriented psychotherapy can have no quarrel with any of these theories about human personality. The focusing philosophy doesn't have any view of its own about the structure of personality; it is concerned rather with the process of change, which in therapeutic contexts means personality change. Focusing is primarily concerned not with the parts of the personality as we now experience them, but with the sensing of where our present conceptualisation of ourselves is stuck, or fails to carry our lives forward. From a focusing point of view there is nothing wrong with thinking of ourselves in terms of 'parts'; what would go against the whole focusing philosophy is the idea that these parts are 'just there', fixed in the sort of way that the parts of a machine are fixed elements in its structure.

For these reasons I think that talk of parts has only a limited usefulness. Why then make it central to focusing, as some focusing teachers do? The obvious answer is that 'parts talk' links with talk of disidentification. In focusing we want to distinguish between 'I am angry' and 'There is anger there.' 'I am angry' identifies us with the anger and prevents us from getting a proper look at it. To get a proper look we need to 'stand back' from the anger-making situation. Now saying 'part of me is angry' can help in this standing back. 'Part of me is angry' is not a natural way of expressing anger — it moves us into a position of describing rather than expressing what is going on. But it is this distinction between expressing and describing which is important, and not the part/whole distinction. I can imagine someone who uses the parts terminology a lot coming to use *it* to express anger. They stomp around and say 'Part of me is just so angry about this.' Here the angry part, rather than the whole person, is expressing itself, but the person is not standing back from their anger. Conversely, one can stand back not just from a part of oneself but from one's whole self. People do this when they say such things as 'I'm really going to look at who I am, and what my life is all about, the whole thing.'

As I hinted earlier, I think that to speak of identifying with an emotion or attitude can be misleading. The situations to which we are applying this terminology are not really situations where *we are identifying* with something; rather, they are situations in which we are caught up in (ensnared by, entangled by . . .) something. It is misleading to speak of 'identifying' here because the normal sense of identifying with something (such as a political cause) involves us in being active. It is true that we may identify ourselves not only with external causes but with aspects of our own nature. For example, one may have conflicting desires and finally align oneself or identify oneself with one of these rather than the other. That is what is involved in making decisions. Identifying with some aspect of oneself is something active; it amounts to incorporating that attitude into one's self, making it something about which one can wholeheartedly say 'This is me, this is something I value.' It is quite different from being 'caught up in', 'entangled in' or 'overwhelmed by' something, which are the phrases I would prefer to use for the situations with which we are concerned.

Similarly, although I have used the terminology of 'disidentification' in earlier parts of this paper, I don't think the word is really appropriate. What has been called disidentification from one's experiencing is better described simply in terms of being aware of one's experiencing, or more metaphorically as 'standing back' from it.

Let me conclude by stating my belief that it is important for focusing to keep in touch with its philosophical roots. Focusing is not just one therapeutic technique amongst others. It is not on a level with dream work or two-chair work, for example. It is rooted in a profound philosophical analysis of the relationship between experiencing and symbolisation, which in turn is central to our understanding of what it is to be a human being. If focusing-oriented psychotherapy is to flourish there needs to be not only the refinement of practice, but also a deepening understanding of what is involved in the process. The *experience* of working with focusing needs to be adequately *symbolised*; in short, we need to apply focusing to itself, to focus on focusing.

REFERENCES

Cornell, A. W. (1995). Relationship = distance + connection. *The Folio: A Journal for Focusing and Experiential Therapy, 15*(1).

Cornell, A. W. (1996). *The Power of Focusing*. Oakland, CA: New Harbinger Publications.

Cornell, A. W. (1998). The power of inner relationship: A response. *The Focusing Connection, 15*(6).

Frankfurt, H. (1971). Freedom of the will and the concept of a person. *Journal of Philosophy, 68*, 5–20.

Gendlin, E. (1962/1997). *Experiencing and the Creation of Meaning*. Evanston: Northwestern Univ. Press.

Gendlin, E. (1981). *Focusing*. 2nd edn. New York: Bantam Books.

Gendlin, E. (1984). Imagery, body and space in focusing. In A. A. Sheikh (Ed.) *Imagination and Healing*. New York: Baywood Publishing.

Hadamard, J. (1954.) *The Psychology of Invention in the Mathematical Field*. New York: Dover.

Hinterkopf, E. (1998). Finding a certain distance: A helpful and even life-saving technique. *The Focusing Connection, 15*(6).

Mearns, D. (1999) Person-centred therapy with configurations of the self. *Counselling, 10*, 125–30.

Popper, K. R. (1959). *The Logic of Scientific Discovery*. London: Hutchinson.

Purton, C. (1998). Unconditional positive regard and its spiritual implications. In B. Thorne and E. Lambers (Eds.) *Person-Centred Therapy. A European perspective*. London: Sage.

Purton, C. (2000a). Empathising with shame and guilt. In J. Marques-Teixera and S. Antunes (Eds.) *Client-centred and Experiential Psychotherapy*. Linda a Velha, Portugal: Vale and Vale.

Purton, C. (2000b). Introjection and the aliens within. *Person-Centred Practice, 8*, 15–20

Stern, D. N. (1985) The *Interpersonal World of the Infant*. New York: Basic Books.

Wittgenstein, L. (1963). *Philosophical Investigations*. Oxford: Blackwell.

Edwin Kahn PhD

Queensborough Community College, The City University of New York

Heinz Kohut's Empathy

In a paper comparing himself to Heinz Kohut and Milton Erickson, Rogers (1986) describes two contrasting ways that Kohut conceived of empathy. First, he quotes Kohut in the following way:

> Empathy, the accepting, confirming, and understanding human echo evoked by the self, is a psychological nutrient without which human life as we know and cherish it, could not be sustained. (Kohut, 1973/1978, p. 705)

Rogers says that this description is beautiful and he feels very much in tune with it. But then he quotes Kohut in another way:

> Empathy is employed only for data gathering; there is no way in which it could serve us in our theory building. In the clinical situation, the analyst employs empathy to collect information about specific current events in the patient's inner life. After he has collected these data with the aid of empathy, he orders them and gives the patient a dynamic or genetic interpretation. (Kohut, 1980, pp. 483–4)

Rogers (1986) comments, 'Here is where we part company. This cold, impersonal use of the capacity for understanding is abhorrent to me' (p. 129). Unfortunately, Brian Thorne (1992), in his book on Rogers, repeats *only* Rogers 'abhorrence of Kohut's apparently cold and impersonal use of empathy as a means of "collecting information" about the patient's inner life.' Thorne then says Rogers, in contrast, 'reaffirmed in the strongest possible terms his own conviction that empathy is in itself a powerful healing agent' (p. 39). From Thorne's comments, it sounds like Kohut used empathy only in a cold way, which is obviously incorrect. Kohut clearly distinguished between empathy as a healing agent, and empathy as a scientific tool (Kohut, 1973/1978, p. 705; 1980, p. 482; 1982, p. 397). I think this is an example of how distortions about each other's approach have permeated the self psychology and client-centered literature. I have described elsewhere how these two approaches, client-centered therapy and self psychology, are very similar at their core (Kahn, 1996; Kahn and Rachman, 2000).

Kohut, who had been referred to as Mr. Psychoanalysis by his colleagues, was deeply tied to classical psychoanalysis, and the changes he began to make in theory were very difficult for him and involved much struggle. His new ideas threatened the orthodoxy of the psychoanalytic establishment, and he was criticized and shunned by the people he most admired, such as Anna Freud and Kurt Eissler (Strozier, 1985, pp. 10–11; Strozier, 2001, pp. 269–71). He wrote about 'having to make a scientific step that . . . would arouse strong controversy among my colleagues and require the mobilization of all my intellectual and emotional resources for the rest of my life' (Kohut, 1984, p. 89).

Kohut (1982) realized that there was something fundamentally wrong with Freud's theory of sex and aggressive instincts, and the need to tame these instincts by the influences of civilization. For Kohut this psychobiological theory had evolved into a moral system, and therapeutic analysis became an educational procedure, where patients were taught to control their inborn instincts (that is, their pleasure-seeking and destructive tendencies), adapt to society, and become independent. Kohut (1982), echoing Rogers' philosophy, said, the unacknowledged presence of these Freudian values 'interferes with the analyst's ability to allow his analysands to develop in accordance with their own nuclear programme and destiny' (p. 399).

Wolf (1990) commented on the historical significance of Kohut's use of empathy as an observational tool:

> The Cartesian split of mind from body has had a tremendous influence on the development of science. On the one hand, by restricting scientific data to what is publicly replicable, and by freeing science from superstitions and myth, Descartes made possible the great achievements of the natural sciences that have given us our modern world of technological wonders. On the other hand, other avenues to knowledge — for example, inferences from history or from the humanities and the arts — having been measured by the criteria of natural science, were downgraded as unreliable and unscientific. The study of the inner life of men and women became scientifically not respectable and was relegated to the poets and their kind. Western civilization has paid for our sophistication in the mechanics of the world with a renewed ignorance of our own inner selves. (pp. 423–4)

Freud, trained in the scientific tradition of the nineteenth century, was greatly influenced by the objectivist epistemology of that time. As a result, Freud's science of the mind was closely associated to biology (the sex and aggressive instincts) and sociology (the ego as a structure, or 'mental apparatus,' which facilitated adaptation to society). Mid-twentieth century psychoanalysis in America was single-mindedly concerned with objective truthfulness in the form of an exact interpretation (Miller, 1990, p. 379). Concepts such as analytic neutrality, and the analyst as a blank screen were developed because the theoretical ideal 'was total objectivity, that is, the removal of the influence of the observer on the observed' (Kohut, 1984, p. 37).

It was in this intellectual climate that Kohut, in 1959, defined psychoanalysis as the scientific study of complex mental states (Kohut, 1959/1978). Wolf (1990) said, 'in terms of the development of science and of psychoanalysis, Kohut's greatest merit, in my opinion, lies in his having shown the scientific validity and necessity of using empathy as a tool for obtaining data about the inner life of men and women' (p. 426). I describe the above history to demonstrate that Kohut's use of empathy for scientific purposes was not a trivial or unimportant matter.

In 1981, with only three more days to live, and barely surviving the previous night, Kohut, with adrenaline dripping into his weakened heart, was taken by ambulance, with a stop at a McDonald's hamburger restaurant for lunch (Strozier, 1997), to an appreciative self psychology audience in Berkeley, where he gave his final address, without notes, titled 'On Empathy.' In this talk he outlined three functions of empathy (Kohut, 1981/1991).

The first function, already discussed, is what Kohut called the epistemological function of empathy. Introspection and empathy (which he called vicarious introspection) were definers of the field, the field of 'pure psychology,' a psychology of complex mental states. Just as the physical sciences use extrospection (observation of the external world) to collect data, psychoanalysis uses the tools of introspection and empathy to collect data for a science of the mind. Kohut (1959/1978) said that theories of the mind, such as Freud's, were formulated from the data collected through introspection (Freud, by observing his own experiences, such as his dreams, explored aspects of the unconscious) and empathy (by listening to his patients Freud also learned about mental life). For Kohut (1977) 'psychoanalysis is a psychology of complex mental states which, with the aid of the persevering empathic-introspective immersion of the observer into the inner life of man, gathers its data in order to explain them' (p. 302). Interestingly, Kohut used introspection to study aspects of his own self pathology. It is now accepted that Kohut's (1979) well-known *'The Two Analyses of Mr. Z'* was a case history of himself (Strozier, 1997; 2001).

The second function of empathy was that it serves as a guide to action. If we want to help someone, we must know them and understand them before we can take appropriate action (or maybe inaction). Even to hurt someone, Kohut commented, we must first know them and their vulnerability. Kohut (1981/1991) said,

> Introspection and empathy should be looked at as informers of appropriate action. In other words, if you understand, 'put yourself into the shoes of,' think yourself appropriately into the inner life of another person, then you can use this knowledge for your purposes. Now . . . these purposes can be of kindness, and these purposes can be of utter hostility. If you want to hurt somebody, and you want to know where his vulnerable spot is, you have to know him before you can put in the right dig. (p. 529)

In an unusual emphasis, Kohut stressed that when empathy is used destructively it is more beneficial than the indifference of 'emotional absence.' Kohut (1981/1991) said,

> The presence of empathy in the surrounding milieu, whether used for compassionate, well-intentioned therapeutic, and now listen, even for utterly destructive purposes, is still an admixture of something positive. In other words, there is a step beyond an empathy-informed hatred that wants to destroy you; and an empathyless environment that just brushes you off the face of the earth. (p. 530)

Elaborating, Kohut (1981/1991) goes on,

> The worst suffering I've seen in adult patients is in those very subtle, and difficult to uncover, absences of the mother — because her personality was absent . . . In one of my patients, it was the mother's hiding behind bridge cards. Whenever he came, there were those bridge cards between him and her. But she had nothing to give. It is this emptiness that leads to the worst sufferings later in life. (pp. 531–2)

The third function of empathy is that its mere presence is therapeutic. Kohut (1981/1991) said, 'empathy, per se, is a therapeutic action in the broadest sense . . . [S]ince it is true, and I know it is true, and I've evidence for its being true, I must mention it' (p. 530). On other occasions Kohut (1977, p. 85; 1980, p. 478; 1984, p. 47) said that just as oxygen is required for our physiological survival, the empathic presence of others, throughout life, is necessary for our psychological survival.

Kohut (1981/1991) described disintegration anxiety as the loss of an empathic environment. He said, 'What leads to the human self's destruction, however, is its exposure to the coldness, the indifference of the nonhuman, the nonempathically responding world . . . It is not physical extinction that is feared, however, but the ascendancy of a nonhuman environment . . . in which our humanness would permanently come to an end' (Kohut, 1984, p. 18). Interestingly, while Kohut was describing the devastating effect of the absence of human contact, Rogers was saying that it is the human quality of the therapist that is most healing.

In this context, it seems to me that Kohut had a special empathic understanding for disorders of the self, that is clients who are seriously developmentally arrested (what Warner, 1991, has called fragile process). Kohut described with emotion and vividness clients who suffered from a deep sense of vulnerability, and an inability to sustain a positive and stable sense of self. Interestingly, Kohut viewed psychosis as a relative term, that is, such a label was partially a function of the empathic limits of the clinician. Kohut (1981/1985) said, 'Insofar as you can truly build a bridge of empathy to a person, to that extent he is not psychotic . . . Once you are with him and have built this bridge, he has ceased to be psychotic' (p. 250). Thus, for Kohut, the more empathic the clinician, the less the need for a psychotic diagnosis.

At this point, Kohut's (1984) definition of empathy may be useful. He said empathy was 'the capacity to think and feel oneself into the inner life of another person. It is our lifelong ability to experience what another person experiences, though usually, and appropriately, to an attenuated degree' (p. 82). Kohut (1980) also noted that empathy was neutral and 'must, therefore, not be confused with either sympathy or compassion. Empathy is surely a necessary precondition for our ability to experience compassion; and compassionate acts, in order to be effective, must be guided by the accurate empathic assessment of the recipient's needs'(p. 483). John Shlien (1997), too, has noted that empathy, without sympathy, can be used for cruel purposes (p. 63). Shlien emphasizes the importance of sympathy and understanding (rather than empathy) in psychotherapy.

> Sympathy — 'feeling for' — is a type of commitment. Empathy is not . . . In my view, (sympathy) works at a higher stage of moral development than empathy. In fact, empathy may have no more moral status than does the circulatory system. Understanding is a volitional effort and a service that empathy is not; if there is 'empathic' understanding, then it is the understanding that promotes the healing from within. (p. 67)

Donna Orange (1995), a self psychologist, also distinguishes between empathy and empathic understanding. Empathic understanding is something more — it includes, first, a helpful response, such as adjusting the heat and light for a patient's comfort or a parent protecting a child from mistreatment (Orange, 1995, pp. 22–3). Furthermore, empathic understanding is intersubjective — your subjectivity and my subjectivity 'assume their particular shape in our relatedness' (p. 24). The therapeutic relationship, for Orange, consists of 'the therapist's subjectivity, the patient's subjectivity, and the emerging and changing sense of the "we"' (p. 24), a 'we' which emerges with novelty and surprise, and has both a history and emotional qualities (p. 9). Shlien (1997) referred to this experience of 'we' as 'reverberative' empathy (p. 75), and described it as 'I understood, he understood — we understood, in a series of "bouncing between us" consequences, for each and for both' (p. 77). This changing sense of the 'we' seems characteristic of Martin Buber's 'I-thou' relationship, and also evolved in

Rogers' conceptualization of empathy (Shlien, 1997).

Kohut's ideas on empathy may relate to the issue of non-directivity in client-centered therapy. Kohut (1984) noted that severely traumatized patients require very long periods of just understanding or attentive silent listening — they cannot yet tolerate the otherness, separateness, or foreignness of the therapist (p. 177, p. 105). Kohut's (1971, p. 288) well-known patient, Miss F, who became very upset at Kohut's analytic interpretations, and from whom Kohut learned to see things more completely from the patient's perspective, is an example of such a severely traumatized patient. However, according to Kohut (1984, p. 185), more mature patients, who have a clear awareness of their separateness from the analyst, may benefit, in different ways, from the interpretations of the therapist. Kohut (1981/1991) said:

> There is always the question of how to treat people with very serious self disturbances, who cannot possibly benefit from interpretations, I believe. It's too soon, and for many years, they do need an empathic understanding on the closest level that we can muster. And it does not mean that one cannot move naturally, slowly, and gradually into higher forms of empathy and explaining, much, much, much later on. (p. 534)

In the therapeutic interaction, clients occasionally report that they want their therapist to be more active and directive. Bohart (1998), in describing such a client, who was a colleague of his, said,

> Yet when she sees a therapist she wants the therapist to argue with her, debate with her, express opinions, suggest techniques, and so on, *while* respecting her self-directed growth process and autonomy. In no way does an active, 'directive' therapist squelch her self-directed growth process. To the contrary, it seems to contribute to it. (p. 69)

Perhaps severely traumatized clients, such as the ones Prouty (1994) describes in his work with Pre Therapy, require constant mirroring and validation of their frame of reference, while higher functioning clients, whose sense of self is more stable and mature, appreciate empathic input from the therapist's frame of reference. This controversial topic was material for different manuscripts (Kahn, 1999a; 1999b; 2002).

REFERENCES

Bohart, A. C. (1998). Book Review of C. H. Patterson and S. Hildore, *Successful Psychotherapy: A caring, loving relationship*. *Person-Centered Journal, 5*, 66–70.

Kahn, E. (1996). The intersubjective perspective and the client-centered approach: Are they one at their core? *Psychotherapy, 33*, 30–42.

Kahn, E. (1999a). A critique of nondirectivity in the person-centered approach. *Journal of Humanistic Psychology, 39*, 94–110.

Kahn, E. (1999b, July). On the concept of non-directivity in the PCA. Presented at the Second World Congress for Psychotherapy, Vienna, Austria.

Kahn, E. and Rachman, A. (2000). Carl Rogers and Heinz Kohut: A historical perspective. *Psychoanalytic Psychology, 17*, 294–312.

Kahn, E. (2002). A way to help people by holding theory lightly: A response to Bozarth; Merry and Brodley; and Sommerbeck. *Journal of Humanistic Psychology, 42*, pp. 88–96.

Kohut, H. (1959/1978). Introspection, empathy, and psychoanalysis: An examination of the relationship between mode of observation and theory. In P. H. Ornstein (Ed.), *The Search for the Self, Vol. 1*, New York: International Universities Press, pp. 205–32.

Kohut, H. (1973/1978). The psychoanalyst in the community of scholars. In P. H. Ornstein (Ed.), *The Search for the Self, Vol. 2*, New York: International Universities Press, pp. 685–72.

Kohut, H. (1971). *The Analysis of the Self.* New York: International Universities Press.

Kohut, H. (1977). *The Restoration of the Self.* New York: International Universities Press.

Kohut, H. (1979). The two analyses of Mr Z. *International Journal of Psychoanalysis, 60*, 3–27.

Kohut, H. (1980). Reflections on advances in self psychology. In A. Goldberg (Ed.) *Advances in Self Psychology*. New York: International Press, pp. 473–554.

Kohut, H. (1981/1991). On empathy. In P. H. Ornstein (Ed.) *The Search for the Self: Selected writings of Heinz Kohut: 1978–81, Vol. 4*, Madison, CT: International Universities Press, pp. 525–35.

Kohut, H. (1982). Introspection, empathy, and the semi-circle of mental health. *International Journal of Psychoanalysis, 63*, 395–407.

Kohut, H. (1984). *How does Analysis Cure?* (A. Goldberg and P. E. Stepansky, Eds.). Chicago: University of Chicago Press.

Miller, J. P. (1990). The corrective emotional experience: Reflections in retrospect. *Psychoanalytic Inquiry, 10*, 373–88.

Orange, D. M. (1995). *Emotional Understanding: Studies in psychoanalytic epistemology*. New York: Guilford Press.

Prouty, G. (1994). *Theoretical Evolutions in Person-centered/Experiential Therapy: Applications to schizophrenic and retarded psychoses*. Westport, CT: Praeger.

Rogers, C. R. (1986). Rogers, Kohut and Erickson: A personal perspective on some similarities and differences. *Person-Centered Review, 1*, 125–40.

Shlien, J. M. (1997). Empathy in psychotherapy: A vital mechanism? Yes. Therapist's Conceit? All too often. By itself enough? No. In A. C. Bohart and L. S. Greenberg (Eds.) *Empathy Reconsidered: New directions in psychotherapy*. Washington, DC: American Psychological Association, (pp. 63–80).

Strozier, C. B. (1985). Glimpses of a life: Heinz Kohut (1913–81). In A. Goldberg (Ed.) *Progress in Self Psychology, Vol. 1*. New York: Guilford Press, (pp. 3–12).

Strozier, C. B. (1997). Death and the self. *Kohut Memorial Lecture*. Presented at the 20th Annual Conference on the Psychology of the Self, Chicago.

Strozier, C. B. (2001). *Heinz Kohut: The making of a psychoanalyst*. New York: Farrar, Straus and Giroux.

Thorne, B. (1992). *Carl Rogers*. London: Sage.

Warner, M. S. (1991). Fragile process. In L. Fusek (Ed.) *New Directions in Client-centered Therapy: Practice with difficult client populations*. Chicago: Chicago Counseling and Psychotherapy Center.

Wolf, E. S. (1990). Clinical responsiveness: Corrective or empathic? *Psychoanalytic Inquiry, 10*, 420–32.

Nathaniel J. Raskin
Northwestern University, USA

Rogers' Empathy: A revolutionary innovation[1]

When Carl Rogers introduced his approach in 1940, therapists generally saw themselves as useful because of the guidance they gave or the interpretations they were able to make. The therapist was an expert. The client explained the problem; the therapist provided the solution. Rogers was distinctive in seeing himself as the facilitator of a process driven by the client.

As client-centered theory and practice developed in the 1940s and 1950s at Ohio State University and the University of Chicago, a far-reaching body of research on a more refined hypothesis grew up: that if the therapist offered, and the client experienced, a particular kind of relationship characterized by genuineness, unconditional positive regard, and empathy, a self-directed process of growth would follow. In this process, individuals could be trusted to set their own goals, to monitor their progress toward these goals, and to decide when to terminate.

In 1951, Rogers formulated a systematic foundation for this trust, a theory of personality and behavior consisting of a set of nineteen propositions (Rogers, 1951, pp. 481–533). These were basically phenomenological in character, relying heavily on the concept of self as an explanatory construct, and on the internal frame of reference, that is, the perceptual field of the individual, the way the world appears to the person and the meanings he or she attaches to experience and feeling. Rogers believed that this provided the fullest understanding of why people behave as they do, superior to external judgments of behavior, attitudes, and personality.

These developments took place in the 1940s and 50s. When, a few years ago, over four decades later, the American Psychological Association organized a videotape series project to demonstrate twelve different orientations, the client-centered therapist was still uniquely not an expert who would show the client the way. I was asked to represent the client-centered approach, and while it was not my finest hour, it turned out that I was the only therapist among the twelve who did not assume the expert role, and I was shocked by the extent of the directiveness of the therapist with whom I was paired, who was supposed to be demonstrating the psychoanalytic method.

The heart of what I did do was to try to be empathic, in the client-centered sense, that is, to follow what the client was trying to communicate to me, to be in touch with his or her frame of reference, and to respond with no embellishment, but with simple understanding. The idea meant a lot to me and I wrote a paper on it in 1947 entitled 'The Nondirective Attitude'. It was never published but Rogers quoted from it in his book, *Client-Centered Therapy*, (1951) citing this passage:

---

[1] Paper presented as part of a panel on 'Fernczi, Rogers, and Kohut on Empathy'.

> At this level, counselor participation becomes an active experiencing with the client of the feelings to which he gives expression, the counselor makes a maximum effort to get under the skin of the person with whom he is communicating, he tries to get within and to live the attitudes expressed instead of observing them, to catch every nuance of their changing nature; in a word, to absorb himself completely in the attitudes of the other. And in struggling to do this, there is simply no room for any other type of counselor activity or attitude; if he is attempting to live the attitudes of the other, he cannot be diagnosing them, he cannot be thinking of making the process go faster. Because he is another, and not the client, the understanding is not spontaneous but must be acquired, and this through the most intense, continuous and active attention to the feelings of the other, to the exclusion of any other type of attention. (p. 29)

This indicates that, for Rogers and his associates, empathy is thoroughgoing and valued for itself; Rogers termed it 'an unappreciated way of being'. He wrote:

> The way of being with another person which is termed empathic has several facets. It means entering the private, perceptual world of the other and becoming thoroughly at home in it. It involves being sensitive, moment to moment, to the changing felt meanings which flow in this other person, to the fear or rage or tenderness or confusion or whatever, that he/she is experiencing. It means temporarily living in his/her life, moving about in it delicately without making judgments, sensing meanings of which he/she is scarcely aware, but not trying to uncover feelings of which the person is totally unaware, since this would be too threatening. (Rogers, 1980, p. 142)

It is clear, then, that for Rogers, empathy is not a technique used to gather information as a basis for making interpretations later, which was how Heinz Kohut employed it. As deeply as Kohut valued empathy, he wrote the following, as quoted by Goldberg in 1980:

> Empathy is employed only for data gathering; there is no way it can serve us in our theory building. In the clinical situation, the analyst employs empathy to collect information about specific current events in the patient's inner life. After he has collected these data with the aid of empathy, he orders them and gives the patient a dynamic or genetic interpretation.

On October 4, 1981, four days before his death, an emaciated but still passionate Heinz Kohut gave a talk on empathy at the Self-Psychology Conference in Los Angeles. He described his work with a very depressed and suicidal woman. He did something he said he would not recommend but did only because he was desperate, 'I gave her two fingers to hold. I immediately made a genetic interpretation to myself. It was of the toothless gums of a very young child, clamping down on an empty nipple . . . I wouldn't say that it turned the tide, but it overcame a very difficult impasse at a dangerous moment.' Kohut writes that the analysis went on for years and was reasonably successful.

Rogers commented on this event:

> It seems clear that in this interaction Dr. Kohut is experiencing desperation, caring, and compassion. He found a beautifully symbolic gesture that enabled him to express something of what he was feeling. Yet he is apologetic about this, about giving her his fingers to hold. Even more astonishing — and sad — is his interpretation to himself that he is giving her a dry nipple. He appears unaware that by giving something of himself — of his own deep and

persistent feelings — he is giving her the nourishing human caring and compassion that she so desperately needs. Being thus openly feeling with her is most therapeutic. Yet he seems dubious and apologetic about his action. He appears to be unaware that being openly himself in the relationship was the most healing thing he could have done. It is obvious that I differ deeply from Dr. Kohut in the value I give to being one's own whole person in the relationship. (Rogers, 1986, pp. 132–3)

I hope that I have succeeded in clarifying the nature of empathy in the client-centered approach, and to have distinguished it from the views of analyst Heinz Kohut.

REFERENCES

Goldberg, A. (Ed.) (1980). *Advances in Self-psychology.* New York: International Universities Press.
Raskin, N. J. (1947). The non-directive attitude. Unpublished manuscript.
Rogers, C. R. (1951). *Client-centered Therapy.* Boston: Houghton Mifflin.
Rogers, C. R. (1980). *A Way of Being.* Boston: Houghton Mifflin.
Rogers, C. R. (1986). Rogers, Kohut and Erickson. *Person-Centered Review, 1*(2), 125–40.

Gerhard Stumm
Vienna, Austria

The Person-Centered Approach and Self Psychology[1]

Abstract. After explaining my motives for undertaking this comparison this paper deals with some biographical aspects of the two founders, which also yield insights into their principal theoretical concerns. Thereafter, it reviews the philosophical background of the two approaches, and comments on their personality theory (mainly their concept of the self, but also their view of aggression and sexuality) and their therapeutic theory (in particular, the role of empathy, and the view of transference and interpretation), thereby also illustrating the correspondence of the therapeutic relationship and therapeutic techniques. This account, and the propositions derived from it, show that, despite significant differences in theory and practice, there are also some significant similarities. Self psychology — which regards itself as modern psychoanalysis — adopts positions first taken by Rogers a few decades earlier, for instance stressing the importance of subjective experience and empathy. Finally, I will highlight some concepts of self psychology that in my opinion offer valuable aspects for client-centered psychotherapy.

After training in person-centered therapy, for personal reasons I was in psychoanalysis for about six years, not with a self psychologist, but with a psychoanalyst who, in my belief, introduced elements of self psychology. For a while I had supervision for my practical work as a person-centered psychotherapist with Erwin Bartosch, a self psychologist[2]. For a short time I had the opportunity to participate in lectures and discussions in the self psychological group in Vienna, and took part in seminars given by Anna and Paul Ornstein as well as Frank Lachmann, disciples of Heinz Kohut, the founder of self psychology.

It is worth mentioning that I have been comparing psychotherapeutic approaches on an overall level for a long time (Stumm and Wirth, 1994; Stumm and Pritz, 2000). Though the presented topic had already been taken up by some authors, including Rogers himself (1984; 1987), Stolorow (1976), Kahn (1985; 1989a; 1989b; 1996), Kahn and Rachman (2000), Bohart (1991), Tobin (1991) and Korbei (1997), I wanted to focus on it once more from a person-centered perspective.

This comparison of the two approaches is merely a rough outline. Further distinctions emerge from the fact that both schools have a number of specific directions and developments. In person-centered therapy, for instance, there is the view of psychotherapy as *personal encounter* (represented for example by Raskin, Brodley, Bozarth and Schmid), as well as Gene Gendlin (1978) and Hans Swildens (1991) inspired by an existential orientation, and approaches marked by a stress on cognitive information theory and experiential concepts (cf. Keil and

[1] Translation by Roy Fox
[2] I'd like to thank Erwin Bartosch and Edwin Kahn for their helpful feedback on my paper.

Stumm, 2001). Within the self psychology movement, too, a number of different tendencies are identifiable: the emphasis on infancy research, the intersubjective orientation (Stolorow and Atwood, 1976), and the work that leans on systems theory.

1. PERSONALITIES OF THE FOUNDERS

Despite the contributions of colleagues, the two approaches discussed here cannot be viewed in isolation from the personalities of the founders, who made decisive contributions to the development of the bodies of theory in question, and left an indelible mark on them. It thus makes sense to begin with a comparison of the personal development of Carl Rogers and Heinz Kohut (for their biographies see for example Thorne, 1992; Kirschenbaum, 1995; Siegel, 1996; Butzer, 1997).

Some passages in Carl Rogers' (1902–1987) autobiographical texts (1961 Chapter 1; 1973) indicate that he was a very withdrawn and shy child, and that his parents — especially his mother — gave him a very religious upbringing. This is probably one of the roots of his belief that the relationship, and a particular psychological climate, is the key to psychotherapy. Trust in the actualizing tendency and the individual's capacity for self-regulation, rather than external influences and manipulation by others, is axiomatic to Rogers' fundamental beliefs. By the way this can be seen as a counterprogram to standards in psychology and education, when Rogers received his professional training.

Kohut's (1913–1983) Vienna childhood has been described as 'sad' and characterized by 'loneliness' (Strozier, 1985, p. 4; Hexel, 1994; Butzer, 1997). There is some evidence that this was the origin of Kohut's theoretically postulated, lifelong need for selfobjects. The loss, in 1937, of his father, who was important to him, may have played a significant part in the position of the father as a selfobject in the developmental concept he was to formulate. He himself probably idealized Freud.

Kohut's reputed 'narcissistic personality structure' (Butzer, 1997, p. 32) may be regarded as motive for his theoretical concern with narcissism ('self-relatedness'), and also for his relatively 'autistic' approach to the development of his theories, witnessed in his failure to draw on other sources (e.g. Winnicott and Balint). As a European, an Austrian and a Jew, Kohut lived through the tragic developments on the continent which, among other things, led to his being uprooted in 1938, when he had to flee Austria at the age of 26.

While Kohut, an only child, is said to have been 'self-centered' (Strozier, 1985, p. 8) and 'special' (verbal communication from Arnold Goldberg to Strozier, 1985, p. 12), what struck people about Rogers, who was one of six children, was his charismatic modesty. I twice had the opportunity to experience his loving, warm and authentic charisma in encounter groups, when he visited Austria in 1981 and 1984. Put in self psychological terms, Rogers met my need for idealization in the sense of idealizing selfobject transference.

While Kohut dedicated himself, in both his practical and his theoretical work, entirely to the psychoanalytical situation, Rogers' practical and theoretical interest also focused on groups, particularly in the last 20 years of his life.

As a medical practitioner and a psychiatrist, Kohut did not reject the medical model of illness. Carl Rogers avoided expressions such as 'patient', 'diagnosis', 'illness', 'treatment' and 'healing'. His attitude to diagnoses was one of great reservations. There are, however, quite a few exponents of the person-centered approach who would not go along with the sharply critical and provocative position towards schematized diagnostic categories taken in his historic article of 1957. Kohut, by contrast, had no aversion to diagnostic categories, but used them in a differentiated manner, having regard to their specific self-pathology, and distinguishing between psychosis, borderline, schizoid and paranoid personality disorders, narcissistic personality disorders, and narcissistic behavioral disorders (the latter two categories being seen as treatable by psychoanalysis).

On the other hand, Kohut in his research methodology only recognized the psychological methods of 'introspection' and 'empathy' (as vicarious introspection) for capturing internal psychological data.

Rogers' theoretical framework and hypotheses were influenced by existential philosophy and the philosophy of encounter (above all his dialogue with Martin Buber). His psychotherapeutic interviews were based on a phenomenological perspective, but in his research during his academic career the psychologist Rogers used statistical methods to test his hypotheses, and in this sense he was a pioneer of empirical research into psychotherapy, whereas Kohut opposed these as inadequate to the object of investigation, the human psyche. Introspection and empathy were the only research methods Kohut was prepared to accept as suitable for this purpose (see Rogers' criticism of Kohut's view of research in his comparative article, 1987, p. 309).

Rogers distanced himself from psychoanalysis at a very early stage, and his attitude to its concepts ranged from skepticism to outright rejection. Meanwhile, Kohut — a man who so personified the classical analyst that he was nicknamed 'Mr. Psychoanalysis' — only departed from orthodox, mechanistic concepts (the primacy of drive theory, the idea of a general validity of Oedipus complex, and the structure and conflict model) relatively late in life (Kohut, 1971, 1977). The result was that he only partly abandoned some classical stances (Kohut, 1984). This applies to the essential continuity of his view of the therapeutic relationship as one of transference, his effective retention of the abstinence principle, and his reintroduction of metapsychological concepts such as the selfobject, selfobject transferences, the bipolar self, and the complementarity of self psychology and drive theory. The more radical surmounting of Freudian orthodoxy by the intersubjective approach of Stolorow and Atwood brings it thus even closer to the Person-Centered Approach (see Kahn, 1996).

Rogers remained largely undisputed in the PCA community until his death. Kohut — former President of the American Psychoanalytic Association — in the course of elaborating his self psychology — progressively departed from classical psychoanalytical positions, especially as regards drive theory and the ego, ultimately emphasizing the therapeutic climate while assigning lesser importance to insight as compared to consolidation of the self. He largely broke with the psychoanalytical establishment, and was increasingly ostracized by colleagues, including Kurt Eissler, whose wife Ruth was his analyst while in training. Only recently, a friend of mine who is a classical psychoanalyst said with some vehemence that self psychology was something entirely different from orthodox psychoanalysis.

Beyond their own work, both fostered co-operation and exchanges with groups of associates, whose reactions and ideas made a significant contribution to the development of their theories: In self psychology, for example, the role of E. Wolf, Paul and Anna Ornstein, M. Basch, A. Goldberg, and Paul and Marian Tolpin is worthy of mention. Goldberg (1985, p. IX) sees in them colleagues 'who allowed and perhaps encouraged his emancipation from the constraints of orthodox psychoanalysis'. Rogers worked in teams, in Chicago and Wisconsin as well as on the west coast. His companions, at least part of the way, included Gene Gendlin, Nat Raskin, John Shlien, John Wood and Doug Land.

A comparison of the two men's state of health shows that Kohut's physical constitution was less sound. He suffered cancer of the lymph cells at the age of 58, had a bypass operation in 1979, and in 1980 contracted pneumonia. This took a heavy toll on his own narcissism and challenged him to contemplate the limits of his existence. Kohut died at the age of 68, only some ten years after his departure from an orthodox psychoanalytical orientation. What would have happened if he had lived longer? What new directions would he have brought to self psychology? What developments would he have fostered? Rogers reached the age of 85 and remained relatively fit until then. Despite (or perhaps because of) the fact that he considered his life's work to have been completed, he continued to stress his growth experiences and his almost stoical attitude to death.

Kohut and Rogers never met, though both lived and worked in Chicago at the same time (1945–1957). In the final version of an article, which he had revised many times, Rogers (1984) mentioned Kohut's approach in a short paragraph on empathy. At a conference on the 'Evolution of Psychotherapy', which took place in Phoenix, Arizona, in 1985, he discussed Kohut at greater length (Rogers, 1987). Kohut (1979, p. 15) refers to Rogers' client-centered therapy in connection with Stolorow (1976) whose article draws a comparison between Kohut's and Rogers' concepts as one of many examples of similarities between his theory of narcissism and other authors. Tobin (1991, p. 11) notes that, to the best of his knowledge, Kohut's wife Elizabeth — a psychiatric social worker — influenced him on a theoretical as well as a clinical plane.

Kohut is described as an aesthete with cultural interests, but also as a sportsman. He wrote about the psychological importance of music and literature. This indicates characteristics connected with his middle-class origins. Rogers, with his rural background, loved nature and local customs. Here, too, we can find links with the emphasis on the actualizing tendency, the organismic valuing, and Rogers' phenomenological stress on reliance on experience.

True to his commitment to humanistic traditions, Rogers' tone in his publications was highly personal. In later life he became very open about himself in his publications and practice. He never abandoned his gentle way of tuning in with his clients, whilst remaining in the background. Kohut, both in his writings and in his therapeutic style, adopted a more detached manner.

In a sense, both were self-taught, as neither Rogers nor Kohut had a master. However, Freud was long an example to Kohut, or in self psychological terms an idealized selfobject. Rank — one of the sources of psychoanalysis, albeit an unorthodox one — was relatively important to Rogers (see Pfeiffer, 1990). According to Stolorow and Atwood (1976), Kohut also owed a debt to Rank (see Kohut, 1977, p. 16).

Strozier (1985, pp. 8–10) considers Kohut to have had four personal goals: 'to be an excellent analyst' and an 'effective teacher', and 'to achieve leadership of the psychoanalytic community' and 'as a researcher and original thinker'. Kohut attained all these objectives. The same can be said of Rogers. His work as a therapist and facilitator was documented on many videotapes and numerous witnesses, observers and clients attested to its impressiveness and beneficial nature. His leading role in the client-centered movement remains undisputed, though he himself disliked and rejected the role of a 'guru'. His reputation as a researcher, and as a creative and independent spirit, is legendary. Both men revised and reevaluated their work, providing striking confirmation of the view that scientific thinking is a continuous process of evolution. Rogers' work as a teacher in the traditional sense is of less importance, as his person-centered view of teaching and learning made him skeptical of brilliance in a teacher. He wanted his 'students' to tap and develop their own knowledge and potential. As a teacher he set out only to inspire and encourage.

2. PHILOSOPHICAL BACKGROUND: VIEW OF HUMAN NATURE AND SCIENTIFIC THEORY

2. 1. The view of human nature taken by the client-centered approach and self psychology

While self psychology is based on depth psychology, the person-centered approach, with its links to a philosophy of existence, self-organization, and encounter, is ultimately a classic example of humanistic psychology, despite its acknowledgement of the value of a psychodynamic perspective. Its recurrent themes are Man's nature as an essentially trustworthy, constructive, progressive and growth-directed, holistic and social being (see Rogers, 1957b), capable of self-reflection, self-determination and empowerment. Individuals cannot be controlled from outside; they require the right climate to develop, and at times also a stimulus to do so. This belief is distilled into a wonderful formulation: 'We cannot give the truth to others, but we can find it together with them' (Trüb, 1951, p. 103; cit. Pfeiffer, 1981, p. 220; translated into English). Rogers sees self-actualization, with its striving to maintain and enhance the human organism, as a creative tendency which justifies his commitment to 'a life-affirming way of being' (Rogers, 1981, p. 84; retranslated into English).

In many ways Kohut's thinking also implies a humanistic-existential view of the individual. He ascribes 'primary hope' and a 'challenging wholeness' to Man, and does not consider him to be a 'bundle of isolated biological drives' which need to be tamed. Bartosch (1999, p. 49) mentions the 'self-healing power', a 'tendency towards development' and 'a core self that is directed towards development because of its innate vitality'. Kohut though acknowledging influences from the past rejects a mechanistic or pure deterministic view of mankind. The fundamental human motivation is — just as with Rogers — that of preserving and enhancing the self.

Kahn (1985, p. 893) considers the self psychological concept a 'bridge between psychoanalysis and humanistic psychology'. Tobin (1990) dedicates a whole article with this title to the sides of self psychology that constitute this bridge and justify the attribution of at least some aspects of self psychology to the existential-humanistic paradigm. Among these he cites the holistic view of Man, the stress on introspection and empathy, the phenomenological approach to the human psyche, the placing of the therapeutic situation in a field-theoretical, intersubjective frame of reference, and the belief in human nature as positive in its core, as well as the emphasis on the importance of free will and respect for the client's values. Yet none of these affinities arises from an explicit philosophical current, and Kohut never referred to any such authority.

In connection with the complementarity of self psychology with drive and conflict psychology, whereby he attempts to take account of both the primary narcissistic needs and the drive needs, Kohut distinguishes between the 'guilty' and the 'tragic' person. In both cases there is an evident link with existentialism. In the one, the pleasure principle is to the fore, whereas in the other, which transcends pleasure, the emphasis is on the joy that comes from a reinforced self. However, Kohut, with his European roots, is less optimistic than the humanistic concept of self-actualization, and tends to regard this aspect as a Sisyphean task.

Rogers did not consider it necessary to look at individual (substantial) motivations separately from the general developmental principle, which he posited as the actualizing tendency. Sexuality was important to him at a personal level (see Rogers, 1981, p. 35), but he made no specific mention of it in his theoretical writings. He often treated destructive aggression as a secondary, reactive phenomenon, which was not rooted in human nature (Rogers, 1957b; Rogers, 1961, Chapter 8). Here, the perspectives are similar. In self psychology specifically *destructive aggressions* and *sexual perversions* are regarded as a response of the self to a narcissistic injury. They are seen as a means of compensating for inner emptiness and threat — in short, a way to feel alive again. Here, Kohut both highlighted the phenomenon of *sexualization*, and discussed in great detail the symptoms of *narcissistic rage* with its insatiable thirst for revenge and its latent or manifest hostility, contrasting this with *assertiveness* as adjustment and the expression of a strong, self-confident self (Kohut, 1972; Ornstein and Ornstein, 1990; Wolf, 1996, pp. 104–13; Lachmann, 1999).

The differences between the views of human nature in self psychology and client-centered therapy can, in part, be summarized as follows:

• Both approaches stress the incalculable importance of the 'psychological climate' — the 'ambience' of the therapeutic relationship — but in self psychology responsibility for the process, that is, for interpretation, remains with the analyst, who facilitates curative processes by offering interpretations. Here, Kohut is closer to the medical or expert model than is Rogers.
• While according to Kohut values are acquired through the idealization of selfobjects, in Rogers' approach values, as part of the organismic experience, are an 'internal locus of evaluation' (cf. Kahn, 1985, p. 900; Raskin, 1986, p. 236).
• Kohut, with his concept of the 'tragic person', was less optimistic than Rogers about Man's ability to actualize his potential.

2. 2. Approaches to research

For Kohut, introspection and empathy (as vicarious introspection) were the only acceptable methods of acquiring data. He therefore largely dispensed with the metapsychology of classical psychoanalysis, and in particular rejected mechanistic concepts as inappropriate to the object of research. He rejected empirical examination of his theoretical concepts (e.g. his theory of the bipolar self) out of hand. This led to the criticism of his theoretical work as impressionistic and speculative, which Rogers himself (1991b, p. 309) also voiced in connection with Kohut. Kohut was indeed skeptical about the ability of natural science to investigate the self.

Rogers took a strong interest in phenomenological, experience-near theory and practice. When testing his hypotheses (especially those of his theory of therapy), however, he did apply common empirical scientific methods, which led to his being labeled the 'father of empirical psychotherapeutic research'.

3. PERSONALITY, MOTIVATIONAL AND DEVELOPMENTAL THEORY

3. 1. Personality theory

The self is a central concept for both Rogers and Kohut. There are similarities between the two approaches, for instance in the holistic view of the self as an organizational principle permitting the perception and processing of experience. Rogers speaks of the 'true self', by which he means the essence of a person in its deeply organismic being, and thus the 'organismic self'. In a narrower, phenomenological sense, however, he defines the self as a perceptual structure, object and *gestalt* — in a manner of speaking, self-representation — and thus also uses the expression 'self-concept' as a synonym for the self (Rogers, 1959). As such, the self is neither an agency, nor is it located in any given place. The self, in this sense, does not do anything. Rather, it is a perceived self, not a *center of activity* or reflection as with Kohut. Rogers is mainly concerned with self-development (the dynamics of the self). Personality structure is of far less importance to him. To Kohut, the self is structural in two senses: firstly, it is the 'structured organization of experience'; and secondly, it is the center of activity and initiative, and as such has the connotation of spatial extension and of the motivational states that Rogers ascribes to the organism (which is synonymous with the person). 'In certain mental states the self may extend far beyond the bounds of the individual, or may contract to become identical with just one of its actions or goals' (Kohut, 1975a, pp. 141f.; retranslated into English). In his comparison of the concepts of empathy in the client-centered approach and self psychology, Bohart (1991, p. 44) uses the following metaphors: he describes Kohut's self, with its structural character, as a 'house' and Rogers' self, with its process character, as a 'river'.

In his description of the characteristics of the self, Kohut ascribes to it a bipolar — and thus, again, authoritative and experience-distant — character (see Kahn's [1985] diagrammatic representation of the self, its structural elements and the needs related to them, as well as Emery's criticism [1987] of this and Kahn's reply [1987]). The self comprises:

1.   The pole of the ambitions, the exhibitionistic and grandiose sector (the 'grandiose self'), is fed by mirroring selfobject experiences ('the gleam in the mother's eye'), and is the locus of the need for mirroring and approval, from which self-assertiveness, vitality, pleasure in independent activity, initiative, self-esteem and self-regard may grow (generally a healthy narcissism or 'striving for power and success'; Wolf, 1996, p. 51).
2.   The pole of values and ideals: It arises from idealizing selfobject experiences, and is the locus of the need for idealization, and the accompanying wish to admire and to merge with the strong selfobject. For Kohut, the strong, powerful caretaker calms and soothes the child, which will become internalized by the child as the capacity for self-soothing. When the child gets older, it will also internalize the ideals, morals, and values of the strong, idealized caretaker.
3.   The tension arc between the two poles is the locus of the talents and abilities. It is here that the alter ego or 'twinship' needs are situated.

According to Kohut the self, as the 'core of the personality', thus consists of the pole of the ambitions, which in a manner of speaking 'pushes' the person, and the pole of the ideals which 'pulls' him/her. Between the two lie the innate talents and acquired abilities, which are mobilized by the 'tension arc' created by the twin poles.

Common to both concepts is the overriding importance of the self, as an interface for encounters with others and the world. Kohut subsumed under his psychology of the self both the organismic self — which as the center of initiative is capable of organismic evaluation — and the self as an object of perception ('organized perceptions about the self'), which under favorable conditions will permit the internalization of experience as self-experience.

The unconscious and defense

In the client-centered approach the unconscious is not topical, but rather unnoticed, lying outside of awareness; yet it is subliminally perceived by the entire organism. By contrast, self psychology attaches great importance to the investigation of repressed biographical data. Stolorow (cf. Orange, Atwood and Stolorow, 1997, pp. 7–8) distinguishes between three forms of the unconscious: the pre-reflective, the dynamic (the repressed), and the unvalidated.

The two approaches use the concept of defense in a similar fashion: Rogers is chiefly concerned with the denial of experience and the distortion of awareness in order to maintain and secure the self-concept. Defense is a protective function, a 'wise' reaction of the organism, mainly aimed at preserving the self-concept from inundation and collapse. For Kohut, too, defense is adjustment in the interests of the survival of the self.

3. 2. Primary motivations

With his acceptance of a 'need for positive regard' and a 'need for positive self-regard', Rogers to some extent departed from his line of desisting from naming specific human motives and only assuming one general developmental principle, the actualizing tendency. According to self psychology, the primary motivation of human beings is strengthening the self and repelling threats to it. In Kohut's theory, drives like sexuality and aggression no longer have the primary character assigned to them by classical psychoanalysis.

3. 3. Developmental theory

While Kohut traces highly precise vectors of development of the (disturbed) self, the phenomenologist Rogers only deals with developmental questions in very general terms, and consciously refrains from speculation about them. The findings of modern research into infantile psychology, to which self psychology has paid close attention, have provided empirical evidence which is also of relevance to client-centered theory and disorders (e.g. Biermann-Ratjen, 2001).

In self psychology, individual development is seen as critically dependent on the fulfillment of the needs associated with the various sectors of the self, that is, mainly on the empathic understanding and answering of the need for grandiosity and subsequently — in what Kohut also regarded as a *second chance* — those for idealization and the experience of essential sameness. In self psychology the term 'selfobject' does not refer to a person but to the function fulfilled by that person — that of facilitating and stimulating certain experiences, namely selfobject experiences. 'Selfobjects . . . are the subjectively experienced aspect of a function exercised in a relationship' (Wolf, 1996, p. 77; retranslated into English). In extreme cases the (archaic) selfobject entirely loses the character of a dialogue with an opposite number, and virtually becomes an apersonal function for the client, which has its parallel in the depersonalized alter ego found in the early Rogers. This may be the reason why a psychoanalyst friend of mine, after his teaching analysis with a self psychologist, complained that the latter had not been enough of another as a partner. While such an attitude is understandable in highly sensitive clients, it is clearly less so where more robust individuals are concerned. In self psychology archaic selfobjects are distinguished from mature selfobjects, the first serving as self-object functions for rather 'immature' persons, the latter as self-object functions for 'mature' persons. These not only have to be provided by other persons but can also take the form of symbols or ideas.

4. THE THEORY OF DISTURBANCE (CONCEPTS OF ETIOLOGY, ILLNESS AND HEALTH)

4. 1. Etiology

The counterpart of the Freudian *conflict model* in self psychology is a *deficit model* which stresses developmental deficits in early childhood. It is assumed that selfobjects arise from the inadequate functioning of parents. In client-centered psychotherapy we encounter a dissociation model. Due to the (unconditional) need assumed by Rogers for positive regard and self-regard, 'conditions of worth' imposed by significant others cause a denial or distortion of organismic experience, and thus incongruence between self and experience. Here, too, interpersonal processes give rise to deficits and inner tensions that result from the dissociation of organismic experience on the one hand, and conscious experience and symbolized needs on the other.

4. 2. Concept of illness and health

By contrast to the concept of incongruence and lack of organismic valuing in the terminology of the Person-Centered Approach, in self psychology the category relevant to pathology is that of the fragmented, disharmonious and enfeebled self.

Instead of an ability to work, love and enjoy or the formula, 'Where It was, I shall become,' both well-known goals in classical psychoanalysis, self psychology sees the 'healthy' person as someone with a coherent, vital and harmonious self and an ability to acquire the responsiveness of mature selfobjects. Coherence means inner cohesion and continuity of self-experience, while harmony stands for freedom from contradictions and inner peace, and vitality for an energetic bent, dynamism and flexibility. Self psychology aims not for consciousness or catharsis but for consolidation and strengthening of the self, which may also be reflected in a restructuring of the self.

In person-centered terms, this can be reformulated as follows: harmony calls for congruence, that is, agreement between experience(s) and self-representation. Vitality is fed by openness to experience, and the constant nourishment provided by satisfactory relationships (and hence positive self-regard). Coherence is akin to the 'consistent *gestalt*' of a self, and to the integration and mutual reinforcement of differing experiences, which result in strength — but not rigidity — and structural order.

In the client-centered approach, the ideal of health is the growth of the 'true self' ('to be that self which one truly is'; Rogers, 1961 in reference to Kierkegaard) — the notional 'fully functioning person' in the sense of a personality that is developing fully and is characterized by openness to experience and existential freedom of choice. Pfeiffer (1995, p. 57) notes that while a changing self-configuration due to openness to experience may be an expression of flexibility, a healthy person also has a need for continuity and stability, for delimitation. This is a dialectic of which Kohut partly takes account, with his concept of a vital yet consistent self.

While Rogers' goal is the autonomous subject, capable of growth under favorable social conditions, Kohut stresses lifelong dependence on empathic selfobjects (the selfobject matrix as 'oxygen') for 'psychological survival', and for renewal and replenishment of the psychic structure.

5. THERAPEUTIC THEORY

5. 1. Basic attitudes and ambience as foundations of the relationship

Client-centered therapeutic theory is based on six interacting *necessary and sufficient conditions* that define an intersubjective field or relationship (Rogers, 1957a). I take these as given here. The relationship offered by the psychotherapist corresponds to predefined attitudes that are also referred to as therapeutic principles (see Finke, 1994), but not as guides to action. Therapeutic techniques (see *inter alia* Finke, 1994; Swildens, 1991; and Sachse, 1999) certainly delimit behavioral possibilities, yet these should always be judged by the attitudes they reveal, and in no way be a fixed component of therapeutic theory or practice. Interpretation, dream interpretation, resistance and transference analysis, and key elements of self psychological work, may all in some circumstances help to express basic attitudes, even at the behavioral level. Provided that the basic attitudes translate into fulfillment of the necessary conditions in such a way that they are actually experienced, and that no techniques are forced on the client (principle of 'nondirectiveness') there are no limits to the spectrum of treatment practice. In general, however, expert-oriented intervention is given a low priority because of the trust placed in the client's potential for self-actualization.

In self psychology as in classical psychoanalysis, it is probably the case that such a basic attitude, in the sense of a general therapeutic factor, serves to create 'favorable transference and working conditions' (Biermann-Ratjen, Eckert and Schwartz, 1995, p. 41) ('necessary but not sufficient'), to which specific therapeutic actions are allied, e.g. resistance analysis, transference work and interpretation. However, the stress on the exceptional importance of the therapeutic ambience and the analyst's responsiveness is strikingly close to the client-centered approach. Kohut came to accept that both the 'corrective emotional experience', and 'healing through relationship' or 'empathy even as a therapeutic agent' were useful and valid.

Both in the Person-Centered Approach (PCA) and in self psychology, the relationship is seen as the space for activity and experience, and as the fertile ground that nourishes the client's growth. There are, however, shades of difference as regards the greater weight given by PCA to here-and-now experience and dialogue, and in self psychology in the view of the past when seen from the angle of the origins of becoming, as well as the role of the transference relationship.

It also seems to me that the concept of 'corrective emotional experience' is differently understood and applied. While client-centered therapy sees the real, new experience (which may include need fulfillment) as beneficial, in self psychology it is optimal responsiveness (including optimal frustration, empathic lapses, disruption and restoration) in the working through (often mourning; so to speak, taking leave of 'Paradise') of earlier experiences (disappointments, traumas, etc.) that is seen as corrective.

I am critical of the tendency in self psychology, when discussing parental failure, to assign blame. What is at issue is the subjective experience of the client, which must certainly be valued, but without making judgements as to the objective situation. It is often sufficient to recognize the client's plight. I also find that the value of frustration is overdone in some passages in the self psychological literature.

Genuineness and abstinence

If the early Rogers (1951) depicts the psychotherapist as a rather impersonal alter ego, the later Rogers gives prominence to the 'person-to-person' relationship, and in the PCA genuineness actually becomes the most important condition. Meanwhile, the self psychological analyst remains largely abstinent, though — in the interests of pair psychology, in which the analyst emerges from the role of an observer — this principle is somewhat less rigorously applied than in classical analysis, mainly in order to avoid causing additional injury to the vulnerable self of the client.

In PCA, the main purpose of the therapist's transparency, which is the other side of the congruence coin, is to give the client feedback on arrestive states. Client-centered psychotherapy does not, as such, demand abstinence. The guideline is that the psychotherapist should not put words in the client's mouth, despite the client's being expected to enter into a dialogue of equals. Because of this, person-centered therapists have great reservations about interpretation. As a self psychologist (verbal communication by Paul Ornstein) put it, 'Rogers was phobic about adding anything to the client.'

During a seminar moderated by Frank Lachmann in Vienna, he discussed an analysand whom he had had in analysis for many years and for whom the separation was very hard. Because of this he gave her a parting gift of a marble egg, probably as a symbol of the enduring nature of the relationship and the shared experience. I suspect that he did this almost guiltily ('One shouldn't do it, but in this case I decided to'). A client-centered therapist would probably not find a gesture like this so hard to make. If anything, the stress on the realness of the therapeutic relationship as a dialogue makes it questionable not to give way to such impulses and to place them in a transference context. Rogers' comments (1987) on Kohut's approach point in this direction. The fact that Kohut once said to an analysand who had been speeding in his car on the way to the session, in a worried tone, 'You're a damned idiot' merely qualifies the general difference, rather than removing it.

Positive regard

According to Rogers, the adoption of an attitude of acceptance will largely exclude the sense of threat created by interpretation, abstinence and valuation. Psychoanalysts are normally mistrustful of this view of the therapist's commitment to the client, and in consequence they are often reputed to be cool and distant. Kohut took a humanistic line, believing that empathy and warmth played a crucial role in the creation of a strong, 'real' relationship that would spark 'the gleam in the mothers' eye'. However, Kahn (1985, p. 895) follows Stolorow in pointing out that, what for Rogers was prizing the client, to Kohut was mirroring, which served to promote transference, rather than constituting a fundamental admiration for the client. On the other hand, Kohut was entirely open to 'appreciation' of the client, regarded it as correct 'to indicate, when a patient was making progress' (Miller, 1985, p. 20), and on a wider plane believed in expressing regard for the client's inner resources and tendencies towards health, provided that this did not obstruct transference.

Empathy

Rogers and Kohut are in agreement on the overriding importance of empathy to the therapeutic process, and in their view of its essence as understanding the client from the client's point of view, meaning that it has both an *emotional* and a *cognitive-understanding* side. Sight should not be lost of the 'as if' character of Rogers' 'alter ego' relationship or of Kohut's 'vicarious introspection'. This is a matter of 'trying to sense meanings of which the client is only barely aware, but not to uncover feelings of which the person is unconscious, which would be threatening' (Rogers, 1980b, p. 79; retranslated into English). 'Reflection of feelings' or even 'verbalization of emotional experiential contents' is certainly a technique frequently used to express the empathic stance, but it is by no means the only way of communicating empathic understanding.

For Kohut, empathy is a creative extension of the self. He argued that the accepting and understanding human echo is 'psychological nutrition' and 'oxygen' without which it would be impossible to live a satisfying life. This sounds very much like Rogers. What Kohut called the 'self-pathologies' are for him the 'result of a lack of empathy in the selfobjects' (Kohut, 1977, p. 85; retranslated into English).

Empathy lapses, which Kohut regards as virtually inevitable because highly disordered people find it particularly difficult to attune in this way, present both a danger to the stability of the relationship and an opportunity. In the process of restoration the client discovers that the therapist is prepared to get back onto the track that was being pursued and place himself entirely at the client's service by sharing his/her world as much as possible. In this way the client learns that disruptions can be overcome. This is also the meaning of Rogers' statement that even the striving for empathy can have a sustained beneficial effect.

Differences can be identified in the view of the function of empathy. While Kohut principally sees this as a method of observation aimed at the collection of data, which in turn lays the basis for the dynamic and genetic interpretations that constitute the higher form of empathy (the lower form is understanding), for Rogers it is intrinsically therapeutic (see Rogers, 1991b, pp. 302–3) — a view that Kohut, however, increasingly came to share (cf. Bohart and Greenberg, 1997, a book which is dedicated 'to Carl Rogers and Heinz Kohut, two pioneers in the study of empathy', including contributions by Shlien, Bozarth and Barrett-Lennard from a client-centered perspective, and a few articles from a psychoanalytic-self psychological perspective).

5. 2. Some aspects of technique

Silence and questioning

I suspect that, in a therapy session based on self psychology, the analyst will on average be more inclined to remain silent than in one based on client-centered therapy. This is confirmed by the advice of my self psychological supervisor, when supporting me in a difficult therapeutic process, to 'say less'. But maybe that is more a question of personal style than of the applied method.

Neither approach sets great store by systematic questioning by the psychotherapist. Instead, what is called for is *constant attentiveness*, leading to immersion in the client's world, so as to be better able to understand him/her.

Regression

Kohut may not have had a high opinion of the therapeutic efficacy of regression, but in view of the analytical setting, its importance as a component of the analytical cure should not be underestimated. By contrast, the PCA probably gives far more weight to promoting the progressive, adult perspective — sometimes, perhaps, too much. The PCA seeks not to encourage dependence on the therapist, but to respect the client's free will and capability for self-reflection, which also have an impact on the frequency and duration of the therapy. Naturally, choice and decision-making as expressions of free will are often only possible after the processing of emotions and strengthening of the personality. Only by understanding him-/herself will the client be able to express a view.

Interpretation

In his comparison of his position with that of Kohut, Rogers (1987) said that the intention behind an understanding reaction differed from Kohut's to the extent that he (Rogers) focused on agreement with the client, on ensuring that he had understood and that the client approved of what he was doing, whereas Kohut aimed to ascertain whether the client was ready for the interpretation, i.e. was capable of accepting it. In other words, Kohut tested the inner frame of reference of the client to see whether an interpretation from the outer frame of reference (that of the psychotherapist) appeared appropriate. As far as possible, Rogers remained within the inner frame of reference of the client, only occasionally interposing minor additions, some of them coming from the psychotherapist's inner frame of reference. For Kohut, (genetic) interpretation and the systematic working through of the client's biography (going back as far as possible) were of cardinal importance. Rogers stressed the value of the reality experienced by the client, rather than external ascriptions by the psychotherapist, which the client would wrongly take to be actual events. Here, Rogers' radical proposition that the client's experience was the 'highest authority' should be recalled. The crucial difference probably lies in the fact that, for Kohut, interpretation was a higher form of empathy, and understanding thus a first step towards the explanation of a phenomenon. However, for all his stress on interpretation and skill at it, Kohut differed from classical psychoanalysis in advocating confronting phenomena 'in a 'straight' manner' (Miller, 1985, p. 15) and 'as it is presented' (ibid., p. 20).

Transference

Self psychology continues to regard work with transference and counter-transference as the highroad to therapeutic success. However, unlike the libidinal transferences of classical psychoanalysis, narcissistic transferences, which he later called 'selfobject transferences', are central to Kohut's thinking (cf. chapter 3.1.):

- The mirror transference corresponds most closely to Rogers' alter ego relationship, with its focus on empathy and 'positive regard', which is often linked with a 'mothering' function.
- The idealizing transference does not have any equivalent in the PCA. Stolorow (1976) takes the view that Rogers did not see this as a separate component of the relationship. For Kohut, idealizing selfobject-experiences are an opportunity to develop the capacity for self-soothing (as the strong, powerful care taker calms and soothes the child, which later gets internalized).
- The alter ego transference in the narrow sense of the term, which Kohut also referred to as the 'twinship transference', is that most likely to contain those elements of dialogue to which client-centered therapy attaches such importance. Bartosch (1999) takes the view that efforts towards a maximum of equality are doomed to failure, and speaks of the 'principle of minor deviation' — a qualification with regard to the 'I–Thou' relationship in the therapeutic setting for which Buber, too, argued in his memorable dialogue with Rogers.

The focus on the 'transference relationship' represents a marked difference from client-centered therapy. Rogers, among other such remarks, referred to the transference concept as a 'highly intellectual framework' in his comments on his conversation with Gloria. His contribution to the debate in the Person-Centered Review in 1987, touched off by Shlien, reaffirmed the position taken in 1951, when he said that the emergence of a transference relationship or worse still, a transference neurosis, was undesirable. He argued that, instead of leaving the matter open and keeping the client in ignorance of the therapist's thoughts and feelings, the therapist's observations and the transparent revelations of his congruent experiences were needed as feedback, and sometimes as a 'correction' or alternative to the client's — or the therapist's — perception of the situation, though there should naturally be no suggestion of dogmatism or knowing best. Rogers is closer to Jung's view that healing is in spite of, and not because of, transference.

Transference, resistance, interpretation and 'working through', like optimal frustration and transmuting internalization, are, then, concepts which may present a fruitful challenge for client-centered psychotherapy but do not form part of the theory, conceptual armory or methodological repertoire of the client-centered approach.

5. 3. On the range of applications

Both self psychology and person-centered psychotherapy are well suited to working with clients with severe mental disorders, though self psychological psychoanalysis according to Kohut is not indicated for patients with psychosis, schizoid and paranoid personality disorders, and borderline personality disorders. Kohut extended psychoanalysis to clients with so-called 'narcissistic disorders', and expressed the opinion that the insights thus gained also provide important guidelines for work with persons with neurotic problems. Because of its practical approach, outlined in the section of this paper on therapeutic theory, (e.g. basic attitudes and the technique of explanatory relationships), client-centered psychotherapy has a good record of success with clients with so-called personality disorders (cf. Biermann-Ratjen et al., 1995, p. 167).

6. LESSONS OF SELF PSYCHOLOGY FOR CLIENT-CENTERED PRACTICE

For reasons of space, I shall not extend this comparison into the areas of indication, setting, applications in psychotherapy and elsewhere, or dissemination, development and training. Instead, I shall now turn to the question of what lessons client-centered therapy can draw from self psychology. Particularly as regards comparison of the intersubjective and the person-centered approach, readers are referred to the work of Kahn (1996). With the continued development of self psychology as an intersubjective approach, the phenomenological position emerged in a still more rigorous form. This is apparent in the skepticism towards diagnoses and constructs remote from experience, e.g. that of Kohut's self (see Tobin, 1991, p. 16), and towards the concept of 'optimal frustration' (ibid., p. 20). Thus, for Stolorow the self is 'the individual's organization of his or her self-experience in the world' (see Tobin, 1990, p. 25). However, Stolorow's method ('active empathic inquiry') appears to involve a more active investigation of the client's inner life by the therapist than is the case with client-centered therapy.

The question is to what extent the person-centered approach can learn and profit from self psychological theory and practice:

1. One lesson is that we should not merely respond with respect and understanding to idealization of the therapist by the client as the need arises, but see it as the expression of a deep-seated need which requires space to unfold and should not be relativized by misconstruing it as a tendency towards dependency or lack of self-esteem.

2. Particularly when working with severely disturbed people who are incapable of tolerating much frustration, the 'injured self' — as a theoretical concept — can be extremely helpful in achieving a basic understanding of the demands of the client — especially those made on the therapist — and an understanding of the client's reactions when attempting to cope with stressful situations. Kohut's theory, in situations that are hard to understand empathically, does not stand in the way of the relationship, but might be a precondition of entering into it. The knowledge of the theory of a vulnerable self, for example, can help the therapist to stay empathic and prize clients even when they are hard to understand, hostile, or apparently 'strange'. This could spare many therapists the sense of inadequacy engendered by what they see as their insufficient capacity for empathy or unconditional positive regard. This theory offers the therapist guidelines to provide optimal responsiveness and perhaps even gratification of the client's needs.

3. The concept of narcissistic rage may also be helpful in the aforementioned sense, as a means of understanding and coming to terms with the vehemence of clients' reactions. It is a characteristic of narcissistic rage that its intensity does not diminish when the (present) threat has in reality already been removed.

4. Sexualization: Taking this aspect into account helps sensitize one to sexual undertones. According to the client-centered view, this would reveal an incongruence manifested by the fact that the experience did not arise primarily from the actualizing tendency, but was a question of distortions required by the self-concept.

5. Disruption and restoration: This concept can also help us to understand and accept disruptions of the therapeutic relationship field as transitional phases, and as a means of attaining a more solid basis.

6. A further lesson is the need to take more account of the narcissistic needs of the therapist, for instance when nothing he/she does is felt by the client to be helpful.

7. FINAL REMARKS

To take up Paul Bergman's contention (Rogers, 1981, p. 46) that no one has more than one pathfinding idea in the course of a lifetime, the rest are merely variations on a theme: in the case of Rogers this would be his proposition of the 'necessary and sufficient conditions for personality development through psychotherapy' (1957). In that of Kohut it would be his recognition of the outstanding importance of narcissistic strivings and the introduction of the theoretical constructs of the 'selfobject' and 'selfobject transferences', i.e. the need for mirroring, and also for idealization and equality. Common to both is the central role they accord to the experiencing subject and his/her social needs in therapeutic work.

Self psychology tends to leave more space for inner experiences; while client-centered therapy offers more opportunities for interpersonal encounter and the experiences connected with it. This is also true for Stolorow's approach to intersubjectivity involving the relationship between two interacting subjectivities, and therefore this theory is very much a two-person psychology. The client-centered therapist is an expert in offering a particular kind of relationship which may give rise to changes. The self psychologist is also an expert in interpreting phenomena and fitting them into the client's biographical structure.

The *therapeutic goal* of client-centered therapy is the reorganization of the self, and it may also seek to achieve personality development. The aim is not healing but self-development, which may also be manifested in increased self-empathy, in congruent perception of the self and positive self-regard. I do not share the assessment of Kahn (1985, p. 897) and Tobin (1991, p. 28) that Rogers, like Freud, attached more importance than Kohut to widening of consciousness. Instead, like Bohart (1991, p. 41) I refer readers to the words of Rogers himself, who saw the expansion of consciousness as a by-product — albeit an important one — of empathic accompaniment of the stream of experience, and not as its purpose. Thus Rogers (1951/1972, p. 144) said that 'change in the self tends to precede the rediscovery of denied or repressed material rather than to follow it' (retranslated into English). For him, the process orientation of the therapeutic relationship from 'moment to moment' is of central importance, and psychotherapy is 'a way of being with' which calls for openness to (new) experiences. This accords with the experiencing concept, which has little room for cognitive understanding, and still less for dynamic or genetic interpretations. Unlike Kohut, Rogers wished to dispense with these altogether, as procedures aimed at cognitive insights, though this was mainly because of his faith in clients' capability for self-exploration. Explanation as a therapeutic agent is more characteristic of the early Rogers (1942).

For all the differences that I have attempted to detail, the watershed in Kohut's thinking resulted in an affinity to Rogers' approach in the 1940s–50s, and introduced an approach within psychoanalysis that has much in common with Rogers' radical — and often ridiculed — positions. I am not ashamed to say this, despite the widespread denigration of client-centered psychotherapy, even by its own exponents. In place of the sense of inferiority that one not infrequently encounters, I should like to plead for sufficient self-confidence to acknowledge the strengths and lessons of other approaches, without overestimating them as sometimes occurs in relation to psychoanalysis.

REFERENCES

Bartosch, E. (1999). *Auf dem Weg zu einer neuen Psychoanalyse. Charakterentwicklung und Therapie aus der Sicht der Selbstpsychologie.* Vienna-New York: Verlag Neue Psychoanalyse.

Biermann-Ratjen, E-M., Eckert, J. and Schwartz H.J. (1995). *Gesprächspsychotherapie.* 7th edn. Stuttgart: Kohlhammer.

Biermann-Ratjen, E-M. (2002). Die entwicklungspsychologische Perspektive des Klientenzentrierten Konzepts. In W. Keil and G. Stumm, G. (Eds.) *Die vielen Gesichter der Personzentrierten Psychotherapie.* Wien-New York: Springer, pp. 123–45.

Bohart, A. C. (1991). Empathy in client-centered therapy: A contrast with psychoanalysis and self psychology. *Journal of Humanistic Psychology, 31*(1) 34–48.

Bohart, A. C. and Greenberg, L.S. (Eds.) (1997). *Empathy Reconsidered. New directions in psychotherapy.* Washington, DC: American Psychological Association.

Butzer, R. J. (1997). *Heinz Kohut zur Einführung.* Hamburg: Junius.

Emery, E. J. (1987). Empathy: Psychoanalytic and client-centered. *American Psychologist, 5,* 513–15.

Gendlin, E. T. (1978). *Focusing.* New York: Everest House.

Goldberg, A. (1985). Preface. In A. Goldberg, (Ed.) *Progress in Self Psychology. Vol. 1.* New York: The Guilford Press, pp. VII–X.

Finke, J. (1994). *Empathie und Interaktion. Methodik und Praxis der Gesprächspsychotherapie.* Stuttgart: Georg Thieme.

Hexel, M. (1994). Heinz Kohut. In O. Frischenschlager, (Ed.) *Wien, wo sonst! Die Entstehung der Psychoanalyse und ihrer Schulen.* Vienna: Böhlau, pp. 161–73.

Kahn, E. (1985). Heinz Kohut and Carl Rogers: A timely comparison. *American Psychologist, 40,* 893–904.

Kahn, E. (1987). A reply to Emery's comments. *American Psychologist, 5,* 515–16.

Kahn, E. (1989a). Carl Rogers and Heinz Kohut. On the importance of valuing the 'self'. In D. W. Detrick and S. P. Detrick, (Eds.) *Self Psychology. Comparisons and contrasts.* Hillsdale, NJ: The Analytic Press, pp. 213–28.

Kahn, E. (1989b). Carl Rogers and Heinz Kohut: Toward a constructive collaboration. *Psychotherapy, 26,* 4, 555–63.

Kahn, E. (1996). The intersubjective perspective and the client-centered approach: Are they one at their core? *Psychotherapy, 33*(1), 30–42.

Kahn, E. and Rachman, A.W. (2000). Carl Rogers and Heinz Kohut. A historical perspective. *Psychoanalytic Psychology, 17*(2), 294–312.

Keil, W. and Stumm, G. (2002). *Die vielen Gesichter der Personzentrierten Psychotherapie.* Vienna-New York: Springer.

Kirschenbaum, H. (1995). Carl Rogers. In M. Suhd, (Ed.) *Positive Regard. Carl Rogers and other notables he influenced.* Palo Alto: Science and Behavior Books, pp. 1-102.

Kohut, H. (1971). *The Analysis of the Self. A systematic approach to the psychoanalytic treatment of the narcissistic personality disorders* (in German: *Narzißmus. Eine Theorie der psychoanalytischen Behandlung narzißtischer Persönlichkeitsstörungen.* Frankfurt: Suhrkamp, 1973).

Kohut, H. [1972] (1975). Überlegungen zum Narzißmus und zur narzißtischen Wut. In *Die Zukunft der Psychoanalyse.* Frankfurt: Suhrkamp, pp. 205–51.

Kohut, H. [1966] (1975a). Formen und Umformungen des Narzißmus. In *Die Zukunft der Psychoanalyse. Aufsätze zu allgemeinen Themen und zur Psychologie des Selbst.* Frankfurt, Suhrkamp, pp. 140–72.

Kohut, H. (1977). *The Restoration of the Self* (in German: *Die Heilung des Selbst.* Frankfurt: Suhrkamp, 1979).

Kohut, H. (1984) *How does Analysis Cure?* (in German: *Wie heilt die Psychoanalyse?* Frankfurt, Suhrkamp, 1987).

Korbei, L. (1997). Der Personzentrierte Ansatz und die Psychoanalyse. In C. Korunka, (Ed.) *Begegnungen: Psychotherapeutische Schulen im Gespräch.* Vienna: Facultas, pp. 38–58.

Lachmann, F. M. (1999). Aggression: reaktiv und transformiert. In E. Bartosch, H. Hinterhofer and E Pellegrini, (Eds.) *Aspekte einer neuen Psychoanalyse. Ein selbstpsychologischer Austausch.* Vienna-New York: Verlag Neue Psychoanalyse, pp. 9–20.

Miller, J.P. (1985). How Kohut actually worked. In A. Goldberg, (Ed.) *Progress in Self Psychology. Vol. 1.* New York: Guilford Press, pp. 13–30.

Orange, D. M., Atwood, G. E. and Stolorow, R. D. (1997) *Working Intersubjectively. Contextualism in psychoanalytic practice.* Hillsdale, NJ: The Analytic Press.

Ornstein, P. and Ornstein, A. (1990). Assertiveness, anger, rage, and destructive aggression: A perspective from the treatment process. In R. A. Glick and S. P. Roose, (Eds.) *Rage, Power, and Aggression.* New Haven-London: Yale University Press (in German: (1997) Selbstbehauptung, Ärger, Wut und zerstörerische Aggression: Perspektiven des Behandlungsprozesses. *Psyche 51,* 4, 289–310).

Pfeiffer, W. M. (1981). Der Widerstand in der Sicht der klientenzentrierten Psychotherapie. In H. Petzold, (Ed.) *Widerstand — ein strittiges Konzept in der Psychotherapie.* Paderborn: Junfermann, pp. 209–25.

Pfeiffer, W. M. (1990). Otto Rank und die klientenzentrierte Psychotherapie. In M. Behr, U. Esser, F. Petermann and W. M. Pfeiffer, (Eds.) *Jahrbuch für personenzentrierte Psychologie und Psychotherapie. Vol. 2.* Salzburg: Otto Müller, pp. 8–21.

Pfeiffer, W. M. (1995). Überlegungen zu einer Störungslehre aus interaktioneller Perspektie. In S. Schmidtchen, G-W. Speierer and H. Linster, (Eds.) *Die Entwicklung der Person und ihre Störung. Vol. 2. Theorien und Ergebnisse zur Grundlegung einer klientenzentrierten Krankheitslehre.* Köln: GwG, pp. 41–81.

Raskin, N. (1986). Heinz Kohut and Carl Rogers. A timely comparison (article review). *Person-Centered Review, 1,* 235–8.

Rogers, C. (1942). *Counseling and Psychotherapy. New concepts in practice.* Boston: Houghton Mifflin (in German: *Die nicht-direktive Beratung.* München: Kindler, 1973).

Rogers, C. (1951). *Client-centered Therapy. Its current practice, implications, and theory.* Boston: Houghton Mifflin (in German: *Die klientenzentrierte Gesprächspsychotherapie.* München: Kindler, 1972).

Rogers, C. (1957a). The necessary and sufficient conditions of therapeutic personality change. *Journal of Consulting Psychology, 21*(2), 95–103.

Rogers, C. (1957b). A note on 'The nature of man'. *Journal of Counseling Psychology, 4*(3) 199–203.

Rogers, C. (1959). A theory of therapy, personality, and interpersonal relationships, as developed in the client-centered framework. In S. Koch, (Ed.) *Psychology. A study of a science. Vol. III. Formulations of the person and the social context.* New York: McGraw Hill, pp. 184–256 (in German: *Eine Theorie der Psychotherapie, der Persönlichkeit und der zwischenmenschlichen*

Beziehungen. Köln: GwG, 1987).

Rogers, C. (1961). *On Becoming a Person. A therapist's view of psychotherapy.* Boston: Houghton Mifflin (in German: *Entwicklung der Persönlichkeit. Psychotherapie aus der Sicht eines Therapeuten.* Stuttgart, Klett-Cotta, 1973).

Rogers, C. [1973] (1980a). Meine Philosophie der interpersonalen Beziehungen und ihre Entstehung. In C. Rogers and R. Rosenberg *Die Person als Mittelpunkt der Wirklichkeit.* Stuttgart: Klett-Cotta, pp. 185–98.

Rogers, C. [1975] (1980b). Empathie — eine unterschätzte Seinsweise. In C. Rogers and R. Rosenberg, *Die Person als Mittelpunkt der Wirklichkeit.* Stuttgart: Klett-Cotta, pp. 75–93.

Rogers, C. [1980] (1981). Die Grundlagen eines personenzentrierten Ansatzes. In *Der neue Mensch.* Stuttgart: Klett-Cotta, pp. 65–84.

Rogers, C. [1984] (1991a). Klientenzentrierte Psychotherapie. In C. Rogers and P. F. Schmid, *Person-zentriert. Grundlagen von Theorie und Praxis.* Mainz, Grünewald, pp. 185–237.

Rogers, C. [1987] (1991b). Rogers, Kohut and Erickson: Eine persönliche Betrachtung über einige Ähnlichkeiten und Unterschiede. In J. K. Zeig, (Ed.) *Psychotherapie: Entwicklungslinien und Geschichte.* Tübingen, Deutsche Gesellschaft für Verhaltenstherapie, pp. 299–313.

Sachse, R. (1999). *Lehrbuch der Gesprächspsychotherapie.* Göttingen: Hogrefe.

Siegel, A. (1996). *Heinz Kohut and the Psychology of the Self.* New York: Routledge.

Stolorow, R. D. (1976). Psychoanalytic reflections on client-centered therapy in the light of modern conceptions of narcissism. *Psychotherapy: Theory, research and practice, 13*(1) 26–9.

Stolorow, R. D. and Atwood, G. E. (1976). An ego-psychological analysis of the work and life of Otto Rank in the light of modern conceptions of narcissism. *The International Review of Psycho-Analysis, 3,* 441–59.

Strozier, C. B. (1985). Glimpses of a life: Heinz Kohut (1913–1981). In A. Goldberg, (Ed.) *Progress in Self Psychology. Vol. 1.* New York, Guilford Press, pp. 3–12.

Stumm, G. and Wirth, B. (Eds.). (1994). *Psychotherapie: Schulen und Methoden. Eine Orientierungshilfe für Theorie und Praxis.* Vienna: Falter.

Stumm, G. and Pritz, A. (Eds.) (2000). *Wörterbuch der Psychotherapie.* Vienna-New York: Springer.

Swildens, H. (1991). *Prozeßorientierte Gesprächspsychotherapie. Einführung in eine differenzielle Anwendung des klientenzentrierten Ansatzes bei der Behandlung psychischer Störungen.* Köln: GwG.

Thorne, B. (1992). *Carl Rogers.* London: Sage.

Tobin, S. A. (1990). Self psychology as a bridge between existential-humanistic psychology and psychoanalysis. *Journal of Humanistic Psychology, 30*(1) 14–63.

Tobin, S. A. (1991). A comparison of psychoanalytic self psychology and Carl Rogers's person-centered therapy. *Journal of Humanistic Psychology, 31*(1) 9–33.

Trüb, H. (1951). *Heilung aus der Begegnung.* Stuttgart: Klett-Cotta.

Wolf, E. (1988). *Treating the Self. Elements of clinical self psychology.* New York-London: Guilford Press (in German: *Theorie und Praxis der psychoanalytischen Selbstpsychologie.* Frankfurt: Suhrkamp, 1996).

Martin Van Kalmthout

University of Nijmegen, The Netherlands

The Farther Reaches of Person-Centered Psychotherapy

INTRODUCTION

In this chapter, I will consider the role that psychotherapy in general and the person-oriented approach[1] in particular can play both now and in the future within the domain of the great life questions. My examination will take place within the context of the large socio-cultural changes currently taking place and the consequences of these changes, namely that the traditional meaning systems no longer appear to fulfill their role satisfactorily. The secularization, the individualization, and the psychologization of our culture call for not only a re-evaluation of the function of psychotherapy but also raise the question of the reach of psychotherapy. Maslow (1970) summarized his search for the hidden possibilities of human nature under the beautiful title of his book, *The Farther Reaches of Human Nature*. In analogy to this, I have summarized my search for the hidden potentials of psychotherapy and the person-oriented approach in particular under the title: *The Farther Reaches of Person-centered Psychotherapy*. The question, in this connection, is whether psychotherapy as one of the modern meaning systems can specifically contribute to the age-old life questions. I am not, thus, concerned with the question of whether psychotherapy should be aimed at existential problems nor do I pay attention to the role of religion or spirituality in psychotherapy. The starting assumption underlying my approach is that psychotherapy itself comprises a system of meanings and that psychotherapists are more or less always concerned with the meaning of life — whether they want to be or not. For this reason, I do not assume that the question of the meaning of life arises at the end of therapy, after the 'real' psychotherapeutic problems have been solved; I assume, rather, that questions of life meaning are always present either implicitly or explicitly.

As a result of this basic starting assumption, I am also interested in the consequences of such a conceptualization of psychotherapy for the further development of psychotherapy in general and the person-oriented approach in particular. The consequences may be quite exciting and revolutionary. At the same time, such a conceptualization raises numerous questions, which cannot be so quickly answered. One important question for instance is which sources of inspiration and nourishment should present-day psychotherapy draw upon when indeed construed as a modern meaning system and, as a consequence, attributed new and different functions than when traditionally conceptualized. As a system of meaning, psychotherapy may not be given sufficient inspiration by scientific research and may actually

---

[1] I prefer 'person-oriented' to 'person-centered', because the former is not linked to a particular school of therapy (see: Van Kalmthout, 2000, p. 20).

attain very little inspiration from such research. Similar to most of the other meaning systems, a field of tension exists between psychotherapy and scientific research. So where does the underlying wisdom of psychotherapy come from? Is psychotherapy actually a hidden form of religion ('invisible religion', as Luckmann, 1967, names it), or at least inspired either implicitly or explicitly by such? Or does psychotherapy have enough on its own and therefore not need any external sources of inspiration? The relation between psychotherapy, science, and religion certainly constitutes an important theme in this connection and, against this background, the question of just what the identity of psychotherapy is will continually present itself.

No matter how important these questions may be, I will limit myself in the present chapter to an initial exploration of the topic, in the hope that the numerous questions that the topic elicits will inspire others to discuss them. In the following, I will first position the issue in its actual socio-cultural context, describe my own approach to the issue and relate some of my own experiences from psychotherapeutic practice to the issue. I will then proceed from this wider socio-cultural and psychotherapeutic context to the person-oriented approach proper and attempt to describe it as a modern system of meaning. I will close with a main conclusion and a brief discussion.

PSYCHOTHERAPY IN A CHANGING WORLD

It appears today that we have completely gone off track when it comes to the great life questions. Who dares to say something about the origin, purpose, or significance of life? Who can offer a solution to the immense agony being suffered by people or provide an answer to the question of what the origin of evil might be? Skepticism and cynicism predominate. Natural scientists report no signs of goal-oriented development in biological evolution and that the impressive processes of the universe can be characterized by indifference with regard to the fate of the individual person and even the fate of an entire species, with humans not excluded. This cosmic indifference can be observed when confronted with the occurrence of natural disasters, disease, and death either elsewhere or in our own experience. Fewer and fewer people believe in a protective hand keeping watch over their personal safety and that of those who are dear to them.

Our world has, however, become even less safe as a result of what human beings do to themselves and to others. Since the Holocaust, it has not only become impossible for many to believe in God but also their faith in man has disappeared. More than ever, we appear to be aware of the atrocities that people are capable of committing. Genocide in the most bizarre forms has become a regularly recurring phenomenon in the second half of the twentieth century. War is also not the only form of violence; at the level of the individual, manslaughter and murder are also a part of daily life. Violence (physical or emotional) penetrates all parts of society and even the most intimate sectors such as the family. Sexual misuse of children — sometimes by their own parents, brothers, uncles, friends or neighbors — occurs daily. Even more shocking is the news of cold-blooded massacres of their own age-mates by children and adolescents. Slowly but surely, violence appears to be emerging as the number one characteristic of contemporary culture. This has not made the question of our own identity, who we ourselves really are, much easier.

All of this has made people shy away from philosophies of life that preach the all-embracing significance of our lives, not so much because they do not want to believe in them but because the facts that reach us are so completely and consistently in conflict with such beliefs. A philosophy of life based on the assumption that the cosmos and the history of man have some purpose and that human nature is basically good quickly gives rise to an impression of naiveté. For many people, life today is experienced as purposeless and the question of the purpose or meaning of life has thus become very real.

It is certainly not the case that natural disasters, genocide, and other gruesome deeds are new phenomena in the history of humanity. We can properly assume that (senseless) suffering has always been a part of the human condition. A major difference from earlier times, however, is that the classic sources of consolation and meaning appear to have disappeared forever and new meaning systems only develop with considerable difficulty. The widespread exodus from churches has, for example, left people with a massive ideological emptiness. Religions emerged to explain such suffering, make such suffering endurable and even tolerable, and succeeded with greater and lesser degrees of success. As long as the content and form of their messages appealed to the imagination of man and were perceived as credible, they constituted a clear source of comfort and provided a practical guideline for daily life. The past few centuries have seen a gradual change in this situation via processes that are commonly referred to as secularization and individualization. People are increasingly thinking, feeling, and behaving from their own perspective rather than allowing themselves to be guided by religious or other external institutions. A third cultural change has also emerged, namely the psychologization of human problems. This tendency has arisen with and been greatly reinforced by the emergence of a psychotherapeutic culture, which has contributed considerably to the explanation and practical handling of human suffering for some hundred years now (globally speaking, since the work of Freud). Freud, and the many psychotherapeutic schools and traditions that have arisen after him, localized the origin of human suffering primarily in the individual psyche and also fostered the processes of secularization and individualization thereby.

Modern man is now searching for a new way of giving meaning to this meaningless world. He has learned to enjoy life, is no longer hindered by feelings of guilt or having to do penance, and has become very aware of the fact that it is this life and not the hereafter that is important. In such a manner, the entertainment industry emerged with sport, sex, and unlimited consumption as the most important products. This new system of giving meaning has the important function of distracting man from the grimness of his existence. In an extension of this and as a prerequisite for it, the economy and economic prosperity — both individual and collective — have become the highest good and the measurement criteria for everything.

But 'man cannot live by bread alone'. The need for a meaning system in the stricter sense of the word and not just for distraction continues to be felt. This need has expressed itself in the emergence of all kinds of new religious and spiritual orientations and all kinds of therapies and systems of healing, that are collectively referred to as New Age (Hanegraaff, 1996). Yet another form of modern meaning-giving has emerged in our time, but then primarily within the ideology underlying the care sector and mental health care in particular. Vandermeersch (1996) speaks here and not unjustifiably of 'the ideology of mental health care'. In this connection, some people have wondered whether increasing mental health care and the profession of psychotherapist in particular may not be replacing the vanishing clergy. In this context, psychotherapists have been, and still are, sometimes referred to as 'secular priests' or 'the new clergy' (de Groot, 1995). This is not so strange as it appears at first sight. Thorough examination of the major psychotherapeutic traditions quickly shows them to have all the characteristics of a modern meaning system, without exception.

What has changed just as little as the need for life meaning is the psychological need for safety, security, and something to hold on to. Science, although not intended to serve such a purpose by most scientists, has become something for people to go by and hang on to. Politicians and policy-makers but also individual people are increasingly basing their choices on scientific findings. In such a manner, the term scientific has gradually been equated with the terms 'truth' and 'indisputable'. 'Scientific' is increasingly being taken as the final and exclusive criterion for what is true and good. Science is also increasingly being used to legitimatize what is believed or decided on non-scientific grounds. In so far as science is used in such a manner, we can justifiably speak of science as 'the new religion.'

MY APPROACH TO THE TOPIC

As a psychotherapist, I have wondered what should be understood as psychotherapy for many, many years. During this reflection, it became apparent to me that identification of the goals of psychotherapy is critical for answering this question. The goals determine the domain of psychotherapy: is psychotherapy part of the medical, psychological, religious, philosophical, or spiritual domain? Depending on how one answers this question, one may either come to the obvious conclusion that psychotherapy is a modern system of meaning (and that its practitioners are 'the new priests') or adamantly refute and deny such a conclusion. While the latter will argue that psychotherapy is a treatment method for disorders defined in psychiatric terms, the former will argue that psychotherapy addresses a much broader range of objectives and is inevitably concerned with questions of meaning and the good life. It should be clear that the latter conclusion leads more logically to the assumption that psychotherapy is a modern system of meaning, and the concomitant assumption that the practitioners of psychotherapy are our new spiritual leaders, than does the former conclusion.

Personally, I have always felt attracted to opinions that view psychotherapy as a modern variant of a phenomenon that is as old as humanity. Such an approach is well articulated by the American psychiatrist Jerome Frank in his famous book, *Persuasion and Healing* (1961). For a present-day practicing psychotherapist it might well be a difficult task to consider oneself as a healer as described by Frank. It certainly requires the necessary abstraction capacity to be able to isolate the hard core of present-day psychotherapy and its predecessors and thereby strip it of all its frills. The difficulty in doing this, however, is that not everyone agrees on what is frill and what is hard core. Is, for example, belief in God (which stood central to many of the earlier therapies) a frill? Is the theory concerned with the Oedipus complex (which stands central to psychoanalysis) a frill? Or do the experiments in the psychological laboratory (on which behavior therapy is said to be based) fall within the category of frill? The latter would certainly go too far for many of the modern psychotherapists. Nevertheless, I — myself — believe that the above (and many of the other dogmas of psychotherapy) do not constitute the essence of psychotherapy. This may also be easier for the researcher observing from a distance to see than for the practicing psychotherapist in the middle of things.

What stands out to this observer is that the structure of psychotherapy has something that is of all time. There is a kind of 'healer' who occupies an official function for people in need and people seeking help. The healer has a 'reference framework' that is — when viewed across all history — a mixture of magic, medicine, religion, psychology, and (more recently) science. The therapeutic actions of the healer stem from this reference framework and may change depending on societal circumstances, the culture, and the nature of the problem or problems. For the same reasons, the reference framework itself is equally changeable. Sometimes the framework is pure magic; then it is more psychological or philosophical in nature; sometimes clearly religious and, in our time, clearly scientific. All of this goes to show that both the content of the reference frameworks as well as the design of the therapeutic actions undertaken are strongly determined by the current culture and the actual societal circumstances. This relativizes the content of the framework and urges us to proceed with utmost care when it comes to trying to determine what does and does not belong to the hard core of psychotherapy. What belongs to the core in any case is the presence of a reference framework or system of meaning, and the fact that something is done on the basis of this framework and appears to have a therapeutic effect.

The advantage of the aforementioned approach to psychotherapy is that it helps contemporary psychotherapists to see themselves more easily as the successors to a long procession of healers: shamans, Eastern gurus, Greek-Roman philosophers, Jewish wise men from the mystical traditions, exorcists, hypnotists, and — more recently — priests and ministers. Also, it may well help us, psychotherapists, to be more open to a previously unsuspected definition and function of the profession of psychotherapy. Along the same lines as the theory of Frank are those opinions that explicitly view psychotherapy as a modern variant of religion (e.g., Johnson and Sandage, 1999; Thorne, 1997) or those opinions that assign psychotherapy and religion the same function on the health-and-happiness market within current culture (e.g., Kilbourne and Richardson, 1984). I also feel a close relation to sociological approaches that see psychotherapy as a modern meaning system (e.g., Luckmann, 1967; Hijmans, 1994). In my search for the essence of psychotherapy, I have been particularly intrigued by the aforementioned line of thinking and it therefore constitutes an important starting point in my exploration.

PSYCHOTHERAPEUTIC PRACTICE

My interest in the possible contribution of psychotherapy and the person-oriented approach to the great life questions is also inspired by my work as a practicing psychotherapist. I have noticed that science supplies only a very limited source of inspiration for the work that we do. We psychotherapists have come to a position in which we are confronted with the big life questions, in particular the question of how life should best be lived. On the one hand, I believe that psychotherapists are well-equipped to answer these questions; on the other hand, I think they are also lacking quite a lot. The strong side of psychotherapy is that it is practical and concrete rather than theoretical and contemplative. The weaker side (in my opinion) is that contemporary psychotherapy is often too superficial and quite limited in its objectives. We psychotherapists have, in fact, numerous *implicit* convictions, values, norms, and opinions with regard to what is good and bad. We also all have a particular philosophy of life and man.

These implicit convictions are not well articulated most of the time and I think that we should explicate them as fully as we can. Personally, I experience a great need within my work for a more elaborated philosophy of life, because I think that I cannot function very well without this and certainly cannot help others to live well.

The following two examples from actual practice may serve to illustrate the aforementioned view on the position of psychotherapy in our present society.

Example 1

A woman of 40 years came to me with severely depressive complaints. She said she had been referred by a colleague of mine because I am seen by him 'as being open to the existential dimension'. She uses antidepressants and has visited different psychotherapists with the same complaints over the years and sometimes for more than three years. She has a good job, children, and a good relationship. But, as she says, this is not enough to make her life meaningful. She wrestles with deep feelings of loneliness, which she tries to solve with fusion-like relationships. Because she is afraid of relationships (because of the danger of losing herself), she isolates herself to an extreme degree and feels even more lonely as a result of her heavy longing for the fusion of relationships. In relationships, she only knows two extremes: isolation and fusion; the area in between is unfamiliar territory for her.

Her wrestling with the meaning of her life is accompanied by a crisis of faith. She has strongly started to doubt the existence of God over the past few years and certainly the dogma and dictates of the church. At the same time, her longing for fusion with God is extremely intense. If God should not exist and she could not thus fuse with him, then her life would be absolutely meaningless for her.

This psychotherapy was a challenge for me to help this client with the process of letting go of God and grieving. We first examined what God meant for her. This came down to that it gave her the feeling that there was someone who knew her through and through, someone who had attention for her, and someone with whom she felt safe. I tried to get her to consider the question of why she could not find all this in her actual relations or whether she could imagine finding life purpose in such. In such a manner, we touched upon many important existential themes, including dependency, autonomy, own responsibility, etc.

We next discussed what else there might be in life that could make her life purposeful. In doing this, we regularly considered the senseless suffering in our world and how you can live if God no longer exists and the hereafter also does not exist.

This therapy was conducted, on the one hand, following the familiar methods of the person-oriented approach (empathy, respect, and authenticity). On the other hand, an appeal was made to my own philosophy of life and this was brought into the therapy in an appropriate manner without steering the client in a particular direction. I noticed the more convinced I was of my own person-oriented philosophy of life, the better I could help her with her problems.

It is interesting to report that this therapy lasted no more than 20 sessions and that major changes nevertheless took place.

Example 2

A man of around 60 approached me after reading my book on the person-oriented approach.

In his admission letter, he wrote that he had found himself in an existential crisis for quite some time and that he was wrestling with the question of how he wanted to further his life. For this reason, he wrote, he was in search of a therapist with an eye to the problems of life meaning. In the therapy, it appeared that he was extremely unhappy with the life that he had led. He was somber, dissatisfied, and at times depressed. He missed the capacity to enjoy life. He isolated himself and his relations with others were characterized by detachment.

We first considered the course of his life with, as the central question, how his life could have run the course that it has in fact run. A central theme within this appeared to be his incapacity to choose, which was a consequence of a pattern of trying to please others at the cost of his own needs. The paradox of trying to please others but nevertheless not developing any intimate and satisfying relationships was also considered.

This therapy was a challenge for me: to help someone still find some meaning for his life against the background of a life experienced as lost and with a view to its approaching end. This therapy confronted me as a psychotherapist with the larger life questions and with the question of where I stand with regard to these, and just how far I have progressed with them in order to be able to help others with them.

THE PERSON-ORIENTED APPROACH AS A SYSTEM OF MEANING

I am clear in my opinion that every psychotherapeutic approach can be seen as a modern system of meaning, including cognitive behavior therapy, which is appropriately characterized as a 'behavioral Weltanschauung' by Woolfolk and Richardson (1984). Nevertheless, it cannot be denied that the psychotherapeutic schools in the existential-humanistic direction have a greater affinity with the existential dimension of psychotherapy than other schools; this particularly holds for the person-oriented approach that can clearly and without much effort be worked out into a system of meaning (Van Kalmthout, 1995, 1998a). In the following, I will provide a brief description of the person-oriented approach as a system of meaning by presenting my interpretation of: (1) the underlying assumptions; (2) the concept of personality change from such a perspective; and (3) what the meaning of life is according to the person-oriented approach. I would like to emphasize that there is no attempt to be exhaustive; rather, the intention is to examine the fruitfulness of interpreting the person-oriented approach as a system of meaning and to initiate the discussion of the consequences that this may have for the further development of the person-oriented approach, training in this direction, and the position and function of the approach in the future of society.

I base the following on a book written previously by me in Dutch on the person-oriented approach (Van Kalmthout, 1997).

TWO FUNDAMENTAL PRINCIPLES UNDERLYING THE PERSON-ORIENTED APPROACH

I assume that the person-oriented approach is characterized by two fundamental assumptions or principles:

1. The assumption that human problems can be traced back to the interpersonal field of

tension between the longing for autonomy and the longing for connectedness. This is the interpersonal principle.

2. The assumption that 'experiencing what there really is' must be emulated and that avoidance of this can lead to problems and even psychopathology. This is the experiential principle.

These two assumptions can be seen as universal principles — as applicable in principle to all psychological problems (Van Kalmthout and Pelgrim, 1990). In the following, the principles will be described in greater detail.

Autonomy and connectedness

The complementary pair of concepts — 'autonomy' and 'connectedness' — point to two fundamental human longings or needs and the conflict that not infrequently arises between them: How can I as a person develop my autonomy and at the same time stay connected with others? People want to occupy their own space, develop themselves as persons, and also be respected and valued while doing this. Experience teaches, however, that such a longing for autonomy is often not only unappreciated by others but even punished, because it is experienced as a threat. In many people, this may lead to the longing for autonomy being surrounded by anxiety and feelings of guilt, prompted primarily by a fear of losing one's connectedness with important others. People want not only their own space but also to 'belong'. This double longing leads to an interpersonal field of tension, and all kinds of strategies are developed to solve this fundamental conflict and thereby reduce the tension. We often end up sitting on the fence, with the development of neither autonomy nor connectedness as a consequence. What indeed develops is isolation (also sometimes in the form of a narcissistic personality) or enmeshment with someone (also referred to as fusion or symbiosis). In the first instance, connectedness with other people is lacking, but there is also no real autonomy. In the second instance, autonomy is lacking, but there is also no real connectedness. A person-oriented approach presupposes that human problems emerge within this universal human conflict and that a solution must therefore be sought at that level. My assumption is that the theme of autonomy and connectedness, which has a broad basis of support within the psychotherapeutic tradition, offers a fruitful framework for a person-oriented interpretation of human problems. This also implies that the person-oriented approach is actually an interpersonal approach: it is essentially about human relations (Rogers, 1959).

The person-oriented approach presupposes that the essence of human problems can be described as the underdevelopment of a person, as an incompletely grown individual. It is also presupposed that such underdevelopment is a consequence of specific relations with other people. When it comes to human problems, this means that significant others in the surroundings of children have exerted such an influence on them that they have not been able to become themselves; do not know who they are; do not know what they want, feel, or think; and that they must later learn this — either with or without psychotherapy — as a consequence. It is presupposed that a basic field of tension develops right from birth between the biological given of being an individual (with all the threats associated with this right from the beginning) and the equally biologically given reality of dependence on the environment and other individuals in particular. Rank (1924) gave apt expression to this with the title of his book: *Das Trauma der Geburt* (The Trauma of Birth). A biological birth is, according to Rank, also a psychological birth, because the total fusion with the oceanic environment of the womb is broken at this moment and the young human child can be threatened, frustrated, and left alone for the first time in his life at this point. The threat of the environment at the same time elicits an excessive longing for protection, safety, and connectedness. At birth, thus, not only the seed for the growth of a separate individual is planted but also the grounds for the inner division of this being. The child positions himself in opposition to the environment with all of its threats, but also recognizes that his safety depends on the environment and therefore longs for a deep connection to the environment. Human children can only survive with utmost difficulty when lacking the safety and security of the womb, where they do not have any responsibilities, do not have to make decisions, and do not have to make choices and thereby run the risk of either physical or psychological threat/harm. From the point of birth, however, this situation quickly changes. The physical and social environments make themselves felt, not all of the child's desires are fulfilled, and the influence of the outside environment is sometimes painfully noticeable. In such a manner, the universal field of tension or conflict emerges between the longing to be one's own person and the fear of the risks, dangers, and threats that this inevitably brings with it. The threat can sometimes be so great that the longing for the safety of the cradle completely dominates any desire for freedom or self-fulfillment. This two-sided longing for autonomy and connectedness can give rise to insoluble conflicts in adult-aged people — conflicts that sometimes have the characteristics of a life/death battle: Do I give up my individual being to return to the safety of the womb because the burden of life has become too heavy, or do I still dare to take responsibility for my own life? Existentialists speak, in this connection, of *The Courage to Be*, which is also the title of a famous book by Tillich (1952).

Summarized briefly, we can state that the person-oriented approach encompasses the universal human conflict involving the individual being dependent on other people for his most essential needs, while these same people constitute a direct threat to his becoming an individual.

Experiencing what there really is

The second fundamental principle underlying the person-oriented approach involves the assumption that it is better in the end to experience reality as it is than to live in an illusory world to avoid pain. This assumption is generally referred to as the experience-oriented or experiential.

When it comes to the development of human problems, it can be posited that the root of the problem lies, on the one hand, in the absence of the receiving of love in this life by adults in the immediate environment (principle 1: autonomy and connectedness); on the other hand, a concomitant lack of contact with the inner and outer reality as it is (principle 2: the experiential). The correspondence between the two principles is as follows: in order to learn to experience all aspects of reality and make contact with all of the different aspects of reality, a safe haven is necessary from which this reality can be carefully explored and confronted without too much danger.

Of particular importance in this connection is the opposition between the most personal on the one hand, and what I would like to call the 'conditioned self' or personality, on the other hand. 'Persona' literally means mask, and should be clearly distinguished from the notion of 'person' that we use here and that actually constitutes the opposite (see Schmid, 1991, for a very extensive historical and comprehensible description of the notion of persona). The mask that we display for others (and not infrequently ourselves) during daily life is the product of the individual conditioning of us by others and should not be confused with 'who we really are'. The mask is not of us but of others, and we wear it to hide behind. We also have every reason to do this as it is often the case that, if we should actually allow ourselves to be seen, people would walk all over us or make us feel ridiculous. Just how often the latter is really the case, or follows from our conditioned experience, is often not particularly clear to us.

The person-oriented principle of 'experience reality as it is' pertains to not only our conditioned self (our interpersonal patterns of interacting and our own self-image) but also to our most characteristic core. The latter also refers to all of the as-yet undeveloped possibilities that we have. We rarely experience reality as it is. It is always colored by our conditioning; we look at it through the eyes of others instead of through our own eyes. In such a manner, we do not see ourselves as we really are and also do not see others as they really are; others become a projection of our own self-image, and even the world and society are colored by this.

As already stated, the person-oriented approach assumes that we are better off in the end when we learn to experience reality as much as possible and do not avoid it.

PERSONALITY CHANGE

In popular language use, personality change is understood as the replacement of a troublesome or annoying personality with a 'better' one. It is also typically assumed, however, that very little of the personality or character of someone can be changed; at most, the sharp edges can be smoothed out or made more adaptable. In our terminology, such a definition can be described as the replacement of one mask with another. Even if the latter mask is better adapted than the first mask, one still does not speak within our approach of a personality change in the sense of a fundamental change (Van Kalmthout, 1998b). In both cases, the person still lives on the outside, with his mask or personality, and does not have contact with his internal source of truth. Only in the latter case can we speak of fundamental change or change affecting the very core of someone's personality. The question is just what this involves and what the criteria for such change may be. Starting from the two fundamental principles underlying person-oriented psychotherapy, I will attempt to make this clear in the form of a number of propositions.

1) The truth sets one free

Under 'truth' here, we do not understand the so-called truth of a particular belief or ideology. Nor do we mean the lease on the truth that some people think they have. In fact, these have nothing to do with the truth; they are, rather, the limited religious convictions that people have often invented in answer to their existential anxieties or simply adopted on the authority of others. In this context, 'truth' is understood as the experience of and belief in what really is, as introduced in the second fundamental principle underlying the person-oriented approach. This principle pertains both to the world around me and to myself. The assumption is that by making contact with reality as it is (and not as I fear or hope it is), I will be better off than when all kinds of illusions are maintained about the world and myself. In this sense, the truth constitutes a liberating force.

The preceding is not to say that all kinds of illusions (in the form of positive thinking, for example) do not influence our health, the disappearance of complaints or problems, or even our interest in life (Taylor and Brown, 1988). There is no reason to speak condescendingly of such an influence or suggest that 'it really amounts to nothing'. It should be attempted, rather, to place such effects under the question of what we should and can understand as personality change. According to our definition of personality change, we cannot call this fundamental change, but rather a useful adaptation of a threatened organism. This organism has learned during the endless course of evolution to adapt to environmental circumstances by fighting (when possible) or fleeing (when nothing else is possible). There is no doubt that many people approach life in such a manner and solve their problems in this way. Religions, sects, psychotherapies, alternative medicines and such, all play into such a self-evident adaptation strategy. They provide myths and rituals for people to hang onto in order to survive, and not without success. The need is great and, with some handiness, it can be provided for and even helped, although no one knows for how long.

But all of this has nothing to do with the change process aimed at within the person-oriented approach, as the person-oriented approach has to do with living and all of the risks that this brings with it, rather than with survival. It is also here that the fundamental difference between what Jung referred to as 'kleine und große Psychotherapie' (the little and big psychotherapies: Van Kalmthout, 1991) manifests itself most clearly. It is the difference between living versus survival, exploration versus adaptation, enquiring versus suppressing. Illusions are always a flight from reality; they do not bring reality closer but, rather, they push it further away. Sooner or later, man will again be confronted by it and the threat of this always remains present in the background. While the danger has been averted, it still lurks in the distance. The misery must first be felt before you can really leave it behind you. The pain must first be experienced before you can go on to enjoy life again.

The discovery of the truth about yourself and the world is a long-term process that never really comes to an end. If we dare to undertake this adventure, there is a chance — by falling and then standing up again — of further penetrating the mystery of reality unhindered by preconceived theories, no matter how comfortable they may be. During this process, many things will appear to be more and more of an illusion invented to make life more bearable for us. The truth liberates: Is this the final illusion? The quest for truth requires, in any case, considerable 'faith' that may nevertheless be continually tested against reality. What is the content of this faith? The content of this faith is that reality with all of its atrocities, bizarre phenomena, death, and decay, but also all its beauty and humanity, is ultimately friendly, and can therefore be better approached with an open mind than fled from. This reminds one of Rogers' saying that 'the facts are friendly'.

Personality change, thus and paradoxically enough, should not be understood — as is usually the case — as an actual change of personality (from the one type to the other), but rather as coming into contact with something that was always there. This is an interesting and important view of change. Not as a movement from something that already exists to something that is not yet there (for example, I do not dare to go out into the street and now I have learned to do this), but as a movement towards becoming aware of what is already there (for example, fear of revealing myself to others). We might also say that change from such a perspective means to move inside, as opposed to outside. Or in depth as opposed to surface breadth.

2) Love heals

The second proposition is related to the other fundamental principle underlying the person-oriented approach, namely the struggle for a balanced relation between autonomy and connectedness. Connectedness in its most pure form can be referred to by the term 'love'. The term love is just as tarnished as the term truth and can thus lead to an equal number of misconceptions. One can 'cover something with the cloak of charity', which actually means shutting one's eyes to the truth. Furthermore, all sorts of sentimental feelings can be referred to with the term love. Along these lines are the expressions: falling in love, falling out of love, making love, love of one's fatherland, love blinds, and an act of love or charity. None of these has anything to do with love in the sense that we mean it here. With regard to fundamental change, love has to do with respect and appreciation of what there is. It has to do with giving other individuals and organisms the space to live and respecting, nourishing, and helping them develop their individuality. It has to do with the love that a good gardener feels for his plants, trees, and bushes. It is not aimed at shaping these into his own likeness and exerting his influence on them but, rather, helping their own character blossom.

Many in our world have lost their love in this sense or have simply never known it. They have lost contact with it and thus live alone with their inflated egos. They are not blamed for this, as people cannot give what they do not have. But profound personality change means that this contact must be restored or, in some cases, established for the first time. If this does not occur, they will continue to muddle along. The person will continue to search for the lost treasure and, because he does not know what it looks like, continue to just hang around and become easy prey for all kinds of pseudo or surrogate products.

The foregoing implies that love is something which you really have to experience yourself and not out of books. You can only love someone else when you have really felt that someone has loved you, which means seeing you as you really are and not wanting to make you into his own likeness (or the opposite of this). When you have woken up to this, then you know what it is and that it really exists.

Far too many people, who have not had the luck of someone really loving them, have never learned to love themselves. This is also a dangerous statement because it is frequently used to justify all kinds of indefensible activities. But in the deepest sense, nothing more is meant than what we already said about the love of other people. It concerns respect for who you yourself are, your own desires, your talents and possibilities, your limitations and your weaknesses. Taking yourself seriously without making yourself the middle of the universe (which is neurotic). If the foregoing happens with someone for whom it was not initially the case, then we can speak of a fundamental personality change: the harness of the conditioned self has been broken, the mask has been removed, and contact has been made with reality as it is. Reality appears to be not only a cesspool but also the ground for lilies of the valley and other pretty flowers.

3) *Truth and love*

At first glance, a gigantic field of tension appears to exist between the search for and confrontation with reality, on the one hand, and the love of this reality, on the other hand. The chaotic and criminal world around us calls for a powerless aversion of one's eyes rather than the constant confrontation with the endlessly repeating cycle of perverted power, exploitation, and slaughter. There is very little personal to be seen; it often appears to be complete dehumanization. In the personal sphere, people are also more likely to avoid their dark side than expose it to the light of day or embrace it. 'Loving yourself as you are' is easier said than done.

The person-oriented psychotherapist experiences the field of tension between truth and love when searching for an adequate balance between empathy and authenticity, between understanding and confrontation. This also holds for all personal relationships, where the equilibrium is frequently way out of balance. The question, then, is whether a completely unbridgeable field of tension is involved or not.

While bridging such a gap in actual practice may constitute a real feat, the gap is in principle only the semblance of one. As we often say, true love accepts reality — which includes the other person — as it is. One tries to see the other person for what he or she is, with respect to all idiosyncrasies but also an eye to the hidden possibilities. Without love, acceptance of reality cannot occur; the treatment of reality remains superficial, prejudiced, one-sided, limited, and — in short — does not do justice to the full richness of actual reality. In other words: No truth without love.

Conversely, understanding and empathy can turn into positionless compliance, or a supernatural and thus unreal capacity to empathize, if not to say an ingratiating permissiveness. There is no real contact with reality without confrontation and the collision of souls (and the feelings associated with such). Personal contact asks for the presence of a person of flesh and blood with his own roots clearly perceptible and tangible in the contact as well. This is something very different from an unbolted screen. In the latter case, just as little is revealed about the truth or reality as in the absence of a loving other. In other words: No love without truth.

In conclusion, it can be stated that the core of fundamental personality change within the person-oriented approach is sought in making contact with our inner world, which is of a completely different quality from our conditioned mask. This quality has to do with the capacity to explore reality as it is (the truth) and the capacity of loving acceptance of this reality (love). This inner dimension, as opposed to our conditioned self, is love and truth.

THE MEANING OF LIFE ACCORDING TO THE PERSON-ORIENTED APPROACH

In the preceding, I have briefly described the essence of the person-oriented approach. This basically boils down to people becoming estranged from themselves during the course of their lives as a result of the conditioning that they have undergone in their interactions with others. As a consequence, these people do not grow into harmoniously integrated individuals but, rather, find themselves plagued by a split between the conditioned self and the true self. I have referred to the unconditioned self as 'the inner dimension' and identified 'living in truth and love' as the essence of it. Person-oriented psychotherapy has living in truth and love as its fundamental goal. These are the values underlying the approach, which also thus constitute its 'system of belief', if you like. It is therefore fairly obvious that the answer to the question of the meaning of life can also be found in this essence: to live in keeping with truth and love.

Within this framework, the distinction between autonomy and heteronomy is of particular importance. Within the person-oriented approach, the meaning of life is sought not in the following of others (heteronomy) but in the following of our most inner, personal sources (autonomy). The following of others stems from fear and uncertainty. Fear of seeing reality, for what it is and uncertainty concerning a lack of something to hold on to. Listening to and contemplating our inner sources can be described as lovingly contemplating this reality with all its horrors and poignant beauty. The source of truth within the person-oriented approach is thus sought in the inner source and not in external conditioning. The opposition between the inner dimension and the conditioned self parallels the distinction between autonomy and heteronomy. Within the person-oriented tradition, this contrast is sometimes referred to as the qualitative difference between reality or authenticity and the facade or surface, which also explains why the notion of authenticity occupies such a central position within the person-oriented approach to psychopathology and psychotherapy.

This fundamental contrast is also sometimes referred to using such terms as spontaneity and intuition, which emphasize the unconditioned (spontaneous) and irrational (intuitive) aspects of the inner world. This is also in keeping with yet another characteristic of the inner dimension, namely that it transcends our rational knowledge and the technology arising from this. The terms used to refer to this dimension — such as 'organismic' by Rogers — are primarily pointers to something that we will never completely know and at most continually try to approximate. This is in keeping with the notion that truth and love are absolute entities that we can never fully fathom with our limited knowledge and capacities. William James speaks in this connection of the 'ineffable'. The purpose of life must, according to the person-oriented approach, be found in this dimension. Living in the grip of the conditioned self only leads to feelings of meaninglessness, depression, and other signs of alienation. Living in the 'one', as the existentialists say, is not living. It is, rather, only surviving or living while you are actually dead. They refer to a dimension of existence that can, in principle, be experienced and that has a totally different quality from our conditioned existence, which can be described as a facade. In approaching other people, we usually come no further than this facade, which also holds for how we approach reality and ourselves. But the assumption is that both in the other person, as well as in ourselves and reality as a whole, a totally different quality is hidden. Tillich (1962) refers to this as the 'lost dimension' and experiencing this lost dimension is — according to the person-oriented approach — the purpose of life. Put differently: Without this, we can survive, as many people can be seen to do, but one cannot speak of really living.

According to the person-oriented approach, people experience purposelessness because they themselves are no longer authentic and are caught in an externally imposed conditioning. Given that an authentic life is the purpose of life, psychotherapy is concerned with helping people come into contact with that which is real or authentic in themselves again. This means, on the one hand, a battle against the conditioned self and, on the other hand, being open to the authentic self.

CONCLUSION AND DISCUSSION

In the preceding, I have attempted to describe one system of psychotherapy, namely person-oriented psychotherapy, as a system of meaning. In doing this, I also assumed that psychotherapy is always operating with the existential condition of man in the background and that a psychotherapy that aspires to having some depth simply cannot avoid this question. People enter into psychotherapy with concrete complaints (for example, anxiety or depression), but these are the expression — from the person-oriented perspective — of existential conflicts and dilemmas. The vulnerability of the human organism and the longing of people for safety, structure, and control are always present in the background. Experiencing the absence of such can lead to anxiety, depression, and feelings of meaninglessness. And in intensive psychotherapy, these cannot be avoided or 'therapied away'.

This theme brings us unavoidably to religion, in part because religion has more or less exclusive rights to the theme. Now that large groups of the population has lost their affinity with organized religion, new meaning-giving systems have shown up on the health-and-happiness market, and they include psychotherapy. I have presented person-oriented psychotherapy as such a system. In fact, it involves what Kurtz (1986) refers to as secular humanism. This points to an ideology that combines the critical and based-on-facts fundamental attitude of science with a belief in human potential and possibilities. One might say, an ideology that values the virtues of the intellect just as much as those of the heart. This system of beliefs is based on the assumption that in this limited lifetime on this earth, meaningful goals can be striven for, which people can get within their reach if they want to, can, and have the courage to do so. The critical-scientific attitude implies that everything undergoes examination, that nothing is certain right from the beginning, and that nothing can be excluded. It is typical of the existential-humanistic tradition that people themselves are held responsible for finding meaning in their lives, even though certain values and norms can be considered to apply universally. The person-oriented approach, which constitutes part of this tradition, is not a dogmatic belief and therefore opens its own starting assumptions to discussion. As such, the person-oriented approach contributes to the search for the purpose of life without any pretense of coming up with the only or true answer.

In contrast, one might posit that person-oriented psychotherapy cannot possibly contend with the traditional systems of meaning and their all-encompassing systems of belief precisely because it is standing there with empty hands. This appears to me to be an underestimate of the values and norms implicit in psychotherapy, and simultaneously an overestimate of the meaning-giving power of traditional systems. Modern man is standing in any case with empty hands, and it appears in all respects that psychotherapy fits in better with this modern sense of life than do the traditional churches. This is not to say that psychotherapy alone is going to provide the complete new worldview, but that it will — like it or not — continually make a contribution.

Each of the existing psychotherapeutic schools runs the risk of lapsing into dogma and becoming a new religion as a result. This is inherent in the structure of a particular orientation or school, particularly once it has established itself and has to defend its interests. Allegiance to the truth is difficult to unite with proclaiming and defending the belief with which one identifies. In so far as allegiance to the truth (not to be confused with claiming possession of the truth) is a pillar of the person-oriented approach, the latter can by definition never take on the character of a school or a specific orientation. The same holds for the second pillar of the person-oriented approach, namely the healing power of love. As soon as this is subsumed under the limited construction of a specific orientation or school, we can — by definition — no longer speak of a person-oriented approach. Both pillars point towards a specific attitude or basic philosophy that must be continually substantiated. Neither what someone says nor even what they do is the criterion for this, but who someone is at the present moment. It should be clear that membership in a particular club says nothing in this regard; nor do the beautiful words that someone speaks or writes. The only criterion is whether someone is, at this very moment, loyal to the truth and loving.

All in all, the person-oriented approach finds itself in a paradoxical situation. On the one hand, it is a system of meaning and runs the risk, as such, of degenerating into a dogmatic belief system. On the other hand, it is essential that the person-oriented approach be personal and experience-oriented, which clearly rules out dogmatism. Rogers' wrestle with the question of whether his psychotherapy should constitute a separate school is an example of this paradoxical situation, just as his wrestle with religion and spirituality was too (Van Belle, 1990; Van Kalmthout, 1995). At the end of his life, he appears to have found a satisfactory solution to this problem, a solution that may also help guide the further development of the person-oriented approach as a modern system of meaning. In an interview he says:

> I would put it that the best of therapy leads to a dimension that is spiritual, rather than saying that the spiritual is having an impact on therapy. (Carl Rogers, 1987)

This perspective of Rogers on the relation between psychotherapy and spirituality is in complete accordance with the present description of the person-oriented approach as a modern system of meaning. The point is not that psychotherapy should incorporate elements of spirituality; rather, the best of psychotherapy and of the person-oriented approach is itself a spiritual system of meaning and should be further developed as such. This is an exciting and revolutionary endeavor. What is more, such an endeavor can give the person-oriented approach a new perspective on its future, which has been weakened to such an extent that complete disappearance from the field of mental health and psychotherapy is feared.

REFERENCES

Frank, J. (1961). *Persuasion and Healing: A comparative study of psychotherapy*. Baltimore: Johns Hopkins.

Groot, C. de (1995). *Naar een nieuwe clerus*. Kampen: Kok Agora.

Hanegraaff, W. J. (1996). *New Age Religion and Western Culture*. New York: Brill.

Hijmans, E. (1994). *Je moet er het beste van maken. Een empirisch onderzoek naar hedendaagse zingevingssystemen*. Nijmegen: ITS.

Johnson, E. and Sandage, S. (1999). A postmodern reconstruction of psychotherapy: orienteering, religion, and the healing of the soul. *Psychotherapy, 36*, 1–15.

Kilbourne, B. and Richardson, J. (1984). Psychotherapy and new religions in a pluralistic society. *American Psychologist, 39*, 237–51.

Kurtz, P. (1986). *The Transcendental Temptation*. New York: Prometheus.

Luckmann, Th. (1967). *The Invisible Religion. The problem of religion in modern society*. New York: MacMillan.

Maslow, A. (1971). *The Farther Reaches of Human Nature*. New York: Viking Press.

Rank, O. (1924). *Das Trauma der Geburt und seine Bedeutung für die Psychoanalyse*. Vienna: Internationaler Psychoanalytischer Verlag.

Rogers, C. R. (1959). A theory of therapy, personality, and interpersonal relationships, as developed in the client-centered framework. In S. Koch (Ed.) *Psychology: A study of a science, (Vol. III). Formulations of the person and the social context*. New York: McGraw Hill, pp. 154–86.

Rogers, C. R. (1961). *On Becoming a Person*. Boston: Houghton Mifflin.

Rogers, C. R. (1987). In M. Baldwin and V. Satir (Eds.) *The use of self in therapy. Interview by M. Baldwin*. London: Haworth.

Schmid, P. (1991). *Person-zentriert. Grundlagen von Theorie und Praxis*. Mainz: Grünewald.

Taylor, S. and Brown, J. (1988). Illusion and well-being: A social psychological perspective on mental health. *Psychological Bulletin, 103*, 193–210.

Thorne, B. (1997). Spiritual responsibility in a secular profession. In I. Horton and V. Varma (Eds.), *The Needs of Counsellors and Psychotherapists*. London: Sage.

Tillich, P. (1952). *The Courage to Be*. New Haven, CT: Yale University Press.

Tillich, P. (1962). *Die verlorene Dimension*. Hamburg: Furche.

Vandermeersch, P. (1996). *Uit de hemel gevallen? De levensbeschouwing van de geestelijke gezondheidszorg*. Trimboslezing 1996. Utrecht: NcGv.

Van Belle, H. (1990). Rogers' later move toward mysticism: Implications for client-centered therapy. In G. Lietaer, J. Rombauts and R. Van Balen (Eds.) *Client-centered and Experiential Psychotherapy in the Nineties*. Leuven: Leuven University Press, pp. 47–64.

Van Kalmthout, M. and Pelgrim, F. (1990). In search of universal concepts in psychopathology and psychotherapy. In G. Lietaer, J. Rombauts and R. Van Balen (Eds.) *Client-centered and Experiential Psychotherapy in the Nineties*. Leuven: Leuven University Press, pp. 381–96.

Van Kalmthout, M. (1991). *Psychotherapie: Het bos en de bomen*. Amersfoort: Acco.

Van Kalmthout, M. (1995). The religious dimension of Rogers' work. *Journal of Humanistic Psychology, 35*, 23–39.

Van Kalmthout, M. (1997). *Persoonsgerichte psychotherapie*. Utrecht: De Tijdstroom.

Van Kalmthout, M. (1998a). Person-centred theory as a system of meaning. In B. Thorne and E. Lambers (Eds.) *Person-centred Therapy. A European perspective*. London: Sage, pp. 11–22.

Van Kalmthout, M. (1998b). Personality change and the concept of the self. In B. Thorne and E. Lambers (Eds.), *Person-centred Therapy. A European perspective*. London: Sage, pp. 53–61.

Van Kalmthout, M. (2000). Person-oriented psychotherapy. *Person, 4*, (1), 18–22.

Woolfolk, R. and Richardson, F. (1984). Behaviour therapy and the ideology of modernity. *American Psychologist, 39*, 777–86.

Janet Tolan

John Moores University, Liverpool, UK

The Fallacy of the 'Real' Self: In praise of self-structure

Several years ago, as a trainer and supervisor of client-centred therapists, I began to notice a common thread with many students and supervisees who reported themselves 'stuck' with clients. It was a seeming reluctance in these counsellors to acknowledge and empathise with their clients' self-structure — as though they had received the 'message' from their reading and training that their clients' organismic experiencing was the only valuable and trustworthy aspect of the client's personality.

It set me thinking about the self-structure as originally described by Rogers and his colleagues. Surely it would run counter to the whole philosophical base of client-centred theory to believe that *any* part of the personality had no purpose — no function. What, then, *was* the function of the self-structure? Why had I never read anything which celebrated, which extolled the virtues of, the self-structure?

It is, of course, true to say that the individual's organismic experiencing gives her accurate information about herself and the world around her — information which can be denied or distorted by her self-structure. But over the years, the organismic self has come to be called the *real self,* the *core self* or even the *true self.* The implication inherent in such language is that the self-structure is false, extraneous or unreliable. Have we come to associate the self-structure solely with conditions of worth and introjected values? It is a small step from there to the idea that the whole of the self-structure has been externally imposed upon the person, that it is *bad* and, moreover, that it gets in the way of the actualising tendency.

The therapist who has taken this message from her reading and her training is liable, unwittingly, to convey messages to her clients such as, *'Don't listen to those old introjects. Follow your heart. Be true to your feelings.'* In effect, this can replace old *shoulds* and *oughts* by new ones, imposed — subtly — by the therapist. Rather than accepting himself as he is, the client learns new worries: *'I must learn to think of myself for a change.' 'I shouldn't be bothered so much about what my mother will say.' 'I ought to just leave and not be so afraid of the consequences.' 'I shouldn't be so hung up on earning money'. 'I should only talk about my feelings'.*

There is, of course, a truth to the notion that the self-structure has been imposed from the outside. But the pertinent question is, *To what purpose?* Why does the self-structure come into being and why is it of such importance to the individual that it is maintained?

Organismic experiencing is simply that: the capacity of the organism to experience. We see, we hear, we touch, we smell, we taste, we sense our own inner sadness or happiness,

---

In this paper I have used 'he' or 'she' somewhat arbitrarily when referring to people in general, having found the continual use of 'he or she', 'himself or herself', 'his or hers' to be clumsy and, at times, to obstruct the meaning.

anger or calm. This experiencing is essentially neutral — neither healthy nor unhealthy, neither good nor bad. It simply *is*. Without the self-structure, we would not be able to construe any of this experience or give it meaning.

So the first purpose of the self-structure is to organise our experience — to categorise it. The category which has been most focused upon in client-centred theory is that part of experience which we label 'I' or 'me'. However, I would suggest that the wider category of 'the world-as-I-see-it', including other people, is an equally important component of the self-structure.

To rehearse the entire development of the self-structure would be a paper in itself so the following is a brief, and limited, description. Initially, we construe the world according to others' teaching and modelling. The process by which children acquire language (the main means by which experience is symbolised) involves adults naming the child's experience for them, so that they develop the capacity to identify for themselves and communicate that experience. The child learns to name (*sky, Julie*), to categorise (*car, dog*), to describe (*big, green*) and to value (*dirty, beautiful*) within the particular family, community and culture to which they belong.

If *naming* is important, then *not naming* and *misnaming* are equally so. Some people have never had their emotional experience symbolised and validated through the process of having it named. The child who, when distressed or angry, has been dismissed with the phrase *'You're just tired'* is one example. Another is that of the child who has been abused in the name of 'love'.

If sufficient importance is attached to something by the child's significant others, the child will come to perceive it as a 'truth', and this construction may persist into adulthood. In other words, the individual will subordinate her own experience to maintain the perception of 'truth': *'I am lazy', 'People on Welfare are scroungers', 'Children should grow up in a family with a father and a mother'.*

However, in that area of the personality we term *congruent*, the individual is able to test out the concepts and values she has learned and amend them according to her own perceptions. She might still hold the opinion that *'Children should grow up in a family with a father and a mother,'* but she knows that it is an opinion rather than an absolute truth and has been able to evaluate it according to her own experience.

So although the self-structure can be argued to be highly dependent upon external influences, individuals do have the potential capacity to evaluate and amend it.

Carl Rogers used the terms self-structure and self-concept rather interchangeably, but at several points in his *XIX Propositions* he alludes to the fact that the individual construes the world external to herself in as unique a way as she construes her own self (Rogers 1951, pp. 484–6). Although he writes that there is 'no sharp limit between the experience of the self and of the outside world' (p. 497), I propose to differentiate between the terms *self-structure* and *self-concept*. The self-structure includes the individual's unique *map of the world* (including his assumptions and expectations of others) as well as his beliefs about himself. So the self-structure will be viewed as the whole and the self-concept as a subset of the whole.

There is, of course, a connection between the self-structure as the whole and the self-concept as a part of the whole. The general belief, *There is a God,* is usually allied with, *I believe in God.* The general belief, *Homosexuality is unnatural,* is usually allied with, *I am a heterosexual.* Where such introjected self-structural beliefs conflict with some organismic experiencing (*I am attracted to another man*, for example), the individual will experience anxiety and distress, to the extent that this experiencing is admitted to awareness.

Rigid beliefs, however, have a bearing not only upon the self-concept, but upon the individual's view of the world and of other people. Strongly-held convictions can be perceived as self-evident 'truth'. The person who *knows* that there is a God will see non-believers as misguided or deluded or even wicked. This kind of construing of reality seems to go beyond the self-concept.

Similarly, a woman who holds the view that *men should not cry* is likely to feel uncomfortable and embarrassed in the presence of a tearful man. Such a belief will probably also affect the way she brings up her children. And yet it is not a belief directly about herself, so it makes more *everyday* sense to describe it as a component of her self-structure rather than her self-concept.

That an individual's *worldview* is a part of her self-structure is borne out by how threatened she can become if this is challenged, and how she is able to distort and deny information which conflicts with it. Someone whose belief in racial superiority is based upon introjected values will defend that view in the face of mountainous evidence to the contrary. Employing logic or reason will be ineffectual since any challenge is a threat to the self-structure and will give rise to an emotional reaction.

So why do we have rigidly held beliefs about the world which are not amenable to the evidence of our own senses? How can this be functional?

The wish for love, acceptance, respect, admiration from others — to be valued by others — is very strong in all of us. When we receive it, we experience those emotions which Rogers (1951) described as 'calm' and 'satisfied' (Proposition VI). As young children, we experience the calm, satisfied emotions when we receive love and praise from adults. We experience the uncomfortable, dissatisfied emotions when we receive censure and rejection from adults — and, later, from our peers. The self-structure is built upon our taking account of other people's needs and wishes. So the self-structure *enables us to live in relationship with others*.

Our beliefs about the world are, I would suggest, built into the self-structure as a means of ensuring our acceptance within a particular family, gang, tribe, society or culture and this is one of the main purposes of the self-structure. In this respect, the self-structure fulfils an organismic need — the need to be accepted, valued and loved — to *belong*. If this premise is accepted, then, paradoxically, the counsellor who fails to pay attention to the self-structure is failing to understand her client's struggle to meet this most fundamental organismic need.

When a therapist does not pay attention to or 'receive' certain self-structural aspects of her client, the client himself might come to see them as of less value or even shameful. Furthermore, many clients will begin to censor that part or those parts of themselves which they judge the counsellor not to value. If the counsellor sees any facet of the self-structure as a rather inconvenient barrier to self-actualisation, she may ignore it, try to bypass it, or even attack it (gently, of course, as seems in keeping with the person-centred way!).

'I *can't* cry,' says the client. The therapist hears this as a plea for help. According to her theoretical understanding, her client's inability to express his distress is caused by his conditions of worth. It is entirely logical, therefore, for her to accept the task of helping her client to overcome this barrier to true expression of his feelings.

She comes to supervision and reports being 'stuck' with this client. He seems to be going round in circles and she cannot seem to help him to release his tears. Without realising it, she has fallen into the judgmental trap of valuing his distress more highly than his apprehension. The client knows better. He is of a family, of a workplace and of a society which see men who cry as weak. Realistically, if he were to cry in front of his family members, he, and they, would suffer considerable embarrassment. If he were to cry in front of his colleagues, he would jeopardise his prospects of promotion. Instead of receiving acceptance and understanding from his counsellor, he has received the subtle message that he should learn how to cry. His self-structure is under threat and it has marshalled its defences.

The self-structure is fulfilling its function admirably in ensuring that this client does not receive censure or disapprobation from others. However, the actualising tendency is at work. His uncomfortable feelings are its signal that there is an important matter which needs to be symbolised in awareness and incorporated into his self-structure. By failing to empathise with the self-structure and to accept its validity, the counsellor is failing to provide the climate in which the self-structure can loosen and integrate the distorted or denied material. If this climate were to be provided, '*I can't cry*' could become '*I can sometimes cry, but not in front of . . .*'

In practice, it can be very difficult to accord equal unconditional positive regard to every aspect of a client's self-structure: an anorexic who perceives herself as fat; an abused young woman who is convinced that she is worthless; a convicted criminal who 'knows' that no-one gives a shit, so why should he? How tempting it is to 'show' such clients that they are wrong! But any attempt to do so, however subtle, is an attack upon the self-structure and it will respond by defending itself and becoming more rigid.

Moreover, we can easily collude with the judgements of our clients: '*It's stupid of me to stay with a partner who beats me up.*' Subtly, we can take on the task of helping the client to leave this relationship by giving full empathic attention to those aspects of her experience which seem to us to move forward the 'goal' and failing to pay attention to those which, in our judgement, work against it. The counsellor in this scenario *hears*, for example, his client's fear for her own safety, but does not give empathic weight to her worry that people will condemn her for leaving the father of their children. He can even become impatient with the client's seeming unwillingness to 'move on'. His concern for this client is very real and his intentions are of the best, but he has failed to give full weight to his client's reasons for being in and remaining in this relationship and has not enabled her to grieve her potential losses in leaving. Has he, at some level, categorised her terror of further violence as *real self* and her wish to be seen as a good mother as based upon introjected values and therefore in some way *false*? And yet her need to be accepted by those important to her is also real. Indeed, in some cultures the honour of her whole family might depend upon her staying with her husband. Making aware choices involves all aspects of the self, not solely organismic experiencing.

The self-structure is our way of organising and categorising the world around us. Without a self-structure we would be at a loss. How would we know which ideas and behaviours would be acceptable to others? The self-structure enables us to predict the world and, in particular, to anticipate how people will respond to us. The more this is in awareness, the more choice we have. One person might choose to express a radical opinion at work and risk censure. The same person might choose to keep her opinion quiet at a family gathering, not to avoid censure but out of respect. She will wear clothes she dislikes to a wedding for the same reason. Ultimately, the self-structure helps us to balance our own organismic needs with the needs of others. It enables us to live in a world peopled with others rather than in an isolated world of our own.

Another basic purpose or function of the self-structure is to bring some organisation and categorisation to a complex world and to 'lose' information which is extraneous. We put something of a premium on bringing material into awareness. However, much of the useful work of the self-structure is out of our awareness. In my culture, for example, it is unacceptable for people to spit in public. And yet, there are other cultures in which spitting is not prohibited, where people recognise their wish to spit and do it in an acceptable way. Those of us from a non-spitting society will rarely even be aware of a wish to spit. We do not need to spend energy thinking and making decisions about it. We may be denying an experience to awareness, but it is a functional denial.

Also in my culture, it is polite to say 'Please', when asking for something in a bar or restaurant. In other cultures, this is not the norm — why ask a favour when it is the waiter's job to bring food and drink? Even knowing this, I and my compatriots say 'please' in the appropriate language. We do this automatically and we do it despite the fact that it has been pointed out to us as unnecessary — because it *feels* rude not to say it. This feeling response is the clue that the self-structure is working to maintain itself in the face of a challenge.

Anyone who has ever found themselves in a strange culture will know how disorienting and anxiety-producing it can be when the self-structure is challenged through contact with a different set of values or mores. Indeed, for many people, a counselling course or a racial awareness course is such an experience. So, too, might be a new workplace or a first meeting with a new partner's family. Ways of thinking and behaving which have stood them in good stead for many years might suddenly be met with subtle (or not-so-subtle) disapproval. They struggle to understand what is expected of them — what to say, how to behave.

Upon encountering a different culture, the individual will be able to incorporate the new experience according to the rigidity of the self-structure. One person might have a tendency to hang back — to see how others behave before committing herself. Another might be paralysed by anxiety, sensing others' potential disapproval of her own behaviour or values and not daring to express herself freely. A third might be angry and argumentative, attempting to 'show' others that they are misguided and that her own behaviour is correct and her values the true ones. A fourth might be dismissive, not prepared to or able to engage with the differences. A fifth might see the differences as interesting, neither denying her own values nor condemning others'. In each case, the role of the self-structure in enabling each of us to predict how we will be received by others is evident when we encounter a culture in which our predictions no longer hold true.

That the self-structure enables us to predict other people's reactions to us is important on a daily basis. There is, however, another aspect of the self-structure's role in enabling us to make predictions which becomes evident only in more extreme circumstances. This occurs when the predictability of the world itself is overturned by some extreme event such as an earthquake or a car crash or a personal assault. Again, the challenge here is not predominantly to the person's perception of self, but to the expectations the individual has about the world they live in. A car is no longer an everyday vehicle but a deadly metallic machine. This aspect of the theory needs further expansion and development, but it seems likely that phenomena such as flashbacks and recurrent dreams are a continuing attempt on the part of the organism to symbolise such traumatic events accurately in awareness so that they can be incorporated into self-structural constructs of the external world.

The self-structure *organises* our experience. First, it *symbolises* experience, then it fits the symbols into the patterns and categories it has built up. It learns to *ignore* experiences which seem irrelevant or insignificant. It is our map of the world — heavily influenced, of course, by those significant others who named (or mis-named) our experience as we developed.

Without the self-structure, would we know what 'green' is?

Without the self-structure, would we, at all times, be *feeling* our feet on the ground?

Without the self-structure, would we know how others would receive our behaviour?

Without the self-structure, would we be able to empathise?

Without the self-structure, would we know right from wrong?

The last question is a fundamental one for client-centred therapy, because the theory clearly separates *other people's* 'rights and wrongs' from *the individual's* 'rights and wrongs'. 'Right and wrong' differ from family to family, culture to culture, society to society — and they are continually changing. Fifty years ago, in Britain, it was generally considered 'wrong' to have a baby without being married. Now we are shocked by what we perceive as the 'inhuman' treatment of unmarried mothers and their children which happened in that era. Recognising that 'right and wrong' are not absolute and universal concepts, client-centred theory talks about what is *valued* — it is important for all of us to know what is valued by others. Where the organismic self and the self-structure are in harmony, the person can make his own value-judgements. He can choose to go along with other people's wishes, expectations and demands, or he can choose to follow his own path. He is aware of the possibilities and risks of both options.

In conclusion, then, the self-structure deserves our attention, our respect and, when we are acting as therapists, our empathic understanding. It is as much a *real, core* and *true* aspect of the self as organismic experiencing and if we place a lesser value upon it we shall indeed find ourselves 'getting stuck'.

REFERENCE

Rogers C R (1951). *Client-Centered Therapy.* Boston: Houghton Mifflin.

Michael Behr
University of Education, Schwäbisch Gmünd

Martina Becker
University of Education, Heidelberg

Congruence and Experiencing Emotions: Self-report scales for the Person-Centered and Experiential theory of personality

Abstract. Research proposes that abilities in experiencing and managing emotions ensure mental health and interpersonal skills. A new multidimensional measure for individuals experiencing, valuing and regulating feelings supports and operationalizes the person-centered and experiential theory of personality and recent concepts of emotional intelligence. The seven construct-related scales are Bodily Experience, Overwhelming Emotions, Imagination, Self-Control, Congruence, Lack of Emotions and Regulation of Emotions. Using 46 Items, reliability and validity are very satisfying. Factor structure is stable with gender. Women are more emotional than men. A slight relation with age is found. The experience of overwhelming feelings and regulation shows more impact than theory proposes. This measure is useful for research in clinical and social psychology, in practice during the initial phase of counselling and psychotherapy, and for outcome verification.

Descriptors: client-centered therapy, counselling, emotion, empathy, experiential psychotherapy, personality traits, personality change, person-centered psychotherapy

Being in contact with their emotions enables a person to cope with mental disorders and stress (Rogers 1951; 1959). It furthers interpersonal functioning and social skills in all private and professional domains. On the basis of these ideas it is a goal of person-centered and emotion-focused counselling and psychotherapy processes, to bring feelings into awareness, to support a positive regard of one's feelings and to give help for regulating one's feelings (Greenberg, Rice, and Elliott, 1996). In the past three decades it has become most common to regard feelings when communication problems arise in everyday life. A considerable amount of communication training programs focus on the person's ability to become aware of their feelings and to talk about them (e.g. Aspy and Roebuck 1977; Aspy 1972; Gordon 1970, 1974; Behr and Walterscheid 1995; Greenberg, Kusche, Cook, and Quamma 1995).

The person-centered theory of personality and personality change has created a model of an emotionally incongruent self and of the process of experiencing new feelings (Rogers 1959, 1961). Since then this has accompanied a huge amount of psychotherapy process and outcome research within clinical psychology. In the last decade, emerging from social psychology and psychology of personality, a concept of emotional intelligence (Salovey and Mayer 1990) arose, describing and valuing personality traits nearly identical to those in person-centered theory (Rogers 1963). First measures for some of these traits have already been developed (Mayer and Gaschke 1988; Salovey, Mayer, Goldman, Turvey and Palfai 1995). In regard to psychotherapy/counselling practice and research, as well as the hypothesized impact of these traits for interpersonal functioning, we developed a short and easy to use self-report measure. It will assess central constructs of the person-centered theory of personality, concepts of emotion-focused and focusing work, and some of the constructs of emotional intelligence. This article reports the development and validation of these scales, theoretical and practical implications of our findings and discusses the use in practice and research.

THEORETICAL FRAME

Person-centered and experiential research

The Rogerian theory of personality and personality change (Rogers 1959), visualized in Figure 1, defines major constructs of the therapeutic process: There are individual differences in a person's congruence between experience and self concept. A congruent person will accept their experience-based feelings and use and rely on these feelings for intuition (Rogers 1951, 1963). A less congruent person will symbolize experiences incompletely or not at all. The person is unclear and embarrassed about some feelings. A basic objective of the person-centered theory of personality change and of most of the experiential and emotion-focused psychotherapy-approaches, (Greenberg, Rice and Elliott, 1996) is bringing feelings/experiences into awareness and integrating them into the self by a process of symbolization. Symbolizing an experience means, the person gains a mental representation of an experience within the self-structure that makes sense to them within this structure and can so be regarded as belonging to the self.

Experiences will symbolize within the self, when the person performs self-exploration by talking to a therapist under given core conditions. Concepts have been elaborated to support and enrich this process. Psychodynamic concepts have always stressed the roles of fantasies and dreams in the symbolization process. In addition, the concept of focusing elucidates not only the value of imagination but especially the surpassing role of bodily sensations for symbolizing experiences (Gendlin, 1978). Biermann-Ratjen, Eckert and Schwartz (1997) outline the symbolization process as mainly influenced by the degree to which a person values their own emotions, with the practical consequence that therapy should focus on this valuing process.

Research about person-centered psychotherapy concentrates more on process and outcome than on the underlying theory of personality. Variables under investigation are the core conditions, (Carkhuff 1969; Tausch 1990; Barrett-Lennard 1998) and the client's self-exploration or self-explication (Sachse 1990); for these variables data are often gained by expert-ratings. Outcome measures are gathered by clients' self-reports, concentrating on the decrease of symptoms, increased interpersonal functioning and some personality traits. If one's underlying theory of personality says that the change process is guided and surpassed by a development of the emotional organization of the person (symbolization, more congruence and intuition, experiencing, regulation, and positive valuing of feelings), then it would be confirming as well as valuable for research and practice to assess these constructs directly.

Actually, two measures try to accomplish that. The personal orientation dimensions (Shostrom, Knapp and Knapp 1976; Knapp, Shostrom and Knapp 1977) exists in two versions. The scales of this instrument are derived from the person-centered theory of personality aiming towards definitions and concrete topics of the actualizing tendency. Therefore, life-attitudes and central questions of life-orientations can be rated, and aspects of emotional experiences are only marginal. The Feelings, Reactions and Beliefs Survey (FRBS) of Cartwright, DeBruin and Berg (1991) (Höger 1995) is clearly based on some constructs of the person-centered theory of personality, referring as well to attitudes but also comprising aspects of experiencing emotions. Sample scales for that are 'Focusing Conscious Attention', 'Open to Feelings in Relationships', 'Trust in Self as an Organism' and 'Fully Functioning Person'. The 9 scales require 129 items, and the scales, comprising up to 20 items, cover a broad range of meanings as they try to correspond to the construct described by theory as entirely as possible. Maybe this is the reason why the homogeneity of the scales is quite low; the a-coefficients range between .63 and .86; some scale-intercorrelations are quite high, up to .61, which does not allow the scales to be regarded as independent from one another. Cartwright et al. and Höger thus do not recommend this measure for individual scores or profiles but only for research studies of group data. The search for measures that enable the client to give self-reports about how she or he experiences this emotional organization of the self has recently been facilitated by Rogers' psychology of personality and the concept of emotional intelligence.

Emotional and social intelligence

The much younger concept of emotional intelligence (Salovey and Mayer 1990) proposes a rather wide cluster of constructs like congruence, experiencing, and being in contact to oneself as a form of intelligence. The Rogerian ideal of the 'fully functioning person' (Rogers 1963) describes much of what Salovey and Mayer consider to be emotionally intelligent. In addition to being aware and valuing one's own emotions, Salovey and Mayer conceptualize regulation and utilizing of emotions as well as social skills explicitly as being part of emotional intelligence. They describe their sub-concepts of emotional intelligence as: (1) Appraisal and Expression of Emotions, (2) Empathy, (3) Regulations of Emotions in the Self and in Others, (4) Utilizing Emotions, (5) Social Skills.

This conception aims to cover a very broad range of skills: so broad that there might be little evidence for something like a general or core emotional intelligence factor. In addition, the concept seems to overlap with the construct of social intelligence, which suffers with similar problems and with the inability to discriminate from general intelligence (Riggio 1986). This has led to promising attempts to identify and to measure a number of specific abilities and to construct multidimensional instruments. Thus within the psychology of personality and social psychology many concepts and related measures have been developed concerning human emotionality. A stress has been put on how emotions are expressed. Namely, the scales of Riggio (1986), Kring, Smith and Neale (1994) and especially Gross and John (1998) give an elaborated conceptualization of emotional expressivity and its role in human communication. However, they do not focus on congruence or on the processes of valuing emotions or symbolization. Within the concept of self-consciousness (Fenigstein, Scheier and Buss 1975), the private self-consciousness scale offers a measure of the degree to which people take their own feelings and the self into awareness and consideration, without any focus on the individual valuing-aspect. The subscale 'attention to feelings' of the Trait Meta Mood Scale of Salovey, Mayer, Goldman, Turvey and Palfai (1995) assesses a similar trait. Together with the two other subscales, 'clarity of feelings' and 'mood repair', aspects of the definition of emotional intelligence are covered. Although emerging out of a clinical context with a deficit-orientated point of view, the alexithymia scale of Taylor, Ryan and Bagby

(1985) developed quite similar constructs to the concept of emotional intelligence and to the topics of emotion-focused therapies. The subscales are named 'Ability to identify and distinguish between feelings and bodily sensations', 'Ability to describe feelings', 'Daydreaming' and 'Externally-oriented thinking'. The emotional awareness scale (Lane et al., 1990) clearly assesses a skill described as part of emotional intelligence and is a central aim of emotion-focused therapies. Following in parts a qualitative approach, the practical use is critical, because it requires a time-consuming rating procedure for researchers or practitioners. At the same time the statistical indices do not promise advantages towards standardized procedures.

There are some elaborate measures of perception of emotions, their regulation and the relatedness to social skills, and they are more or less in touch with what the present study aims at. But they too rarely seem to cover the topic of congruence, *valuing* own feelings and the *symbolization*-process, and some of them are too long and time-consuming for use in practice.

PURPOSE OF THIS STUDY

This situation suggests the need for a new theory-based multidimensional measure, that tries to capture central constructs of the person-centered theory of personality that suggest additional and modified concepts, that contribute to the idea of emotional intelligence.

Research in this area might open valuable approaches to assess the process and the outcome of psychotherapy in the future by using the constructs of the person-centered theory of personality themselves. Furthermore, it may provide a tool for various questions in research about personality, counseling or education, and may so verify the value of constructs of the person-centered theory and emotional intelligence in various fields of interpersonal life.

In the practice of counselling and psychotherapy the questionnaire will give quick initial information on how a client experiences and values their own feelings and about specific ways and possibilities of the client's symbolization process. This might, for the first sessions, enable a quicker and more attuned therapeutic behavior towards the client's process of inner functioning and towards some possible therapeutic aims.

A third aim was to provide additional *evidence to the person-centered theory of personality*. We therefore tried to identify construct-related scales that are independent of one another.

Method

Participants took part in several sessions, in each of which the SEE was applied. Except for sample A, only parts of the additional questionnaires were completed as described below.

Participants

Sample A consisted of 89 women and 24 men with an average age of 26.1 years (SD = 8.5). Some of these individuals were undergraduate students in a teacher training college, who took part in a lecture about emotional intelligence. The others were friends or relatives of the students.

Sample B consisted of 117 female and 43 male undergraduates (M age of 27.0 years, SD = 8.0) of the same teachers training college, who took part in general lectures of educational psychology and completed the forms in connection with the lecture.

Table 1
Factor loadings of the SQEVE-Scales

No. Items (paraphrased)	Symbolization by Bodily Experience	Experiencing Overwhelming Emotions	Symbolization by Imagination	Lack of Self-Control	Experiencing Congruence	Experiencing Lack of Emotions	Regulation of Emotions	h^2
1. body reflects feelings	.75					-.25		.64
2. physical corresponds mental state	.70						-.14	.52
3. problems in body correspond mental uneasiness	.69	.22			.11			.54
4. feel unhappy I notice in my stomach	.68	.12				-.25		.55
5. tensions and relaxations help make decisions	.66		.23				.21	.54
6. bodily feelings give idea of what I want	.64	-.16	.23		.16		.14	.53
7. decisions rely on bodily feelings	.55		.13				.21	.38
8. emotions bother me		.69			-.14			.51
9. feelings, which I'd like to get rid of		.66			-.32	.11	-.18	.60
10. so full of emotions that I can hardly stand it	.13	.64	.13	.26			-.18	.53
11. wish I were not so affected by emotions		.64	.15	.29	-.14			.56
12. situations with others, wish I were less emotional		.64		.17		.12		.46
13. switch off thoughts		.58		.10			-.14	.38
14. emotions that I would rather not have		.55			-.29	.18	-.12	.45
15. daydreams useful			.78		.14			.64
16. daydreams give clues as to my needs	.12		.77					.65
17. focus on daydreams helps to cope with stress			.75			-.16		.57
18. feelings clearer through dreams	.24		.74					.62
19. fantasies help to cope with the past	.12		.72					.53
20. dreams give understanding of relationships	.23		.67	.12			.11	.55

	8.79	8.07	7.89	7.68	7.51	7.39	5.99	53.31
21. self-control could be better		.18		.73				.59
22. got control		-.21		-.71	.16			.59
23. regret acting spontaneously		.19		.62			.15	.46
24. can pretend to be calm	-.15			-.62		.12	.35	.55
25. things are bubbling up inside me	.32	.27		.56	.19	-.12	-.17	.51
26. hate quick temper	.10	.34		.54		.24		.44
27. like to control myself better				.54		.24		.48
28. people can't see what is going on inside me	-.30	.11		-.51	-.11	.23	.21	.48
29. manage my emotions well		-.29	-.11	-.47	-.14	.12	.21	.40
30. what I feel is ok		-.20		-.15	.77	-.14	.17	.69
31. emotions have the right to be		-.25			.73			.64
32. right to feelings	.16		.10		.71	-.21		.59
33. stand by feelings	.10	-.12		.10	.68	-.19		.54
34. stick to something embarrassing		-.11			.64		.23	.49
35. don't feel my inner world					-.18	.77		.63
36. wish more aware of my emotions					-.20	.73		.56
37. don't notice what my body is telling me	-.37		.18			.59	-.12	.57
38. like to experience more within myself					.12	.55		.36
39. notice signals in my body	.39		.13		.27	-.54	.17	.55
40. with other people, I'm aware of emotions	.19				.25	-.50		.38
41. physical symptoms split off	-.14	.27	-.16			.49		.36
42. aware of my bodily needs	.17	-.15			.33	-.48	.19	.45
43. know how to calm down	.16	-.14	-.15		.19	-.11	.74	.67
44. have ways of controlling my emotions	.18	-.19	-.18				.72	.63
45. can't do anything about certain moods	.20	.20	.11			.11	-.69	.56
46. more lively mood, I can bring that about.	-.23	-.23			.23	-.13	.68	.59
Variance explained	8.79	8.07	7.89	7.68	7.51	7.39	5.99	53.31

Note: principal-components extraction /varimax rotation. Loadings below .10 are not reported. Statistics related to the German version.

Sample C consisted of 62 female and 10 male undergraduates (M age of 22.5 years, SD = 2.8) of the same teachers training college, who took part in two days' training in person-centered communication in school and completed the forms as part of the training evaluation.

Sample D consisted of 56 female and 15 male undergraduates (M age of 23.4 years, SD = 6.2) of a different teachers training college, who took part in general lectures of educational psychology and completed the forms in connection with the lecture.

Sample E consisted of 22 women and 17 men, who were friends or relatives of undergraduates, who took part in a person-centered communication role-play experiment and completed the forms as part of the evaluation. On average they were 35.7 years old (SD = 12.4).

In sum of all 5 samples 347 women and 109 men (M age of 26.3 years, SD = 8.5) participated, of whom 43 were postgraduates, 288 were undergraduates and 122 had no academic level. All volunteered.

Apparatus

In order to give evidence for convergent validity, a scale must be related to conceptually similar measures and for discriminant validity it must be unrelated to conceptually dissimilar constructs. Thus we chose the measures #2 to #5, which we assumed to be both satisfying and at the same time economical samples of scales representing both criteria. Measures #6 to #8 were additionally chosen to provide information about the relations of concrete emotions and aspects of interpersonal communication towards the SEE-Scales. On the basis of the person-centered theory of personality this might provide additional evidence for validity.

These specific questionnaires were used:
1. A pre-form of the SEE with 106 Items and a 7-point rating scale with anchors from 1 = 'trifft gar nicht zu' [not at all true] to 7 = 'trifft voll zu' [completely true] (fulfilled by all samples).
2. As a Big Five instrument Costa and McCrae's (1992) 60-item NEO Five Factor Inventory (NEO FFI), German version (fulfilled by sample A, scales *neuroticism* and *openness to experiences* by sample B, D and E).
3. The Private Self-Consciousness Scale, German version (Merz 1986; Fenigstein et al., 1975) (fulfilled by sample A).
4. The Trait Meta Mood Scale (TMMS) Scale *Clarity of Feelings* (Salovey et al., 1995), own translation into German (fulfilled by sample A).
5. The Freiburger Persönlichkeits Inventar (FPI) Scales *Lebenszufriedenheit [life satisfaction], Belastung [stress]* and *Somatisierung [psychosomatic reactions]* (fulfilled by. A, B, D and E).
6. A sum of 16 words for basic emotions with a 7-point rating scale indicating the extent to which the emotion plays a role in the person's everyday life in the sense of a trait (fulfilled by all samples). Examples are: Anxiety, Depression, Happiness.
7. A sum of 22 self-constructed items describing a persons behavior in communication and interpersonal relation with a 7-point rating scale (fulfilled by sample A).
8. A slightly modified version of these items being prepared for a peer-rating of the person's behavior in communication and interpersonal relation (fulfilled by sample A).

Procedure

A broad set of items was accumulated. Item generation was guided by the constructs of the person-centered theory of personality, concepts of experiential work, and by major definitions of emotional intelligence. In regard to the theoretical constructs, we formulated items led by the words of psychotherapy clients and encounter group participants when they share feelings and talk about themselves. Items were extensively discussed with colleagues and acquaintances. Two pretests (No. 1 in 1997 with 32 Items and 35 Pn; No. 2 in 1999 with 72 Items and 276 Pn) confirmed, modified and sorted out items.

As the items were accumulated, they were classified into conceptual categories in order to identify repetitive groups of items in large categories and potential items that were missing from smaller categories. Item categories used were: (a) positive valuing of feelings, (b) experiencing too many feelings, (c) experiencing few feelings, (d) reasoning about feelings, (e) experiencing daydreaming as useful, (f) experiencing dreams as useful, (g) experiencing bodily experiences as useful, (h) feeling able to retain emotions and reactions, (i) feeling able to regulate emotions, (j) experiencing intuition. Items within a category were balanced as to direction of response. Each category contained 6 to 14 Items. Although these categories collectively described the item domain, they were not necessarily expected to correspond to the obtained factorial structure.

A final sum of 106 items was given with other questionnaires as described above to the different samples. Pn were briefly informed about the background of the study. In addition, the participants of sample 1 obtained four extra sheets of form #8, in order to perform peer-ratings with friends or partners. As participants were known to both sides before the testing, anonymity was precluded between the peer rater and the person being related concerning form #8. The recollection of the major forms strictly ensured anonymity.

Results

Scale Construction

Previous research with factor analysis about items touching our topic (e.g. Taylor et al., 1985; Salovey et al., 1995; Gross and John 1998) has yielded three to five factors, which corresponded somewhat with constructs of our theoretical orientation towards person-centered and experiential counseling and the concept of emotional intelligence. We thus hypothesized that a similar number of factors would partly represent well-known constructs within this theoretical orientation, and would partly merge in other aspects. Which of the constructs of the major theoretical propositions would emerge? After deleting a few Items not ranging between .20 and .80 in power, we conducted an exploratory factor analysis using principal-component analysis. The scree test was not definite, suggesting 6 to 8 factors; the underlying theoretical constructs were best displayed by the 7-factor solution, which we thus interpreted.

The item selection followed the criteria of Rost and Schermer (1986). In additional stages further items were deleted in order to increase the homogeneity of the scales, and thus maximize instrumental reliability. The result met the aim to develop a short test with as few items as possible. Factor analysis with the remaining 46 Items (Table 1) clearly yields seven factors (eigenvalues 7.7 – 5.8 – 3.3 – 2.3 – 2.0 – 1.8 – 1.5), which explain 53% of variance. The factor structure remains stable whether regarding male or female participants.

The first varimax-rotated factor was defined by items referring to bodily sensations that indicate mental states and feelings which are anchors for intuition. Sample items include 'My body often reflects my feelings,' 'When I make decisions I rely on my bodily feelings,' and 'When I feel unhappy in a situation I notice this for example in my stomach, on my skin, in areas of tension.' This factor describes individuals who perceive their bodily processes and bring them into immediate contact with a possible mental meaning. As this clearly corresponds with a major process assumption within experiential therapy, we labeled this factor *Symbolization by Bodily Experience.*

The items defining the second factor devalue the experiences of many feelings. This factor describes individuals who suffer from an overload of emotions and thoughts, and wish they had less. Examples include 'I'm so full of emotions that I can often hardly stand it,' 'I wish I could switch off my thoughts sometimes,' and 'I've got some emotions that I would rather not have.' Therefore we labeled this factor *Experiencing Overwhelming Emotions.*

The third factor was defined by items regarding fantasies or dreams that were evaluated as useful to understand and cope with a number of mental problems. Sample items include 'My feelings become clearer through my dreams,' 'My fantasies help me to cope with the past,' and 'I consider daydreams to be useful.' Each of these items involves a positive regard for imaginative processes, which help one to understand oneself, and for coping processes. The factor thus stands for a central idea for helpful processes in psychodynamic and experiential psychotherapy and was therefore named *Symbolization by Imagination.*

The fourth factor was defined by items describing individuals who have to sustain emotional impulses which they have difficulty hiding from others. Sample items include 'My self-control could be better,' 'I hate my quick temper,' and 'Normally, other people can't see what is going on inside of me' (negatively keyed). These individuals abhor their lack of self-control and are embarrassed about it. We therefore labeled this factor *Lack of Self-control.*

The fifth factor gathered items expressing a clearly positive regard of own feelings. Examples include: 'I feel what I feel and that's OK,' 'All my emotions have the right to be just as they are,' and 'I stand by all my feelings.' The major construct of congruence within the person-centered theory is clearly represented by this factor. We named it *Experiencing Congruence.*

The sixth factor was defined by items describing individuals being empty of emotions, cut off from their body and regretting this. Sample items include: 'I often wish that I were more aware of my emotions,' 'I don't often notice what my body is telling me,' and 'When I'm with other people, I'm always aware of my fleeting emotions' (negatively keyed). This factor comprehends again a major idea of all emotion-focused counselling work: the individual being split off from her or his feelings and only experiencing an insignificant grumble and lack. We found the label *Experiencing Lack of Emotions* to be appropriate for this factor.

The seventh factor comprises items clearly addressing the individual's ability to regulate their own moods. Sample items include: 'I have ways of controlling my emotions,' 'Most of the time I know how to calm down when I'm het up,' and 'When I'm in certain moods, I can't do anything about it' (negatively keyed). We therefore named this factor *Regulation of Emotions.*

Scale statistics
Table 2 reports the descriptive statistics of the items, Table 3 reports the descriptive statistics of the final version of the seven scales. Although the number of items only ranged between 4 and 9, all scales were found to be highly reliable and satisfyingly homogeneous, with Cronbach's

Table 2 Item-Statistics of the SQEVE

Scales	No.	Items (paraphrased)	M	SD	Item-total r (corrected)	p_i
Symbolization by Bodily Experiences	1.	body reflects feelings	4.43	1.43	.61	.57
	2.	physical corresponds mental state	4.68	1.46	.55	.61
	3.	problems in body correspond mental uneasiness	4.40	1.55	.57	.57
	4.	feel unhappy I notice in my stomach	5.13	1.53	.61	.69
	5.	tensions and relaxations help make decisions.	3.87	1.41	.61	.48
	6.	bodily feelings give idea of what I want	4.31	1.53	.55	.55
	7.	decisions rely on bodily feelings	3.59	1.28	.47	.43
Experiencing Overwhelming Emotions	8.	emotions bother me	4.16	1.40	.55	.53
	9.	feelings, which I'd like to get rid of	3.24	1.58	.61	.37
	10.	So full of emotions that I can hardly stand it	3.65	1.67	.56	.44
	11.	wish, I were not so affected by emotions	4.05	1.70	.59	.51
	12.	situations with others, wish I were less emotional	3.90	1.64	.50	.48
	13.	switch off thoughts	4.43	1.68	.49	.57
	14.	emotions that I would rather not have	3.51	1.62	.50	.42
Symbolization by Imagination	15.	daydreams useful	4.64	1.52	.67	.61
	16.	daydreams give clues as to my needs	4.63	1.64	.64	.61
	17.	focus on daydreams helps to cope with stress	4.12	1.72	.59	.52
	18.	feelings clearer through dreams	3.94	1.71	.68	.49
	19.	fanatasies help to cope with the past	3.96	1.59	.62	.49
	20.	dreams give understanding of relationships	3.28	1.62	.61	.38
Lack of Self-Control	21.	self control could be better	3.11	1.49	.61	.35
	22. (-)	got control	3.56	1.39	.62	.43
	23.	regret acting spontaneously	4.14	1.55	.46	.52
	24. (-)	can pretend to be calm	3.53	1.53	.53	.42
	25.	things are bubbling up inside me	4.08	1.62	.43	.51
	26.	hate quick temper	2.45	1.48	.44	.24
	27.	like to control myself better	3.29	1.54	.49	.38
	28. (-)	people can't see what is going on inside me	3.92	1.56	.38	.49
	29. (-)	manage my emotions well	3.84	1.35	.45	.47
Experiencing Congruence	30.	what I feel is ok	5.43	1.34	.70	.74
	31.	emotions have the right to be	5.31	1.43	.62	.72
	32.	right to feelings	5.62	1.42	.55	.77
	33.	stand by feelings	5.10	1.38	.58	.68
	34.	stick to something embarrassing	4.90	1.27	.56	.65
Experiencing Lack of Emotions	35.	don't feel my inner world	2.50	1.33	.64	.25
	36.	wish more aware of my emotions	3.09	1.54	.52	.35
	37.	don't notice what my body is telling me	2.91	1.41	.61	.32
	38.	like to experience more within myself	3.13	1.45	.32	.36
	39.(-)	notice signals in my body	2.89	1.31	.58	.32
	40.(-)	with other people, I'm aware of emotions	2.91	1.31	.49	.32
	41.	physical symptoms split off	2.71	1.40	.42	.29
	42.(-)	aware of my bodily needs	3.07	1.35	.52	.35
Regulation of Emotions	43.	know how to calm down	4.43	1.39	.68	.57
	44.	have ways of controlling my emotions	4.51	1.27	.64	.59
	45.(-)	can't do anything about certain moods	4.38	1.40	.57	.56
	46.	more lively mood, I can bring that about.	4.55	1.31	.60	.59

Note. (-) indicates negatively keyed items. Statistics related to the German version.

Alpha ranging between .80 and .85. With respect to men, the reliability ranged between .76 and .87 and with respect to women only, the reliability ranged between .79 and .85.

Table 4 reports the intercorrelations among the scales. The highest coefficient is .43, only two further are .41, all others are below .40 and on average .22. The inter-correlations range on a level low enough to consider the scales to be independent from one another.

To test interrelations on a higher level we conducted an exploratory factor analysis of the seven scales. Using principal-component analysis, we found that the scree test indicated two factors explaining 55% of variance. The first varimax-rotated factor includes the scales Congruence (–), Regulation(–), Lack of Self-control, Overwhelming and Lack of Emotions. The second factor includes Bodily Experience, Imagination and Lack of Emotions (–). The first factor thus is defined by scales indicating mental stability vs instability. The second factor is defined by the two symbolization scales and lack of emotions, thus representing some kind of openness for experiential processes.

Differential effects of gender and age

Previous research reports gender differences in some emotional and social dimensions. Women are found to be emotionally more expressive than men (Gross and John, 1998, 1995; Riggio, 1986), score higher on impulse intensity (Gross and John, 1998), and have more emotional and social sensitivity and less emotional control (Riggio, 1986). Figure 2 shows the means of the seven experiencing scales in standard-score metric, to permit an immediate appraisal of effect sizes. Women reported more overwhelming emotions, $F(450)=12.7$, $p<.001$, $d=.39$; more symbolization of bodily experience, $F(450)=8.4$, $p<.01$, $d=.32$; more lack of self control, $F(450)=8.1$, $p<.01$, $d=.32$; and less lack of emotions $F(450)=5.7$, $p<.05$, $d=-.27$. Low correlations are found between age and regulation of emotions, ($r=.14$, $p<.01$), symbolization of bodily experience ($r=.14$, $p<.01$) and symbolization by imagination ($r=.–10$, $p<.05$).

Convergent and discriminant validity

The test was related to the conceptually similar and dissimilar measures mentioned above. They may not represent an exhaustive compilation of measures but they gave satisfying evidence for validity. In Table 5 we see how the SEE-Scales correlate with the personality measures #2 to #5 as described in the apparatus section. As person-centered theory predicts that incongruent people suffer with mental disorders, we expected negative relations of Congruence with Neuroticism, Stress and Psychosomatic Disorders, Anxiety and Depression and positive relations with Openness to Experience, Life-Satisfaction and Happiness. The scales assessing regulation and valuing of emotions should show similar relations, as they focus on specific aspects of Incongruence. The two Symbolization Scales were expected to correlate with Openness to Experience, as theory regards the process of symbolization to be an integration of new experiences into the self-concept.

Actually the Congruence scale correlated positively with the FPI Life-Satisfaction and the TMMS Clarity of Feelings scale, highly negative with the NEO-FFI Neuroticism scale and negatively with the FPI Stress scale, suggesting that individuals who experience congruence are satisfied, clear about their feelings, and don't suffer from stress or disorders.

The Regulation of Emotions scale shows a similar pattern of correlations. The coefficients are still higher in value; in addition a very significant relationship is found with the absence of psychosomatic disorders.

Table 3 Scale-Statistics of the SEE

Scales	No. of Items	M (Total sample)	SD (Total sample)	Cronbachs Alpha Reliability (Total sample)	Cronbachs Alpha Reliability (Men)	Cronbachs Alpha Reliability (Women)
Symbolization by Bodily Experience	7	30.38	7.14	.82	.82	.83
Experiencing Overwhelming Emotions	7	26.95	7.70	.81	.80	.80
Symbolization by Imagination	6	24.66	7.38	.85	.87	.85
Lack of Self-control	9	31.95	8.28	.80	.81	.79
Experiencing Congruence	5	26.50	5.15	.81	.77	.83
Experiencing Lack of Emotions	8	23.36	7.20	.80	.76	.81
Regulation of Emotions	4	17.88	4.32	.81	.80	.81

Note. Statistics related to the German version. n= 439

Table 4 Inter-Correlations of the SEE-Scales

Experiencing Emotions Scale	1	2	3	4	5	6	7
1. Symbolization by Bodily Experience	—						
2. Experiencing Overwhelming Emotions	.05	—					
3. Symbolization by Imagination	.37**	.15**	—				
4. Lack of Self-control	.13**	.43**	.05	—			
5. Experiencing Congruence	.21**	-.38**	-.02	-.11*	—		
6. Experiencing Lack of Emotions	-.35**	.19**	-.08	.08	-.41**	—	
7. Regulation of Emotions	.14**	-.41**	.04	-.31**	.36**	-.27**	—

Note. n= 439   * $p < .05$ ** $p < 0.01$ (two-tailed)

The Overwhelming Emotions and Lack of Self-control scales also show a similar pattern of relations. A high rating on these scales is related to Neuroticism, Stress, Psychosomatic Disorders, lack of Life Satisfaction and lack of Clarity of Feelings, suggesting the factor Overwhelming Emotions to be highly and the factor Lack of Self-control to be moderately related to a sample of measures all indicating disorders and boredom. Overwhelming Emotions is also significantly related to Private Self-consciousness, indicating that some kind of active process may be an element within this experience.

The Lack of Emotions scale is moderately related to Neuroticism too, and negatively to Openness to Experience, Life Satisfaction, Stress, Private Self-consciousness and very strongly negative to Clarity of Feelings. Individuals rating high on this scale in fact do not seem to experience much. The only positive correlation is the one to Neuroticism. Also stress experiences seem to be negatively related.

The Symbolization by Bodily Experience and Symbolization by Imagination scales are moderately related to Openness to Experience and to Psychosomatic Disorders. Symbolization

Table 5 Correlations of the SEE-scales with other personality measures

Personality Subscale	Symbolization by Bodily Experience	Experiencing Overwhelming Emotions	Symbolization by Imagination	Lack of Self-control	Experiencing Congruence	Experiencing Lack of Emotions	Regulation of Emotions
NEO-FFI							
Neuroticism [a].	.13*	.54**	.13*	.31**	-.36**	.23**	-.44**
Extraversion [b].	.14	.04	.01	.18	.14	-.08	.23
Openness to Experience [a]	.20**	-.01	.29**	.02	.18**	-.24**	.16**
Agreeableness [b]	.27*	.10	-.03	.00	-.14	.06	-.19
Conscientiousness [b]	.12	.06	-.00	-.16	.02	.07	.03
FPI							
Life-Satisfaction [c]	-.05	-.44**	-.12*	-.21**	.30**	-.16**	.34**
Stress [c]	.04	.44**	.04	.25**	-.22**	-.22**	-.31**
Psychosomatic-Disorders [c].	.21**	.36**	.17**	.19**	-.12*	.12*	-.30**
TMMS: Clarity of Feelings [b]	.20	-.34**	.00	-.28*	.37**	-.50**	.46**
Private Self-consciousness [b]	.16	.28**	.36**	.11	-.07	-.29**	.03

Note. NEO-FFI = Five Factor Inventory; FPI = Freiburger Persönlichkeits Inventar; TMMS = Trait Meta Mood Scale
a: n= 331. b: n= 64. c: n= 360.
* $p < .05$ ** $p < 0.01$ (two-tailed)

Table 6
Correlations of the SEE-scales with self- and peer-rated communication and with the experience of concrete emotions

	Symbolization by Bodily Experience	Experiencing Overwhelming Emotions	Symbolization by Imagination	Lack of Self-control	Experiencing Congruence	Experiencing Lack of Emotions	Regulation of Emotions
Communication							
Self-rating: Closeness [a]	.03	-.09	.02	.25*	.31**	.13	.28**
Self-rating: Empathy [a]	.20*	-.24*	-.05	-.30**	.34**	-.37**	.22*
Peer-rating: [b]							
Engaged and Dominant	-.05	-.08	.02	.09	.22	-.26*	.20
Partner-rating: Closeness [c].	-.05	-.19	.16	-.20	.36*	-.29	.20
Dominant Emotion							
Anxiety [d]	.12*	.37**	.15**	.14**	-.26**	.08	-.31**
Depression [d].	.03	.30**	.15**	.09	-.20**	.07	-.24**
Happiness (Glück) [d]	.17**	-.11*	.15**	-.01	.34**	-.27**	.24**
Mental vacuum, [d]							
Boredom (Langeweile)	.05	.23**	.07	.13**	-.18**	.27**	-.27**
Shame [d]	.03	.26**	.10*	.09*	-.22**	.11*	-.15**

Note. a: n= 87. b: n= 61. c: n= 30. d: n= 429
* $p < .05$ ** $p < 0.01$ (two-tailed)

by Imagination is also related to Private Self-consciousness, suggesting that a sensitivity for inner processes plays a role in these concepts.

In addition to being related to conceptually similar constructs or to constructs where theory would predict a relation, the scales showed discriminant validity being uncorrelated to conceptually unrelated constructs. As anticipated, the SEE was not related to the big five measures of Agreeableness (with one exception) and Conscientiousness. Surprisingly, they were unrelated to Extraversion, too. We expected correlations assuming that positive valuing of one's emotions would be accompanied by Extraversion and Lack of Emotions would not be. However, these constructs seem to be unrelated and further research is warranted at this point.

Conceptual evidence

Table 6 reports the relations of the SEE-Scales with the trait-experience of concrete emotions and self- and peer-rated aspects of interpersonal communication. Coefficients are in accord with what could be hypothesized on the basis of the person-centered theory of personality. Congruent individuals experience positive emotions, interpersonal closeness and empathy and they are seen this way by others. Individuals experiencing lack of emotions feel neither empathy nor happiness but rather boredom, and others find them lacking in closeness and engagement. Individuals experiencing overwhelming emotions feel negative emotions, shame and less empathy.

DISCUSSION

The main topic of this article was the development of a multidimensional measure for practical use in psychotherapy and research. It represents constructs from the person-centered and experiential theory of personality and suggests new and modified subconstructs for the concept of Emotional Intelligence. Out of an item pool covering a broad range of ideas about experiencing, valuing and regulating emotions, independent scales were constructed with very satisfying statistical scores. The sum of only 46 items allows uncomplicated and timesaving use. Three main aspects of our findings can be pointed out.

Theory development

Some of our findings suggest extensions of the person-centered theory of personality. The SEE subscale *Experiencing Overwhelming Emotions* represents a cluster of individual experiences that are not directly covered by a construct. The theory more likely describes the individual as not being in contact with an important range of feelings (*Experiencing Lack of Emotions*) and becoming aware of them in a self-directed process of symbolizations (Rogers, 1951), one of the core-concepts of all experiential psychotherapy (Greenberg 1993). The correlations matrices (Table 5 and 6) show, concordant with theory, that an individual without contact with feelings turns out to be unhappy, unclear about feelings and not in contact with others. On the other hand, measures indicating mental disorders in a more clinical sense, for example: neuroticism, stress, psychosomatic problems, anxiety and depression, show the strongest relations with the scale *Experiencing Overwhelming Emotions*. These correlations are in part consistent with the findings of Gross and John (1998, p 180–3), who also report very significant but lower relations with neuroticism measures with their 'Impulse Intensity Scale'.

Furthermore, these findings are consistent with the work of Greenberg, Rice and Elliott (1996), who elaborate how person-centered experiential psychotherapy is more than accessing previously unknown feelings.

Who suffers more, individuals experiencing lack of emotions or overwhelming emotions? Physiological and more clinical data would be needed. But already the present findings suggest what psychotherapists in practice know by intuition: that the experience of being overwhelmed by emotion is a primary and common problem in many psychotherapy processes. An extension of the person-centered theoretical model is required, explaining more directly personality facets and the process of symbolization for these individuals.

This notion is still supported by the fact that three out of our seven scales deal with problems concerning overwhelming emotions, self-control and regulation. Of course a factor structure depends on which items are used initially. Recent research as well as our experiences as practitioners gave us the idea to fill in items addressing the regulation aspect. However, we did not expect it to have so much weight.

Practical value

The issue of controlling and struggling with too much emotion raises a discussion about a core idea of all person-centered-experiential psychotherapy approaches, which brings feelings into awareness and enables a person to experience feelings. Does it always enrich individuals feeling overwhelmed by emotions, when we help them to actualize their feelings and experiential processes? Maybe we need more differentiated approaches for a subgroup of clients.

It is of course helpful to explicitly attune psychotherapeutic interventions to this level of inner functioning, and we have no doubt that psychotherapists do this automatically, once they gain deep enough empathy for their clients' process of exploration and valuing. However and in general we argue that information about these issues via clients' self-reports will help any therapist in the initial sessions to be better and more accurately attuned. It will allow a more immediate insight into the client's meta experiences of emotions, her or his ways of symbolizing, and possible therapeutic interventions on this level of emotional functioning.

Assessing the scales during and at the end of a therapy will provide verification about whether or not only symptoms or general personality traits (e.g. depression) have changed, as well as the emotional organization of the person that is postulated within the person-centered theory of personality.

Impact for research

Outcome and process studies might use this measure additionally to prove clients' developments, concerning the very traits that the underlying theory of personality postulates. Maybe effect sizes will be increased.

Furthermore, our scales provide an additional and modified measure in regard to the diverse concepts contributing to the wide cluster of abilities subsumed under Emotional Intelligence. Our findings already suggest that the person-centered and experiential constructs elucidate the relation between the individual's ways of emotional experiencing and valuing on the one hand, and mental health, interpersonal skills and life satisfaction on the other hand. This suggests using these constructs as underlying theory for research in the fields of Social Psychology, Psychology of Personality and Educational Psychology.

Future research might first of all cover (1) further and improved validation of the scales, in contexts of counselling and psychotherapy and with more appropriate clinical measures; (2) outcome studies; and (3) investigations on relations between the person-centered constructs of personality, social interaction skills and attitudes of the individual.

REFERENCES

Aspy, D. N. and Roebuck, F. N. (1977). *Kids Don't Learn from People They Don't like.* Amherst, MA: HRD Press.

Aspy, D. N. (1972). *Toward a Technology for Humanizing Education.* Champaign: Research Press Company.

Barrett-Lennard, G. T. (1998). *Carl Rogers' Helping System.* London: Sage.

Behr, M. and Walterscheid-Kramer, J. (1995). *Einfühlendes Erzieherverhalten* (4. Aufl.). [Empathy in Education] Weinheim: Beltz.

Biermann-Ratjen, E., Eckert, J. and Schwartz, H. (1997). *Gesprächspsychotherapie — Verändern durch Verstehen* (8. Auflage). [Person-centered Psychotherapy — Change through Empathy] Stuttgart: Kohlhammer.

Carkhuff, R. R. (1969). *Helping and Human Relations (Vols I+II).* New York: Holt, Rinehart and Winston.

Cartwright, D., DeBruin, J. and Berg, S. (1991). Some scales for assessing personality based on Carl Rogers' theory: Further evidence of validity. *Personality and Individual Differences, 12*(2), 151–6.

Costa, P. T. and McCrae, R. R. (1992). *Revised NEO Personality Inventory (NEO-PI-R) and NEO-Five Factor Inventory (NEO-FFI) Professional Manual.* Odessa, FL: Psychological Assessment Resources.

Fenigstein, A., Scheier, M. F. and Buss, A. H. (1975). Public and private self-consciousness: Assessment and theory. *Journal of Consulting and Clinical Psychology, 43*(4), 522–7.

Gendlin, E. T. (1978). *Focusing.* New York: Everest House.

Gordon, T. (1970). *Parent Effectiveness Training.* New York: Wyden.

Gordon, T. (1974). *T.E.T. Teacher Effectiveness Training.* New York: Wyden.

Greenberg, L. S. (1993). Emotion and change processes in psychotherapy. In M. Lewis and J. M. Haviland (Eds.) *Handbook of emotions* (499–508). New York: Guilford Press.

Greenberg, L. S., Rice, L. N. and Elliott, R. K. and (1996). *Facilitating Emotional Change: The moment-by-moment process.* New York: Guilford Press.

Greenberg, M. T., Kusche C. A., Cook, E. T. and Quamma, J.P. (1995). Promoting emotional competence in school-aged children: The effects of the PATHS curriculum. *Development and Psychopathology, 7*(1), 117–36.

Gross, J. and John, O. (1998). Mapping the domain of expressivity: Multimethod evidence for a hierarchical model. *Journal of Personality and Social Psychology, 74*, 170–91.

Höger, D. (1995). Deutsche Adaption und erste Validierung des Feeling, Reactions and Beliefs Survey (FRBS) von Desmond S. Cartwright. [German Adaptation and first Validation of the Feeling, Reactions and Beliefs Survey (FRBS) of Desmond S. Cartwright.] In J. Eckert (Ed.) *Forschung zur Klientenzentrierten Psychotherapie. Aktuelle Ansätze und Ergebnisse,* [Research in client-centered Psychotherapy. New Approaches and Results.]. Köln: GwG, pp. 167–83.

Knapp, R. R., Shostrom, E. L. and Knapp, L. (1977). Assessment of the actualizing person. In P. McReynolds (Ed.) *Advances in Psychological Assessment, Vol. 4.* San Francisco: Jossey-Bass, pp. 103–40.

Kring, L. A., Smith, D. A. and Neale, J. M. (1994). Individual differences in dispositional expressiveness: development and validation of the Emotional Expressivity Scale. *Journal of Personality and Social Psychology. 5*, 934–49.

Lane R. D., Quinlan, D. M., Schwartz, G. E., Walker, P.A. and Zeitlin, S. B. (1990). The level of emotional awareness scale: A cognitive-development measure of emotion. *Journal of Personality Assessment, 55*, 124–34.

Mayer, J. D. and Gaschke, Y. N. (1988). The experience and meta-experience of mood. *Journal of Personality and Social Psychology, 55*, 102–11.

Merz, J. (1986). SAF: Fragebogen zur Messung von dispositioneller Selbstaufmerksamkeit [SAF: Questionnaire for Assessment of Dispositional Self-Consciousness]. *Diagnostica, 32*, 142–52.

Riggio, R. E. (1986). Assessment of basic social skills. *Journal of Personality and Social Psychology, 51*, 649–60.

Rogers, C. R. (1951). *Client-centered Therapy*. London: Constable.

Rogers, C. R. (1959). A theory of therapy, personality and interpersonal relationships, as developed in the client-centered framework. In S. Koch (Ed.) *Psychology: The Study of a Science, Vol. 3 Formulations of the Person and the Social Context*. New York: McGraw-Hill, pp. 184–256.

Rogers, C. R. (1961). *On Becoming a Person*. Boston: Houghton Mifflin.

Rogers, C. R. (1963). The concept of the fully functioning person. *Psychotherapy: Theory, research and practice, 1*, 17–26.

Rost, D. H. and Schermer, F. J. (1986). Strategien der Prüfungsangstverarbeitung. [Strategies of coping with exam nerves.] *Zeitschrift für Differentielle und Diagnostische Psychologie, 7*, 127–39.

Sachse, R. (1990). The influence of processing proposals on the explication process of the client. *Person-Centered-Review, 5*, 321–44.

Salovey, P. and Mayer, J.D. (1990). Emotional intelligence. *Imagination, Cognition and Personality, 9*, 185–211

Salovey, P, Mayer, J.D., Goldman, S., Turvey C. and Palfai, T (1995). Emotional attention, clarity and repair: Exploring emotional intelligence using the trait meta-mood scale. In J.W. Pennebaker (Ed.) *Emotion, Disclosure and Health*. Washington D.C.: American Psychological Association, pp. 125–54.

Shostrom, E. L., Knapp, R. R. and Knapp, L. (1976). Validation of the personal orientation dimensions: An inventory for the dimensions of actualizing. *Educational-and-Psychological-Measurement, 36*, 491–4.

Tausch, R. and Tausch, A. (1990). *Gesprächspsychotherapie* (9. Auflage). [Person-centered Psychotherapy.] Göttingen: Hogrefe.

Taylor, G. J., Ryan, D. and Bagby, R. M. (1986). Toward the development of a new self-report alexithymia scale. *Psychotherapy and Psychosomatics, 44*, 191–9

We would like to thank Mary Kilborn (+) and Sandra Pedevilla for translating the items into English; Isabella Hübner, who translated the items into Spanish; and Ludwig Merle, who revised the article concerning language.

For a complete version of the items please write to the authors. Correspondence concerning this article should be addressed to Michael Behr, Department of Psychology, Pädagogische Hochschule, D-73525 Schwäbisch Gmünd, Germany. Electronic mail may be sent via the Internet to michael.behr@ph-gmuend.de

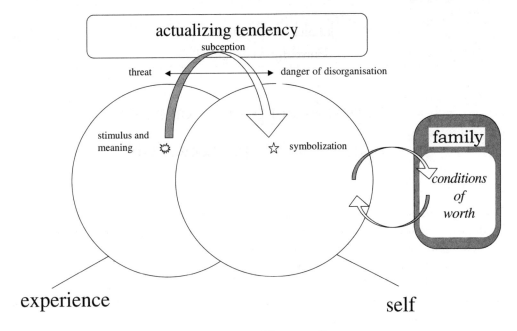

Figure 1. The Person-Centered Theory of Personality

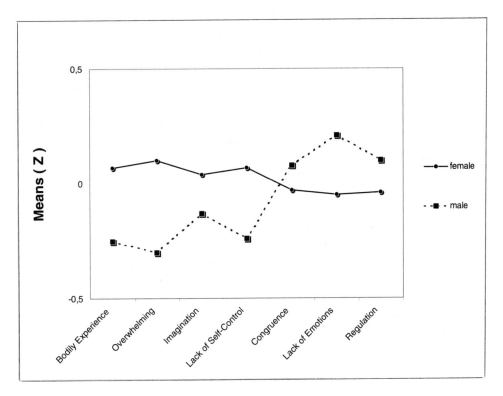

Figure 2. Gender differences on the seven experiencing scales.

Jerold D. Bozarth PhD

University of Georgia, USA

Empirically Supported Treatments:
Epitome of the 'Specificity Myth'[1]

This chapter identifies Empirically Supported Treatments as the epitome of the 'Specificity Myth', and as representative of the fallacious premise in the treatment of psychiatric conditions.

The term 'Specificity Myth' refers to treatments that are based upon the premise that there are specific treatments for specific dysfunction. This myth has been perpetuated by the medical model and by behavioral treatment models for mental dysfunction. It is found in extreme form in the attempts to identify Empirically Supported Treatments (EST) (previously 'Empirically Validated Treatments' (EVT)).

The argument between EST advocates and others reflects the differences in the fundamental views of the nature of human beings. O'Hara (1993) summarizes the two most prominent views of human nature as the deterministic view and the view of humans as beings in the process of actualization. She identifies the determinsitic view as suggesting that '. . . the only valid knowledge is scientific knowledge; hence, human life is predictable, explainable and controllable' (p. 9). The view of the actualizing human being suggests '. . . a process by which the natural inner being is set free from the stunting effect of civilization to realize itself and to actualize its highest potentials' (p. 8). Kuhn (1962) argues another difference in relation to 'inter-theoretical' choice. He points out that the criterion for choice between competing theories is not logical. Such terms as 'truth' and 'proof' cannot be applied in inter-theoretical contexts, because there is neither a neutral language of observation nor a basic vocabulary shared by the competing theories. The EST Syndrome is predicated upon a particular theoretical context (or more precisely is based upon an a-theoretical context of behaviorism) that is identified as the deterministic view.

The deterministic view currently dominates mental health treatment with the illusion of scientific verification. This view adopts major aspects of the medical model for treatment of physical illness, a model that has dominated mental health treatment and propels the assumption that there are viable specific treatments for specific dysfunction in human behavior.

This following discourse reviews the questionable credibility of diagnosis, the deceiving pattern of psychotherapy outcome research, and the conclusion of five decades of psychotherapy outcome research. Several intrinsic flaws in the reported evidence for Empirically Supported Treatments are identified and discussed.

[1.] Also Presented as: Bozarth, J. and Schneider, C. (August, 2000). The Specificity Myth: The Fallacious Premise of Mental Health Treatment. Paper presentation at the *American Psychological Association*, Washington, DC.

DIAGNOSIS

Psychiatric diagnosis and empirically supported treatment are predicated upon the same assumption. The logic is that the assumptions are integrally related to science and are true; hence, not open to critique. It is critical that the veracity of the assumptions be determined since this is the foundation of the entire system. Diagnosis involves two assumptions. First, it is assumed that there is a relationship among certain phenomena (discovered by researchers) from which the concept of a diagnostic label can be determined. Second, it is assumed that there is binding of the clusters identified by researchers. The validity of both of these assumptions is sorely lacking in relation to psychiatric diagnoses. For example, it was clear from my (Bozarth, 1999) personal observations in the 1950s and my personal studies in the 1960s that a particular diagnosis or even psychological description was more related to the diagnostician or author of the descriptive reports than to the characteristics of the 'patients'. It became common knowledge among psychiatric hospital personnel that the diagnosis of 'schizophrenia' in the 1950s was a catch-all for those who did not fit other diagnostic categories.

Boyle (1990) presents a compendium of arguments that schizophrenia is a 'scientific delusion'. Boyle (1999) states that '. . . there is no evidence whatsoever that the original introduction of the concept of schizophrenia was accompanied by the observation of a meaningful relationship amongst the many behaviors and experiences from which the concept was inferred' (p. 80). Statistical studies of groups diagnosed as schizophrenic show no evidence of the symptoms clustering together in a meaningful way (Bentall, 1990; Slade and Cooper, 1979). Similar lack of evidence of other diagnostic concepts has been found in studies of depression (Hallett, 1990; Wiener, 1989); panic disorder (Hallam, 1989); agoraphobia (Hallam, 1983); borderline personality disorder (Kutchins and Kirk, 1997); self-defeating or masochistic personality disorder (Caplan and Gans, 1991). Boyle (1999) presents an extensive discussion of these critical points; i.e., the previous 'discovery' of patterns by researchers and the existence of underlying processes, which she contends has been seriously questioned in relation to psychiatric diagnoses. Boyle concludes that:

> The assumptions behind psychiatric classification are extremely problematic, which is hardly surprising as they were developed by medicine to suit bodily processes not people's behaviour and experience. Non-diagnostic approaches demand a very different set of assumptions, which in turn demand a different set of social and therapeutic responses. (p. 88)

These problematic assumptions are the basis of the current mental health treatment system. The problems with these assumptions are virtually ignored in the development of the diagnostic manuals. Rather, the attention is directed to the benefits of the manual for the purpose of providing '. . . clear descriptions of diagnostic categories . . .' (American Psychiatric Association, p. xxvii). Further, these diagnostic categories are to enable investigators '. . . to diagnose, communicate about, study, and treat people with various mental disorders' (p. xxvii). This is about it! There is a noticeable absence of designated treatment for diagnoses. When we come to the basic purpose of diagnosis; that is, determination of the most appropriate treatment for a particular dysfunction, there is a notorious lack of recommendations in the diagnostic manuals. Why is this? Is it that the coalitions of therapeutic approaches could not agree upon uniform treatment for any particular diagnosis? Is it that the social zeitgeist is much of the determinant of psychiatric diagnoses? Is it that the adherence of the model to find specificity simply ignores findings which are not compatible with the method? Caplan (1995) and Kutchins and Kirk (1997) document the deceptive political process of the development of the DSM among others. Is the system creating new mental illnesses within the facade that such illnesses are being scientifically discovered? The classic example of the influence of societal views on the development of diagnosis was the diagnosis of homosexuality in the earlier diagnostic manuals. Homosexuality was once a diagnostic category that required treatment for deviant pathology. 'Gay and Lesbian Issues' is now a division of the American Psychological Association.

> In fact, the lack of scientific evidence, so badly ignored by the adherents, gave way to the pressure of political groups. (However, the diagnosis of homosexuality was actually kept; first, referring to 'ego dystonic homosexuality', and finally in the DSM-IV providing the catch-all sexual deviancies with the diagnoses of 'Sexual dysfunction not otherwise specified' and 'Paraphernalias not otherwise specified'.) A notable gay physician, Howard Brown, aptly commented upon the DSM Board vote deleting homosexuality as a diagnosis. He stated, 'The board vote made millions of Americans who had officially been ill that morning officially well that afternoon. Never before in history had so many people been cured in so little time.' (Cited in Minton, 2002, p. 261)

Simply removing the diagnostic category from the manual is a remarkably efficient way to eliminate pathology.

PATTERN OF PSYCHOTHERAPY OUTCOME RESEARCH

A subtle twist of scientific method research in psychotherapy outcome studies is the shift towards specificity research. The drive for more rigor, more precision and more focus on specific operational variables has resulted in failure to build on the outcome findings of the last four decades. This is reflected in the reviews reported later. However, the study of patterns of psychotherapy efficacy research by Stubbs and Bozarth (1994) depicts a sobering picture. The pattern suggests the pervasive bias of specificity guiding the unsubstantiated direction of psychotherapy outcome research.

In the article dubbed, 'The Dodo Bird revisited: A qualitative study of psychotherapy research', five temporal categories characterized the evolution of psychotherapy outcome research. The title was adopted from Luborsky, Singer and Luborsky's (1975) review of comparative studies of psychotherapy. Luborsky et al. concluded that the effectiveness of all therapies was equivalent. They used the Dodo Bird metaphor from 'Alice in Wonderland' where there was a race to help the animals dry off after they had become wet with Alice's tears. The animals ran in different directions, and finally the race was just stopped. The Dodo bird was asked, 'Who has won?' He finally exclaimed, 'Everybody has won, and all must have prizes.' Luborsky et al. (1975) used this statement to convey the idea that all therapies are equally effective. The 'Dodo Bird' article suggests that common factors are likely to be the source of this equivalence. The categorical themes discovered by Stubbs and Bozarth were the following:

Category 1: *Psychotherapy is no more effective than no psychotherapy (1950s and 1960s) (Eysenck, 1952; 1966).*

Eysenck's hypothesis that psychotherapy is no more effective than no psychotherapy stimulated considerable reaction and criticism (Bergin, 1971). Somewhat unheralded and unrealized, the research on Rogers' (1957) hypothesis of the necessary and sufficient conditions became an important part of the responses to Eysenck. This is elaborated upon in Category 3. Re-analyses of Eysenck's data in addition to other findings refuted Eysenck's contention. Psychotherapy was generally found to be effective. Later studies using meta-analysis confirmed the general effectiveness of psychotherapy.

Category 2: *The 'core conditions' (empathic understanding, unconditional positive regard and congruence) are necessary and sufficient for therapeutic personality change (1960s and 1970s).*

This category revealed that a large number of studies were directly related to Rogers' hypothesis of the 'conditions therapy theory' (Barrett-Lennard, 1998) or 'integration statement' (Bozarth, 1998, pp. 103–10). Rogers' hypothesis was consistently supported (Lambert, DeJulio and Stein, 1978; Truax and Mitchell, 1971) and continued to be supported through the latter 1970s and 1980s (e.g. Orlinsky and Howard, 1986; Patterson, 1984) in the face of more equivocal reviews to be noted next. Truax and Mitchell (1971) presented fourteen studies (eight of which were individual therapy) consisting of 992 subjects. They identified 125 specific outcome measures favoring the hypothesis (66 of 158 were statistically significant). They report an analysis of the long-term effects of higher and lower levels of empathy, warmth and genuineness experienced by chronic hospitalized clients in the Wisconsin Project (Truax and Mitchell, 1971, p. 329). Their data examined over nine years indicates that patients seen by therapists low on the common conditions tended to not get out of the hospital, and those who were released tended to return.

Lambert, Shapiro and Bergin (1986) conclude in their review of the outcome research that the attitudinal qualities: 'seem to make up a significant portion of the effective ingredients of psychotherapy' (p. 202). Likewise, Orlinsky and Howard (1986) concluded that: 'generally, 50 to 80 per cent of the substantial number of studies in this area were significantly positive, indicating that these dimensions were very consistently related to patient outcome' (p. 365).

A series of studies in Germany orchestrated by Reinhard Tausch and colleagues (1990), as well as other studies in Europe, provide additional strong support for Rogers' (1957) hypothesis of the necessary and sufficient conditions for therapeutic personality change (see Bozarth, Zimring and Tausch, 2002).

There were also studies that investigated the conditions as secondary variables that support this theme. For example, the effects of focused versus broad-spectrum behavioral therapy with problem drinkers in an effort to control their alcohol consumption was studied by Miller, Taylor and West (1980). They collected data on therapist empathy as a secondary inquiry and found that the level of therapist empathy was highly correlated ($r = .82$) with outcome.

The National Institute of Mental Health (NIMH) survey which was conducted to compare various treatments for depression (Blatt, Zuroff, Quinlan and Pilkonis, 1996) reported another example of the importance of relationship variables in the study. They compared the effects of the administration of a drug (imipramine), cognitive behavioral therapy, interpersonal therapy and 'ward management' which served as a placebo. The placebo effect involved a therapist who spent time talking to patients about ward management. There were no significant differences between the effects of the three active treatments. The best prediction of success at the end of any of the active treatments was whether the patient perceived the therapist as empathic at the end of the second interview. Even drug treatment was significantly more successful if the patient viewed the therapist as empathic after the second interview.

Category 3: *Psychotherapy is for better or for worse (early 1960s).*

Therapists who were higher on the conditions were found to have clients related to positive outcome, while therapists lower on the conditions have more clients related to deterioration. As mentioned above, this was a strong argument against Eysenck's assertions that no psychotherapy was as effective as psychotherapy.

Several reviewers pointed to the adverse effects of some therapists. Truax and Carkhuff (1967) concluded that psychotherapy was 'for better or for worse' (p 143). The review by Truax and Mitchell (1971) included a call for attrition in the ranks of 'psychonoxious practitioners' while increasing the number of helpful counselors (p. 301). The deleterious effects of some therapists were highlighted.

Based upon a separate research review, Bergin (1971) concluded that the previous four decades of the practice of psychotherapy has had an effect that is modestly positive, adding: 'However, the averaged group data on which this conclusion is based obscure the multiplicity of processes occurring in therapy, some of which are now known to be either unproductive or actually harmful' (p. 263).

Lambert, Shapiro and Bergin (1986) also found evidence to support the position that psychotherapy is for better or for worse; indicating that some therapists are detrimental as reflected in outcome data.

It is interesting that research on this rather dire finding, which suggests that therapists low on the attitudinal conditions were detrimental to their clients, virtually disappeared with the advent of the thrust for 'specificity' studies in the 1980s and 1990s.

Category 4: *The core conditions are necessary but NOT sufficient for therapeutic personality change (late 1970s and early 1980s).*

Several of the reviews during the middle 1970s through the 1980s offered equivocal conclusions for Rogers' hypothesis of the necessary and sufficient conditions. Change in the direction of research began in the middle 1970s, paralleling these equivocal reviews. Several reviews critiqued the research designs suggesting that: (1) 'more complex relationships exist among therapists, patients and techniques' (Parloff, Waskow and Wolf, 1978, p. 273); and that (2) the conditions have not been adequately investigated (Bozarth, 1983; Mitchell, Bozarth and Krauft, 1977; Watson, 1984). Issues that needed resolution were cited by Beutler, Crago and Arismendi (1986) in their recommendation for finding 'an acceptance of an optimal level of therapeutic skill, common methods of measurement, and the creation and control of levels of the facilitative skills' (p. 276).

Opinions rather than design critique included the view that the core conditions were 'nonspecific' and similar to placebo effect (Luborsky, Singer and Luborsky, 1975; Shapiro, 1971); and that 'the conditions are neither necessary nor sufficient although it seems clear that such conditions are facilitative' (Gelso and Carter, 1985, p. 220).

The data-based equivocal reviews pointed to the need for more extensive examination of the complex phenomena of Rogers' postulates and called for more rigorous methodological investigation.

There was virtually *no* support for the category of the conditions being necessary but *not* sufficient. There was not one study that supported the assertion that the conditions are not sufficient. Nevertheless, the assertion of these reviews did affect (or perhaps served as a rationalization for) the direction of research. The research shifted from examining the attitudinal conditions to investigating 'specificity'. This shift was clearly *not* predicated upon previous research results.

Category 5: *There are specific techniques that are uniquely effective in treating particular disorders (late 1980s and 1990s).*

The search for the effectiveness of techniques and for specificity virtually extinguished published studies on the Rogerian hypothesis of the necessary and sufficient conditions. On the face of it, studies in client-centered therapy and the conditions therapy theory were no longer viable inquiries in the United States.

After the middle 1980s, the Rogerian (1997) hypothesis was investigated by only a dozen outcome studies which emphasized therapists' empathy (Sexton and Whiston, 1994). These studies were all positive. They included a study of therapist variables that found that emotional adjustment, relationship attitudes and empathy were most predictive of effective therapists (Lafferty, Beutler and Crago, 1989). Positive therapy outcome in several studies was linked to such constructs as 'understanding and involvement' (Gaston and Marmar, 1994), 'warmth and friendliness' (Gomes-Schwartz, 1978), and similar constructs (Bachelor, 1991; Gaston 1991; Windholtz and Silberschatz, 1988). Empathy was strongly related to improvement for depressed clients who were being treated by cognitive-behavioral therapy (Burns and Nolen-Hoeksema, 1992). Despite the many positive findings, the few equivocal reviews of the research on the attitudinal conditions were used to buttress the rationale for research on 'specificity' of treatment. The focus on 'specificity' research replaced inquiry on Rogers' hypotheses and on common factors in general.

CONCLUSIONS OF PSYCHOTHERAPY OUTCOME RESEARCH

Stubbs and Bozarth (1994) concluded that: 'Over four decades, the major thread in psychotherapy efficacy research is the presence of the therapist attitudes hypothesized by Rogers' (p. 120). Concomitant to their conclusion of psychotherapy outcome research, Duncan and Moynihan (1994) independently analyzed psychotherapy outcome research. Their report titled, 'Intentional utilization of the client's frame of reference' reviewed outcome research to develop a treatment model. They conclude that the major operational variable was that of intentionally utilizing the client's frame of reference. This article was associated with an explosion of psychological literature that identifies the common factors of relationship and client resources as the basis for most psychological improvement (Asay and Lambert, 1999; Duncan, Hubble and Miller, 1997; Hubble, Duncan and Miller, 1999; Lambert, 1992; Miller, Duncan and Hubble, 1997).

From 1987 to 1999, the investigations of specificity research have ironically returned full cycle to the pervasive influence of the common factors. That is, the reviews of outcome research by various reviewers reveal that: (1) Effective psychotherapy is predicated upon the relationship of the therapist and client in combination with the inner and external resources of the client (common factors) (Hubble, Duncan and Miller, 1999); (2) Type of therapy and technique add little to the effect of the relationship and client resources if not accompanied by common factors (Hubble et al., 1999); and (3) Relationship variables that are most often related to effectiveness are the conditions of empathy, genuineness and unconditional positive regard (Bozarth, 1999; Stubbs and Bozarth, 1994). Current reviews now substantiate Patterson's (1984) penetrating analysis of the reviews of research on Rogers' postulate of the necessary and sufficient conditions.

The clear message of five decades of outcome research is that it is the relationship of the client and therapist in combination with the resources of the client (extratherapeutic variables) that, respectively, account for 30% and 40% of the variance in successful psychotherapy. Techniques account for 15% of the success variance, comparable to 15% success rate related to placebo effect.

INTRINSIC FLAWS OF EMPIRICALLY SUPPORTED TREATMENTS

The current efforts in the United States and Europe to involve endorsement of specific psychotherapies by accrediting bodies are predicated upon the specificity myth. Those treatments to be approved are those which are 'empirically supported'. It is important to remember that the EST syndrome (previously referred to as the Empirically Validated Treatment or EVT by the Task Force of Division 12, Clinical Psychology, of the American Psychological Association) is founded upon the assumption that there are specific treatments for particular dysfunction (Task Force on Promotion and Dissemination of Psychological Procedures, 1995). The task force, in fact, is determined to find such treatments.

The advocates have already assumed the veracity of their claim. Their task now is to convince others; especially those who are in positions to influence policies, of the veracity of their belief. The postulate of specificity is accelerated through the use of manuals that delineate specific procedures.

Advocates of EST argue that their assumption is supported by 'efficacious' empirical research. The arguments for EST are primarily seven points. These points are that: (1) much is already known about the effectiveness of specific treatments with specific dysfunction; (2) patient care will be improved; (3) the research will influence policymakers; (4) better training will be fostered; (5) therapy research will be encouraged; (6) it will be more fair because of the professionals who have been consulted in developing the criteria; and (7) the project is intended to encourage guidelines and lists for effective treatments that can be useful to the field. It can be noted that, like the arguments for diagnosis, six of the assertions are based upon the assumption that their first argument is true. The assertion that 'much is already known' is followed by the six assertions that have to do with influence, strategies and factors other than the validity of the EST stance. The only substantial argument is whether or not there are effective treatments for particular dysfunction. The bold assertion is affirmative according to advocates (Barlow, 1996; Chambless, 1996). The Institute for the Study of Therapeutic Change (www.talkingcure.com, 2000) succinctly responds to this assertion about EVT (Since designated as EST):

> Unfortunately, they (the members of the Task Force) are dead wrong when they link therapeutic effectiveness to so-called empirically validated treatments (EVTs). In drawing their conclusions, members of the Task Force of Division 12 have ignored the conclusion of nearly 40 years of sophisticated outcome research. (See Psychotherapy (1997, *33*(2)); and American Psychologist (1996, *51*(10))

With such a difference in views, it behooves us to look a bit further at the assumptions and developmental process of EST.

The words 'efficacy' and 'effectiveness' were interchangeable until recent years. The dictionary definitions are synonymous. Recently, the term 'efficacious' has come to identify the results of 'gold standard' studies (Seligman, 1995). These are studies that have been traditionally identified as true design studies; that is, studies which are randomized, double-blind and have an adequate number of subjects as well as adequate controls for therapists. Appropriate replications of such studies are also required. The rationale for 'efficaciousness' is that causation can be more accurately determined with this type of study. Efficacious studies are actually rare in the bulk of research in psychotherapy outcome. EST (EVT at the time) initially intended to identify the most effective treatments through 'efficacious studies'. This point is quite often confused, to suggest that there are 'efficacious' treatments that are more potent than 'effective' treatments. The reality is that certain treatments are considered more effective because they are considered to meet the criteria of 'efficacious' designs in contrast to the less rigorous 'non-gold standard' designs. However, the premise of efficacious designs turns out to be questionable in the machinations of the EST syndrome. The following conclusions attend to major flaws of the assumption and process of EST:

Conclusion 1: *There is considerable variation of the design criteria from the assumption of 'Gold Standard' studies as implied by the advocates. The quality of the designs is no more rigorous than many of those representing the previous five decades of research.*

It turns out that the 'efficacious' or 'gold standard' studies identified by the APA task force are not quite as efficacious as implied. The Task Force, in one publication, identified 36 studies of 'Empirically Validated Treatments and another 32 studies of 'Probably Efficacious Treatments' (Chambless et al., 1996). The general criteria for acceptance as efficacious studies include case study design experiments with N's greater than 9. These experiments are part of the 36 recommended studies. The task force guidelines for the criteria of EST now define their 'Well Established Treatments' in less than rigorous terminology. (Task Force on promotion and dissemination of psychological procedures, 1995). Rather than referring to true design studies, they refer to the need for 'At least two *good* (authors' emphasis) group design studies . . .' Such loose terminology is symbolic of the deviation from the original intention to utilize 'efficacious' studies as the criterion. The criteria for efficacious designs have been severely altered.

A thorough critique of the empirically validated treatment studies is presented in the journal of Psychotherapy Research (Bohart, O'Hara and Leitner, 1998).

Conclusion 2: *Five decades of research have been disregarded because those studies are not viewed as appropriately measuring the specific behaviors of the therapist, or else because they do not fit the clusters of client dysfunction which have been 'reliably' agreed upon (but not validly determined) by those who recommend the categories for the DSM-IV.*

It is somewhat baffling how the task force conclusions could be reached after examining psychotherapy outcome research over the past five decades. It turns out that the five decades of research have been summarily disregarded for somewhat obscure reasons. The dismissal is, according to Garfield (1996), that there are now instruments (i.e., training manuals) that identify more specific behaviors and standardize the therapy; and to the idea that there are reliable diagnoses (via the DSM-IV) to which treatment can be directed. As noted previously, it is interesting that neither the DSM-III-R nor DSM-IV actually recommend treatments for the supposedly 'reliable' diagnoses of the DSM-IV.

A specific example of dismissal of research findings is the renowned Smith et al. (1980) analysis of 475 studies which concludes that psychotherapy of all kinds is generally more effective than no treatment. The study is disregarded primarily on the basis that it pre-dates the Beck et al. Manual and DSM-III (Garfield, 1996). The faux pas of dismissing the 1980 analysis has been raised anew by a meta-analysis in the November, 1997 issue of the Psychological Bulletin (Wampold et al.) which reconfirms the Smith et al. study. Elliott (1997) also reconfirms these findings in his meta-analysis of outcome research. Nevertheless, these recent studies are not acceptable to EST advocates because they do not meet the criteria of the 'gold standard', a criterion that applies to all studies except those used to support the EVT position.

Conclusion 3: *The findings of five decades of psychotherapy outcome research have discovered that the client-driven/client-resources paradigm accounts for the major success variance for clients.*

The most cogent conclusions of this research are:
• That the type of therapy and technique is largely irrelevant in terms of successful outcome;
• That there is little evidence to support the position that there are specific treatments for particular disabilities; and
• That the influence of treatment models pales in comparison to the personal qualities of the individual therapist. (Luborsky et al., 1986).

The most clear research evidence is that effective psychotherapy results from the resources of the client and chance factors related to the client (extratherapeutic variables) and from the person-to-person relationship of the therapist and client. As previously mentioned, Duncan and Moynihan (1994) cite reviews of quantitative research (e.g. Lambert, 1992; Lambert, Shapiro and Bergin, 1986) that offer data to develop a model for clinical practice. It bears repeating that these reviews conclude that 30% of the outcome success variance is accounted for by the common factor of the client-counselor relationship, and 40% of the variance is accounted for by extratherapeutic change variables (factors unique to the client and her/his environment). That is, 70% of the successful therapy is accounted for by therapist and client variables. Techniques account for only 15% of the success variance and that is similar to the 15% accounted for by placebo effect. Such research findings suggest the viability of intentionally utilizing the client's frame of reference, 'courting' the client, and going with the client's direction in therapy.

Conclusion 4: *The precise functional practice of specific treatments for a particular dysfunction is questionable.*

How does the concept of EST relate to efficacious treatment? Here is one response: The question is: what do you mean by efficacious treatment? The client comes for a panic attack: maybe they have some other things to say; maybe you tell them something of what you know about managing anxiety or whatever; but do you inhibit their talking about related or non-related topics?

Right now I have a woman who has panic after a traffic accident. It turns out that her sister who was the closest person to her died suddenly a few years earlier. She went to the hospital for a 'simple but delicate procedure . . .', her leg had to be cut off and three weeks later she was dead. My client was broken hearted and in shock. This was her primary focus in the session. Now what do I do? Do I treat her for the panic attack from the road accident, which is the reason for the referral? Or listen to her more pressing concerns as she talks about the rest of it? Do I stop her from talking about what she expresses as her more basic difficulty?

How can it be so simple? . . . what is the definition of efficacious? What is withholding treatment? How do you know what the problem is, anyway, even if you're intent on fixing it; if you close off the avenue of talking about it before you begin? The doctor hadn't even heard about the sister . . . that is how efficacious he is . . .

This is just one of maybe five panic attack cases I have right now . . . all with tails that wag the dog. (Source unknown)

The efficacy of treatment becomes a bit confounded in the real world.

The myth of EST is further compromised in the violation of the fundamental premise. The primary premise is that there are certain procedures that will ameliorate or diminish a particular dysfunction. It is so certain that this is the case that the procedures are identified via treatment manuals. In fact, EST is not even possible without a treatment manual. This might be considered to be pretty good, because what it means is that anyone who is reasonably intelligent can follow the procedures and the result will be positive. In the 1960s, we did this with behavior modification procedures that were integrated into hospitals and schools for the mentally retarded and mentally ill. Ward attendants, many with less than high-school education, could follow these procedures with reported successful results as long as the procedures were followed. Many of these procedures are still in the institutions in spite of serious questions about the validity of the results. But, if it works as asserted, let's do it. However, somehow we find that it requires a doctoral-level psychologist to apply the technical manual. Why is this? If the procedure is, in fact, the point of the whole thing, then why do we need the clinical psychologist as a treatment phenomenon? If the premise of specificity (that there are particular treatments for particular dysfunction) is correct, the specific treatment is the thing. But now we have an intervening variable present. That is, we need a licensed clinician in case there are clinical judgments that the procedure is not working. This means that we must be ready to change the procedure at any given moment if the treatment is not working. The procedure, which is the thing, must be open to be tailor-made to the particular client. The fact that five decades of psychotherapy outcome research has been ignored in the search for specificity as highlighted by the EST proposals is further compounded by the murkiness of 'good' research designs which support procedures that cannot be trusted without the murkiness of licensed clinical judgment.

SUMMARY

An examination of the questionable credibility of diagnosis, the pattern of psychotherapy outcome research, the conclusion of five decades of psychotherapy outcome research, and the intrinsic flaws in the reported evidence for Empirically Supported Treatments suggest a radical conclusion. This conclusion is that the foundation of the mental health system in the United States is predicated upon a myth; that is, the myth that there are specific treatments for particular dysfunction. This myth is exemplified and perpetuated by the EST syndrome, that ignores psychotherapy outcome research. The solution for this misguided direction calls for a radical restructuring of the mental health system to accentuate the demonstrated therapeutic variables related to success. These are the common factor variables of therapist/ client relationship and emphasis of client resources and the client's frame of reference.

REFERENCES

American Psychiatric Association. (1994). DSM-IV. Washington, DC: American Psychiatric Association.

Asay, T. P. and Lambert, M. J. (1999). The empirical case for the common factors in therapy: Qualitative findings. In M. A. Hubble, B. L. Duncan and S. D. Miller (Eds.) *The Heart and Soul of Change: What works in therapy*. Washington, DC: APA, pp. 23–55.

American Psychological Association Task Force on Psychological Intervention guidelines. (1995, February). *Template for Developing Guidelines: Interventions for Mental Disorders and Psychosocial Aspects of Physical Disorders*. Washington, DC: American Psychological Association.

Bachelor, A. (1991). Comparison and relationship to outcome of diverse dimensions of the helping alliance as seen by client and therapist. *Psychotherapy: Theory, Research and Practice, 28,* 534–49.

Barlow, D. H. (1996). The effectiveness of psychotherapy: Science and policy. *Clinical Psychology: Science and Practice, 3,* 236–40.

Bentall, R. P. (1990). The syndromes and symptoms of psychosis. In R. P. Bentall (Ed.) *Reconstructing Schizophrenia*. London: Routledge.

Barrett-Lennard, G. T. (1998). *Carl Rogers' Helping System: Journey and substance*. London: Sage.

Bergin, A. E. (1971). The evaluation of therapeutic outcomes. In A. E. Bergin and S. L. Garfield (Eds.) *Handbook of Psychotherapy and Behavior Change*. New York: Wiley, pp. 217–70.

Beutler, L. E., Crago, M. and Arismendi, T. G. (1986). Research on therapist variables in psychotherapy. In S. L. Garfield and A. E. Bergin (Eds.) *Handbook of Psychotherapy and Behavior Change* (3rd edn.) New York: Wiley, pp. 257–310.

Blatt, S. J., Zuroff, D. C., Quinlan, D. M. and Pilkonis, P. A. (1996). Interpersonal factors in brief treatment of depression: Further analyses of the National Institute of Mental Health treatment of depression collaborative research program. *Journal of Consulting and Clinical Psychology, 64,* 162–71.

Bohart, A. C., O'Hara, M. and Leitner, L. M. (1998). Empirically violated treatments: Disenfranchisement of humanistic and other psychotherapies. *Psychotherapy Research, 8,* 141–17.

Boyle, M. (1990). Schizophrenia: A scientific delusion? London: Routledge.

Boyle, M. (1999). Diagnosis. In C. Newnes, G. Holmes and C. Dunn, (Eds.) *This is Madness*. Ross-on-Wye: PCCS Books, pp. 75–90.

Bozarth, J. D. (1983). Current research on client-centered therapy in the USA. In M. Wolf-Rudiger and H. Wolfgang (Eds.) *Research on Psychotherapeutic Approaches: Proceedings of the 1st European Conference on Psychotherapy Research*. Trier, Germany: Peter Lang, pp. 105–15.

Bozarth, J. D. (1999). *Person-Centered Therapy: A revolutionary paradigm*. Ross-on-Wye: PCCS Books.

Bozarth, J. D., Zimring, F and Tausch, R. (2002). Client-Centered Therapy: Evolution of a revolution. In D. Cain and J. Seeman (Eds.) *Handbook of Research and Practice in Humanistic Psychotherapies*. Washington DC: America Psychological Association.

Burns, D. D. and Nolen-Hoeksema, S. (1992). Therapy empathy and recovery from depression in cognitive behavioral therapy: A structural equation model. *Journal of Consulting and Clinical Psychology, 60,* 441–9.

Caplan, P. J. (1995). *They Say You're Crazy: How the world's most powerful psychiatrists decide who's normal*. Reading, Mass.: Perseus Books.

Caplan, P. and Gans, M. (1991). Is there empirical justification for the category of Self-defeating Personality Disorder? *Feminism and Psychology 1*, 263–78.

Chambless, D. L. (1996). In defense of dissemination of empirically supported psychological interventions. *Clinical Psychology: Science and Practice, 3*, 230–35.

Chambless, D. L., Sanderson, W. C., Shoham, V., Johnson, S. B., Pope, K. S., Crits-Christoph, P., Baker, M., Johnson, B., Woody, S. R., Sue, S. Beutler, L., Williams, D. A. and McCurry, S. (1996). An update on empirically validated therapies. *The Clinical Psychologist, 49*, 5–18.

Duncan, B. L., Hubble, M. A. and Miller, S. D. (1997). *Psychotherapy with 'Impossible' Cases: The efficient treatment of therapy veterans*. New York: Norton.

Duncan, B. L. and Moynihan, D. (1994). Applying outcome research: Intentional utilization of the client's frame of reference. *Psychotherapy, 31*, 294–301.

Elliott, R. (1997). Are client-centered/experiential therapies effective? A meta-analysis of outcome research. In U. Esser, H. Pabst and G. W. Speierer (Eds.), *The Power of the Person-Centered Approach*. Kln, Germany: GwG Verlag, pp. 125–38..

Eysenck, H. J. (1952). The effects of psychotherapy: An evaluation. *Journal of Consulting Psychology, 16*, 319–24.

Eysenck, H. J. (1966). *The Effects of Psychotherapy*. New York: International Science Press.

Garfield, S. L. (1996). Some problems associated with 'validated' forms of psychotherapy. *Clinical Psychology: Science and practice, 3*, 218–29.

Garfield, S. L. and Bergin, A. E. (Eds.) (1986). *Handbook of Psychotherapy and Behavior Change* (4th edn.) New York: Wiley, pp. 190–228.

Gaston, L. (1991). The reliability and criterion-related validity of the patient version of the California Psychotherapy Alliance Scale. *Journal of Consulting and Clinical Psychology, 3*, 68–74.

Gaston, L. and Marmar, C. (1994). The California Psychotherapy Alliance Scales. In O. Horvath and L. S. Greenberg (Eds.), *The Working Alliance: Theory, research and practice*. New York: Wiley, pp. 85–108.

Gelso, C. J. and Carter, J. A. (1985). The relationship in counseling and psychotherapy: Components, consequences and theoretical antecedents. *The Counseling Psychologist, 13*, 155–433.

Gomes-Schwartz, B. (1978). Effective ingredients in psychotherapy: Prediction of outcome from process variables. *Journal of Consulting and Clinical Psychology, 46*, 196–97.

Hallam, R. S. (1983). Agoraphobia: Deconstructing a clinical syndrome. *Bulletin of the British Psychological Society 36*, 337–40.

Hallam, R. S. (1989). Classification and research into panic. In R. Baker and M. McFadyen (Eds.) *Panic Disorder*. Chichester, UK: Wiley.

Hallett, R. (1990). Melancholia and depression. A brief history and analysis of contemporary confusions. Unpublished Masters Thesis, University of East London, UK.

Hubble, M. A., Duncan, B. L. and Miller, S. D. (1999). *The Heart and Soul of Change: What works in therapy*. Washington DC: American Psychological Association.

Kuhn, T. (1962). The structure of scientific revolutions. Chicago: Chicago University Press.

Kutchins, H. and Kirk, S. (1997). *Making us crazy: DSM: The psychiatric Bible and the creation of mental disorders*. New York: The Free Press/Simon Schuster.

Lafferty, P., Beutler, L. E. and Crago, M. (1989). Differences between more and less effective psychotherapists: A study of select therapist variables. *Journal of Consulting and Clinical Psychology, 57*, 76–80.

Lambert, M. J. (1992). Psychotherapy outcome research. In J. C. Norcross and M. R. Goldfreid (Eds.) *Handbook of Psychotherapy Integration*. New York: Basic Books, pp. 94–129.

Lambert, M. J., DeJulio, S. J. and Stein, D. M. (1978). Therapist interpersonal skills: Process, outcome, methodological considerations and recommendations for future research. *Psychological Bulletin,*

85, 467–89.

Lambert, M. J., Shapiro, D. A. and Bergin, A. E. (1986). The effectiveness of psychotherapy. In S. L. Garfield and A. E. Bergin (Eds.), *Handbook of Psychotherapy and Behavior Change*, 3rd edn. New York: Wiley, pp. 157–212.

Luborsky, L., Crits-Cristoph, P., McLellan, T., Woody, G., Piper, W., Liberman, B., Imber, S. and Pilkonis, P. (1986). Do therapists vary very much in their success? Findings from four outcome studies. *American Journal of Orthopsychiatry. 56*, 501–611.

Luborsky, L., Singer, B. and Luborsky, L. (1975). Comparative studies of psychotherapies: Is it true that 'everyone has won and all must have prizes' ? *Archives of General Psychiatry, 32*, 995–1008.

Miller, S. D., Duncan, B. L. and Hubble, M. A. (1997). *Escape from Babel: Toward a unifying language for psychotherapy practice.* New York: Norton.

Miller, S. D., Taylor, C. A. and West, J. C. (1980). Focused versus broad-spectrum behavior therapy for problem drinkers. *Journal of Consulting and Clinical Psychology, 48*, 590–601.

Minton, H. L. (2002). *Departing from Deviance.* Chicago: University of Chicago Press.

Mitchell, K. M., Bozarth, J. D. and Krauft, C. C. (1977). A reappraisal of the therapeutic effectiveness of accurate empathy, non-possessive warmth and genuineness. In A. S. Gurman and A. M. Razin (Eds.), *Effective Psychotherapy: A handbook of research. New* York: Pergamon, pp. 482–502.

O'Hara, M. (1993). Association for humanistic psychology: Ethics project. AHP Ethics Study Group Paper. Headquarters of AHP.

Orlinsky, D. E. and Howard, K. J. (1986). Process and outcome in psychotherapy. In S. L. Garfield and A. E. Bergin (Eds.) *Handbook of Psychotherapy and Behavior Change*, 3rd edn. New York: Wiley, pp. 311–81.

Parloff, M. B. Waskow, I. E. and Wolfe, B. E., (1978). Research on therapist variables in relation to process and outcome. In S. L. Garfield and A. E. Bergin (Eds.) *Handbook of Psychotherapy and Behavior Change An Empirical Analysis.* 2nd edn. New York: Wiley, pp. 233–82.

Patterson, C. H. (1984). Empathy, warmth and genuineness in psychotherapy: A review of reviews. P*sychotherapy, 21*(4), 431–8.

Rogers, C. R. (1957). The necessary and sufficient conditions of therapeutic personality change. *Journal of Consulting Psychology, 21*(2), 95–103.

Sexton, T. L. and Whiston, S. C. (1994). The status of the counseling relationship: An empirical review: Theoretical implications and research directions. *The Counseling Psychologist, 22*(1), 6–78.

Slade, P. D. and Cooper, R. (1979). Some difficulties with the term 'schizophrenia': An alternative model. *British Journal of Social and Clinical Psychology, 18*, 309–17.

Seligman, M. E. P. (1995). The effectiveness of psychotherapy. The *Consumer Reports* study. *American Psychologist, 50*, 965–74.

Shapiro, A. K. (1971). Placebo effects in medicine, psychotherapy and psychoanalysis. In A. E. Bergin and S. C. Garfield (Eds.) *Handbook of Psychotherapy and Behavior Change: Empirical analysis.* New York: Wiley, pp. 437–73.

Smith, M. L., Glass, G. U. and Miller, T. J. (1980). *The Benefits of Psychotherapy.* Baltimore: John Hopkins University.

Stubbs, J. P. and Bozarth, J. D. (1994). The dodo bird revisited: A qualitative study of psychotherapy efficacy research. *Journal of Applied and Preventive Psychology, 3*(2), 109–20.

Task Force on Promotion and Dissemination of Psychological Procedures. (1995). Training in and dissemination of empirically validated psychological treatments: Report and recommendations. *The Clinical Psychologist, 48*, 3–23.

Tausch, R. and Tausch, A. M. (1990). *Gesprechspsychotherapy.* (9th edn). Guttingen: Hogrefe.

Truax, C. B. and Carkhuff, R. R. (1967). *Toward Effective Counseling and Psychotherapy: Training and practice.* Chicago: Aldine.

Truax, C. B. and Mitchell, K. M. (1971). Research on certain therapist interpersonal skills in relation to process and outcome. In A. E. Bergin and S. L. Garfield (Eds.) *Handbook of Psychotherapy and Behavior Change.* New York: Wiley, pp. 299–344.

Wampold, B. E. (1997). Methodological problems in identifying efficacious psychotherapies. *Psychotherapy Research, 7*, 21–43.

Watson, N. (1984). The empirical status of Rogers' hypothesis of the necessary and sufficient conditions for effective psychotherapy. In R. F. Levant and J. M. Shlien (Eds.), *Client-Centered Therapy and the Person-Centered Approach: New directions in theory, research and practice.* New York: Praeger, pp. 17–40.

Weiner, M. (1989). Psychopathology reconsidered: Depression interpreted as psychosocial interactions. *Clinical Psychology Review, 9*, 295–321.

Windholtz, J. J. and Silbershatz, G. (1988). Vanderbilt psychotherapy process scale: A replication with adult outpatients. *Journal of Consulting and Clinical Psychology, 37*, 369–76.

Barbara Temaner Brodley PhD

Illinois School of Professional Psychology;   Chicago Counseling and Psychotherapy Center

Observations of Empathic Understanding in Two Client-Centered Therapists[1]

INTRODUCTION

This paper reports a study of empathic responses in twenty-two client-centered (CC) therapy sessions conducted by Carl Rogers and in twenty sessions by the writer. The basic question addressed by the study is 'what specifically does empathic understanding, in CC therapy, appear to be understanding?' The study addresses this question by examining responses made by Rogers — the creator and a master of the approach — and by the writer who has had long experience as a CC therapist. The specific aim of the study was to identify certain elements in the therapists' empathic responses on the basis of theory about empathic understanding, to determine the frequency of the elements, and compare the empathic responses of the two therapists. The paper presents my view of empathic understanding in CC work and some of Rogers' elucidating views about it. I shall describe the study and its findings, and discuss the observations in the context of Zimring's (2000) theory of the *targets* of empathic understanding in CC therapy.

ACCEPTANT EMPATHIC UNDERSTANDING

As a nondirective, client-centered therapist, a*cceptant empathic understanding* (AEU) is my fundamental attitude in relation to clients. My immediate and constant goal in therapeutic interactions with clients is to experience and maintain this complex *attitude*. Logically, to have a therapeutic effect, I must behave such that the attitude is communicated to the client. According to Rogers' (1957; 1959) theory of therapy, the client must perceive or experience the therapist's AEU in order to experience therapeutic benefits from the relationship. Therefore, with most clients, the therapist must deliberately communicate AEU. Empathic responses are primarily *explicit* communications — expressed in words representing the therapist's understanding of the client's intended communications and expression. Acceptance, however, is communicated indirectly by the therapist's tone and manner, and by the absence of evaluative or judgmental elements (Brodley and Schneider, 2001) in empathic responses.

    Communication of the acceptant empathic attitude usually takes place through an interaction — the *empathic understanding response process* (EURP) (Temaner, 1977) — between the client and the therapist. The EURP is also referred to as the *empathy cycle* by Barrett-

---

[1] Thanks to Charley Knapp, Julie Roe and Christine Badger, who made transcripts and reliability ratings for the study.

Lennard (1981). The following segment from a session illustrates the EURP in CC therapy.

CLIENT 1: *I expected to get a severe rejection. I expect this all the time. I don't know why this is, but even if I go up to somebody and ask for the time, the thing that I'm really bracing myself against is a severe rejection of me, even if it is realistically and completely unlikely. I really have to brace myself against something as strong as that just to ask for the time.*

THERAPIST 1: *Even in the most trivial kind of relationships the feeling is . . . 'Here comes rejection!'*

CLIENT 2: *Here comes . . . some tremendous danger. And physical violence doesn't even get the danger in it . . . although I do fear physical violence a lot. That's the same kind of thing . . . That if whatever the worst that can happen can be, that's what I feel most concerned about.*

THERAPIST 2: *That's almost a better phrase for it than* rejection. *That the point is, you're expecting* the worst. *Exactly what the definition of* worst *is, may not be too easy to know. But you just know . . . 'This will be* catastrophe.'

CLIENT 3: *Yeah. And the idea that it's not so, is very hard. But somehow I even feel it with you. Or at least this is what I kinda have ta' be ready for, and if I do something which seems like it might make it a little more possible, then I have to . . . sorta compensate . . . to make sure it's all right again.*

THERAPIST 3: *So it's in this relationship too. There is the feeling that . . . 'Look out if I do something a little out of line . . . the world will fall in on me.' Or something like that.*

CLIENT 4: *(Very long pause, 35 seconds) It's hard to talk about it because I don't know quite . . . or it's that I want to be so good with you somehow, you know . . . ?*

THERAPIST 4: *Uhm, hm.*

CLIENT 5: *I want to be the best I can possibly be with you . . . kinda like that . . . But that somehow ties with this idea that you . . . of feeling so good with . . . you were my father. That I just try to do good for you.*

THERAPIST 5: *You want to be the* best possible *here in* my *terms. Is that the way you mean it?*

CLIENT 6: *Yeah. It would feel good being that way. But it was somehow a past need that I had to be the best possible for you in your terms. (Pause) But there was some negative side to the idea I was picking up somehow . . . (Pause)*

THERAPIST 6: *But anyway, that doesn't quite catch the present feeling.*

CLIENT 7: *I kinda still have to work through that . . . work through the feeling of being a little boy . . . feeling good pleasing his father.*

THERAPIST 7: *Uhm, hm.*

CLIENT 8: *That's sorta one of the stages I'm at somehow.*

THERAPIST 8: *That sorta, that has felt good. Is this the stage you're in or about to leave . . . or something?*

CLIENT 9: *I just don't know exactly what it is. (Long pause, 25 seconds) That this idea of needing to please . . . of having to do it . . . that's the same thing again. That's really been kinda (weeps) . . . been a basic assumption of my life . . . kinda the very unquestioned axiom that . . . I have to please . . . I have no choice; I just have to . . . (Rogers, circa 1950)*

All of the therapist's responses in the segment are empathic understandings (or acknowledgements, e.g. therapist #4 and #7). They are *following-the-client* responses. They are expressed tentatively and they are open to correction by the client. Therapist response number 8, that appears to be a question addressed to the client, is an empathic response expressing the therapist's sense of the question the client is considering.

As the segment suggests, in order for the EURP to happen, the client must be minimally motivated to reveal, and capable of expressing, something of his or her inner world or life experiences to the therapist. In the EURP, the therapist expresses (a) an intention to pay authentic attention to the client, (b) an intention to accurately understand the client's immediate experience as the client intends that it be communicated, (c) an intention to seek verification or correction of inner understandings by representing them to the client. Nondirective following also expresses the therapist's unconditional positive regard (UPR) for the client. In this activity the CC therapist is not gathering information about the client's phenomenology in order to make effective interpretations, but engaging in understanding for its own value. The ultimate purpose of this empathic understanding is the therapeutic benefit that is found to be inherent in the understanding interaction and relationship.

The therapist's responses include simple acknowledgments of following — nodding or vocal gestures such as 'uhm hm' — as well as articulate following responses that represent part of what the client has expressed or communicated to the therapist. Articulate following responses may consist only of *information* that the client communicates or they may be AEU responses. True empathic responses contain expression of *the client's relation to what he or she is talking about* that often involve personal meanings or feelings. The therapist's reason for making an articulate empathic or other following-type response is to check his or her inner, subjective accuracy of understanding, to find out if it is correct according to the client (Rogers, 1986; Brodley, 1997b).

The therapist's verbal and expressive behavior that communicates the AEU attitude typically has several additional qualities. It represents portions of a close following of the client's narrative and *related* vocal and non-verbal expressive behavior. It represents the client's *immediate* focus and communicative intentions. It communicates the therapist's *inner* AEU of the client as accurately as possible. The CC therapist's behavior does not involve intentions to point the client towards any goal originating from the therapist regarding content or process. The therapist's intention in relation to the client is to understand what the client is getting at. The therapist maintains an acceptant attitude towards the client and usually experiences warm feelings towards him or her while listening and responding.

The CC therapist intends to remain integrated, relaxed, attentive and undistracted by irrelevant stimuli in order to accomplish AEU. The therapist is open to awareness of his or her own associations and emotional reactions, as they are needed for the purpose of discriminating her personal reactions from the client's intended communications. The interaction consisting of the client's self-disclosures and expressive behavior and the therapist's acceptant, following behavior builds empathic understanding of the client in the therapist's mind and promotes the client's sense of being understood and accepted by the therapist — the components of an evolving CC therapeutic relationship. Through this interaction process therapeutic change occurs in the client (Patterson, 1985).

Acceptant empathic understanding in CC therapy is a particular kind of understanding. Unless informed otherwise, the therapist assumes it is the kind of understanding that the client is expecting or hoping to receive when entering the therapy situation — an uncritical understanding especially of the client's personal thoughts and feelings. Thus, if the assumption about the client's expectations is correct, AEU is intrinsically a nondirective following. The

CC therapist intends to remain non-judgmental and acceptant towards all of the client's communication and expressive behavior. The therapist is listening to understand all of the client's communications. He or she, however, is especially interested in and responsive to certain aspects of it in order to understand *empathically*.

Zimring (2000) uses the term *targets* to refer to the particular aspects in clients' communications that CC therapists strive to grasp in listening to clients, in order to experience *accurate* empathic understanding. Rogers described targets of empathic understanding in his explanations, without referring to the term. Rogers (1959) wrote as follows:

> Being empathic, is to perceive the internal frame of reference of another with accuracy and with the emotional components and meanings which pertain thereto . . . Thus it means to sense the hurt or the pleasure of another as he senses it and to perceive the causes thereof as he perceives them, but without ever losing the recognition that it is *as if* I were hurt or pleased. (pp. 210–11)

Rogers' targets of AEU in this description involve (a) 'emotional components' which would include basic feelings such as *fear* or *anger*, and also (b) more complex experiences having affective qualities, such as *conflicted* or *perplexed*. The targets also involve (c) personal 'meanings', as they appear in one client's statement, 'I feel *we're so isolated*,' or in her statement, 'There's *a big hollow of things* that aren't there,' or in another client's statement 'I developed obsession and then tension in the back of my head and then *it centralized in one spot like a hook*.' Rogers also suggests that the targets include (d) the person's explanations and interpretations of his experience such as the statement 'I'm doing something to push people away.'

In a later formulation, Rogers (1980) emphasized that empathy is a process, not a state. Through *interaction* between client and therapist the therapist enters 'the private perceptual world of the other and becomes thoroughly at home in it' (p. 142). According to Rogers, empathy involves 'frequently *checking with the person* [italics mine] as to the accuracy of your sensing, and being guided by the responses you receive' (p. 142).

Rogers' writings, as well as his own therapy behavior, reveal that the experience of empathic understanding involves inferential processes, as is true of understanding in any context. A mother of small children describes, in a tired tone of voice, a list of chores she accomplished today. The listener responds with the remark, 'You must be worn out' or he says, 'Would you like me to take the kids so you can get a break?' The woman's point has been inferred by the combination of words and expressive behavior. Similarly, the empathic therapist is not focused on understanding in the sense of knowing what a client said so the literal words may be reproduced. The therapist is trying to grasp the meanings and experiences that the client *seems to intend* to be understood by the listener. Rogers reveals this focus when he uses the phrases 'sense the hurt or the pleasure of another' above, and when he describes the therapist's responses as ones 'pointing to the *possible* [my italics] meanings in the flow of another person's experiencing' (p. 142).

The therapist expresses his AEU in a manner that is likely to result in the client having the experience of *feeling understood*. This latter part of the goal is implied in Rogers (1959) sixth condition 'that the client perceives . . . the empathic understanding of the therapist' (p. 213). In other words, the goal is accurate empathic understanding of the client, and the client determines what is accurate. The forms of the therapist's communication, consequently, depend in part upon a client's characteristics — the client's vocabulary, style of speech, flow — that become apparent as the therapist interacts with the client.

Previous analyses of Rogers' therapy behavior (Brodley and Brody, 1990; Brody, 1991; Brodley, 1994; Nelson, 1994; Brodley, 1996; Diss, 1996; Merry, 1996; Bradburn, 1996) have contributed to my formulation (Brodley, 1996) concerning the elements the therapist especially attends to in the process of empathic understanding. Studies of transcripts of Rogers' therapy behavior, from the mid-1940s until his death in 1987, for example, reveal he produces (a mean of) approximately ninety percent empathic responses in his therapy interviews. Most of these responses explicitly or implicitly communicate that Rogers is understanding the client as an *agent or actor*, as *an active and reactive person*, and as *a source of meanings, feelings, reactions and other experiences about self or about the external world*. Words for feelings, however, are only contained in approximately twenty-five percent of Rogers' empathic responses according to past studies. Thus clients' feelings that the therapist can express in single words have been observed to be only part of Rogers' focus.

The evidence from Rogers' sessions and impressions of other CC therapists suggests that client-confirmed empathic understanding responses usually emphasize the client as an *agent, actor* or *source of actions*. Rogers' clients show an almost ubiquitous explicit approval of his AEU responses. These responses tend to show his understanding of their *agency*. It appears that clients feel well understood when he has grasped and communicated to them that their talk expresses their *intentions* and relates to their self as an *agent, an actor,* or *a source* of thoughts, feelings and actions. If one follows Rogers as a model, to empathically understand very accurately, the therapist should aim to recognize the client's *intentions* in his communications and relate the client's feelings, meanings, perspectives, explanations and reactions to those intentions. This conception of the aim in AEU is similar to the recent formulation by Zimring (2000).

THE STUDY

The specific aim of the study is to determine the frequency of CC therapists' representations of certain elements of their clients' communications and expressive behavior in empathic responses. The study is based on two samples of therapists' responses — one sample of responses selected unsystematically from transcripts of twenty-two interviews conducted by Carl Rogers and another sample from twenty interviews I have conducted. Various ratings and counts were made on the selected responses in order to produce a summary picture of salient features of each therapist's empathic responses.

The following features of empathic responses were rated: words or phrases that express emotions or feelings; words or phrases with vivid or evocative qualities; phrases without feeling or evocative qualities; words for specific cognitive processes; words that point to subjective experiences; responses that speak for the client in the first-person; dramatic-form responses that represent third persons' remarks to the client; references to the therapist; responses that represent the client as having a *want*; responses that represent the client as *trying*; and sentence units that represent the client as agent or actor. The reliability ratings of the features studied were either inter-rater or test-retest type, depending upon the availability of raters. All were in the 85%–98% range of agreement; I personally resolved all differences.

The Interviews

The two sets of interviews consist of client-therapist interactions in which eighty-five percent to one hundred percent of all the therapists' responses are empathic following responses. All the sessions of both sets combined show a mean of ninety-one percent empathic following responses. Responses to clients' questions were omitted on theoretical grounds (see Brodley, 1999b). The two sets of interviews are similar in the percentage of total words spoken by the therapists — twenty-nine percent by Rogers and twenty-seven percent by Brodley. Both sets include interviews with regular clients and with clients who volunteered for demonstrations. The clients are persons living in the community, with the exception of several of Rogers' clients who were hospitalized mentally ill persons.

The Rogers sample

The Rogers sample of empathic responses is from twenty-two sessions conducted by Carl Rogers (the CR sample) — many of them not previously studied. Altogether, one hundred and thirty-one responses were selected, culled from the beginning, middle and end of each session. In my reading of the empathic interactions and viewing of videotapes, Rogers is obviously attempting to represent his understanding of the clients' immediately previous communications and expressive behavior. Also, clients' immediate reactions to the responses selected for the sample showed that the clients accepted all Rogers' responses as representing their prior intended communications. There were no disagreements voiced by his clients to any of the selected responses.

The BTB sample

The empathic responses from my twenty interviews were selected on the basis of clients' strong confirming responses. When clients perceive that a therapist's empathic understanding response is adequately accurate, they may make several types of response that confirm the therapist's accuracy. Often, client statements immediately following a therapist's empathic response imply confirmation by the way they continue or further develop what he or she has been expressing prior to the therapist's response. Or, clients nod their affirmation and then elaborate or expand on their point. At other times clients first make a vocal gesture, such as 'ah haw', 'uh huh' or 'uhm hm' and then continue their narrative. Alternatively, clients will say 'yes', or 'right', or 'yeah' before they continue their narrative. Sometimes they repeat the point the therapist expressed, using the therapist's words, in that way indicating their confirmation.

The BTB sample consists of responses eliciting the clients' *strongest* explicit confirmations in the twenty interviews. These strong confirmations included the following responses: 'Yeah! Yeah!'; 'Absolutely, absolutely'; 'That's exactly right'; 'Yes I do. Right! Absolutely.' The selection was based on the assumption that strong confirmations indicate that the therapist's preceding empathic responses were accurate and possibly especially meaningful to the clients. The BTB sample consists of eighty-six therapist empathic understanding responses that elicited the clients' strong confirmations.

Observations and Comments

Words-for-feelings

Using single words-for-feelings in empathic responses is one way a therapist may communicate his or her understanding of clients' feelings. The first observation involves the frequency of words-for-feelings that the therapist expresses. (See Rosenberg, 1983 for lists of feeling-words.) The words rated exclusively represent the feelings of the client, not third persons. In the CR sample, Rogers expressed fifty-three feeling-words (1.1% of all therapist-words) including 'rage', 'afraid', 'hurt', 'desire'. In the BT sample there are thirty-six feeling-words (1.3% of all therapist words) including 'tense', 'joyful', 'furious', 'calm'. The two samples are almost identical in frequency of feeling-words.

Feeling-words pertaining to the client sometimes occur more than once in an empathic response in a particular *natural unit of interaction* between client and therapist. A word is repeated, or different words-for-feeling may be expressed in the same response. When a CC therapist is closely following, the variation in the frequency of feeling-words in specific responses to clients is closely related to the individual client's complexity of expression of experiences that may be accurately represented by such words. In the CR sample, for example, the range is zero to seven occurrences of feeling-words within particular empathic responses. In the BTB sample, the range is zero to five occurrences.

A different approach to assess the frequency of words-for-feelings (as well as for assessing the incidence of other features of an interview), instead of counting the words to find percentage of total words, is to count the natural interaction units in which at least one feeling-word occurs. Using this method, in the CR sample we find feeling-words occur in thirty percent of Rogers' responses; in the BTB sample, feeling-words occur in thirty-one percent of the responses. The two samples are almost identical in respect to frequency of occurrence of words-for-feelings (30% versus 31%; D = 1%); they appear in slightly less than one-third of all empathic responses.

The striking point of the observation is that the clients in both samples are responding with confirmations — always with strong confirmations in the BTB sample — to over two-thirds of the therapists' responses (70% in the CR sample and 69% in the BTB sample) that contain *no words-for-feelings*. Although these two therapists perceive and respond to clients' communications that include such 'hot feelings' (Zimring, personal communication), it appears that both therapists' clients seem able to feel empathically understood much of the time without hearing responses containing feeling-words. This observation supports the idea that the therapists are frequently empathically understanding and communicating *other experiences* that may involve more subtle or complex feelings or cognitive components.

Words or phrases that allude-to-feelings

The second observation involves the frequency of words or phrases that express experiences that involve feelings (of the client, not third persons) that are not feeling-words. These words or phrases refer to experiences that involve a feeling quality, but are more subtle or complex than *hot* feelings, or that may involve cognitive elements. They are words or phrases that express dispositions, evaluations, volitional states and other experiences. Examples of words and phrases for these experiences include 'ignored', 'pleading', 'resisting', 'very careful', 'subjective', 'worried', 'intimate aspect', 'don't feel good', 'not feeling safe', 'care', 'closeness', 'merged', 'dissatisfaction', 'confusing'. Words or phrases are included in the category if the rater *senses feelings in his or her self* while introspecting on the word or phrase. The high — 96% — inter-rater reliability for the rating of alluding-to-feeling is surprising, given the extremely subjective criterion for rating.

In the CR sample, approximately one percent of Rogers' total words are words or phrases alluding-to-feelings, whereas these elements occur in approximately six percent of total words in the BTB sample. The counts include single words and words in short phrases, consequently this method may make counts aimed to measure incidence artificially vary in the two samples. The alternative method used for assessing incidence of words-for-feelings counts empathic response units that include one or more words or phrases that allude-to-feelings (but are not words for feelings). This method gives a more accurate picture of the incidence and the difference in the two samples.

Forty-five percent of the empathic responses in the CR sample contain words or phrases alluding-to-feelings, fifty-nine percent in the BTB sample (45% versus 59%; D = 14%). This fourteen percent difference in percent responses containing alluding-words between the two samples is a surprise given that the percentage of units containing feeling-words was almost identical in both samples (31% versus 30%). Although there is a difference in the two samples, Rogers is still verbalizing alluding-to-feeling words in almost fifty percent of his responses. I have no speculations to account for the difference.

Combining the samples, compared to the pure or *hot* feelings in the therapists' empathic responses, both therapists together express these complex feelings more frequently to represent their understandings of clients (30.5% words-for feelings versus 52% alluding-to-feelings words; D = 21.5%). Approximately half of all AEU responses contain alluding-to-feelings words. This observation is consistent with the view that empathic understanding is an attempt to understand much more than clients' simple feelings.

Combining words-for-feelings and words or phrases that allude-to-feelings

Empathic responses that include feeling-words and/or alluding-to-feeling-words were counted to obtain a picture of the therapists' responsiveness to feeling-experiences that they perceived in their clients' communications. If a response had at least one feeling-word or at least one word or phrase that alludes to feelings it was counted. In some instances a response had only one feeling-word or one alluding-to-feelings word or phrase. In others it had more than one of the same kind of element or it had both feeling-words and a words or phrases alluding-to-feelings. An example of an empathic response that combines a feeling-word and an alluding-to-feeling word is 'You feel *sad* about *not feeling safe.*' The word 'sad' was rated as a feeling-word, and 'not feeling safe' is a phrase classed as alluding-to-feeling.

This method of counting occurrences reveals that sixty-one percent of the total AEU responses in the CR sample and seventy-three percent in the BTB sample contain both, or either, words-for-feelings and words-alluding-to-feelings. There is a twelve percent difference in the two samples (61% versus 73%; D = 12%). Thus it appears that I perceive my clients as communicating their feeling experiences more frequently that Rogers.

Examining both samples together and putting aside the difference in them, a large majority (67%) of responses include reference to clients' feeling experiences using feeling-words or alluding-to-feelings words or phrases. Almost two-thirds (61%) of Rogers' empathic response units and almost three-fourths (73%) of my response units include one or more reference to clients' feeling experiences. The majority of the references in both samples are to states and experiences that are a mixture of cognitive and affective elements rather than to relatively pure or *hot* feelings such as 'fear', 'anger' or 'joy'.

This observation is consistent with the results of a study of twenty-five of Rogers' sessions by Bradburn (1996; Brodley, 1999a) that showed a substantial portion of his empathic responses *do not* reveal affective features. She found that twenty-seven percent of a randomized sample of Rogers' clients' statements were *without* affective features and that Rogers' empathic responses tracked those absences. Twenty-four percent of his responses did not include affective features compared with the larger percent (39%) without affective features in the present CR sample. In the current BTB sample, twenty-seven percent responses were without affective features — close to the observation in the Bradburn sample. In the Bradburn study, the seventy-six percent of Rogers' responses *with affective features* did track the presence, quality and intensity of his client's affect.

Figures-of-speech

Figures-of-speech are common, short metaphors that contribute to the vividness and liveliness of speech. They serve various expressive functions although they often refer to *what is happening to the person* or *what the person is doing* in their life. The figures-of speech, 'drain on your life', 'take a lot out of you', 'part of you is torn away', 'that pulls you down', 'you give weight', 'lost your ground', 'in a black hole', 'clam up', 'it's before your eyes', and so forth, illustrate this function. Figures-of-speech require variable numbers of words. Consequently, a count of empathic responses containing figures-of-speech is more informative than word frequencies.

The frequencies of responses containing figures-of-speech were high and similar in the two samples (Rogers: 61% and BTB: 66%; D =5). These therapists are frequently — in approximately two-thirds of their empathic responses — expressing their clients' experiences in an idiosyncratic and lively manner.

Almost all figures-of-speech are brief elements in the responses using only a few words. There are no similes and only a few semi-extended metaphors in the CR sample. One metaphor quotes the client's homily, 'Poor man throws away and rich man puts in his pocket.' In a response to another client Rogers creates the following metaphor: 'You'll be glad to wash the dust of Madison off your feet.' In response to another client he says, 'It's so risky, coming from the lighted spot into the darkness, into the unknown.'

Rogers' use of figures-of-speech is rich and varied. They include, 'root it out', 'touch the core', 'you had an eye on him', 'shut it out of mind', 'bright world', 'the dark side', 'a little shaky', 'wave a magic wand'. The figures-of-speech in the BTB sample are similar to those of Rogers, such as 'stand up and fight', 'open the gate', 'people jump in', 'your spirits went up', 'in a black hole', 'clam up', 'your impotence', 'pull back', 'doesn't hold water'. In the BTB sample there are two similes — 'like the ground were suddenly up there', and 'like a camera that won't go into focus'. There are no extended metaphors whatsoever in the BTB sample, only brief figures-of-speech. Neither therapist appears likely to coin an extended metaphor in an empathic response. Sometimes they do pick up on a client's own metaphor and carry it or an element in it forward, such as use of the words 'octopus' and 'tentacles' in one of Rogers' client's metaphor for his mother. With only a few exceptions, in both therapists, their figures-of-speech are not picked up from their clients. They are spontaneous expressions of part of their empathic understanding of their clients.

The vividness of even common figures-of-speech, that often use visual images (e.g., 'crossed the line', 'let down a step'), may contribute to clients' perceptions of therapists' personal presence — to the perception that the therapist is emotionally alive in the relationship. Rice (1974) discusses figures-of-speech as evocative *technique*. My impression of Rogers is that his use of figures-of-speech in empathic responses is spontaneously expressive, and not a deliberate technique to stimulate the client. I am certain that in my own therapy I do not express figures-of-speech as technique. I do not intend them to evoke the client's feelings or emotions, but they may tend to have that evocative effect. Phrases such as 'going too far', 'wound your pride', 'damned', 'pulled out from under you', and 'seeps into you' are stimulating and probably convey a liveliness in a therapist's understandings more than similar meanings not communicated with figures-of-speech.

Combining feeling-words, words or phrases that allude-to-feelings and figures-of-speech

Three kinds of elements — feeling-words, the words or phrases that allude-to-feelings and the words or phrases that compose the figures-of-speech together express most of the emotional, feeling, and evocative or stimulating qualities in the therapist's responses. Using feeling-words plus using alluding-to-feeling words or phrases are the main ways the therapists capture their clients' feeling-experiences in empathic responses. Figures-of-speech sometimes express clients' feelings but they also capture what CC therapists understand is happening to or impacting their clients. To get a picture of the presence of all these emotion/feeling/evocative elements in AEU responses, I employed the method of counting instances of empathic responses in which one or the other, or many, or all of these elements occur. A response was counted if any one or any combination of the elements was found in the response.

The following response is an example of an empathic response that includes all three elements — feeling-words, an alluding-to-feeling phrase, and a figure of speech: 'In expressing some of the *stress* of this and some of your *upset* feelings, people *jump in* with solutions that *don't feel good to you.*' The words 'stress' and 'upset' are rated as feeling-words, the phrase 'don't feel good to you' is rated as an alluding-to-feeling phrase, and 'jump in' is a figure of speech. It is a complex empathic response; it tells what the client does (she reveals some feelings to others), it expresses her reactions (she feels imposed on by their solutions), and it states the client's feelings (she doesn't feel good). A lot of information is expressed in the response; but at the same time it has a vividness that suggests the therapist's close presence in the relationship.

The percentage of empathic responses containing any or all of the three elements were found to be equal in the two samples. In both the CR sample and the BTB sample eighty-five percent of the units contain at least one feeling-word and/or at least one word or phrase that alludes to feelings and/or at least one figure-of-speech (CR: 85% and BTB: 85%; D = 0%).

Responses that have no feeling-related words or phrases (no feeling-words, no words or phrases that allude to feeling, and no figures-of-speech) relating to, or about, the client

In both samples, fifteen percent of the therapists' responses are devoid of feeling-related or evocative words or phrases. These responses consist of three kinds of statements. One kind is about a third person's wants, feelings or reactions such as, 'But he clearly wants you, he really wants you.' A second is a statement about facts or information such as, 'The ones that follow from earlier choices.' Or, 'Such a good thing after all, and natural, and it kills him.' A third is a response that expresses conceptual, rational or cognitive experiences such as, 'You knew that quite well.' Or, 'That decided it for you.' Or, 'Every calculation makes it less important.' These responses that express no feeling or evocative experiences, nevertheless contribute to the EURP. They elicited clients' confirmations — strong confirmations in the BTB sample. Consequently, I infer they are accurate understandings of the clients' immediate communicative intentions.

Responses that include specific words for cognitive processes
Words for cognitive processes such as 'think', 'interest', 'consider', 'means', 'implies', or 'aware' occur more frequently in the natural response units in the CR sample than in the BTB sample (35% versus 28%; D = 7%). Many empathic responses in both samples contain words or phrases that express feeling experiences or evocative experiences and also express cognitive experiences such as 'a *desire* [feeling-word] to *wave a magic wand* [figure-of-speech] and have it be *true*' [cognitive word]. Some responses contain only cognitive words such as 'You're coming to the only possible *conclusion*' [cognitive word]. Although representations of feeling-experiences are most frequent, found in two-thirds of responses, the therapists also understand their clients' cognitive experiences in one-third of their empathic responses.

Responses that include the words 'feel', 'feeling', 'feels', 'felt'.
The words 'feel', 'feeling', 'feels', 'felt' occur in thirty-seven percent of the responses in the CR sample and in twenty-six percent of the responses in the BTB sample (37% versus 26%; D = 11%). This eleven percent difference in the two therapists' use of these words is not surprising to me given the fact that I consciously tend to avoid the terms 'you feel', 'it feels' etc. if my response refers to what the client thinks, believes, imagines or to other cognitive activities. I prefer to use the words that explicitly describe the mental activity the client expressed, rather than employ 'you feel' etc. to point to those mental activities. My preference shows up in our difference in respect to juxtaposing 'feel', etc. with cognitive words.

The CR sample includes more responses combining 'feel' etc. with cognitive words than the BTB sample (CR: 48% versus BTB: 4%; D = 44%). Only four percent of my responses that contain 'feel' words also include specific words for cognitive experiences. This is a small portion of all empathic responses — only one percent. It contrasts with the eighteen percent portion of all responses (containing 'feel' etc., plus a cognitive word) in the CR sample (CR: 18% versus BTB: 1%; D = 17%). Examples of these responses from both samples include 'You feel it's kind of *characteristic* of you,' 'You feel that it's just a *mystery* to you,' 'You feel as though you *can understand*,' 'That is the feeling,' 'If they really *knew* . . . ', 'You feel that's kind of the same *pattern*,' 'You're trying to feel out the *implications*,' 'It feels *overdone*,' and 'It just feels it was *clear*.'

In pointing to cognitive experiences with the words 'feel' etc., Rogers apparently uses these words as a pointer to clients' internal processes more frequently than I am inclined to do this. Nevertheless, Rogers uses 'feel' etc. as a specific reference to feeling-experiences in the majority of instances of using 'feel' etc. words (CR: feeling-words 8%, alluding-words 31%, and figures-of-speech expressing feelings 13% = 52% words for feeling-experiences versus 48% cognitive words).

In both samples, the words 'feel' etc., occur in relation to feeling-experiences expressed by words-for-feelings or words alluding-to-feelings. Examples are 'you feel very *tense*', '*panicky* feeling,' 'a feeling of *despair*,' 'you feel you are being *disapproved of*,' 'you feel *hopeless*,' and 'you feel *persecuted*.' As discussed in an earlier paper (Brodley, 1996) Rogers' use of the words 'feel' etc. often appears to signal that he is understanding clients' experiences that cannot be accurately communicated by words for feelings, but are ones that convey a quality of underlying or associated feelings. This observation is supported in the current CR samples by Rogers' use of words-for-feeling (such as 'sad' or 'afraid') as the object of 'feel' etc. in only eight percent of his empathic responses containing 'feel' etc. thus in only three percent of all responses. This is in contrast to his use of words or phrases alluding-to-feelings in thirty-one percent of his responses containing 'feel' etc. thus in twelve percent of all his empathic responses. He also uses figures-of-speech that characterize feeling states (for example, 'the *hole* that you feel', or 'you feel *tiny* and *shriveled*,' or 'you do feel a little *bitter*') in thirteen percent of his responses containing 'feel' etc. thus in five percent of all responses. The portions are small, but alluding-to-feeling words and figures-of-speech expressed as the objects of 'feel' etc. appear more frequently in Rogers' total empathic responses than the purer words-for-feelings (CR: 3% words-for-feeling versus 17% other words or phrases referring to feeling-experiences; D = 14%).

Some uses of the words 'feel' etc., refer to an experience that may have been mentioned previously by the therapist or the client. The following examples are of this type: 'A preoccupation with your feeling', 'When you're feeling that way', or 'You have some feelings on this side.' Granted a variety of usages, with feeling experiences and with cognitive experiences, reference to 'feel' etc. often signals to the client that the therapist's response pertains to clients' subjective experiences that are complex or subtle. When the words 'feel' etc. are voiced in an empathic response, they sometimes have the effect of focusing the client inward, towards the *subjective experiences* that are the source of meanings and feelings that may be expressed in language. They may have the effect, in the terms of Gendlin's (1964; 1974) *experiencing* theory, of focusing the client's attention towards his or her *felt sense*.

First-person empathic responses

An immediate or dramatic way to express an empathic response is to employ the first-person and state the response exactly as one thinks the client would express it. This is a form of empathic understanding response observed in earlier studies of Rogers' therapy behavior (Brodley and Brody, 1990; Brody, 1991; Brodley, 1996; Merry, 1996). Merry found a mean frequency of 10% (range of 5% to 14%) of first-person empathic responses in the ten Rogers sessions he studied. The current Rogers sample includes the following responses: 'How am I going to deal with it within myself?' 'I need maturity to live with that fear within myself,' 'Where am I going? What is my purpose? What do I want to make of my life?' First-person empathic responses also appear in the BTB sample: 'I must be empty,' 'I have to find something to bring him to me,' 'God damn it!', and 'I don't think it's always been this way for me.'

Twenty-nine percent of the empathic response units in the CR sample include a first-person statement compared with fourteen percent of the response units in the BTB sample (29% versus 14%; D = 15%). This makes twice as many first-person responses in the CR sample as in the BTB sample and three times as many first-person responses in the current CR sample compared to the earlier sample of Rogers' responses studied by Merry.

The greater frequency of this form of response in the current Rogers sample compared to the Merry sample (29% versus 10%; D = 19%) is probably because the Merry sample consists solely of demonstration interviews conducted by Rogers. The present CR sample from twenty-two sessions, in contrast, consists of responses from eighteen sessions with regular clients. A CC therapist is likely to feel more confident in the context of an ongoing relationship that his or her empathic responses will not be confusing to clients when expressed in the first-person form. The fifteen percent difference in the two current samples may also be accounted for by the fact that the BTB sample of responses was taken from twenty interviews of which eleven (55%) were demonstration interviews. Nevertheless, the first-person-form of empathic response conveys a sense of the therapist's close participation in the client's world. In the current samples, Rogers expresses this immediacy in approximately one-third of his empathic responses, while I do so only half as often, in only one-sixth of my responses.

Together, the greater frequency of 'feel' etc. being related to cognitions, and the greater frequency of 'I-form' responses in the CR sample suggests that Rogers is subtly orienting his clients towards their immediate subjective experiences or *felt sense*. Rogers is responding less frequently than I am to *feeling-experiences,* consequently it appears he is not biased towards feeling-experiences in particular. But the use of 'feel' etc. about cognitive experiences may suggest to clients that there is more to know, or be revealed to them, if they attend more closely to their subjective processes. In contrast, I am consciously motivated to represent clients' experiences as *what they seem to be to them* rather than alluding, by voicing 'you feel . . .', to the inner source of the experiences. In this difference, it appears that I am responding to my clients *slightly* more nondirectively than Rogers is responding to his clients.

Third-person dramatic empathic responses

Another dramatic form of empathic response is a statement representing a third person — not the client or the therapist — presented as a quote of the person. These are rare in Rogers' behavior and rare in mine, but they do occur in both. In the CR sample, one speaks for the client's parent: 'I don't like this, so you mustn't, because you're a part of me.' Another speaks for the client's old acquaintances; 'That reminds you of those days when they asked, "What's new?" doesn't it?' There are two such responses in the BTB sample. The following example occurs in my Client E interview. Therapist: You get blamed — *'Well, if you hadn't'.* The second example is in my client Q interview: Client: You know, 'She'll have a career and have great children and all of that, but she'll be alone' (laughs). Therapist: *'And celebrate* (C: laughs) *for ten years* (C: laughs) . . . *not five or six'.* The response to client Q picks up on the client's third-person dramatic form. Third-person-form responses usually capture something happening in the client's personal relationships that are having an impact on the client.

Third-person dramatic-form responses may also speak for a client's invented persona or a *non-self experience.* In the CR sample there are three of these. In one, the client has referred to an experience of himself as a 'little boy' and Rogers speaks for the 'little boy'. 'The little boy feels, "this feels good to me, it's satisfying to me to me to do this".' In a response to another client, Rogers speaks for the 'deep thing' in the client. He speaks dramatically: 'Look out, this might be another octopus.' In the third instance, Rogers speaks for the client's hallucinatory voice, saying 'If you are feeling desperate . . .' The therapist usually makes up the piece of dialogue that captures the third person's attitude toward the client, although sometimes it is an elaboration on the client's use of dialogue. Like figures-of-speech and the first-person dramatic-form of response, these third-person statements give variety and vitality to the flow of empathic responses. The dramatic quality of these responses may help the client experience the therapist's engagement and presence (Brodley, 2000a) in the relationship.

Therapist references to self

When CC therapists are following a client, making empathic understanding responses, and thus not representing their own frame of reference, they usually make no references to themselves. In the context of empathic following, therapist self-references are almost exclusively expressions of the therapist's tentativeness or uncertainty about the accuracy of his or her empathic responses. They usually preface the empathic response or follow it and they often form a question. The following statements from the two samples are explicit expressions of the therapists' tentativeness or uncertainty about their empathic understanding: 'I guess the impression I get is . . .'; 'What I hear you saying there is . . .'; 'If I get it . . .'; 'I guess you're saying there . . .'; 'If I understand that . . .'; 'If I sense some of your feeling there — let's see if I am . . .'; 'Ah, it strikes me that what you're saying is . . .'; 'But there too, I guess I get the feeling . . .'; 'I don't know if this is right, but it seems . . .'; 'You've been saying to me . . .'; 'So, I guess . . .' The following examples of uncertainty are in the form of questions: 'Is this what you're saying . . . ?'; 'Am I getting this right?'; 'Would it be overstating it too much . . . ?' Therapists also make self-references as an acknowledgment response to the client, such as 'I see' or 'now I understand', followed by an empathic response.

The tentativeness- or uncertainty-type of self-reference is found in twenty percent of Rogers' empathic responses and in nine percent of responses in the BTB sample (20% versus 9%; D = 11%). Rogers is explicitly communicating his tentativeness or uncertainty in one-fifth of his responses, twice as frequently as BTB.

Although I explicitly indicate my tentativeness to my clients when I am very unsure, Rogers has impressed me as especially scrupulous in indicating uncertainty when he feels it is beyond the basic tentativeness of all CC empathic responses. Care to be explicit about uncertainty expresses Rogers' sincere desire to accurately understand his clients and not impose his interpretations on their meanings. Rogers goes to lengths to make it clear he has a strongly felt uncertainty about his accuracy in the following empathic response: '*In the way I'm understanding that, though I'm not quite sure*, is . . . you would want to be the best possible here in my terms. *Is that the way you mean it?*'

Rogers and I are both likely to be particularly careful to explicitly signal our uncertainty if the empathic response expresses the client's feelings *about us* or the client's perception of his or her *relation to us*. Explicit expressions of uncertainty, of course, are not a strategy. They are not aimed to produce an effect (see Brodley, 2001) in clients. Nevertheless, there probably is a serendipitous effect on the client's sense of the therapist's presence as a personal participant when owning their imperfections as a listener.

The client as agent or actor

Empathic understanding is a complex, ongoing process of listening to clients, of sensing clients' perceptions and experiences that they represent to the therapist, and of representing some of these to the client for their correction or confirmation. As mentioned earlier, I have speculated that the major focus for empathic understanding of clients' verbal and expressive communications is primarily clients' statements about themselves as an agent or actor, as an active force — as a *source* of intentions, experiences, actions and reactions.

The empathic therapist's particular focus of attention is on the client's reactions to, feelings about, thoughts about, and intentions in respect to, what the client is talking about. It follows that the therapist statements that should be productive to scrutinize in studying therapists' empathic understanding behavior are the words, expressions, phrases or sentences that communicate about the client's agency. These statements would be ones that represent the client's intentions, experiences (including feeling experiences), actions, reactions, or the client's role as a source of directed actions, as well as what is happening to the client. Examples of empathic responses whose structure and content (note italics) express the client's pro-active or re-active agency are as follows: '*You want to find* some way of coming out of this hole, of really resolving a relationship, not just having it chopped off.' 'You were always *trying to find some way to win* him.' 'You're *worried about* the impact on your child.' 'It's *a preoccupation* with your feelings.' '*What you want is a relationship* with someone *that will strengthen you* to fight what's in your mind.' The following empathic response illustrates both the client's pro-active and re-active agency: 'There's one link *that you sense* [pro-active]. That one time when you felt your internal *sexual organs were being hooked and manipulated*' [reactive].

The words 'want', 'wanting', 'wants', 'wanted'

Remarking that 'I want . . .' is a straightforward expression of the speaker as an agent or actor toward or away from something. Empathic responses that explicitly represent the client as *wanting* something are an obvious choice to examine in studying the frequency of agency elements. In the CR sample nine percent of the therapist's AEU responses contain the word 'want' etc., and in the BTB sample eight percent of the AEU responses contain these words. The samples contain almost identical frequencies of 'want' etc. (9% and 8%; D = 1%), although the less than ten percent usage indicates these words obviously are not the only way the therapists represent their clients' expressions of their agency.

The words 'try', 'trying', 'tries', 'tried'

A remark that 'I am trying . . .' is another straightforward expression of the speaker as an agent or actor towards or away from something. In the CR sample 'try' words appear in four percent of Rogers' empathic responses and in two percent of the responses in the BTB sample. The occurrence is small and similar in both samples (4% and 2%; D = 2%). Together, 'want' and 'try' words occur in thirteen percent of Rogers' responses and ten percent of mine (13% and 10%; D = 3%). In both samples they appear in only slightly more than one-tenth of all AEU responses, thus there must be other ways the clients' agency gets expressed in empathic responses.

The sentence-units for observing agency.

Empathic responses in natural interactions are often complex responses, containing more than one sentence or more than one complete statement in response to the client. The following example of an empathic response in a natural interaction, containing several sentence-units, comes from one of Rogers' interviews:

> CLIENT: *Another thing about the hook [in her head] is when I get too confused. When like I got up this morning and I felt so discouraged about the job and so discouraged about B [husband]. And I also felt that something was oppressing me — the feeling of being*

> *dominated and oppressed. I went to have my coffee and I just sat and I thought really if I did what I feel like doing I'd just sit here and I wouldn't move. (T: Uhm, hm) And I think maybe I put the hook in, as an alternative to something worse. (T: Uhm, hm, uhm, hm) (Pause 5 seconds) The hook, the hook was once an organization.*
>
> THERAPIST: *I don't think I get that. So the feeling was, 'I'm discouraged — about various things. What I really feel like doing is just sinking into apathy'. And you feel maybe that's when you put the hook in yourself. That the hook, really, in one sense, stands for . . . I don't know, for making yourself be organized, something like that. (Rogers, circa 1955).*

The therapist's response has four statements within it, as well as several indications of his uncertainty.

Taking the complexity of many empathic responses into account, the responses in the sample were divided up into their sentence-units. There are 1.4 sentence-units per empathic response in the CR sample and 1.8 sentence-units per empathic response in the BTB sample.

Non-agency sentence-units

Only seven percent of the sentence-units in the CR sample and eight percent in the BTB sample contain *no expression of the client as an agent or actor* (CR: 7% and BTB: 8%; D = 1%). These non-agency sentence-units are usually of two types. They are always part of the therapist's empathic responses, but one type consists of statements about someone other than the client such as, 'He must have been very careless to get this,' 'He thought you had an eye on him.' 'She's got some outlet that doesn't criticize her,' and 'There's a point beyond which they disagree.' Other non-agency sentence-units are statements of fact, or information: 'Everybody is low key in terms of approval responses'; 'Those are the qualities valued here'; 'The gifts are unevenly distributed in the world'; 'That's the way it is.' The non-agency sentence-units, like the agency units, either make-up entire therapist natural response units or they are *sentence-units* that are parts of whole complex empathic responses.

The sentence-units-containing agency

The samples are almost identical in the percentage of sentence-units describing clients' agency features. Ninety-three percent of the sentence-units in the CR sample and ninety-two percent in the BTB sample (93% versus 92%; D = 1%) contain an expression of the client as an agent or actor — either pro-active or re-active. Both therapists are making responses more than nine-tenths of the time that represent the client as an agent, actor or source of experiences, actions or reactions. This dominant feature of empathic responses encompasses representations of clients' feelings, meanings, perceptions, explanations, intentions and what is happening to them — all representing the clients as active personalities.

The observations indicate that most empathic responses wholly or in part represent clients as active personalities. The italicized elements in the following *clients' statements* emphasize this active quality that the therapists' attempt to represent in their empathic responses: '*It feels* oftentimes that *it's just too much for me*. Then *I build up* notion*s* . . .'; '*I mix it up* and *I can't separate* well enough what's in my head, what is an objective upset . . .'; '*I resent* it because since I was seventeen *I've been doing* everything for her'; '*I can be attracted* to women and yet *I don't know*. It just *doesn't seem to be* the real thing. There's *no real attraction*'; '*I think about* buildings. *I try to picture* them but *I can't. I can't remember* them'; '*I feel* like a broken record.'

The therapists' representations of this important feature of clients' narratives — in their empathic understanding responses, or in parts of them, are illustrated by the following examples: 'It [referring to the client's behavior] *feels overdone* [to the client] and it's even *boring to you* at a certain point'; 'You were always *trying to find* some way to win him'; 'You *doubt*, because it *doesn't feel* like the right place; you *don't like* your job, you *don't like* your boss . . .'; 'You're somewhat *too quick* with it, even though you're *discriminating*'; 'You definitely *expected* . . . and then all of a sudden that was pulled out from under you.'

Agency to the external, agency to the internal

I distinguished whether the therapist's agency-type sentence-units expressed the client's *self* (a) in relation to something or someone external to him or her, or (b) in relation to subjective experiences of himself or herself. In both categories, the clients have revealed something about their subjective self-life (feelings, thoughts, wants, etc.). The difference is in the object of the self-life — whether it is about something outside the self, or within the person's subjective processes. Examples of responses that contain elements indicating (a) an external object of self are as follows: 'You were feeling ignored *in relation to your father.*' 'It's damned inconvenient *to have to stay here* all day' [an implied other]. 'You wonder about *the authority.*' 'You care *about her* and you want to be close *to her* . . .' 'You want to influence *your husband* . . .' 'As long as *he has that reaction* you can't turn to him'. The following examples express the client's self about inner experiences: '*Deeply within you* there's a tremendous *sense of vulnerability*'; 'When *you try and think, it just doesn't come clear to you*'; 'This *sense of yourself* as not good enough'; 'It's *a felt need* to get more order'; 'Those *sensations* give you a whole other *level of stress*'; 'It's a *conflict of feelings.*'

In the CR sample, sixty-one percent, in the BTB sample sixty-five percent of agency-type sentence-units are expressions of clients' self *in relation to something or someone outside the self* — the (a) type (61% versus 65%; D = 4%). Accordingly, in the CR sample thirty-nine percent, in the BTB sample thirty-five percent of the sentence-units *related clients' self towards subjective experiences* — the (b) type (39% versus 35%; D = 4%). The two samples are very similar. Given that all the therapists' clients confirmed accuracy of all the empathic understanding responses, the similarity of the samples in this observation is telling.

It appears that CC clients' engagement in therapy is *more* about their thoughts, feelings and reactions to persons and situations outside of themselves (two-thirds of the time) than to their intrapsychic world (one-third of the time). At least for the most part, it appears that these two CC therapists' clients are not focusing on their experiences in the sense of exploring their own inner feeling phenomenology. Instead they are mostly expressing their emotional and thoughtful actions towards, or reactions to, things going on in the external world that are having some impact on them or that are important to them. The similarity of the two samples in regard to their proportions is surprising and telling, because one would expect differences on the grounds of clients' individual differences and because the samples are small.

CONCLUDING DISCUSSION

The interviews

The sets of therapy interviews from which the samples of empathic responses were drawn are similar in a number of respects. This is not surprising, given the fact that I developed my approach to therapy on the basis of Rogers' writings and client-centered consultants. Predominantly, Rogers and I closely follow our clients, making empathic responses from time to time. Both have written that the reason we verbalize our inner understandings to clients is in order to find out whether or not we understand correctly according to the clients (Rogers, 1996; Brodley, 1997b). Our tone, manner and expressive behavior, revealed in the interview transcripts, and in video or audiotapes of some of the sessions, appears to be consistent with our expressed rationale. Our clients indicate they disagree with our understandings in less than one percent of our responses. The sets of interviews are almost the same in the percent of the words spoken by the therapist versus percentage spoken by the client.

Similarity of the therapists' empathic responses

The observations reveal that the two therapists' *empathic responses* are similar in a number of ways. Rogers and I are usually making empathic responses that represent clients' relatively complex experiences including feelings, thoughts, and personal meanings, including their explanations and interpretations as well as memories, and their future hopes or expectations. We tend to express relatively complex feeling-experiences — that are subtle or that involve cognitive elements — much more frequently than pure or *hot* feelings. We both represent clients' cognitive-experiences in approximately one-third of all our empathic responses. Other evidence of our similarity is in the observation that most of our responses represent clients as agents or actors, acting or reacting in relation to their own subjective experiences, or towards or away from someone or something. In these responses we show the same proportions of self-agency relating to subjective experiences and relating to something outside the person. Several observations in the study show that both therapists are personally expressive in their empathic responses. Probably both, in this way, stimulate a strong sense of their presence (Brodley, 2000) in their clients' perceptions

Some differences in the therapists

Rogers expressed fewer words or phrases that allude-to-feelings and more cognitive words than I do. This difference is carried out in the observation that Rogers expresses the words 'feel' etc. more frequently than I in relation to cognitive experiences. Rogers also utilizes the first-person form in his empathic responses more frequently than I do.

There appears to be a subtle difference in the two therapists in the way their empathic responses orient to their clients' subjective experiences. Both therapists are profoundly nondirective. Rogers, however, tends more than I do to make responses that may stimulate the client to attend to the subjective source of feelings and meanings. I tend to aim towards a precise representation of the ways clients express what they are subjectively experiencing or doing. It is not apparent whether our slight behavioral difference reflects a somewhat different conception of the empathic task, or if it is a stylistic difference.

Applying the Zimring theory to the study

The study is based on the idea that the contents of therapists' client-validated empathic responses reveal an answer to the question 'what is being understood in empathic understanding?' Fred Zimring (2000) addressed this question in his explication of the *targets of empathic understanding*. Zimring's answers are based on an underlying theory of change that he developed from earlier formulations (Zimring, 1995; 1990a; 1990b). His theoretical context for ideas about the targets includes the view that 'it is the involved, acting self involved in a transaction that is central . . . The person [*or self*] is not a separate object or entity, but rather is a part of an interacting system' (Zimring, 2000, p. 103). Consequently, 'what we do or say is not determined by an inner state or entity, but rather is part of the transaction in which we are engaged' (p. 104). He further explains that a person's actions result from the *self* as part of transactional activity rather than from intra-psychic content. Actions involve *intentionality* or *purposiveness* and persons are constantly involved with and reacting to their world as they see it in order to fulfill intentions.

Zimring distinguishes two self-states; one is the 'Me' state, when mental representations are about the objective world and transactions concern the objective world. In this state we perceive ourselves as objects. In the 'I' transactional self-state, transactions are concerned with subjective representations. 'We interact with representations of feelings and meanings; here one sees one's self as the initiating actor' (p. 106). Following from this theory, Zimring posits three targets for empathic understanding. One is 'the speaker's self-sense and self-reactions'. Second is 'the speaker's intentions within the transactions in which he or she is engaged'. Third is 'the nature of the representations that are the context in which these intentional transactions are occurring' (p. 108). Zimring asserts that in general, the client-centered therapist primarily responds not to what the person may be feeling or experiencing, 'but rather to the person's intention, to what the person is trying to convey to you about what is happening to him or her' (p. 110).

Although I did not analyze the two samples of empathic responses from the perspective of Zimring's conception of the targets of empathic understanding, the observations, nevertheless, lend support to his views. Clients' *self-sense* and *self-reactions* are found in part among the feeling-words, for example 'it hurts', 'aloneness', 'fear'. They are also found among the alluding-to-feeling words or phrases, such as 'dilemma', 'shaky', 'undigested lump', and among the agency sentence-units in which the therapist represents the client relating directly to his or her own inner experiences, for example '. . . it comes to you as sort of a hole,' 'you're getting calmer,' 'you just feel a kind of helpless rage.'

Representations of clients' *intentions within their transactions* are found in the agency sentence-units that make up most empathic responses. Clients' intentions are represented in the following sentence-units: 'You do *want to do something* about the problem.' 'You are *trying to help*.' 'You *think its time* to go ahead.' 'You're *working to find* some way.' 'You're *determined* to keep apart from her.' 'You *have to* say things that this woman is not going to like to hear.' *Intentions* in the agency sentences are also expressed by figures-of-speech such as 'you want to *stand up and fight*,' 'you want to keep your *battery charged*,' or 'you want to *run away*,' and many others.

The therapists' responses expressing clients' representations that are *the context in which transactions are occurring* also are found among the agency sentence-units. Words or phrases expressing context are in italics in these examples. '*After that* you realize . . .' 'Even *in the most trivial kind of relationship* the feeling is rejection.' '*He asked you questions* that would make you think of certain things that had happened, and you'd start to cry.' 'Your spirits went up, *thinking that brown is beautiful*.' 'It has hurt you, even though *you haven't been the victim much compared to many people*.'

Many of the agency sentence-units include *what is happening to the client*. For example, 'you get support,' 'something happens in your gut,' and 'you are being disapproved of.' Figures-of-speech that are prevalent in the agency units often express *what is happening to* the client, such as 'that label really *destroys* you as a person,' 'you *lost your ground*,' 'it's an *act of war*,' 'you were in *a black hole*,' 'that was *pulled out from under you*,' 'you *explore various alleys* and they all have *stone walls* at the end of them.'

Zimring's view that, in general, the CC therapist responds to the person's intentions and to what the person is trying to convey about what is happening to him or her, not pointedly to feelings, seems to be supported by the study. Judging by both therapists' responses, clients often talk about what is happening to them. What is happening to them may include their feelings or other experiences that have feeling components as in the response, 'That's been hurting you and weakening you for years, but *now . . . you still suffer*, but *you resist her* and *stand up for yourself*.' Sometimes, however, *what is happening* to clients does not in itself involve feeling-experiences. It may set the stage for their feeling-experiences, as in the empathic response, 'that's the tension you feel *when you're with people*.' References to feeling-experiences are an important part of empathic understanding, but they usually appear in complex contexts of the clients' intentions and of experiences that are happening to them, as shown in the following complex empathic response: 'You feel sad about not feeling safe to tell her what your intentions are because she might not accept them. And yet you care about her and you want to be close to her and keep that closeness. And yet you feel like you have to keep apart from her to protect your own direction — the direction that feels like the right one for you at this time.'

Projects using different CC therapists' transcripts could contribute to understanding of the empathic understanding attitude and its verbal expression in client-centered therapy. I intend to do further analyses of such transcripts. Many of Rogers' preserved transcripts of sessions have not been studied, so there is more of that fascinating material to explore. None have been examined from the explicit perspective of Zimring's concept of the targets of empathic understanding — a provocative future project.

REFERENCES

Barrett-Lennard, G. T. (1981). The empathy cycle: refinement of a nuclear concept. *Journal of Counseling Psychology*, *28*, 91–100.

Bradburn, W. M. (1996). *Did Carl Rogers' positive view of human nature bias his psychotherapy? An empirical investigation*. Unpublished doctoral dissertation, Illinois School of Professional Psychology, Chicago.

Brodley, B. T. (1990). Client-centered and experiential: Two different therapies. In G. Lietaer, J. Rombauts, and R. Van Balen (Eds.) *Client-centered and Experiential Psychotherapy Towards the Nineties*. Leuven, Belgium: Leuven University Press, (pp. 87–108).

Brodley, B. T. (1991). The role of focusing in client-centered therapy. Presented in *A dialogue concerning the role of focusing in client-centered therapy between Ann Weiser Cornell and Barbara Temaner Brodley*, at the meeting of the Association for the Development of the Person-Centered Approach, Coffeyville, KS (May).

Brodley, B. T. (1994). Some observations of Carl Rogers' behavior in therapy interviews. *Person-Centered Journal, 1*(2), 37–48.

Brodley, B. T. (1996). Empathic understanding and feelings in client-centered therapy. *The Person-Centered Journal, 3* (1), 22–30.

Brodley, B. T. (1997a). The nondirective attitude in client-centered therapy. *The Person-Centered Journal, 4* (1), 18–30.

Brodley, B.T. (1997b). Criteria for making empathic responses in client-centered therapy. *The Person-Centered Journal, 5* (1), 20–8. Also (1984 Published under Barbara S. Temaner), *Renaissance, 2* (1).

Brodley, B.T. (1999a). Did Carl Rogers' positive view of human nature bias his psychotherapy? (Based on the research doctoral dissertation (1996) by Wendy M. Bradburn). Paper presented at the Second World Congress for Psychotherapy, Vienna, Austria (July). Also (2000, July) Presented at the meeting of the Eastern Psychological Association, Baltimore, MD.

Brodley, B.T. (1999b). Reasons for responses expressing the therapist's frame of reference in client-centered therapy. *The Person-Centered Journal, 6* (1), 4–27.

Brodley, B.T. (2000a). Personal presence in client-centered therapy. *The Person-Centered Journal, 7* (2), 139–49.

Brodley, B.T. (2000b). Client-centered: An expressive therapy. *Client-centered and Experiential Psychotherapy*. Linda a Velha, Portugal: Vale and Vale Editores, (pp. 133–149).

Brodley, B. T. and Brody, A. F. (1990). *Understanding client-centered therapy through interviews conducted by Carl Rogers*. Paper presented at the annual conference of the American Psychological Association, Boston, August.

Brodley, B.T. and Schneider, C. (2001). Unconditional positive regard as communicated through verbal behavior in client-centered therapy. In J. Bozarth and P. Wilkins (Eds.) *Unconditional Positive Regard*. Ross-on-Wye: PCCS Books.

Brody, A. F. (1991). *Understanding client-centered therapy through interviews conducted by Carl Rogers*. Unpublished Doctoral Dissertation. Illinois School of Professional Psychology, Chicago.

Diss, J. W. (1996). *Facilitative responses leading to client process disruption in Carl Rogers' therapy behavior*. Unpublished doctoral dissertation. Illinois School of Professional Psychology, Chicago.

Gendlin, E. T. (1964). A theory of personality change. In P. Worchel and D. Byrne (Eds.) *Personality Change*. New York: Wiley.

Gendlin, E. T. (1974). Client-centered and experiential psychotherapy. In D. A. Wexler and L. N. Rice (Eds.) *Innovations in Client-centered Therapy*. New York: Wiley, (pp. 211–46).

Merry, T. (1996). An analysis of ten demonstration interviews by Carl Rogers: Implications for the training of client-centered counselors. In R. Hutterer, G. Pawlowsky, P. F. Schmid and R. Stipsits (Eds.) *Client-centered and Experiential Therapy: A paradigm in motion*. Frankfurt am Main: Peter Lang, (pp. 273–84).

Nelson, J. A. (1994). *Carl Rogers' verbal behavior in therapy: a comparison of theory and therapeutic practice*. Unpublished doctoral dissertation, Illinois School of Professional Psychology, Chicago.

Rice, L. N. (1974). The evocative function of the therapist. In D. A. Wexler and L. N. Rice (Eds.) *Innovations in Client-centered Therapy*. New York: Wiley, (pp. 289–311).

Rogers, C. R. (circa 1950). Transcript of Carl Rogers' interview with Mr. Necta. The Carl R. Rogers

Archive, Library of Congress. Washington, DC.

Rogers, C. R. (circa 1956). Transcript of Carl Rogers' interview with Mrs. ROC. The Carl R. Rogers Archive. Library of Congress. Washington, DC.

Rogers, C. R. (1957). The necessary and sufficient conditions for therapeutic personality change. *Journal of Consulting Psychology*, *21* (2), 95–103.

Rogers, C. R. (1959). A theory of therapy, personality, and interpersonal relationships as developed in the client-centered framework. In S. Koch (Ed.) *Psychology: A study of a science* (Vol. 3). New York: McGraw-Hill , (pp. 184–256).

Rogers, C. R. (1980). Empathic: An unappreciated way of being. In C. R. Rogers, *A Way of Being*. Boston: Houghton Mifflin, (pp. 137–63).

Rogers, C.R. (1986). Reflection of feelings. *Person-Centered Review*, *1*(4), 375–77.

Rosenberg, M. B. (1983). *A model for nonviolent communication*. Philadelphia, PA: New Society Publishers.

Temaner, B. S. (1977). The empathic understanding response process. *Chicago Counseling and Psychotherapy Center Discussion Papers*.

Zimring, F. M. (1990a). Cognitive processes as a cause of psychotherapeutic change: self-initiated processes. In G. Lietaer, J. Rombauts and R. Van Balen (Eds.) *Client-centered and experiential psychotherapy in the nineties*. Leuven, Belgium: Leuven University Press, (pp. 361–80).

Zimring, F. M. (1990b). A characteristic of Rogers' response to clients. *Person-Centered Review*, *5*, 433–48.

Zimring, F. (1995). A new explanation for the beneficial results of client-centered therapy: The possibility of a new paradigm. *The Person-Centered Journal*, *2*(2), 36–48.

Zimring, F. (2000). Empathic understanding grows the person. *The Person-Centered Journal*, *7*(2), 101–13.

Leslie S. Greenberg and Rachel Rushanski-Rosenberg

York University, Toronto, Ontario, Canada

Therapists' Experience of Empathy

A major problem with investigating empathy in psychotherapy is the lack of an agreed-upon definition of empathy (Bohart and Greenberg, 1997). It is difficult to train people in empathy and to develop measures of empathy without a clear understanding of what empathy is. Most would agree with an informal definition of empathy as 'putting oneself into the shoes of the other', but beyond that definitions diverge both conceptually and operationally.

Carl Rogers' (1980) describes empathy as:

the therapist's sensitive ability and willingness to understand the client's thoughts, feelings and struggles from the client's point of view. [It is] this ability to see completely through the client's eyes, to adopt his frame of reference . . . (p. 85)

It means entering the private perceptual world of the other . . . being sensitive, moment by moment, to the changing felt meanings which flow in this other person . . . It means sensing meanings of which he or she is scarcely aware . . . (p. 142)

This definition reveals the essential complexity of the empathy process, which entails several related therapist cognitive and experiential activities: For example, perceiving what the client is feeling, understanding the client's communication, imaginatively entering the client's world, and comprehending what it is like to be them (Bohart and Greenberg. 1997).

Barrett-Lennard (1981) has described empathy in terms of three cyclical connected phases: therapists' empathic resonance (therapist experience); expressed empathy (therapist observable behavior); and client received empathy (client experience). In this paper we will explore the empathic resonance phase. Empathic process in therapy in this cyclical view involves a complex process in which one attends to the client with a genuine interest in understanding the world from the client's point of view, respecting the client's subjective world and the client as an authentic source of experience. In the resonance phase of this process one needs to perceive what the client is feeling, imaginatively enter their world, attempt to understand their communications, and engage in a complex process of comprehending what it is like for that person to be that person. This is a full-bodied integrative experience in which multiple sources of information, including cognition and affect, are used, possibly including one's own feeling, one's own prior experiences, as well as any current feeling one might have through the process of imaginative entry. This comprehensive process is both an experiential and a conceptual process.

As suggested in *Empathy Reconsidered* (Bohart and Greenberg 1997) empathy in the expressed phase 'is not a singular act but varies according to that which is being understood in the moment'. Thus empathy may at one time involve understanding and communicating a feeling ('you felt really alone'), or at another time understanding a complex narrative of a person's perception of an event ('it was somehow the way he looked at you that led you to feel so small and led you to react so angrily'), or capturing a high level synthesis of complex experience ('and this was the final rejection'), or at still another time it may involve identifying an idiosyncratic meaning ('this meant "I've finally proved it"'). The type of processing the therapist is involved in at each point differs — at one point it is affect perception, at another narrative reconstruction, at a third articulation of the immediate and emerging implications in what the client is saying, and at still another more of an abstract synthesis. The empathic process thus is not a simple or singular thing. However, what is most characteristic of empathy, in our view, is that whatever empathic expression occurs it is based on a therapist's bodily felt experience of what is being understood rather than a purely conceptual understanding.

A controversy does exist however with regard to the nature of the bodily felt experience. Rogers (1957), in describing empathy, wrote that it involves the ability 'To sense the client's private world as if it was your own but without ever losing the "as if" quality . . . To sense the client's anger, fear, or confusion as if it were your own, yet without your own anger, fear or confusion getting bound up in it' (pp. 99). It is unclear whether therapists when empathizing with a client's feeling actually feel a little bit of the same feeling as if it were their own, or whether what they feel is something more complex.

Based on the above multicomponent, experiential view of empathy we set out to investigate therapists' experience of empathy to try and shed some light on the actual experience of being empathic and to clarify the nature of the as if quality. To do this we interviewed a number of therapists on their experience of being empathic.

METHOD

Participants

Eight therapists ranging in therapeutic experience from 1 to 27 years, with a mean of 6 years, and a mode of 3 years of experience, were interviewed. One therapist was interviewed on two different clients. Sessions came from nine clients with major depressive disorder. The sessions came from 16 to 20 sessions of Client-centered and Experiential treatments, and the location of the sessions studied ranged from between session 5 to 17.

Procedure

Using an interpersonal process recall (IPR) method, therapists received at least two key moments in an audio- or videotape that they had selected as moments in which they remembered feeling particularly empathic. The tapes were reviewed, as soon after the session as possible, some directly after the session but within forty-eight hours of the session. Therapists were asked to review the segments chosen and to stop the tape whenever they chose and report on what they could recall of their internal experience in the session in the segment of tape reviewed. The questions asked by the IPR interviewer at this time (shown in appendix 1) focused on inquiring into the therapist's internal process while being empathic.

Using a grounded theory approach, the transcripts of the therapists' responses in the

IPR sessions were analyzed and a set of categories were constructed. Grounded Theory method is a phenomenological qualitative research methodology, which values individual experience and the ability of the individual to access and articulate their conscious awareness of an experience (Colaizzi, 1978). It is a systematic method for the interpretive analysis of people's verbatim accounts of their experience and focuses not just on the participant's verbalization, but also on their implicit meanings.

The Grounded Theory method used involved several steps. Initially, participants, in this case therapists, were interviewed on their experience. The interviews were transcribed and protocols were then categorized by dividing them into meaning units, that is, sortable portions of data, which captured individual concepts or ideas conveyed by the participants. Meaning units were decided by shifts in topics introduced into the interview by either the participant or the interviewer. Each meaning unit was then condensed into a one- or two-line summary, and subsequently sorted into clusters on the basis of the embedded meaning of the item. As more categories emerged, constructed categories were generated to explain the descriptive categories and the relationship between them. Throughout this process ideas about the data, categories, and theory were written down, so as to enhance and record the conceptualization process as it was forming. Once the point of saturation of categories was reached, that is, when the analysis of additional protocols failed to yield new categories, a theory was formed based on conceptual material that emerged from research memos, about the categories and the relationship between them. A model of the process of the therapists' inner experience while being empathic, was constructed.

RESULTS

From analysis of the transcripts it was clear that, at the self-identified points of heightened experience of empathy, several complex processes were occurring within the therapists, often a number occurring at the same time. All the therapists reported a multifaceted process of trying to capture and convey to clients an understanding of their unique experience. Therapists reported using their own feelings, bodily responses, and even personal experiences as calibrating tools to allow for the most accurate empathic experience. Often therapists were also feeling compassion, were accepting and containing clients' feelings, while trying to facilitate specific processes to encourage a shift in clients' processes.

Based on the grounded analysis of therapists' accounts, a model consisting of three categories of different classes of the experience of being empathic was constructed. These categories were: Therapists' internal experience relating to their processing of the client's experience; therapists' internal experience relating to their processing of their own experience; and therapist's feelings and intentions toward their clients. These categories of therapist experience were labeled: About Client's Experience, About Therapist's Experience: Toward Client. These categories were formed from the subcategories shown in Table 1 and described below.

About client's experience
This major category involved those internal experience(s) the therapists described relating to their processing of the client's experience. This category was constituted by four subcategories,

Table 1. Therapists' inner experience of empathy

About Client's experience	*About Therapist's experience*	*Toward Client*
Actively trying to understand	Being on the mark	Facilitating specific process
Imagining	Responsive bodily reactions	
Sensing client's experience	Feeling (feeling a bit of the client's feeling)	Compassion (Touched by client's pain)
A thinking process	Drawing on personal experience (memory)	Accepting client's feelings

Actively trying to understand; Imagining; Sensing Client's Experience; and Thinking. These are described below with varied examples provided in associated tables to provide a thick description of these subcategories.

1. Actively trying to understand:

Therapists reported that they actively attempted to capture and reflect back to the client an understanding of the client's unique experience. The process of actively trying to understand, in the words of one of the therapists, involves being 'aware of really trying to capture (the client's) experience . . . a sense of understanding . . . of trying to understand (the client) . . . absorbed in that moment trying to reflect back to her what her experience was'.

There were several subcategories of actively trying to understand, shown in Table 2, and they describe ways therapists made an effort to understand their clients. They understood through listening to core feelings. They synthesized a meaning out of the client's words, and this sometimes evoked a feeling the therapists tasted, to help form an understanding of what the client might be feeling. Therapists also reported that they: drew on their own experience in order to understand; that they understood the client through a general understanding of human experience; and that they built a progressive understanding of the client. Thinking and sensing also were used to enhance understanding. Examples of therapist statements under the lower-level categories are shown in Table 2.

Regarding therapist statements on the degree to which the therapist felt the client's feeling we found that, according to the therapists, the understanding process seemed to focus mainly on the client's feelings, without the therapist actually feeling what the client is feeling. For example one therapist said: 'I certainly don't recall having feelings. I guess I would have had feelings in the sense of the feeling of being close to, well, close to my client, but more than that, close to his experience. And a sense of, maybe the sense you have when something kind of hits you, as the kind of that's the essence of it or that, or that captures that, and there is sort of excitement that goes along with feeling like you really understood. So I guess that's what it is. But it didn't have the feeling . . . I certainly didn't feel vulnerable, I didn't feel like I was subject to being attacked. I didn't feel exposed . . . So I didn't have his experience.'

Another said: 'I am understanding that it's hard for her to look at me and say what she

---

Table 2. Actively trying to understand

1. Understanding through listening to core feelings:
   - 'I try to listen carefully . . . to what it is that she's actually feeling. What's the core feeling state that would be generating these words'. Or: 'I feel like all of me is listening . . . and it feels very finely tuned. Trying to get where it fits'.
2. Synthesizing a meaning out of the client's words, which may evoke a feeling the therapist tastes, to form an understanding of what the client may be feeling:
   - 'I am, synthesizing a meaning . . . understanding of what she's saying . . . I am translating that into a feeling. 'So there is no hope.' But then I say, no hope, and that generates a feeling in me. I am generating an experience, and then trying to taste it.'
   - 'I am just going to try and summarize my understanding of what she's saying. So I am actually doing some kind of summary, repeating and tying together.'
3. Drawing on the therapist's own experience in order to understand:
   - 'I said then what was the antidote? I had a very clear image that the antidote [to loneliness] for me was having somebody. So I said I can use that, at least to try to get at what was it for her. It's been on my mind with hers. I guess that helped me. I have a big chunk of personal experience that parallels her. I guess implicitly that I understood it because I understood what I had gone through.'
4. Understanding the client through a general understanding of human experience:
   - 'So, I am putting together both current and general understanding to form the understanding of what she's saying.'
   - 'I am kind of drawing on understanding the general experience of what it's like to feel rejected to help me understand.'
5. Building and drawing on a progressive understanding of the client:
   - 'I am also synthesizing it with my global understanding of her and what's going on in her life with him.'
   - 'So it must be things that I'm processing on an automatic level. Things from other sessions that I heard her say.'
   - 'So here I'm building a bigger and bigger map or model of what's going on for her, isolation, hopeless. I am building a picture or a model of her internal world, over time, and it's elaborating.'
   - 'And I was thinking more about her past relational experiences that she described in the session, and just thinking about some of her reactions and feelings that she had described to me in the past. I guess I use that prior information to help guide me in terms of what I thought she was feeling.'

---

feels. I mean, there I am not feeling anything. I am not feeling her feeling at all.'

Another said, 'Ok, so she feels hopeless here, that's very real. I guess that's what she does feel. I mean I don't feel hopeless (I: you are thinking it?) I am understanding, and it's making an impact on me.'

2. Imagining

One of the most comfortable and direct entry points into clients' experiences was through the process of imagining. From a number of therapists' accounts, and in the words of one therapist, it seems that 'the more they (the clients) use imagery the easier it is to get into their experience,' and 'When my client uses images it is a lot easier for me to get in.' The therapists reported that they did not become the client in the images, but rather sensed through the image what the client was feeling. One said, 'It is always an image. It's always in relation to an

Table 3. Imagining

1. Images are conjured up by the therapist in response to the client's narrative:
   - 'I just kept getting an image of her very young and just holding herself back from, somehow protecting herself from being hurt. I'm not sure exactly. She didn't really talk about exactly what happened in those childhood experiences, how she was hurt, but the image I kept getting of her was that she was very young and I felt even more.'
   - 'It was the sense of the children and the school yard, all huddled in a circle and pushing her out and it was her on the outside.'
   - '. . . As she talks I have a picture of her mother old and helpless, and I sense . . . it's like I'm seeing a movie. And then I'm seeing that the mother is helpless. And I'm seeing her feel helpless. I'm feeling inside there is a lot of helplessness in her.'
   - 'In her family (the client's) achievement is very emphasized . . . in my head I'm playing this movie of comments about so and so is so wonderful . . . and she's doing this. And I suppose, almost a sense of what's it like sitting at a table like that, in a shrinking way, that drains the light out of you. How do you shine when everyone around you is so luminous?'
2. Body language is translated into an image:
   - 'She usually is quite open non-verbally . . . so that (the client holding both hands across her abdomen) cued me that she might have some tightness there. So I kept having this image of her holding herself in and that was what I was trying to understand. What is she protecting?'
3. Translating images into words that reflect the therapist's understanding:
   - 'So when she was painting this picture for me, the world of the child was happy and light and in my head, I had this contrast of a dark, heavy, drudgery of being adult. So, I try to capture that when I say this is this other place, the world we're in.'
4. Client's narrative evokes an image, which helps the therapist empathize with the client's feelings:
   - 'It definitely evoked a kind of biblical thing, I have this image . . . I sort of have an image of a desert and somebody going out into the desert and being banished.'
   - '. . . at this point I begin to try to get into her internal frame of reference. What it is really like for her. And I start searching inside myself for what this is like. I'm imagining what is happening for her here that she feels this pain and stress. Somehow I come up with the idea . . . there is a kind of imaginative part to this. I think I have a picture in my head . . .'
   - 'I had this image in my head of, I know I'm in this place and I could imagine her house and imagine the people there. And in my head I'm playing this movie of the comments about, so-and-so is so wonderful and he's so great and he has this Ph.D. and she's doing this. And I suppose, almost a sense of what it's like sitting at a table like that, in a shrinking way.'
   - 'In this moment I had a strong sense of what it was like to be him, to feel so vulnerable. I had an image of him on the river in this canoe; his hand kind of literally dangling. And it was a very vivid image. And I was able to respond to that feeling.'
   - 'Her whole expression there has led to me having an image, and it's tied to this directionless. So I sort of have an image of her . . . So I sort of have an image of her, me, but not really me, but of the state of waiting for this call. The image is filled with this feeling of unknowing expectance, or expectation.'
5. The image evokes further images:
   - 'I sort of have an image of her, me, but not really me, but of the state of waiting for this call. The image is filled with this feeling of unknowing expectance, or expectation, and of just waiting. And then I try to put that image into words and I say "hanging in limbo", which is sort of another metaphor which evokes another image almost in me of "hanging in limbo".'

image. There is still an "as if" quality'.

Another said, 'There was that image of a nine-year-old child and how invalidating that would feel to be . . . authority figure screaming at you, and how could you have not known, and how little you would feel. That was very intense. That's when I had an image, not that I was the child, but what it would feel like to be the child.'

There were several ways therapists experienced images: These are given in the lower-level categories in Table 3. Images were conjured up by the therapist in response to client's narrative; Body language was translated into an image; images were translated into words that reflected the therapist's understanding; the client's narrative evoked an image, that helped the therapist empathize with the client's feelings; an image evoked further images. Examples of therapist statements under these lower-level categories of imagining are given in Table 3.

3. Sensing client's experience

Some therapists talked about having a sense of what their client's experience was, or what the client's felt sense was, that had not yet been put into words. This is a body sensing that results in meaning without explicit thinking process. For example therapists said:

'I don't feel ridiculed and left out, I just have a sense of what her sense of isolation, a sense of feeling lost in a school yard, a sense of being alone.'

'At times I'm sensing some of what it universally feels like to feel rejected or hopeless or powerless, but I'm not feeling it myself, but I have some way of sensing what it feels like to feel hopeless.'

' I'm in no way feeling helpless. But I'm sensing that she feels . . . As she talks I have a picture of her mother, old and helpless, and I sense . . .'

There were several ways in which sensing worked in the empathic process as shown in the lower-level categories in Table 4. These were: Sensing what the client is experiencing through body language; Sensing what the client is experiencing by cognitively going through the events that the client went through; Sensing what the client is experiencing by translating the client's body language into an image. Examples of therapist statements under lower-level categories are shown in Table 4.

4. A thinking process

Thinking was most often used to recalibrate therapists' understandings and to help decide what to do at choice points. There were several ways in which thinking was involved, as shown in the lower-level category headings in Table 5: Actively trying to understand what is going on for the client by thinking; Deciding to be empathic; Inferring from client's narrative what the client experienced, and symbolizing in words understanding of client's feelings; Listening carefully and sorting out nuances of understanding. Examples of therapist statements under lower-level categories of thinking are given below in Table 5.

About therapist's experience

This major category involved those internal operations the therapists described relating to their processing of their own experience. These involved sub-categories of: Being on the Mark; Feeling; Responsive Bodily Reactions; and Drawing on Personal Experience. The subcategories are described below.

Table 4. Sensing Client's Experience

1. Sensing what the client is experiencing through body language:
    - 'I had a suspicion that she was afraid of something and she wasn't giving it voice, because of this non-verbal shift in her posture.' (Ann-Marie)
      'I hear her voice. I hear the powerlessness, the tearfulness. Now somehow that touches me. Why bother, I know, is a feeling: I sense a feeling of hopelessness.'
    - 'I am actually responding to her face and voice. She looks and sounds plaintive . . . A lot I think, had to do with her non-verbal expression looking kind of powerless. There was more going on than just the words. It was the manner.'
    - 'I guess I noticed on her face that there was a lot of pain and sadness and that gave me an internal sense that she was experiencing that.'
2. Sensing what the client is experiencing by cognitively going through the events that the client went through:
    - 'That's why there I was feeling really, wow, this sense of betrayal. There was this woman and your father . . . sort of this charade. And you thought things were a certain way. That you were lied to. But then what I didn't say, but was in my head 'cause then she started talking again, was how devastating that must have been.'
3. Sensing what the client is experiencing by translating the client's body language into an image:
    - 'Throughout it, I kept having this image of her physically holding herself. Physically protecting herself and that, as long as I was still having that image, I knew we were still dealing with fear.'

---

1. Being on the mark

Therapists receive cues from the client and experience being on the mark with their understanding. This experience of being accurately on target comes from a variety of processes as depicted in the lower-level categories of Table 6. Therapists know they are on the mark when: Clients are able to make further meaning and differentiate their own experience; The clients' reactions indicated that a statement that the therapist made reflected their experience accurately. Clients may verbally let the therapist know that the word he/she put on the client's experience fits. The therapist may also receive cues internally of being on the mark, for example by: Sensing that the bond with the client fluctuates with the degree of therapist being on the mark: Feeling 'with' the client vs. wandering around; Having a physical sensation of having captured the client's experience by feeling alert and excited, and: Having an internal sense of capturing the client's experience. Examples of therapist statements under lower-level categories of being on the mark are given in Table 6.

2. Feeling

With regard to whether therapists felt their clients' experiences therapists, at times, did report feeling similar feelings to those expressed by clients, or those generated by clients' internal issues. But at the same time they reported knowing that they were imagining what the feeling was, rather than actually experiencing it first hand. One for example said, 'I am also feeling anxious because it's obviously some anxiety problem.' Another therapist said, 'I know that I'm imagining it, that's the difference . . . I do feel a lonely yearning, but I know I'm not in it. As if I were you, as if I was in the picture.' Some therapists said that feeling came always in relation to an image they had: 'I actually feel. But it is always an image. It's always in relation to an image.' Thus the 'as if' quality in there, and feeling what the client is feeling, is clearly different from simply feeling one's own feeling. The therapist who said she felt anxiety because

Table 5. A Thinking Process

1. Actively trying to understand what is going on for the client by thinking:
    *   'I feel very actively engaged in understanding this. This part is very much about trying to find the key, what is this about, how can we shift this?'
    *   'One of the things I must have been thinking as well, gee, it must be very difficult to feel like this. Must be hard to write a term paper under this kind of pressure.'
    *   'I am actually doing this quite cognitively. I am just conceptually understanding that this is a conflict. There is something scary or something difficult about discussing the issue.'
    *   'And I recall having those thoughts within myself, thinking what she could be experiencing, what is really going on and working that out in my head.'
    *   'So, I think yes, part of the difficulty is you avoid . . . Then I think, yes, but I guess that's 'cause it's scary. And so I restate and I say I guess it's scary. So I am actually thinking.'
    *   'So I'm doing kind of thinking about what is the real experience here and how can I get to it.'
2. Deciding to be empathic:
    *   'There, I'm being empathic because I realize she needs to know that I know she's okay. She's trying . . .'
    *   'But here I am heading in with an agenda to try to really be empathic. I mean I set myself with an agenda, which is not unusual . . . I am saying to myself I'm really going to try and understand, and see if she can use this, 'cause she's quite a difficult client. She's quite avoidant, and then I often get more directive. So I am setting myself an agenda, not to be too directive. So I am actually trying to be empathic.'
3. Inferring from client's narrative what the client experienced, and symbolizing in words the understanding of the client's feelings:
    *   'When she was telling me this, I said 'betrayal'. But it started as the feeling of impact when the realization is there, that somebody has lied to me — way, like your father's having an affair with your mother's best friend who is also your friend. And then the other piece to it, which I didn't say, was also part of that chest hurt feeling.'
4. Listening carefully and sorting out nuances of understanding:
    *   'I'm doing a lot of understanding with sort of trying to get at the nuances of understanding of what exactly was it like.'
    *   'What is funny is I could have told you that in the first five minutes of the session. And actually I think so could she. There are sort of different ways of knowing. I mean I could have told you conceptually that she . . . I guess it is more differentiated . . .The refined understanding.'
    *   'She didn't say, 'Something's wrong with me.' She said something is wrong or what is wrong. When I heard that wrong word, I heard, "I'm wrong." There's something wrong with me. I did that constructing myself.'
    *   'When I say I'm thinking is actually listening very, very carefully for the nuance, not for the easy understanding. So I 'm actually listening. But listening is a very cognitive understanding thing. I am not feeling anything. I am listening and I am trying to sort out the nuances of understanding.'
    *   'So it's like there is something here . . . What exactly is it? That's differentiating meaning or facets of meaning to get at exactly what the experience is.'

it is an anxiety problem, for example, was not herself feeling anxious but was feeling a higher-order representation of what it feels like to feel anxious. Therapist statements falling under the lower-level categories of: Feeling a bit of the feeling; Feeling the client's feeling but not being debilitated; and Using own feelings as a gauge, are given in Table 7.

Table 6. Being on the Mark

1. The therapist knows he/she is on the mark when the client is able to make further meaning and differentiate own experience:
   - 'It was a good empathy segment because what developed is more meaning-making on her part, and she was able to sort through a few things. Although it was more on a conceptual level she was able to further differentiate some of what she is experiencing.'

2. The reaction of the client gives the therapist the indication that the statement he/she made reflected the client's experience:
   - 'I just have a sense of what her sense of isolation, a sense of feeling lost in a school yard, a sense of being alone . . . I'm sensing what it might be like to be that person . . . Now I notice that veering away from everything but her voice also begins to change. Her vocal quality, beginning to be more thoughtful, more turned inwards.'
   - 'I think the reaction of the client gives me an indication that statements I've made reflected her experience. She was very emphatic in agreeing with what I said. Also in particular what I said brought her back to her emotional experience, where she was more in the story-telling mode. It allowed her to draw into her emotions.'

3. The client lets the therapist know that the word the therapist put on his/her experience, fits:
   - 'She gives that "Yes that's a good word," right. So somehow that's a prototypic empathic process of putting a word on somebody's feelings that they feel fits.'

4. Sensing that the bond with the client fluctuates with the degree of therapist being on the mark:
   - 'And there is this feeling in my body that I'm on the mark. And I can also feel her coming close to me. There is something about the energy of the other person. It's like she moves towards me somehow, or the attachment is stronger.'

5. When the therapist is on the mark, he/she feels 'with' the client vs. wandering around:
   - 'There is a kind of a "with" quality to it. I feel like I'm really with her, and somehow I really gone to where she is. I'm where she is, I'm not wandering around. It's like coming around the corner and her actually being right there, instead of me talking to her and she's somewhere in the bushes there, and I'm making contact with her but I'm not standing next to her. In those moments I feel she's right in front of me and I really see her.'

6. The therapist has a physical sensation of having captured the client's experience:
   - 'I feel very certain of what I'm saying. And there is this feeling in my body that I'm on the mark.'
   - 'When I'm on the mark there is actually a physical sensation I get with that . . . I feel it in my body (showing on gut). Yeah, I feel it in my body. It's an actual feeling of being on the mark. I don't know how to express it; it's a physical sensation of having landed on it.'

7. The therapist feels alert and excited, when capturing the client's experience:
   - 'I feel there is a part of me . . . I feel it down my back. That tenses almost as if, I'm not in pain, but I know there is a resonance somewhere in me that goes, "Ssss," that's sore. So, I feel a mix of that alertness, which is a body thing.'
   - 'I become more alert. I feel slightly more emotionally activated, aroused. I hear the plea.'
   - 'The sense you have when something kind of hits you, as the kind of that's the essence of it or that, or that captures that, and there is sort of excitement that goes along with feeling like you really understood.'

8. The therapist has an internal sense that he/she is capturing the client's internal experience:
   - 'I know that I get a sense of being on the mark.'
   - 'At that point, fully in her experience, that's always the point where I know okay, we're in the groove now. I know where she's coming from.'
   - 'There was also an internal sense that I was mirroring her experience . . . I just had this

internal sense that it was what she was experiencing. So it was almost like an internal knowing that I was accessing her internal experience.'
- 'I was aware of, it's hard to explain, but like I said before it was almost like a knowing that I was right on, that I was on the right track.'
- 'I felt that in this segment things I just really was understanding what she was talking about. I have an internal sense of that.'

Table 7. Feeling (Feeling a bit of the Client's Feeling)

1. Feeling a 'bit' of the feeling:
   - 'I sort of taste the hopelessness . . . I'm not feeling frozen myself, I'm not feeling hopeless myself, but I am having an experiential sense of what hopelessness feels like. It's kind of second-level emotional experience. I'm not hopeless, but I have a sense of what hopelessness feels like.'
   - 'I just feel how stuck she is . . . I don't feel stuck. I hear how stuck she is. I do feel something. I do feel a little bit of helplessness . . .'
   - 'I do actually feel something, but it's once removed. I mean this is the "as if".'
   - 'I never did feel like I was fully, like I was in a state of betrayal. It was something familiar. Some signal went off or something that was somehow familiar.'
2. Feeling the client's feelings but not debilitated by it:
   - 'I am not feeling debilitated by it.'
3. Using own feelings as a gauge to client's feelings:
   - 'It seemed like she was very discouraged and I had a feeling in myself also of are we getting anywhere . . .'

Table 8. Responsive Bodily Reactions

1. The client's pain produces body movements in the therapist:
   - 'There I had an image of a nine-year-old kid being screamed at. That was very strong, I mean, you can see my reaction. It was like, 'Oh my God.' And I actually moved back in my chair. Feeling the impact of that . . . the moving back was the physical action of needing to get away from that yelling or whatever it was.'
   - 'Something about loss that touched me in my chest and then I moved forward in the chair and then it was like it drew me forward toward her or something, I was drawn toward her.'
2. A physical sensation in the therapist's body in reaction to/or anticipation of the client's pain:
   - 'This is a point where, again, I feel resonance down here. In my gut. This image of her having to extinguish herself.'
   - 'And the physical sensation almost, of anticipating someone else's pain. Yeah, it's a sensation that I get down my back.'
   - 'I feel it down my back. That tenses almost as if, I'm not in pain, but I know there is a resonance somewhere in me that goes, "Ssss, that's sore. . ." I have a sense that's there's hurt in that point in time.'
3. The client's narrative is translated into sensations and then words that capture the client's feeling:
   - 'It starts as a sensation or often it does; in this case it did. And then I'm in it and words are coming out of it.'
   - 'It doesn't start as an articulated feeling. I feel it as sensation. It's usually in here and then it's like I'm putting words to that.' (Janice)
   - 'It's like it hit me like an impact in my chest. And the word that came to mind, 'betrayed,' it came from that feeling.'

Table 9. Drawing on Personal Experience

1. The client's narrative evoked memory of the therapist's own experience:
   - 'It was also around when she said she had moved and I had a similar experience as a child. So, it was of like I was it for a moment, in my own . . . like I remember that image of myself in the car driving away.'
   - 'But it has been on my mind with her. I guess that helped me. I have a big chunk of personal experience that parallels hers.'
   - 'I guess implicitly that I understood it because I understood what I had gone through.'
   - 'I really think empathy is a complex emotional task. So much of it is high-speed synthesis. And you cannot be empathic with something that you can't read. You're the most empathic with things that you have some . . . you've tasted somehow, It's like, "Oh I know what you are. This is what it's like." and you describe the flavour of it, the taste of it and you're like, "Yeah, that's exactly what it's like".'
   - 'In a way, I wasn't consciously doing that but I know it. I have felt that feeling of being broken and being judged by my injury. I feel like I'm privileged. I have a privileged perspective in a way.'
2. The image that the client painted evoked a memory of the client's own experience:
   - 'I see that image, I actually see it. Then I evoked . . . a memory of my own experience.'
3. Putting oneself 'into' the client in the image evokes a memory:
   - 'And I also saw an image, very clear, of her walking along the rows. And I think I did put myself into her. And then I remember thinking of my own experience.'
4. Drawing on personal experience to interpret the therapist's physiological reactions as hint to what is going on for the client:
   - 'I'm drawing on my own wisdom of having similar triggers to evoke that physiological feeling . . . I'll have this awareness of like, usually it's my abdomen or my shoulders that are tight. If it's abdomen, it's usually fear in a room and if it's shoulders, it's anger. It's just how I've learned to use my own bodily keys as a hint to what's going on.'

3. Responsive bodily reaction

Therapists often use their responsive bodily sensations as a clue to what is going on for the client. One therapist said, ' I can actually feel some sympathetic symptoms. Like, I felt tightness in my own abdomen. I can actually experience what they're experiencing. When it works with clients, yeah, it's not every session. But I happened to have quite a good connection with her. So, it can be evoked in me.' Often the responsive bodily reaction also helped the therapist focus on what needed to be worked on. One therapist for example said, 'What's happening in my body is always just a clue to re-enter with a client. It's like she's telling me this and I'm feeling this and this is really what's in the room, or what I'm going to work with now.' The lower-level categories: Client's pain produces body movement in therapist; Physical sensation in the therapists bodily; and Client's narrative translated into sensations and then words are given in Table 8.

4. Drawing on personal experience

There were several ways therapists drew on their personal experience. These are shown in Table 9. The client's narrative either evoked a memory of the therapist's own experience, or the image that the client painted evoked a memory of the client's own experience, or the therapists, by putting themselves 'into' their client's image, evoked a memory. In addition therapists drew on personal experience to interpret their own physiological reactions as a hint to what was going on for the client.

With respect to what therapists were feeling in drawing on their own personal experience, or when a memory of their experience was evoked by the client's narrative, therapists reported that remembering an emotion or a painful experience was not the same as feeling it. There was both a distance and a separation from the feeling. One therapist said, 'I mean there's a distance from it. There's a separation. It's I remember me feeling it, it's not like I feel it happening now . . . I didn't feel lonely at the moment, but I remembered feeling lonely. And that's the difference. I remember my experience from the image; that is not the same as feeling it. Remembering an emotion for me is not the same as feeling an emotion.'

Once the memory of an experience or an emotion surfaced, the therapist distinguished between his or her own experience, and emotions, and those of the client, and does not draw a complete parallel between the two. One therapist said, 'I might have used more of my own experience. But somehow I know that that feeling is a propensity of mine, and it may not be hers. So I've learned something about when my own feelings are a good indicator of somebody else's feelings, or may be just more my own. So there was a lot I thought in there about my own experience.'

On another occasion the therapist said, 'So she paints an image and I see that image . . . Then I actually did evoke a memory of my own experience, which quite matched that, you know. I just remembered, I remembered feeling so yearning and alone, that's right. So I drew on a lot of my internal experience. And I also saw an image, very clear, of her walking along the rows. And I think I did put myself in to her. And then I remember thinking of my own experience . . .'

Toward the client

There were several ways in which therapists had feelings toward the client's experience.

The therapists on occasion reported a current feeling toward the client such as feeling touched by the client's pain. At other times therapists reported that in being empathic they

---

Table 10. Compassion

1. Sensing client is hurt and feeling tenderness/compassion towards him/her:
   - 'Now, I feel tremendous compassion. She struggled, she feels stuck.'
   - 'When she started talking about the childhood experiences, I started really feeling a lot of compassion for her.'
   - 'I had this image in my head of, I know I'm in this place and I could imagine her house and imagine the people there. And in my head I'm playing this movie of the comments . . . And I suppose, almost a sense of real concern.'
   - 'This image of her having to extinguish herself. Again, that makes me feel Tender.'
   - 'I feel . . . a tenderness because I have a sense that's there's hurt in that point in time.'
   - 'So now I know that I just felt a rush of compassion. Of how sad, yes, I understand how awful. Now, there I feel compassion.'
2. Feeling touched by clients' pain:
   - 'I mean I am feeling what I would call really empathic. And there, firstly, I am feeling touched by her pain.'
   - 'I hear the powerlessness, the tearfulness. Now somehow that touches me. It touches me emotionally, definitely.'

Table 11. Accepting Client's Feelings

1. Containing the client's perceived negative feelings about therapist or the therapy process:
   - 'I felt her in this space where nothing was working and I'm not getting anywhere. And I realize that therapy is part of that . . . that was how she was feeling. Being willing to contain that, her feeling of that, along with everything that meant for me.'
   - 'It's like I knew what she felt and I just stopped defending myself on it. It was like, this is how she feels and I was like, "Okay." Inside I was like, "Okay, if that's how you feel, I'm going to permit it."'
   - 'I was willing to contain her feelings of these sessions aren't working.'
2. Willing to go 'down the road' with the client although wanting to 'run away':
   - 'I'm running away from it and then I go, "I'm willing to go down in there."'

---

were trying to facilitate a specific process or experience in the client: There were three major categories: Compassion; Accepting Client's Feelings; and Facilitating Specific Processes. These are described below.

1. Compassion

This is feeling for the client's suffering. Compassion is defined in Buddhist terms as the heartfelt wish that others be free from suffering and the causes of suffering. Three forms of compassion are defined in this perspective. One is described as 'How nice it would be if the other would be free of suffering and its causes'. The second perspective is defined as 'May the other be free of' and the third as 'I will free them from' suffering and its causes (Hopkins, 2001). The later form does not appear in therapy. Therapist experience is probably best characterized as a sincere wish for the other to be free of suffering. The therapist statements in lower-level categories of compassion, Sensing client is hurt and feeling tenderness/compassion, and Feeling touched by client's pain, are shown in Table 10.

2. Accepting client's feelings

Being empathic also involved accepting the client's experience, even if it may involve feelings that the therapist perceives as negative for some reason. For example, the therapist might struggle with accepting the client's feelings, if he or she perceives that those feelings are connected in a negative way to the therapist's performance, or to the success of therapy. In another example, the therapist experienced some initial difficulty 'going down the road' with the client into the depths of her experience because the client's experience 'triggered' difficult feelings for the therapist. The initial difficulty was examined by the therapist, processed, and a decision to go 'down the road' with the client was made. This illuminates the process of accepting clients' feelings and experience while being empathic. Therapists' statements of the lower-level categories of: Containing the client's perceived negative feelings, and Willing to go 'down the road' with the client, are shown in Table 11.

Facilitating specific processes

Finally the understanding of the client that is gained in the process of being empathic is at times used as a part of a conscious decision on the part of the therapist, to encourage, or facilitate, certain processes in the client. The therapist's intent will vary with different clients and at different times in the therapeutic process. This is indicated by the lower-level categories shown in Table 12. The therapist uses understanding to: Remain on an important topic; Not intervene; Encourage differentiation; Unpack experience; Articulate; Shift the client's frame; Reaffirm client's understanding; Encourage client to stay with an experience; Validate the client; Encourage the client to say things out loud; and to Emphasize and focus on something.

CONCLUSION

From this grounded theory study, although no core category emerged to capture the essential experience, it appears that the experience of being empathic is a multicomponent experience. Many things are going on inside in the process of being empathic. Although no core category emerged, it did appear that an experiential process of having a bodily felt experience of some type was central to experiencing empathy. Being empathic involves feeling something in one's body along with an understanding, thinking, imagining, sensing, remembering and intending. The important process of understanding was difficult to unpack into more fundamental processes. The sub-processes of understanding appear predominately to be automatic and inaccessible to awareness.

It became clear that therapists in this sample when empathizing with a client's feeling did not feel their own feelings or, for that matter, their client's feelings projected into them (as analytic therapists believe occurs in projective identification). They did feel something, but even when it was a feeling that matched the client's feeling, what therapists experience is more like understanding, knowing or remembering what that feeling feels like rather than feeling it. There is a real difference between feeling sad (or a little sad) and experientially knowing what it feels like to feel sad. In being empathic it is this later, higher-level form of experiencing in which therapists engage. They feel something, but what this is, is a feeling of knowing experientially what something feels like. Thus experientially knowing what it is like to feel humiliated, sad or angry does not produce the action tendency in the therapist that these emotions normally would produce if experienced as the therapist's own emotion. Thus the therapist does not experience wanting to shrink into the ground, cry out or withdraw, or thrust forward (not even a little bit).

Table 12. Facilitating Specific Processes

1. Using the understanding to remain on topic that seems important to figure out:
   - 'It flashes like don't follow that, that's the frustration. And I'm also saying yeah, this is important . . . So let's keep trying to get at it. So I'm sort of coaching myself not to go off in different directions. And just stay with trying to get at it.'
2. Using the understanding to not intervene:
   - 'And I was thinking of doing a linking interpretation, and than tying that back to her mother and father, and her abandonment. Then deciding I wouldn't do that at this point because it was sort of too beyond what she's dealing with right now.'
   - 'There were a few points where I felt like I could have made an empathic reflection but she was . . . I don't know. I just made a decision to let her tell the whole thing, rather than derail her from her story.'
3. Using the understanding to encourage the client to differentiate his/her experience:
   - ' I am trying to get her to differentiate, to stay with. So I have a number of intentions. Try

Table 12 (cont.)

> to stay with it, open it up, and differentiate. And then I'm trying to see the different facets of her experience, of the situation.'

4. Using the understanding to encourage the client to unpack the experience or for the therapist to unpack the client's experience:
   - 'I'm intentionally trying to open out that experience.'
   - 'Unpacking it and unfolding . . . So I have a number of intentions. Try to stay with it, open it up.'
   - 'Let's try to unpack this experience, so I repeat evocatively.'

5. Using the understanding to encourage the client to articulate his/her experience:
   - 'I didn't know it was fear for sure but I felt like there was something that she needed to articulate.'

6. Using the understanding to shift the client's frame:
   - 'Just trying to understand her frame. Trying to shift it.'
   - 'So, my intent right through this tape is to try and shift, with the use of empathy, just a different pace that we can get different perspectives on this anxiety and maybe, find a way out.'

7. Using the understanding to reaffirm the client's understanding:
   - 'Here, my goal is to reaffirm, try and make this new understanding take root.'
   - 'Okay, again, I'm still empathically trying to affirm that she's okay the way she is. That this is a difference, not a good or bad thing.'

8. Using the understanding to encourage the client to stay with his/her experience:
   - 'I'm trying to, very gently, and as empathetically as I can, recreate what her experience was like. To get her to stay with it.'
   - 'So for me, empathy is really trying to get them out of their heads and into their experience'.
   - 'And so now, I'm really trying to get her to experience it.'
   - 'I said, 'So you felt really shut out, ridiculed at school' . . . we've veered from the pain. [inaudible] before bringing her back.'
   - 'I am trying to get her to differentiate to stay with. So I have a number of intentions. Try to stay with it.'
   - 'I'm aware let's stay there. I'm trying to get her to stay in this "hanging in limbo" experience. There is some intention as well, that it would be good to slow down and taste this experience. Because that's central to what she's finding difficult.'
   - 'Need to remember, that's what she's really feeling. Now let's try and really stay with that feeling rather than not feeling it. So I am going through, it's like a theoretical . . . Then I go into a strategy, a therapeutic technique.' (Les)

9. Using the understanding to validate the client:
   - 'I am working on a theoretical understanding. Understanding that this is important to bring us into being validated . . .'
   - 'I just validated her, basically. It's like, yeah, why wouldn't you want that? Like, it's okay to have irrational desires.'

10. Using the understanding to encourage the client to say things out loud:
    - 'I thought she really feels this is not working yet, and I wanted her to be able to say that'.
    - 'I have the sense of her underground kind of despair was that nothing is working. And that sessions were part of that that nothing is working. And I just wanted to give her permission to say that out loud.'

11. Using the understanding to emphasize and focus the client on one piece:
    - 'I'm trying to have her experience fully that she just doesn't like it. So actually I am emphasizing something.'
    - 'And I'm emphasizing haven't owned, don't believe. This is obviously what we need to change, then. So, this is the key, changing her belief in herself.'

APPENDIX 1: EMPATHY IPR INTERVIEW

Everybody has perceptions about what empathy is supposed to be. In this interview we are not concerned with your personal definition of empathy. We are, however, trying to get as close as possible to your own personal experience of what actually happened within you when you felt you were being empathic. For this purpose we ask you to please drop all preconceptions about empathy, and just report as accurately as you can what you were experiencing (thoughts, feelings, images) inside when you felt you were being empathic to your client. Don't worry if you don't know or are unsure; just do the best you can.

    1. What about this particular moment /segment makes you feel that you were being empathic?

    2. What were you experiencing internally when you were being empathic? (Were you feeling, thinking?)

REFERENCES

Barrett-Lennard, G.T. (1981). The empathy cycle: Refinement of a nuclear concept. *Journal of Counseling Psychology, 28* , 91–100.

Bohart, A. C. and Greenberg, L. S. (1997). Empathy: Where are we and where do we go from here? In A. C. Bohart and L. S. Greenberg (Eds.) *Empathy Reconsidered: New directions in psychotherapy.* Washington, DC: American Psychological Association, pp. 419–50.

Colaizzi, P . (1978). Psychological research as the phenomenologist views it. In R. Valle and M . King (Eds.) *Existential-phenomenological Alternatives for Psychology.* New York: Oxford University Press, pp. 48–71.

Hopkins, J. (2001). *Cultivating Compassion: A Buddhist perspective.* New York: Broadway Books.

Rogers, C. R. (1957). The necessary and sufficient conditions of therapeutic personality change. *Journal of Consulting Psychology, 21,* 95–103.

Rogers, C. R. (1980). *A Way of Being.* Boston: Houghton Mifflin.

James R. Iberg
Illinois School of Professional Psychology, Chicago, USA

Psychometric Development of Measures of In-session Focusing Activity: The *Focusing-oriented Session Report* and the *Therapist Ratings of Client Focusing Activity*

Abstract. The *Focusing-oriented Session Report* (the FSR) and the *Therapist Ratings of Client Focusing Activity* (the TRCFA) have been under development for some years. Elsewhere (Iberg, 2000), the initial factor analyses and relationships between these two measures and a symptom checklist are available. In this article, I present an introduction to the measures which grounds them in the philosophy of E. T. Gendlin (2000). Then data from a new sample of psychotherapy sessions are presented. After these sessions we used a revised (expanded) version of the FSR, and the original version of the TRCFA. Factor analyses were performed on the new data, and these and the correlations between subscales from the two data sources (client and therapist) are reported. We find good support in these data for convergent and discriminant validation of the client-rated focusing activity subscales by the therapist-rated subscales. Causal relationships between in-session focusing activities and client satisfaction with the session were examined from both the client and therapist perspectives, and the results are in close agreement. Better focusing attitudes contributed to client satisfaction indirectly by raising levels of opening of feeling and carrying forward. More opening of feeling contributed to client satisfaction indirectly by raising levels of carrying forward and also directly. More carrying forward directly led to more client satisfaction with session. Directions for further research are also discussed.

GENDLIN'S PROCESS MODEL

The *Process Model* (Gendlin, 2000) is a philosophy that starts with interaction processes as the basic concept, rather than starting with uniform mathematical units of space and time as the 'givens' upon which other concepts are built. How this enriches our map of reality shows up early in Gendlin's model, where he distinguishes four types of 'environment' for a living body.

Four types of environment

Gendlin's notation is intended to remind us of the reciprocally defining and essential interrelatedness of body (b) and environment (en) which applies to all four of the types he distinguishes:
  b-en#1, the spectator environment.
  b-en#2, body and environment as one process event.
  b-en#3, the environment as arranged by b-en#2 processes, including physical body structures.

b-en#0, things 'in the world' that have never yet been part of b-en#2, but could be.

The spectator environment is the familiar way we usually think about the environment. It's the three-dimensional space filled with things that can be measured in equal units on a measuring device. A scientist watches things happen in this type of environment, measuring and correlating, often considering him- or herself to be a minimal influence (or none at all) on the objects or animals being studied.

The second kind of environment is less intuitively obvious, and yet it is quite natural to understand. Living processes are always in interaction with their surroundings. Such interaction is fundamental and not something which can be taken away without altering the living process. Breathing is a good example. The lungs and the blood flowing through them must be in constant interaction with the air pulled in by the muscles and diaphragm. The lung tissue and the air are different aspects of one event. Without the air, the basic structure of the lungs will begin to change, and in a short time the changed tissue will no longer support breathing properly. Living processes generally have this relationship to environment which is much closer to — actually one with — the environment, than we grasp when thinking in terms of the spectator environment. Notice too that other parts of the organism are b-en#2 to a particular process we might focus on: the blood and capillary system are this one-with-the-process kind of environment to the gaseous exchange which occurs at the lung surface.

The third kind of environment is the one built by the ongoing life processes which occur in b-en#2, and within which the b-en#2 goes on. A simple example is the spider's web, which is something produced by the living spider that serves certain functions for the ongoing living of the spider, but which is not, once built, actively b-en#2 for many of the spider's life processes. Physical body structures themselves are another example of this kind of environment to the living processes. B-en#2 processes go on in and with the b-en#3 environment they have created.

The fourth type of environment includes things unknown that have the potential to enter into b-en#2, but that have not yet done so. Things not yet discovered that could, and may one day, enter b-en#2 are b-en#0.

Functional cycles, bodily implying, and carrying forward

An important feature of many life processes is that they are cyclical. An example is ingestion of food, which includes procuring food, preparing it, eating, digesting, absorbing water and nutrients, eliminating wastes.

Each b-en#2 in such a cycle implies the next step, and all the others, in an intricate order that cannot be rearranged arbitrarily.

When an aspect of environment needed to further a functional cycle is missing, the process is 'stopped' in that regard. The body carries such a stoppage with it in how the remaining processes go on differently because of the stopped one. In this way the body itself 'knows' what is needed: what isn't right and what would resolve the dilemma is implied in the tissues of all the ongoing processes as they are changed. This 'implying' of the body is a central concept in Gendlin's model. Bodily implying is very intricately determined by many interwoven processes and only certain things will allow the stopped process to proceed properly. And yet what will allow the process to proceed is open-ended in many ways, so that numerous variations in the environment can carry the process forward. Certain special occurrences change the bodily implying in just the way it implies itself changed. Other occurrences, although they may affect the body, fail to enable the process to properly proceed, and the implying remains active in the body. When the special events occur which change the process as the body needed it to be changed, we say the process is 'carried forward'. This is another important term in Gendlin's model.

Therapeutic interaction and the intent of the FSR and the TRCFA

In therapy, people come with problems they want to change. If we are able with them to create the right b-en#2, then their own implying-bodies will find steps forward where movement has not been happening to their satisfaction. As steps forward happen in the therapy interaction, the client is empowered to also find features in their b-en#2 beyond the therapy situation that will carry forward his/her living. My goal with the FSR and the TRCFA is to assess client introspective activities crucial to those delicate moments when a stopped process, in a therapeutic environment, finds a way to move ahead. Since carrying forward is the bodily experience of movement where there was stoppage, we expect these interpersonal/ introspective activities to be associated with client satisfaction with the session.

We have three constructs and associated subscales for assessing these interpersonal/ introspective activities, and another subscale for assessing client satisfaction with the session.

The Focusing attitude

One peculiarly human characteristic is that a person can have complex relationships with him/herself. One 'part' of a person may disapprove of or criticize another part, as in 'self-evaluative splits' (Greenberg, Rice and Elliott, 1993). Sometimes what one finds in experiencing is inconsistent with how one thinks of oneself (what Greenberg, Rice, and Elliott have called a 'problematic reaction'. Also see Rogers, 1959, on 'incongruence'.) Habitual attitudes one has toward one's bodily experiencing are part of the b-en#3 which is the product of earlier life processes.

The quality of such 'inner relationships' (Cornell, 1996) is highly pertinent to the ease or difficulty with which one's living carries forward in the face of the inevitable challenges encountered throughout life (also see Gendlin, 1996; Greenberg, Watson and Lietaer, 1998; Iberg, 1996). Through years of work teaching people a manner of relating to experiencing associated with positive outcomes in psychotherapy (Gendlin, 1969, 1981; Klein, Mathieu-Coughlan and Kiesler, 1986), certain attitudes toward one's experiencing have been identified as generally productive of insight and other kinds of carrying forward. These attitudes can be summarized as curious, friendly, gentle, patient, accepting, expectant of new developments, receptive to what comes, and we might say 'democratic' in relation to the various parts and voices that may be present in one's experiencing. These attitudes seem to allow troubled feelings to open up and change. We expect therapeutic interaction which enables the client to adopt these attitudes toward experiencing to be productive of therapeutic change. Our Focusing Attitude scales assess the degree to which, during the session, the client held this set of attitudes toward bodily felt experiencing.

Opening of feelings (actuality of trust)

This construct refers to an event in which effective therapists participate often, in therapeutic interaction. After being heard (and hearing oneself) about a problem, at certain moments, something happens viscerally for the client and the issue becomes immediately felt. Feelings 'well up' in the client. Freud (1895/1952) implied that such moments were an essential development for psychotherapy to alleviate hysterical symptoms: 'Recollections without affect are almost utterly useless. The psychic process which originally elapsed must be reproduced as vividly as possible so as to bring it back into the *statum nascendi,* and then thoroughly "talked out."' (p.25) In Gendlin's language, we refer to such moments as the formation of a 'bodily felt sense', although to fully qualify as a bodily felt sense, in addition to the bodily activation of immediate sensory/affective experience, the client must hold Focusing Attitudes toward the visceral event. These are moments of special opportunity to symbolize quite directly from bodily implying.

Opening of Feelings is seen as a fundamentally interactive event: it happens when trust is actualized between the parties to the therapeutic interaction. It seems to be the result of the contact between therapist and client having qualities of empathy, genuineness, and respect for the individuals to the point that the client experiences the trust necessary for complex, not-fully-known feelings to surface. This development is in itself seen as therapeutic and as leading to subsequent insight or relief (carrying forward). Thus, we expect opening of feelings to be associated with client satsfaction. Our Opening of Feelings scales aim to measure the extent to which trust was actualized in the therapy session and bodily felt senses formed for the client.

Carrying forward

As discussed above, carrying forward is defined by change in the person's bodily sense of distress, and a new ability to live forward in ways that were stopped. Easing in the bodily sense of distress is primary evidence of carrying forward. There could hardly be a better source than the client of information regarding whether or not the bodily sense has eased. The therapist can also, if attentive, observe some of the things that come with carrying forward: the client's body may relax, breathing may deepen, sighs may indicate relief, tears of release may come, and insights may appear in the client's thinking, for example (see Leijssen, 1998, p. 138, for more description). With carrying forward, people often become less self-protective and more sympathetic to the perspective of others. Our Carrying Forward scales aim to measure the degree to which such changes have taken place.

Our primary interest in this study is to build psychometric support for the subscales reflecting these focusing activities. In addition to that, we explore how client satisfaction with the session is influenced by the symptom level coming into the session and by the amounts of the three measured types of focusing activity which occurred in the session.

OUTCOME AS PREDICTED BY FOCUSING ACTIVITIES: CLIENT SATISFACTION WITH THE SESSION

From the Process Model perspective, the three types of focusing activity in a therapy session reflect the productivity of the session. We consider the subjective experience of clients to be one important indicator of productivity. Therefore, the focusing activities should be predictive of client satisfaction with the session. How the three focusing activities defined above are interrelated is of great interest as well. To begin to explore these matters, we will examine some causal analyses of the relationships of the focusing activity variables to each other and to client satisfaction with the session.

We expect focusing attitude to be an important influence on how much of the other two focusing activities occur: the more good focusing attitudes are present, the more opening of feeling and carrying forward we expect. Focusing attitude may also have a direct effect on the client's satisfaction with the session, since people report valuing the 'disidentification' characteristic of focusing attitudes (Cornell, 1996) even when little opening of feelings and no carrying forward seem to have occurred.

Opening of feelings, which involves direct reference to a bodily felt sense, should promote carrying forward in the session, and thereby indirectly increase the client's satisfaction with the session. Also, people often talk about the formation of a bodily felt sense in terms like 'getting more in touch with myself', and 'discovering how I really feel', which are satisfying developments. Therefore we expect a direct positive effect of opening of feelings on satisfaction with session.

Finally, the amount of carrying forward in the session should be directly productive of client satisfaction with the session, for reasons already articulated.

These relationships could conceivably vary depending on the client's level of distress coming into the session. We will estimate a recursive causal model for the relationships of these variables to client satisfaction with the session, assuming symptom distress at the start of the session is first in the causal sequence (exogenous to what happens in the session). Next in the causal sequence is focusing attitude, followed by opening of feelings, and finally carrying forward.

Method

Participants

Listeners. We had 18 listeners — 7 therapists and 11 focusing guides. Therapists ranged in age from 45 to 70, with an average of 54. Four therapists (57 %) were male. The 11 focusing guides were Canadians, all of whom were involved in a training program on Focusing. They were all professionally involved in counseling or psychotherapy, but we do not have detailed demographic information on these listeners. 82% (nine) of the Canadians were females.

The seven professional therapists were an experienced group (averaging over 14 years since licensure for independent practice) in the Chicago area. Three of the professional therapists are Focusing trainers, the other four have little or no training in Focusing-oriented psychotherapy. One of these four is a longtime therapist with eclectic training and methods. Another is a longtime client-centered therapist. Another is psychoanalytic in orientation, and the fourth is cognitive-behaviorally trained and certified.

Clients. There were 54 clients or focusers of whom 42 were private practice clients. Age ranged from 19 to 70, with a mean of 38, s.d. of 10.6. For the private practice clients, who were in ongoing outpatient psychotherapy, at the first session in the study the average symptom level on the OQ™-45.2 (see below) was 70.4, above the clinical cutoff point of 63 on that instrument, and roughly at the level of the 'EAP Clinical Services' normative group (Lambert, Hansen, Umpress, Lunnen, Okiishi and Burlingame, 1996).

Instruments

Focusing-oriented Session Report. The FSR (see Appendix A), rated by clients immediately after sessions, has 33 rating-scale items anchored with descriptive phrases. It was initially patterned after Orlinsky and Howard's (1975) 'Therapy Session Report' (the TSR). Some items (1 and 5) were taken directly from the TSR, with others devised to be more specifically relevant to Focusing activity. Three items (numbered 14–16 on the FSR) were inspired by conclusions drawn by Elliott and James (1989) that three dimensions underlie much of the variance in client experiences of sessions: evaluation — affiliation; controlled — independent; and interpersonal — task-focused.

Analysis of an earlier 15-item version of the FSR assessed internal consistency of subscales related to focusing, and a subscale measuring general session satisfaction (Iberg, 2000). Internal consistency was excellent for a 3-item general satisfaction scale, Client Satisfaction with Session (CSS: alpha = .85). It was good for a 4-item Carrying Forward scale (alpha = .75). It was marginal for a 3-item Opening of Feelings scale (alpha = .51). A single item was included on that version of the FSR for Focusing Attitude, called Attitude to Feelings. In that study we found significant positive within-client (between session) associations between the Focusing subscales and client satisfaction with session: more of the focusing-related activities assessed by the scales was associated with more satisfaction. Between-client analysis showed that better (lower) symptom levels on the OQ™-45.2 were associated with higher levels of focusing activity.

The expanded version of the FSR used in this study had additional items added to improve reliabilities on the focusing-related subscales. Respondents mark the spots on unnumbered rulers that best characterize their experience. The rulers are anchored with brief verbal descriptions to establish the range covered by the question. Scoring templates are used with the questionnaire to scale the items numerically, with higher scores indicating more of the focusing-related activity or outcome. The items in Appendix A appear in the sub groupings relevant to subscales (item numbers indicate the order in which they appeared on the questionnaire and + and – indicate the sense of each item).

Therapist's Ratings of Client Focusing Activity (Iberg, 2000). The TRCFA consists of six theoretically based (Iberg, 1996) items rated by the therapist immediately after the session. These items assess, from the therapist's perspective, six variables pertinent to the amount and quality of focusing-related activity the client demonstrated in the session. The items of the TRCFA appear as Appendix B with subscale groupings indicated. These items ask therapists to mark rulers numbered from 0–10, with higher scores indicating more of the focusing-related activity. Factor analysis of these items in an earlier, smaller sample (Iberg, 2000: N = 86) identified one factor. The associated scale averaging the six items had an excellent reliability coefficient (alpha = .92). A new factor analysis based on the present data set (N = 148) is reported below.

The OQ™-45.2 The Outcome Questionnaire (Lambert, Hansen, Umpress, Lunnen,

Okiishi and Burlingame, 1996) was used to characterize the sample of clients, and to explore whether symptom level at the beginning of the session related to client satisfaction with the session directly, or indirectly through the focusing activities reflected in the FSR. This one-page instrument (the OQ) comprises 45 statements describing feelings, how the client relates to others, and other mental health status indicators. The written instructions tell the client to rate each statement for its prevalence during the past week on a five-point scale from 'never' to 'almost always'. The authors established the clinical cutoff total score of 63 to differentiate between scores more typical of clinical samples than community samples. Higher scores indicate worse symptomatology. The authors present data which showed, for a sample of 76 university outpatient clinic patients, a downward approximately linear trend in the first seven sessions of therapy, from an average score of 85 at intake to an average score of 67 at seven weeks of therapy. They also presented a student sample (in a psychology class, not in therapy) over a similar time period in which the scores were approximately level at an average of about 43. Thus the scale appears to be sensitive to the kind of change which typically occurs in the first two months of therapy. The three subscales (Symptom Distress, Interpersonal Relations and Social Role) may be useful to identify the area in which a client's concerns are greatest, but these subscales correlate highly with the total score. It is the total score we use here.

Procedure

The bulk of the data was gathered as part of an ongoing process-monitoring system used by a private practice group in the Chicago area. Seven participating therapists collected the measures at the first session and about every fourth session thereafter. Permission for anonymous analysis of the data was granted as part of the initial agreement between therapists and clients.

For this study, 13 additional sets of questionnaires were collected from a Canadian group of therapists in a training program. The Canadians did not complete the OQ, but contributed FSR and TRCFA data for those factor analyses. Altogether, subjects completed 165 sessions at which questionnaires were completed. 152 of these (92%) were sessions with the private practice clients.

These data were collected naturalistically, rather than in the more common way of structuring a study so selected therapists conduct comparable numbers of sessions with the same number of clients at the same point in therapy. To clarify how this procedure actually occurred, statistics descriptive of procedural features are reported here rather than in the Results section. The average number of observations collected per client was 3.06, with a range of 1 to 19 (s.d. = 3.6). Twenty-five subjects provided one observation only (eight of these were in the Canadian Group). Twelve provided two observations. Fourteen provided between 3 and 8 observations, and three provided between 11 and 19 observations. This corresponds to therapy durations between one session and two years in the study, with some study participants well under way in their therapies.

The OQ was completed by private practice clients at the beginning of each data collection session. The FSR and TRCFA were completed at the end of those sessions, without discussion of the respective ratings at that time, and the therapist forwarded them to the author on a monthly basis.

Private practice therapists had a range of 1 to 20 clients contributing data to the study, with a mean of 6.14 clients and s.d. of 7.15 (3 had one client each, one had 2 clients, one had 8, one 10 and one 20).

Data analysis

Subscale construction

Items loading .40 or above on orthogonally rotated factors were standardized and then summed for each subscale we created.

The FSR. The three item Client Satisfaction Scale (CSS), which had very good internal consistency in earlier data analysis (alpha = .85), was used without change. These items were not included in the present factor analysis (but do appear in Appendix A), to avoid spreading limited data over more items than necessary.

Twenty-nine items thought to be related to focusing activity were factor analyzed, and new subscales were defined to reproduce the previously defined focusing-activity subscales with additional items to improve reliability.

The TRCFA. The six items of the TRCFA were factor analyzed on this new sample. As a result, we defined three subscales of two items each from the TRCFA. These subscales were evaluated for internal consistency.

Subscale validation

Therapist-client corroboration. In the first step of hierarchical regression, between-client variance was partialled out by constructing indicator variables for clients with effects coding (Cohen and Cohen, 1983). The FSR focusing subscales were regressed at later steps onto the TRCFA subscales, to assess the degree to which therapist-based indicators agreed with and were specific to client ratings of the different kinds of focusing activity measured by the FSR subscales.

Causal analysis of client satisfaction with session. Hierarchical regression was used to estimate direct and indirect effects on CSS (within clients) of 1) OQ at session start, 2) Focusing Attitude, 3) Opening of Feelings and 4) Carrying Forward, in that order. All variables were standardized before this analysis, so their effects would be scaled in standard deviation units (path coefficients: Cohen and Cohen, 1983).

Results

FSR factor analysis

We intend the FSR to be used to detect within-client, between session variation in focusing activity. Thus the session is our unit of analysis. Table 1 displays the results of the Principal Components factor analysis of the FSR items after orthogonal rotation (N = 137 sessions with complete data on all items). Although there were 8 factors with eigenvalues greater than 1 in the full factor analysis, examination of the scree plot suggested that four were more important than the rest (eigenvalues of 1.72 and above). Four factors explain 53% of the variance, and were more interpretable than eight. The item loadings which appear in bold indicate subscale items. After rotation, there was good simple structure. Only 'Solutions'

Table 1. *Means, Standard Deviations, and Principal Component Factor Analysis of the Focusing-oriented Session Report*

Item (question #)	M	SD	1	2	3	4	Communality
				Rotated Factors			
Doorway to Feelings (2)	61.2	23.4	.009	−.751	−.199	.130	.622
Therapist Influence (3)	29.2	15.5	−.067	.049	−.141	**.624**	.417
Understanding (4)	62.4	17.2	.238	−.595	.188	−.104	.457
New Perspectives (6)	57.1	19.3	**.546**	−.305	.004	.397	.548
Right Topics (7)	78.1	19.2	.115	−.687	−.348	.019	.607
Feel Better? (9a)	35.2	22.9	**.763**	−.295	.034	.069	.675
Emotional Intensity (10a)	62.2	20.7	−.145	−.733	.220	.184	.640
Intensity Duration (10b)	55.4	20.8	.115	−.661	.057	−.141	.473
Attitude to Feelings (11)	57.8	22.0	.230	−.163	−.673	.099	.543
Solutions (12)	68.1	28.6	**.513**	−.095	−.408	.346	.558
Specific Actions (13)	58.1	27.1	**.449**	−.066	−.308	.209	.345
Acceptance (14)	72.8	23.8	.355	−.393	.288	−.350	.486
Guidedness (15)	32.6	25.0	−.141	.378	−.186	**.570**	.522
Task Orientedness (16)	42.0	27.5	.005	.217	−.516	.273	.388
Complexity (17)	66.9	19.8	.157	−.576	−.379	−.040	.502
Congruence (18)	65.8	21.9	−.088	−.067	−.653	−.074	.444
Witnessing (19)	55.6	22.1	.069	−.087	−.711	−.081	.524
Surrender (20)	62.1	19.2	.235	−.226	−.638	.210	.557
Self Among Equals (21)	72.6	18.8	.327	−.358	−.260	−.363	.434
Safe From Criticism (22)	79.9	17.4	.509	−.532	−.052	−.164	.571
Relaxation (23.1)	15.0	24.7	**.867**	−.091	−.094	−.023	.770
Calmness (23.2)	15.0	24.2	**.775**	−.201	.007	−.119	.655
Sensory Awareness (23.3)	12.4	15.4	.060	−.287	.098	**.496**	.341
Breath Depth (23.4)	7.8	18.0	.354	−.235	.059	.293	.269
Body Warmth (23.5)	6.3	18.8	**.400**	.177	−.144	.384	.359
Pain Reduction (23.6)	4.7	16.6	**.705**	.029	−.128	.222	.563
Body Solidity (23.7)	12.0	22.8	**.870**	−.103	−.067	−.128	.789
Less Tearful (23.8)	4.7	21.8	**.700**	.033	−.101	−.096	.511
Less Vulnerable (23.9)	7.2	24.9	**.784**	−.059	−.077	−.221	.673
% Variance			21	14	10	08	53

Note: N = 137. The four-factor solution, orthogonally rotated, accounted for 52.6% of the variance. Numerals in boldface indicate substantial factor loadings and items included in associated scales. Scale 1 = Carrying Forward; Scale 2 = Opening of Feelings; Scale 3 = Focusing Attitude.

(question #12) and 'Safe from Criticism' (question # 22) loaded above .40 on more than one factor. In both of these cases, the item was included only on the scale corresponding to the factor on which it loaded the highest.

Although 'Acceptance' (question 14) had loadings above .40 on no factor, it loaded .393

on factor 2, and theoretically acceptance is expected to be associated with Opening of Feelings, so it was included on that scale. Two other items, 'Self Among Equals' (question 21), and the change in 'Breathing Depth' (question 23.4), loaded at a maximum of .36 on any factor. These two items were not included on any subscale.

Carrying Forward subscale. Eleven items make up this subscale, including the four which made up the subscale by the same name in a previous study (Iberg, 2000): New Perspectives (question #6), Feel Better (question 9a), Solutions (question 12), and Specific Actions (question 13). The seven new items added to this subscale are all from ratings of how the client's body felt compared to how it felt at the beginning of the session: these were Relaxation (question 23.1), Calmness (question 23.2), Body Warmth (question 23.5), Pain Reduction (question 23.6), Body Solidity (question 23.7), Less Tearful (question 23.8), and Less Vulnerable (question 23.9).

Internal consistency for this subscale is excellent (coefficient alpha = .89).

Opening of Feelings subscale. Eight items make up this subscale, including Doorway to Feelings (question 2), Understanding (question 4), and Emotional Intensity (question 10a). These three are the same items that defined the subscale by this name in a previous study (Iberg, 2000). Five additional items which also loaded on this factor were: 1) Right Topics (question 7), 2) Intensity Duration (question 10b), 3) Acceptance (question 14), 4) Complexity (question 17) and 5) Safe from Criticism (question 22).

Internal consistency for this subscale is excellent (alpha = .81).

Focusing Attitude subscale. Five items make up this subscale, including the Attitude to Feelings (question 11) which was used as the indicator of Focusing Attitude in the previous study. The four additional items are: 1) Task Orientedness (question 16), 2) Congruence (question 18), 3) Witnessing (question 19) and 4) Surrender (question 20).

Internal consistency was adequate for this subscale (alpha = .71).

Table 2. *Means, Standard Deviations, and Principal Component Factor Analysis of the Therapist Ratings of Client Focusing Activity*

			Rotated Factors			
Therapist-rated Item	M	SD	1	2	3	Communality
complexity	5.97	1.39	**.83**	.20	.25	.79
body feelings	5.78	1.40	**.79**	.35	.22	.79
congruence	6.21	1.40	.49	.07	**.77**	.83
witnessing	5.48	1.57	.14	.31	**.88**	.89
surrender	5.23	1.57	.39	**.81**	.08	.81
self-am-equals	5.68	1.38	.15	**.86**	.30	.84
Variance			1.74	1.64	1.57	4.95
% Variance			29	27	26	83

Note: N = 148. The three-factor solution, orthogonally rotated, accounted for 82.5% of the variance. Numerals in boldface indicate substantial factor loadings and items included in associated scales. Scale 1 = 'Opening of Feelings$_{Tx}$'; Scale 2 = 'Carrying Forward$_{Tx}$'; Scale 3 = 'Focusing Attitude Tx.'

Factor 4. Three items loaded above .40 on this factor: 1) Therapist Influence (question 3), 2) Guidedness (question 15) and 3) Sensory Awareness (question 23.3).

Internal consistency was poor for these three items (alpha = .32). Because of poor reliability, no further scale construction or analysis is reported related to this factor.

TRCFA factor analysis

Principal Components Factor analysis was done on the TRCFA items (N = 148 sessions). The 75% variance rule (Gorsuch, 1983) resulted in three factors with good simple structure after rotation. Table 2 shows the results of the orthogonal rotation. Only one item (congruence, # 3) loaded more than .40 on more than one of the factors. This item was included only in the subscale corresponding to factor three, on which it loaded much more heavily (.77 *cf.* .49 on factor 1).

Opening of Feelings$_{Tx}$ subscale. Two items make up this subscale: 1) the therapist's rating of the client's articulation of internal and external complexity related to feelings worked on and 2) the extent to which the therapist saw the client experience the formation and opening up of bodily feelings.

Internal reliability was good for this subscale (alpha = .76), especially considering it is a two-item scale.

Carrying Forward$_{Tx}$ subscale. Two items make up this subscale: therapist assessments of 1) the extent to which the client was able to loosen existing ideas and self-conception and open up to the unknown and change and 2) the extent to which the client's attitude toward self and others became more humble and considerate of other perspectives, rather than narrow and self-oriented.

Internal reliability was good for this two-item subscale (alpha = .76).

Focusing Attitude$_{Tx}$ subscale. Two items make up this subscale: therapist assessments of 1) client's ability to accurately represent his or her true feelings in words and self-image and 2) client's ability to acknowledge his or her full range of feelings without favoring some feelings and resisting others.

Internal consistency was good for this two-item subscale (alpha = .78).

FSR–TRCFA agreement

Agreement between the therapist and client perspectives was examined in two ways: first by directly correlating the scales from the two perspectives, and then by comparing separate causal analyses of Client Satisfaction with Session for each of the two perspectives.

Hierarchically regressing FSR subscales on TRCFA subscales. The hierarchical sequence for comparing Focusing Activity variables was the same for each of the focusing activities: first the therapist-rated target subscale, then the other two therapist-rated subscales.

A preliminary step involved regressing on the set of client indicator variables (effects coded) so that we could partial out between-client variance: we are interested in the variance within clients (between sessions) for establishing the validity of the FSR and the TRCFA.

In step two, an FSR subscale was regressed on the corresponding TRCFA subscale, to

Table 3. *Hierarchical Regressions of FSR Subscales on TRCFA Subscales*

	B	R²	F	d.f.	I	F_I	d.f.
I. *Focusing Attitude*							
Step							
1. Client set		.528	2.55***	47,107			
2. Focusing Attitude_Tx	.629*	.554	2.75***	48,106	.026	6.179*	1,106
3. Opening of Feelings_Tx	–.084						
Carrying Forward_Tx	.098	.556	2.60***	50,104	.002	.234	2,104
II. *Opening of Feelings*							
Step							
1. Client set		.609	3.54***	47,107			
2. Opening of Feelings_Tx	1.33***	.693	4.98***	48,106	.084	29.003***	1,106
3. Focusing Attitude_Tx	.785*						
Carrying Forward_Tx	.618*	.723	5.44***	50,104	.030	5.632**	2,104
III. *Carrying Forward*							
Step							
1. Client set		.448	1.85**	47,107			
2. Carrying Forward _Tx	1.94***	.513	2.33***	48,106	.065	14.148 ***	1,106
3. Focusing Attitude_Tx	.678						
Opening of Feelings_Tx	.659	.535	5.44***	50,104	.022	2.460	2,104

Note: N = 155
* $p < .05$
** $p < .01$
*** $p < .001$

evaluate agreement between the client-originating and the therapist-originating indicators of the target focusing activity.

We explored the discriminant validity of the scales in step three: the other two therapist subscales were added, to assess the relative contributions of each therapist subscale, controlling for the other therapist subscales. This gives the partial correlation of each of the therapist subscales on the client subscale being analyzed, controlling for the other two.

Focusing Attitude. See Table 3 for detailed statistics. Fifty-three percent of variance in Focusing Attitude scores was due to between-client differences. Adding Focusing Attitude_Tx in step 2 increased explained variance by 2.6%, a significant amount ($p < .05$). This represents 5.5% of within-client variance, a medium effect by Cohen's suggested standards (Cohen, 1988).

Adding Opening of Feelings_Tx and Carrying Forward_Tx in step 3 added .002 to explained variance, a non-significant increase. Neither of these variables approached the .05 level individually, and Focusing Attitude$_{Tx}$ was still significant at .05 with the other two partialled out.

Opening of Feelings. See Table 3 for detailed statistics. Sixty-one percent of variance in Opening of Feelings scores was due to between-client differences. Adding Opening of Feelings$_{Tx}$ in step 2 increased explained variance by 8.4%, a significant amount ($p < .001$). This represents 21.5% of within-client variance, a very large effect (Cohen, 1988).

Adding Focusing Attitude$_{Tx}$ and Carrying Forward$_{Tx}$ in step 3 added .03 to explained variance, a significant increase ($p < .01$). Focusing Attitude$_{Tx}$ and Carrying Forward were each significant at .05. Opening of Feelings$_{Tx}$ remained the most strongly associated with Opening of Feelings (B = .883, $p < .01$) with the other two therapist scales partialled out.

Carrying Forward. See Table 3 for detailed statistics. Forty-five percent of variance in Carrying Forward scores was due to between-client differences. Adding Carrying Forward$_{Tx}$ in step 2 increased explained variance by 6.5%, a significant amount ($p < .001$). This represents 11.8% of within-client variance, a medium-large effect (Cohen, 1988).

Adding Opening of Feelings$_{Tx}$ and Attitude to Feelings$_{Tx}$ in step 3 added .022 to explained variance, a non-significant increase. Neither of these variables approached the .05 level

Figure 1 Causal Analysis of Client Satisfaction with Session (within client variance)

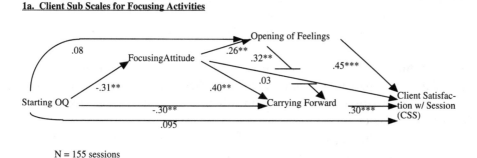

1a. Client Sub Scales for Focusing Activities

N = 155 sessions

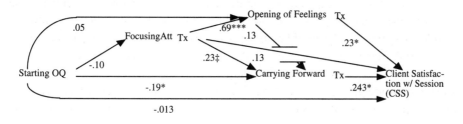

1b. Therapist Sub Scales for Focusing Activities

N = 150 sessions

‡ *p< .10*   * *p< .05*   ** *p< .01*   *** *p< .001*

individually, and Carrying Forward$_{Tx}$ was still significant at the .01 level with the other two partialled out.

Causal analysis of client satisfaction with session.

Prior to the causal modeling, all variables were standardized, so that coefficients are in standard deviation units to facilitate interpretation. The first step was to regress CSS scores on a complete set of indicator variables for clients, to partial out between client variance. The subsequent causal analysis is therefore of within-client (between-session) variance. Figure 1. illustrates the results. Numbers under the lines indicate size of effect (beta weight, or 'path coefficient:' Cohen and Cohen, 1983) of a variable on the next in the sequence, with all variables prior in the sequence controlled for.

Using subscales based on client-ratings. Part 1a. shows the analysis using client-based subscales for focusing activities. We see that higher symptom levels at the beginning of the session tended to depress the levels of Focusing attitude (ß = −.31, p < .01) and Carrying forward (ß = −.30, p < .01). Starting symptom level did not have significant direct effects on Opening of Feelings or on Client Satisfaction with Session.

Focusing Attitude promoted both Opening of Feelings and Carrying Forward (ß = .26, p < .01, and ß = .40, p < .01, respectively), but had no direct effect on Client Satisfaction with Session.

Opening of Feelings directly promoted Carrying Forward (ß = .32, p < .01) and Client Satisfaction with Session (ß = .45, p < .001).

Finally, Carrying forward directly promoted Client Satisfaction with Session (ß = .30, p < .001).

The preceding results, with the addition of the indirect effects of the variables, are summarized in Table 4 part a. The symptom levels of clients at the beginning of sessions had a negligible effect on satisfaction with session, whether directly, or indirectly through the focusing activity variables.

Here we see that the Focusing Attitude effects on CSS, nearly all indirect, were about evenly split through Opening of Feelings and Carrying Forward.
Opening of Feelings had an indirect effect by promoting Carrying Forward, but this was relatively small compared to its direct effect (which was nearly five times bigger).

Using subscales based on therapist-ratings. Figure 1b. shows the analysis for therapist-based subscales for focusing activities. We see that higher symptom levels at the beginning of the session tended to depress the levels of Focusing attitude (ß = −.10, *n.s.*) and Carrying Forward (ß = −.19, p < .05). Starting symptom level did not have significant direct effects on Opening of Feelings or on Client Satisfaction with Session.

Focusing Attitude promoted both Opening of Feelings and Carrying Forward (ß = .69, p < .001, and ß = .23, p < .10, respectively), but had no significant direct effect on Client Satisfaction with Session.

Opening of feelings had a positive but not significant direct effect on Carrying Forward by the therapist measures (ß = .13, *n.s.*) Opening of Feelings directly promoted Client Satisfaction with Session (ß = .23, p < .05).

Finally, Carrying forward directly promoted Client Satisfaction with Session (ß = .24, p < .05).

Table 4.

Summary of Direct, Indirect, and Spurious Effects on Standardized Client Satisfaction with Session (within clients)

	Zero-order ß	Spurious	Direct	Indirect	Total
a. *Client-rated Focusing Activity Subscales as Predictors*[†]					
OQ Total Score (standardized)					
via Focusing Attitude				−.090	
via Opening of Feelings				.043	
via Carrying Forward				−.093	
	−.045	—	.095	−.140	−.045
Focusing Attitude (standardized)					
via Opening of Feelings				.143	
via Carrying Forward				.120	
	.279**	−.014	.030	.263	.293**
Opening of Feeling (standardized)					
via Carrying Forward				.096	
	.592***	.042	.454***	.096	.550***
Carrying Forward (standardized)	.423***	.120	.303***	—	.303***
b. *Therapist-rated Focusing Activity Subscales as Predictors*[††]					
OQ Total Score (standardized)					
via Focusing Attitude$_{Tx}$				−.002	
via Opening of Feelings$_{Tx}$				.014	
via Carrying Forward$_{Tx}$				−.045	
	−.045	.001	−.013	−.033	−.046
Focusing Attitude$_{Tx}$ (standardized)					
via Opening of Feelings$_{Tx}$				.182	
via Carrying Forward$_{Tx}$				.056	
	.371**	.008	.125	.238	.363**
Opening of Feeling$_{Tx}$ (standardized)					
via Carrying Forward$_{Tx}$				.032	
	.336***	.072	.232*	.032	.264*
Carrying Forward$_{Tx}$ (standardized)	.351**	.108	.243*	—	.243*

Notes: [†]$N = 155$. [††]$N = 150$. *$p < .05$. **$p < .01$. ***$p < .001$

These results, with the addition of the indirect effects of the variables, are summarized in Table 4b. Symptom levels of clients at the beginning of sessions had a negligible effect on satisfaction with session either directly or indirectly through the focusing activity variables.

In this table we see that as perceived by therapists, the Focusing Attitude effects on CSS operated more through Opening of Feelings and directly, and less by promoting Carrying Forward.

Opening of Feelings had a small indirect effect through Carrying Forward, with a much larger direct effect (more than seven times as large).

FSR–TRCFA agreement in the causal analyses. Overall, the pattern of path coefficients agrees almost completely between the therapist-rated measures and the client-rated measures. There are differences in magnitudes, but no differences in sign on any coefficient except the one between starting symptom level and CSS, and this one is not significantly different from zero in either case. In general, magnitudes of effect are a bit smaller when using the TRCFA. One exception is the effect of Focusing Attitude on Opening of Feelings, which was stronger as rated by therapists than as rated by clients. The other exception is the direct effect of Focusing Attitude on CSS, which is higher in the therapist ratings, but in neither causal analysis was this effect significant, so it is probably not a real difference.

The patterns of indirect effects vary only in that Focusing Attitude as rated by therapists operated less through it's effect on Carrying Forward than it did when rated by clients.

DISCUSSION

Factor analysis of the expanded version of the FSR replicated the clustering of the items which had been the basis of three focusing activity subscales from a previous factor analysis. Additional items improved the reliability of the three scales: Focusing Attitude, Opening of Feelings and Carrying Forward. A fourth factor suggested a fourth scale, but internal consistency was poor, and no further scale construction or analysis was undertaken related to that factor. Two items of the expanded FSR did not load at .40 on any factors, and could be revised, replaced, or dropped. Replacing these with additional items reflecting Focusing Attitude might be a good idea to further improve its reliability.

Factor analysis of the TRCFA on this sample resulted in three factors of two items each, with good reliabilities. The three associated subscales were easily named to correspond with the FSR subscales, which permitted a straightforward examination of therapist-client agreement regarding focusing activity.

The corroboration of the FSR by the TRCFA on within-client (between-session) variance was very good in two ways. First, the direct correlations between the two sources of measurement were positive and significant. The therapist Focusing Attitude scale was significantly associated with the client scale for this activity (5.5% of within-client variance, a medium effect), and when the other two therapist scales (Opening of Feelings$_{Tx}$ and Carrying Forward$_{Tx}$) were added to the hierarchical regression at step 3, neither was significantly associated with the client Focusing Attitude scale, indicating cross-perspective discriminant validity (see Table 3).

The therapist Carrying Forward subscale was strongly associated with the client subscale for this activity (11.8% of within-client variance, a medium-large effect). Adding the other two therapist subscales resulted in a non-significant increase in explained variance, so we have evidence of cross-perspective discriminant validity for the Carrying Forward subscale of The FSR.

The therapist Opening of Feelings subscale was strongly associated with the client subscale for this activity (21.5% of within-client variance, a very large effect). Adding the other two therapist subscales resulted in significant associations of both of these therapist scales with the FSR Opening of Feeling subscale. Therapist ratings blur the distinction of Opening of Feelings from Focusing Attitude and Carrying Forward with client ratings of Opening of Feelings as criterion. Nevertheless, with all three therapist subscales in the regression equation, the Opening of Feelings$_{Tx}$ subscale remained the most strongly associated of the three with the FSR Opening of Feelings subscale (ß = .88 for Opening of Feelings$_{Tx}$, p < .01, ß = .78 for Focusing Attitude$_{Tx}$, p < .05, and ß = .62 for Carrying Forward$_{Tx}$, p < .05).

Some blurring of these distinctions may be the result of the small number of items and the specific item content on the TRCFA. One of the two Carrying Forward$_{Tx}$ items asks about the degree to which the client opened up to the unknown and the unexpected. One of the two Attitude to Feelings items asks about the extent to which the client was able to acknowledge the full range of feelings without favoring some and resisting others. When a client experiences the formation of a felt sense — the hallmark of Opening of Feelings — these things are often going to be part of what happens. Having only two items for each therapist subscale means such overlap will naturally reduce the discriminative power of the therapist subscales. For this reason, the FSR is a more precise measure than the TRCFA for Opening of Feelings. With these considerations in mind, it is impressive that with two of the three FSR subscales we found good discriminant validation with the non-target TRCFA subscales.

These results are quite encouraging about the meaningfulness of these subscales as measures of three distinct theoretically meaningful focusing activity variables. This may represent a further differentiation of the construct of Experiencing, which is usually measured as a one-dimensional quantitative scale closely associated with Focusing, especially at higher levels of Experiencing (Klein, et. al., 1986; Hendricks, in press).

Our second corroboration of The FSR by the TRCFA is the close agreement in the causal analysis of client satisfaction with session (CSS) computed for the two perspectives on client focusing activity. These causal analyses illuminate how focusing activities affect session-level outcomes. Symptom distress level at the beginning of the session, as reflected by total score on the OQ in the range of our sample (from 29 to 103), did not significantly influence CSS either directly or indirectly through the focusing activities. Worse symptomatology did suppress Focusing Attitudes and Carrying Forward, resulting in some indirect downward pressure on CSS.

The focusing activities all had significant positive influences on Client Satisfaction with Session after controlling for effects due to starting symptom level. Focusing Attitude had its influence through Opening of Feelings and Carrying Forward: better Focusing Attitudes made positive contributions to CSS by promoting Opening of Feelings and Carrying Forward. If neither Opening of Feelings nor Carrying Forward were to occur, good Focusing Attitudes by themselves would not assure detectable satisfaction effects in a sample of this size.

Opening of Feelings promoted satisfaction with session mostly directly, with a relatively small indirect effect through its influence on Carrying Forward. If Carrying Forward did not occur, the client could still derive satisfaction from the session as a result of Opening of Feelings.

Finally, Carrying Forward directly promoted satisfaction with session beyond the contributions attributable to Focusing Attitude and Opening of Feelings. For given levels of Focusing Attitude and Opening of Feelings, more satisfaction with session comes with insight and bodily relief than when that relief does not happen. Although not surprising, this finding affirms that Carrying Forward is a distinct step in the therapeutic process beyond Focusing Attitude and Opening of Feelings.

Overall, the results reported here support the psychometric status of the FSR and the TRCFA and the importance of focusing activities for session satisfaction, as far as we have gone. The two instruments are in good agreement with each other, showing cross-perspective convergence and discrimination on the three subscales (less strong discrimination with Opening of Feelings than with Focusing Attitude and Carrying Forward). The FSR factor analysis reported here reproduced, expanded, and improved the reliabilities of the scales that were defined based on a separate factor analysis conducted on a different occasion with different clients and mostly different therapists (the author was a therapist in both samples). In addition, we found a meaningful pattern of associations between these subscales and Client Satisfaction with Session.

Some weaknesses of the study point to further research. The CSS scale is derived from the same instrument as the client-rated focusing activity scales (The FSR). Thus halo effects may increase positive correlations among the FSR subscales and between FSR subscales and CSS. Still, in the causal analysis we found clear distinctions in how the subscales are related to CSS, which cannot be explained by halo effects, which would apply equally to all subscales. The fact that the causal model based on therapist subscales agrees so closely with the model based on the FSR subscales also alleviates this concern. Halo effects *could* explain the generally higher magnitudes of association with CSS for the FSR subscales when compared to the TRCFA subscales in the causal analyses. Adding an independent measure of client session satisfaction would build confidence in these findings.

Another weakness is that we have not included other widely recognized measures to assess the relationship of the focusing activity scales to other process measures. This must be done, and clearly begins to lay out the objectives for further study. Foremost is to validate these scales with the Experiencing Scale. We would also expect positive correspondence between Carrying Forward and the Helpful Impacts subscale of the Session Impacts Scale (Elliott and Wexler, 1994), and a negative correlation between their Hindering Impacts subscale and our index of Opening of Feelings. Similarly, we would expect greater 'Depth' on the Session Evaluation Questionnaire (Stiles, 1980) to be associated with Opening of Feelings, and post-session 'Positivity' seems likely to correlate with Carrying Forward.

In this study, we included sessions from the first through very late in therapy (as much as two years). It is possible that the relation between CSS and Focusing activities changes at different points in therapy: perhaps after the first few sessions CSS depends more heavily on Opening and Carrying Forward than at the beginning. This is an issue for further exploration.

Also of great interest would be how these focusing activities relate to longer-term outcome in therapy. Although the OQ total scores might be useful in this way, in this sample we had only 24 clients with two or more observations on the OQ, so power for such testing was weak. Another problem is that some of these clients had been in therapy for some time prior to the study. A good test of the relationship of change on the OQ and focusing activities should have enough clients to have adequate power, and these clients should all start the study at the same point in therapy, preferably the beginning. The relationship between immediate session effects and longer-term outcome is complex. For example, Elliott and Wexler (1994) found no relationship between Session Impact Scales and change on the week-to-week measure they used. Still, this matter is one of utmost interest, since a predictive relationship to ultimate therapeutic outcome is one criterion by which valid and reliable in-session process measures could be deemed useful, especially in today's cost-conscious market.

In conclusion, we found empirical results highly consistent with predictions derived from Gendlin's Process Model concepts. This underscores the continued promise of that philosophically based perspective for illuminating psychotherapy process-outcome relationships.

REFERENCES

Cohen, J. (1988). *Power Analysis for the Behavioral Sciences.* Hillsdale, NJ: Erlbaum.

Cohen, J. and Cohen, P. (1983). *Applied Multiple Regression / Correlation Analysis for the Behavioral Sciences* (2nd edn.). Hillsdale, NJ: Erlbaum.

Cornell, A. W. (1996). Relationship = distance + connection: A comparison of inner relationship techniques to finding distance techniques. *The Folio: A Journal for Focusing and Experiential Therapy, 15*(1) 1–8.

Elliott, R. and James, E. (1989). Varieties of client experience in psychotherapy: An analysis of the literature. *Clinical Psychology Review, 9,* 443–67.

Elliott, R. and Wexler, M. (1994). Measuring the impact of sessions in Process-Experiential Therapy of depression: The session impacts scale. *Journal of Counseling Psychology, 41*(2) 166–74.

Freud, S. (1895/1952). The psychic mechanism of hysterical phenomena. Written in collaboration with Joseph Breuer, translated as the first of several 'Selected papers on hysteria'. In R. M. Hutchins (Ed.) *Great Books of the Western World, 54.* Chicago: Encyclopaedia Britannica.

Gendlin, E. T. (1969). Focusing. *Psychotherapy: Theory, Research and Practice, 6,* 4–15.

Gendlin, E. T. (1981). *Focusing* (2nd edn.) New York: Bantam.

Gendlin, E. T. (1996). *Focusing-oriented Psychotherapy: A manual of the experiential method.* New York: Guilford Press.

Gendlin, E. T. (2000). *A Process Model.* Available at http://www.focusing.org/philosophy

Gorsuch, R. L. (1983). *Factor Analysis* (2nd. edn.) Hillsdale, NJ: Erlbaum.

Greenberg, L., Rice, L.and Elliott, R. (1993). *Facilitating Emotional Change: The moment-by-moment process.* New York: Guilford Press.

Greenberg, L., Watson, J. and Lietaer, G. (1998). *Handbook of Experiential Psychotherapy.* New York: Guilford Press.

Hendricks, M. N. (in press). Research basis of experiential/focusing-oriented psychotherapy. In D. Cain (Ed.) *Research Bases of Humanistic Psychotherapy.* Washington: APA Press.

Iberg, J. R. (2000). The *Focusing-oriented Session Report* and the *Therapist's Ratings of Client Process*: The development of new measures of client experiencing. Unpublished manuscript.

Iberg, J. R. (1996). Finding the body's next step: Ingredients and hindrances. *The Folio: a Journal for Focusing and Experiential Therapy, 15*(1) 13–42.

Klein, M., Mathieu-Coughlan, P. and Kiesler, D. (1986). The experiencing scales. In L.S. Greenberg and W. M. Pinsof (Eds.) *The Psychotherapeutic Process: A research handbook.* New York: Guilford Press.

Lambert, M. J., Hansen, N. B., Umpress, V., Lunnen, K., Okiishi, J. and Burlingame, G. M. (1996).

Administration and Scoring Manual for the QC™-45.2. Stevenson, MD: American Professional Credentialing Services LLC.

Leijssen, M. (1998). Focusing microprocesses. In L. Greenberg, J. Watson, and G. Lietaer, (Eds.) *Handbook of Experiential Psychotherapy.* New York: Guilford Press.

Orlinsky, D. E. and Howard, K. I. (1975). *Varieties of Psychotherapeutic Experience.* New York: Columbia Teachers College Press.

Rogers, C. R. (1959). A theory of therapy, personality and interpersonal relationships as developed in the client-centered framework. In S. Koch (Ed.) *Psychology: A study of a science.* New York: McGraw-Hill.

Stiles, W. B. (1980). Measurement of the impact of psychotherapy sessions. *Journal of Consulting and Clinical Psychology, 48,* 176–85.

APPENDIX A. SUBSCALE ITEMS OF THE FOCUSING-ORIENTED SESSION REPORT

Three 'Client Satisfaction with Session' (CSS) Subscale items:

1. How do you feel about the session which you have just completed?
   THIS SESSION WAS: +   -| Perfect.
                            -| Excellent.
                            -| Very good.
                            -| Pretty good.
                            -| Fair.
                            -| Pretty poor.
                       −   -| Very poor.

5. How helpful do you feel your listener was to you this session?
   +   -| Completely helpful.
          -| Very helpful.
          -| Pretty helpful.
          -| Somewhat helpful.
          -| Slightly helpful.
   −   -| Not at all helpful.

8. In the context of all the therapeutic conversations you've ever had (with therapists or friends), how does this one compare?
   THIS SESSION WAS   −   -| Terrible. It was worse than any other I have had.
                            -| Poor. It ranks among some of the worst I've had.
                            -| Below average.
                            -| Average.Comparable to many. Useful,but not great,nor
                               lacking in any major way.
                            -| Better than average.
                            -| Excellent. It was one of the best I've ever had.
                       +   -| Superlative. It was better than any other I have had.

Eleven 'Carrying Forward' Subscale items:

6. How much did the session leave you with changed or new perspectives on the matters you talked about?
   +   -| Extremely much.Things look dramatically different to me now.
          -| Very much. There has been a definite shift in my perspective.
          -| Some. My view is slightly different than before the session.
          -| Not much. My views are pretty much the same.
   −   -| Not at all. Everything seems just as it was.

9. Please rate how you felt after and before the session. a. Do you *feel* any better after this session?

    –   -| No. I feel worse.
            -| No. I feel just the same.
            -| A little better, but not much.
            -| Yes, there is some relief or improvement in how I feel.
            -| A lot. I feel distinctly better.
    +   -| A great deal. I *really* feel better than I did before the session.

12. Did the session result in your coming up with any solutions to your problems?

    +   -| Yes.
            -| Not really.
    –   -| Definitely not.

13. Do you now have any specific actions you intend to take which will be steps forward on your issue(s)?

    –   -| No, no actions that I can think of.
            -| I have a sense of what I need to do, but it's not very specific in action terms.
    +   -| Yes, I have a very specific picture of what action steps to take next.

23. Please mark the spots on the rulers below which indicate how your **body** feels now compared to how it felt at the beginning of the session (we understand that it might have been different in the middle of the session, but please compare how your body *ended up* with how it *began*).

```
                                     no difference
- more tense    |----|----|----0----|----|----|   more relaxed   +
+ calmer        |----|----|----0----|----|----|   more agitated   -
+ warmer        |----|----|----0----|----|----|   cooler          -
+ reduced pain  |----|----|----0----|----|----|   increased pain  -
+ more solid    |----|----|----0----|----|----|   more shaky      -
- more tearful  |----|----|----0----|----|----|   less tearful    +
- more vulnerable |----|----|----0----|----|----| less vulnerable +
```

Eight 'Opening of Feelings' Subscale Items

2. To what extent did the 'doorway' to your feelings open in this session?

    –   -| Not at all. I felt closed and guarded.
            -| Slightly. At least once in the session I definitely felt something.
            -| Quite a bit. At a few points, I was in touch with feelings.
            -| A lot. Several times in the session, some feelings opened up.
    +   -| Extensively. Deep feelings opened up and moved me in unexpected ways.

4. How well did your listener seem to understand what you were feeling and thinking this session?

MY LISTENER + -| Understood exactly how I thought and felt.

-| Understood very well how I thought and felt.

-| Understood pretty well, but there were some things he/she didn't seem to grasp.

-| Didn't understand too well how I thought and felt.

− -| Misunderstood how I thought and felt.

10. Please rate the following two aspects of the emotional intensity of the session:

a. How intense was the most intense emotion you felt?

+ -| extremely intense

-| very intense

-| mildly intense

-| not very intense

− -| not at all intense

7. To what extent do you feel you were able to talk about what was valuable for you to discuss?

+ -| Completely. Everything covered felt important/valuable to talk about.

-| Very much. Most of the session was very valuable to me.

-| Pretty much. Some of the discussion was very good, some so-so.

-| Somewhat. Some stretches of the session were not so useful to me.

-| Not much. We didn't talk about much of real importance to me.

− -| Not at all. We talked about things of minor or no importance to me.

10b. Sometimes people keep their more intense feelings to themselves for various reasons. How much of this session was spent talking about or openly expressing the most intense emotions you felt?

− -| none

-| very little

-| some

-| pretty much

-| very much

+ -| nearly all

14. The attitude of my listener seemed more

− Evaluative |−−|−−|−−|−−|−−|−−| Unconditionally accepting +

17. To what extent were you able to express the full complexity of your situation and your feelings about it?

+ |−−−−|−−−−−|−−−−−|−−−−−|−−−−|−−−−−|−−−−−|−−−−−|−

Completely, with all   Medium: there is   Not much:I was unable to articu-
nuances, subtle relation-   more to it than I   late many important things that
ships, and inner feelings   was able to bring out   relate to these concerns

22. Compared to everyday life, how safe from criticism did you feel during the session?

$-$ |$----$|$-----$|$-----$|$----$|$-----$|$-----$|$-----$| $+$

Unsafe: I felt criti-	Not very safe:	More safe than	Extremely safe:
cized in many ways	even though I wasn't	usual. I felt rela-	I felt unusually free
	explicitly criticized,	tively free of nega-	of any sense of
	I feel I was being judged	tive evaluation	criticism or negative
			evaluation

Five 'Focusing Attitude' Subscale Items:

11. To what extent were you able to hold an attitude of friendly curiosity toward the emotions, feelings, and thoughts you experienced during the session?

- $-$ -| Not at all. I had a lot of disapproval, dislike, or self-criticism about them.
-      -| Barely. There were only moments of friendly curiosity.
-      -| Pretty much. But there were a few times I was unable to have a friendly attitude.
-      -| Nearly the whole time.
- $+$ -| Completely. I didn't waver from friendly curiosity toward my feelings and thoughts.

16. The spirit of our relationship in this session seemed to be more like:

$-$ interpersonal contact |$--$|$--$|$--$|$--$|$--$|$--$| task-oriented work on my issues $+$

18. How much did you feel anxious or uptight or self-conscious related to what you might discover or reveal about yourself?

$-$|$----$|$-----$|$-----$|$-----$|$----$|$-----$|$-----$|$-----$| $+$

A great deal: I was	At some points in the	Not at all: I remained relaxed
worried in this way	session I felt anxious	and comfortable with myself
throughout the session	about what might come out	and not at all defensive

19. To what degree were you able to observe your own feelings and experiences with neutrality, witnessing what was there without getting caught up in evaluative reactions?

$-$|$----$|$-----$|$-----$|$-----$|$----$|$-----$|$-----$|$-----$| $+$

None: I was caught up	I was able to observe	Very much: I felt solidly
in evaluative reactions to	most things without	grounded in a 'witnessing'
everything I said and felt	thinking of them as	part of myself and was not
	'good' or 'bad'	identified with my
		evaluative reactions

20. Please rate the extent to which you felt able to 'let go' to change and the 'unknown'.

$-$|$----$|$-----$|$-----$|$-----$|$----$|$-----$|$-----$|$-----$| $+$

Not at all. I felt very	Medium	A great deal: I was not
self-protective and resistant		defensive or self-protective
to being changed		and could surrender to new
		things

Three 'Sense-pointing by Therapist' Subscale Items:

3. In approximately what proportions did you and the listener influence the course of the session? (i.e. decide what to talk about, change the subject, do the talking, etc.)

- −   -| 20% listener – 80% me
-          -| 40% listener – 60% me
-          -| 50% listener – 50% me
-          -| 60% listener – 40% me
- +   -| 80% listener – 20% me

15. I had a sense that:

  – I led the way |−−|−−|−−|−−|−−|−−| I was guided or led by my listener +

23. Please mark the spots on the rulers below which indicate how your **body** feels now compared to how it felt at the beginning of the session (we understand that it might have been different in the middle of the session, but please compare how your body *ended up* with how it *began*).

no difference

− more numb |−−−−|−−−−|−−−−0−−−−|−−−−|−−−−| more sensory awareness +

APPENDIX B: THERAPIST RATINGS OF CLIENT FOCUSING ACTIVITY

Two 'Opening of Feelings $_{Tx}$' Subscale Items:

'complexity':

1. To what degree did client articulate the full complexity, including internal and external aspects, related to the feelings worked on today?

```
0           2           4           6           8          10
|——|——|——|——|——|——|——|——|——|——|
minimal                 average                 full articulation
```

'body-feelings':

2. To what extent did the client experience the formation and opening up of immediate, viscerally felt feelings?

```
0           2           4           6           8          10
|——|——|——|——|——|——|——|——|——|——|
no occurrences          some bodily             several bodily felt feelings
of bodily feeling       feeling but             formed and most opened up
                        little opening
```

Two 'Focusing Attitude Tx' Subscale Items:

'congruence':
3. To what extent today, in your judgment, was the client able to accurately and fully represent his/her true feelings in words and self-image?

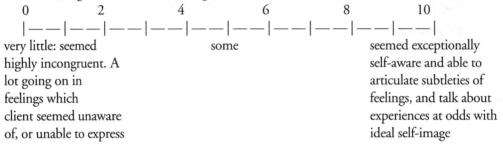

| 0 | 2 | 4 | 6 | 8 | 10 |

very little: seemed
highly incongruent. A   some   seemed exceptionally
lot going on in   self-aware and able to
feelings which   articulate subtleties of
client seemed unaware   feelings, and talk about
of, or unable to express   experiences at odds with
                                                                                ideal self-image

'witnessing':
4. To what degree was the client able to acknowledge his/her full range of feelings without favoring some feelings and resisting others?

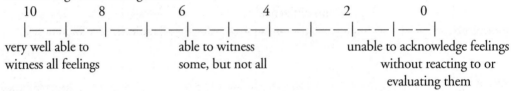

| 10 | 8 | 6 | 4 | 2 | 0 |

very well able to   able to witness   unable to acknowledge feelings
witness all feelings   some, but not all   without reacting to or
                                                                            evaluating them

Two 'Carrying Forward Tx' Subscale Items:

'surrender':
5. To what extent in this session did the client seem able to loosen existing ideas and self-conceptions, to 'sense the unknown', thus opening up to things unexpected or unfamiliar in feelings and experiencing?

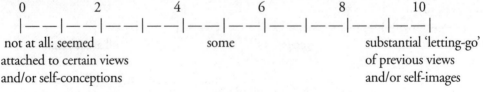

| 0 | 2 | 4 | 6 | 8 | 10 |

not at all: seemed   some   substantial 'letting-go'
attached to certain views   of previous views
and/or self-conceptions   and/or self-images

'self-among-equals':
6. By the end of the session, did the client's attitude toward self and others seem more narrow and self-oriented, or more humble and considerate of perspectives broader than his/her own?

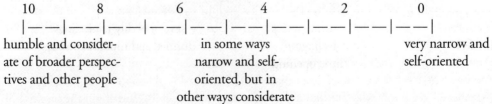

| 10 | 8 | 6 | 4 | 2 | 0 |

humble and consider-   in some ways   very narrow and
ate of broader perspec-   narrow and self-   self-oriented
tives and other people   oriented, but in
                                       other ways considerate

Kevin C. Krycka and Deb Lambo
Seattle University, Washington State, USA

Gendlin's 'Edge': Making fresh sense of gay and lesbian experience

Abstract. By asking: 'What more can emerge after my research is completed?' any researcher can follow strands of truths implicit in their work to new and fresh understandings. This chapter elaborates on Gendlin's 'responsive order' (1997d) and explores what remained implicit after a recent phenomenological research study investigating gay and lesbian experience was completed. Structural-thematic statements from the study form the backdrop and starting point for this discussion. We suggest that when researchers 'think at the edge' (Gendlin, 1997c) of their own conclusions, something more than was originally found or anticipated can come. The 'more' that emerges then carries the project forward (backwards, in and out, even crossing and dipping conceptual-disciplinary lines here and there) resulting in a fresh understanding of the phenomenon investigated.

Making sense of a completed research project involves more than logical or even intersubjective agreement with colleagues. It involves using the more-than-logical and more-than-intersubjective. Making sense requires that the felt complexity of the question under investigation be followed, carried forward if you will, to its fresh new beginnings.

What starts off most research is a felt-sense of some 'thing' needing to be further explored, explained, or defined. The originating felt-sense occupies a large part of the very first movements of any research project. If not protected in some manner, the felt-sense, with its nascent structural future, will be dislodged from its centrality and relegated to the outskirts, or even the trash bin, of our activities. If protected and nurtured, the surviving felt-sense inevitably encounters other, often disparate, considerations. This is not usually a problem. In fact, having other voices partake in our 'thing' can be exciting to it and invigorate the entire process of research.

We could probably all agree that research comes into existence out of a host of influences located within and outside the researchers. The original felt-sense, in the best of situations, is present during the project's development and is able to be accessed by the researcher at every step of the way. Of course the felt-sense is transformed and shaped along the way by our theoretical leanings and other demands that more pragmatic concerns placed upon us, such as our employer, the government, or the subjects of the question. However, even after the project is completed, for some, the felt-sense will continue to raise its voice and call us on to further action (Gendlin, 1990). Such was the case with us. In the following pages, we explain what happened regarding the felt-sense of a completed research project and how the felt-sense came forward again forming a new, fresh understanding of gay and lesbian experience.

Anyone who has been involved in research will more than likely relate to this chapter on a personal level. We know what it's like to sit with what remains to be said about the original idea or felt-sense of the project, long after it's finished. We know what it's like to ponder the conclusions not yet articulated. However, anyone can relate to what it feels like to sense the pull of an idea that needs to be put down into words, concepts, or even theory. Under the special circumstance of a research setting, the leftover felt-sense of the project serves to draw the researcher into new situations and new questions. It's fair to say many of us have had this very experience.

The authors collaborated on taking an already-completed qualitative research project on gay and lesbian experience and following its conceptual and felt-sense edges toward a point where we could be done with it. Kevin Krycka had concluded the original project in the year prior to his asking Deb Lambo, a partner on past research projects, to help think through his sense that the work was not yet done. As we had worked together on other focusing-oriented research projects, we were familiar with each other's style of approaching understanding experience and the processes involved in doing research. So, it didn't take long for us to admit to being somewhat compelled to take the research through its next steps and see what would come of it.

Kevin recalled about one of our first meetings that 'Graciously, Deb sat with me as I went over my 'findings' with her. She sympathized with me as I complained about a nagging feeling I had about the themes I had articulated from the project. She was intrigued more by my not being finished than with the themes of the finished project. I thought that was a hopeful sign. To me, and now to her, the project wasn't yet over.'

Nevertheless, a conceptual block stood in our way that stemmed from our own graduate schooling. We had both been taught that the general goal of doing research is to construct a study in such a way that you could come up with final conclusions based on the data. You weren't supposed to keep going after you made your final statements. The prevailing wisdom of doing research held that when you were done with a research project, you were done and you should move on to something else.

This did not satisfy us in the least. We had to get around our own hesitance to see and honor what was unsaid as an indicator of there being more to do, more to say about being gay and lesbian. To help jostle our thinking, we took up re-reading the contemporary works of Eugene Gendlin that pertained to grounding understanding in the body, particularly his latest body of work referred to under the rubric, 'The Philosophy of Entry into the Implicit'. (Gendlin, 1991b, 1992b and 1992c).

As we reviewed Gendlin's works and shared our responses to it, we quickly realized that Gendlin's emphasis on the role of the 'more than words can say' played an important part in our next step with the project. We discovered that following the edge of our bodily complexity regarding the finished research project indeed could lead us to new articulations and extensions of the project itself.

Philosophically, the foundation for this project rests on Gendlin's core philosophical works beginning with *Experience and the Creation of Meaning* (1962/97a) and continuing through in his later works 'Thinking Beyond Patterns' (1991b), *A Process Model* (1997c), 'Thinking at the Edge', or TAE for short, and those on language (1997b). In these works, Gendlin revolutionizes philosophy and psychology by explicating the responsive order of experience.

This order is present in every part of our existence, in fact, the responsive order itself forms a hermeneutic through which knowledge is discovered. Gendlin brings together praxis with theory in a way that makes central the felt-sense (felt-referent), a concept he pioneered through Focusing (Gendlin, 1982) and his work as a psychotherapist (Gendlin, 1996a, 1996b, 1990 and 1984). He insists we marry thinking with feeling, so that new ideas and concepts can flow from that place where precise thinking and explicit bodily felt-knowing come together.

For our part, we have a rather modest agenda in regard to Gendlin's larger philosophical project. We simply hope to show how we came to form new concepts out of an emergent bodily sense. Our specific goal for this chapter is to show how implicit intricacy might work in research, and how a project on gay and lesbian experience was carried forward beyond thematic statements to more precise and fresh languaging of gay and lesbian experience that is faithful to experience itself.

The concepts that were ultimately formed found their way to daylight through the use of TAE. We don't pretend to be experts on TAE in the least; rather, we see this chapter as one example of how research can be carried forward where there was previously an unfinished sense.

At the heart of what we have done lies an appreciation for the psychological and philosophical concepts and models of human experience present in phenomenology. Again to quote Gendlin, 'Philosophy can reopen the old assumptions and conceptual models if we think with our more intricate experiencing as well as with logic. Our more intricate experiencing may carry it forward, but is not thereby replaced. It (models, concepts, forms) is always freshly there again, and open to being carried forward in new ways, never arbitrarily, but always in quite special and precise ways' (Gendlin, 1962/97a, p. xxi).

Perhaps a little about the initial project is in order at this point. The next section is written in Kevin's own voice so that the reader can be more closely connected to what pulled him to contact Deb. Perhaps you will discover for yourself a felt-sense of the initial research project.

DESCRIPTION OF THE INITIAL STUDY

I began almost five years ago with a sense for a gap in the psychological and sociological literature on what it means to identify oneself as gay or lesbian as we approach midlife. The various deconstructions of identity frankly left me cold inside. There was ample evidence that I probably should have stopped with the conclusions of Foucault, Derrida, and Plummer, who say identity, among other things, is really a politics; not a mutable or changeable form, but a form itself that is determined —by one's culture, race, gender, class, and history — and which is played out in the social arena.

In my social-cultural neighborhood of Seattle, no one I knew really acted as if they were a product of their culture or their past. It seemed more true to me that who we are as gays and lesbians cannot be solely located within specified disciplinary domains or the contextual elements of our current times or those preceding us. Indeed, my company of friends, my lover, and my colleagues, showed something quite different. I sensed an action within the common body of theories about gay identity (or identity in general) that was not reflected in my world at all. So I sat with an uneasy, somewhat irritated felt-sense about my reading of those theories. I knew something was absolutely right about what they said, but something was also absolutely missing as well.

Stumbling forward with this 'something's missing' sense, I took up the methodological tools I'm most familiar with from phenomenological psychology and posed a task to 15 gay men and women. Their task was to 'Describe how you know you are gay/lesbian.'

These individuals were asked to describe their knowing in body-sensing terms, their felt-sense of the task. What came were elaborate descriptions of many defining moments of what it's like to be gay or lesbian at midlife.

You might predict that such an open-ended question would yield a discordant picture of gay identity. At first glance it seemed so. After all, there are many different kinds of tales to tell about oneself, all gripping in detail and meaning. But a thorough phenomenological analysis revealed something different. Recall that phenomenological analysis asks of the investigator to let the underlying experiential structure of the thing being studied speak loudest (Halling, 1984). In my case, analysis revealed what I believe to be rather provocative answers to what it is to be gay and lesbian at midlife. Below are the major thematic findings from the initial study.

- The experience of being a gay person is most basically one of difference.
- Gay life is one marked by hope, which is the ambiguous balance between passion and committed action.
- Ethicality in gay life emerges from one's difference and sense of hope.

These three sentences can further be reduced to three words, 'difference, hope, and ethicality'. Again, I present these findings as a basis for our further discussion of employing TAE when research refuses to finish. In the following section, we will briefly review the basic background to TAE and explain how we employed it.

WHAT IS 'THINKING AT THE EDGE'?

> Thinking at the edge arises through an intuitive understanding of the subject that can only come with experience. It includes a sense of urgency or opportunity, a sense of necessity which brings a pressure or drive to articulate and communicate this understanding. What it is may still be inchoate — fertile with possibility but still unformed and unclear.' (Gendlin, 1997e, July)

When we first read this statement from the Focusing Institute's summary of the first TAE conference, we were drawn and excited. The first conference happened just after Kevin had finished the project on gay/lesbian identity at mid-age.

When we sat down together at one of our very first meetings to discuss going further with the research, we both felt Gendlin's paragraph tugging at our insides. Like the restless quality that helped form the initial research project, we found the project was not finished yet. Ostensibly, it was done, but not finished.

When we finally sat down to work further with the research, we noticed distinct felt-senses emerge. First was the sense that 'more could be said'. This came in relation to the individual themes. The second distinct sense that came in a felt-sense way was the realization that the larger importance of the project was 'yet to be discovered'. For us this was certainly true, but we also felt it may be true for others who would someday read that original study. The sense of 'yet to be discovered' is both inviting of further research projects, but more importantly for us, is characteristic of Gendlin's edge.

He said at the first TAE Conference in 1997 some notable things. Below are a few excerpts from some of Gendlin's full-group sessions. In their entirety, they can provide an overview of the entire TAE process.

- In you, arising from and relating to your work, there is a knowing. It is out of this knowing that a new expression of your work can seek to come.
- In the edge of this knowing, you can touch something as yet unclear. You sense the never-yet-said quality of this unclear something, and its value to others.
- So you make a place to listen to this something, and you hold it carefully but strongly, protecting it as words to speak from it come.
- You step outside yourself and look at each main word, but none of them yet say what this something in you means to say.
- But in seeing how they don't work, you insist that they say what you want them to say, and so make them come alive.
- As you listen, you begin to pull out strands from this something, and what was vague begins to take form.
- The strands cross, and bring out their intricacy and become able to contain a world of new meaning. The crossing generates sentences.
- Your particular becomes universal, and your knowing is carried forward.
- Then you write your theory.

In order to help you get a sense of the importance of staying with the felt-sense, let's review the first theme. Here again is the first statement from the original research project: THE EXPERIENCE OF BEING A GAY PERSON IS MOST BASICALLY ONE OF DIFFERENCE.

See if you can find your felt-sense of this statement. What is there for you right now as you re-read the above statement? It may be inchoate, it may be very defined. See if you can find your own sense of this statement. Whatever it is, your sense has an intuitive edge about it. That's where TAE works. It works with deeply already-known places and draws us beyond its (our own) initial felt-sense and the parameters, forms, constructs, meanings, and classifications we use in explaining. Below is a brief re-creation of a meeting where a clear felt-sense emerged regarding this research statement.

We reread the entire first statement and then remained still for quite a few moments. Attending to our inner workings, we were each on our own finding our felt-sense about the statement. Deb indicated first that she had something. 'I don't know, but it seems not right.' Almost inevitably this is how a felt-sense emerges. There indeed is something not quite right going on. She persisted, 'It's like I want to add some more words.' Kevin then helps the unclear find words or senses by saying, 'There's more that wants to be said?' By posing a question here the process of Deb leaning into her unclear sense starts to move forward. The unclear now has an edge. Deb then said, 'I don't like it. Who says gays and lesbians have a corner on feeling different? Isn't it just plain wrong to say that? I get all tight inside. Something's not right here.'

Reference to being 'tight inside' is a bodily signal that Deb has long ago learned to pay attention to. The bodily signal is now invited to come a bit forward and say more in its own right.

'The tight seems like a jealousy thing. Yeh, that's it. It's twisted up there. Hum. Tight and jealous go together. Yes, that's right.'

At this point Kevin is acting as an active listener. Since he knows Deb is proficient at finding her way with felt-senses, he sits back and watches the sense unfold for several more minutes.

'Wow! Reading that gays and lesbians feel so different makes me feel defensive, tight, and wanting to contradict it or . . . no, not contradict it. I feel this pulling going on that is more like wanting to join it and say, 'Hey, I know that feeling too.' So, if I make a place for *that* . . . ah, then it eases.'

Deb found that the sense of being different at a very basic level wanted to be owned by her. In our time together we unpacked the subtle but powerful rendering of the word 'different' so that it eased; it no longer presented a huge blocking to sensing what more could be said about gay and lesbian experience of difference.

If you're like us, you may have had a negative reaction to this statement as well. The statement, 'gays are different,' may seem to you (as it did to us) very problematic on a number of levels, levels associated with what is *already known* — or stated — about gays and their identity. But, Gendlin's work says we can go beyond what is already known and beyond the given patterns, assumptions, and categorizations lying underneath that knowledge. We can go to the fresh, the emergent, and the revealing. He encourages us to enter into our original research again and again with our felt-sense at any step. That is what we did and then further built upon this one statement with more concepts that came from the experiential edge of our thinking.

We should note that TAE is an evolving process based in a likewise-evolving new theory of being human. The steps of TAE are the more mechanical aspects associated with how we can develop new theory. Like the steps of Focusing (Gendlin, 1981), TAE has an order that is always in service of the felt-sense itself. The marriage of thinking and feeling in TAE and Focusing rely upon our interest in maintaining congruence with our ever-changing experience and not to let a somewhat arbitrary form, like steps, interfere with discovery and idea creation.

We also note that the steps of TAE have grown since we finished the bulk of our work together from nine steps (below) to now fourteen steps as of the summer of 2000. Here are the nine steps of TAE that we used in our working out what was implicit still in thinking about what it means to be gay or lesbian at midlife.

SUMMARY OF THE NINE STEPS

Step 1 — Get a felt sense.

Step 2 — Notice how this thing is in some way not logical.

Step 3 — Notice that no words fit. Explore the felt sense as you do so. Pull out these key words.

Step 4 — Make the words mean what you want them to mean.

Step 5 — Notice that each time you use a different word to mean what you mean you pull out something different from the felt sense.

Step 6 — Collect facets.

Step 7 — Write a sentence for each facet that makes no sense at all unless it is understood

the way you mean it.
Step 8 — Cross the structure of two facets.
Step 9 — Write some real sentences about your thing.

There are many, many things that could be said about the steps themselves, but for now, let us proceed with an example of how the nine steps came into use in regards to just the first thematic statement about gays, saying they are different. If you would like a further and more in-depth discussion of the steps of TAE, please go to the Focusing Institute's web site (http://www.focusing.org). For now, let us make a few general observations about using the TAE steps.

Steps One and Two: Unpacking our thing

> In you, arising from and relating to your work, there is a knowing. (Gendlin, 2000, July)

In steps one and two, we went back to the original wording of the themes and played with them and let our felt-sense be the guide. In the TAE process, the first two steps are critical. Without consistently referencing the felt-sense and noticing how it shifted and changed as we discussed the themes, we believe it would have been very difficult, if not impossible, to carry forward our concepts beyond the original wording and assumptions about difference and being gay. We aired our objections over phrasing and our troubles with the buried meanings the words themselves give to each other. We used the first two steps over and over to help us get underneath the given quality of that first statement.

At times it wasn't easy to stick with this process. We wanted to short-cut TAE and make it more 'efficient'. It was taking too long, we said to each other on many occasions. There is no doubt that working with TAE is exacting, but we know now just how powerful a process it is.

In practical terms, we each sat with the themes from the study and let our felt-sense of each come. We talked together about our felt-sense and let each inform and even change the other at times. The organic feel to this part of the process was exciting. It really helped us clarify our positions and involve the other in the discovery process itself. We stopped this part of TAE only when we felt all of the felt-sense was known.

Steps Three, Four, Five: Inching us forward

> It is out of this knowing that a new expression of your work can seek to come. In the edge of this knowing, you can touch something as yet unclear. You sense the never-yet-said quality of this unclear something, and its value to others. So you make a space for it and let it speak up. (Gendlin, 2000, July)

In Steps Three, Four, and Five we took apart the three themes from the original study and played around with various wordings, being diligent to stay in touch with our felt-sense in the process. The key to these steps is to let your felt-sense guide you and keep you honest. We decided to work on each theme separately and then all at once. It seemed to us that each concept was different enough to warrant being worked on alone, but we were uncomfortable with not tying each back to the other. Keeping the sense of the whole research project was very important to us, even though keeping the whole created its own confusions.

Along the way, we were comforted by Gendlin's various writings where he encourages us to go beyond traditional patterns of understanding (language, etc.) in our thinking. We came to realize that by seeing how things don't work, how words don't say what we mean, we became free to make words work for us, or as Gendlin says, 'make the words say what you mean them to say' (Gendlin, 2000, July).

Again, using the first concept-statement as an example, we pulled out various words from it and tried to insert new ones. For instance, we took out the word 'basically' and worked on it a little. We tried substituting 'substantially' and 'eventually' because these words held something of their own that needed to be said. We also found that each tried-out word conveyed more than was said in 'basically', particularly if you add a prefix or suffix to them. Basic (the core of basically) became briefly 'basicnessing'. In the end, we kept 'basically' just as it was. There was genuine excitement at attempting to forge new words, weird ones in fact, that followed the leading edge of our felt-sense.

Steps Six and Seven: Filling-out

> You find however, that if you step outside of it, some of it doesn't work all that well. You insist that your thing say exactly what you mean it to say. (Gendlin, 2000, July)

Gendlin asks in these steps that we first collect instances of the concepts. We discuss these steps together because step six came right along with step seven for us in practice. For this part of the process, we went our separate ways for a while, each collecting our own personal stories of being different, for instance. This was a personally challenging time. It caused us to delve deeply into our own histories and feelings. It engaged us further in the concepts by demanding that we use our own experiences as a sort of tool for the refinement of the concept itself.

We believe these two steps to be two of the most powerful in Gendlin's TAE process. It called us first to go inside our own experiences and recall times from our own lives that resonated to the particular concept or part of the concept we were working with at the time, and then to write down these facets. The act of writing something powerful down, knowing it will be eventually shared, was necessary if we were going to pull out the fresh and leading edges of our work that could be shared. So we wrote down instances, we collected various facets for each of the three concepts from the original study.

When we came back together to go over our facets, we noticed how much similarity there was between us. Our personal life stories yielded many of the same kinds of feelings and memories. In the end, we found this to be a very powerful time in our work together. It enabled us to share deeply from our own history and listen intently to that of the other. Of course, Focusing helped out a great deal here for it provided a practical tool for us when we got stuck in our sharing or in understanding each other.

One kind of instance that poked through many of our personal instances was that of embodiment. Difference was (is) a thing felt in the body. Yes, it could be a kind of thought or intellectual endeavor, but it was mostly for us a felt experience. We recalled the feelings of being called names at school or simply feeling not 'normal' in adolescence, like just about everybody has. We shared how that sick feeling in our guts would almost come spontaneously when discussing the very word difference. We also recalled the times when difference was a badge of honor and the associated feelings were ones of power and location in life. Under whatever circumstance it arose, difference was very present for us in a physical way.

It should be noted too that this word embodiment is laden with various meanings in the philosophical and psychological literature, so much so that we almost threw it out. We decided to keep it primarily because it was accessible to so many who might read our words later, and the fact that it fit our felt-sense of difference.

Steps Eight and Nine: Finalizing our thing

It begins to take new form. You are now ready to share it with the outside world. (Gendlin, 2000, July)

We worked with TAE for about a year with the thematic statements. We met regularly to sit with and move with the first statement, then the others. Neither one of us was satisfied with the statements, even though they were the major findings of the original project. When it came time to actually write out our new understandings we were intimidated a little. Upon reflection, it seemed to us that writing something down could potentially close it off too soon. But, if we checked back with the felt-sense regarding our new sentences, we generally found our felt-sense was indeed okay with the new phrasing.

Below is an example of a preliminary sentence created at this stage. The sentence relates to the first theme produced in the original study. Here's the sentence.

QUEER DIFFERENCE IS MARKED BY AN EMBODIED UNDERSTANDING THAT INVOLVES A DISTINCT KIND OF PRESENCE-IN-THE-BODY.

You can see how we were now using words in traditional ways. 'Difference' reappears here in recognizable form, but we also added several new words that change the original theme dramatically. Now difference comes to be about embodiment that involves distinctiveness.

What's so important about Gendlin's theory making process in TAE, is that the goal is to produce a new understanding, perhaps an entirely new theory, regarding the thing we know and are working with. In this case, difference comes to mean more than originally thought. Difference is distinctly about the manner in which it is embodied in the gay and lesbian person. Our theme becomes a theory now, because it is stated as one and holds up to the truth of experience and logic.

Is it reasonable to see being gay or lesbian as essentially about being different? Maybe. Is it plausible that queer people see and experience themselves and the world in a uniquely embodied way? Sure. This is a new theory. Of course it remains to be tried out and tested, but it is a new theory on queer difference.

PARTING THOUGHTS

We worked the steps, not religiously, but rigorously. Sometimes we'd go off in what you might call tangents, setting down those strings of associations for what would come into the slot created by an unfinished sense from within the work. Setting down strings became just as important to notice as did realizing when a set of words actually did stick.

We found staying with the felt-sense amazingly helpful. We would often become caught up in something or another and then need to be brought back to the felt-sense to see if the tangent was part of what was emerging. The steps provided a method for our searching and in that way were invaluable to use. At times we felt lost in our own process or in the giddy potentials that lay ahead. In the end, we relied upon the felt-sense to guide us.

We frequently went back to Step Seven for instance. We forced ourselves to live with the not-fitting facets. In our dialogue, we crossed our 'opposing' facets Step Eight, and eventually found out more that did fit the blank but pregnant slot facing us.

Coming to joint resolution took quite a while. As was said earlier, about a year. There were many weeks between our meetings. Plenty of time for our concepts to be reformed by further readings and conversations. Each facet was interfered. The interfering could not, nor should not, be stopped. It was part of it — part of the discovery of the fresh understanding yet to come, but somehow implied already.

In closing, we would like to share another statement we generated that is fuller, dramatically so, and ripe with big words strung together just so, compared to the original theme on ethicality. Here it is.

AS REGARDS GAY EXPERIENCE EMBODIED — A PRIMARILY A DIALOGAL PHENOMENON — IT INHABITS PLACES THAT REACH OUT FROM FLESHY BOUNDARIES TO OTHERS IN WHAT CAN BE UNDERSTOOD AS POINTING TOWARD A TRANSHUMAN ETHICAL LIFE.

You can see this statement (probably not yet fully explored) has much more life in it than the theme 'Ethicality in gay life emerges from ones difference and sense of hope.' It has movement (pointing toward) and anchoring (embodied). The old concepts, being different and hope, still exist in this one. The old ones have not been supplanted totally. No, the new statement pays tribute and even honors a little the old way of seeing things.

Gay experience now becomes alive again. From the stale, no-flesh, deconstructions and constructions of concepts familiar to us, this last statement resonates as something original, something not quite said before in this exact way with these exact intentions packed into each word.

Of course, it remains for us to suffer the slings and arrows of disagreement and conjecture that inevitably will come. But, that is part of entering into the public discourse, isn't it? Any discourse on a 'truth' will be debated. But that is not in fact why we thought of presenting this work to you.

Rather, we wanted to demonstrate how TAE works in the revolution of concepts and ideas, some near and dear to us, which ultimately can produce new knowledges that, given a space, will provoke further intricacies and clarifications.

> Our culture primarily uses two thinking systems. What seems to be needed most in this historical moment is the capacity to join the precision of logic which comes from the use of the intellect with the groundedness-in-experience contributed by our intuitive, experiential side: in short, a system of thought that can help mediate between the felt-sense of what one knows, and the public language in which one must communicate. (Gendlin, 1997e, July)

Thinking at the Edge is a risky business. On the one hand, it does not deny the usual frameworks of words and meanings, and on the other hand, it rearranges and transforms them to suit the very specific needs of the emergent in our thinking and experiencing. As Gendlin says, there is benefit to thinking at the edge. It mediates between the felt-sense of what one knows and the public language in which one must communicate. This benefits us with fresh understandings, intricacy beyond original concepts, with original ways of thinking and communicating. It is revolutionary in the kindest of ways and leads us to new ground where structures change and excitement for thinking can be found again.

REFERENCES

Gendlin, E. T. (1982). *Focusing*. New York: Bantam.

Gendlin, E. T. (1984). The client's client: The edge of awareness. In R. L. Levant and J. M. Shlien (Eds.) *Client-centered Therapy and the Person-Centered Approach. New directions in theory, research and practice*. New York: Praeger, pp. 76–107.

Gendlin, E. T. (1990). The small steps of the therapy process : How they come and how to help them come. In G. Lietaer, J. Rombauts and R. Van Balen (Eds.) *Client-centered and Experiential Psychotherapy in the Nineties*. Leuven: Leuven University Press, pp. 205–24.

Gendlin, E. T. (1991a). On emotion in therapy. In J. D. Safran and L. S. Greenberg (Eds.) *Emotion, Psychotherapy and Change*. New York and London: Guilford Press, pp. 255–79. Also in *The Folio*, 1990, *9*(1), 1–49, under the title 'On emotion in therapy' (1990 revision).

Gendlin, E. T. (1991b). Thinking beyond patterns: body, language and situations. In B. den Ouden and M. Moen (Eds.) *The Presence of Feeling in Thought*. New York: Peter Lang, pp. 25–151.

Gendlin, E. T. (1992a). Celebrations and problems of humanistic psychology. *Humanistic Psychologist*, *20*(2–3), 447–60. Reprinted in *The Folio*, 1994, *13*(1), 27–37.

Gendlin, E. T. (1992b). Meaning prior to the separation of the five senses. In M. Stamenov (Ed.) *Current Advances in Semantic Theory*. (Published as Vol. 73 of the series 'Current issues in linguistic theory'). Amsterdam/Philadelphia: John Benjamins, pp. 31–53.

Gendlin, E. T. (1992c). The primacy of the body, not the primacy of perception. *Man and World*, 25 (3–4), 341–53.

Gendlin, E. T. (1996a). *Focusing-oriented Psychotherapy. A manual of the experiential method*. New York: Guilford Press.

Gendlin, E. T. (1996b). The use of focusing in therapy. In J.K. Zeig, (Ed.) *The Evolution of Psychotherapy*. New York: Brunner/Mazel.

Gendlin, E. T. (1962/97a). *Experience and the Creation of Meaning: A philosophical and psychological approach to the subjective*. Chicago, IL: Northwestern University Press.

Gendlin, E. T. (1997b). How philosophy cannot appeal to experience, and how it can. *Language beyond Postmodernism: Saying and thinking in Gendlin's philosophy*. Chicago, IL: Northwestern University Press, pp. 3–41.

Gendlin, E. T. (1997c). *A Process Model*. Spring Valley, NY: Focusing Institute.

Gendlin, E. T. (1997d). The responsive order: A new empiricism. *Man and World. 30*, 383–411.

Gendlin, E. T. (1997e, July). *Thinking at the Edge*. Presented at the annual Thinking at the Edge workshop, Spring Valley, NY.

Gendlin, E. T. (2000, July). *Thinking at the Edge*. Presented at the annual Thinking at the Edge workshop, Spring Valley, NY.

Halling, S. and Leifer, M. (1991). The theory and practice of dialogal research. *Journal of Phenomenological Psychology, 22*(1), 1–15.

Arthur C. Bohart

California State University, Dominguez Hills
and Saybrook Graduate School and Research Centre

A Passionate Critique of Empirically Supported Treatments and the Provision of an Alternative Paradigm[1]

Kuhn (1977) has noted that it is difficult for those speaking from different paradigms to understand one another. The EST approach is based on an implicit paradigm of what psychotherapy and research on psychotherapy is about. From the point of view of that paradigm, the EST approach seems so logical that its advocates have difficulty grasping the objections of those of us who do not ascribe to the paradigm. EST advocates fail to recognize the paradigmatic nature of the objections, and so assimilate and deal with them from within their paradigm. Those of us who ascribe to alternative paradigms are undoubtedly guilty of the same thing. ESTers probably feel misunderstood by us as well. Nonetheless in this paper I present a view of what the EST paradigm looks like from a different paradigmatic perspective.

When confronted with objections EST proponents typically respond in one of two ways. First they assume that the motivation of opponents is to inappropriately defend 'unscientific' practice. Therefore, the answer for these opponents is to manualize and do the randomized controlled clinical trials (RCTs) that show that their approaches work. Second, EST advocates argue that objections can be dealt with from within the EST paradigm. Lampropoulos (2000), for instance, thinks it is a matter of showing those of us opposed to the EST paradigm how our ideas can fit into that paradigm. This, however, is a little like a Republican telling Democrats that their concerns (e.g., poverty, gun control) can be handled within the Republican paradigm. This is true. In some sense, *all* issues and ideas can be handled from within any paradigm. However the framing of issues is different in different paradigms. So, in another sense, this is not true. As I shall argue below, while it may be true that analogues of certain therapies can be created within the EST paradigm, it is not true that the real spirit of them is captured within these analogues.

While it may be that science progresses when one paradigm is accepted by a field (Kuhn, 1970), it is not wise to prematurely impose a paradigm on a field, especially when that paradigm was not decided upon by a consensus in the field, but rather was created by a small minority of scholars in a particular division of the American Psychological Association. Further, the impetus to the development of the EST standards is economic and political, more so than it is scientific (Beutler, 1998; Nathan, 2000). Therefore, those of us who subscribe to alternative paradigmatic assumptions perceive the attempt to make EST assumptions the

---

[1] This paper is a revised, expanded version of a paper originally published in *Psychotherapy Research*, (Bohart, 2000). Various versions were also distributed at the Conference of the Society for Psychotherapy Research, Chicago, June, 2000; the International Conference on Client-Centered and Experiential Psychotherapy, Chicago, June, 2000; The Convention of the American Psychological Association, Washington, DC, August, 2000.

'law of the land' as an illegitimate, hegemonic attempt to impose a world view on both science and practice.

I shall not rigorously define 'paradigm,' especially since Kuhn (1970) himself has identified a number of different uses/meanings of the term. In general, though, I take a paradigm to be a fundamental model of the phenomena being studied which underlies specific theories. It shapes the kinds of theories that are developed, how research is done, and what is to be considered as research-based knowledge. In psychotherapy a paradigm might include a fundamental model of what a psychological problem is (e.g., thought of as a syndrome or disorder analogous to a medical problem, versus a family-systemic problem or a problem in living), a model of what the process of providing help is (e.g., therapy as treatment versus therapy as interpersonal encounter, dialogue, and consultation), and an underlying metaphysical model which influences both practice and the conducting and use of research (e.g., a modernistic Newtonian view of the universe, with a goal of increasing control of dependent variables by specification of independent variables; versus a postmodern systemic universe where we can never know or totally predict or control the phenomena being studied and where science is used by the practitioner but does not determine practice).

In this rejoinder to EST proponents I will (a) make a brief paradigmatic comment on the dodo bird verdict, (b) present what I perceive, from within my paradigm, as the implicit but unspelled-out logic of the paradigm underlying the EST approach, and (c) present the implicit logic of an alternative possible paradigm. I hope to use this to argue (a) there are alternative viable paradigms underlying psychotherapy practice within which the EST criteria make at best limited sense, (b) both the research and practice of psychotherapy should remain open to alternative paradigms until through the slow, steady accumulation of results, one or another paradigm becomes dominant, and (c) there are evidence-based ways of practicing that do not rely on the EST philosophy. In so doing I shall focus primarily on the issue of manualization. Those of us who ascribe to alternative therapy models may also have reservations about RCTs, believing them to be useful but not the 'gold standard' (Persons and Silberschatz, 1998) for investigating how therapy works. However, it is manualization which is the most objectionable part of the EST criteria.

THE DODO BIRD: AN EXAMPLE OF PARADIGM CLASH

Perhaps no issue is more pivotal in highlighting the difference between competing paradigms of psychotherapy than the Dodo bird verdict that all therapies, for the most part, are equally effective for most disorders. For proponents of the EST paradigm the Dodo bird verdict, if true, would be instant death. First, there would be no point in developing and studying different treatments for different disorders. Second, the EST paradigm is a technological view of therapy—it places its bets on technology as the primary cause of change. Developing and testing specific technologies, manualized for different disorders, is what it is about. Even the therapeutic relationship is treated as a kind of technology, to be studied and then differentially 'provided' for different disorders. Therefore it is not surprising that EST advocates are quick to conclude that the Dodo bird verdict is 'flawed' (Lampropoulos, 2000) or that it has been superseded (Task Force, 1995).

For proponents of alternative paradigms, such as the one I propose below, therapy is fundamentally an interpersonal/dialogical process. Technology may or may not be used, but it is secondary in importance. As a result, it is no surprise to advocates of these paradigms that different therapeutic approaches may have only minimal differential treatment effects. Therefore proponents of this paradigm find it easy to accept the Dodo bird verdict and to try to build on it.

Because the willingness with which one accepts the Dodo bird verdict is paradigm-based, it is unlikely this issue will ever be resolved until one or the other paradigm (or some entirely new paradigm) triumphs. As a proponent of an alternative to the EST approach, my view is that the evidence for the Dodo bird verdict is so compelling that, were its conclusions in accord with people's beliefs and theories about therapy, it would long ago have been accepted as one of psychology's major findings and built upon, instead of being continually debated (Bohart and Tallman, 1999). Therefore, I object to Lampropoulos' (2000) comment that therapists such as myself should not be allowed to '. . . rest exclusively on the therapeutic relationship, powerful placebos and other ill-defined common factors, which seems to be a major assumption shared by most of the EST opponents.'

I shall not try to debate all the issues involved in the Dodo bird issue here. I will simply make this point: the opposite of the dodo bird verdict, the contention that differential treatment effects have been demonstrated, has equally been criticized. Wampold (1997) has pointed out that the number of such findings do not exceed what one would expect by chance. Additionally, findings of experimenter allegiance effects further cast doubt on any differential treatment finding. Therefore, while a positive affirmation of the Dodo bird (all therapies work about equally well for most disorders) may be criticizable, the safest, most conservative scientific conclusion concerning the idea of differential treatment effects is a weak version of the Dodo bird that there is still no compelling evidence of differential effects either. Therefore, those of us who choose to pursue an alternative view of psychotherapy from the medical-model-based differential treatment model, and to rest our view on things like 'ill-defined common factors' are on as solid grounds as are EST proponents.

THE EST PARADIGM FROM THE PERSPECTIVE OF A NONBELIEVER

I now sketch out what I take to be the underlying logic of the EST paradigm, realizing that this is from within my perceptual universe and that EST advocates may feel I have misunderstood them. The EST paradigm is both a particular model concerning the nature of psychotherapy, and a more general metaphysical model, which includes within it implicit assumptions about science and knowledge. These levels are intertwined.

The practice model

From a practice point of view, psychotherapy is viewed through an analogy to the medical model (Bohart and Tallman, 1999; Orlinsky, 1989; Stiles and Shapiro, 1989). By this I do not mean simply that it relies on DSM diagnoses, nor that it necessarily has to focus on pathology. What I mean is that the focus is on *treatment*, and treatment packages, which are viewed as analogous to drugs (Stiles and Shapiro, 1989). The treatment is *applied to* the problem or disorder. It is the treatment which carries the load in causing change. As in medicine, the more specifically tailored the treatment is to the disorder, the more likely it will be to be effective. Because there is an a priori belief in the principle that differential treatment must be more effective than 'nonspecific' treatment, research becomes a matter of discovering and demonstrating differential treatment effects. Therapy is therefore fundamentally a technological enterprise. As noted by Johnson and Sandage (1999), therapists are viewed as ' . . .' behavioral engineers" rather than storytellers or moral guides' (p. 4).

Because therapy is viewed as the application of treatment, treatments must be described as specifically as possible in conducting research. They should be standardized in their application. Ergo manualization. While I have yet to encounter a clear definition of a manual, various writings of ESTers imply that specificity is the ideal. The manual is to be more than a general statement of therapeutic principles which could be operationalized by different practitioners in different ways (if this were so it would be impossible to research 'the treatment'). EST advocates acknowledge and accept that not all current therapy manuals have the specificity of cognitive-behavioral manuals (Task Force, 1995). However the 'operational logic' underlying the rationale for utilizing manuals in research would seem to imply a drive for greater and greater specificity as further research is conducted.

Further, regardless of the fact that some manuals are not highly specific (primarily psychodynamic and humanistic ones), the *metaphor* of manual-driven therapy implies certain things. It implies an approach where the practitioner follows rules and where the rules are reasonably specific. This is the meaning that the metaphor of 'the manual' brings to mind to most people (at least based on my informal survey). A manual, in contrast to a book which may describe a set of philosophical principles, is a set or relatively specific rules and prescriptions for doing something, a 'how to' book or a rule book of operating procedures. One need only think of marriage manuals or the American Psychological Association Publication Manual to get a feel for what the metaphor of 'manual' typically suggests to most people. It is this guiding metaphor of therapy as manual-driven that many of us feel is in contradiction to our intuitions about the nature of therapy and how therapy should be conducted (and accordingly researched).

The underlying metaphysical model and its relation to research

The EST research paradigm is based on traditional natural science experimental logic. First one tries to specify an independent variable, control all other variables, and use standardized measures of the dependent variable, so that one can demonstrate a linear causal relationship between the independent variable and the dependent variable. Underlying all this is an implicit linear causal, mechanistic view of how psychotherapy operates. Stiles, Honos-Webb and Surko (1998) have distinguished between a *ballistic* view of therapy and a *responsive* view. In the ballistic view, a treatment is applied to a disorder, and everything then follows in a chain-reaction way. In contrast, in a responsive view, therapy is an ongoing interaction, where things emerge and change in response to what has gone before. Key to true responsiveness is that the treatment is invented in part as therapist and client go along in response to emerging contingencies. Stiles et al. note that the ballistic view is how we often write about therapy, even when we actually practice in a responsive way. In my view, the ballistic perspective represents the underlying logic of the EST approach, even though its advocates argue for responsiveness and flexibility in practice.

Using the experiment as a model, and based on the analogy to medicine, the randomized controlled clinical trial (RCT) is seen as the 'method of choice'. Because the RCT is the 'gold standard' in medicine, it a priori is also assumed to be the gold standard in psychotherapy research (e.g., Persons in Persons and Silberschatz, 1998), even though it may not be a particularly valid or useful tool for the study of complex ecological systems (e.g., DeGreene, 1991). In medicine, one wants to control as tightly as possible the independent variable (i.e. the purity of the drug being administered). Therefore in psychotherapy one wants to manualize. In medicine, one wants to identify the active ingredients in the medication. Therefore in psychotherapy research one wants to do dismantling studies to identify operative ingredients. Finally, underlying this model is the assumption that the best way to practice is to discover general laws and then to treat individual cases as specific instances of these general laws or categories (Schon, 1983).

Following traditional experimental logic, the treatment is the independent variable, which is being applied to the 'dependent variable,' the client (or the client's disorder). Following 1930s operationism, the goal is to 'operationalize' the treatment clearly and specifically. As in any experiment, the more precisely the independent variable can be operationalized, the better for plotting linear causal relationships between it and the dependent variable. ESTers often speak with disdain of 'ill-defined common factors', such as the relationship, because they have not been specified as a series of specific therapist behaviors or strategies. In this they appear to be, once again, following a kind of 1930s logical positivism in dismissing as meaningless concepts that cannot be easily and simply operationalized.

It is because of the underlying operational logic that I believe it is fair to say that the EST enterprise implies a goal of more and more specific manuals. It is recognized that manuals, at the present time (especially those written by humanists and psychodynamicists), cannot be as standardized as a drug trial. However, that is merely seen as a matter of time. Further research, using dismantling studies and so on, will specify more and more precisely the relationship between various components of treatment and outcome. Further research will more specifically identify just which patients are benefitted by which specific forms of treatment as well. Findings that the relationship plays a role will lead to a technologizing of the relationship. It too will be studied so that it can be 'manipulated' as a form of treatment.

Ultimately, the satirically absurd endpoint of this paradigmatic project would be, somewhere in the dim future, nearly perfect predictability: an immensely complex manual, where each step in the therapy process could be schematized in the form of a series of decision rules of the form: 'If the client says, does, this . . . consult decision rule X1.' Perhaps the practitioner would have a microchip in his or her brain. A little recording device would track the ongoing interaction, feed it into this data bank of complex decision rules, and feed back to the practitioner just what to say at each point to maximize 'treatment effects'. This would include whether to ask a question, what question to ask, whether to interpret, reflect, or utilize a technique. In a sense the practitioner would not be there at all. Eventually a mechanistic equivalent of Stiles' et al. (1998) responsiveness could thus be achieved. Of course this is absurd, but this would appear to be the ultimate logical culmination of this vision of therapy and research.

The EST people, at least through my eyes, live in a modernist, mechanistic, linearly determined world, where perfect predictability is at least in principle attainable. Underlying this model appears to be a traditional Newtonian world view of the universe as a giant clock. It can be taken apart and how each part contributes to the operation of the whole can be figured out. Using a simple additive model of main effects and interactions, ultimately the whole clock can theoretically be known, and its workings completely predicted and controlled. Further, because it is a completely deterministic universe, with cause conceived of ballistically, the goal of research is to establish the independent variable's *control* over the dependent variable. The client is truly a 'dependent variable' (a live dependent variable, to be sure) on which the independent variable is operating to 'cause' its effects.

AN ALTERNATIVE PARADIGM

I present an alternative paradigm derived from two approaches: client-centered therapy (Bozarth, 1998), and 'constructive' therapies (e.g., strategic/solution-focused therapy and its descendants — Berg and Miller, 1992; Duncan, Hubble, and Miller, 1997; Miller, Duncan, and Hubble, 1997; Hoyt, 1994; Rosenbaum, 1994). As with the EST paradigm, there is both a practice level and an underlying philosophical or metaphysical level.

The nature of therapy: practice level

Client-centered therapy and strategic therapy differ somewhat in how they proceed, but they share similar assumptions. Both adopt a holistic attitude: the therapist is working with a whole person to help that person remove obstacles to living a better life. This is in contrast to a model in which a treatment is being applied to dysfunctional parts of the person (egos, schemas, conditioned responses, etc.). Second, the therapist relies on clients' own capacities for self-healing, and works within the client's frame of reference. The client's generativity is an integral part of the process, and solutions emerge out of therapist and client interaction, rather than being dictated a priori by a cookbook list of treatments matched up to problems, conditions, or diagnoses. Third, the practitioner is guided by a set of principles. These can be embodied or actualized by different practitioners in interaction with different clients in different ways. The resultant therapy will therefore look different from one therapist–client pair to another,[2] while still being principle-guided. In this respect the therapist is similar to an architect, who must use principles of science and construction to design buildings, but can design many different viable buildings given different contingencies of space, soil, terrain, and the wishes of the consumer. Further, different architects might design quite different viable 'solutions' to the same problems of space, terrain, and need.

Despite the fact that some practitioners who share this paradigm use the words 'treatment' (e.g., Duncan et al., 1997), therapy is not really seen as a treatment in the medical-like sense of that word. In contrast to the idea that the therapist is 'treating' a disorder, therapy is a dialogue between two (or more) intelligent living beings. As Johnson and Sandage note, referencing Martin (1994), '[Therapy] is a practice composed of sustained conversations with the aim of assisting another to resolve or cope better with circumstances' (p. 2).

Therefore, the guiding metaphor for this approach is conversation and dialogue. Therapy is no more a medical-like treatment than this article is a 'treatment for EST-Belief Disorder'

---

[2] In this regard client-centered therapy is not to be equated with the reflective method, which Rogers himself was critical of late in his life. As early as the 1960s different therapists began to embody client-centered principles in different ways in practice (Hart, 1970).

(rather this article is part of a conversation or dialogue). To try to manualize a dialogue is contrary to what most of our intuitions tell us a genuine dialogue is. Therefore, the metaphor of manualization is antithetical to the guiding metaphor of this approach.

Additionally, since therapy relies crucially on clients' active creative intelligence to fashion solutions, interventions are tools used by therapist and client to fashion solutions (Bohart and Tallman, 1999). They are not 'independent variables' which operate on 'dependent variables' (clients) to produce 'effects'. Solutions are not applied to clients like salves. From a systemic perspective two clients with 'the same' problem (for instance: depression) may differ considerably in how the problem was generated, how it is maintained, and how it interacts with their life spaces (Kleinman, 1988). Solutions accordingly vary and it would not be in-paradigm to apply a standardized solution to them. Rather, solutions emerge out of an intelligent interactive dialogue and are in that sense emergent and idiosyncratic.

With client-centered therapy in particular, it is the 'being' of the therapist and client in relationship which is therapeutic, not specific 'therapist operations'. There may be a potentially infinite set of different ways different therapists could embody and actualize warmth, empathy, and genuineness with different clients. Therapy 'works' through the interactive presence of the therapist[2], rather than through specific technological operations. According to Lewis, Amini and Lannon (2000), who share this view, 'The dispensable trappings of dogma may determine what a therapist *thinks* he is doing, what he talks about when he talks about therapy, but the agent of change is who he *is*' (p. 187). It is difficult to imagine how one could manualize 'being yourself' in therapy. Yet there is now some empirical support for this view of therapy (Lewis et al., 2000).

Finally both approaches place responsiveness first. They rely on moment-to-moment sensitivity to the emerging process, and on their ability to respond appropriately in that moment.

Consider as an example of the strategic/solution-focused approach the following case of Hoyt's (1995). He worked with a 67-year-old man who met Hoyt in a wheelchair. The man had been referred by his internist because he had had a stroke and now was afraid of falling when he walked, although he could walk. In chatting with the man Hoyt ascertained that he was a practical man. Additionally, it turned out that he was a baseball fan. He mentioned that he wanted to go to an upcoming baseball game with his sons, but he had to get over his great fear of falling. These discoveries were used in Hoyt's interventions. Hoyt's main intervention was to suggest that Hoyt be the client. The client was then to instruct Hoyt on how to get up if he fell on the floor. With that Hoyt threw himself on the floor. The client instructed him on how to get up. This was repeated several times. Then the man was given a choice of trying it himself either there in the office, or later at home. The man chose 'at home'. Hoyt then asked the man to show him how he was able to walk as he left the office, and as they were walking out, Hoyt painted a vivid word picture of the man and his sons going to the ball game, and emphasized what a good remembrance it would be for his sons to have later on. Hoyt mentioned how such memories with his own father had left an impact

---

[3.] EST proponents would probably see this as 'ill-defined' as indeed would most advocates of drug metaphor therapy. They would like 'interactive presence' to be specified and broken down. But again I point out that that amounts to imposition of one paradigm on another. These words make perfect sense to someone who lives in the universe of a nonmechanistic paradigm of therapy and views the interaction between persons holistically and systemically. Such complex interactions which are not easily broken down into simple input-output terms. The challenge to those of us who believe in this paradigm is to find ways of meaningfully studying these more complex concepts.

on him. Hoyt also hinted that by overcoming his fear of walking the man would also be able to get his wife, who was being overly watchful, off his back. In two weeks the man returned, proudly walking into the office on his own. Subsequently he did go to the game with his sons, and began to get involved in other activities.

In this case Hoyt used a number of standard strategic/solution-focused principles and interventions. First, as a general operating principle, Hoyt drew on the client's potential for self-healing and strength. Then he adopted a future orientation and focused on developing a solution rather than on analyzing the nature of the problem (see Nadler, Hibino and Farrell, 1995). Next he relied on the client's own intelligent capacities by reversing roles and having the client coach him. Giving the client the 'choice' of practicing in the therapist's office or at home is a strategic intervention called the 'illusion of alternatives', and was originally pioneered by Milton Erickson. Getting the client to walk from the office into the hallway was done in a way that made it a subtle, hypnotic induction.

However, while certain general principles were employed and some relatively standard strategic-solution-focused interventions were used, the most important point is that the interventions and techniques chosen were based on the stuff of life of this individual client, intersecting with this therapist, and emerged out of the dialogue with this client. The example is a good one of the therapist utilizing resources in the moment. The client's problem was not treated merely as an instance of a more generalized category of disorder (e.g., some kind of anxiety disorder). Nor was any standardized 'treatment' for this kind of disorder applied to him. Completely different interventions might have been used with a different client with 'the same' fear, depending on the client and the client's life. Further, a different strategic therapist, working with the same client, might have productively utilized entirely different interventions, while still being faithful to general strategic principles and still being effective.

It has been argued by EST proponents (e.g., Lampropoulos, 2000) that solution-focused therapy can be manualized. Yet it is difficult to see how the approach I have presented above could be manualized in any way that fits what most people take to be the meaning of the word. If we consider any clear, coherent statement of principles and therapeutic strategies a manual, then it is probably true that solution-focused therapy can be manualized in that sense. But it is also true that then it already has been in the numerous books written on it. Similarly, we would have to consider any of Carl Rogers' books in which he describes client-centered practice as 'manuals'. It seems unlikely, though, that an EST proponent would consider *On becoming a person* or *Client-centered therapy* as manuals because they are not written in the specific 'operational' kind of 'if-then' 'do-this, do-that to have this or that kind of effect' type of language that the concept of manual implies.

If one does not consider a statement of principles and strategies a manual, but wants something more specific, it is difficult to imagine how the approach described above can be manualized in any meaningful sense.

The EST approach when applied to something like solution-focused therapy almost seems like trying to map higher level moral reasoning (stages 5 and 6 on Kohlberg's scale, principled moral reasoning) into a stage four rule-based approach. Further, I would argue that the concept of manualization is incompatible with the experimental, interactive, responsive flavor of this approach. In other words, there is 'metaphor clash'. To say that these approaches can be manualized is to ignore the fact that this and other approaches do not accept the premises of the EST paradigm. Spokespersons for solution-focused disagree that it can or even should be manualized (e.g., Rosenbaum, 1994). To quote Rosenbaum (1994), 'Therapy requires a constant, ongoing process where the therapist adjusts to the client, and the client adjusts to this adjustment. This makes the manualizing of therapy precisely the wrong strategy for psychotherapy research' (p. 248).

It is true that, in a sense, client-centered therapy has been manualized (Greenberg and Watson, 1998). I have personally seen these manuals. They are very well done, but what they create is an excellent *analogue* of client-centered therapy mapped into a different intellectual universe. They do not fully represent client-centered therapy as I understand it. Again, the very concept of following a manual is antithetical to the basic nature of client-centered therapy. To manualize an approach like client-centered therapy reminds me a little bit of Cinderella's sister who tries to fit into the glass slipper by cutting off part of her foot. One can do it, and one can even make it fit, but would it not be better to find a scientific glass slipper that truly fits the phenomenon being studied instead of mangling it to fit it into one that doesn't?

Following is an example of a helping situation of empathic witnessing compatible with client-centered therapy. It is instructive to consider this in the context of manualization.

During the early 1970s, in my second and third years at medical school, I encountered several patients whose powerful experiences . . . fixed my interest on the intimate and manifold ways by which illness comes to affect our lives.

The first patient was a pathetic seven-year-old girl who had been badly burned over most of her body. She had to undergo a daily ordeal of a whirlpool bath during which the burnt flesh was tweezered away from her raw, open wounds. This experience was horribly painful to her. She screamed and moaned . . . My job as a neophyte clinical student was to hold her uninjured hand, as much to reassure her and calm her as to enable the surgical resident to quickly pull away the dead, infected tissue in the pool of swirling water, which rapidly turned pinkish, then bloody red . . . I tried to distract this little patient from her traumatic daily confrontation with terrible pain. I tried talking to her about her home, her family, her school . . . Then one day, I made contact. At wit's end . . . uncertain what to do besides clutching the small hand, and in despair over her unrelenting anguish, I found myself asking her to tell me how she tolerated it, what the feeling was like of being so badly burned and having to experience the awful surgical ritual, day after day after day. She stopped, quite surprised, and looked at me . . . then, in terms direct and simple, she told me. While she spoke, she grasped my hand harder and neither screamed nor fought off the surgeon or the nurse. Each day from then on, her trust established, she tried to give me a feeling of what she was experiencing. By the time my training took me off this rehabilitation unit, the little burned patient seemed noticeably better able to tolerate her debridement . . . She taught me a grand lesson . . . about the actual experience of illness, and that witnessing and helping to order that experience can be of therapeutic value. (Kleinman, 1988, pp. xi–xii)

This account is wholly in keeping with client-centered therapy in its emphasis on a *human* act of contact and witnessing. Let us consider trying to study this from an EST frame of reference, again taking the principles underlying the EST philosophy to their logical extreme. What Kleinman did would be considered an intervention, and we would want to manualize, operationalize, and standardize it so that it could be 'provided' over and over as an intervention for this 'disorder'. Ideally we would have to do an RCT. We would have to locate 60 such little girls, randomly assign them to a treatment and control group. Then we would have to manualize what Kleinman did — his reaching out and holding her hand, asking about her experience, and then respectfully listening. (Perhaps we would even manualize what she did — encouraging her to hold the therapist's hand at just the right level of tightness, and tell her that the intervention is for her to tell us how she is experiencing the situation.) We would then train our therapists all to repeat these actions in a similar fashion with the 30 little burned girls in the treatment group. Once we had established that this 'intervention' worked, we would then want to do dismantling studies — just how long should the therapist hold her hand? How much pressure? Is hand-holding necessary? Perhaps we would do parametric variations on various combinations of hand-holding, gaze, tone of voice, and phrasing. We would want to do such parametric research in order to be able to 'provide' this intervention, dismantle it to find the 'effective ingredients', so as to better be able to 'cause' the effect we want.

This scenario of course was designed to be absurd. Yet it hopefully helps get at what I and others object to in the EST paradigm. First, to call what Kleinman did an intervention seems to bastardize it in ways that distort the human, experienced meaning of it on both sides: Kleinman's and the little girl's. In the moment when Kleinman did this, he wasn't deliberately doing it to 'intervene'. He was genuinely interested and curious. This was no more treatment than the audience's interest in listening to what I have to say is an intervention or treatment, or my interest in listening to my daughter's experience of college is an intervention. Second, to deliberately try to manualize it and 'provide' it *as* intervention equally seems to distort its true meaning. It seems particularly absurd to think of 30 therapists all trying to 'provide' the same 'intervention' in a standardized fashion, when what was so clearly healing about it was its natural spontaneity and human quality.

Yet there is an important lesson in this example: genuine interest and listening to another person's experiencing — witnessing, as Kleinman calls it — can be very healing. We certainly can encourage therapists, through example and experiential training, to witness, in their own ways, individualized to respond to the uniqueness of each client, without considering them 'interventions' in the mechanistic sense of ESTs. We must come up with meaningful ways to study client-centered therapy in its 'natural setting', rather than to distort its nature by manualization to fit into a paradigm whose nature is really alien to it.

Metaphysical level

At the metaphysical or philosophical level there are two components of this alternative paradigm.

The nature of professional practice and the uniqueness assumption
First, psychotherapy is conceived of as a *practice* (see also Johnson and Sandage, 1999). There are many different practices: law, medicine, psychotherapy, architecture, farming, and art. The kinds of knowledge and the way knowledge is utilized in a practice are different from the goals of acquiring scientific knowledge (Schon, 1983). The goal of scientific knowledge is to formulate general laws, while the goal of practice is to focus on the unique, particular individual case. Scientific knowledge is used in this enterprise, but forms only a part of what is done.

The model of practice of client-centered and solution-focused therapy given above is therefore highly compatible with what a number of writers have described as the real nature of professional practice in all professions (Bourdieu, 1990; Schon, 1983; Sundararajan, 2000). Practice of any profession is fundamentally different from the model of practice implied by the EST approach (Bourdieu, 1990; Schon, 1983; Sundararajan, in press). The manualization idea is an instance of what Schon calls technical rationality, and is an example of the traditional model of how science is to be applied to practice. However, based on Schon's studies of practitioners in a variety of professions, it does not represent how expert professionals actually practice, even professionals who utilize scientific knowledge, such as architects and engineers. The manualization model (and EST in general) is also an example of what Nadler et al. (1995) in their studies of how professionals creatively solve problems in business call the 'traditional' problem-solving model, and does not represent how creative business professionals develop effective solutions to problems either.

According to Schon, Nadler et al., and others, effective professionals treat each new problem or case as unique. In contrast, the manualization idea starts out with the assumption of similarity (this case is an instance of a general category) and only moves to uniqueness when the manual fails.[4] In real life it is frequently not the case that one case is sufficiently like another to lead to the mechanistic generalization of a rule from one case to another. Manualized generalizing may work sometimes, but in all cases it is the judgment of the practitioner which transcends and supersedes the application of such rules. Consider, for instance, a trial judge being asked to support an objection by the defense lawyer. The judge must *judge* to what degree this particular instance conforms to the general principle. New law is made precisely because lawyers challenge old interpretations and argue for new interpretations of old principles.

Uniqueness exists in the real world because each individual case is a complex combination of many different variables. Phenomena in the real world are characterized by '. . . complexity, uncertainty, [and] instability' (Schon, 1983, p. 39). To quote Robert Sternberg, 'Real problems are often poorly structured and hard to define . . .' (Sternberg, 1987, as quoted in Nadler et al., 1995, p. 273). In medicine, for instance,

> . . . family practitioners and internists all know that patient care is seldom a simple matter of prescribing precise treatments for distinct disease states. Patients present as polysymptomatic; complaints are often vague and emotional; and neat, clearly identifiable syndromes and diseases often fail to emerge from the review of systems. For example, Sobel (1995) summarized data that showed that when patients present with 1 of the 14 most common symptoms reported in outpatient clinics . . . in less than 16% of the cases is a probable cause established. In these situations the physician uses intuition, follows a hunch. (Scovern, 1999, p. 287)

Schon notes, 'An ophthalmologist says that a great many of his patients bring problems that are not in the book. In 80 or 85 percent of the cases, the patient's complaints and symptoms do not fall into familiar categories of diagnosis and treatment . . .' (p. 64). In business Nadler et al. (1995) report the example of two hospitals of similar size, in similar areas, where each had to generate its own unique solution to a similar problem, because the complex ecological dependencies were different in each case.

The uniqueness assumption means that the practitioner focuses on the particulars of each individual case rather than on how this case fits into a general category (Schon, 1983). General principles and prior knowledge are used to help understand the unique case, but do not override the necessity of dealing with the uniqueness. Schon notes that the practitioners

---

[4.] I consider 'manualized flexibility' to be an oxymoron. The point I am making here is that one can never manualize flexibility sufficiently to deal with the complexity of individual cases.

he studied sought '. . . to discover the particular features of his problematic situation, and from their gradual discovery, [design] an intervention' (p. 129). He also notes that '[The practitioner] is not dependent on the categories of established theory and technique, but constructs a new theory of the unique case . . .' (p. 68).

Actual solution-finding in real-life situations therefore involves a blend of nomothetic knowledge, use of prior exemplars, and considerable tacit knowledge gained through experience, all applied to understanding this unique case. Additionally, practice involves an ongoing experimental self-correcting *dialogue* with the situation. Through this dialogue solutions are frequently forged which at the least are creative modifications of old solutions, and at the best are often entirely new solutions that are discovered through that dialogue (emergence).

Schon notes: 'There are more variables — kinds of possible moves, norms, and interrelationships of these — than can be represented in a finite model. Because of this complexity, the designer's moves tend, happily or unhappily, to produce consequences other than those intended. When this happens, the designer may take account of the unintended changes he has made . . . by forming new appreciations and understandings and by making new moves. He shapes the situation . . . the situation 'talks back,' and he responds . . .' (p 79). Schon's description of an architect solving a design problem is illustrative. Initially the architect imposes one trial solution on the problem. Then through thought experiments the situation 'talks back' to the architect, who then revises the solution and in the process, makes a new discovery (emergence) which leads to a reframing of the whole design.

This description of practice is compatible with the description of practice I have given above of both client-centered and strategic/solution-focused therapy. In my alternate paradigm of practice the expert therapist treats each case as unique. This does not mean he or she does not use nomothetic knowledge, nor that he or she treats the case as entirely unique. Instead what it means is that each case is its own unique blend of what is similar to other cases and what is different. The solution developed must be developed by a process of ongoing experimentation and *judgment* by the professional (and client) wherein prior knowledge and ideas are tested, modified, and so on, until new solutions are developed. Standardized nomothetic knowledge is one component of what might be used to develop a solution with the individual client. EST- and RCT-based information would be one source of information factored in to the professional's and client's decision-making process, but there would be no automatic assumption that just because a particular treatment has been manualized and found through an RCT to work for that disorder, that this is what the professional and client would necessarily use in this particular instance. In this regard, Goldfried and Wolfe (1996) have said about the relationship of therapy research to practice: 'Although we strongly believe that clinical practice should be informed by outcome research, it is quite another thing for it to be dictated by such findings. Group designs, in which patients are randomly assigned to treatment conditions, simply do not generalize to how we practice clinically' (Goldfried and Wolfe, 1996, p. 1015).

Given that the description of practice I have presented is compatible with how Schon (1983) and others have found that practitioners *in general* function, it would seem that this is an entirely reasonable way to conceptualize a way of practice, even if it is antithetical to manualization. Accordingly, if we wish to really learn how to be effective practitioners, it will be counterproductive to force both research and practice into a mold which does not even represent real, effective practice. To quote DeGreene, 'much laboratory-style research may be irrelevant, misleading or downright wrong. The concept of clearly definable and correlatable independent, intervening and dependent variables may be completely inappropriate in a dynamic, mutually causal world' (DeGreene, 1991, as quoted in Nadler, p. 89).

Tacit knowledge and role of the practitioner

Another key principle of practice from this paradigmatic perspective and how it differs from how ESTers think therapy should proceed has to do with the nature of expertise, particularly with the issue of tacit knowledge. Experts do not practice by following manuals. Dreyfus and Dreyfus (1982) argue that it is only novices who follow rules. Experts learn how to use their intuition to transcend rules. Searle (1983) has written about skiing that 'As the skier gets better he does not internalize the rules better, but rather the rules become progressively irrelevant' (p. 15). This is because through practice practitioners gradually acquire a much more subtle and differentiated tacit knowledge of the terrain of practice than can ever be expressed in explicit rules. For instance, Christine Padesky (Beck and Padesky, 1990) tells of her first seeing a film of Aaron Beck doing cognitive therapy and being disappointed because he did not follow the manual she had been studying (e.g., Beck, Rush, Shaw and Emery, 1979). She observed that initially she thought he wasn't a very good cognitive therapist. It was only with experience that she came to realize how good he really was. Similarly, I have heard from EMDR trainers how Francine Shapiro creatively violates her own protocols on occasion.

Therefore once again the manualization idea misrepresents the nature of practice. Not only should expert practitioners not practice by following manuals, but they don't. In fact, it is unlikely that practice in any EST research project is actually guided by manualization either. Rather it is guided by the considerable tacit learning that has occurred through training, and then through ongoing supervision by experienced practitioners. It is precisely the claim, despite manualization, that the newly trained cognitive therapists in the NIMH study (Elkin, 1994) were not adequately supervised, which has been used by Beck and his colleagues (e.g., Hollon and Beck, 1994) to explain why cognitive therapy fared relatively poorly in that study. I personally have observed Leslie Greenberg train therapists for his manualized study of process-experiential therapy versus client-centered therapy (Greenberg and Watson, 1998), and it was clear that Greenberg was using considerable tacit, fine-grained understanding in training his therapists in subtleties that went well beyond the descriptions in the training manual.

Manuals, therefore, represent the illusion of the specificity sought after by researchers, but are actually 'pretend science'. Further, it is illusory to believe that the immense degree of tacit knowledge conveyed by experts in their tutoring process will ever be specified well enough in manuals to make practice as 'scientific' as those who advocate ESTS seem to be pursuing (Schon 1983). Despite manualization, it will be expected that experts will practice differently, as they do in all other professions. The same melody played by two different guitarists or two different conductors is always different. The player matters a lot. Therefore there is no standardized 'treatment' which is being applied even in the case of manualized therapies. In our paradigm, a starting assumption is that each practitioner — client pair will generate its own unique solutions. Different practitioners will embody practice principles in different ways (Sundararajan, in press). In all cases of practice, the role of the practitioner is crucial.

Role of science

Realizing that therapy is the *practice* of a profession leads us to view the role of science in it in a different way. As a practice it shares things in common with other practices, such as those of architect, physician, lawyer, and artisan. In a practice view of what therapists are doing, science is an aid to the practice, an important component, but the practice itself is not, nor can it ever be, mechanistically scientific (e.g., the quotation from Goldfried and Wolfe, 1996, previously given). Consider as examples how artists and artisans use science. A potter uses scientific knowledge of materials, firing, and so on. In a similar manner, my high-school friend, the artist James Turrell (Anonymous, 2000) intensively studied the optics of light and the psychology of perception, in order to create the light installations for which he has become famous. Gardeners too must use science. I have already mentioned the example of architects. However science is used inventively by such practitioners to solve real-life problems. It is not manualistically applied.

Therefore scientific investigation serves a somewhat different purpose in this account than in the drug metaphor paradigm. Imagine a world where my alternative paradigm were accepted—no one might even think of doing ESTs. They would ask very different research questions. They might want to know about the principles of change involved in helping, and how expert practitioners blend tacit and explicit knowledge to make productive decisions for individual clients. They might be interested in questions concerning sensitivity to individual cases. And they might be interested in how practitioners learn from and adjust to ongoing feedback in sessions. This knowledge would not then be manualized, because it would be understood that practice knowledge is different from (but includes) scientific knowledge (Schon, 1983; Sundararajan, 2000). Rather, this research might then be used to improve training programs. This kind of research would be done instead of writing theory-based treatment manuals and then engaging in RCTs to test these theory-based treatment manuals for standardized disorders.

Research instead, following Goldfried and Wolfe (1996), would investigate principles and processes of change. For instance, what would be useful to practitioners might be to study the tacit knowing processes used by successful practitioners and see if they can be explicitly increased. Beginning attempts have already been done in this regard in therapy. We can say, for instance, with some degree of scientific backing, that therapists who (a) are adept at facilitating the formation of a good therapeutic alliance; (b) are adept at dialoging with the client, empathically listening, and taking the client's frame of reference into account (Duncan et al., 1997); (c) who are adept at supporting client involvement (Bohart and Tallman, 1999) and mobilizing their hope and optimism (Duncan et al., 1997; Greenberg, 1999; Snyder, Michael and Cheavens, 1999); (d) adept at fostering the developing of insight, development of new perspectives, and clarification of the problem (Grawe, 1997); (e) who allow or foster problem actuation in the learning environment of therapy (Grawe, 1997); and (f) who provide the opportunity for mastery experiences (Grawe, 1997) will be more likely to be successful. In this sense, practitioners who do these things could be said to be practicing therapy in an empirically supported fashion, although they do not necessarily practice empirically supported treatments. If it turns out that these are the qualities that are more important than standardized treatment packages for specific disorders, then the whole EST approach has been an unfortunate distraction and detour.

Nature of the phenomena

At a deeper level, the alternative paradigm is more compatible with postmodern, nondeterministic views of the universe than with nineteenth century Newtonian mechanics. There is a degree of indeterminacy in principle in the universe, and things will never be known with 100% predictability, not because we simply can't learn everything (a practical problem), but because of the nature of knowing itself. Complete predictability is not even in principle possible.

Our model adopts a systems view compatible with Stiles et al.'s (1998) responsiveness. Therapy is two complex systems interacting, and this interaction is itself a complex, dynamic ongoing system. These two complex systems influence one another in a multitude of ways: verbally, nonverbally, emotionally, cognitively, perceptually, behaviorally. The multiple paths of influence cross and recross in dynamic, circular causal ways. A 'meeting of persons' is a complex holistic phenomenon which cannot be dismantled into component, linear causal parts. There are too many ways two individuals can 'meet', and 'meeting' even within the system of the same two individuals can vary from moment to moment and time to time as these two systems themselves change, mutually influence one another, evolve, and change some more (sometimes within minutes). Consider as an example the many different ways a parent and child may 'meet' and feel in tune with one another and share when the child has painful experiences at school: one day meeting may be talking about the painful experience, another day it may mutually feel congruent to sit together in silence, still another day it may feel sharing to get away from it all and go out together to a movie, yet another day doing homework together, and so on. Further, all these examples may be examples of not meeting as well depending on the kind and quality of connection established, which may depend on how each party has 'eased into' the connection in that given instance. What works to establish a connection one time may produce the exact opposite at another time, and so forth. Talking about 'meeting' may seem too 'ill-defined' to EST advocates, but that is because it is a complex, interlocking, shifting phenomenon, not reducible to easily specified behaviors or their combinations. That doesn't mean it doesn't exist.

Because of the mutual, ongoing reciprocal influence of the dynamic system which is a therapy interaction, there is no operationalizable independent variable in therapy research. Manualization may present the illusion that there is, but from this point of view that is just that: an illusion. When complex systems interact it is philosophically impossible to chart simple linear causal relationships between input from one system to another system. Interventions do not map in a one-to-one fashion into client effects, but rather set up perturbations in complex ecological systems where, at best, all we will ever be able to expect are partial correlations between inputs and ultimate outputs. Predictability is possible, but is inherently imperfect and probabilistic. You will philosophically never get perfect predictability. Further, because of the systemic nature of the interaction, along with the phenomenon of emergence, the very meaning of any intervention shifts and changes as an ongoing function of its place in that evolving complex system. Therefore the drug metaphor model is not a good one from this point of view.

Because we realize we can never have perfect predictability, and that there is no necessary standard solution for a given problem, we need to try things out, experiment, and self-correct. This leads us to operating *intelligently*. Because of this, in practice and in research, it is important to *consult* with the system being worked with. One works *with* the system, not *on* the system. Therefore, the systems involved must be viewed as self-correcting systems —

both therapist and client. The process is inherently discovery-oriented, including creative generation of new solutions through processes of dialoging with the problem, and then correcting in an ongoing way. Ultimately each solution will be unique to that system's interaction, sometimes in very large ways, sometimes in relatively subtle ways. This implies also that there is no one solution to the problem. Many different solutions may 'fit' the problem. As De Shazer (1985) says, the solution must fit: it need not match.

Therefore, this model is much more based on metaphors of responsiveness and resonance. Responsiveness and resonance are primary, not additions to a standardized format. The client is not a 'dependent variable' to be operated on by an 'independent variable'.

EMPIRICALLY SUPPORTED PSYCHOTHERAPY PRACTICE (ESPP)

From this paradigm, then, research-informed or scientifically-based practice is conceived of differently from in the EST paradigm. There are at least four approaches that ascribe to evidence-based practice, but can be taken to mean something different by it than do EST people. They, too, can claim to practice in an empirically-supported way, although we would not necessarily follow an 'empirically-supported-*treatment*' approach. Rather they could describe their approaches as 'empirically supported psychotherapy practice' or 'empirically corroborated therapy'.[5] For space limitations I will not describe them in detail, but simply note them. They are all based on the idea of using principles of practice that have been shown to relate to outcome. First, Norcross (2000), as president of Division 29 of the American Psychological Association, is forming a commission to describe 'empirically supported relationships', as a partial refutation of the EST approach. Norcross' project is based on findings that the relationship accounts for more of the variance in therapy than do techniques and procedures. Second, Walsh and McElwain (in press) delineate the research support for the following existential principles: freedom and responsibility, intersubjectivity, temporality, and becoming; existential, anxiety, guilt, and authenticity; relationship, understanding, liberation, and flexibility. Third, Duncan, Miller and Hubble (Duncan, Hubble and Miller, 1997; Hubble, Duncan and Miller, 1999; Miller, Duncan and Hubble, 1997) have developed what they call variously an evidence-based or outcome-informed practice based on research that supports the following principles: relationship, utilizing resources in the client's life space, utilizing the client's strengths, utilizing the client's frame of reference and theory of change, mobilizing hope and optimism, utilizing client's attributions of the causes of problems, and so on. Finally, Grawe (1997) argues for an evidence-based approach based on research support for three key principles of learning: clarification and/or cognitive insight; problem actuation; mastery experiences.

CONCLUDING COMMENTS

From my perspective the culprits in the EST paradigm ultimately appear to be twofold: the underlying mechanistic assumptions upon which the EST paradigm appears to be based,

---

[5.] I thank Robert Elliott and Michael Mahoney for these suggested alternatives.

which presume that greater and greater specificity will lead to better and better predictability and control, based on the research model wherein an independent variable is manipulated to 'control' the dependent variable; and the metaphorical comparison of psychotherapy to drugs (e.g., Stiles and Shapiro, 1989). In regards to the former, I have argued that the EST paradigm is based on a traditional Newtonian view of the universe, in which it is conceivable (if not actually possible) to know everything so that one can predict and 'control' everything. In this model science is only imperfect because one does not know everything yet. But in principle complete predictability is possible. In contrast, I have suggested that in a complex, systemic, nonlinear view of the universe, more compatible with postmodern thought, one will never even in principle be able to know with complete certainty how A affects B in any case where complex systems are involved. Therefore simple input-output models of research, while perhaps useful as 'rough cuts', are actually misleading in understanding the complex nature of the phenomena involved. When two complex nonlinear systems 'bump up' against one another, one can hope for research to show an increase in probability that an input A will lead to an effect B, but the idea that one can successively dismantle the phenomenon and move closer and closer to complete mechanistic predictability is unrealistic. In sum pro-EST advocates live in a modernist universe, and anti-EST advocates live in a postmodern one.

The second culprit appears to be the drug metaphor. In medicine, when a new drug comes along, RCTs are done to test its effects. However, when a physician encounters a patient with a problem, he or she does not mechanistically apply the drug and do nothing else. The drug, which has been validated in a drug trial, is used as a *part* of treatment. But the whole course of treatment itself is not manualized. In contrast, because the whole course of a treatment (e.g., a treatment for a disorder) is analogized to a drug in psychotherapy, in the psychotherapy domain those who want to use the drug metaphor *manualize the whole course of treatment*. However, based on how professionals really practice, a more appropriate analogy would be that if research showed that assertion training is a useful procedure for depression (e.g., Goldfried and Wolfe, 1996), the therapist would consider that research and likely incorporate assertion training into a course of therapy for a person who is depressed. But the whole treatment would not be manualized as if it were a drug.

The debate over ESTs is a good example of the sociology of science. A paradigm, designed primarily to answer socio-economic threats, threatens to override and dominate other paradigms of both doing psychotherapy and researching psychotherapy. Framed as a paradigmatic issue it is clear that the kinds of questions the EST criteria are designed to answer are not questions of meaning or relevance in at least some alternative paradigms. Therefore it becomes a form of scientific hegemony to suggest that all research should be done within the EST paradigm. It is equally hegemonous to argue that practice should be based on therapies that meet EST criteria, or to argue that it is unethical if one does not use an RCT-supported therapy where appropriate (e.g., Persons, in Persons and Silberschatz, 1998).

I can imagine ESTers raising objections to what I have said. First, they might object that the research findings cited by those suggesting alternative models of empirical support or corroboration have been collected through the use of RCTs. This is partially true; however, some studies have used more naturalistic methods. In any case there is nothing in principle to dictate that the data would have had to be collected that way, and advocates of the alternative paradigm are not opposed to RCTs; they just view them as only one of many methods to explore the effectiveness of therapy.

Second, ESTers might suggest a head-to-head test of a manualized empirically supported treatment versus therapy done from the alternative paradigm. But that will not do. The troubling question would be: which set of research criteria from which paradigm would be used to answer the question? It is likely that framing the question in a way that would satisfy advocates of the EST approach would not satisfy advocates of the other approach, and vice versa. In any case based on what we know about therapy research the most likely outcome would be the Dodo bird. Even if one approach did show itself superior to the other, advocates of whichever one 'lost' would argue that the test wasn't fair. A far better way to proceed is for researchers from different paradigms to pursue their varying ends, and somewhere down the road, the slow, steady accumulation of results will decide the issue. Let the games begin!

REFERENCES

Anonymous (2000, March/April). Back page: Light odyssey. *Utne Reader* (No. 98), 120.

Beck, A. T. and Padesky, C. (1990). *Cognitive therapy of personality disorders.* Presentation at the Second Evolution of Psychotherapy Conference, Anaheim, CA.

Beck, A. T., Rush, A. J., Shaw, B. F. and Emery, G. (1979). *Cognitive therapy of depression.* New York: Guilford Press.

Berg, I. K. and Miller, S. D. (1992). *Working with the Problem Drinker: A solution-focused approach.* New York: Norton.

Beutler, L. E. (1998). Identifying empirically supported treatments: What if we don't? *Journal of Consulting and Clinical Psychology, 66,* 113–20.

Bohart, A. (2000). Paradigm clash: Empirically supported treatments versus empirically supported psychotherapy practice. *Psychotherapy Research, 10,* 488–93.

Bohart, A. and Tallman, K. (1999). *How Clients Make Therapy Work: The process of active self-healing.* Washington, DC: American Psychological Association.

Bourdieu, P. (1990). *The Logic of Practice* (R. Nice, Trans.). Stanford, CA: Stanford University Press.

Bozarth, J. (1998). *Person-centered Therapy: A revolutionary paradigm.* Ross-on Wye: PCCS Books.

DeGreene, K. B. (1991). Rigidity and fragility of large sociotechnical systems: Advanced information technology, the dominant coalition, and paradigm shift at the end of the 20th century. *Behavioral Science, 36,* 64–79.

De Shazer, S. (1985). *Keys to Solution in Brief Therapy.* New York: Norton.

Dreyfus, H. and Dreyfus, S. (1982). *Mind over Machine.* New York: Free Press.

Duncan, B. L. and Miller, S. D. (2000). *The Heroic Client.* San Francisco: Jossey-Bass.

Duncan, B. L., Hubble, M. A. and Miller, S. D. (1997). *Psychotherapy with 'Impossible' Cases: The efficient treatment of therapy veterans.* New York: Norton.

Elkin, I. (1994). The NIMH Treatment of Depression Collaborative Research Program: Where we began and where we are. In A. E. Bergin and S. L. Garfield (Eds.) *Handbook of Psychotherapy and Behavior Change* (4th edn.). New York: Wiley, pp. 114–42.

Goldfried, M.R. and Wolfe, B. E. (1996). Psychotherapy practice and research: Repairing a strained alliance. *American Psychologist, 51,* 1007–16.

Grawe, K. (1997). Research-informed psychotherapy. *Psychotherapy Research, 7,* 1–20.

Greenberg, L. S. and Watson, J. (1998). Experiential therapy of depression: Differential effects of client-centered relationship conditions and process-experiential interventions. *Psychotherapy Research, 8,* 210–24.

Greenberg, R. P. (1999). Common psychosocial factors in psychiatric drug therapy. In M. A. Hubble,

B. L. Duncan, and S. D. Miller (Eds.) *The Heart and Soul of Change: What works in therapy.* Washington, DC: American Psychological Association, pp. 297–328.

Hart, J. T. (1970). The development of client-centered therapy. In J. T. Hart and T. M. Tomlinson (Eds.) *New Directions in Client-centered Therapy.* Boston: Houghton-Mifflin, pp. 3–22.

Hollon, S. D. and Beck, A.T. (1994). Cognitive and cognitive-behavioral therapies. In A. E. Bergin and S. L. Garfield (Eds.) *Handbook of Psychotherapy and Behavior Change* (4th edn.). New York: Wiley, pp. 428–66.

Hoyt, M. F. (Ed.). (1994). *Constructive Therapies.* New York: Guilford Press.

Hoyt, M. F. (1995). Brief psychotherapies. In A. S. Gurman and S. B. Messer (Eds.) *Essential Psychotherapies.* New York: Guilford Press, pp. 441–87.

Hubble, M. A., Duncan, B. L. and Miller, S. D. (Eds.), *The Heart and Soul of Change: What works in therapy.* Washington, DC: American Psychological Association.

Johnson, E. L. and Sandage, S. J. (1999). A postmodern reconstruction of psychotherapy: Orienteering, religion and the healing of the soul. *Psychotherapy: Theory, research, practice, training, 36,* 1–15.

Kleinman, A. (1988). *The Illness Narratives: Suffering, healing, and the human condition.* New York: Basic Books.

Kuhn, T. S. (1970). *The Structure of Scientific Revolutions* (2nd ed.). Chicago: University of Chicago Press.

Kuhn, T. S. (1977). *The essential tension: Selected studies in scientific tradition and change.* Chicago: University of Chicago Press.

Lampropoulos, G. K. (2000). A reexamination of the empirically supported treatments critiques. *Psychotherapy Research, 10,* 474–87.

Lewis, T., Amini, F. and Lannon, R. (2000). *A General Theory of Love.* New York: Random House.

Miller, S. D., Duncan, B. L. and Hubble, M. A. (1997). *Escape from Babel.* New York: Norton.

Nadler, G., Hibino, S. and Farrell, J. (1995). *Creative Solution Finding: The triumph of breakthrough thinking over conventional problem solving.* Rocklin, CA: Prima Publishing.

Nathan, P. E. (2000). The boulder model: A dream deferred — or lost? *American Psychologist, 55,* 250–1.

Norcross, J. C. (2000). President's column: Empirically supported therapeutic relationships: A Division 29 Task Force. *Psychotherapy Bulletin, 35*(2), 2–4.

Orlinsky, D. (1989). Researchers' images of psychotherapy: Their origins and influence on research. *Clinical Psychology Review, 9 ,* 413–42.

Persons, J. B. and Silberschatz, G. (1998). Are results of randomized controlled trials useful to psychotherapists? *Journal of Consulting and Clinical Psychology, 66,* 126–35.

Rosenbaum, R. (1994). Single-session therapies: Intrinsic integration? *Journal of Psychotherapy Integration, 4,* 229–52.

Schon, D. A. (1983). *The Reflective Practitioner: How professionals think in action.* New York: Basic Books.

Scovern, A. W. (1999). From placebo to alliance: The role of common factors in medicine. In M. A. Hubble, B. L. Duncan, and S. D. Miller (Eds.) *The Heart and Soul of Change: What works in therapy.* Washington, DC: American Psychological Association, pp. 259–96.

Searle, J. R. (1983). *Intentionality.* Cambridge: Cambridge University Press.

Snyder, C.R., Michael, S.T. and Cheavens, J. S. (1999). Hope as a psychotherapeutic foundation of common factors, placebos, and expectancies. In M. A. Hubble, B. L. Duncan, and S. D. Miller (Eds.) *The Heart and Soul of Change: What works in therapy.* Washington, DC: American Psychological Association, pp. 179–200.

Sobel, D.S. (1995). Rethinking medicine: Improving health outcomes with cost-effective psychosocial interventions. *Psychosomatic Medicine, 57,* 234–44.

Sternberg, R. J. (July 30, 1987). Think better. *Bottom Line/Personal.* As quoted in Nadler, G., Hibino, S. and Farrell, J. (1995). *Creative Solution Finding: The triumph of breakthrough thinking over conventional problem solving.* Rocklin, CA: Prima Publishing, p. 273.

Stiles, W. B. and Shapiro, D. A. (1989). Abuse of the drug metaphor in psychotherapy process-outcome research. *Clinical Psychology Review, 9,* 521–44.

Stiles, W. B., Honos-Webb, L. and Surko, M. (1998). Responsiveness in psychotherapy. *Clinical Psychology: Science and Practice, 5,* 439–458.

Sundararajan, L. (2002). Humanistic psychotherapy and the scientist-practitioner debate: An 'embodied' perspective. *Journal of Humanistic Psychology, 42*(2), 34–47.

Task Force on Promotion and Dissemination of Psychological Procedures, Division of Clinical Psychology of the American Psychological Association (1995). Training and dissemination of empirically-validated psychological treatments: Report and recommendations. *The Clinical Psychologist, 48,* 3–23.

Walsh, R. and McElwain, B. (2002). Existential psychotherapies. In D. J. Cain and J. Seeman (Eds.) *Humanistic Psychotherapies: Handbook of research and practice.* Washington, DC: American Psychological Association. pp. 253–78.

Wampold, B. E. (1997). Methodological problems in identifying efficacious psychotherapies. *Psychotherapy Research, 7,* 21–43.

Soti Grafanaki Ph.D
St Paul University, Ottawa, Canada

On Becoming Congruent: How congruence works in Person-Centred Counselling and practical applications for training and practice

Abstract. The primary objective of this presentation is to offer a better understanding of the experiential processes that occur during moments of congruence and incongruence, and the possible impact and meaning of such moments on the quality of therapy interaction. Client and counsellor accounts from six person-centred counselling cases (12 sessions each) were collected using Brief Structured Recall interviews. Participants were interviewed on their experience during helpful and hindering moments of therapy. The analysis revealed that participants experienced congruence in a variety of ways, suggesting that the construct does not describe a unitary phenomenon. Different types of congruence and incongruence emerged. Moments of incongruence seemed to capture important experiential and process shifts in therapy, including ruptures in the therapeutic alliance. The practical implications of the findings are discussed and future directions for training and practice are considered.

Despite the fact that congruence represents a central concept in the development of client-centred and experiential approaches to psychotherapy, relatively little attention has been given to its systematic study. Nevertheless, congruence represents an important construct in understanding therapy interaction and can capture important personal, interpersonal and relational aspects of that interaction. As a phenomenon congruence not only deals with what we feel, think and do, but also with how we see and relate to others and how others respond to us. Therefore, congruence has the potential to capture the quality of the therapeutic relationship and the degree that participants are real and present in this relationship.

A detailed review of the research literature on this construct (Grafanaki, 2001) is beyond the scope of this presentation; however it is important to mention that most of the research done on congruence has followed two different paths. First, a group of researchers has examined the validity of the Rogers' (1957) hypotheses concerning the 'necessary and sufficient conditions' (Rogers, 1957) for therapeutic change (e.g. Truax, Wittmer and Wargo, 1971; Smith-Hanen, 1977; Hermansson, Webster and McFarland, 1988; Gallagher and Hargie, 1992). Much of this research has looked at process-outcome linkages by inviting clients to complete the Barrett-Lennard Relationship Inventory (BLRI; Barrett-Lennard, 1964/1973) following sessions. Second, several researchers have looked at the portrayal of congruence through verbal and non verbal messages and have conducted experimental studies on the impact of mismatch between verbal and nonverbal messages on therapy interaction (Haase and Tepper, 1972; Graves and Robinson, 1976; Tepper and Haase, 1978; Fretz, Corn, Tuemmler and Bellet, 1979; Seay and Altekruse, 1979; Reade and Smouse, 1980; Hill, Gronsky, Sturniolo and Fretz, 1981; Tyson and Wall, 1983). Past research has mainly supported the idea that congruence represents an important element of successful psychotherapy; however it has not provided a clear understanding of how congruence works in ongoing therapy. There is a considerable gap in our understanding of how clients and counsellors experience and express their congruence and incongruence during therapy. Examination of reviews of the relevant literature (e.g. Bergin and Garfield, 1994) reveals an absence of recent research on congruence. Given the importance of congruence within the humanistic-experiential approach to counselling, it is clearly necessary to find new ways to engage in constructive critical inquiry about this construct.

The aim of this presentation is to share some of the findings from a recent qualitative investigation (Grafanaki, 1997) that tried to explore and describe client and counsellor experience of being congruent within the boundaries of ongoing person-centred therapy. In this study congruence was operationally defined as a phenomenon which consists of personal, interpersonal and relational components. Congruence was defined as: 'the degree to which one person is functionally integrated in the context of his relationship with another, such that there is absence of conflict or inconsistency between his total experience, his awareness, and overt communication in this relationship' (Barrett-Lennard, 1962, p. 4).

METHOD

The methodology used in this study will be presented only briefly, in order to allow more time for sharing the findings and some of the practical applications that these findings suggest. For a more detailed account of methodology, please refer to Grafanaki, 1997 and Grafanaki and McLeod, 1999.

A multiple-case study methodology was used for studying client and counsellor experiences of congruence and incongruence. Data were collected from six cases of person-centred, time-limited counselling (12 sessions). Participants were interviewed three times during the course of therapy (after their first, sixth and last sessions). The interviews were conducted at the beginning, middle and end of therapy in an effort to find out if the experience of being congruent or incongruent changed over the course of therapy. At the same time, the use of repeated interviews was considered as a good way of building a strong research alliance with participants, ensuring in this way more truthful responses and co-operation. Each participant's narrative accounts of congruence were collected through Brief Structured Recall Interviews (BSR; for more details on this method please refer to Elliott and Shapiro, 1988; 1992). The interviews focused on moments that the client had identified as the most helpful and hindering of that particular session. During the interviews participants reported what kind of feelings, thoughts, verbal and nonverbal messages, and things were left unexpressed during the most helpful and hindering moment of the session. They also revealed any reasons that kept them from sharing their internal experience with the other party of the interaction. All therapy sessions were video-recorded. All research interviews were tape-recorded and fully transcribed. In total 36 interviews (18 interviews with clients and 18 interviews with counsellors) were conducted. Client and counsellor accounts were analysed using a method of analysis that combined grounded theory and narrative analysis elements (SNAPS: Structured Narrative Analysis of Psychotherapy Segments, Grafanaki, 1997). This method of analysis also allowed clients and counsellors to comment on the accuracy of the reports produced. It is important to mention that during the course of therapy clients and counsellors completed a number of measures (e.g. SEQ, BLRI, HAT, WAI, GHQ) that provided important contextual information about therapy process and outcome. Detailed information on the psychometric validity of these measures can be found in Grafanaki, 1997. This presentation will focus on the knowledge generated from the Brief Structured Recall interviews.

FINDINGS

The analysis of client and counsellor narrative accounts revealed that participants' moments of congruence and incongruence were triggered by different experiential states, which affected the quality and intensity of congruence that was experienced in therapy. During the research interviews clients and counsellors shared a number of different types of congruence and incongruence that took place during helpful and hindering moments of therapy. In more detail:

Counsellors

All counsellors reported that they were in a state of congruence during moments they experienced themselves as being fully engaged in the therapy process and present in the therapeutic relationship. This type of congruence was accompanied by a strong sense of *direction in therapy process*. The analysis revealed that during such moments of congruence the counsellors were able to empathetically listen to their clients and effectively direct the therapy process in a way that was helping the client focus and process important material.

> Example: Talking about the most helpful event of the final session, Tony reported:
> *I was asking him to focus into the past, to get some idea of how it might have started, this idea of putting different parts of this life into boxes. I asked him a question . . . I was very interested in finding out more. During that moment voice, words and body language were all reinforcing each other and everything was happening 'quite naturally'.*

Counsellors experienced a more intense sense of congruence during moments they were able to become *emotionally involved* in the client's story. Those moments the counsellors were able to be present for the client not only with their 'heads' but also with their 'hearts'. Usually such moments were accompanied by powerful images related to the client's story and deep empathic understanding.

> Example: Reporting about the most helpful event of the first session, Mary said:
> *I had very strong images of her sitting in that cart and going around and being inside her skin and looking out, but just seeing other people, who looked as if they had a close relationship and she didn't. All she had was this stuff in her bag, so I have this very clear image of that, and how difficult that is and how lonely that is. And I wanted to let her know that I was sharing it. And actually I do not think there was any conflict. I think I was actually so much a kind of in her seeing it through her eyes.*

A different type of counsellor's congruence emerged during moments that clients shared stories, which triggered the memory of *personal material that counsellors had achieved some resolution* of in their own life. During such moments the counsellors reported feeling closer to the client, and more able to understand the client's issue.

Example: Talking about the most helpful event of the sixth session, Lisa reported:
He said that he has moved 20 times in his life and I can remember a very transient thought about how. Because I have moved only four times and I have found it incredibly painful and difficult, and I suppose my transient thought which I remember having was: Fancy, moving so much! This was a transient thought. Otherwise I am engaged on how to make sense of what is happening. I do not recall being in any conflict between what I was feeling and what I was expressing.

Finally, counsellors reported being in a state of congruence during moments that they were embarking at some *personal or process disclosure* in their effort to provide feedback to the client, clear a misunderstanding or correct an inappropriate intervention.

Example: During the most hindering event of the first session, Jenny used an image as a tool to reflect on what the client had shared with her. Jenny described this moment:
I was trying to see if this (image) could clarify the problems, and when I found that it was not helpful, I tried to stop it. I directly told her 'That's my image'. I felt she needed to feel that I could let it go, and she did not have to try. I tried to be congruent.

On the contrary, counsellors' incongruence was usually present during moments they were not able to stay connected and engaged with their clients, and had difficulty in entering the client's frame of reference. Counsellors reported experiencing the most intense incongruence during moments when they felt confused, judgmental or were having *negative feelings toward the client*.

Example: Talking about the most hindering event of the last session, Tony said:
He was telling me about his skills as a designer and I was wondering if there was a contrast between how he presents himself to me as a skilled designer and to what extent this might be unreal. I was wondering if his perception matches with reality. Part of what I was thinking was: 'Can I trust you? Can I believe you? Is that true or fantasy?' But when he showed me his design work afterwards, it was really good stuff! During that moment in the session I was not transparent, because I was actually questioning his honesty; I was questioning his degree of self-knowledge. My transparency was very low and I hope it didn't show, because it could have been very hurtful, and an offensive and destructive thing.

A different type of counsellors' incongruence was related to feelings of *boredom and disengagement* during moments when there was a sense that the client was not really sharing important material and simply wasting time by talking about trivial things.

Example: About the most hindering event of the last session Jack reported:
He was talking, and I am aware of my frustration: 'How can I enter into this? It is like a package.' At the time it was quite hard for me to hear all that. It was not a track that was going anywhere. I was pretending to listen. Well, I was listening, but I was pretending that it was really interesting and all-right stuff, but it was not entirely right.

Counsellors' incongruence was not always generated by what the client was contributing to the interaction. At times incongruence was the result of counsellor's *physical tiredness, fatigue, busy schedule* or *counsellor's unresolved personal material*. At these moments the counsellor was experiencing him/herself as trying too hard to do his/her job properly and there was some sense of professional incompetence.

> Example: At the end of the first session, Jack reported:
> *There was at least one moment where I drifted away and I remember I was sitting over there and I thought: 'I am thinking about work or that research proposal I am doing, and I am not thinking about the client at all.' I felt there was a discrepancy between what I was thinking and what I tried to convey to the client.*

Finally, three of the counsellors reported being in a state of incongruence during moments when they were uncertain about what the best course of action was as prescribed by their *professional role* in their interaction with their clients. During such moments the counsellors stopped themselves from reacting the way they felt was true to their experience out of *fear of violating the therapeutic boundaries.* (e.g. touching a client, hugging a client, etc.)

> Example: Talking about her experience before the most hindering event of the 6th session, Mary reported:
> *Before we started the session, when I came into the room and I said 'Happy New Year' to you (researcher) and gave you a hug, I sort of became very aware of my client and that this is something she doesn't get very much in her life. And it did occur to me. That you know I wish I have been in a position to give her a hug, when I met her, and then I was thinking in my mind whether that was appropriate or not. It is the client's role and not wishing to - not exactly jeopardise, but not compromise it in any way.*

Clients

Similarly, clients felt congruent during moments when they were engaged with the therapy process and were actively contributing to the therapy interaction. At these moments there was a willingness to allow parts of their experience to be known to the counsellor. During such moments they were either *sharing meaningful material* about their life or they were *disclosing simple information about self or significant others*. Whereas in both cases clients were experiencing congruence, sharing meaningful personal material required higher levels of connection with the counsellor and more willingness to be open and connected with their own experience, even in the presence of some very difficult emotions. Such moments of congruence were experienced by clients as promoting understanding and connectedness/ relatedness with counsellors.

> Example: Talking about the most hindering event of the first session, Alex reported:
> *I was nervous about my relationship with my boyfriend and I wished that it was the abuse as a child that made me what I am, and now I can be cured; and then when I met my boyfriend I realised that it was not. I was a gay anyway. And I was nervous about talking to her about that, because I did not know what she was thinking. And I am telling her about my relationship. And I am showing my nervousness.*

An important finding of this study was that clients were congruent and honest when they were giving *feedback* to the counsellor *about the therapy process*. However, this was true when this process disclosure was client initiated and not something that the counsellor had asked the client to share without having informed the client in advance.

Example: For the most helpful event of the last session, Lora reported:
I was telling the counsellor that the picture she had of me was an accurate one. So I was giving her feedback. And I think I was happy to give Jenny the feedback she deserves. And there was not any sort of tension there. I was sharing my recollections. I was not feeling anxiety to do that; I was feeling calm, without any sort of tension.

On some occasions, clients shared that they particularly enjoyed it when their counsellors shared with them some personal information and experiences and allowed parts of themselves to be seen. During such moments there was a sense of *personal* rather than professional *connection with the counsellor.* Timing seemed to play an important role in these kinds of disclosures and clients seemed to appreciate more these kinds of revelations towards the end of therapy.

Example: Talking about the minute following the hindering event of the first session, Alex reported:
I asked her some questions. I wanted her to share something about herself with me, rather than me giving all the stuff. I wanted something back. And I felt she accepted me, because she was sharing something with me. And I felt good about that. I felt closer to her. With my body I was showing her, 'Give me more.' And I was quite pleased about that.

Clients' moments of incongruence were usually present when they were experiencing difficulties in expressing themselves in therapy. At these moments clients were experiencing the session either as hard going or a waste of time. During such moments of incongruence they either were *sharing material that was never shared before* (i.e. warded off material) or *material that was considered trivial and unimportant.* This difference in the quality of the material shared had an impact on the quality of incongruence experienced by clients. When warded-off material was shared the impact of the moment was considered highly therapeutic and helpful, whereas in the second case the sharing of trivial material was considered as hindering and unhelpful in promoting any meaningful change. For example: When warded-off material was shared, clients were usually in touch with their pain; however they were not sharing its intensity with the counsellor, but rather they were trying to show a 'brave face' by joking or minimising its impact on their life. These kind of revelations were considered as highly therapeutic by the clients, despite the fact that during such moments there was a discrepancy between their internal experience and the way they were talking about the issue. On the contrary, when clients shared trivial material they usually considered those moments as hindering: more a way to escape from going deeper rather than focusing on a real issue. Clients' moments of incongruence seemed to reflect the level of readiness of the client to deal with specific, usually problematic issues in his/her life and his/her ability to allow him/herself to be vulnerable during the therapeutic interaction.

Example: Talking about the most helpful moment of the final session, Nick reported:
So I told him about the dream, which I have never sort of said to anybody, because people would think I am weird. It was the first time and I just sort of blasted it out and it was quite a big sort of thing to say. And I was in [conflict] because I laughed and I tried to pass it on. I tried to sort of mask it.

An interesting finding of this study was that at times clients experienced incongruence during helpful moments of therapy when they were able to achieve some *insight or new awareness.*

The findings revealed that clients did not always share their insights with their counsellor, especially those ones that forced them to deconstruct the way they see themselves and/or their problem(s).

    Example: Regarding the most helpful event of the 6th session, David said that he: *tried to mask his surprise and uncertainty when he came to realise that he does not want to work for other people any more. David said: I know I am uncertain, I know I am surprised, but I also know that I need to control it, because that's part of me, part of how I react in situations that surprise me or I am uncertain about. So I displayed cool, calm and controlled. It is an automatic response; it is 30 years of practice.*

In most of the cases clients showed *deference* to counsellors' suggestions and rarely challenged counsellors' perceptions. In such moments clients were not willing to be congruent and reveal how they felt or what they thought about the topic under discussion, because they did not want to hurt the counsellors' feelings or undermine the counsellors' efforts to help them with their problem. This type of incongruence was present even in good therapeutic alliances, suggesting that clients are aware of the differential power issues involved in therapy interactions even in encounters in which the counsellors are operating from a person-centred framework.

    Example: Talking about the most hindering event of the first session Alex shared that: *There was a silence. It sounded to me like ages. I don't think it was, but it sounded like that. I was feeling just uncomfortable. It was too quiet. I felt as though everything was put into a fullstop, and I wanted her to say something. But I didn't tell her that I wanted her to say something. I didn't want to impose what she has to do, probably if we had spoken after [the session] like we are talking now [I would have asked her to say something], but there in the session is difficult, because she is a professional.*

The above counsellor and client types of congruence and incongruence suggest that congruence and incongruence are not a unitary phenomenon; rather they are triggered by different personal, interpersonal and relational processes. The experience of being congruent or incongruent varies in intensity, depending on the severity of the discrepancy between what the person is experiencing internally and what he/she decides to express and/or share with the other party of the interaction.

    Furthermore, a closer look at the words clients and counsellors used in order to describe their experience during moments of congruence (e.g. relaxed, in tune, flowing, relieved, in control) and incongruence (e.g. bored, tired, uncomfortable, nervous, stuck, disengaged) revealed that congruence/incongruence is a bodily felt phenomenon. Hence, participants' awareness of their own bodily sensations may represent the most accurate referent for detecting/ recognising the presence or absence of congruence in a therapeutic encounter.

    One major theme that seemed to emerge from the interviews was that during moments of congruence clients and counsellors experienced the therapy process as 'flowing', whereas during moments of incongruence they experienced an 'interruption of flow' that made the whole process seem much harder. It is important to highlight that moments of 'interrupted flow' were not related always to hindering moments of therapy. On the contrary there were moments that were highly therapeutic, despite the fact that the client was not allowing part of his/her experience to be seen by the counsellor (e.g. during moments that warded-off material was shared).

CONGRUENCE RECONSIDERED

Client and counsellor narrative accounts (Grafanaki, 1997) highlighted that:

1. The concept of congruence/incongruence is a complex phenomenon, which appears in many different qualitative experiential states/types and levels of intensity.

2. Congruence and/or incongruence includes personal, interpersonal and interactive/relational aspects. The interactive/relational aspects of congruence suggest that each participant's state of congruence/incongruence is affected by the other participant's state/contribution to the interaction and vice versa.

3. Moments of counsellor incongruence are present even in the most successful therapies and strong therapeutic alliances.

4. Moments of incongruence usually represent 'markers' for personal, interpersonal and/or relationship tasks for participants. If acknowledged, they provide unique opportunities for further self-development and enhancement of the therapeutic relationship.

5. Congruence is an active process of working out more creative ways of relating with others and one's self.

6. Moments of incongruence are experienced as an interruption to the flow of therapy process; however they provide the opportunity for participants to break conventional, non-facilitative patterns of communication.

7. The quality and depth of the client's sharing has a catalytic impact on the counsellor's ability to be congruent during that moment.

8. The counsellor with his/her own commitment to the process and willingness/ability to be available and present for the client affects the quality of the client's sharing.

9. Being congruent/incongruent involves choice and selection of one specific course of action over another. It involves a dynamic and dialectic process between the person and his/her environment. This process is not just an intellectual process, but it is also a 'lived' sense of what 'feels' appropriate at the time, in the light of what the person perceives that his/her counterpart is contributing to the interaction.

Applications for training and practice

The understandings and realisations that emerged from the intensive interviews on client and counsellor experience during helpful and hindering moments of therapy suggest that congruence is a complex phenomenon, more *a process, rather than a product* (Barrett-Lennard, 1962, 1986). In this process of becoming congruent, brief moments of incongruence can play a very important role in highlighting the areas and directions on which the person needs to focus, in order to achieve higher levels of self-awareness and self-integration.

The most important learning generated from these six counselling dyads was that incongruence is inevitable. Even experienced therapists do not always feel congruent in their interactions with clients. In the course of therapy the therapist's ability to be congruent fluctuates and the client plays an important role in those fluctuations.

The message that this study wants to convey to the practising therapist is that by discussing our moments of incongruence openly, we begin to work in the direction of resolving them, and at the same time we move towards understanding better what is happening in therapy and within ourselves when we are in therapy.

Training programmes in counselling/psychotherapy need to encourage counsellors to ask clients more often what they are experiencing and to offer them opportunities to provide feedback about the therapy process (Hill, Nutt-Williams, Heaton, Thompson and Rhodes, 1996). This would be particularly important when therapists feel intense stuckness, interruptedness and lack of progress in the way therapy is proceeding.

In this study it was found that when therapists feel frustrated and disappointed with their clients, or with the therapy process, clients experience similar feelings as well. Therefore, therapists need to check with their clients their feelings about therapy so that they can intervene before their dissatisfaction or disappointment reaches a crisis stage. Asking clients about their feelings, or using forms which invite clients to share their feelings and reactions to the therapy process, can help clients articulate some of the possible difficulties they face in therapy. In addition, counsellors can seek supervision early when they start feeling stuck or frustrated with the therapy process, so they could be able to further clarify some of the issues involved in this stuckness (Hill et al., 1996).

The study showed that clients were quite willing to reveal negative reactions and moments of incongruence during the research procedures and were able to locate them and connect them with specific processes that were taking place at that point of the interaction. This contributes to understanding that the quality of client incongruence is not an unconscious process, where the client is unaware of what is taking place. Rather in many instances it is a deliberate act during moments when the client does not feel that it is appropriate or safe to disclose his/her feelings to the counsellor. This highlights the importance for the counsellor of being aware of his/her own contribution to the client's reaction and the significance of providing and asking for feedback, especially during moments when the counsellor has a strong sense that there is a rupture in 'relatedness'.

Counselling training programmes need to focus not just on how to teach specific behaviours to beginning counsellors, but on how to help counsellors become aware of the cognitive and affective dimensions of such behaviours and their appropriateness in therapy interaction (Gallagher and Hargie, 1992). The findings of the study have suggested that appropriateness cannot be assessed without taking into consideration the impact of specific behaviours on both people involved in the counselling enterprise.

Counsellors in training need to be encouraged to share not only their verbal and nonverbal aspects of behaviour, but also their internal experience, the vulnerable spots, and the difficulties faced during their interactions with clients (Lietaer, 1992). It is important that training assists counsellors to know themselves, their strengths and weaknesses, their conflicts and personal issues that get activated in therapy relationships. Training needs to provide the opportunity for the counsellors to be aware of vulnerable areas, as well as the resources they possess (McConnaughy, 1987).

Finally, in counselling training it is important to highlight the idea that everyone's way of expressing him/herself is unique and captures specific personal characteristics and style. Thus, the expression of congruence or incongruence will be expressed in a way that feels right for the person. The aim is not how to teach specific ways of being congruent or how to teach techniques to avoid incongruence, but how to be able to learn to be attuned to one's self and able to recognise signals of incongruence and to respect them. Instead of training counsellors with the notion that incongruence needs to be avoided, it is important to focus on how to increase the person's ability to be in a relationship and what might stop him/her from making the most of that relationship. Training programmes need to emphasise that coming closer to one's own experiential world does not develop only through exposure to therapy and supervision or more practice, but also through intensive 'living' with other people such as partners, friends, family, etc. (Leijssen, 1990).

Training programmes need to encourage new counsellors to increase their body awareness as a means for encouraging congruence. Corcoran (1981) has made similar suggestions for encouraging development of experiential empathy. The close interrelation of these two concepts (Lovejoy, 1971) seems to highlight the importance of body work for the development of the counsellor's awareness of his/her own experience, which in turn seems to increase the counsellor's ability to be in tune with the client's experience. Counselling training should endorse bodywork activities, which would give the opportunity to the beginning counsellor to learn how to respond to his/her own inner experience, and to be able to recognise the signals of discomfort or uneasiness on his/her own body.

According to Leijssen (1990) denying or ignoring persistent sensations/feelings experienced during the session or work with a particular client (i.e. feeling restless, disengaged, bored, etc.) leads to lack of congruence and authenticity in the relationship and could lead to persistent incongruence in the client. Thus, it is considered as important in counselling training and practice that the counsellor remains receptive to his/her own bodily experiencing (Safran and Greenberg, 1991) and to how particular incidents or therapy interactions affect/touch him/her and in what ways he/she can be in touch with those feelings/sensations and be able to verbalise them. Personal therapy and supervision can be valuable in facilitating the above process of counsellor's 'attunement' with his/her own experiencing and the meanings attached to it. Thus, body work is not a replacement for therapy and/or supervision, but an additional tool in the service of the counsellor's self-development.

The findings of the study stress the importance of training specifically designed to sensitise counsellors to the idea that therapy process and outcome is co-constructed by both parties of the therapy interaction. The therapist's ability to respond accurately to the demands of the therapeutic relationship may be blocked by relational issues (Horvath and Luborsky, 1993) or by unresolved personal material, which in some cases may be activated by what the client is contributing to the interaction.

Most of the therapists indicated that their own unresolved personal issues made them feel vulnerable in moments when the client shared a similar issue, and that this represented an important source of incongruence. This further encourages the need for taking into serious consideration the counsellor's personal issues as an important component in the counsellor's ability to be present for the client. As has been suggested in an investigation in the area of 'impasses in psychotherapy', personal issues have the potential to cloud the counsellor's judgement in their work with clients (Hill et al., 1996). Thus, training programmes need to teach counsellors to deal with their personal issues to reduce the potential negative impact in therapy.

Personal therapy seems to enhance the counsellor's ability to experience and display congruence (Peebles, 1980). Personal therapy provides the opportunity for the counsellor to work on him/her self and to become more attuned to his/her own experience. Working in depth on personal issues lets the counsellor become more aware of his/her own capabilities and limitations. Tolerating vulnerability represents part of the counsellor's commitment to promoting his/her own personal growth by confronting unresolved issues in his/her own life and appreciating their impact on his/her way of interacting in therapeutic and other interpersonal encounters.

Asking for feedback from clients, colleagues, partners and friends and having ongoing supervision represent ways of increasing self-understanding and sharpening our ability to be in touch with our own selves and others.

Supervision can help the counsellor to make sense of his/her experience of the client (Mearns, 1995) and become aware of the possible discrepancies in his/her behaviour during the session. However, supervision needs to become a sufficiently safe place for the counsellor to bring issues related to difficulties experienced in his/her work with clients. The use of therapy recordings in the process of supervision can be quite helpful for the counsellor (Kirschenbaum and Henderson, 1989; Mearns, 1995). Especially, the use of video-recordings of therapy can provide feedback to the counsellors and give them the opportunity to observe what happened during the session, without having the pressure to be 'present' for the client.

Participation in qualitative process research studies can be very helpful for the counsellor in providing him/her with feedback about his/her practice. To be specific, the use of session-recall methodologies (such as IPR or BSR) can offer additional knowledge to the counsellor by identifying commonalities of perception with the client and reassuring the counsellor that he/she is in touch with what is going on in therapy. These kinds of study have the potential of being highly informative and educational for the therapist (Elliott and Shapiro, 1992). It is important to acknowledge that this process can only be beneficial if the therapist can be respected and not judged about the way he/she reacted in the therapy sessions. Only when the counsellor feels sufficiently secure will he/she take the risk of examining and exploring the personal and interpersonal aspects of therapeutic work (Lietaer, 1992), and provide information not only on what he/she did, but also how he/she felt during the time of a particular intervention.

Finally, the types that emerged from this investigation presented here by no means represent absolute responses that the practising therapist needs to fit in. These types can be used in training only as a way of communicating some aspects of our experience and starting to appreciate some of the complexities and richness of this phenomenon. However, we need to remember that our experiencing would not always fit so neatly under pre-decided categories and the richness of our experience can not be exhausted by this small number of different types. More is still to be discovered on the process of 'becoming congruent', on the process of staying connected with ourselves without losing touch with the other person that is sitting across from us.

REFERENCES

Barrett-Lennard, G. T. (1962). Dimensions of therapist response as casual factors in therapeutic change. *Psychological Monographs, 76* (43), p. 562.

Barrett-Lennard, G. T. (1964;1973). *Barrett-Lennard Relationship Inventory*. MO-64, OS-64 forms. Available from the author.

Barrett-Lennard, G. T. (1972). Notes on congruence. Unpublished manuscript.

Barrett-Lennard, G. T. (1986). The relationship inventory now: Issues and advances in theory, method and use. In L. S. Greenberg and W. M. Pinsof (Eds.) *The Psychotherapeutic Process: a research handbook* (pp. 439–75). New York: Guilford Press.

Bergin, A. E. and Garfield, S. L. (1994). *Handbook of Psychotherapy and Behavior Change*. New York: Wiley.

Corcoran, K. (1981). Experiential empathy: a theory of a felt-level experience. *Journal of Humanistic Psychology, 21*, 29–38.

Elliott, R. and Shapiro, D. (1988). 'Brief Structured Recall': a more efficient method for studying significant therapy events. *British Journal of Medical Psychology, 61*, 141–53.

Elliott, R. and Shapiro, D. (1992). Client and therapist as analyst of significant events. In S. Toukmanian and D. Rennie (Eds.) *Psychotherapy Process Research: Paradigmatic and narrative approaches*. London: Sage, pp. 163–86.

Fretz, B., Corn, R., Tuemmler, J. and Bellet, W. (1979). Counsellor nonverbal behaviours and client evaluations. *Journal of Counseling Psychology, 24*, 304–11.

Gallagher, M. and Hargie, O. (1992). The relationship between counsellor interpersonal skills and the core conditions of client-centred counselling. *Counselling Psychology Quarterly, 5*, 3–16.

Grafanaki, S. (1997). Client and counsellor experiences of therapy interaction during moments of congruence and incongruence: Analysis of significant events in counselling/psychotherapy. Unpublished Doctoral Dissertation, Keele University, UK.

Grafanaki, S. (2001). What counselling research has taught us about the concept of congruence: Main discoveries and unresolved issues. In G. Wyatt (Ed.) *Rogers' Therapeutic Conditions: Vol. 1, Congruence*, Ross-on-Wye, UK: PCCS Books, pp. 18–35.

Grafanaki, S. and McLeod, J. (1999) Narrative processes in the construction of helpful and hindering events in time limited person-centred therapy. *Psychotherapy Research, 9*(3),289–302.

Graves, J. and Robinson, J. (1976). Proxemic behaviour as a function of inconsistent verbal and nonverbal messages. *Journal of Counseling Psychology, 23* (4), 333–8.

Haase, R. and Tepper, D. (1972). Nonverbal components of empathic communication. *Journal of Counseling Psychology, 19*, 417–24.

Hermansson, G., Webster, A. and McFarland, K. (1988). Counsellor deliberate postural lean and communication of facilitative conditions. *Journal of Counseling Psychology, 35*, 149–53.

Hill, C., Gronsky, B., Sturniolo, F. and Fretz, B. (1981). Nonverbal communication and counselling outcome. *Journal of Counseling Psychology, 28*, 203–12.

Hill, C. E., Nutt-Williams, E., Heaton, K. J., Thompson, B. J. and Rhodes, R. H. (1996). Therapist retrospective recall of impasses in long-term psychotherapy: a qualitative analysis. *Journal of Counseling Psychology, 43* (2), 207–17.

Horvath, A. and Luborsky, L. (1993). The role of the therapeutic alliance in psychotherapy. *Journal of Consulting and Clinical Psychology, 61*, 561–73.

Kirschenbaum, H. and Henderson, V. (1989). *Carl Rogers: Dialogues*. Boston: Houghton Mifflin.

Leijssen, M. (1990). On focusing and the necessary conditions of therapeutic personality change. In G. Lietaer, J. Rombauts and R. Van Balen (Eds.) *Client-centred and Experiential Psychotherapy in the Nineties*. Leuven, Belgium: Leuven University Press.

Lietaer, G. (1992). Helping and hindering processes in client-centred experiential psychotherapy. In S. Toukmanian and D. Rennie (Eds.) *Psychotherapy Process Research : Paradigmatic and narrative approaches*. London: Sage, pp. 134–62.

Lovejoy, L. (1971). *Congruence Intrapersonal or Interpersonal*. Unpublished Doctoral Dissertation, University of Waterloo, Australia.

McConnaughy, E. A. (1987). The person of the therapist in psychotherapeutic practice. *Psychotherapy, 24*, 303–14.

Mearns, D. (1995). Supervision: a tale of the missing client. *British Journal of Guidance and Counselling, 23* (3), 421–27.

Peebles, M. J. (1980). Personal therapy and ability to display empathy, warmth and genuineness in psychotherapy. *Psychotherapy: Theory, research and practice, 17* (3), 258–62.

Reade, M. and Smouse, A. (1980). Effect of inconsistent nonverbal communication and counsellor response mode on client estimate of counsellor regard and effectiveness. *Journal of Counseling Psychology, 27*, 546–53.

Rogers, C. (1957). The necessary and sufficient conditions of therapeutic personality change. *Journal of Consulting Psychology, 21*, 95–103.

Safran, J. D. and Greenberg, L. S. (Eds.). (1991). *Emotion, Psychotherapy and Change.* New York: Guilford Press.

Seay, T. and Altekruse, M. (1979). Verbal and nonverbal behaviour in judgements of facilitative conditions. *Journal of Counseling Psychology, 26*, 108–19.

Smith-Hanen, S. (1977). Effects of nonverbal behaviours on judged levels of counsellor warmth and empathy. *Journal of Counselling Psychology, 24*(2), 87–91.

Tepper, D. and Haase, R. (1978). Effects of nonverbal communication of facilitative conditions. *Journal of Counseling Psychology, 25*, 35–44.

Truax, C. B., Witmer, J. and Wargo, D. G. (1971). Effects of the therapeutic conditions of accurate empathy, non-possessive warmth, and genuineness on hospitalised mental patients during group therapy. *Journal of Clinical Psychology, 27*, 137–42.

Tyson, J. and Wall, S. (1983). Effect of inconsistency between counsellor verbal and nonverbal behaviour on perception of counsellor attributes. *Journal of Counseling Psychology, 30*, 433–7.

Paul Wilkins and Zinnia Mitchell-Williams
Manchester Metropolitan University, Manchester, UK

The Theory and Experience of Person-Centred Research

INTRODUCTION

This paper arises from the thought and experience of a group of people working together to conduct research in a person-centred way. Although there are only two authors, we draw heavily on the experience and thought of our collaborators and we wish to publicly acknowledge their contribution. One of us (PW) has been working with student groups for some years now with the intent of developing an approach to research which is rooted in his person-centred philosophy and which is genuinely 'participant-centred'. ZM-W was a member of the collaborative research group which met in the academic year 1999/2000. As well as contributing to the theoretical sections of the paper, hers is the principal voice of practical experience.

THE PERSON-CENTRED APPROACH TO RESEARCH

Wood (1996, p. 163) characterised the person-centred approach as 'a psychological posture, a way of being, from which one confronts a situation'. It follows that this psychological posture may be adopted when investigating phenomena; that is, it is possible to be person-centred as a researcher. By definition, such an approach to research values the subjective experience of the participants and depends for its effectiveness upon the communication of Rogers' (1957, p. 96) necessary and sufficient conditions. It involves a willingness of the initiator(s) of the research to share power with everybody else involved and to engage with them, the research question and findings as a whole and present person. That is, the research is not 'led' by any one individual but all are co-researchers. The effectiveness and validity of a person-centred approach to research depends upon the expression of the actualising tendencies of the co-researchers.

There is little research which conforms fully to person-centred principles and yet there is a deeply-felt need on the part of some people committed to the approach to employ its values in researching. For example, Wolter-Gustafson (1990, pp. 221–22) writes:

> I needed a method that would involve my whole being, including intellect, intuition, feelings, and spirit. To honor and reclaim as strengths my emotions, sensitivity, and creativity was to claim my wholeness as a researcher.

She concludes that person-centred theory and practice offers strategies to enable this. Similarly,

Ulph (1998, p. 27) writes:

> As I unravel it I come to see that I do not want to tamper with other peoples' experience. I have a sense within me which is enhanced by my commitment to a person-centred way of being that I want to be entirely respectful to the data I have gathered.

This desire to be 'respectful to the data', that is to accept the stories of the co-researchers with empathic understanding and to represent them in a way which is free from artifice and the imposition of the views and values of the researcher, agrees with person-centred philosophy. One of us (PW) was driven by a similar desire to find a way of doing research which is compatible with a person-centred approach. This is the story of the theory behind his evolving approach and how it has been experienced (and modified) by the co-researchers.

'Research' has always been important in person-centred therapy and one of the major claims for its legitimacy is that from the outset theory has been derived by researching practice (see, for example, Rogers and Dymond, 1954; Rogers, 1961, pp. 199–270). All of this early research and much that has followed was conducted in the positivist paradigm. Rogers himself appears to have questioned this and came to doubt the usefulness of 'scientific' research. O'Hara (1995, p. 44) reports that, originally, Rogers 'aspired to a highly precise, positivistic science'. She (p. 40–53) explores his journey from positivist to 'unwitting postmodernist pioneer', recording that this involved Rogers in encountering a contradiction. Rogers (1961, p. 200) wrote:

> The better therapist I have become (as I believe I have) the more I have been vaguely aware of my complete subjectivity when I am at my best in this function. And as I have become a better investigator, more 'hard-headed' and more scientific (as I believe I have) I have felt an increasing discomfort at the distance between the rigorous objectivity of myself as scientist and the almost mystical subjectivity of myself as therapist.

O'Hara (1995, p. 49) shows that Rogers' output of positivistic research ceased in the mid-1960s and that 'he had crossed over an invisible line between one kind of human inquiry and another.' In her view, Rogers had become much more inclined towards valuing personal accounts. She considers that:

> What he needed, but had arrived at his understanding of the relationship between science and subjectivity too soon for, was a methodology that could elucidate and critically evaluate the link between his own inner reality and the external reality to which he was attending.

It is our contention that such a methodology can be derived from person-centred theory and that its implementation is beneficial to all those involved in the research.

Any approach to research incorporating Wood's criteria could be person-centred. In research into human experience, other aspects of person-centred theory offer useful elements. These are based in Rogers' (1959, pp. 221–40) model of the person and predicated on the recognition that 'persons are basically motivated to seek the truth' (Mearns and Thorne, 1988, p. 16); that is, it is human nature to investigate phenomena and to construct meaning. This tendency of human beings to inquire and to 'learn' is well understood by person-centred practitioners and, with the axiomatic belief that 'expertise' does not rest with one individual, leads to the assumption that research into the human condition *must* involve all concerned with the research as equals. This agrees with Rogers' concept of 'authentic science' of which

Hutterer (1990, pp. 60–1) writes:

> To be engaged in authentic science means that investigators are involved as subjective human beings, committed to their values and intrinsically motivated to investigate a specific area of interest. Authentic science involves subjects as respected partners in the research process, incorporating their interests and interpretations as a part of the investigatory process.

Rogers (in Kirschenbaum and Henderson, 1990, p. 270) records his belief:

> that the human organism, when operating freely and nondefensively, is perhaps the best scientific tool in existence, and is able to sense a pattern long before it can consciously formulate one.

When people approach phenomena with minimal reference to previous knowledge and preconceptions, are willing to consider any seemingly relevant data, however small, and trust their total sensing (for example, instinct and intuition as well as cognition) then they are most likely to discover significant meaning. Rogers also stated (ibid., p. 274) that 'the more nearly the individual comes to being a fully functioning person, the more trustworthy he is as a discoverer of truth.'

It is the active demonstration of the core conditions which promotes 'free and nondefensive' behaviour in co-researchers. Just as the ability of person-centred therapists to be accepting of their clients while remaining authentic is dependent on their ability to be self-accepting, so the ability of the person-centred researcher is similarly restricted. Part of person-centred research therefore must be attention to the personal development of each co-researcher and to the process of the group as a whole, otherwise the research may be limited. Marshall (1986, pp. 194–5) has pointed out some of the dangers of developing defensive attitudes and how they may be avoided:

> Research can be a wonderful way of not finding out, of avoiding central issues — by erecting a facade of academic theory, for example, I can become estranged from my concerns and deal with them as if they are purely aspects of the outside world.
>
> Embracing the personal nature of research means I live through each project, balancing my engagement with others with attention to my own processes, always with the aim of using my involvement creatively.

However, the validity of person-centred research does not depend upon its participants being 'fully functioning'. What is important is that they freely enter into the research, that they are motivated (that is, it has purpose, relevance and meaning for all concerned) and they are encouraged and supported in it by person-centred attitudes.

There are strong links between new paradigm methods which seek to co-operatively explore human experience and person-centred therapy. Such methods include heuristic inquiry (Moustakas, 1990) and co-operative experiential inquiry (Reason and Heron, 1984). For example, Barrineau and Bozarth (1989, pp. 465–6) consider that 'qualitative researchers may benefit from developing and fostering the attitudinal qualities Rogers postulated to be necessary and sufficient conditions for therapeutic personality change.' These conditions and (*ibid.* p. 468) the 'atmosphere of open inquiry' which is fundamental to the person-centred approach are appropriate to heuristic research. In their comparison of heuristic inquiry and the person-centred approach, they argue that the difference between therapy and heuristic research is slight: both promote growth. This echoes the view of O'Hara (1986, pp. 172–84) who argues that person-centred therapy *is* heuristic inquiry. She states (p. 174) 'Client-centered therapy is, itself, a heuristic investigation into the nature and meaning of human experience.'

Mearns and McLeod (1984, p. 372) offer five key characteristics of a person-centred approach to research which 'when taken as a whole, define a distinctive and powerful perspective on the research act'. Similarly, Barrineau and Bozarth (1989, pp. 472–3) characterise person-centred research as requiring that the researcher holds particular attitudes: these are essentially those required of a person-centred therapist.

The characteristics of person-centred research

Drawing on our own experience, the previous models of person-centred research and related methodologies, we propose that person-centred research has the following characteristics. It is:

Phenomenological
It is based in the subjective experience of all those involved. The focus is on the wholeness of experience and meaning is discerned from that, not from measurement or abstraction. Becker (1992, pp. 10–11) emphasises that 'experience is a valid and fruitful source of knowledge.' This requires an openness to the experience of others. Intuition, emotional reactions, sensations and flights of fancy are to be listened to with as much respect and regard as 'rational' thought.

Empowering
The 'subjects' of research are also co-researchers and contribute equally to the discovery and construction of meaning. This process empowers all co-researchers because value is placed on each individual's wealth of experience and opinion. We use the term 'co-researchers' to include all members, including the facilitator or initiator of the research, to reflect the equal importance of each member. The product is co-owned and the responsibility for the research is shared. When talking about 'power' with respect to person-centred research, we do not mean power in an authoritarian sense, but rather personal or collaborative power. Natiello (1990) discusses the characteristics and implementation of both personal and collaborative power (see below).

Permissive and elective
Participation is by invitation and (except in the most extraordinary circumstances) anyone volunteering with understanding of the process and the commitment involved is likely to be able to offer something of relevance. This is different from research conducted with 'informed consent' in that the potential co-researchers are proactive. To rule anyone in or out complicates the process of getting as wide a spectrum of experience as possible. Co-researchers are encouraged to contribute to the research in personally meaningful ways. It is a role of the research community to support each other in these efforts.

Inclusive
Person-centred research seeks to include the views and experiences of all involved (co-researchers make a deliberate effort to lay aside their frames of reference when considering the contributions of others — see Mearns and McLeod, 1984, pp. 376–7) but it is inclusive in other ways. Co-researchers participate in the data processing and formulation of conclusions

and contribute to the presentation of the research. Reason (1988, p. 38) writes 'Presumably co-operative inquiry leads to co-operative reporting, and the writing of any report should be a shared business.' This is true for person-centred research, the results of which are always co-owned. Who actually undertakes the task of writing is less important than that every participant agrees that the final report reflects their experience. It is the tendency to mutuality and the open and continual sharing about the process of research which is conducive to the production of jointly owned findings.

Involves empathy, unconditional positive regard and congruence

This is axiomatic — it is fundamental to person-centred research that empathy, acceptance and congruence are encouraged and promoted throughout. When co-researchers experience themselves to be deeply understood and accepted by authentic co-researchers, however naive, wild or silly they may fear their views to be, they are likely to be encouraged further in their explorations and so to offer more of the totality of their experience. This considerably enriches the 'data'.

A 'real world' approach

Person-centred research is not concerned with the control of variables — it deals with actual situations, complex inter-relationships and commonplace reality. Becker (1992, p. 11) states that 'our everyday worlds are valuable sources of knowledge'. Person-centred research is inductive and synthetic. It attempts to achieve an understanding of individual and collective reality.

POWER AND THE PERSON-CENTRED APPROACH TO RESEARCH

In any human inquiry, power is an issue. Much of PW's concern in developing person-centred research strategies has centred on how to 'democratise' the research process. This is especially a problem if the research is conceived and implemented by one person — that is if there is a 'researcher' and several co-researchers.

Mearns and Thorne (1988, p. 127) argue that, as the person-centred therapeutic relationship develops, so there is a developing reciprocal trust between counsellor and client. This leads to the development of 'mutuality', which is a central process in the person-centred relationship. Mutuality is highly desirable in person-centred research and it is a particular strength of the approach that it is likely to lead to the development of trust. Whereas the therapeutic relationship clearly has potential advantages for the client, if research is initiated by someone who will directly profit from its successful completion but other research participants will not, this may militate against the development of a committed community of collaborative researchers.

As well as inequality with respect to who profits most directly, there are other power imbalances of various kinds. For example, 'researchers' have 'power' in as much as they, consciously or unconsciously, have a major influence over the direction of the research and who participates in it; but they are dependent upon the active co-operation of the other participants who, through their action or inaction, have the 'power' to determine whether or not the research proceeds to completion. Marshall (1986, p. 196) writes of the importance of 'engagement with people' as part of the research process stating:

> I seek a measure of equality and wish to be non-alienating in relationships. This involves telling participants what the project is about; discussing its aims and uncertainties; at times revealing where I stand and what I find puzzling and contradictory about the issues raised; and allowing participants to shape the research direction. Whilst as the researcher, I have a different stake in the project from others, I expect to meet other people's needs as well as my own.

That the researcher, while having definite and apparent personal needs of the research, will be open to and have the expectation of meeting the needs of others is an essential element in the equalising of power in person-centred research.

Marshall (1984, pp. 107–8) argues that there are four dimensions to power and that, as an alternative to the notion that 'power is competitive, a matter of individual ownership, motivated towards control and expressed through doing', 'power can be co-operative, based in joint ownership, directed towards influence and expressed in individuals' quality of being.' She (*ibid.* p. 110) defines co-operative power as originating 'in a wide attunement to the interests of the . . . community.'

Natiello (1990, p. 272) states 'the concept of collaborative power is inherent in the theory of the person-centered approach'. Collaborative power is at the very heart of person-centred research and it is essential that an atmosphere conducive to its development is promoted. 'Personal power', defined by Natiello (1987, p. 210) as:

> the ability to act effectively under one's own volition rather than under external control. It is a state wherein the individual is aware of and can act upon his or her own feelings, needs, and values rather than looking to others for direction.

Power which Marshall (1984, p. 231) sees as conferring flexibility and choice, is also important both because empowerment is an aim of the process and because co-researchers who sense their personal power are more likely to contribute to the fullest. In the core conditions, there is a powerful tool with which to promote an atmosphere of collaboration and an increasing sense of personal power (see Rogers in Kirschenbaum and Henderson, 1990, p. 182).

What evidence is there for all this? Drawing on PW's work as a collaborative researcher, feedback suggests at least some success. For example, co-researchers commenting on PW's role (see Wilkins et al., 1999, p. 12) say:

> Ultimately Paul's inductive naturalistic and flexible style of facilitation meant we were all responsible for the content and direction of the group and though this was at first disconcerting, it became very empowering. The sense of shared responsibility was very important in terms of taking away a sense of strengthened self.

and:

> In the end, when facilitation moved away from Paul to other group members, it appeared to me as if his role of 'expert' had been replaced by his role as 'equal'.

PERSON-CENTRED RESEARCH IN ACTION

In this section, we explain something of our actual experience as person-centred researchers. Six undergraduate students (including ZM-W) and PW (as facilitator or convenor) met weekly for six months to conduct a 'human inquiry'. Because it represents the voice of the group, the rest of this section is written in the first person plural.

As members of this research group, we were free to determine the focus of this inquiry and our way of working together. It was never suggested that we must approach the research in a person-centred manner (although PW did mention this as one of several possibilities). Chiefly, we drew on the co-operative experiential inquiry method of Reason and Heron (1986) and we were influenced by ideas from heuristic inquiry (Moustakas, 1990). We were also deeply affected by the person-centred philosophy of PW, but how we were together became much more important than any theoretical understanding. Although it was unspoken, we recognise that our research was person-centred and our mutual history and our personal and group needs led us inevitably to our way of working. We think that our experience contributes to an understanding of what it means to be a person-centred researcher and offers a basis from which others may develop their own approaches.

Our chosen methodologies implicitly involved person-centred values in our way of working. These included an openness towards one another, attempting to understand things from the other person's frame of reference, accepting the views and experiences of others and also being honest in our communication with one another. These things we knew were important to us from the outset and we could just as well have declared that we were going to work in a person-centred way. For whatever reason, we soon all become 'person-centred' in our approach to understanding and interacting with each other. In a way, we were already well grounded in the approach because PW had introduced the rest of us to its values, both explicitly in (for example) his teaching of a counselling skills course the previous year and implicitly through his application of person-centred philosophy to his teaching. Perhaps we were so deeply imbued with these values we took them for granted.

Our topic came about as a result of collaborative choice. In the early part of the research, we got to know each other and to understand what was important in each person's life, sharing the important events and feelings of the week with one another. Our discussions led directly (although not quickly!) to the topic of 'life stages', which we studied by sharing stories, anxieties and future projections about our lives. As we were open with one another, listening to ourselves and others, there was an organic flow into this subject. Somehow something directly relevant to our lives emerged (most of us were about to leave university and saw ourselves as on the verge of change). This process of reaching a mutual decision about the focus of the research we came to call 'pre-propositional knowing' because, when working in a consensual way, it is a necessary precursor to 'propositional knowing' (see Reason and Heron, 1984, p. 458). In this respect our research was person-centred because it was designed by all participants to meet the needs of us all. We continued to work together in a variety of ways, becoming so committed to our process that we voluntarily put in more time and effort than was required of us. We refined our interests, answered our questions and formulated others. We were attentive to one another, argued, celebrated, got stuck, were inspired (severally and together) and sometimes indulged ourselves (for example, by sneaking out of college to a coffee shop just before Christmas — although our conversation soon became centred on 'Christmases Past, Present and Future' which, of course, was directly relevant). We did come up with 'findings' but in many ways this was a less important part of our process. Towards the end of our time together, we presented our research as a departmental research seminar — a most unusual step for undergraduates. Rather than make a formal presentation of our methods and interim findings, we chose to give an active demonstration of our way of being together as a research group. This presentation itself became part of the research.

Each of us tells how important this research was in terms of our development. For example, one wrote:

> *Heron (1996, p. 100) compares co-operative inquiry to renaissance art in that outcomes are a combination of a way of being present in the world, the propositions that articulate it, and the practices that transform it. This is the way that I would see the outcome of this research, as a way of being, and a way of conceptualising life stages to enable us to trans-form through these stages . . . It feels like we have made the blueprints of our lives together and we have aided each other in developing the skills we need to cope.*

and another:

> (the research) *has enabled me to grow as a person and understand 'who I am' (I feel that this point is perhaps the most significant outcome of the research).*

On one level, this was a straightforward 'informative' exploration — we were seeking to discover and understand patterns in the lives of people in the communities to which we belonged, drawing on our own experience, the experience of others to whom we had access, the literature (fiction, biography and academic), etc. But there was a deeper meaning to this research. Why should a group of people, most with relatively little experience of life and its stages, be so interested in these patterns? It was clearly linked to what most of us saw as an imminent (and perhaps radical) change in our own lives. The investigation had a subsidiary (and at first unexpressed) aim of helping group members through this change. By understanding life stages in general, we would be better equipped to understand and deal with the changes which were happening to us.

We do not think that any one of us would claim to be 'fully functioning' and that alone may be seen as limiting our potential to discover 'truth'. However, we did grow to trust each other and our collective wisdom. One of us recorded what she believed to be the 'good points' of the research. These were:

> *1. There was a great level of respect for all the group members as personal thoughts and feelings were shared.*
> *2. The group didn't seem competitive in any way.*
> *3. The level of trust in the group was high due to sensitive issues being discussed.*
> *4. The group worked extremely well on the research issues.*
> *5. We all seemed to have a good time.*
> *6. People were honest about life experiences and personal thoughts on certain matters.*
>   *Also the group was able to confront each group member freely.*

These comments are about the climate we engendered and in which we worked. Her negative points dealt with a different, less personal quality, for example '*there was only one male in the group*'. Others too state that an important element of this research was 'the way in which we worked'. One described our way of working in the form of a poem which begins:

> We sit in companionable silence
> Waiting for the first voice
> The strands of our uniqueness
> Stretching out like tentacles
> To discover new truths.
>
> In sharing we discover new truth between us
> But in our silence we discover the truth within
> Each moment of silence is a form of growth
> But the growth is fed by our struggling words
> Words of questioning
> Words of encouragement
> Words of wisdom
> Or just words starting on their own journey
> And we each discover the truth within ourselves.

In terms of person-centred theory, it is the active demonstration of Rogers' conditions which promotes 'free and nondefensive' behaviour in the co-researchers. Sceptics may assume that, as the experienced person-centred practitioner, PW had a major role to play in this. Although a typical comment is 'Paul's style of facilitation gave all the members a sense of responsibility and confidence in directing the research', what strikes us most is that in the reports of our process, we pay much more attention to how we collectively did this for each other. For example, one records that even in our disputes there was 'a deep respect and understanding of the other person's point of view'; another, discussing the importance of 'authentic collaboration'; writes 'all members of the group were very supportive and accepting of what everybody had to say'; and a third states 'our faith in each other's opinions, feelings and intuition . . . has developed through the time we have spent together and through the natural development of person-centred characteristics'.

Person-centred research, then, offers much more than 'information'. The experience can bring great personal benefit to all co-researchers. As in our case, the focus of the energy of the researchers may become so attuned to the process that the subject of the research becomes secondary in importance. Although we do not believe that 'person-centred research is therapy' is a necessary corollary of O'Hara's (1986, p. 174) view that person-centred therapy is heuristic inquiry, we do find that it is inevitably growth-promoting. Whatever its subject, it is difficult to see how person-centred research can exclude a focus on 'self' and the interactions between co-researchers because its nature invites people to be themselves, and share that self with others. This, together with the provision of a climate in which the actualising tendency is fostered, leads inexorably to personal development.

Heron (1996, p. 48) described co-operative inquiry as being either transformative or informative — that is, either exploring practice within some domain of experience and being transformative of it, or being descriptive of some domain and informative or explanatory about it. Person-centred research can be either, or (like co-operative inquiry) can combine these approaches, but it has another dimension in that it can change the participants. In our study of life changes, we found that our research aided us in making the transition from one way of being to another. This and an awareness of other ways in which we had changed, led us to an understanding that research can also be 'developmental'.

In feedback from groups such as ours, members talk about the importance of learning more about themselves, being able to take the time for that focus, and how learning about the self then aids sharing that new understanding with others. The research group becomes a community where each person is developing their understanding of self and others. In essence it is the process of becoming 'fully functioning' through which we all become more comfortable with ourselves and gain an insight into the way we, ourselves, approach the world.

Person-centred research leads to an understanding of the self through reclaiming the strengths, emotions, sensitivity and creativity that Wolter-Gustafson (1990, p. 222) sees as necessary to her 'wholeness as a researcher. Participants are facilitated towards becoming 'whole' as a person, allowing inhibitions to fall away. For us, it was almost like returning to childhood — a state in which we truly sensed our 'selves' and were able to express what we felt. Such expression offers infinite richness to the research. When the people involved in a research project are encouraged to discover more about themselves as they share their views with others, the research can only benefit. It becomes richer both in its informative or academic outcome and in its 'developmental' outcome. In our experience, for the co-researchers it is the process of researching themselves, sharing their findings through which something of incredible depth, interest and validity can be added to the understanding of human life, the human mind and human behaviour. This is at once intensely personal and of great value in that respect, but it also offers something to the sum total of knowledge of the human condition.

APPROPRIATENESS OF PERSON-CENTRED RESEARCH

A person-centred approach is most appropriate where the aim is to achieve a deep understanding of the experience of research participants. It is a way of comprehending *personal* meaning and of transforming this to achieve a consensus understanding. It is most fitting when the basic questions are 'How?' or 'What?' rather than 'Why?' For this reason, it is unlikely to be appropriate when some measure of 'effectiveness' is required. Mearns and McLeod (1984, p. 384) point out that:

> The person-centred approach fulfils the requirements of research that involves, or may lead to, a *developmental* aspect. The open-ended nature of person-centred investigations increases the likelihood that new perspectives will be identified that can be assimilated into the developmental process.

Person-centred research depends for its success upon the commitment of the participants to *encounter*. This means that attention must be paid not only to the research process but to the relationships between participants (hence the importance of the core conditions). This is demanding but, as Mearns and McLeod (p. 384) state, 'it is also offset by the fact that this personal commitment tends to be reciprocated'. It is from the wellspring of encounter that person-centred research draws its strength. If the intending co-researcher finds the process of encounter difficult, or for some other reason foresees that this level of personal commitment is unlikely, then a person-centred approach to research may be unsuitable.

Because person-centred research is collaborative and because it seeks to explore the frames of reference of the participants, it is impossible to dictate its course or even the manner in which it is conducted. Mearns and McLeod (1984, p. 385) write:

> As one avenue is explored, others open up. The researcher, with due regard to his proposal, must make choices as to which should be explored during this 'unpredictable journey'.

Such choices are made by the research community as a whole. It is unlikely to serve if there is an intention to move towards a definite endpoint or if there is a particular question which *must* be answered.

Person-centred research is appropriate when, for example, the aim is to reach an understanding of process in therapy, what clients value or the experiences of therapists. It is equally appropriate to working towards an understanding of consciousness, for exploring social needs or in reaching some assessment of educational strategies. It will never lead to an 'objective' understanding but it is singularly effective if the intention is to find out what people really think, feel and/or sense in any given situation. It also has a role to play when change is a potential objective, whether this is developmental change or a transformation of the type which may be sought through participatory action research. Undoubtedly it has other applications. All it needs is the inspiration, dedication and determination of the co-researchers.

REFERENCES

Barrineau, P. and Bozarth, J. D. (1989). A person-centred research model. *Person-Centred Review, 4* (4), 465–74.

Becker, C. S. (1992). *Living and Relating: An introduction to phenomenology.* London: Sage.

Heron, J. (1996). *Co-operative Inquiry: Research into the human condition.* London: Sage.

Hutterer, R. (1990). Authentic science: some implications of Carl Rogers's reflections on science. *Person-Centred Review, 5*(1), 57–76.

Kirschenbaum, H. and Henderson, V. L. (Eds.) (1990). *The Carl Rogers Reader.* London: Constable.

Marshall, J. (1984). *Women Managers: Travellers in a male world.* Chichester: Wiley.

Marshall, J. (1986). Exploring the experiences of women managers: towards rigour in qualitative methods. In S. Wilkinson (Ed.) *Feminist Social Psychology: Developing theory and practice.* Milton Keynes: Open University Press.

Mearns, D. and McLeod, J. (1984). A person-centered approach to research. In R. F. Levant and J. M. Shlien (Eds.) *Client-Centered Therapy and the Person-Centered Approach: New directions in theory, research and practice.* New York: Praeger.

Mearns, D. and Thorne, B. (1988). *Person-Centred Counselling in Action.* London: Sage.

Moustakas, C. (1990). *Heuristic Research: Design, Methodology, and Applications.* Newbury Park, CA: Sage.

Natiello, P. (1987). The Person-Centered Approach: From theory to practice. *Person-Centered Review, 2*, 203–16.

Natiello, P. (1990). The Person-Centered Approach, collaborative power, and cultural transformation. *Person-Centred Review, 5*(3), 268–86.

O'Hara, M. (1986). Heuristic inquiry as psychotherapy. *Person-Centered Review, 1*(2), 172–84.

O'Hara, M. (1995). Carl Rogers: Scientist and mystic. *Journal of Humanistic Psychology, 35,* (4), 40–53.

Reason, P. (1988). The Co-operative Inquiry Group. In P. Reason (Ed.) *Human Inquiry in Action: Developments in new paradigm research.* London: Sage.

Reason, P. and Heron, J. (1984). Research with people: the paradigm of co-operative experiential inquiry. *Person-Centered Review, 1*(4), 456–76.

Rogers, C. R. (1957). The necessary and sufficient conditions of therapeutic change. *Journal of Consulting Psychology, 21*, 95–103.

Rogers, C. R. (1959). A theory of therapy, personality, and interpersonal relationships, as developed in the person-centered framework. In S. Koch (Ed.) *Psychology: A study of a science. Vol. 3 Formulations of the person and the social context.* New York: McGraw-Hill.

Rogers, C. R. (1961). *On Becoming a Person: A therapist's view of psychotherapy.* London: Constable.

Rogers, C. R. and Dymond, R. F. (1954). *Psychotherapy and Personality Change.* Chicago: University of Chicago Press.

Ulph, M. (1998). *Stolen Lives: The effects on the development of self of men who have experienced sexual abuse in childhood.* MA Dissertation, University of East Anglia.

Wilkins, P., Ambrose, S., Bishop, A., Hall, R., Maugham, P., Pitcher, C., Richards, E., Shortland, J., Turnbull, A., Wilding, S. and Wright, N. (1999). Collaborative inquiry as a teaching and learning strategy in a university setting: Processes within an experiential group — the group's story. *Psychology Teaching Review, 8*(1), 4–18.

Wolter-Gustafson, C. (1990). How person-centered theory informed my qualitative research on women's lived-experience of wholeness. *Person-Centred Review, 5*(2), 221–32.

Wood, J. K. (1996). The Person-Centered Approach: Toward an understanding of its implications. In R. Hutterer, G. Pawlowsky, P. F. Schmid and R. Stipsits (Eds.) *Client-Centered and Experiential Psychotherapy: A paradigm in motion.* Frankfurt am Main: Peter Lang.

Jeanne C. Watson and Meghan Prosser
OISE/University of Toronto, Ontario, Canada

Development of an Observer-rated Measure
of Therapist Empathy

ROGERS' VIEW OF EMPATHY

Rogers defined empathy as the ability to 'perceive the internal frame of reference of another with accuracy and with the emotional components and meanings which pertain thereto as if one were the person, but without ever losing the 'as if' condition' (Rogers, 1959, p 210). This definition highlights empathy both as an emotional and a cognitive process. Rogers saw empathy as the ability to see the world through someone else's eyes so as to sense their hurt and pain and to perceive the source of their feelings in the same way as they do. In this regard he was careful to distinguish identification from empathy. Identification occurs when one loses a sense of boundaries and the other's perceived reality becomes one's own.

One way Rogers suggested that therapists could demonstrate empathy was through trying to reflect people's feelings. However this activity was often misconstrued as merely parroting the client's words or repeating the last thing the client said (Rogers, 1975). This view reflects a misunderstanding of empathic responding, which is a sophisticated and highly complex way of being with a client. The task of listening empathically to get at the heart of clients' communications, and to distill the essence and centrality of their messages, is a taxing and demanding exercise. Research studies have shown that therapeutic empathy is correlated with therapists' cognitive complexity. The attention required to listen and process sensitively what clients are saying is a sophisticated exercise of critical deconstruction in the moment.

The simplistic way in which empathy came to be understood deterred Rogers from discussing it further until his landmark article in 1975. In his 1975 paper, Rogers returned to the subject of empathy and tried to define it more precisely. At that time Rogers saw empathy as a process, rather than a state of being. This process can be described as an ongoing attempt to enter the private, subjective world of the other, while at the same time being sensitive to the changes in meaning so that they can be tracked accurately. The process of trying to understand the subjective world of the other is done with careful attention to nuance so as to be able to sense meanings of which the person may not be fully aware. However, this does not mean uncovering or reporting on feelings and sensations of which the person has no awareness. Moreover, attempts to understand what clients are saying are always done tentatively and constantly checked with clients, who remain the final arbiters of whether their therapists have understood them correctly or caught a meaning of which they were not fully aware. Rogers (1975) saw empathy as a way to evoke self-directed change and to empower the person. Thus he was at pains not to appear the expert with clients in therapy, so that they would assume responsibility for their own change processes and behaviours, and come to see themselves as the best judge of their own needs and feelings.

Empathy has been found to be related to positive outcome across different therapeutic modalities (Bohart, Elliott, Greenberg and Watson, in press; Bohart and Greenberg, 1997; Burns and Nolen-Hoeksma, 1991; Raue and Goldfried, 1994; Rogers, 1974). A recent meta-analysis of studies relating empathy to psychotherapy outcome showed that empathy accounted for 10% of the outcome variance compared to other process variables (Bohart et al., in press). Horvath and Symonds (1991) also report an effect size for empathy that is of the same order of magnitude as the relationship between the therapeutic alliance and outcome . In spite of these findings numerous researchers have noted that research on empathy has diminished over the last few decades, as interest in the alliance has grown (Duan and Hill, 1996). Two other reasons posited for a decline in the number of studies that examined empathy were the difficulties encountered with defining the construct (Bohart and Greenberg, 1997) and the research tools that were available to measure therapist empathy in the session (Barkham and Shapiro, 1986; Duan and Hill, 1996; Sexton and Whiston, 1994).

Empathy has been measured from three different perspectives: observers, clients and therapists. Observer-rated measures were developed by Truax and Carkhuff (1967) and Berenson (1967). These scales have observers rate the content of therapists' responses on a 10-point scale to determine whether they detract from the client's response, mirror it, or carry it forward by attending to the underlying feelings and live edges. A review of research studies on empathy shows this to be one of the most common ways of measuring empathy from an observer's perspective (Duan and Hill, 1996). However, these scales have been critiqued as measuring only specific empathic responses or reflections and thus being inadequate reflections of the client-centered conception of empathy as an attitude or process of being with a client (Bohart et al., in press). To the extent that they are limited to specific response modes, they are not suitable for measuring empathy in other therapeutic approaches (Lambert, De Julio and Stein, 1978).

Elliott, Filipovicch, Harrigan, Gaynor, Reimschuessel and Zapadka (1982) sought to broaden Truax and Carkhuff's measure of empathy using a wider definition of empathic responses. Elliot et al.'s (1982) measure breaks empathy down into nine component elements including whether the therapist stays within the client's frame of reference, captures the centrality of the client's message, adds something to the exchange that the client has not yet said, is accurate in his/her response, attends to the clients' current experience, uses rich, vivid, metaphorical language, has an expressive and empathic vocal quality, an exploratory manner, facilitates as opposed to blocking and restricting the clients' exploration, and introduces new material. The authors reported good interrater reliability for the whole scale and seven of the nine components. A factor analysis yielded two underlying factors, Depth Expressiveness and Empathic Exploration. Some evidence for the measure's validity was found with small but significant correlations with clients' ratings of being understood; however this measure has not been used in psychotherapy outcome research.

Another way of measuring empathy has been from the client's perspective using the Barrett-Lennard Relationship Inventory (Barrett-Lennard, 1962). This is a self-report measure that asks clients to rate the extent to which they experienced their therapists as genuine, prizing and empathic during the session. Although other methods have been developed, this is the most widely used measure for rating clients' sense of the relationship conditions (Asay and Lambert, 2001).

Previous reviews have noted that client-perceived empathy predicted outcomes better than observer- or therapist-rated empathy. There is also a therapist version of the Barrett-Lennard Relationship Inventory. However therapist ratings of the extent to which they provided the relationship conditions have not predicted outcomes nor have they correlated with client or observer ratings of empathy (Barrett-Lennard, 1981; Gurman, 1977).

Studies that have attempted to validate different measures against each other have yielded very low or nonexistent correlations. It appears that ratings by external judges of the content of therapist responses are different from clients' experience of their therapists. (Bohart and Greenberg, 1997; Kurtz and Grummon, 1972). A study by Kurtz and Grummon (1972) demonstrated the lack of agreement between different measures of empathy. They correlated six different measures of empathy and found no significant correlations between any of the measures. The highest correlation found was r = .31 between clients' ratings on the Relationship Inventory (Barrett-Lennard, 1962) and observers' ratings using Carkhuff's Empathic Understanding Scale, a revised version of the Accurate Empathy Scale (Truax and Carkhuff, 1967). The correlation between client and therapist ratings of empathy was even lower (r = .21).

In a recent review of the research on empathy Watson (2001) noted that there were a number of reasons that might account for the discrepancies among the measures. One is that external raters and clients are attending to different cues on which to base their evaluations of therapeutic empathy. Most raters are limited to audio recordings or transcripts of therapy sessions and are not able to attend to or use therapists' non-verbal behaviour in their ratings of empathy (Duan and Hill, 1996; McWhirter, 1973). A study by Caracena and Vicory (1969) provides support for the view that raters and clients attend to and evaluate different behaviours as empathic. They found that verbal dominance and verbosity was rated as empathic by raters but not by clients.

Measures of empathy have failed to adequately capture the complexity of Rogers's definition. Moreover, as Bachelor (1988) found, while clients identify therapists' understanding of their affective states as empathic, they identified a number of other behaviours as empathic including cognitive understanding, therapist self-disclosure and nurturing behaviours. To the extent that empathically understanding another means not only having access to their emotional worlds but also to their goals, intentions, and values, then it seems important to be able to incorporate these in order to adequately capture the multi-faceted and complex nature of the construct. Lietaer (1974) and (1977), in their factor analysis of the components of empathy found that it included six and five factors respectively. Other components of empathy included respect, unconditional positive regard, transparency, directivity, and congruence. In order to experience another as empathic it is not sufficient to feel that the other cognitively understands you, but in addition there must be some sense that the other is involved and receptive to your concerns. Moreover, given that empathic understanding is likely to shift over time as more information becomes available, it seems important for therapists to be responsively attuned moment by moment to the client's narrative and its evolving meanings.

BEHAVIOURAL CORRELATES OF EMPATHY

If we are to capture the complexity and interpersonal dynamic of empathy, then it is important to determine the criteria that people use to ascertain whether another is empathic or not. In a previous review of the research on empathy Watson (2001) noted that a number of studies had attempted to identify the behavioural correlates of empathy (Barkham and Shapiro, 1986; Barrington, 1961; Caracena and Vicory, 1969; D'Augelli, 1974; Gardner, 1971; Tepper and Hasse, 1973; Westerman, Tanaka, Frankel and Khan, 1986). These studies have investigated four different areas associated with the communication of empathy: (1) therapists' non-verbal behaviours; (2) therapists' speech characteristics; (3) therapists' response modes; and (4) therapists' characteristics. Researchers have found a relationship between certain therapist non-verbal behaviours and perceptions of empathy. Tepper (1973) observed that direct eye contact and a concerned expression contributed to therapists being perceived as empathic. In a similar study investigating therapist kinesic and proxemic cues, D'Augelli (1974) found that a forward trunk lean and head nods conveyed an empathic stance (Watson, 2001).

An examination of therapists' speech characteristics found that similarity between clients and therapists in their rate of speech, i.e. the number of words spoken per minute was positively related to clients' judgements of therapists' empathy (Barrington, 1961). Vocal tone has also been found to affect clients' perceptions of empathy. A tone that communicates an expression of interest and as much emotional involvement as the client is feeling reflects empathy, while a tone that is bored and detached does not (Caracena and Vicory, 1969; Tepper and Hasse, 1973). Interruptions by the therapist are also seen as indicating less empathy (Pierce, 1971; Pierce and Mosher, 1967). In fact Staples and Sloane (1976) found that successful patients spoke more often and had a longer total speech time than less successful patients and that this was significantly related to therapists' empathy and warmth in the session. Moreover, a decrease in therapist verbosity from first to second interview was positively associated with clients' perceptions of empathy (Barrington, 1961). It has also been observed that there is a significantly shorter pause time following therapist speech with successful patients who respond more quickly to their therapists' comments than less successful patients (Staples and Sloane, 1976; Westerman et al., 1986). This is a good measure of the degree of synchrony, understanding and comfort between the participants.

Further support for the importance of vocal quality was provided by a study of therapists' lexical styles conducted by Rice (1965). She found that distorted therapist vocal quality characterised by marked pitch variation and a sing song quality was related to poor outcome in therapy. Another important dimension of therapist behaviour has to do with clarity of expression. Disorganised speech can be confusing and may convey incongruence to the receiver. The more clearly a message is communicated the more understood clients feel (Bohart and Greenberg, 1997; Caracena and Vicory, 1969; Sachse, 1997).

Specific types of therapist response modes are related to clients' perceptions of their therapists' level of empathic understanding. An increase in the percentage of emotional words used by the therapist was positively related to client perceptions of their therapists' empathy (Barrington, 1961). Barkham and Shapiro (1986) found that clients found exploratory therapist responses, characterised by reformulated reflections and 'inside exploration', in which the therapist tries to represent how the client might be feeling in response to a specific event, as more empathic than general advisements. The latter were in fact negatively correlated with empathy, as was reassurance (Watson, 2001).

More recent studies have sought to examine the therapeutic relationship looking at specific therapist responses as classified by the Structural Analysis of Social Behaviour (Benjamin, 1974). These studies have found that successful outcome cases across different modalities are characterised by a high proportion of therapist statements that express understanding, attentive listening and receptive openness to the client's perspective (Henry, Schacht and Strupp, 1986; Watson, Enright and Kalogerakos 1998). In contrast, numerous studies report that critical, hostile and controlling statements are negatively associated with successful outcome in psychotherapy (Henry et al., 1986; Lorr, 1965; Watson et al., 1998).

A number of studies have sought to look at specific therapist qualities and their relationship to empathy. Cahoon (1968) and Tosi (1970) both found that dogmatic counsellors, as determined by the Rokeach Scale, were seen by their clients to provide a relatively unfavourable therapeutic climate. In a more recent study, Nerdrum (1997) found that those therapists who had very high internal locus of control scores were less empathic than those who had lower internal locus of control scores, indicating more balance with an external orientation. In their study contrasting more and less effective therapists, Lafferty, Beutler and Crago (1989) found that less effective therapists placed more importance on having a stimulating and prosperous life than more effective therapists. The latter valued intelligence and reflection indicating a more intellectual orientation. Similarity is another variable that has been found to relate to empathy in the developmental literature (Feshbach and Roe, 1968). A number of studies have investigated the relationship between therapists' similarity to their clients and empathy in terms of race and gender. Numerous studies using both non-participant ratings and participant ratings have found that more facilitative relationships are established between intra racial dyads than interracial ones (Gardner, 1971; Orlinsky and Howard, 1986; Sattler, 1970). With respect to gender, it has been observed that female clients experience female therapists as warmer than male therapists (Gurman, 1977).

If we are to facilitate our understanding of empathic processes in the therapeutic relationship and enhance training then we need to spend more time researching and identifying the specific behaviours that communicate empathy to others. Other than studies that have looked at therapist and client interactions using SASB, little attention has been paid to refining our operational definitions of empathy, in spite of numerous reviews indicating its importance (Barkham and Shapiro, 1986; Gurman, 1977; Orlinsky and Howard, 1986).

The objective of the current study was to develop an observer-rated measure of empathy based on the behavioural correlates identified in previous research and to validate it with clients' perceptions of their therapists' level of empathy with the Barrett-Lennard Relationship Inventory (BLRI; Barrett-Lennard, 1962).

Method

Data Set
Archival data borrowed from the York Psychotherapy of Depression Research Project (Greenberg and Watson, 1998) was used in the current study. This data consisted of 40 videotaped sessions (2 per client) taken from the middle to late phase of therapy, the accompanying transcripts, and the scores from the perceived empathy scale of the Barrett-Lennard Relationship Inventory (Barrett-Lennard, 1962).

Measures
Measure of Expressed Empathy (MEE —Watson, 1999): An observer-rated measure of therapist-communicated empathy was developed for use in the current study. The measure evaluates

therapists' verbal and non-verbal behaviours, speech characteristics, and response modes. It consists of 22 items that are rated in terms of frequency on a nine-point Likert scale ranging from 0 (never) to 8 (all the time). Ratings are made after each five-minute segment.

Barrett-Lennard Relationship Inventory, Perceived Empathy Scale (OS form) (BLRI — Barrett-Lennard, 1962): the client's perception of the therapists' empathy was obtained from the BLRI. This scale consists of 16 statements such as '(insert therapist's name) tries to see things through my eyes', and 'understands my words but not the way I feel.' The client indicates three degrees of agreement or disagreement with each statement, with no neutral position provided. This measure has been shown to have excellent psychometric properties (Barrett-Lennard, 1962).

Procedure

The raters were trained on the measure by Dr. Watson. Training consisted of rating pilot data, and discussing these practice ratings. Ratings were made through the use of videotapes and transcripts. Raters met once a week for approximately 10 weeks. Practice ratings and pilot data consisted of sessions from the York Psychotherapy of Depression Research Project that were not being used in the current study as well as sessions from masters therapists (i.e., Rogers, Greenberg, Beck, Perls, Strupp and Ellis). A reliability check on pilot data consisting of two five-minute segments from eight different sessions rated at the end of training showed interrater agreement to be at the .91 level. Each rater rated two-thirds of the data.

The data from 20 clients was used in this study. Clients were randomly selected whenever possible; however, often it was determined by the availability of both videotapes (some were missing or ruined) and transcripts. For each client sessions 7 and 16 were rated in order to comply with Barrett-Lennard's suggestion that ratings of empathy be done after the fifth session (Gurman, 1977). Furthermore, in response to the common criticism that the traditional four-minute segment is not long enough to reliably assess therapist empathy, twenty-minute segments from the middle of each session were selected for assessment. This twenty-minute segment was then broken up further into four five-minute segments which were rated on all 22 components of the scale. Thus, there were four sets of ratings for each session, a total of eight for each client. The raters rated the segments independently and were blind to the perceived empathy ratings given by clients on the RI.

Results

Reliability
Interrater Reliability: Interrater reliability for empathy was calculated on approximately one-third of the data, equalling a total of 16 sessions (2 sessions per client). The raters' scores on each five-minute segment were correlated resulting in an n of 64 (4 segments x 16 sessions). Pearson's product moment correlation was then computed and resulted in an r of .84 (p<.01).

Interrater reliability (Pearson's r) was also calculated for each item on the scale (see Table 1). The reliability coefficient was derived by calculating a mean score for the ratings on each item across sessions for both raters. This resulted in an n of 16 (2 sessions x 8 clients). Sixteen of the 22 items reached the .7 level or higher and most were in the .80 to 1.0 range. Four of the items failed to achieve significance (items #1, 2, 8, and 13).

Table 1   *Interrater Reliability for Components*

Items	Interrater Reliability Correlation coefficient
Rate of Speech	-.08
Interruptions	.41
Hijacks	.92**
Voice Conveys Concern	.85**
Expressive Voice	.85**
Tentativeness	.78**
Captures Intensity	.66**
Clarity	.17
Fresh Language	.82**
Speaks More	.81**
Warmth	.72**
Attuned	.73**
Emotional Words	.36
Looks Concerned	.85**
Attentive	.70**
Leans Forward	.98**
Eye Contact	.86**
Responsive	.79**
Controls Direction	.86**
Emotional Understanding	.72**
Cognitive Understanding	.51*
Exploratory	.86**

**. Correlation is significant at the 0.01 level (2-tailed).
*. Correlation is significant at the 0.05 level (2-tailed).
Note. n = 16

Inter-item Reliability: Inter-item reliability (Cronbach's alpha) for empathy (components summed across raters) was .88, indicating a high degree of internal consistency for the scale (see Table 2). Therapists maintained direct eye contact and a similar rate of speech with their client throughout the session and therefore they all received the same score.

Validity
Differential validity: Although we did not specifically look at differential validity, it should be noted that during training on the measure our ratings of master therapists did provide some indication of differential validity. Rogers received a score of 7.18 out of 8, Greenberg 6.56, Beck 4.28, Strupp 4.52, Perls 2.91, and Ellis 1.78.

Correlation of MEE with BLRI: The validity of the scale was tested by correlating the observer ratings on the Measure of Expressed Empathy (Watson, 1999) with client ratings as measured by the Barrett-Lennard Relationship Inventory (Barrett-Lennard, 1962). In order to ensure independence of observations the empathy scores for sessions 7 and 16 were combined and a mean score was calculated for each measure. Initial examination of the data revealed a restricted range of scores resulting in negatively skewed distributions on both measures. The level of skewness was calculated for the RI and MEE and resulted in scores of -1.20 and -1.11

Table 2   *Reliability Analysis - Scale (Alpha)*

Items	Corrected Item-Total Correlation	Alpha If Item Deleted
Rate of Speech	.2425	.8799
Interruptions	-.2316	.9014
Hijacks	.5257	.8757
Concerned Voice	.8025	.8624
Expressive Voice	.7820	.8620
Tentativeness	.7158	.8649
Captures Intensity	.8841	.8628
Clarity	.3926	.8777
Fresh Language	.5184	.8728
Speaks More	.3068	.8764
Warmth	.8162	.8621
Attuned	.8467	.8622
Emotional Words	-.0327	.8864
Looks Concerned	.8303	.8638
Attentive	.6934	.8703
Leans Forward	.0796	.8903
Eye Contact	.1335	.8808
Responsive	.7200	.8685
Controls Direction	.1766	.8860
Emotional	.6850	.8679
Cognitive	.6405	.8706
Exploratory	.4650	.8751

Reliability Coefficients: Alpha = .88   N of Cases = 20   N of Items = 22

respectively. These scores were well outside the acceptable range of between +0.50 and -0.50, indicating a significant deviation from normality. In order to obtain the normal distribution required to meet the assumptions necessary for a Pearson's correlation, outliers with a z-score greater than 2 were removed as well as cases in which the ratings were suspected to be biased. In each of these cases the therapist being assessed was the raters' current supervisor and had received much higher scores than the clients had given. Removal of this data resulted in a normal distribution and an n of 15. A bivariate correlational analysis using Pearson's r was then calculated on the two sets of empathy scores. This analysis resulted in a non-significant correlation of .44.

Correlation of components with client ratings: In order to grasp a better understanding of what exactly clients are assessing when determining therapist empathy, the correlations between each of the components and the Relationship Inventory were examined (see Table 3). Only three of the items correlated significantly with client ratings of empathy and one other item approached significance.

Correlation of revised scale with client ratings: In order to add validity to the component correlations, the scores on the MEE were recalculated to include only the ratings on those components, which had correlated with the RI at the .36 level or higher. This resulted in a scale consisting of nine items. These included: does the therapist's voice convey concern? Does the therapist's vocal tone or response capture the intensity of the client's feelings? Is the

Table 3   *Correlation of Components with the RI*

Items	RI	Significance
Rate of Speech	.12	.666
Interruptions	-.40	.144
Hijacks	.19	.501
Voice Conveys Concern	.62*	.014
Expressive Voice	.40	.138
Tentativeness	-.02	.953
Captures Intensity Of Feelings	.68**	.006
Clarity	-.21	.448
Fresh Language	.18	.526
Speaks More	.09	.739
Warmth	.41	.133
Attuned	.60*	.019
Emotional Words	-.11	.688
Looks Concerned	.42	.123
Attentive	-.14	.610
Leans Forward	.27	.325
Eye Contact	-.28	.322
Responsive	.36	.187
Controls Direction	.06	.840
Emotional Understanding	.39	.152
Cognitive Understanding	.46	.088
Exploratory	-.16	.561

**. Correlation is significant at the 0.01 level (2-tailed).
*. Correlation is significant at the 0.05 level (2-tailed).
Note. n = 15

therapist's response attuned to the client's inner world; does the therapist's response convey an understanding of the client's cognitive framework and meanings? Does the therapist look concerned? Does the therapist convey warmth? Is the therapists's voice expressive? Does the therapist communicate an understanding of the client's feelings and inner experience? Is the therapist responsive to the client? A bivariate correlational analysis was computed using Pearson's r. The results showed a significant and large correlation between the RI and the revised MEE at .66 (p<.01).

DISCUSSION

This study introduces a measure comprised of specific components related to therapist-expressed empathy. The MEE is a useful as a way of operationalising empathy from a third-party perspective. The results show that the scale is internally consistent and demonstrate that both the whole scale as well as its components can be reliably rated. Although the original scale failed to correlate significantly with clients' ratings of empathy the correlations for individual components led to a refinement of the measure. This revised scale correlated significantly with clients' ratings of empathy, despite the small sample size, providing some initial evidence for the validity of the scale. This represents a potentially important breakthrough given the difficulty researchers have had trying to correlate observer-rated scales with self-report measures in the past (Haft and Slade, 1989).

A limitation of this study is the small sample size. Although the correlation between the two measures was quite large, the findings may not hold across larger samples nor was it possible to factor analyse the scale, which may have proved helpful in eliminating overlap between items. A slight ceiling effect was noticeable on both scales, in particular the BLRI, which may have resulted from a somewhat biased sample. The therapists being rated had undergone extensive training in both client-centered and process-experiential therapy, both of which require high levels of empathy. Thus these therapists were probably more empathic than the average therapist that a client might encounter, which may have accounted for the high ratings. It will be important to replicate these findings with a larger sample using therapists from different modalities.

The scale has implications for future research and training. Not only will it advance our understanding of empathic processes in the therapeutic environment and contribute to process and outcome research, it will also facilitate the training of empathy.

A number of studies have shown that experienced therapists are generally more empathic than less experienced therapists (Lafferty et. al., 1989; Marangoni, Garcia, Ickes, and Teng, 1995; Mullen and Abeles, 1971), and Nerdrum's (1997) research supports the idea that therapist empathy can be increased with training; however the trainee requires a basic level of empathy upon which to build. The MEE can facilitate the training process to the extent that it can provide feedback to individuals on different aspects of their behaviour. Especially as trainees have difficulty providing reliable self-reports of their own behaviour Marangoni et al. (1995). The measure is easy to learn and a number of raters observed that the process of learning the scale was useful in terms of improving their level of empathy. Other advantages of the scale are that it measures specific components of expressed empathy, does not rely on content solely and can be used across different modalities. Currently, the revised scale is being tested on a larger, more diverse sample of process experiential and cognitive-behavioral therapists to determine its relationship to both client outcome and their ratings on the BLRI. In future work it would be important to examine the relationship between this new scale and other related constructs such as the working alliance, emotional intelligence, and emotional regulation.

REFERENCES

Bachelor, A. (1988). How clients perceive therapist empathy: A content analysis of 'received' empathy. *Psychotherapy, 25*, 227–40.

Barkham, M. and Shapiro, D. A. (1986). Counselor verbal response modes and experienced empathy. *Journal of Counseling Psychology, 33*, 3–10.

Barrett-Lennard, G. T. (1962). Dimensions of therapy response as causal factors in therapeutic change. *Psychological Monographs, 76*, 1–33.

Barrett-Lennard, G.T. (1962). The empathy cycle: Refinement of an unclear concept. *Journal of Counseling Psychology, 28*, 91–100.

Barrington, B. L. (1961). Prediction from counselor behavior of client perception and of case outcome. *Journal of Counseling Psychology, 8*, 37–42.

Bergin, A. E. and Jasper, L. G. (1969). Correlates of empathy in psychotherapy: A replication. *Journal of abnormal Psychology, 74*, 477–81.

Bergin, A. E. and Suinn, R. M. (1975). Individual psychotherapy and behavior therapy. In M. R. Rosenzweig and L. W. Porter (Eds.), *Annual Review of Psychology.* Palo Alto, CA: Annual Reviews.

Bohart, A. C. and Greenberg, L. S. (1997). Empathy and psychotherapy: An introductory overview. In A. Bohart and L. S. Greenberg (Eds.) *Empathy reconsidered.* Washington: APA Books.

Bozarth, J. D. and Grace, D. P. (1970). Objective ratings and client perception of therapeutic conditions with university counseling center clients. *Journal of Clinical Psychology, 26*, 117–18.

Caracena, P. F. and Vicory, J. R. (1969). Correlates of phenomenological and judged empathy. *Journal of Counseling Psychology, 16*, 510–15.

Carkhuff, R. R. and Burstein, J. W. (1970). Objective therapist and client ratings of therapist-offered facilitative conditions of moderate to low functioning therapists. *Journal of Clinical Psychology, 50*, 103–12.

Cross, D. G., Sheehan, P. W. and Khan, J. A. (1982). Short- and long-term follow-up of clients receiving insight-oriented and behavior therapy. *Journal of Consulting and Clinical Psychology, 50,* 103–12.

D'Augelli, A. R. (1974). Nonverbal behavior of helpers in initial helping interactions. *Journal of Counseling Psychology, 21*, 360–3.

Duan, C. and Hill, C. E. (I 996). The current state of empathy research. *Journal of Counseling Psychology, 43,* 261–74.

Elliott, R., Filipovich, H., Harrigan, L., Gaynor, J., Reimschuessel, C. and Zapadka, J. K. (1982). Measuring response empathy: The development of a multi-component rating scale. *Journal of Counseling Psychology, 29*, 379–87.

Elliott, R. (1986). Interpersonal Process Recall (IPR) as a psychotherapy process research method. In L. S. Greenberg and W. M. Pinsof (Eds.) *The Psychotherapeutic Process.* New York: Guilford Press.

Feldman, R. and Greenbaum, C. W. (I 997). Affect regulation and synchrony in mother-infant play as precursors to the development of symbolic competence. *Infant Mental Health Journal, 18* (l), 4–23.

Gardner, L. H. (1971). The therapeutic relationship under varying conditions of race. *Psychotherapy: Theory, research, and practice, 8*, 78–87.

Gurmnan, A. S. (1977). The patient's perception of the therapeutic relationship. In A. S. Gurman and A. M. Razin (Eds.) *Effective Psychotherapy: A handbook of research.* New York: Pergamon Press.

Haft, W. L. and Slade, A. (1989). Affect attunement and matemal attachment: A pilot study. *Infant Mental Health Journal, 10* (3), 157–72.

Isabella, R. A. and Belsky, J. (1991). Interactional synchrony and the origins of infant-mother attachment: A replication study. *Child Development 62*, 373–84.

Kahn, E. and Rachman, A.W. (2000). Carl Rogers and Heinz Kohut: A historical perspective. *Psychoanalytic Psychology, 17* (2), 294–312.

Kiesler, D. J., Klein, M. H. and Matthieu, P. L. (1965). Sampling from the recorded therapy interview: The problem of segment location. *Journal of Consulting Psychology, 29* (4), 337–44.

Kurtz, R. R. and Grummon, D. L. (1972). Different approaches to the measurement of therapist empathy and their relationship to therapy outcomes. *Journal of Consulting and Clinical Psychology, 39*, 106–15.

Lafferty, P., Beutler, L. E. and Crago, M. (1989). Differences between more and less effective psychotherapists: A study of select therapist variables. *Journal of Consulting and Clinical Psychology, 57*, 76–80.

Luborsky, L., Crits-Christoph, P., Mintz, J. and Auerbach, A. (1988). *Who will Benefit from*

Psychotherapy?: Predicting therapeutic outcomes. New York: Basic Books.

McCluskey, U., Hooper, C. and Miller, L. B. (1999). Goal-corrected empathic attunement: developing and rating the concept within an attachment perspective. *Psychotherapy, 36*(1), 80–90.

McWhirter, J. J. (1973). Two measures of the facilitative conditions: A correlation study. Journal of *Counseling Psychology, 20,* 317–20.

Nerdrum, P. (1997). Maintenance of the effect of training in communication skills: A controlled follow-up study of level of communicated empathy. *British Journal of Social Work, 27,* 705–22.

Orlinsky, D. and Howard, K. I. (1986). Process and outcome in psychotherapy. In A. Bergin and S. Garfield (Eds.) *Handbook of psychotherapy and behavior change.* New York: Wiley and Sons.

Orlinsky, D., Grawe, K. and Parks, B. K. (1994). Process and outcome in psychotherapy. In A. Bergin and S. Garfield (Eds.) *Handbook of Psychotherapy and Behavior Change.* New York: Wiley.

Patterson, C. H. (1984). Empathy, warmth, and genuineness in psychotherapy: A review of reviews. *Psychotherapy, 21,* 431–8.

Pierce, W. D. (1971). Anxiety and the act of communicating and perceiving empathy. *Psychotherapy: Theory, research, and practice, 8,* 120-3.

Pierce, W. D. and Mosher, D. L. (1967). Perceived empathy, interviewer behavior, and interviewee anxiety. *Journal of Consulting Psychology, 31,* 101–4.

Rice, L. N. (1965). Therapist's style of participation and case outcome. *Journal of Consulting Psychology, 29,* 155–60.

Rogers, C. R. (1957). The necessary and sufficient conditions of therapeutic personality change. *Journal of Counseling Psychology, 21,* 95–103.

Rogers, C. R. (I 975). Empathic: An unappreciated way of being. *The Counseling Psychologist, 5,* 2–10.

Sachse, R. (1997). Experiential empathy. In A. Bohart and L. S. Greenberg (Eds.) *Empathy Reconsidered.* Washington: APA Books.

Sattler, J. M. (1970). Racial experimenter effects on experimentation, testing, and psychotherapy. *Psychological Bulletin, 73,* 137–60.

Sexton, T. L. and Whiston, S. C. (1994). The status of the counseling relationship: An empirical review, theoretical implications, and research directions. *Counseling Psychologist, 22,* 6–78.

Smith-Hanen, S. S. (1977). Effects of nonverbal behaviors on judged levels of counselor warmth and empathy. *Journal of Counseling Psychology, 24,* 87–91.

Staples, F. R., and Sloane, R. B. (1976). Truax factors, speech characteristics, and therapeutic outcome. *Journal of Nervous and Mental Disease, 163,* 135–40.

Stem, D. N. (1985). *The Interpersonal World of the Infant.* New York: Basic Books.

Tepper, D. T. and Haase, R. F. (1978). Verbal and nonverbal communication of facilitative conditions. *Journal of Counseling Psychology, 25,* 35–44.

Truax, C. B. and Carkhuff, R. R. (1967). *Toward effective counseling and psychotherapy.* Chicago: Aldine.

Van der Veen, F. (1967). Basic elements in the process of psychotherapy: Research study. *Journal of Consulting Psychology, 31,* 295–303.

Van der Veen, F. (I 970). Client perception of therapist conditions as a factor in psychotherapy. In J. H. Hart and T. M. Tomlinson (Eds.) *New Directions in Client-centered Therapy.* Boston: Houghton Mifflin; pp. 214–22.

Warner, M. (1997). How does empathy cure? In A. Bohart and L. S. Greenberg (Eds.), *Empathy Reconsidered.* Washington: APA Books.

Watson, J. C., Goldman, R. and Vanaerschot, G. (1998). Empathy: A postmortem way of being? In L. S. Greenberg, J. C. Watson, and G. Lietaer (Eds.) *The Handbook of Experiential Psychotherapy.* New York: Guilford Press.

Watson, J. C. (1999). Measure of Expressed Empathy. Unpublished measure. Toronto: OISE/UT.

Watson, J. C. (2001). Re-visioning empathy: Reflections and conjectures. Theory, research and practice. In D. Cain and J. Seeman (Eds.) *Handbook of Research in Humanistic Therapies.* Washington: APA.

Marijke C. L. Baljon

Mental Heath Care, Drenthe, Assen, The Netherlands

Focusing in Client-Centred Psychotherapy Supervision: Teaching congruence[1]

I find that when I am closest to my inner, intuitive self, when I am somehow in touch with the unknown in me, when perhaps I am in a slightly altered state of consciousness in the relationship, then whatever I do seems to be full of healing . . . (Rogers 1980, p. 129).

The experienced therapist learns to listen to his feelings; they are as useful to him as a microscope to a microbiologist. If he feels impatient, frustrated, bored, confused, discouraged — any of the entire panoply of feelings available to an individual — he considers these valuable data and puts it to work, if appropriate (Yalom 1975, p. 149).

Abstract. The importance of congruence, of being in touch with one's own feelings while practising psychotherapy, is generally accepted. However, how to obtain this skill is seldom discussed. It is often seen as a talent that future psychotherapists already possess, or else the problem is avoided by assuming that congruence is developed during personal therapy. In this article I will show how focusing, as developed by Gendlin, can be used for teaching congruence within the context of psychotherapy supervision.

INTRODUCTION

In the quotations cited above, two experienced psychotherapists describe a fundamental attitude they adopt in psychotherapy: being in contact with their own feelings. Rogers (1957) saw congruence as an essential aspect of the attitude of the therapist, together with empathy and unconditioned positive regard. In his view, therapists should be aware of the emotions they go through in the here and now, and should be capable of really experiencing these emotions and of communicating them whenever this might contribute to the therapeutic process of the client. There is an interior and an exterior side to this congruence. The interior side, the extent to which therapists are in touch with their own inner experience, will be referred to as congruence in this article. The exterior side, the way in which therapists communicate their experience, will be referred to as transparency (Lietaer, 1991, p. 29).

To what extent psychiatrists and psychotherapists in training are used to being in touch

---

1. This paper is a translation of an article first published in Dutch in 1999 in *Tijdschrift voor Clientgerichte Psychotherapie, 36*, pp. 21–31, with permission of the publisher. Translation: Krijn Peter Hesselink.

with their inner experience varies widely. Bloemsma and van den Hoofdakker (1990) describe two anti-therapeutic attitudes, which many novice therapists will have to abandon. Firstly, there is the pseudo-scientific idea that therapists need to understand a problem completely before they can act on it. Secondly, there is the view that there is no need for therapists to become personally involved in the conversations with their clients. The question is: 'How can these doctors and psychologists, blinded and frightened by professionalisation, be dragged out of the morass, how can they be helped to look at people open-mindedly again, with curiosity and affection?' Such a change of attitude is not easily achieved and requires great patience and tenacity of supervisors. According to Bloemsma and van den Hoofdakker, a feeling of safety within the supervision relationship is of vital importance, since supervisees are very vulnerable with respect to the way they function as professionals. Lambers (2000) explores supervision as a relationship which supports the therapist in the development of her *congruence* in relation to her client. She acknowledges the ethical issues involved when the supervisee makes mistakes. *Glickauf-Hughes* (1994) discusses characterological resistances in psychotherapy supervision.

The professional identity is an important aspect of the self, and therefore trainees are extremely sensitive to criticism on their conduct as therapists. Warner (1991) describes the fragile process of clients who experience core issues at very low or very high levels of intensity. In these cases, there is some inner experience, but it is very fragile, because feeling is strongly associated with shame and vulnerability. These persons have difficulty focusing on the perceptions of others while at the same time remaining in contact with their own inner experience. This fragile process is most prominent in clients with personality disorders, but neurotic clients have to deal with it as well when experiences are at stake that concern the core of the self.

Focusing was developed by Gendlin (1981; 1996) for clients who have difficulty coming into contact with their inner experience. This technique can be used in psychotherapy supervision too. Supervisees can learn to stay in touch with their own feelings in work situations by focusing on situations from the psychotherapy under supervision.

ROGERIAN BASIC ATTITUDES AND FOCUSING

In 1957 Rogers formulated the necessary and sufficient conditions that in his view any psychotherapist had to meet to be able to realise constructive personality change: congruence, unconditional positive regard and empathy. The importance of these Rogerian core conditions is now generally accepted for all forms of psychotherapy; the so-called common factors. In most training in counselling and psychotherapy they are given proper attention (Ivey and Authier, 1978). However, I notice time and again, when teaching psychiatrists and psychotherapists, how difficult it is for trainees to sustain these core conditions .

According to Vanaerschot and van Balen (1991, p. 98) being empathic means 'applying yourself in such a way that you are maximally responsive to what is offered by the client'. This asks for 'the capacity to defy the desire for knowledge, the capacity to endure insecurity and confusion'. When therapists make themselves receptive to the emotional experience of their clients, their own experience keeps participating on an implicit level. Of course, psychotherapists should not let themselves be carried along by their emotions. If they are occupied too much by experiences that arise from their own lives, they will not be able to focus sufficiently on the experience of their clients. Therefore, psychotherapists should free themselves of their personal preoccupations, but in such a way that their emotional responsiveness is not affected. Therapists who lock away their emotions and approach their clients rationally create too much distance, but therapists who pick up the emotional vibrations of their clients, without conceiving their own experience as distinct from that of their clients, have too little distance (Leijssen, 1996).

These dynamics can be understood as a process involving several steps by using focusing as developed by Gendlin (1981;1996). Although focusing has generally been described as a process for clients, it can be applied equally well to psychotherapists who have to learn to distinguish their personal preoccupations from what their clients evoke in them. When focusing, people concentrate on an internal point of reference, on a physically felt sense. Generally, this 'sense' is vague at first and only acquires significance through active questioning. A first step is to create an inner space. Instead of working on their problems, people put everything that occupies them at a distance at this stage. This results in a physically experienced sense of relief. The second step is to concentrate on a certain problem area. For psychotherapists this might be their clients' experience. While contemplating, they record their own inner experience. They might, for instance, become aware of a lump in the throat or a turning of the stomach while listening to a client. This experience is what Gendlin calls the 'felt sense'. It is something vague at first, but it has meaning nevertheless. It is not the sum of explicit aspects of a situation but an intuitively grasped totality (Depestele, 1984). Already-acquired knowledge, in the case of psychotherapy both about the client in question and about psychopathology and psychotherapeutic skills in general, is thus integrated with emotional experience (Gendlin, 1974). In the next four focusing steps Gendlin explains how the meaning of the 'felt sense' can be deciphered through an inner dialogue.

SUPERVISION AS AN EDUCATIONAL METHOD

The training of psychotherapists in the Netherlands rests on three pillars: theoretical and technical courses, personal therapy, and supervision. In the theoretical and technical courses the ideas of the main schools of psychotherapy are discussed and therapeutic techniques are practised through role-playing and the like. The obligatory personal therapy focuses on the personal development of the students. And lastly, by doing psychotherapy under supervision the students acquire the necessary practical skills. Following Hanekamp (1993), I consider supervision as a guided individual learning process. Supervision offers excellent opportunities to integrate the acquired theoretical and technical knowledge with personal professional development. An example can clarify how theoretically acquired knowledge only starts to live when trainees experience for themselves how they can act on problems by making contact with their inner experience.

> *Jack started conducting his first psychotherapy a year after he began his training as a psychiatrist. Despite all the teaching he had received he said he did not have the slightest idea of what psychotherapy entailed. He had just had a first meeting with his personal therapist and said that he did not know what to expect from that either. His endearing honesty and his sincere curiosity about the phenomenon of psychotherapy made a fruitful supervision contact possible. His client turned out to be a very talkative one who seized the*

opportunity to think aloud in the psychotherapy situation. Jack observed that it was apparently effective 'just to listen', but he felt ill at ease and insecure about it. Support and explanation could not take away this feeling. I suggested that he should focus on something that occupied him to illustrate in this way what psychotherapy was all about. Jack told me that he had some problems with the ward where he was in training at the time. He was angry about all sorts of ward rules that in his view hindered rather than supported treatment. The relationship with his supervisor on the ward became more and more hostile and competitive, and he experienced it as unsafe. I interrupted his indignant account and asked him to relax physically and to focus on how it felt within when he thought about the ward. Jack became calmer. He made a mental picture representing the extent to which he felt in a fix. By talking about it in metaphors he experienced more space and he realised who he might turn to to help solve the deadlock in the relationship with his coach. Jack was surprised about what he had just experienced and began to understand a little bit better how psychotherapy works. In later supervision sessions, it turned out that Jack had difficulty taking space in ways other than through action. This problem was not restricted to psychotherapy alone. Jack talked about it in his personal therapy and began to see a connection with the way he had dealt with growing up in a large family. By then, the situation on the ward had brightened up, and Jack observed to his own surprise that the ward rules did not annoy him anymore, even though he still disagreed with some of them. He began to discover the joy of conducting psychotherapy.

This is a beginning supervision. Hogan (1964) and Stoltenberg and McNeill (1997) divide the supervision process and the professional development into four phases. In the first phase beginning therapists are still very dependent. In the second phase the growth of the supervisees is characterised by a dependency-autonomy conflict. They start to adapt the method to their own personalities. In the third phase they become more self-confident. There is either denial of remaining dependency or insightfully continuing dependency. Level four is characterised by the development of creative interaction between skills and intuition that is the characteristic of the mature professional. In the case rendered above the characteristics Hogan (1964), Stoltenberg and McNeill (1997) attribute to the first phase are clearly recognisable. The supervisees are dependent in many ways at this stage: of the method, of the supervisor, of the client. They are very motivated to learn, partly in the hope that they can ameliorate their insecurity through study and practice. In this phase the typical interventions are to instruct and to teach. The supervisors give directions or concrete suggestions what to do in actual practice, and if necessary they add some background information about theory or method.

As a supervisor I focus primarily on the realisation of a working relationship between my supervisees and their clients at this stage. At the same time I try to help the supervisees to discover the joy of conducting psychotherapy. Supervisees become more relaxed and self-confident when they observe that they are really in touch with their clients and that their clients benefit from the sessions. The motivation to learn increases when the supervisees start deriving gratification from conducting psychotherapy.

Although Jack's first therapy got off to a good start, the basic interventions for this phase, explaining and encouraging, proved insufficient for taking away his insecurity. Only when he got in touch with his own inner experience through focusing, did his theoretical knowledge come to life for him emotionally and practically.

METHODICALLY DEVELOPING THE CAPACITY TO UTILISE PERSONAL EMOTIONAL REACTIONS

The professional literature gives little attention to the question of how the capacity to employ personal emotional experience can be developed during psychotherapy education. Psychoanalysts have developed the concept of the parallel process for supervision to indicate that the problems that are encountered in psychotherapy can be re-enacted in the supervision sessions (among others Manassis and Traub -Werner 1994). This phenomenon is supposed to be based on processes like projection and projective identification. From a focusing perspective: The supervisee talks about the client and in the way he is talking his experience of the client is implied. The supervisor listens and has a felt sense about the story.

Van Praag-van Asperen (1993, pp. 95–121) gives a systematic dissertation about learning to acknowledge, accept and apply the emotional reactions of psychotherapists in the context of psychotherapy supervision. She sees a direct connection between systematically fostering the progress of the psychotherapy under supervision and on the basis of that fostering the professional development of the supervisee. Just as psychotherapists apply their personal emotional reactions to get in touch with their clients, supervisors apply their own congruence to get in touch with the experience of their supervisees. The process begins with an emotional reaction of the supervisor to something the supervisee tells. Her supervisor focuses his attention inwards and asks the question whether this emotional reaction is relevant to the supervision at hand. If so, the supervisor tries to make it explicit in such a way that both the therapy and the professional development of the supervisee benefit from it. A next step is to explore what emotional reactions the client evokes in the supervisee. After that, attention should be given to formulating conjectures about what problems might lie at the bottom of the client's emotional appeal and to anticipating the next therapy session and the future course of the therapy.

In Jack's case I felt a certain irritation because I could not reach him with my explanation, and I was worried about his lack of direction in his therapeutic acting. I tried to explore Jack's emotions about the therapy, but he was unable to formulate anything more specific than a vague sense of insecurity. My hypothesis was that Jack was insufficiently in touch with his own experience. Therefore, I inserted an intermediate phase during which I tried to help him with this by letting him focus on a professional problem. Because this was supervision, not personal therapy, I did not go into it deeply. When Jack indicated that he understood, I returned to exploring the emotions the client evoked in him. Jack was now more receptive to this and we could move on to discussing how these emotions could be used in therapy.

LEARNING TO FOCUS IN PSYCHOTHERAPY SITUATIONS

An example of a process that took about a year might help to illustrate how the intended change of attitude can be achieved little by little.

> *Jill had learnt to focus in a course about client-centred psychotherapy. The course had consisted of group exercises, derived from the course model of Coffeng (1985), and apart from that the students had practised with each other in smaller groups. Jill had not experienced much physically and was insecure about her capacity to apply focusing in actual practice.*

She considered this a deficiency, and therefore she brought it up in personal therapy. Her personal therapist focused with her, and it turned out that she saw all sorts of mental images when she focused on what she felt inside. The experience that she was able to focus after all gave her the confidence she needed to keep her mind open to it. Parallel to this personal therapy she conducted a client-centred psychotherapy under my supervision. It became apparent that as a therapist she tended to take on the attitude of a supporting doctor whenever things threatened to become emotional. Initially she waved aside my suggestions when I tried to draw her attention to this. On the other hand she was intrigued by what an experiential psychotherapeutic attitude might yield. When I asked her to focus on the client, she would quickly get in touch with the emotions that were relevant for the client, but she used this too little during the psychotherapy sessions. It was a difficult situation for me. My confrontations seemed to intensify her fear of failure. When I played it safe, we would have civilised conversations, from which she learned too little in my view. Moreover, I regretted that the therapy remained relatively superficial. I adopted a middle course by giving support and explanation, and at the same time confronting her cautiously with the problem. After nine months of supervision the following conversation occurred. Jill apologised for the fact that something went wrong with the tape-recording of the session she wanted to discuss. She regretted this because she was insecure about the session.

J.1   *The problem is that the problems of the client seem so understandable to me.*
• This is an intriguing remark, so I go into it a little bit further.

S.1   *What do you mean by 'understandable'?*
J.2   *Well, he has been declared unfit and his income will now seriously decline and he is worried whether he will be able to pay the costs of his mortgage and the like.*
• I still do not understand what Jill's problem is and ask about its personal significance.

S.2   *But what does that mean to you?*
J.3   *I think I have the feeling that I should be able to solve these problems for him, which is impossible of course.*
• Now I recognise a field of tension Jill struggles with often. Her automatic tendency is to give support and advise in such cases. The first half of the next intervention is in keeping with the cognitive style of the supervisee to create a framework for the experience-centred interventions that follow.

S.3   *Yes, that is a field of tension in this profession. You empathise with how someone gets in a fix through practical circumstances and you cannot do anything about it. But what do you feel, when you think about it for a minute, when you realise what the client is going through?*
J.4   *Of course, this is my doctor-attitude again, my desire to help find a practical solution.*
S.4   *Yes, but think about what you feel inside yourself for a minute when you consider the financial situation of your client, now that he has to live on a disability insurance.*
• Jill starts to focus.

J.5   *Some sort of tension.*

S.5   *Where do you experience this tension?*

• Jill imagines how it would be to be the client and focuses on what emotions this evokes in her.

J.6   *Here on my breast, as if a stone is weighing down on it.*

S.6   *As if you bear a burden?*

J.7   *No, not like that, it doesn't weigh down on my back. I think it is extra difficult for me because there are children involved.*

• The next intervention sprang forth from my perception of Jill's facial expression.

S.7   *You seem to feel something like sorrow now as well.*

J.8   *Yes . . . now I remember, that is what the client needs, that he can express his emotions about this, that these emotions are allowed to exist.*

S.8   *Yes, now you've got it again.*

• Apparently, I sounded like a teacher here who was pleased that her pupil had learnt her lesson well, because Jill answered as a pupil who was brought to account.

J.9   *I think I approached it more or less in the same way in the session, but I became insecure afterwards whether that was okay.*

S.9   *That can very well be true.*

• Jill went back to her physical experience.

J.10   *Now a sort of heavy feeling rises to my head.*

S.10   *Can you breathe towards that feeling?*

J.11   *What do you mean?*

S.11   *You know, let the feeling be there, and breathe calmly.*

J.12   *It is still as if it is not allowed, as if that is not my job, as a therapist, being occupied with my own feelings that way . . .*

S.12   *How does it feel to realise that these messages keep emerging inside of you, saying that you should be rational?*

J.13   *I feel something like . . . not exactly sad . . .*

S.13   *It moves you.*

J.14   *More a feeling as of a child that is not allowed to do something, a bit of, a bit of . . . yes, sadness after all.*

S.14   *Yes.*

Jill expressed her enthusiasm about what she had just experienced. We went on discussing how to deal with the inner critic (Gendlin, 1996, pp. 247–58) for a while. Jill knew from her personal therapy what was at the bottom of it in her case. I emphasised that she need not hurry, that she can learn little by little to stay in touch with her own feelings and not to let herself be dominated by the inner critic. In this part of the supervision session I chose to take on a didactic attitude. If we had explored the personal significance of Jill's emotional experience further, we would have entered into the realm of personal therapy.

    In the second year of the supervision she became aware that she felt more free in her contact with clients and that her interventions started to be more creative. The client-centred therapy she conducted under my supervision became less superficial in the last phase. At an evaluation she said that the above-mentioned session had been a peak experience for her, a turning point in her personal development. While imagining to be the client, she had had an intense sensation in her breast, which had given greater depth to her experience. For the first time she had understood what a 'felt sense' was. She had experienced how she could be in touch with herself and with the client at the same time, without losing sight of the distinction between her own feelings and those of the client. She no longer saw that many mental images when focusing now, but made contact with her physical experience instead. She emphasised that time had been a very important factor for her in the supervision. She had been enabled to discover what was meant by congruence in her own time.

This example clearly shows that the learning process has both a continuous and a discontinuous side. The trainee made what might be called a 'learning leap', during which a fundamental insight suddenly dawned upon her (De Block, 1960, quoted in van Praag-van Asperen, 1993a, p. 31):

> The learning leap is a crystallisation point in a learning process. It has the following characteristics:
> • it is an individual and internal event which should not be disturbed;
> • there is something magical about such a leap that can hardly be explained to someone who has not been through it;
> • it is experienced as something definite, as something 'no-one can take away from me';
> • it is explosive: the way the world is perceived is suddenly radically altered;
> • it is a transferable experience that can be applied to a multitude of situations, an insight that can have consequences for private life, though it might have arisen during a supervision session.

DISCUSSION

Supervision is not personal therapy. This need not keep supervisors from applying their psychotherapeutic techniques for the benefit of the professional development of their supervisees. In the cases mentioned above, this development stagnated because of personal problems of the supervisees. The supervisor's interventions were process-centred. Nevertheless, personal problems came up during the supervision sessions, in Jack's case his difficulty to space, in Jill's case inner voices stemming from her upbringing that said she should be rational. In both cases, personal therapy and supervision proved complementary. The personal and professional aspects of the personality of a supervisee are distinct but not independent of each other.

As Pols (1993) pointed out, supervision should not be confused with practical instruction. In practical instruction the supervisor gives advice on how to behave towards the client. Supervision strives to encourage the professional development of supervisees through in-depth reflection on actually conducted therapies, concentrating not on the patient but on the person of the therapist. Supervisors should be wary, however, not to go into the personal problems of their supervisees too deeply, though this might be very tempting at times, because this might lead supervisees to confuse their professional roles as therapists with the roles they have in their private lives. In personal therapy regression is possible to a greater extent than in supervision. Another danger is that the attention to personal problems might be at the expense of acquiring the technical aspects of the profession. Personal development is not the goal of supervision, but it can be a welcome side effect. In the context of supervision, personal problems should only be explored when they are related to difficulties the supervisees encounter while conducting psychotherapy.

There are opportunities and risks to applying personal emotions, both in supervision and in psychotherapy. Supervisees should ask themselves continuously to what extent their personal problems and peculiarities influence their emotional reactions. This reflection should not be limited to the sessions only, but should be complemented by exchanging experiences with colleagues. By being transparent about the way they reflect on the supervision, the supervisors show their supervisees how they can reflect on their therapeutic interventions. Thus, they function as a model with regard to an important aspect of a psychotherapist's functioning (van Praag, 1993).

Trainees are only at the beginning of their psychotherapeutic development when they have gone through the process discussed in this essay. This process forms the basis for learning how therapists communicate their empathic insights, and how they test them by getting in touch with the experience of their clients (Vanaerschot and van Balen, 1991).

CONCLUSION

It is often amazing to see with what ease experienced psychotherapists place interventions that hit the mark exactly. It seems more like an art form than like an obtainable skill. Nevertheless, psychotherapy can be taught to persons sufficiently talented. It turns out that even the skill of taking on a congruent attitude can be taught, with the help of focusing. What is at stake in the supervision of therapies conducted by trainees is learning to apply what has been learnt and experienced in theoretical and technical training and in personal therapy. If supervisors establish an intimate and safe relationship with their supervisees, in which attention is given to the emotions that the therapies evoke in the supervisees, the supervisees can learn to stay in touch with their own emotions on the spot. This can only succeed, of course, if the supervisors are in touch with their own inner experience during the supervision sessions as well.

REFERENCES

Bloemsma, F. and van den Hoofdakker, R. H. (1990). Over de (on)opleidbaarheid van psychotherapeuten: Een beschouwing vanuit een Rogeriaans kader. *Tijdschrift voor Psychotherapie, 16,* 241–7.

Coffeng, A.M. (1985). Focussen, een cursus als pre-therapie. *Tijdschrift voor Psychotherapie, 11,* 402–9.

Depestele, F. (1984). Ervaringsgerichtheid en Gendlin's begrip 'felt sense'. In G. Lietaer, Ph.H. van Praag and J.A.C.G. Swildens (Eds.) *Client-centered Psychotherapie in Beweging. Naar een procesgerichte benadering.* Leuven: Acco, pp. 87–110,

Gendlin, E.T. (1974). The role of knowledge in practice. In G.F. Farwell, N.R. Garnsky and F.M. Coughlan (Eds.) *The Counsellors Handbook,* 269–297. New York: Intext.

Gendlin, E.T. (1981). *Focusing* (2nd ed.) New York: Bantam Books.

Gendlin, E.T. (1996). *Focusing-oriented Psychotherapy: A manual of the experiential method,* New York: Guilford Press.

Glickauf-Hughes, C. (1994). Characterological resistances in psychotherapy supervision. In *Psychotherapy, 31*, 58–66.

Hanekamp, H. (1993). De praktijk als leerstof: ervaring opdoen en ervaren worden. In H. van Praag-van Asperen and P.H. van Praag (Eds.) *Handboek Supervisie en Intervisie in de Psychotherapie.* Amersfoort: Acco, pp. 35–50.

Hogan, R.A. (1964). Issues and approaches in supervision. *Psychotherapy, 1*, 139-141.

Ivey, A.E. and Authier, J. (1978). *Microcounseling, Innovations in Interviewing, Counseling, Psychotherapy and Psychoeducation.* Springfield: Charles C. Thomas.

Lambers, E. (2000). Supervision in person-centred therapy: Facilitating congruence. In D. Mearns and B. Thorne (Eds.) *Person-Centred Therapy Today: New frontiers in theory and practice.* London: Sage , pp. 197–211.

Manassis, K and Traub-Werner, D. (1994). The occurrence of mirroring in psychotherapy supervision. *Psychotherapy, 31*, 363–7.

Lietaer, G. (1991). Authenticiteit en onvoorwaardelijke positieve gezindheid In J. C. A. G. Swildens, O. P. de Haas, G. Lietaer and R. van Balen (Eds.) *Leerboek Gesprekstherapie. De cliëntgerichte benadering.* Amersfoort/Leuven: Acco, pp. 27–64.

Leijssen, M. (1996). Characteristics of the healing inner relationship. In R. Hutterer, G. Pawlosky, P. F. Schmid and R. Stipsits. (Eds.) *Client-centered and Experiential Psychotherapy. A paradigm in motion.* Frankfurt am Main: Peter Lang, pp. 427–38.

Pols, J. (1993). Meester-gezel relatie of werkbegeleiding? De stagesupervisie in de opleiding tot psychiater. *Tijdschrift voor Psychiatrie, 35,* 122–31.

Praag, P. H. van (1993). Reflecteren en interveniëren in supervisie. In H. van Praag-van Asperen and P. H. van Praag (Eds.) *Handboek Supervisie en Intervisie in de Psychotherapie.* Amersfoort: Acco, pp. 79–94.

Praag-van Asperen, H. van, (1993a). Supervisie: een didactische methode. In H. van Praag-van Asperen and P.H. van Praag (Eds.) *Handboek Supervisie en Intervisie in de Psychotherapie.* Amersfoort: Acco, pp. 21–34.

Praag-van Asperen, H. van, (1993b). Emotionele reacties van de psychotherapeut: Leren erkennen, accepteren en hanteren. In H. van Praag-van Asperen and P.H. van Praag (Eds.) *Handboek Supervisie en Intervisie in de Psychotherapie.* Amersfoort: Acco, pp. 95–108.

Praag-van Asperen, H. van, (1993c). Emotionele reacties van de supervisor; leren onderkennen en hanteren In H. van Praag-van Asperen and P.H. van Praag (Eds.) *Handboek supervisie en intervisie in de psychotherapie.* Amersfoort Acco, pp. 109–21.

Rogers, C.R. (1957). The necessary and sufficient conditions of therapeutic personality change. *Journal of Consulting Psychology, 21,* 95–103.

Rogers, C.R. (1980). *A way of being.* Boston: Houghton Mifflin.

Stoltenberg, C.D. and Mc Neill, B. W. (1997). Clinical supervision from a developmental perspective: Research and practice. In C.E. Watkins (Ed.) *Handbook of Psychotherapy Supervision.* New York, Wiley.

Vanaerschot, G. and van Balen, R. (1991): Empathie, In J.C.A.G.Swildens, O. P. de Haas, G. Lietaer and R. van Balen (Eds.) *Leerboek Gesprekstherapie. De cliëntgerichte benadering.* Amersfoort/Leuven: Acco, pp. 93–137.

Warner, M.S. (1991). Fragile process. In L.Fusek (Ed.) *New Directions in Client-centered Therapy: Practice with difficult client populations (Monograph Series 1).* Chicago: Counseling and Psychotherapy Center, pp. 41–58.

Yalom, I.D. (1975). *The Theory and Practice of Group Psychotherapy.* New York: Basic Books.

Ton Coffeng
Leeuwarden, The Netherlands

Two Phases of Dissociation, Two Languages

Abstract. From a person-centered/experiential perspective, the therapy of dissociating clients seems to have two phases: a pre-experiential and an experiential phase. Initially clients process traumatic feelings in a pre-experiential and pre-symbolic way. Their process is slow. Their trauma cannot yet be told. The therapeutic language of 'Pre-Therapy' and 'Pre-Symbolic Process' (Prouty, 1994) fits this phase. The approach uses slow, literal and descriptive reflections. It assists clients to recontact reality and their affect, and it facilitates their communication. Consequently their inner process is supported. As this develops gradually into an experiential and symbolic process, they enter the second phase. The trauma is no longer experienced as fragments but as a whole. It can be expressed with symbolic language, and become integrated. The two phases were illustrated with video-clips taken from actual sessions. A third video showed the shift from the first to the second phase.

1. INTRODUCTION

Clients who were traumatized in childhood often have dissociative symptoms (Marmar, Weiss and Metzler, 1998). Some have a 'Dissociative Identity Disorder' (DID, formerly Multiple Personality Disorder): a severe form of dissociation in which their identity is split into several 'personalities' (identities, alters), with different age, character, memory and behaviour (Ross, 1997). These personalities, separated by dissociative barriers, are not aware of each other. One of them comes to the foreground during a switch in consciousness. Clients have no control over this. They are handicapped, as awareness of time and continuity is disrupted; they lose track of time, forget appointments, and don't remember where they have been; they have amnesia for recent and past events; and concentration and daily tasks consume much energy and time. These clients suffer also from a Post Traumatic Stress Disorder (PTSD), with flashbacks of the trauma, and alternating episodes of stress and numbness. Their memory of trauma is fragmented: they re-experience a part without remembering the whole. It makes them unsure about the traumatic origin of their suffering.

Traumatization is complex and multilayered (Herman, 1992; v. Ravesteyn, 1978). It influences the development of children, leaving scars on their personality (Coffeng, 1996a). It requires therapy of the whole person (Adshead, 2000). The officially accepted treatment of dissociation, which used to be directive and focused on symptoms, has become open to other orientations recently, introducing concepts such as transference and attachment (Steele, 1995). I missed, however, a client-centered approach: clients should be asked what they need. As survivors, they can show the way to therapists. I also looked for a process-oriented approach, which respects dissociation and other symptoms as ways to cope with trauma and intrusive memory. Prouty (1976, 1977, 1981) showed such respect. He has a trust in the process of clients, whether psychotic or not. His approach is process-oriented and phenomenological. This facilitates a development in which psychotic material can change. Hallucinations changed and began to explain themselves: they appeared to refer to previous trauma!

Fascinated by this work, I realized that dissociative clients had a similar process and that Prouty's approach would fit them, so I adapted it for traumatized borderline and dissociating clients (Coffeng, 1994, 1995, 1996a, 1996b, 1997, 1998, 1999, 2000a and b). Looking at their therapy, I observed that it had two phases, each with a typical tune and pace. Each phase needs a specific therapeutic language. I call the first phase 'pre-experiential and pre-symbolic', the second: 'experiential and symbolic'.

It seems crucial to recognize this biphasic pattern. It helps to find the tune and pace of the client. The phases will be discussed below. A separate paragraph will be spent on the shift from the first to the second phase: a critical episode, in which many things change in short time.

2. PHASE I

A. Pre-experiential process: a slow process

Initially, the memory of dissociative clients is 'traumatic': they have flashbacks as if the trauma is recurring. It's different from 'narrative' memory, when one remembers an event and realizes it is about the past (v. d. Kolk, 1996). Their trauma memory is also split by dissociation into fragments and amnesic gaps. Clients suffer but cannot relate to their feelings or express them in understandable language. They have alexithymia: the suffering has no words (Hyer, Woods and Boudewyns, 1991). They fail to communicate their trauma or to work it through and they become retraumatized if asked to do so. On the other hand, they wish to share their trauma and to get rid of it. It is not just their trauma memory that is affected by dissociation, but also their whole experiencing. Due to switches in consciousness, they lose track in therapy. Sentences are interrupted by voices in their head and clients lose what they said before. It takes effort and time to keep their track and to retrieve what they wanted to say. It is a slow process needing a slow approach. In addition, clients are not at ease, as they had no safe relationships before. Therapists, confronted with the changing appearance of the client, don't feel at ease either.

I characterize this phase as 'pre-experiential'. The term was given to the process of psychotic clients by Prouty (1976). '*Pre*-experiential' means that it precedes experiential process. It is different: it is a slow and repetitive process. It was missed by researchers, who thought psychotic clients were not experiencing (Rogers, 1967). These clients are 'pre-expressive' (Prouty, 1998): their expressions are concrete and not yet symbolic. Prouty developed ways to support and facilitate their slow process. He noticed that it evolved gradually into experiential functioning: clients started to have feelings and to express them with symbolic language.

Psychological contact

Therapy did not work for psychotic clients, because one condition was lacking: they had no 'psychological contact' (Prouty, 1976; Rogers, 1957). Prouty distinguished three dimensions of psychological contact: *reality contact* (with the world, people, places, events); *affective contact* (with one's self, one's feelings); and *communicative contact* (ability to express experience to others). Psychotic clients have poor contact with reality. Occupied by hallucinations, they are not aware where they are, and hardly notice other people. They don't notice their body, body posture, or how they are dressed. They have poor awareness of themselves, their thoughts and feelings. They are unable to communicate properly with others by words or gestures. Dissociating clients have similar handicaps. Their process is slow. They lose contact with reality. Awareness of time is interrupted, they forget where they have been. During flashbacks or switches, they think they are in another time. They are confused from their switches in consciousness. Others don't understand their contradictory behaviour, find them crazy and avoid them. Clients have poor affective contact: their feelings are either numb or very strong. They do everything not to feel, by switching or self-mutilation. Their 'experiencing is frozen' (Gendlin, 1964). They have also difficulty in expressing feelings in understandable language.

Therapeutic language of pre-experiential phase

The first phase is characterized by its slow process. The client needs time to stay in touch with it. Therapists should not respond quickly, but repeat slowly what the client said. They assist by keeping track, especially when clients are interrupted by switches. The process has very tiny steps. Traumatization is so complex and multilayered, that change can only happen in small steps. Every step has many consequences inside the client. The process is also cyclical and repetitive as aspects of trauma come back, as well as behaviour and interaction due to the multilayering of trauma. Prouty underlined the importance of repetition. It may seem at a standstill, but it is a cyclical recurring of something which seeks to be expressed. While the same words are used, each repetition subtly reveals another aspect of the same content. The cyclical pattern is like a screw for metal, which needs many turns to get deeper. The first phase requires patience, but clients expect miracles. They want relief as they have suffered for a long time. They try to work hard, but fear their trauma at the same time. One explains to them that their suffering needs relief, but that change can happen slowly. I use the image of a dance group. When the whole group turns, the dancer in the middle (pivot) turns slowly, lest dancers at the outside will be thrown out of the circle. I shall listen to all. We need a safe relationship first, which needs time. In the context of a relationship, the trauma can be told and change can happen. I call it 'pacing and extrapolation': I try to gain time, and to postpone intensive work to a later phase.

Another aspect of the first phase is its communication. Utterances of clients are pre-expressive, and have not yet meaning in the usual sense. They become understood later in therapy. These need just literal reflections, without change, addition or interpretation. This technique involves a typical language. The few words are only those the client can utter. They are preserved as scarce jewels and reflected literally. Clients become confused when one asks questions about what they said. They get put off track by any straight question. It leads to discussion of personalities inside. Their process becomes interrupted. Whenever I need to ask something, I ask the question aloud to myself: 'I wonder what happened that you did not come last week.' I leave space for the client to respond, or to the personality inside who wants to speak. There is space to respond or not, and also space in time: I am not in a hurry. Sometimes I begin to answer the question myself and I imagine what could have happened. It gives space to the client to correct my hypothesis.

Pre-Therapy

The process of the first phase is assisted by 'Pre-Therapy' (Prouty, 1976, 1994). Pre-therapy addresses the client's lack of psychological contact. It 'anchors' the client with environment, therapist and herself (Van Werde, 1998a). It restores contact, which enables the client to have feelings. Pre-therapy consists of *'contact reflections'*. They contain Rogers' attitudes, using the language of confused clients. They respond to rudiments of contact clients still have, and are offered at their level. Contact reflections point to aspects of the client's experience, behaviour or existence: to reality, affective and communicative contact. *'Situational reflections'* point to reality: 'We are sitting in this room,' 'It is cold here.' The client may nod, look outside, or not respond. We trust that a vague awareness of reality is supported. *'Body reflections'* point to body awareness: 'You are sitting upright,' 'Your body is very stiff,' 'Your hands are on your knees.' The therapist can take the same posture with his body: 'body mirroring', and add verbal body reflections. It assists the awareness of the client's body, contact with self and with reality. Other reflections are *'facial reflections'*: 'You look surprised.' One reflects what is visible on the client's face. It is a neutral description without interpretation or suggestion. It helps the client to contact feelings. *'Word-for-word reflections'* are literal repetitions of the client's words. You said: 'darkness', and then 'away'. Literal reflections support the client's damaged ability to communicate. Dissociative clients are interrupted often by internal voices. 'Word-for-word-reflections' help to get back what they were saying. The last type of reflections are *'reiterative reflections'*. Those reflections that were followed by response or change of the client are repeated. One assumes that there was a move in process. Reiterative reflections reinforce that move. When a client looks at you (contact) after a body reflection, you repeat that body reflection, and you reflect the following eye-contact.

Repetition is a typical aspect of pre-therapy. A client who was elsewhere with his/her mind and who missed reflections hears them at a later moment. Other characteristic is are its slow speed and the time between reflections. Clients need time to hear, to process, and to respond. Moreover, the pre-experiential process is not linear. One does not see direct responses after reflections; it takes time. Then responses one did not expect come from the client. Sentences don't seem to connect with previous utterances. It can confuse therapists since it is unlike a therapy, in which responses follow interventions and can be discussed. It is more like minimal music. The same applies to the effect of pre-therapy. The bucket needs many drips before it is full. Recently, Prouty (1999) stressed that pre-therapy is not just a technique; rather it is an attitude. Its core is the therapist's human presence.

Prouty's contribution has implications for the whole field of therapy. Not only psychotic clients could profit from it. Contact reflections are basic, and support other interventions. They are helpful to trauma clients, when they need a basis from which to endure strong feelings. Summarizing: the general character of pre-therapy is slow, repetitive and literal; it's specific quality is it's focus on contact.

B. Pre-symbolic process: a concrete process

Prouty called an hallucinatory image: a 'Pre-Symbol' (Prouty, 1977; 1986; 1991). 'Pre-' refers to its primitive nature. A Pre-Symbol (hallucination) does not symbolize or mean anything in the usual sense. It is a concrete phenomenon: it just means itself. It needs concrete language. An hallucination is not a projection like images in dreams, but an *extra*-jection: a split-off part of the client's ego. It doesn't refer symbolically to previous experience, and cannot be interpreted. It refers to itself. Prouty watched hallucinations as phenomena, without interpretation: to his surprise, a process started and hallucinations began to change. They became realistic and evolved into previous traumatic experience, which had been frozen. Hallucinations began to make sense, and contained fragments of real experience. First, they were 'pre-expressive' utterances (Prouty, 1998): they announced a message, which became understood later.

This approach of hallucinations is called: '*Pre-Symbolic Process*'. It has four stages. The first is the 'self-indicating stage', in which a hallucination becomes present.[1] The client sees a hallucinatory image. He looks at the corner of the room; his eyes are directed to there. The therapist reflects: 'You look over there. You see something.' The client describes the image (colour, shape): 'It's big, round and yellow.' The therapist reflects that: 'image reflecting'. Image reflections are repeated. It assists to get the hallucination stable. Then, the client enters the second, 'self-emotive stage': he observes affect in the image: 'It's big, round and yellow, and it has anger in it.' The therapist reflects both image and affect. Reflections of image are balanced with those of affect. Slowly, the image loses its abstract or strange shape and becomes a realistic image of persons or events: it is the third or 'self-processing stage'.

The hallucination is still outside, but the client begins to have feelings inside. He is puzzled seeing something there and feeling inside too. Gradually, the hallucination changes into a former real experience, often a traumatic flashback (Prouty, 1983). Clients are shocked to realize that something happened to them. The therapist reflects all these aspects. There is onset of symbolic and experiential language. Instead of being frightened by the strange hallucination, the client is impressed by the old repressed or split experience. Time is needed to integrate it. This happens in the fourth or 'self-integrating stage', when the process has become experiential, and the language symbolic. The therapist facilitates integration with client-centered/experiential reflections.

Dissociating clients have a similar process, especially in the first phase of therapy. They are attacked by flashbacks, over which they have no control. They cannot express or process them either. Due to dissociative barriers and fragmentation, they don't recognize flashbacks as part of *their* trauma. Flashbacks are also split in dimension (Braun, 1986): clients have physical sensations of strangulation without an image of the event; they see a dangerous scene without feeling anything. They don't understand. Flashbacks recur, like hallucinations of psychotic patients. Traumatic flashbacks frighten and evoke strong emotions. Clients don't talk about it: they expect not to be believed, as they never were before. They fear they are crazy, and suffer in isolation. Contact-reflections create a climate where flashbacks are welcome. These reflections support another aspect too. The emotional impact of flashbacks is not only due to the severity of the trauma, but also to the fact that clients suffer alone. They lost contact with the environment, other persons and themselves; they fear they might explode, and switch into another identity who doesn't feel. They reacted this way during the trauma and do so afterwards during flashbacks. With contact-reflections, one assists clients to endure strong feelings. One reconnects the client and does not run away.

[1.] Hallucinations attack clients like nightmares and 'daymares' (Prouty, 1994). They come and go. Clients don't talk about it, fearing more medication if they do. It needs an open attitude. Prouty stressed a second precondition. To enter a process, hallucinations need to be present and stable, for which Pre-therapy provides a basis (Prouty, 1990). When the client feels contact, the hallucination can stay, and a process can follow.

The stages of the Pre-Symbolic Process are observable with dissociating clients. First, there are mere fragments; or parts of fragments: sensations without image, images without feelings. It is the 'self-indicating stage'. One reflects what is expressed, without inquiring about the traumatic event. That story will come. One picks up fragments and gives them a number as an archeologist. Gradually feelings become connected with images, and fragments get more fragments. This is typical for the second 'self-emotive stage'. Clients become curious about what happened and about the origin of their suffering.

A client hallucinated her father (perpetrator) whenever she came home from therapy. He stood in the corner of the room. She was frightened and puzzled, as he had died. I dropped my inclination to control the hallucination, and attended to it. The hallucination appeared in the therapy room and it changed: now she felt her fathers' presence in her body with physical sensations.

Memories and context come back. Flashbacks become complete and become a story of trauma. Clients are shocked to realize that they have been traumatized, but begin to understand the reason for their complaints. This is reassuring: they were not stupid, and their memory is still there. The process follows the 'self-processing stage' of Prouty, which will be called here 'the critical episode'. Clients are no longer split into alters. They suffer, facing the trauma fully, and they realize its impact on their life. They have difficulty integrating all the facts they somehow knew. Integration will be realized in the second, experiential phase, which parallels Prouty's 'self-integrative stage'.

The concept of 'Pre-Symbolic Process' fits into the therapy process of dissociating clients. Its first two stages can be observed during 'phase I' (pre-experiential, pre-symbolic). One does not enter into the content of trauma fragments but attends to them in a concrete an phenomenological way. One trusts the process. Trauma fragments will tell their story in a later phase. Contact reflections provide a basis; slow and concrete pre-symbolic reflections support the process, having the effect of 'pacing and extrapolation'. One slows down the hectic experience of flashbacks, and facilitates a process which the client can digest.

3. SHIFT TO INTEGRATING: A CRITICAL EPISODE

When clients leave the first phase, they enter a no man's land. They begin to have feelings, but are not yet able to stay with them. This episode, between phase I and II, is what Van Werde (1998b) calls 'the grey-zone'. Clients become able to feel and to express feelings in symbolic language but they cannot practice it yet. It is totally new to have feelings, and to be in a climate where feelings are accepted. Moreover, clients begin to remember. Amnesic gaps become smaller and memory less fragmented. They can no longer ignore facts or doubt the reason for their suffering: they must admit they were traumatized. They cannot switch as easily as before. Switching loses its purpose, as dissociative barriers become transparent. Alters cannot persist to deny the trauma. Switching becomes a burden rather than a help, and the clients want it to stop. Although clients are improving, they have difficulty handling the trauma, and are not ready to integrate it. First, they still tend not to feel. Second, they never had feelings in the presence of a person who is safe. Third, they are afraid to face the trauma, because they were brainwashed. They were supposed not to believe they were abused. They were threatened (with abandonment, death, or hell) not to tell what happened. They fear betraying and losing their parents, if they admit that their parents betrayed or abused them. They are confused. Moreover, their full memory of the trauma comes back as a flashback. New details are so fresh that the trauma seems to recur. It is shocking and too much. Clients enter a period of severe crisis and need support. Therapists don't expect it, as their clients were improving. They should not go on leave without replacement. Extra calls or sessions are needed; sometimes a short admission. During the critical episode, contact-reflections (pre-therapy) assist clients to remain connected. One can return to slow literal reflections (pre-experiential and pre-symbolic language) which slows down their hectic process. Symbolic language is reflected, without exploring the trauma. Integration will happen in the second, experiential phase.

4. PHASE II

A. Experiencing and focusing: healing from the body

When clients enter the second, experiential phase, they have contact with their feelings. They remember the trauma, have to face it and to work it through. Their traumatic memory has to change into a narrative memory (v. d. Kolk, 1996). Flashbacks in which the trauma recur, become trauma events which *have* happened. It becomes the past. Then clients can look at it as a story which they remember. They can describe it with words without drowning. The trauma has to get a place and meaning, and must become integrated. Intensive cathartic sessions are not necessary. Integration can happen with small experiential steps. When one is assisted to stay with an anxiety-provoking situation and to feel the crux of it, one feels relief (Gendlin, 1964). The secret of experiential psychotherapy lies in its tiny steps (Gendlin, 1990). When one makes an experiential step with a single word, a problem feels totally different. Attending to the felt complexity ('felt sense') of a problem and finding the right word for it, gives a 'felt shift'. One feels that the problem is moving towards its solution. It feels as a relief. It is different from 'dead-end thinking', or being submerged in 'dead-end feelings' (Gendlin, 1996). A nice illustration was given recently by Elliott and colleagues with a therapy fragment. A change in the client's voice could be heard when she said: 'So the fear is like a thing!' Something fell into its place. It sounded like a turning point (Elliott, Slatick and Urman, 2000).

Focusing (Gendlin, 1981) helps clients to attend to their felt sense. The felt sense is a vague physical feeling, in the middle of the body, about a problematic situation. It becomes clear if one attends to it. It is both feeling and understanding the problem: it is the felt crux of it. Traumatization is so complex that it cannot be described with a single word. But it can be felt at one spot in the body. When clients attend to this felt complexity, they catch the core and they feel relief. *Then* they have a catharsis with release of emotions, which is different from abreactive catharsis. Therefore, clients are encouraged to focus, which they could not do in the first phase. Clients find it important to capture the typical atmosphere in which the trauma happened (Coffeng, 1992a, b and c). It is the 'flavour' of their experience. Experiential words and responses fit with the complexity and specificity of traumatization. The therapeutic language changes from pre-experiential to experiential (Gendlin, 1968).

The body

A benefit of focusing is its trust in the body. The trauma happened to the body of the client. Physical and emotional abuse was felt in the body. The body carries the traces (Terr, 1994; Putnam, 1999; van der Kolk, 1996). It is the source of memory and has the hallmark of facts: it is the center of truth (Pesso, 1990). When the client reconstructs her trauma experience from the different traces (images, sensations, diary, witnesses), she can check with her felt sense if it happened. The body also has the hallmark of another truth. It has a moral blue-print (Gendlin, 1991/92/94, 1993), which tells us that the trauma should not have happened; it knows what should have happened. Moreover, the body is the source of healing. Recovery comes from the body with small steps which are felt. Trauma clients denied their body and avoided feeling. As soon as they can stay with their feelings, they realize that what they felt was true. They begin to trust feelings, and discover that their body knew it. They feel that the process moves forward, and become confident. They notice improvement and discover more facts. A client re-experienced being raped when she was four. She described strong feelings: it burst in her pelvis, her heart pounded as if it exploded, it went to her head, she fell in a black hole, and then she died. I reflected that it felt as if she died. She shouted: 'I had died!' She believed she had died. Afterwards, she asked with surprise: 'But I did not die for real, did I ?'

Focusing language: body language

As the body is crucial, it is important to communicate with it. Focusing language points to the client's bodily felt sense. Questions of the therapist are directed to the client's body. The client repeats these questions inside, and waits for the body's answer. The answer is translated into language the therapist can understand. The body is the client's client (Gendlin, 1984). When clients begin to trust their body, they dare to practice focusing. The first step, clearing a space, gives a time-out when feelings are overwhelming. It is a moment to feel good, a safe place from which to watch their trauma. It helps to pace. The second step, getting a felt sense, makes a distinction between strong emotions and vague experiential feelings. The last carry the core of their trauma, and are felt under strong emotions. A client noticed a vague feeling under her strong emotions. It was the first time she had contact with it. She knew it had been there, and recognized it now as a 'felt sense'. Before, she was scared to feel and got upset by focusing words. Now she felt what was under the emotions: she had contact with her integrated self. The third step, finding a handle, gives the key to the felt sense. Clients feel strength and relief when they can name the crux of their trauma. By the fourth step, resonating, they feel a reinforcement of that relief, and a shift. They feel they are surviving and are getting further. The fifth step, asking, helps to ask new questions: what did really happen and what did matter, instead of what they had to believe. The sixth step, receiving, reinforces the experiential step (shift), and it helps to pace. Clients are vulnerable just after a shift, and may become 'structure-bound' (Coffeng, 1991; Iberg, 1981). Critical voices in their head destroy the shift. It happens often to trauma clients. The experiential shift is so new that they become anxious and tend to split again. Dominating alters take over. The sixth step is a break. One stays with the last felt shift and blocks the door against critical voices or top-alters.

Holding and containment.

It is hard for clients to stand strong feelings when they face their trauma. They fear they may explode and lose control. For such situations Pesso offers a holding technique. Group members hold the client. They form a container for strong feelings and connect the client with the ground. They protect the client's boundaries and form an 'ego-wrapping' (Pesso, 1988). It enables the client to process feelings. Such group members are absent in individual therapy, and the only one who could hold is the therapist. Physical contact, however, is condemned by many therapists, who suppose it would do harm to the symbolic or professional nature of therapy. Others distinguish between therapeutic and non-therapeutic contact, and they argue that physical contact can be symbolic, professional and a skill. They give guidelines and preconditions, so that contact becomes therapeutic and safe (Bohun, Ahern and Kiely, 1990; Durana, 1998; Hunter and Struwe, 1998; Pesso, 1984; Prouty, 1983). One precondition is the client's boundary (Olsen, 1982/83). Clients have their territory with a spatial boundary around it: it can be felt. By moving their chair clients can assess the boundary between them and therapist. They feel and check which distance is right. Focusing helps to define it (Gray, 1988). The therapist promises not to cross their border without their explicit permission. When clients experience this respect and feel they are in charge, they will ask the therapist to come near or to hold them when needed. Therapists should verbalize every step before doing it, and the client can check it. Whenever a client indicates to stop, or when it is unclear, the therapist steps backwards. Respect of the boundary makes holding safe.

Anxiety, pain and sadness

Three affective modes become apparent in the second phase. At first, confrontation with the trauma evokes shock and anxiety. Clients can no longer split when they face the event. It is followed by intensive pain when they refeel the abuse and see their beliefs collapse. Afterwards they enter a period of sadness and grief. They realize that emotionally they lost their parents, their innocence, childhood, and many following years due to their suffering. Before, they held to the belief that their parents loved them. When therapists recognize the affective mode, they find the right tone of support and understanding. Anxiety needs a specific support; pain needs a different response, and so does sadness. The pattern of these three affective modes can be observed in subsequent sessions, sometimes within one session.

B. Symbolic experiencing: the power of images

In the second phase of therapy, the memory of clients about the trauma is no longer fragmented. Meanwhile, their process has become symbolic as well. It corresponds with the 'self-integrating stage' of Prouty's Pre-Symbolic Process. Instead of dissociating, clients feel the crux of their experience and they can give words to it. They can express what it did to them. It is different from what they believed. They find different words. Words and images become symbolic: they have a meaning and capture the emotional and cognitive aspects of the client's experience. The right words bring relief and have an experiential effect: they carry the client's experiencing forward. They need experiential reflections (Gendlin, 1968), which convey not only compassion, but also sensitivity of the context of the trauma. The therapeutic language is symbolic.

In this phase, previous words of the clients come back, but now with a meaning: they have become symbolic. The therapist begins to understand what previous pre-symbolic words meant, and the events to which they referred. In the first phase the client was still 'pre-expressive' (Prouty, 1999) and could use only condensed telegraphic words. Words which were strange before begin to make sense now and appear to have been a key. Previously frozen words come alive and have meaning. It is the most interesting aspect of the Pre-Symbolic Process.

Imagery

Not only the traumatic events can be expressed in symbolic and semantic language; the recovery from the trauma needs symbolic language as well. Imagery is a powerful instrument. Words have a limitation, as they are associated with thinking. Clients tend to think what they were supposed to think. Criticized by internal voices, they become entangled in 'structure bound' or 'dead-end' functioning (Gendlin, 1996). Olsen introduced imagery (Gendlin and Olsen, 1970). Images and symbols often catch the crux of a felt sense better than words. At the same time they leave space for different meanings. They give also emotional space and perspective. Imagery, which was helpful for clients with grief, appears to fit trauma clients as well (Coffeng, 1992; Santen, 1993). They discover its power and their own symbolic energy.

Reconstructing the past

A precondition for recovery is to re-establish the truth: to confirm that the trauma happened. Clients were forced to deny the truth. There was no witness. It is crucial for them to have a person who can testify what happened. Pesso (1990) introduces a group member who acts as a witness: he confirms what happened and expresses that it was bad. Symbolically he is a witness who should have been present at the time of the trauma. He supports the client to believe her eyes and her felt sense. In individual therapy a witness can be imagined. The therapist verbalizes what a witness would say. The image can be extended into a court, where a witness testifies before the judge. The client is shocked to believe her memory, but she is reassured that what she felt was true.

Gendlin (1991/92/94, 1993) introduced the concept of the 'blue print'. It is the body's sense of what is needed. Not only physically (food) or emotionally (contact), but also the need for truth. The blue print knows what happened. A child knows if something is correctly named or not. Clients were forced to disbelieve what they felt and to suppress their blue print. When the truth can be said, the blue print gets air. It confirms what happened. The 'blue print' has also to do with moral rules. It knows what is right or wrong. Children should not be abused, the truth not be distorted, lies not be believed. The body knows what should not, and what should have happened. This inner morality was suppressed, as clients had to accept false rules from people on whom they depended. It is important to restore the 'blue print' with proper moral rules. One says: 'It (trauma) should not have happened!' Clients are asked: 'What should have happened?' When they don't know, therapists assist to imagine it and clients check inside. Their 'blue print' is the basis. This way, there is no risk that therapists impose new rules.

Gendlin (1994) mentions two realities. One reality is that the trauma happened. This statement is relieving: what the client felt was true. Another reality is that it should not have happened and to find out what should have happened. Clients are mixed up by these two realities. They are loyal to false rules of caregivers, and cannot believe normal parents exist. They think all parents are like their parents. It helps to make a distinction between the reality of what happened and the reality of what should have happened. It is done by the following statements: 'It did happen. It is bad that it happened. It should not have happened.' Then one asks: 'What should have happened?' Clients consult their blue print and make it concrete with an image.

Clients need alternatives for the trauma and its context, having no idea of a normal and safe family. In Pesso-therapy, group members act as 'ideal parents', saying what normal parents should say. Clients can feel contact with normal parents. This new experience restores the blue print. In individual therapy, clients must imagine ideal parents with their fantasy. Therapists assist to make it concrete. They verbalize what normal parents would do and say. Clients check inside if it fits. Reconstruction is the bulk of the second phase. Clients have strong loyal ties with former caregivers and perpetrators. They cling to their lies. It takes time and repetition to correct it and to rephrase proper moral rules.

Symbolic energy

The second phase has two sides. It is heavy, as clients face the full reality of the trauma. Having strong feelings, they try to understand how it could have happened, realizing the betrayal. On the other hand, they feel their feet on firm soil, since the truth is confirmed. They discover the power of imagery. They can imagine what should have happened, which was suppressed before as an illusion. Clients have a tremendous symbolic energy. They need hardly to be encouraged. They bring dolls to act as witnesses. They have dolls to protect them at home. They use a towel as an 'ego-skin'. They make drawings when talking is difficult. They bring tapes with music they find comforting. One client showed a drawing of her foot. She had made it after a dream in which she was invisible. Before, she made herself invisible by walking on her toes. Now, the drawing symbolized that she could stand on her feet and be present. While the integration of the trauma takes much energy, energy comes back with imagery.

Integration

Grief and sadness dominate the second phase. Clients realize they have had no proper care-givers and no safe childhood. A whole part of their life is wasted by the consequences of the trauma. When a child, there was no one to whom they could express their grief. Now, there is a place for it. Grief feelings can be channelled with focusing and imagery. Clients imagine ceremonies in which they part from perpetrators, caregivers, and other aspects of their past. They find consolation. They realize it is the past. They no longer have anxiety about the present or future. Instead of frightful flashbacks, they have a narrative memory of the traumatic past. It is an important change. Tears become the water to clean false concepts and to clear the way to new concepts and new persons with whom to relate. Much has to be integrated. Clients have become capable of doing so since they can focus. They find trust in their feelings: what they felt was right. They find power in symbols and images. With the help of imagery, words become cleaned from their old meaning and get new meanings and perspectives.

5. CONCLUSION

Different modes of experiencing have been described, which correspond to sequential therapy phases of dissociative clients. In the first phase, the process is pre-experiential, pre-symbolic, repetitive and slow. Dissociation is prominent. A critical episode announces the second phase, in which the process becomes experiential and symbolic. The client's affect changes from anxiety and pain to sadness. When these phases are recognized, one can adapt to the client's process with one's tone, language and speed. Words which are used in a symbolic way can be taken literally by the client. If therapists adjust their language in time, crises can be prevented. In fact, crises may give feedback about previous interventions.

The presented model differs from the official treatment model of dissociation (van der Hart, van der Kolk and Boon, 1998). The latter is phasic too, but rather it is a program to be followed, than one that follows the client's process. The therapy of multiple trauma has many other aspects. The relationship and (counter-)transference have special qualities (McCann and Coletti, 1994). There are techniques to contact the different identities of DID-clients (Chu, 1994). This therapy, intensive and long lasting, has to be embedded in a network. Therapists need co-therapists; clients need friends or others for assistance. All these aspects could not be discussed here, but they can be found elsewhere (Kluft and Fine, 1993; Putnam, 1989; Ross, 1997).

REFERENCES

Adshead, G. (2000). Psychological therapies for Post-Traumatic Stress Disorder. *British Journal of Psychiatry*, *177*, 144–78.

Bohun, E., Ahern, R. and Kiely, L. (1990). The use of therapeutic touch. Unpublished paper, 7th Annual. Conference on Dissociation and Multiple Personality Disorder, Chicago.

Braun, B. G. (1986). Issues in the psychotherapy of multiple personality disorder. In B. G. Braun, (Ed.) *Treatment of Multiple Personality Disorder*. Washington DC: American Psychiatric Press.

Chu, J. (1994). The rational treatment of multiple personality disorder. *Psychotherapy*, *31* (1), 94–100.

Coffeng, T. (1991). The phasing and timing of focusing in therapy. *The Folio, J. for Focusing and Experiential Therapy*, *10* (3), 40–50.

Coffeng, T. (1992a). Focusing and grief. The *Folio*, *11* (2), 41–8.

Coffeng, T. (1992b). *Recontacting the Child*. Video, International Focusing Conference, Chicago.

Coffeng, T. (1992c). Recontacting the Child. *The Folio*, *11* (3), 11–21. *GwG-Zeitschrift*, *25* (93), 5–12.

Coffeng, T. (1994). *The delicate approach to early trauma*. Video, ICCCEP, Gmunden, Austria.

Coffeng, T. (1995.) *Multiple traumatization and dissociation*. Blueprint for a therapeutic approach. Unpublished paper.

Coffeng, T. (1996a). The delicate approach to early trauma. In R. Hutterer, G. Pawlowsky, P. F. Schmid and R. Stipsits (Eds.) *Client-centered and Experiential Psychotherapy; a paradigm in motion*. Frankfurt am Main: Peter Lang, pp. 499–511.

Coffeng, T. (1996b). Experiential and pre-experiential therapy for multiple trauma. In U. Esser, H. Pabst and G-W. Speierer (Eds.) *The Power of the Person-centered Approach*. Köln: GwG, pp. 185–203..

Coffeng. T. (1997a). *Pre-experiential contact with dissociation*. Video, ICCCEP, Lisbon, Portugal.

Coffeng, T. (1998). Pre-experiencing: a way to contact trauma and dissociation. In H. J. Feuerstein, D. Müller and A. Weiser Cornell (Eds.) *Focusing im Prozess*, pp. 51–61. Köln: GwG, pp. 51–61. (German, 2000).

Coffeng, T. (1999). *Two phases of dissociation*. Video. Netherlands Trauma Conference, Amsterdam.

Coffeng, T. (2000b). *Two phases of dissociation, two languages*. 3 videotapes. ICCCEP, Chicago, USA.

Coffeng, T. (2000c). *Rogerian aspects of recovery from trauma*. Lecture Leuven, Belgium. Flemish Association Client-centered Therapy.

Durana, C. (1998). The use of touch in psychotherapy: ethical and clinical guidelines. *Psychotherapy*,

35 (2), 269–80.

Elliott, R., Slatick, E. and Urman, M. (2000). 'So the Fear is Like a Thing.' A significant empathic exploration event in Process-Experiential Therapy for PTSD. In J. Marques-Teixeira and S. Antunes (Eds.) *Client-Centered and Experiential Psychotherapy*, pp. 179–204. Linda a Velha: Vale and Vale, pp. 179–204.

Gendlin, E. T. (1964). A theory of personality change. In P, Worchel and D. Byrne (Eds.) *Personality Change*, 4. New York: Wiley, pp. 100–48.

Gendlin, E. T. (1968). The experiential response. In E. Hammer (Ed.) *The Use of Interpretation in Treatment*. New York: Grune and Stratton, pp. 208–28.

Gendlin, E. T. (1981). *Focusing*. New York: Bantam

Gendlin, E. T. (1984). The client's client. In R. F. Levant and J. M. Shlien (Eds.) *Client-Centered Therapy and the Person-centered Approach*. New York: Praeger, pp. 76–107.

Gendlin, E. T. (1990). The small steps of the therapy process: how they come and how to help them come. In G. Lietaer, J. Rombauts and R. Van Balen (Eds.) *Client-centered and Experiential Psychotherapy in the Nineties*. Leuven: Leuven University Press, pp. 205–24.

Gendlin, E. T. (1991, '92, '94). *Focusing in the interactional space*. Therapists workshop, Chicago and Weingarten, Germany.

Gendlin, E. T. (1993). *Focusing ist eine kleine Tür*. Würzburg: DAF, Focusing Bibliothek, Band 4.

Gendlin, E. T. (1996). *Focusing-oriented Psychotherapy*. New York: Guilford Press.

Gray, L. (1990). The function of the boundary in facilitating experiential focusing. *The Focusing Folio*, 9 (3), 112–27.

Hart, O. van der, Kolk, B. van der and Boon, S. (1998). Treatment of dissociative disorders. In J. D. Bremner and C. R. Marmar (Eds.) *Trauma, Memory and Dissociation*. Washington DC: American Psychiatric Press, pp. 253–83.

Herman, J. J. (1992). *Trauma and Recovery*. New York: Basic Books.

Hunter, M. and Struwe, J. (1998). *The ethical use of touch in psycho-therapy*. London: Sage.

Hyer, L., Woods, G. and Boudewyns, P. (1991) PTSD and alexithymia: Importance of emotional clarification in treatment. *Psychotherapy*, 28, 129–38.

Iberg, J. R. (1981) Focusing. In J. R. Corsini (Ed.) *Handbook of Innovative Psychotherapies*. New York: Wiley, pp. 334–61.

ICCCEP Video, International Conference Client-centered and Experiential Psychotherapy, Stirling, UK.

Kluft, R. P. and Fine, C. G. (Eds.) (1993). *Clinical Perspectives on Multiple Personality Disorder*. Washington DC: American Psychiatric Press.

Kolk, B. van der (1996). The body keeps the score. In B. van der Kolk and A. C. McFarlane, A.C. (Eds.), *Traumatic Stress*. New York: Guilford Press, pp. 214–41.

Marmar, C. R., Weiss, D. S. and Metzler, Th. (1998). Peritraumatic Dissociation and Posttraumatic Stress Disorder. In J. D. Bremner and C. R. Marmar (Eds.) *Trauma, Memory and Dissociation*. Washington DC: American Psychiatric Press, pp. 229–52.

McCann, I. L. and Coletti, I. (1994). The dance of empathy. In J. P. Wilson and J. D. Lindi (Eds.) *Countertransference in the Treatment of PTSD*. New York: Guilford Press, pp. 87–121.

Olsen, L. (1982/83). How I do body work. *The Folio*, 2 (3), 1–8.

Olsen, L. (1983). *Focusing and Imagery*. Breda, Netherlands: Workshop Breda.

Pesso, A. (1984). Touch and action — the use of the body in psychotherapy. *Bewegen en Hulpverlening*, 1 (4), 254–9.

Pesso, A. (1988). Sexual abuse, the integrity of the body. *Bewegen en Hulpverlening*, 5, 270–81.

Pesso, A. (1990). Center of truth, true scene and pilot in Pesso system/psychomotor therapy. *Bulletin Netherlands Association Pessotherapy*, 6 (2), 13–21

Prouty, G. F. (1976). Pre-Therapy, a method of treating pre-expressive psychotic and retarded patients.

Psychotherapy: Theory, *Research and Practice, 13* (3), 290–4.

Prouty, G. F. (1977). Proto-symbolic method: A phenomenological treatment of schizophrenic hallucinations. *Journal of Mental Imagery, 1* (2), 339–42.

Prouty, G. F. (1981). *Pre-therapy and Proto-symbolic Method.* Workshop 1st International Focusing Weeklong, University of Chicago.

Prouty, G. F. (1983). Hallucinatory Contact: a phenomenological treatment of schizophrenics. *Journal of Communication Therapy, 2* (1), 99–103.

Prouty, G. F. (1986). The Pre-Symbolic structure and therapeutic transformation of hallucinations. In J. Shorr and L. Krueger (Eds) *Imagery.* London: Plenum, pp. 99–106.

Prouty, G. F. (1990). A theoretical evolution in the person-centered/experiential psychotherapy of schizophrenia and retardation. In G. Lietaer, J. Rombauts and R. Van Balen, R. (Eds.) *Client-centered and Experiential Psychotherapy in the Nineties.* Leuven: Leuven University Press, pp. 645–85.

Prouty, G. F. (1991). The pre-symbolic structure and processing of schizophrenic hallucinations: the problematic of a non-process structure. In L. Fusek (Ed.) *New Directions in Client-centered Therapy. Practice with difficult client populations.* Chicago: The Chicago Counseling Center, pp. 18–40.

Prouty, G. F. (1994). *Theoretical Evolutions in Person-Centered/Experiential Therapy. Applications to schizophrenic and retarded psychoses.* New York: Praeger.

Prouty, G. F. (1998). Pre-Therapy and the Pre-Expressive self. *Person-Centered Practice, 6* (2), 80–8.

Prouty, G. F. (1999). *Restoration of Contact.* Symposium and workshop. Leeuwarden, The Netherlands.

Putnam, F. W. (1999). *The long-term psychobiological effects of child abuse.* Netherlands Trauma Conference, Amsterdam.

Putnam, F. W. (1989). *Diagnosis and Treatment of Multiple Personality Disorders.* New York: Guilford Press.

Ravesteyn, L. van (1978). De gelaagdheid van emoties. *Tijdschrift voor Psychotherapie, 4* (4), 175–85.

Rogers, C.R. (1957). The necessary and sufficient conditions of therapeutic personality change. *Journal of Consulting Psychology, 21* (2), 95–103.

Rogers, C.R. (Ed.) (1967). *The Therapeutic Relationship and its Impact.* Madison: University of Wisconsin Press.

Ross, C. (1997). *Dissociative Identity Disorder.* New York: Wiley.

Santen, B. (1993). Focusing with a dissociated adolescent. The *Folio, 12* (2), 45–58.

Steele, K. (1995). *Traumatic Memory: Concepts and treatment techniques.* Workshop, 5th Annual Conference of the International Society of the Study of Dissociation. Amsterdam.

Terr, L. (1994). *Unchained Memories: True stories of traumatic memories, lost and found.* New York: Basic Books.

van Werde, D. (1998a). 'Anchorage' as a core concept in working with psychotic people. In B. Thorne and E. Lambers (Eds.) *Person-centred Therapy, A European perspective.* London: Sage, pp. 195–205.

van Werde, D. (1998b). Prä-Therapie im Alltag einer psychiatrischen Station. In G. Prouty, D. van Werde and M. Pörtner (Eds.) *Prä-Therapie.* Stuttgart: Klett-Cotta, pp. 87–158. (English trans., 2002. Ross-on-Wye, UK: PCCS Books.)

Ned L. Gaylin PhD
University of Maryland College Park

The Relationship: The heart of the matter[1]

INTRODUCTION

Following a workshop on Person-Centered Family Therapy last year, I had, thanks to one of the participants, an epiphany. It was at lunch on the last day and we were chatting about what I might have omitted, should have added, or could have done better. In general the participants were exceedingly kind. But repeatedly I was gently remonstrated for what I inferred was my condescending attitude. That is, I was told that the participants were well-trained seasoned therapists; they had no need to go over basics. What they needed and wanted was help in understanding the methods and techniques unique to my work with children and families.

I was puzzled and a tad hurt by the comments. I was hurt, because I did not feel one whit of superiority and thus felt misunderstood. This was an exceedingly well-trained group — many with much experience. My respect and admiration for them and their teachers, I thought, was evident. I was puzzled, because I could not figure out what I had done to convey this erroneous attitude. On the plane home it occurred to me that what the group perceived as basic — 'old ground' — was material that I considered essential to understanding what Person-Centered Family Therapy is about: the necessary and sufficient conditions for psychotherapeutic change. Despite the fact that, on the surface, family therapy appears so different from individual therapy, methodologically it is not.

When working with children, couples, and families there is little that I do differently from that which I do when working with individuals. Actually, what *is* different is the conceptual extension of the conditions as they apply to more than one person in the intimate context of the family, which in turn amends my focus and attitude. Therefore, I continually return to the essential fundamentals to remind myself how the process is framed.

The conditions serve to keep me on track when I tend to stray. Their richness continues to edify me as I explore their meaning and ramifications. Thus, I begin virtually all of my work by reviewing them. This is all by way of explaining that I do not mean to be simplistic or presumptuous when I present the conditions now.

[1.] A version of this chapter was first published in Gaylin, N. L., (2001). *Family, Self, and Psychotherapy: A person-centred perspective.* Ross-on-Wye: PCCS Books. Reprinted by permission of the author and publisher.

THE CONDITIONS[2]

The conditions are:
1. Two persons are in psychological contact.
2. The first, whom we shall term the client, is in a state of incongruence, being vulnerable or anxious.
3. The second person, whom we shall term the therapist, is congruent or integrated in the relationship.
4. The therapist experiences unconditional positive regard for the client.
5. The therapist experiences an empathic understanding of the client's frame of reference and endeavors to communicate this experience to the client.
6. The communication to the client of the therapist's empathic understanding and unconditional positive regard is to a minimal degree achieved (Rogers, 1957, p. 96).

My primary focus today is upon the first of the six conditions: that of psychological contact — the relationship. This condition has been virtually overlooked. Yet in my work as a family therapist it stands out as lynchpin for all the rest, not so much because I behave differently with families than with individuals, but because my thinking and attitude are extended to all family members and their interrelationships.

Moreover, as I began setting down my thoughts for today's presentation I reminded myself that the conditions are an integral whole, none separable from the others. What's more, invariably I am taken aback when I see some theorists and practitioners telescope the classic six conditions into three, namely genuineness, unconditional positive regard, and empathy. What is continually omitted in this cryptic summary are the first two and last conditions. For me, these three neglected conditions — particularly the first and the last — are central to our understanding of how and why psychotherapy works.

I think the reason we have focused on the conditions of genuineness, unconditional positive regard and empathy is that that they relate to the conduct of the therapist. Indeed, these three conditions encapsulate the single method of the Person-Centered approach. As therapists we are more or less in charge of these behaviors: we can observe them in research, teach them in training, and critique them in supervision or consultation. Thus, it makes sense to concentrate on those conditions that we presume drive the therapeutic process and over which we ideally should have some control. [3]

Penultimately we attend to the second condition — that which impels our clients into therapy — their incongruence. The first and the last conditions, however, we tend to disregard. So did Rogers. There is little elaboration of them in the original statement and little exegesis regarding them since.

[2.] It is worthy of note that a seminal paper by Jules Seeman (1951, reprinted 1994) predates Rogers' and contains all of the therapist conditions.

[3.] A therapist variable, the condition of therapist congruence is an inherent characteristic and less obviously manipulable than both unconditional positive regard and empathy. It also is somewhat more vague. We attempt to explain it by calling it *genuineness, presence, transparency,* and if feeling unshakably incongruent in the hour, concern ourselves with the need for self-disclosure. It should be emphasized that even in this condition, the first is alluded to. It does not state that the therapist is congruent, but rather that the therapist is congruent *in the relationship.*

THE THERAPIST IN THE RELATIONSHIP

About the first condition — the relationship — Rogers, in his classic 1957 paper, mused that 'perhaps it should be labeled an assumption, or a precondition.' Although he noted that without it, the others would have no meaning — indeed, he elaborated that the following five conditions really define the first. In so saying he placed this condition as central. Until recently, I do not believe I had ever fully attended to the one statement that makes the first condition so interesting and complex. Rogers notes that what he means by *psychological contact* is that client and therapist 'each makes some perceived difference in the experiential field of the other.' He later even qualifies the word *perceived*, settling for *subceived*. The bottom line is the reciprocal interaction between client and therapist.

By reciprocal I do not mean that the interaction is either parallel or equal. It is not. I am there to serve my clients in a professional capacity. There are generally rather formal contractual arrangements. We meet at a prescribed scheduled hour for a given period of time, and clients generally compensate me. All of these constraints, and more, set the therapeutic relationship apart from most others. But the key issue is my clients' impact upon my experiential field. Despite the excellence of my didactic teachers, my clients were those from whom I learned the most.

Indeed, my first client at the University of Chicago Counseling Center was perhaps my best mentor. We were both graduate students, she in a different department than I. She was a couple of years ahead of me in school, a few years older, and a whole lot smarter. She continuously challenged my thinking about what I was doing and why. Shortly after we began our sessions together, one of her first admonishments was: 'You're nothing but a goddam whore — selling your love for money.' No matter that as an intern I received no money for my services, I felt hurt and humiliated. I was too young to realize that I might have been gratified that she sensed my caring, my *unconditional positive regard* for her. I remember going with anguish to Jack Butler, my supervisor at the time. He looked at me with a somewhat wry smile and unhelpfully replied, 'What's the matter with being a whore — if you're a good one?' My priggishness aside, it took a few years for me to come to grips with the fact that it was my time that was being procured. My love carried no price and could only be freely given. Nevertheless, questions of what the therapist does and what the therapeutic relationship is have led me to the conclusion that, among other things, psychotherapy clearly is an activity with profound moral implications.

This same client also taught me about pacing. Following one of my overzealous reflections of feelings, she snapped, 'It took me 30 years to develop these problems. Who the hell do you think you are to try to solve them in 30 minutes?' Each client has a pace that is comfortable and that pace varies, not just from client to client but for the same client at different times. The therapist needs to be empathic not only with the client's frame of reference or worldview, but also the style and tempo of the client's readiness for hearing even empathic responses. This is a subtle point often lost on beginning therapists who are eager to effect change as rapidly as possible, and for whom silence is consequently often unbearable.

Similarly, regarding style, pacing, and communication in the relationship, children are perhaps the best instructors of therapists. Even when disturbed, children exhibit little guile, though they may be wary. They are direct rather than oblique and, even when nonverbal, are very communicative. Thus, another of my best teachers was an eleven-year-old boy, whom I will call Leroy. Leroy was referred because of his deteriorating school performance and growing aggressive behavior with age-mates and authority figures alike. He was a large lad entering adolescence — looking perhaps two or three years older than his 11 years. He was taciturn and wore a perpetual scowl. I can well imagine how he intimidated those around him. I was looking for another Dibs, a butterfly ready to emerge from its chrysalis. At the time, what I thought I got was a slug eating holes in my verdant fantasies about psychotherapy. It took a few years for me to realize that what I had, in actuality, was a young swan masquerading as an ugly duckling.

I saw Leroy twice a week for over six months. During all of the time I was with him he said virtually nothing. In the first weeks, at the beginning of sessions, I would try reflecting what I thought was his mood, which I interpreted from the expression on his face. He would neither validate nor invalidate this effort at reflection. Then we would sit. He would then test me. He would stretch his legs out — I would stretch mine. He would knock the soles of his shoes together — I would knock mine. It became a kind of elaborate non-verbal 'Simon Says.' And I was going crazy. Charlotte Ellinwood, my supervisor, would watch patiently behind the one-way mirror. After the sessions, when I started expressing my frustration, she would calm me by saying we were 'really establishing a relationship' and that I was 'developing rapport.' She apparently saw what I could not.

I had little idea what I was doing and what was happening. I was there — at his service. He never missed a session. As time progressed, reports from his mother indicated that things were improving both at home and at school. Perhaps it was simply maturation. In working with children I have grown increasingly more humble, realizing that we often take credit for God's work. Indeed, the old saw about Virginia Axline and Dibs was that she was as good a diagnostician as therapist, plucking Dibs just at the moment of his flowering. Perhaps this was also true for Leroy.[4]

For years after our formal work together, much to my amazement, Leroy, who lived only blocks away from me in Hyde Park, would pop by my apartment on a Saturday or Sunday. First he came by to show me a new bike or a pair of athletic shoes, later to meet his friends — first male, then female. He still spoke little, but smiled more easily. I began feeling less awkward about our nonverbal interactions, taking pleasure in his initiative and demonstrated desire to have me continue to share in his life in some small way. Clearly, although I might neither have seen nor understood it, something about my relationship with this lad had meaning. The nonjudgmental stance took on new meaning.

It was Carl Whittaker, one my first supervisors in family therapy, who summed it up most elegantly, I think. I casually asked him once how he knew when therapy was over. Without hesitating he replied, 'When the therapist stops growing in the relationship.'

Thus, the relationship is clearly one of growth for both client and therapist. The therapist learns to follow the client — in whatever way that client needs following. I have put it to my students this way:

> *The client is the theory. Come with no preconceptions. You have but one task — to learn from the client. You are there to learn the language of the client, not vice versa. When you lose the notion that you are the servant of the client, it is time to seek help for yourself. We need to be humbled by the enormous confidence and responsibility with which our clients entrust us.*

[4.] Perhaps it is true for the vast majority of our clients. After all, 50 percent improve just from being on the waiting list.

However, if therapists are servants, what rewards for them are inherent in the therapeutic relationship other than learning to serve well? Is the relationship entirely one-sided? What does the therapist's growth in the relationship mean? Although therapists usually receive payment for their time and expertise, there are probably more remunerative and less taxing means of being gainfully employed. As an educator of therapists I am impressed with the drive-like quality — the sense of *calling* that impels our students to apprentice as therapists. The first quality that stands out is giftedness, or talent. Virtually all of our prospective students report experiences wherein others have given them positive feedback for their empathic interactions with them. Friends and family seek them out as 'good listeners.' Reciprocally, our candidates and beginning therapists report feeling good about doing good. There is an allocentric as opposed to egocentric quality that they convey: the most gifted radiate an almost grace-like quality.

I once asked one of Rogers' clients, a therapist himself, what he thought made Rogers such a great therapist. The response (through a telling anecdote) was Rogers' concentration and focus on the client. 'When Rogers is with you, you feel bathed by his attention: The world disappears — and you and he are alone in some special place.' I know that when I am deeply focused within the therapeutic relationship I am my best self — my dark side, my warts and scars, are sequestered. I am conscious of myself primarily as an amplifier of another, but yet I feel whole, at one with myself and very much alive in the moment. It is exactly this quality of wholeness, integration — even at times a sense of *peak experience* — that I think the third condition alludes to when noting 'the therapist is congruent in the relationship.' Indeed, I can go into the hour feeling ill with a headache, but if I can mobilize my concentration and put my focus entirely on the client, my headache disappears — I am not even aware that it has done so.[5] We sometimes refer to this quality of therapist congruence as *presence.* But there is vagueness to this term that somehow eludes me, whereas focus connotes an additional dimension that is easier to convey.

I note, too, that my memory is enhanced. I have a terrible memory, and it is growing worse. It has always been bad for both names and telephone numbers. I am loath to admit that at times I will walk into the therapy hour and, with horror, realize that I cannot retrieve my clients' names. But I can remember details about their lives that amaze both them and me. This is true for clients who return many years later. This is not a skill I have worked at or in any way actively practice. It is there — sui generis. I do know that such recall enhances my empathy and gives me a sense of closeness to my client, adding richness and depth to my feelings for them

Thus, when at my best in the therapy relationship, there is a sense of intimacy — a richness and reciprocity — a fulfillment as therapist that I experience during such periods. I do not believe that any of us can maintain such concentration for extensive periods. Rather, I think the time-limited nature of the therapy hour allows the exertion of a special congruence — a special focus or concentration. This kind of special ability to focus, I believe, is what makes being a therapist experientially gratifying. Such concentration is not unlike that of artists enrapt in the process of their craft, be it sculpting or music-making.

[5.] This is a puzzling phenomenon. If my focus in the hour is true congruence — where I am freely and openly experiencing the totality of my being — then, at some level, I should be aware of my headache: Unless, of course, the headache was a symptom of my previous incongruence.

The importance of the relationship is augmented and takes on added dimension in the Person-Centered Approach to working with families. But unlike other so called *systems approaches,* genuine, caring, empathic responding is the sole method — there is no need for an elaborate paradigmatic shift when moving from working with individuals to working with families. What changes is that all family members are being related to individually in the intimate context of their family. The therapist maintains empathy and caring for each individual both separately as well as in concert.

THE CLIENT IN THE RELATIONSHIP

As therapists, we are expected to be in touch with who we are and what we feel during the therapy hour and in the therapy relationship, but what about the client in the relationship? We do know from our clients' reports that they come to us troubled — incongruent. But we do not always know why. Indeed, some of our clients may not know why they are incongruent. Especially with young children, and the severely disturbed, this is often the case. Even when clients do know why they are impelled to seek help, they do not always tell us — at least not right away. Many, perhaps most, clients may well delay sharing their deepest, darkest secrets until they assess the tenor of the relationship with their therapists and their respective therapists' trustworthiness (Rennie, 1990). Some clients have told me that they *never* disclosed their heart of hearts to their previous therapists.

Here is where the traditional core conditions — namely four and five, unconditional positive regard, and empathy — come into play. These two conditions are more complex than they appear at first glance. Condition four really is two conditions. It is unconditional regard — that is a non-judgmental stance; but it is also positive regard, namely caring, or love. I prefer to think of the two aspects of this condition separately. I believe one can regard someone nonjudgmentally but dispassionately. That is I can be fully open to someone, not placing any valence on that person's behavior, yet not necessarily care about her or him. Conversely I can love someone deeply and still be critical of specific qualities or behaviors. It is just this association between this condition's two aspects that give its totality additive power. We presume that these three qualities of the therapist's stance — that is nonjudgmental, caring, empathy — establish a venue of trust, which enables our clients to shed, or at least lower, their masks.

What is rarely discussed is *how* a relationship can enable healing.[6] This process is articulated most clearly in Rogers' (1959) most comprehensive theory paper, and one of the few theoretical statements that enunciate how deep-seated incongruences develop. The explanation requires the introduction of a key, though rarely discussed, concept in Person-Centered theory — namely, *conditions of worth*. Also, it assumes that we all require positive regard to thrive.

Early in life, the developing individual begins to recognize that certain behaviors elicit approbation — that is positive regard — and certain behaviors elicit disapproval. Thus, there are conditions under which the individual perceives that love is granted and certain conditions wherein love is withheld. Thereby, a person's feelings of self-worth or self-esteem are shaped. Though never stated directly, the implication is that within the therapy hour's interpersonal

---

[6.] Rogers is clear that psychotherapy is not the only relationship which promotes healing (Rogers, 1961)

loving, nonjudgmental, empathic climate, early previously instilled *conditions of worth* can be mitigated and clients may be free to be completely themselves. Hence, the importance of *unconditional* positive regard — love given unequivocally.

Herein lies one of my few difficulties with the Person-Centered framework. The inference too easily allowed for is that *conditions of worth* are inherently derogatory — always having negative impact, impairing the process of self-actualization. Contrarily I would argue that there is, perhaps, greater danger of unconditional positive regard than of regard conditionally given. Civil society and living in concert impose conditions; without such conditions life would be anarchy — hell. Self-entitlement and self-indulgence lead to evil — the self-serving abuse of power. Nonetheless, in the first few months of life and in the state of complete dependency, most infants experience unconditional positive regard and appropriately so. We indulge the neonate because of its total helplessness. Its survival depends upon our full and unreserved attention to its needs. Nature even helps by making neonates of virtually all species utterly adorable.

It could very well be that the sense of total acceptance within the therapy hour is inherently reminiscent of those early months wherein caretakers' unquestioningly and unqualifiedly gave nurture to the infant and the infant experienced total acceptance and gratification of its every need. We infer the neonatal period to be one of virtual total self-centeredness, and perhaps the therapy hour emulates the ability of individuals to be totally focused on their needs — self-indulgently introspective, yet simultaneously within the interpersonal context of a relationship. That was my experience of therapy as a client. I felt swaddled and protected emotionally. I could ramble, have a tantrum, cry — even though 'big boys don't' — could feel and express anything, and my therapist would try — usually quite successfully — to be there and make sense of what I was experiencing. I felt emotionally succored, even indulged. There were times I felt almost literally held and rocked by him.

However, there are experiences that are contradictory to the intense closeness described above. For example there is the *stranger-on-the-plane* phenomenon, where by dint of the knowledge that the individual is not a part of one's life — that one will never encounter that person again, one can unburden oneself of one's troubles. People report feeling driven to go into great detail and feel better after such disclosures. Can these experiences illuminate the psychotherapeutic relationship? Here is another human being — one not anticipated ever again to be a part of one's life — acting as a sounding board, and offering a measure of solace from emotional pain, just by being there. Ironically — it is the knowledge that the relationship is circumscribed and quite limited that appears to enable catharsis and therapeusis. Perhaps it is the very circumscribed nature of the relationship and its promise of anonymity that, at least in part, enables its power. Although as therapists, we respect and make every effort to vouchsafe the client's right of confidentiality, we do not explore it as a variable. Perhaps we should.

As a graduate student in Chicago, over 40 years ago I heard Stan Lipkin give a paper titled 'Round Robin Therapy,' that, like the *strangers-on-a-plane* phenomenon, struck at the heart of the notion of a long-term relationship being crucial to successful psychotherapy. A client who had asked Lipkin to be her therapist could not afford his fee. Rather than turn her down he offered her the opportunity to meet sequentially for one session with each of 20 of Chicago's most prestigious therapists. The client reported the experience as a great success. When questioned about having to tell her tale anew 20 times she reported that she experienced no feelings of redundancy, but rather learned something each time she met with a new therapist.

Similarly, during my training at the Counseling Center, when students were deemed ready to see clients, the senior staff would offer 'experienced' clients whom they had been seeing, the opportunity to meet with a novice therapist gratis. Although new students were initially terrified, invariably clients reported the experiences as positive — sometimes to the experienced therapists' chagrin — requesting additional sessions with the novitiate. Indeed, it may be that a fresh therapeutic presence may offer the client new experiential data via the interaction. Furthermore, like Lipkin's round-robin therapy, the new therapist may, in fact, validate the client's recognition that the healing force — i.e., self-actualization — resides within the client rather than results from the expertise of the therapist.

One final piece of anecdotal data regards clients' reports of their therapy and therapists in a study I read many years ago, regarding therapeutic behavior modification. This was the period when behaviorists held that a neutral stance was de rigueur, and prided themselves on the objective, aloof stance of scientists. Conditioning was the definitive behavioral method — the person of the therapist and the relationship were considered confounding rather than facilitative variables. Assiduous recording and note taking regarding the clients' behavior was mandatory. Clients debriefed following a successful course of therapy reported that what was important to them was their therapist's concern and care, evidenced by their great attention to the clients and their behavior.

This brings us to the seemingly most obvious throwaway condition, the sixth, wherein the client perceives (at least to some degree) the therapist's empathy and positive regard. One might add, even if it isn't there! Or maybe it is there even when the therapist believes it is not.

It is the last condition that truly is the heart of the matter. It is the last condition which makes all therapy client-centered. Lest we forget, the conditions do not define the Person-Centered Approach. Rather, we have adapted our approach to the knowledge that these conditions alone are both necessary and sufficient. What other therapy approaches struggle with is the sufficiency of the conditions — their necessity has generally been conceded. That the worldview of the client is paramount — even if it is what others may consider distorted or erroneous, is what most other therapy models contest.

I recall working with a young 20-year-old man, diagnosed as schizophrenic. When he first came to my office he claimed to have visions of Jesus Christ, who spoke with him. He asked me if I believed him. I hesitated, but answered him by explaining that he and I had two problems. The first was that I was Jewish, and had a difficult time accepting the fact that Jesus was, indeed, the messiah. The second problem was that I had never had such a vision, and found it difficult to put myself in his shoes. But I added that I truly believed that he did have these visions, even though I did not understand them, and that I was interested in their meaning to him — as I truly was. I worried that my response would alienate or offend him. It did not. Rather he proceeded to talk to me about problems he was having with his girlfriend.

If clients believe that their therapist is working on their behalf — if they perceive caring and understanding — then therapy is likely to be successful. It is the condition of attachment and the perception of connection that has the power to release the faltered actualizing of the self. We all need to feel connected, prized — loved. We are a species born into mutual interdependence and there can be no self outside the context of others. Loneliness is dehumanizing and isolation anathema to the human condition. The relationship is what psychotherapy is about.

CONCLUSION

The human condition is one of relationships — of mutual interdependence. There have been healers of the troubled spirit as far back as we know. Their power may have been attributed to magic, the divine, or science. We, as psychotherapists, are but the most recent iteration of such healers. It behooves us to recognize that our clients' mending is a result of a growth motive internal to them; our presence is important only insofar as our clients recognize it as important. Thus, the source of our power resides in our clients and our relationship with them — in their belief in our belief in them

REFERENCES

Rennie, D. L. (1990). Toward a representation of the client's experience of the psychotherapy hour. In Lietaer, G., Rombauts, J., and Van Balen, R. (Eds.) *Client-centered and Experiential Psychotherapy in the Nineties*. Louvain, Belgium: Leuven University Press, pp. 155-172.

Rogers, C. R. (1957). The necessary and sufficient conditions of therapeutic personality change. *Journal of Consulting Psychology, 21*(2), 95-103.

Rogers, C. R. (1959). A theory of therapy, personality, and interpersonal relationships, as developed in the client-centered framework. In Koch, S. (Ed.) *Psychology: a study of a science*, Vol. 3. *Formulations of the person and the social context*. New York: McGraw-Hill, pp. 184-256.

Rogers, C. R. (1961). *On Becoming a Person*. Boston: Houghton Mifflin.

Seeman, J. (1994, originally 1951). Conceptual analysis of client and counselor activity in Client-centered therapy. *The Person-Centered Journal, 1*(2), 5-10.

J. Wade Hannon Ed D
North Dakota State University, Fargo, USA

Will Eckersell M Ed
Counselor, Rexburg, Idaho, USE

Infusing Client-Centered/Person-Centered Counseling into a Traditional Counselor Education Program

Counseling, in the United States of America, (USA) is a changing field of study. We, as a counselor educator (first author) and a recent graduate of a master's program in counseling (second author) have reflected on how the Client-Centered/Person-Centered Approach (CC/PCA) can be (and is) infused into a 'traditional' course of study. We will discuss how counseling and psychology differ in the USA; the evolution of the counseling master's degree; national accreditation requirements; ways of infusing CC/PCA into a program; and our experiences.

Working and facilitating student learning and growth from a CC/PCA perspective is difficult. It requires much openness, honesty, and self-searching, as well as risks (both personal and professional). Yet, there is no other way that we see as viable for us to do this work and be true to ourselves. There are a number of external forces that contribute to these difficulties. First, at least in the USA, there is a major effort to restrict access to mental health care by third-party payers, primarily insurance companies and/or managed care schemes. Counselors who work in community settings see their work challenged by restrictions on the number of sessions, either imposed by the employer (often a governmental unit or non-for-profit agency) and/or an irrational focus on 'outcomes'. These 'outcomes' are often defined in arbitrary and capricious ways that are set up to 'prove' that the counseling 'works' in a very instrumental, positivistic manner. The emphasis is *not* on the person one is working with nor her or his real life experience. Often counselors are little more than agents for maintenance of control for the dominant power structure with a goal of maintaining the status quo.

COUNSELING AND PSYCHOLOGY EVOLUTION

Counseling and psychology are closely related. Psychology grew out of philosophy and counseling grew out of a cross-fertilization of education, sociology, philosophy, and psychology. Some in psychology would contend that counseling is a part of the 'domain' of psychology. Those of us in counseling often view this as an attempt by psychology to 'control' the profession of counseling.

In the USA, psychology has two primary specializations that engage in counseling (or 'psychotherapy') — clinical psychology and counseling psychology. According to the American Psychological Association, for one to be called a 'psychologist' one needs a doctoral degree in psychology (2000). Some counseling psychology programs offer a master's degree in 'counseling.' More often, master's degrees in counseling are offered in departments of counselor education (or some similar names), or are a program within a larger department (often education).

In the USA counseling and psychology have separate professional organizations — the

American Counseling Association (ACA), and the American Psychological Association (APA). Within the APA there is a division called 'Counseling Psychology.' There is often conflict between the two 'professions' over licensure and third-party reimbursement. Licensure for professions is not done at the federal level — rather at the 'provincial' (which are called 'states' in the USA) and in the special governmental unit that houses the federal capital (Washington, District of Columbia [D.C.]). This is a total of 51 governmental units and is rife for much chaos and conflict. Third-party reimbursement — whether from government or insurance — is controlled at the federal, state, county and/or municipal levels, as well as through non-governmental groups (such as employers).

There is also conflict over basic professional identity and control over which does what activities. Fortunately, in the USA CC/PCA tradition, no such empire-building exists (we cannot address how this is in other countries — we are not implying that it does — only that we are not aware enough to make an informed assessment.)

Changes in the Master's degree in counseling in the USA

The training of master's degree counselors in the USA has changed much over the past fifty years. Requirements for the degree have increased from approximately thirty-two semester credits (one-year full-time study) to forty-eight credits (two years' full-time study). A master's degree is considered the entry-level training to practice as a 'professional counselor.' (The USA has, unfortunately, a practice of calling all sorts of occupations 'counselors' — such as 'financial counselor,' 'camp counselor,' 'weight-loss counselor' and so on.

The counseling profession established voluntary national certification in 1983 through creation of the National Board for Certified Counselor (NBCC) and has subsequently added specialty certifications in school, mental health, supervision and addiction. Rehabilitation counseling and marriage and family counseling are certified through separate bodies. Licensure for professional counselors was passed first in the state of Virginia and now only five states do not have licensure (or similar regulation).

National Accreditation of Counselor Education Programs of Study

The Council for Accreditation of Counseling and Related Educational Programs (CAPREP) was founded in 1981 by ACA 'to promote the advancement of quality educational program offerings' (Council for Accreditation of Counseling and Related Educational Programs, 2000).

Program areas that are accredited include: Community Counseling; Marriage and Family Counseling; Mental Health Counseling; School Counseling; College Counseling; Student Affairs Practice in Higher Education (all at the Master's degree level; and, Counselor Education and Supervision (at the doctoral level). Master's programs require at least two years of full-time study and 48 to 60 semester credits (depending on the area), while the doctoral program 'builds on the knowledge and skills gained in the Master's program, [and] a minimum of two additional years of study are required' (Council for Accreditation of Counseling and Related Educational Programs, 2000).

CACREP accreditation also mandates a training program that offers 'a core curriculum of courses [that] provide the minimum knowledge and skills necessary to anyone' in the counseling profession. These courses include: Human Growth and Development; Group

Work; Social and Cultural Foundations; Appraisal; Research and Program Evaluation; Professional Orientation; Career and Lifestyle Development; and, Helping Relationships. Additionally, professional ethics must be included, as well as practicum and internships totaling from 750 to 1050 hours. Also, CACREP requires that all counselor education professors hold a doctoral degree in Counselor Education or a closely related field.

Many of these mandated areas go 'against the grain' of the CC/PCA tradition. One has to 'adapt' one's 'way of being' as best one can to comply with these external requirements. For example, one of the required areas of study is 'assessment', which involves various types of psychological testing that is deemed unnecessary by most in the CC/PCA tradition. The bulk of the emphasis is on content rather than process as well, which can be very frustrating for authentic learning.

One requirement that impacts training in a variety of ways is that the program, its faculty and students abide by the ACA Code of Ethics. One section of this code (11F.2.f. Varied Theoretical Positions) has direct implications for one who aspires to provide CC/PCA focused training. It states, 'counselors present varied theoretical positions so that students and supervisees may make comparisons and have opportunities to develop their own positions. Counselors provide information concerning the scientific bases of professional practices' (American Counseling Association, 2000). The first sentence of F.2.f. poses no problem, if interpreted only to 'present' approaches that are varied as alternatives and allow the counselor educator (or program if one has the luxury of having an all CC/PCA faculty) to focus on CC/PCA as the approach for students to learn. Some might interpret this part to mean that one approach could not be the focus, but we are unaware of any ethical complaint being filed over this. The second sentence of F.2.f. is troublesome if one interprets 'science' in a narrow, positivistic sense. This, unfortunately, is often the way it is seen by many in counseling. Obviously, Rogers' early work was fueled by positivism, but he moved away from it later on (Rogers, 1985). Again, we are not aware of any ethical complaints being filed over this either.

WAYS OF INFUSING CC/PCA INTO A PROGRAM

The first author has been a professor in two different counselor education master's programs for a total of 10 years. During that time he has presented the CC/PCA in three major ways: a) in the introductory practice course (called 'Counseling Techniques'), b) in all courses through readings and discussions, and c) through utilizing a teaching-style that is, as much as possible, consistent with CC/PCA (Rogers, 1969).

Counseling techniques class

In this class, which is required to be taken by all students the first semester, they begin the program (currently this is the summer session). This course is set up to be a practice one where students observe the professor demonstrating CC/PCA counseling, watch videos of counseling, and practice in triads where one student is the counselor, one the client, and the other an observer (these roles rotate regularly with each student being in the three roles). The majority of class time is spent in practice with feedback from fellow students, the professor and the graduate assistant who helps with supervision. Students are asked to read a variety of materials, including ones by Rogers (most recently *On Becoming a Person,* 1961) and other CC/PCA writers and some non-CC/PCA writers (such as Ivey, 1982; Mearns, 1994; and Mearns and Thorne, 1988). They are assigned a short paper on empathy and to do two 45-minute counseling sessions with a member of their triad (one due mid-semester and the other at the end).

Other courses

In whatever course the first author 'teaches' he presents a markedly CC/PCA perspective. Discussions are framed within the theoretical context of CC/PCA and other views are introduced for comparison and contrast. Whenever possible, CC/PCA writers are recommended or required (such as Lago and MacMillian [1999] for the Advanced Group Counseling class and Rogers [1970] for Group Counseling).

Student-centered teaching style

The first author endeavors to be consistent with the CC/PCA tradition within his courses in terms of his way of being. Rogers' 1969 *Freedom to Learn* has been a major influence. The following is included in each course syllabus under the heading 'A Few Notes on Teaching Style':

> It is my belief that the most effective learning is self-directed and self-motivated. I cannot 'teach' you anything, rather, I can help to facilitate your learning, My theoretical orientation to counseling and learning is the Person-Centered Approach (PCA). (See *Freedom to Learn* by Carl Rogers for more details in regards to PCA in learning).
>
> The main 'technique' I can offer you as your 'instructor' is my personhood, my authentic self. Sometimes I may be challenging, sometimes humorous, sometimes boring, sometimes maybe even insightful; but, whatever I may be, it is 'me'. I do not think it very helpful for me to lecture to you. Instead, I find interactions the most useful in learning. You are expected to talk in class. Please ask questions when you don't understand.
>
> There are no 'stupid' questions.
>
> In this class I encourage you to be your real self, as much as you can and/or will and/or feel safe to be. The more we can drop the facades of our institutional roles the more effective we will be in our endeavor. You have every right to speak your mind and share your feelings in here. Don't assume that you can be a 'passive' learner and truly benefit from this experience. I have no 'inspired knowledge' that I can pour into your head. It will help for you to read the materials assigned each week.
>
> Sometimes we may not agree about things and that is fine. I only ask that we strive to understand each other, and that our discussions be based on some sort of logic (or at least some systematic attempt to analyze, critique and synthesize the data at hand). If you find yourself feeling challenged, please share that, too. We can all learn by our human encounters. The success of

your learning is as much your responsibility as it is mine. We are in this together. Hopefully, it will be a valuable experience, and, (dare I say it?) maybe even fun?

Learning, especially significant learning, involves risks. It is up to you to determine how much risk-taking you are ready, willing and/or able in which to engage. My experience has taught me that the more I risk, the more I learn. It is not always easy, and, often unpleasant, but, rewarding. Part of learning is learning what we don't like, don't want to do, or are unable to do. Please speak up in class and ask questions when you don't understand.

If you perceive that you are not getting what you want or need, or believe that you should be getting something else from this class, please talk with me. I'm open to changing what needs to be changed. For me, the process of this whole thing we call 'life' is much more important than the 'task' (which explains, in part, why I like group work so much.)

Should you have any concerns or questions, please talk to me about them—in class if you feel comfortable—or out of class if you prefer. It is best to set up an appointment to assure that I'm available, or take a chance and come in anyway. This invitation extends to concerns, issues, or problems that you might have with me. This is a chance for you to learn to practice direct, honest, face-to-face communication with someone in a position of 'authority' (whatever that means). I value and respect people who come to speak to me when there are concerns.

If you feel the need to challenge something I say or do, please do. Challenging me is not a bad thing to do. I appreciate folks who speak their minds and their guts. Please do not let my size and/or gender interfere — I am a non-violent person. For those of you who are from around here, consider all these things said three times. I am sincere. (Hannon, 2000)

A STUDENT'S PERSPECTIVE

(This section was written by the second author, W.E.)

In the Counseling Techniques course I did not feel that I had to worry about a grade in the class. I was perusing learning for learning's sake. The atmosphere of the class was very accepting. The mode of learning was mostly experiential. Often Dr. Hannon would ask, 'how would you like to use the time today?' We used it generally in one of three ways: (a) discussed the reading and other points of interest (our texts were *Developing Person-centered Counselling,* by Dave Mearns and *Basic Attending Skills* by Ivey, Gluckstern, Bradford); (b) we worked in groups of three as either counselor, observer or client; or (c) as a class watched one person be a client and one person be a counselor and then we discussed the process.

I had significant growth and learning in all the above activities. One of the important areas of learning occurred when I volunteered to be the client in front of the group. Dr Hannon was the counselor. I was feeling tremendous anxiety and worry about my future. It was hard for me to talk about. I began with safe material as the client. I wanted to go deeper and did not think I would but with each confused thing I said I felt understood. I felt connected and while I did not feel perfectly safe I risked sharing my deeper anxieties and worries. I felt real change and in the process something happened to me. There was change, as well as growth and insight. I faced my anxieties and voiced them. I was understood, I was not rejected, judged or evaluated. I experienced a caring listener and that was a significant evidence for me that the person-centered approach works. To paraphrase what Rogers states, experience for me is the highest learning.

One of the assignments that we had was to write a paper on empathy. This was a fortuitous assignment for me because this led me to read *On Becoming a Person.* I was impressed with the honesty of that book. It seemed to me to be the most helpful text I had ever read. I would recommend this as a text for any introductory counseling course (it is now in use as one of the texts for the techniques class).

One of the suggestions made in the techniques class was that we take the opportunity to get counseling ourselves. I still had much worry and anxiety and decided to go to the counseling center on campus. I think that this is a good suggestion for students, to go to counseling themselves, because huge amounts of learning can occur in such short periods of time. For me it was very enlightening. I told the counselor that I wanted a person-centered counselor. She agreed. She was person-centered and the counseling was going great. I was open and honest about my anxiety and worry. On the fourth or fifth session the counselor handed me the Burns anxiety scale and the Beck depression inventory to fill out. I felt betrayed. I quit going. I did not want a label for myself and I did not want to fill out an inventory. I reflect on this experience often when I am told that the person-centered approach is not good enough to stand alone and I wonder 'what do you want to add to it?'

I was glad to read Bozarth's book *Person-Centered Therapy: A revolutionary paradigm,* (1998). I had not read this book when I received a lot of criticism from my internship supervisors. Part of the requirements of the course was to hand in videos of counseling sessions for them to review. I received much negative feedback for my technique. One of the complaints concerning my tape occurred from a situation where the student was talking about a 'shitty' teacher. He was talking about the way a teacher was treating him and the other students. I listened to him and was empathic with him. When the supervisor viewed the tape she asked 'why didn't you stick up for the teacher?' I should have just replied the teacher was not my client, but did not feel comfortable doing so.

I knew how effective the person-centered approach was with this student and I was not about to betray him. I do not want my students to feel the betrayal that I felt with my counselor. I had a lot of trouble staying confident through the criticism. The supervisors of the internship did not want me to graduate and even though I knew that the person-centered approach is effective in a school setting, they did not believe that. Nor did they have confidence in my ability to be a counselor. I was hurt by this and one of the assets that I relied on in those times was the relationship I had with Dr Hannon. He was my advisor and is my mentor. I think that if I had not had this relationship and the encouragement I would have decided to pursue work as a counselor in some other setting than in a school.

Being involved with a professor who is person-centered and who teaches in a person-centered way has been the most growth-facilitating aspect of my education. I have not felt *forced* to do anything or learn anything and what I have learned I believe has been earned. It has not been 'shoved' into my skull. By having an example and advocate of the approach I have learned by watching and listening. Seeing confidence in the person-centered approach has been a strength to me when I find myself wondering if what I am doing is adequate.

In concluding this section I will share an experience I had in my internship that has helped me at times when I am criticized. I was asked by a teacher to mediate between her and a student with whom she could not seem to get along. Before the meeting the teacher talked to the student and reported to me that she had worked things out with her. So I called the student into my office to explain that the meeting was going to be canceled. When she came in I explained that the teacher had told me that they had worked things out so we would not need to meet the next day. I saw that she was reluctant to get up and go back to class and it looked like she wanted to say something. I remembered back to techniques class and reflecting back to client what you hear or see. I said, 'It seems like there might be something you would like to talk about before you go back to class.' This was my novice way of trying to be person-centered. My technique was clumsy, but I really cared about this student and tried to listen empathically. The student left my office 50 minutes later after crying and talking and with me having listened empathically, trying to be congruent and to give unconditional positive regard. Before she left she said, 'Thank you for listening to me no one has ever understood before.' I have heard other professors say, 'You must start with the person-centered approach but then you must develop a plan.' And I have heard other newly graduated school counselors say, 'In schools the person-centered approach just is not practical.'

I was amazed at the powerful effect the person-centered approach had on me, and even more amazed that it could work even when I used it clumsily. I do not think that girl or other students who came into my office thought that the person-centered approach was insufficient.' And if it truly is not practical, well, then practicality is over-rated.

A COUNSELOR EDUCATOR'S PERSPECTIVE

There are other theories of working with people that are very popular in the USA mental health system. These include various kinds of cognitive-behavioral theories and family systems theories. Many (if not most) of these tend to be directive and remedial in their ways of working with clients. Additionally, the medical model is the primary lens for viewing the way that humans behave. None of these theoretical issues are new, it is just that they have carved out a near-hegemony in the mental health arena that tends to leave little room for more humanistic approaches, especially the CC/PCA one.

There is often resistance from counseling students themselves. They resist examining themselves, their feelings and their experiences (which is to some degree, expected). In the USA, people are not encouraged to be open and honest. We are many times 'punished' for being so. Many times students will voice something like 'isn't there more?' to being a counselor than the CC/PCA. In the USA culture we are besieged with media stereotypes of the counselor (or 'therapist') as one who 'fixes' people, who 'solves' problems for them, who 'gives advice' and is somehow 'superior to' her/his clients. Instrumentalism is alive and well with a vengeance here. Often, just to resist this ideology seems quite subversive.

SUMMARY (OR, 'IT AIN'T EASY BEING A CC/PCA COUNSELOR EDUCATOR')

We have shared some of our thoughts, feelings and experiences about how one can infuse the CC/PCA into a somewhat hostile environment. There are many potential obstacles and pitfalls. But, the rewards are overwhelming as well. For those of us who are convinced of the usefulness and validity of an evolving CC/PCA theory and practice of counseling there is no other way.

REFERENCES

American Counseling Association (2000). *ACA Code of Ethics and Standards of Practice.* Available at: http://www.counseling.org/resources/codeofethics.htm

American Psychological Association (2000). *Guidelines and principles for accreditation of programs in professional psychology.* Available at: http://www.apa.org/ed/gp2000.html.

Council for Accreditation of Counseling and Related Educational Programs (2000). *A student's guide to accreditation.* Available at: http://www.counseling.org/cacrep/student.htm.

Hannon, J.W. (2000). *Seminar: Community counseling syllabus.* Fargo, ND: North Dakota State University Counselor Education Program. (Available from author).

Ivey, A. and Gluckstern, N. (1982). *Basic Attending Skills.* North Amherst, MA: Microtraining Associates.

Lago, C. and MacMillian, M. (Eds.) (1999). *Experiences in Relatedness: Groupwork and the person-centred approach.* Ross-on-Wye, UK: PCCS Books.

Mearns, D. (1994). *Developing Person-centred Counselling.* London: Sage.

Mearns, D. and Thorne, B. (1988). *Person-centred Counselling in Action.* London: Sage.

National Board for Certified Counselors (2000). *About NBCC.* Available at: http://www.nbcc.org/aboutnbcc.htm.

Rogers, C. R. (1961). *On Becoming a Person.* Boston: Houghton Mifflin.

Rogers, C. R. (1969). *Freedom to Learn: A view of what education might become.* Columbus, OH: Charles Merrill.

Rogers, C. R. (1970). *Carl Rogers on Encounter Groups.* New York: Harper and Row.

Rogers, C. R. (1985) Toward a more human science of the person. *Journal of Humanistic Psychology,* 25(4), 7–24.

Bala Jaison PhD

Focusing for Creative Living, Toronto, Canada

Integrating Experiential and Brief Therapy Models:
A guide for clinicians[1]

With the advent of managed care and limited funds for long-term therapy, there has been a growing movement toward more short-term, constructive, solution-based approaches to creating change and movement in psychotherapy, especially in the field of Brief Therapy.

Concurrently, there is some doubt on the part of those who practice longer-term, experientially-based psychotherapy, that the Brief Therapy approaches may be more of a band-aid and less of a cure for long-standing issues. Some Experiential clinicians feel that the Brief models, with their emphasis on brevity and their focus on finding solutions, do not take enough time to explore the affective states and experiences of the client; the therapists' skepticism, therefore, is connected to the question: *Can lasting change happen — briefly?*

The solution, so to speak, comes in the form of a both/and approach, rather than an either/or position. There is choice. There is room in the structure of a therapy session for adapting and integrating Experiential components into Brief Therapy models, and conversely, weaving Brief Solution-focused components into Experiential work. The process of integration is natural, fluid, and in fact, very effectively supports the ever-increasing trend toward a holistic mind/body approach in psychotherapy.

This paper is meant as a guide to begin thinking more creatively about new possibilities for therapeutic change by comparing, contrasting, and showing how and where the models are similar, different, and ultimately complementary.

EXPERIENTIAL PSYCHOTHERAPY

The Experiential approach evolved out of the Humanistic Psychology movement of the 1960s. Some of the new buzzwords at that time were: *self-actualization*, living in the *here-and-now*, and being *present* to one's *inner journey* by *experiencing the process*. Humanistic Psychology emphasized sensitivity to feelings, internal self-discovery, exploring one's own individual essence, self-expression, communication, and congruency between one's thoughts and feelings. People talked about *the nature of being*, well summed up by Paul Tillich's famous aphorism 'Being is becoming.'

The work was revolutionary at the time. It represented a huge departure from traditional Psychoanalysis and Behaviorism, with their emphasis on the past and early childhood

---

[1] This chapter is a condensed version of the book, *Integrating Experiential and Brief Therapy: How to do deep therapy — briefly and how to do brief therapy — deeply. A Tool-book for Therapists and Counsellors.*

experiences; the new emphasis was on, 'What is going on inside of me, *right now?*' Even more significant was the importance of empowering and trusting the inner wisdom of the patient/client, another huge departure from the traditional professional-knows-all. The new Experiential models transferred the title of 'expert' over to the client.

Both movements (Experiential and Brief) had their pioneers, the great mentors and leading edge thinkers who influenced the new fields of psychology, and the many clinicians who followed them.

For example, under the Experiential umbrella, Fritz Perls (Perls, 1969), developed Gestalt therapy, and the famous empty-chair process; Virginia Satir (Satir, 1967), with tremendous compassion and humor, used family sculpting and therapists' use of self to model how people related to each other — or didn't; Roberto Assagioli brought a spiritual dimension into psychotherapy by adding the perspective of the Soul (Assagioli, 1975); Carl Rogers (Rogers, 1951) developed *client-centered therapy*. Rogers emphasized the importance of the therapist-client relationship, and the attitude of the therapist toward the client which is based on respect, empathy, and 'unconditional positive regard'. Eugene Gendlin's work on *Experiencing* (Gendlin, 1962) and later *Focusing* (Gendlin,1978) stressed the idea of congruency, and listening inside to what *the body* had to say. His patients learned how to recognize whether what they were thinking, *matched* what they were feeling.

BRIEF THERAPY

There has been a dynamic evolution in the way Brief Therapy is practised as increasing numbers of clinicians have been introduced to the work, and adapted it to meet their specific needs. Brief Therapy was profoundly influenced by Milton Erickson, an extraordinary and imaginative hypnotherapist from Arizona, whose attitude towards effecting change was in its time, most unusual. It is important to recognize that behind all Brief Therapy work, including *Neuro-Linguistic Programming* (NLP), is the genius of Milton Erickson, whose approach has been suitably called 'uncommon therapy'. He didn't invent any therapeutic models; he simply did them. Everything after Erickson is an adaptation by other clinicians of his natural precocity. Some of the early pioneers of family therapy such as Jay Haley, Don Jackson, John Weakland, and Paul Watzlawick visited and consulted with Milton Erickson.

A Brief Therapy project started by Richard Fisch in 1966, within the Mental Health Research Institute at Palo Alto, had a profound effect on the development of the Brief/ Strategic approach to change (Fisch, Weakland, and Segal,1982). Two important works, *Toward a Theory of Pathological Systems*, by Haley (Haley, 1967), and *Pragmatics of Human Communication*, by Watzlwawick (Watzlwawick et al., 1967) made important contributions to the thinking about effecting change. In 1967, Haley joined Salvador Minuchin (Minuchin, 1978) in Philadelphia, where they conceptualized further about structure and hierarchy. The term 'Strategic Therapy' was coined in Haley's influential work: *Uncommon Therapy: The psychiatric techniques of Milton H. Erickson* (Haley, 1973).

Particularly because of its impact on Family Therapy, interest in Brief Therapy spread rapidly in the 1970s, stimulated by Jay Haley's work and two more seminal publications from The Mental Research Institute (MRI): *Change Principles of Problem Formation and Problem Resolution* (Watzlawick *et al.*, 1974) and *Brief Therapy: Focused problem resolution*

(Weakland *et al.*, 1974). Brief Therapy continued to grow through the 1970s and early 1980s with its emphasis on:
- Observable phenomena
- Being pragmatic in effecting change
- The theory that problems are produced and maintained by repetitive behavioral sequences, both personal and interpersonal

Brief therapy evolved from being *problem-* and *present*-oriented, to *solution-* and *future*-oriented with the breakthrough work of Steve de Shazer, *Keys to Solution in Brief Therapy* (de Shazer, 1985), and *Family Preservation: A brief workbook*, by Insoo Kim Berg (Berg, 1991) at the Brief Therapy Institute, in Wisconsin, which they called 'Solution Focused Brief Therapy'.

Berg and de Shazer popularized the deceivingly simple application of their model through the late 1980s and 1990s. While Solution Focused Brief Therapy has now been adapted worldwide, it was initially intended to address a variety of disorders and emergency situations: the borderline criminal element, alcoholics, welfare recipients, and extremely dysfunctional and/or abusive families. The work has proven to be highly effective in terms of making positive changes rapidly.

William O'Hanlon, a colleague of Berg and de Shazer, added his own particular twist to the Solution Focused Brief Therapy model of Berg and de Shazer; he was initially trained experientially, by Carl Rogers in *client-centered therapy*. He called his adaptation *Solution Oriented Brief Therapy*, and wrote his own breakthrough work, *In Search of Solutions: A new direction in psychotherapy* (O'Hanlon and Weiner-Davis, 1989). His work over time evolved further into what O'Hanlon called *Possibility Therapy* (O'Hanlon, 1997) — his way of continually broadening the focus of the work into other realms; for example, by incorporating spiritual components.

The field of Brief Therapy continues to expand; and as it does, so do the variations and new possibilities. Increasingly, working with a solution orientation is becoming more viable, more realistic, and easier to integrate for clinicians practising longer term, in-depth therapy.

The remainder of this paper reflects how I have integrated Focusing Oriented Therapy (Gendlin, 1996), an experientially based approach, and Solution Oriented Therapy, a Brief Therapy approach, into my practice.[1]

The most important word for me, in terms of integrating Focusing Oriented Therapy with Solution Oriented Therapy, is the word 'oriented', which implies *leaning toward, in the direction of, so inclined* (Webster's Dictionary, 1981). Both of these models are *oriented* in a very similar direction: changing how the client *views* (Solution language) or *carries inside* (Focusing language) the problem. Both models might be characterized as *wellness work* (versus paying attention to or emphasizing pathology); thus each model concerns itself with what will be creative, life enhancing, and positive for the client. Focusing often calls it finding 'fresh air'. The parallel in the Solution model is asking the client about what will be 'helpful' (in finding relief from the problem). In Focusing we look for *what feels right,* and in the Solution Oriented model for *works*.

Eugene T. Gendlin frequently uses the analogy of an elevator. He talks about putting

---

[1.] For the sake of clarity, I will generally be comparing and contrasting two specific models: Focusing Oriented Therapy, and Solution Oriented Therapy. However, I will at times, refer to 'Experiential approaches' and 'Brief Therapy approaches' meaning that the comparisons and contrasts apply under the general rubric of 'Experiential' and 'Brief'.

one's attention *in the body*, specifically in the area between the throat, chest, stomach, and lower abdomen, and then traveling *down the elevator* to the floor or level (this aforementioned center area) where he says, the Focusing experience takes place.

Staying with this analogy, we might say that Solution Oriented Therapy (and in fact all Brief Therapy approaches) takes place on a different floor from Focusing (and other Experiential approaches), in this case, taking the *elevator* a bit *higher* up to a more *cognitive* level. Hence, integrating the Focusing Oriented and Solution Oriented models can be easily viewed as heading in the same direction, but on different floors. Another way to view the two models is as functioning on parallel planes or in parallel universes. The important point is that both models are headed in a similar, compatible, and positive direction.

For me, the idea of integrating these two models came as a major epiphany very early in my training in Solution Oriented Brief Therapy. It was immediately apparent to me that the two models belonged together, worked together, complemented each other, and most important, gave each other what I viewed as *missing pieces* (in each model.*)* Hence, I have been committed to integrating Focusing Oriented and Solution Oriented Brief Therapy for well over a decade. In the course of developing this model with Glenn Fleish of California, we came to call it the *SOFT* approach: Solution Oriented Focusing Therapy. Its aim is to effectively integrate (or marry) the two models into a complementary partnership by:

- Keeping the integrity of the Focusing Oriented model intact, so that clients have a rich inner understanding of themselves in relationship to their issues, and remain in touch with their moment-to-moment experience and feelings.
- Streaming the questions that the therapist asks in a Solution Oriented manner, but often in an experiential style, as a way to help the session progress more quickly, and in order to facilitate the change process.

COMPARING AND CONTRASTING

One of the cornerstones upon which the Solution work is built shares a fundamental principle with the Focusing approach: The client has within him/her self enormous resources, strengths, natural competencies, and life experience. Through the use of skilful listening on the part of the therapist, and by validating what the client already knows internally, the client learns to value and access his or her own innate capabilities in the process of moving stuck places forward toward change.

Integrity, in both the Focusing Oriented and Solution Oriented models, is connected to their grounding in firm philosophical foundations: Respecting, valuing, and acknowledging that the client has within a wealth of inner resources, strengths, and experience.

Also, deeply embedded in the philosophical core of each model is the strongly held belief that the client already has the *solution* inside; Focusing calls this 'bodily felt wisdom'; both models operate on the assumption that this inner knowing is already there, just waiting to be tapped. Hence, in theory (certainly regarding the attitude towards clients) both models are client-centered.

Solution Oriented work centers around the concept of change: What makes change, breaking the patterns that inhibit change, and co-creating with clients new actions, or *action steps,* that will support new patterns of change, and consequent behavior. These steps in both models are always small, manageable, and built upon progressively according to the clients' sense of *what works* or *what feels right*. The therapist can also facilitate change by observing and pointing out what the client is *already doing* that is working, and building upon it with action steps.

The significant difference here, between the brief and experiential approaches, is that brief work is primarily interested in change, and uses a variety of modalities to find it: therapeutic paradox, double-bind theory, circularity of systems, disruption of homeostasis, and staying focused on the positive in resolving the presenting problem. Experiential work also looks for change, but change needs to be accompanied as well, by *experiential understanding;* the bodily felt, 'ah-ha' experience, or 'Gestalt' (Perls, 1969).

Another significant feature of all Brief Therapy models is the way it clearly defines current and future goals and expectations. Great care and time is taken to set out and develop manageable goals, whether it be for the future, or for this particular session: 'What would you like to see happen?' 'When it is happening what will it look like?' What will be different for you when this is happening?' The trend of these questions is always toward creating and building a more positive future, i.e. how it *will* be (better) *when*.

Conversely, the Experiential models tend to stay more focused on the present and what the client is experiencing *in the moment*. 'Can you take a minute to sense what's there for you, right now?' or 'Of those three issues, can you sense which has *the most energy* for you, right now?' The purpose of phrasing questions in this way is to find the issue *freshly* and *with aliveness*, as the body carries it *now,* rather than having the client recount the problem to the therapist as s/he remembers it from yesterday.

Another hallmark of the Solution Oriented approach (which evolved from the Solution Focused model of Insoo kim Berg and Steve de Shazer) is the specific intervention of finding the *exception to the problem:* 'When was the last time this wasn't happening?' 'What were you doing differently, then?' or 'What was different, then?' 'Given the incredible stress you've been under, I can't help wondering how you've managed so well up to now.' Or 'How did you manage to even get out of bed to come here today?' The point: looking always for what is right, the tiny exception, the small ray of light that the therapist and client can build upon together, creating the sense of expectation, hope, and a more positive vision of the future. Insoo calls this 'the solution picture'.

One of the purposes shared by all Experiential models, is to help clients experience, in the moment, what they are feeling. The emphasis in the experiential approach, however varied (Gestalt, Bioenergetics, or the work of Carl Rogers, Virginia Satir, and Carl Whitaker), is more on personal growth and inner change rather than symptom relief, which is considered important, but holds a second place to what we might loosely call *being true to oneself* or having *inner integrity.* This means specifically helping clients experience congruency between what they are thinking and saying, in relationship to what they are feeling and experiencing. In Experiential approaches they *must match*. I call this 'think/feel'.

In his 1959 article on 'A Tentative Scale for the Measurement of Process in Psychotherapy' Carl Rogers' states very beautifully his own strongly held feelings about the value of 'Experiencing':

> It involves being in an unknown flow rather than in a clear structure . . . there is, in the act of experiencing, a referent which can be symbolized and checked or rechecked for its further meanings and symbolizations. There is a strong desire for exactness in these conceptualizations.

There may be a dim realization that living in terms of these solid referents would be possible . . . There is full acceptance now of experiencing as providing a clear and usable referent for getting at the implicit meanings of the individual's encounter with himself and with life . . . the recognition that the self is now becoming this process of experiencing.

Eugene Gendlin, Ph.D., both a student and colleague of Rogers, developed a profound process, through *Focusing*, of listening inside oneself to what he has termed the 'felt-sense'. The felt-sense is the body's holistically registered experience of a situation or issue. It is based on the premise that everything we experience from the moment of birth is registered in the body in a cellular way, whether or not we consciously remember it.

By paying attention to, and so called 'keeping company' with the *felt* sense of our experience, and by listening attentively to what this felt-sense has to say, we can get new and valuable information that we could not receive from the linear mind alone.

The Focusing Oriented approach involves a great deal of what is commonly known as 'active listening'. Gendlin calls his listening model 'experiential listening', making the distinction between merely reflecting back the client's words and listening deeply, from the therapist's own felt-sense, for the 'felt meaning' underneath the words.

LANGUAGE

Understanding the (sometimes) complex linguistics of each model, especially their different views on precision vs. imprecision of language is fascinating — if somewhat challenging at first.

In Solution Oriented work, language is very specific, pinning down exactly what the client will do, and when, and how often. Language is also specifically used. There is an emphasis on words like 'will', 'when', 'yet' and 'then': 'How *will* it be for you *when* you are less depressed and more positive?' 'Although it hasn't happened, *yet*, imagine a time in the future *when* the problem is solved . . . what you *will* be doing, *then* . . . ?' It is geared toward change and positive expectation about how it *will be when* these new changes occur.

The Solution model, which evolved from a systemic context, also includes in its language the presence of others (spouses, children, co-workers, etc.) whether or not they are in the room: 'So who will be the first to notice the changes you are making?' 'Who else?' or 'What will let you know that your wife has noticed these changes?' 'What will she be telling you, then, that she is not telling you now?'

The Focusing model is less concerned with the inclusion of others, and pays far more attention to the *inner relationship:* what the client is experiencing internally, in the moment. There is also emphasis on the relationship the client has with various inner parts of the self: the child-part, the critic, the part that feels some particular way (sad, troubled, scared, etc.)

Further, the language of the Focusing Oriented model is quite different in two major respects. First, it is oriented in the present and focuses on how it feels inside, *right now.* For example a client says: 'There is a real sinking feeling for me with this issue.' An *experiential response* might be: 'Can you just let that sinking feeling know that it is OK for it to be here, *right now?*' allowing the time for feelings and senses to develop more fully. The Solution approach might ask: 'When this sinking feeling isn't there — or is less than it is now — what do you imagine you *will be* experiencing instead?'

Second, unlike the Solution model, which is very specific, and focuses on the future ('What exactly will be happening when . . .') the Focusing Oriented model is anchored in the present, and often uses language that is intentionally vague and fuzzy; it leaves lots of blanks, pauses, and (purposeful) uncertainty in order to let the client fill in the *felt* blanks: 'So it's something like . . .' and the therapist pauses here, allowing the client to fill in the exact right word.

Perhaps it is 'anger' or 'sadness' or 'heavy'. The therapist simply reflects, for example: 'So there's a feeling . . . *there* . . . of sadness' (the word 'there' is pointing to the *felt-sense*.) And the client might respond 'Well yeah, it's something like sadness . . .' The therapist in this model will stay with (what is called in Focusing) 'the more' of it, until the client gets it exactly right in a bodily felt way. Therapist: 'So it's something like sadness . . . but that's not quite it . . . can you just spend some time with that *something-like-sadness* place . . . and sense . . . what *comes inside* . . . maybe a word or image that . . . just *fits with* . . . what you are *feeling* . . . inside, right now.'

The value of using vague and fuzzy language lies in the scope it gives to the client, allowing him or her to search and *internally grope* for the exact right fit that invites congruency between thought and feeling.

Curiously, the exactness of language in the Solution model achieves the very same result, by *pinning down exactly* what the action steps will be between now and the next session, to move toward change.

For example, the therapist might say, 'What is one small thing you can do between now and the next session, that will help you feel a little less sad and a little more upbeat and like yourself?' Perhaps the client says, 'I need to start exercising again.' The Solution Oriented therapist will pursue this statement in minute detail. Therapist: 'So realistically speaking, how many times do you imagine you'll get to the gym between now and the next time we meet?' Perhaps the client says (usually without thinking it through), 'Five times, and I'll take the weekend off.' This is a wonderful *integration spot* for the therapist to double-check experientially. He or she might say: 'Can you take a moment here, to really ask inside, what your 'body buys' about how often it is willing to exercise . . . take your time . . . and just *sense* what *feels* realistic . . . ?' And the client finally says, 'I know I can do it two times in a week . . . maybe three.' Therapist: 'So you know you can do it two times . . . can we agree on that? . . . and if you do it three times you can consider it a bonus!' After the client agrees, it would not be at all unusual for the therapist to take the action step even further by checking: what time of day, what days, how long, etc. Clients generally feel motivated and uplifted by having something concrete to do between sessions.

Experiential work is less concerned with the action steps, and far more interested and focused on *internal realization,* and how the body carries around the issue. The emphasis is on what feels right or wrong, and taking the time to delve into what the felt-sense is of the next right step.

For the client, the act of *setting* a goal, and also taking the time to *sense* the *felt rightness* of the goal, provides a much wider perspective, and highlights the both/and experience — *doing* and *feeling*.

For the therapist, interfacing the two models gives the clinician a way to reach clients more quickly by following what we might call their 'line of least resistance'. Some clients respond better to doing and action steps, and others to sensing and experiencing; integrating the models gives more choice — both to the therapist and client.

DIALOGUING

Another interesting aspect to explore in joining these two psychological models is in the area of *dialoguing*. This includes dialoguing with self, dialoguing *interactionally* (Klein, 1999) with couples and families, dialoguing in imagery with people who are not actually in the room, or dialoguing with the therapist during the session.

The Experiential models, with their emphasis on staying present to and in touch with the self, tend to *internalize* the dialogue. Focusing in particular, is very specific about not posing direct questions to the client, but rather requesting that the client *ask him or her self*. For example, let's imagine that the question in the therapist's mind is: 'I wonder what she plans to do about it?' In Focusing Oriented language the question might be phased: 'Can you *ask yourself* "So what's my sense of what needs to happen, right now . . . a right next step that will fit for me?"' Another example: The therapist wonders, 'What is the cause of all this pain?' This might be verbalized as, 'Can you ask this *inside place* to sense . . . "What is this pain connected to in my life, right now?"' or 'Ask yourself, "What is it that makes all this discomfort *in here?*"' And the therapist waits patiently, following the process, while the client gropes for just the right *felt word* or *image* that fits their uniquely personal *meaning*.

The value of this approach is in the implicit message clients receive: They know the way and the next right steps to take along the way. This message gives the client a strong sense of empowerment.

In the Solution Oriented model either the dialogue is *externalized* directly with the therapist, who is asking very specific questions; or the client is coached by the therapist to speak with/for a person who is not in the room: 'So if your husband was here with us now, what do you imagine he might say?' And perhaps the client replies, 'He would say that I nag him too much.' 'Oh, I see, ' says the therapist, 'So can you ask him now, how it would make a difference to him if you were nagging him less?' And the client responds, 'He says he wouldn't avoid me so much and would be more attentive' (which was the presenting problem in the first place!)

Thus, the dialogue continues in a circular fashion — what she would say, what he would say, and how each new alteration in action/behavior will affect the other — until the client arrives (often seemingly magically) to an '*Ah-ha*' place, which happens in both models. This type of externalized circular questioning is also used with inner parts. 'So, if the insecure part could speak, right now, what would she say she needs from you?' or 'What would she say that you could do, that would be helpful to her?' When the 'part' expresses its needs, the dialogue continues with 'And how will that be?' or '. . . affect you?'

The value in this approach is in helping clients get a better understanding about the nature of an interaction: How what we do and say impacts upon others, and vice versa. This approach also models concrete positive steps that encourage new patterns of behavior and help heal dysfunctional interactions.

WHICH MODEL IS MORE EFFECTIVE IN THE CHANGE PROCESS?

The argument for whether change needs to happen from the outside in, or the reverse, is a moot debate at best. *It doesn't matter!* Both orientations work, and the success of either is entirely dependent upon

(a) the natural orientation and inclination of the client, couple, or family, and what they respond to best in therapy

(b) the natural orientation and training of the therapist. As professionals, we ultimately do and say whatever works best (therapeutically) in the moment. If the outer condition changes, something inside will most certainly change as well.

Conversely, if the inner viewing of the issue changes, consequent outer changes will occur. Therefore, rather than promoting any particular theory of change, I like to use whichever model incorporates the natural orientation and inclination of the particular client(s); it is usually some combination of both.

In the case of couples, where one partner is perhaps relaxed and fluid in manner, while the other might be more precise and exacting, it is advantageous for the therapist to be fluent in both 'languages': what I think of as being *bilingual* (or *multilingual* if you are integrating yet other approaches) in order to be able to address people in a manner that speaks to their 'line of least resistance'.

PROCESS

The Focusing Oriented model is generally more inclined to follow *the process* of the client, in whatever organic direction that process happens to take. It is non-directive, and follows rather than leads, as a general rule. While the Solution Oriented model (and all brief approaches, in fact) respects the clients' process, the Solution Oriented therapist takes far more responsibility in keeping the sessions 'on track' by maintaining a focus or 'directionality' in the type of questions s/he is asking. The clinician keeps in the forefront of awareness, the client's *stated goals* — whether that is for this session only, or for the whole course of therapy in general.

The Client-centered and Experiential approaches tend to allow the client to direct the theme and structure of the session, and encourage more autonomy in terms of the direction that the session will take; the therapist trusts the process and outcome of the session by allowing the client to do whatever he or she *feels-to-do* with the therapy hour.

The downside of this approach is the lack of a fall-back position if the work is going nowhere: for example, the session is not progressing, change is not happening, the dialogue between the therapist and client is stuck, or the therapist finds him or herself covering with the client, the same old territory — again. The clinician then needs to step in and *do something* — offer some skilled direction to move the process forward, and in that stuck spot, some well placed Solution Oriented questions can move clients forward quite masterfully, toward change. To mention Erickson again, he had a true genius for being directive and extremely powerful in his myriad of interventions and strategies, and yet simultaneously managed, through the gift of innate wisdom, to be ever respectful, accepting, and genuinely empowering others.

USE OF AFFECT IN THERAPY

The biggest gap between the two models, and the most interesting to attempt to interface, is around the use — or not — of affect. The two models are particularly complementary in this area:

- The Focusing Oriented approach takes as much time as necessary for the development of the inner process and *felt experiencing*.
- The Solution Oriented approach sometimes bypasses affect and keeps the client focused on the *action steps* necessary to reach the desired goals.

In examining how each model regards the use of affect, it might be useful to return to the idea of parallel universes or parallel planes. The Solution work tends to be cognitive and imaginative, using the mind to *see* new possibilities. Similarly, but on another level (of the elevator), Focusing specifically pays attention to how one *feels* about *all that*. Therefore, the question that the therapist is posing, depending upon whether it is couched in Focusing or Solution language, may be *similar in orientation*, but reaching a different level of awareness inside of the client:

Focusing: 'Can you *sense* what it *feels* like when it is right?'
Solution: 'What do you *imagine* you will be *doing* when it is right?'
Focusing: 'Can you sense inside what *feels* like a step toward fresh air or relief?'
Solution: 'What small steps can you take that *will be* helpful to you in bringing some relief to this issue?'

In addition, if a client says: 'I am depressed' the orientation in Focusing is to 'make room' for the part that is depressed. The therapist will first reflect back, 'So there is a *part there* that is feeling depressed, right now'; this phrasing makes a clear separation between *the part* that feels depressed and the intact *Self* that is 'all OK'. Further, *based* on the holistic philosophy underlying the work, it is essential that the 'depressed part' is allowed to be there, because it is a component of the whole; healing in this model is not possible unless every (inner) part gets a hearing, feels valued, and becomes integrated into the entirety of the person; ultimately everyone (inner parts) wins.

The Solution approach might completely bypass acknowledging the presence of the 'depressed part' by asking: 'When are the times that you notice you are less depressed and feeling more positive?' or 'What do you suppose . . . or imagine . . . you will be *doing differently* when you are less depressed and feeling better?' Through the responses, for example, 'I will be more productive and creative,' or 'I will start writing again,' the therapist will pursue how that will *make a difference* to being less depressed and 'more productive and creative' or 'writing again'. 'And when you are writing again and feeling more creative, how will that make a difference to you?' and, 'Who in your life will be most affected by these new changes in you?' or 'Who will be the first to notice?'

HOW DO WE KNOW WHICH MODEL TO USE WHEN?

Again, there is no right or only way. Generally, it is a hunch based on the clinician's intuition in the moment — a therapeutic judgment call. Sometimes you notice that the client is talking about the issue, but is not really experiencing what he or she is talking about. This may be the juncture to stop, slow down, and take the time to: *be with, process, pay attention to, sit with,* and not immediately try to *fix the problem.* Something fresh and new may need to come from a deeper place inside of the client.

Conversely, if the client is experiencing the same old thing that you've been over together many times before, a question phrased in Solution Oriented language can be very useful for pattern interruption: 'What will it look when it is right, and no longer a problem?'

The ideal solution, and the juncture where the models exquisitely complement each other, is to weave the language of both models together in a way that allows the client to both *have* a goal and *experience* having a goal: 'How will it look . . . feel . . . be?' or 'what will you be telling yourself when it is right, and no longer a problem?' The words 'look', 'feel' and 'telling yourself' allow clients to respond in the way that is most natural to them: visual, kinesthetic, or auditory. Or, if the Solution question is: 'What will you be doing differently when you are handling this better?' and the client responds 'I will be more organized and efficient with my time,' the therapist will find great value in adding on an experiential version of the question: 'Can you take a moment, now . . . to *sense* . . .what it *feels like* to be you . . . being more organized and efficient with your time?'

Finally, the client can also serve as a guide to knowing which direction to take. I have experienced clients actually asking for what they need at both ends of the (Focusing and Solution) spectrum: If I have used a solution-oriented question *at the wrong moment,* I have had the client say, 'I'm not ready to find a solution, yet. I just want to explore this more . . . take some time to be with it.' On the other side, I have offered an experiential *time-to-be-with* moment, and had the client say, 'You know what, I'm sick to death of this; I don't really care what it's about anymore, I just need a solution!'

SOME HELPFUL TIPS FOR THE PRACTITIONER

1. Become fluid in both languages so that the bilingual (or multilingual) process becomes seamless.
2. Trust your own therapeutic style, how you speak, and how you naturally connect with each of your clients. Authenticity is the bottom line of all good therapeutic work.
3. Be flexible and ready to adapt. I have had the experience during a session of adjusting my tone, speed, and model of language mid-sentence, if I sense in the moment that the client is not responding to something that I am doing.
4. Trust your clients. They are the ultimate guides.

Some clients are most naturally cognitive and cerebral, and an experiential approach and style of language needs to be introduced slowly and over time. Other clients are more naturally experiential, and take to processing easily. In that case, solution-oriented questions phrased in an experiential style can be highly effective. The two coupled together allow for:
• Time in a session to more fully experience an issue.
• Efficiency in a session to keep the process on track, by using streamlined questions.

Both models use the term, and honor the process of *taking small steps.*

WHERE FOCUSING-ORIENTED AND EXPERIENTIAL MODELS WORK BEST

1. Exposing clients to the act of processing: experiencing the *bodily felt-sense* of an issue, and taking the necessary time to learn how to *keep company* with inner feelings.
2. Exposing clients to the language and friendly *attitude* (in Focusing, it is called, the 'Focusing attitude') toward the self: safety; inner space; making room for . . . (places that are hurting, negative, stuck); non-judgment; permitting and allowing whatever feelings come, to *just be there.*
3. Giving clients an awareness of inner parts: critic, inner child, and holistic self.
4. Learning how to listen: both internally and externally to others.
5. Teaching the above explicitly.

WHERE SOLUTION-ORIENTED AND BRIEF THERAPY MODELS WORK BEST

1. Interrupting Patterns:
    • Helping the client break out of old, negative, worn-out patterns and behaviors, that are so embedded, the client doesn't notice that they are there;
    • The client has the awareness of being stuck, but doesn't know how to break free of old programming, and gets repeatedly stuck in the same-old-thing.
2. Creating Change: Learning how to consciously reconstruct problems and issues into positive new realities ('the solution picture') that *are* and *feel,* different, fresh, and new.
3. Managing overwhelming and uncontrollable feelings that impede clear thinking and creative intelligence.
4. Having limited time and/or funds to pursue long-term therapy.
5. Shifting attention away from what doesn't work into to *what is possible.*

INTEGRATING BOTH

What Experiential work gives the Solution approach:

1. Grounding in the knowledge and awareness of the *experience of processing*, and taking the time to explore the felt-sense of an issue.
2. Time and permission to work with *what doesn't work*, what's wrong (instead of what would be right); resistance, negativity and stuck places.

What Solution-oriented work gives to the Experiential approach:

1. Directionality, purpose, intention, and better understanding of what exactly the client *can* and *will* do toward creating positive change.
2. A way to lower the volume on affect when it is too intense, by adding cognitive and behavioral components.

The beauty of the Focusing Oriented model is in its gentleness, respectfulness, and explicit teaching of an 'attitude' toward the self that is caring, empathic, and willing to listen. The process permits and allows whatever wants to unfold, to do so, in a safe and nurturing inner environment that promotes healing and growth. Focusing honors the wisdom of the felt-sense, and works actively with various parts in order to integrate them into the whole.

The beauty of the Solution Oriented model is in its respectful, positive, and non-problem focused approach. The model provides a safe structure in which to explore and create new, more constructive possibilities, and consequent realities. The skillful use of language allows clients to access in a brief and time-efficient manner, what they *do want*, rather than what they don't want.

The integration of the two models allows the client to experience the gentle process of Focusing with a Solution orientation, resulting in both an increased awareness of self, and an enhanced sense-of-hopefulness in finding workable and manageable solutions to seemingly impossible situations.

The purpose of this integrative or SOFT approach is in *making room for both!*

REFERENCES: BRIEF THERAPY

Berg, I. (1991). *Family Preservation: A brief workbook*. London: BT Press.

deShazer, S. (1985). *Keys to Solution in Brief Therapy*. New York: Norton.

Fisch, R., Weakland, J. and Segal, L. (1982). *The Tactics of Change*. San Francisco: Jossey Bass.

Haley, J. (1973). *Uncommon Therapy: The psychiatric techniques of Milton H. Erickson*. New York: Norton.

Haley, J. (1967a). Toward a theory of pathological systems. In G. H. Zuk and I. Boszormeny-Nagy (Eds.) *Family Therapy and Disturbed Families*. Palo Alto, CA: Science and Behavior Books, pp. 11-27.

O'Hanlon, W. H. and Weiner-Davis, M. (1989). *In Search of Solutions: A new direction in psychotherapy*. New York: Norton.

O'Hanlon, W. (1997). *A Guide to Possibility Land*. New York: Norton.

Watzlawick, P., Weakland, J. and Fisch, R. (1974). *Change: Principles of problem formation and problem resolution*. New York: Norton.

Weakland, J. H., Fisch, R., Watzlawick, P. and Bodin, A. (1974). Brief therapy: Focused problem resolution. *Family Process, 13*, 141–68.

Webster's Dictionary for Everyday Use. (1981). Baltimore: Ottenheimer.

REFERENCES: EXPERIENTIAL PSYCHOTHERAPY

Assagioli, R. (1975). *Psychosynthesis*. London: Turnstone Books.

Gendlin, E. T. (1962). *Experiencing and the Creation of Meaning*. New York: Free Press. (Reprinted by Macmillan, 1970).

Gendlin, E. T. (1978). *Focusing*. New York: Bantam Books.

Gendlin, E. T. (1996). *Focusing-oriented Psychotherapy*. New York: Guilford Press.

Jaison, B. (2002). *Integrating Experiential and Brief Therapy: How to do deep therapy — briefly and how to do brief therapy — deeply. A tool-book for therapists and counsellors*. Toronto: Focusing For Creative Living and Cavershambooksellers.com

Klein, J. (1999). *The Interactive Method: The path of healing through empathy and compassion.* Combined edition. The Center for Compassionate Empathic Communication, 62 North Lakeshore Drive Hypoluxo, FL. 33462.

Perls, F. S. (1969). *Gestalt Therapy Verbatim.* Lafayette, CA: Real People Press.

Rogers, C. R. (1951). *Client-centered Therapy.* Boston: Houghton Mifflin.

Satir, V. M. (1967). *Conjoint Family Therapy.* Palo Alto, CA: Science and Behavior Books.

Claude Missiaen

Faculteit voor Mens en Samenleving, Turnhout, Belgium

Client-Centered Group Psychotherapy: Six theses of the theory put to the test. A contribution from practice

After 15 years of practice as a group psychotherapist I decided to put some theses from the theory of client-centered group psychotherapy to the test. The psychotherapeutic groups I am working with are groups with neurotic people, sometimes a borderline client.

In the setting where I do group psychotherapy there are several formulae: some groups gather for 12 evenings with two sessions of one hour and a half; other groups meet during four weekends with an interval of one month; others stay together for a whole week with a follow-up weekend, one month later. The first year of our client-centered psychotherapy training consists of eight weekends with the same group, once a month. This group has several therapists.

Several authors in the Dutch literature (especially Lietaer and Dierick, 1993, 1996; and Berk, 1991) point out that in the client-centered/experiential school of thought there is not an extensive theoretical frame for group psychotherapy. It seems as if principles from individual therapy are transferred from individual to the group setting, yet it is quite a different context. Swildens (1979) argues that a group, phenomenologically speaking, uses the plural mode instead of the dual mode (in the dyadic therapeutic relationship). *I-you*, or should I say *I-thou* becomes *I-group*, or *I-group psychotherapist*. There are reasons to think that this transposition is naive.

In this contribution I select 6 theses of client-centered psychotherapy and put them to the test in practice. Two concern *the group*, two deal with *the therapist in the group* and two with *the therapeutic processes* in the group.

The theses are:

The group
1. The group has, just like any other organism, an actualizing tendency (Rogers, 1970).
2. The group is an interpersonal laboratory in the here-and-now (Lietaer and Dierick, 1993, 1996; Berk, 1991; Yalom, 1985).

The group psychotherapist
3. The therapist is transparent and is present as a real person (Rogers 1970; Lietaer and Dierick, 1993, 1996).
4. The therapist has a phenomenological attitude and uses the Rogerian core conditions as his/her most important instruments.

Therapeutic processes in the group

5. Client-centered group psychotherapy is not individual therapy in the group (Lietaer and Dierick, 1993, 1996). It is psychotherapy in and by the group (Berk, 1991).
6. The safety in the group enables all kinds of emotions and experiences to come forward. (Rogers 1970; Berk, 1991; Lietaer and Dierick, 1993, 1996).

For didactic reasons, the illustrations I use to support my findings consist of different situations from one and the same group. It's a special group situation of twenty friends who lost five of them in a tragic accident on a joint holiday abroad. A few months after the accident, eleven of the group of friends asked for an expert facilitation to help them make a space for their feelings and emotions concerning their collective loss. A female colleague and myself are the therapists of this group; therapy lasted three days, in a secure residence. The six men and five women have a very distinctive relationship to the deceased friends: most of them were with them when the accident happened, others were at home, some lost their very best friend, others lost someone whom they hadn't known for a long time. One woman lost her partner. All group members are between twenty-five and thirty years old. I will refer to them as the 'mourning group'.

Thesis 1: The group has, just like any other organism, an actualizing tendency

Carl Rogers (1970) says about the therapeutic group: ' I trust the group, given a reasonably facilitating climate, to develop its own potential and that of its members . . . This is undoubtedly similar to the trust I came to have in the process of therapy in the individual, when it was facilitated rather than directed. To me a group seems like an organism having a sense of its own direction even though it could not define that direction intellectually . . . A group recognizes unhealthy elements in its process, focuses on them, clears them up or eliminates them, and moves on toward becoming a healthier group. This is my way of saying that I have seen the 'wisdom of the organism' exhibited at every level from cell to group.'

This is an example of the transposing of a supposition from the individual therapeutic field to group psychotherapy. No doubt a group has its own identity, its own culture, group climate, its norms — but a private actualizing tendency?!

Here we see the naive Rogers with his unlimited faith in people and groups of people. For me as a practitioner of group therapy this is an extreme proposition. It forced me, however, to develop my trust in a group and their processes over and over again. Group psychotherapists who can't give their group the necessary trust, 'create' a group that doesn't allow its own potential. And conversely: the therapist who has the courage to delegate his power to his group cooperates in the development of an autonomous and trustworthy group.

The issue here is not about the number of interventions of the group psychotherapist, but about the inner basic attitude of trusting the developing group processes. It does not mean that the therapist just withdraws and doesn't feel responsible for the group. He is and remains the caring parent of the group and as such his interventions intend to provoke the potential of this group.

Of course, this isn't an easy job to do. Groups not only contain growth and actualizing tendencies, but also destruction, chaos, violence, disintegration . . . In many of these situations the obvious thing to do is to have the group psychotherapist use other qualities than just being the fellow-traveller or -pilgrim. Sometimes the therapist is a manager in times of crisis, for instance when a group member gets extremely overwhelmed by his emotions or when a straight fight or another major crisis foreshadows itself, or just happens; or when one group member suffers from excessive self-destruction.

Is the psychotherapy group able to remove its own *unhealthy* elements? (Is this the purpose of group psychotherapy anyway, to split off in order to become healthier?). Is the group able to organize its selfhealing (in Dutch: *genezen*: from Greek *ganisan*: to bring home safely)? Or is it the task of the therapist to take care of the safe homecoming of all members of the group?

I admit that this remains a dialectical tension. I don't share the extreme trust of the group that Carl Rogers taught. However, it remains challenging to not drop the trust concept, and to communicate — mostly non-verbally — my faith in the group, over and over again. I am often very much surprised to notice that a group that receives trust and confidence from its therapist also begins to behave like an autonomous and trustworthy group.

Let me illustrate this with some aspects of the mourning group.

> *In the beginning some of the members mentioned the role of the facilitators of the group. There was resistance; some of them spoke scornfully about what was going to happen. One member gives words to the attitude of the whole group: 'I hope you will be the police officers who regulate and control the traffic in our group.' The facilitators were asked to facilitate what comes up in the group, and to channel the conversations: not more, not less. Very soon, it became clear that facilitating means: structuring, making a space, slowing down and sometimes deepening the material in the group. The common intercourse of these friends is fast, with a high level of interaction, more covering what is there than discovering. The traffic becomes very hasty, with a lot of overtaking manoeuvres, sometimes a small collision, and taking a little time to park for a while.*
>
> *The process of the group belongs to the group, and to no one else, that is the lesson of the group to the therapists. 'Keep your hands off, it's ours,' or 'please don't you try to tell us how we should go into mourning, keep your theory for yourself!' At the end of the three-day session, one client says: 'I want to mention something about the therapists; it may sound negative, but I mean it as a compliment: often during this group I didn't notice that you were here, and yet we met each other in a totally different way than outside the group sessions.'*

Thesis 2: The group is an interpersonal laboratory in the here-and-now

In the absence of our own theory about groups and interactions in groups, the client-centered psychotherapy borrowed a lot of insights from the interactionally oriented group therapist Yalom, who wrote some books of great value concerning group psychotherapy.

The group is a social microcosm in which people get the opportunity to repeat their own personal histories. Group members interact with the other group members as with others from their social environment. The great advantage of the group therapy situation is that the interpersonal patterns can be explored and eventually adapted.

Although this is a very meaningful way of looking at groups, I try to define a group in terms of the concept of *space*, a common concept among experiential therapists (Gendlin, 1981, for instance). I mean that client-centered group therapy and also individual therapy have as their main objective making space for 'what wants to come up'.

I like to distinguish the concept of space in four aspects:

1. *An intrapsychic space* in which the clients can stand still, and can dwell on 'it' (whatever that is, for instance the intrusive loss) a little longer. This is the focusing space of Gendlin (e.g. 1981). Clearing a space also means cleaning up the inner room and looking for the optimal distance between 'myself' and 'my experience' (Weiser, 1996). *Indeed, some group members are overwhelmed by all kinds of intense emotions like grief, anger, or yearning for the deceased friends.*

   Others functioned totally differently, and didn't even start to feel anything at all; there is a big gap between themselves and their inner feelings.

2. To make a space in this context also means an *interpsychic space*. Gradually, groups build an interpsychic space, a new way of interacting with each other. Group members begin to embark on a new 'between', based on and sometimes falling back on the usual interaction patterns, but with an extra dimension that is enabled by the 'police officers'.

   For our mourning group this means: in a group of friends who have known each other for many years there are patterns of interaction that do not always allow them to discuss some topics on a deeper or experiential level. In this specific group humour is an element of cement. The very cordial and sharp humour gives support and connection. At the same time this humour stands in the way of focusing on the themes of grief and mourning for a longer period of time.

   It is as if in the house of the group of friends one more room is entered, a room that usually stays closed. I give an example: in 'normal' circumstances a group member who cries, has very soon an arm around his or her shoulder. Now the same person 'sits alone' with his or her grief. The usual consolation patterns fail to appear, and from that more space originates. It becomes possible to stand still, to explore what is there, and to give expression to what really lives in that person.

3. Psychotherapy groups are influenced by the *physical space*, the setting in which the group takes place. I notice, for instance, major differences between a group that has its sessions in the living-room of a restored little farm on the lonely Flemish countryside, as opposed to in a narrow room in a long corridor of rooms in a very busy university building.

   Experienced group therapists agree on this subject; nevertheless it is an underestimated theme in the group therapeutic literature.

   For the mourning group: the group members created a physical mourning space. The group remained for three days in an informal and secure environment. Very quickly, they appropriated this place. The first evening they built a kind of small altar. Photos of the five deceased friends were posted, clearly visible. The photos were accompanied by five spirit-stoves which were, as symbols of hope, light and presence, very impressive in their simplicity. Beside them lay a voluminous sheaf of press cuttings about the accident, the chaos afterwards, the judicial procedures, the funerals of the five young people.

   Installing a physical space, protected against all kinds of worries from the outside, seems to me an essential condition to help the unfolding of group processes.

4. The last meaning of 'space' for me is the *existential space*. Sharing feelings of grief and loss in a group confronts us with our own finiteness. Existential aspects like being alone and isolated, being responsible for our own life, the senselessness of our earthly existence . . . all come very close to the group members and the facilitators.

   Entering together this existential space (in which also the facilitators are reminded of their existential concerns and pains) is a very intense and connecting occurrence. It sharpens and shapes the realizing of the unpredictability of life, acceptance of the intolerable, the meaninglessness of it all . . .

A special issue here is dreams. Very often when I stay with a group in a residential house I dream about them at night. In my dreams I meet a lot of these existential topics. Dreams seem to be very accurate messengers of existential themes.

In this case I dreamed about the meaning of friendship, my responsibility in this group, my own sense of fluctuating between being all alone and being very close to another when I have to face an emotional crisis.

Thesis 3: The client-centered group psychotherapist is transparent and is present as a real person

Just as in individual therapy, the group psychotherapist is not supposed to be present as a cold professional who keeps at a distance, but as a real person, transparent and entering into the feelings of the group members. For that; he uses his presence. His deeper intuition can show him the way sometimes; he can give personal feedback, he can look at how he takes part in some incidents in the group; he can share some very private life experiences. There is no doubt this is a very powerful therapeutic factor. Also for the group therapist it is often very enriching to participate in this personal manner in the group process. An important condition is that he realizes that he is *not one of the boys,* and that he will never become one of the boys (Lietaer and Dierick, 1993, 1996). Many clients report that they appreciate the openness or the selective authenticity of the therapist. It gives them the feeling that the therapist really cares about them and is not just playing a role; rather they feel supported by the therapist, and that confrontation comes out of a real caring.

Nevertheless, there is another side to the picture, and this is, in my opinion, underexposed in the client-centered theory. I met this seamy side at the very beginning of my working as a (naive) group psychotherapist.

A group meets for the first time. After getting acquainted with each other, one of the female clients says about the therapist that she never met a cold person like this one here. Immediately after, another female client says that she did not know that this kind of person existed on earth: so warm, so receptive, so cordial and welcoming.

The least I could learn from this situation is that I have (indeed) a reserved quality, and that I have a warm aspect, but I feel that this extreme bipartition must also say something about the two ladies concerned. And yes, indeed, when we explored it further, their very early and also their more recent histories were involved. Early history was about the lack of appreciation by the father or being acknowledged; recent history was about a very painful divorce and a young (and thus still happy) marriage.

This incident was the motive for me to make a profound study of the phenomenon of *transference.*

As a group psychotherapist I often experienced that I am not only a person, congruent, transparent, present with all that I am and with all that I'm not, but also a symbolic figure or character, a symbolic representation of all kinds of relationships from the history of the clients. To say it in a disrespectful metaphor: the group psychotherapist often is like a dummy that is dressed and undressed according to the history or the needs of the clients.

Just like any other psychotherapist in any other kind of therapy, the client-centered group psychotherapist is an object on which clients can project their transferential feelings and desires. Group therapists collect lashing criticism that is only partly meant for them; they collect erotic adoration that is only partly meant for them. Appreciation or disapproval, love or hate: very often it concerns an aspect of the therapist, but the emotional loading in it often finds its roots in the life history or the context of the client.

I think it is nonsense to start a beginning client-centered therapist with the reassurance that he will be able to manage to balance his personal presence with the core conditions. Beginning therapists should be prepared for the phenomenon of transference, and taught how to handle this complex therapeutic event. This is even more important for group practitioners who often are confronted with multiple transferences (from different group members) or with group transference (for example, when the whole group is resistant).

Thesis 4: The group psychotherapist has a phenomenological attitude and uses the Rogerian core conditions as his most important instruments

The phenomenological basic attitude requests that the object of study appears as it is, in the context in which it shows itself to us. In terms of Gendlin (1970, 1973) we talk about the unity of body and mind as one system in interaction with other people (the body-mind-not-yet-split). The interactional unity of the organism-in-his-world is further explored in experiential Gestalt therapy. In my opinion, client-centered therapy emphasizes the unified body and psyche, and less attention is paid to the individual-in-his/her-context.

I feel more attracted to this aspect of Gestalt therapy in which also the core conditions are looked at as an interactional event. Empathy is not seen as something that one person has and gives to the other, but is defined as *inclusion*: partially fusing with the client (Buber, 1965; Wollants and Lietaer, 2000). The therapist doesn't put himself in shoes of the client, as if he were the client; but he becomes the client, while he stays on his own track of experiencing. This makes it possible to co-experience: the client and the therapist. Starting from this shared experience in contact, the therapist can help to find words for the yet inexpressible.

Another more relational concept is *percolate*, like a percolator, to make coffee. The client brings the raw materials, the therapist takes care of the hot water: thus they develop from the materials something new. Here also the interactional process of co-experiencing is emphasized. In everyday practice, these concepts and ours are very similar.

I have a more fundamental criticism of the extrapolation from the individual to the group context. I don't agree with the proposition of Lietaer and Dierick (1993, 1996) that the training of client-centered therapists prepares them very well to do group psychotherapy, because of the comprehensive training in the core conditions and interpersonal skills.

In my opinion, a psychotherapy group is in the first place a *group*, and in the second place a psychotherapy group. A group has its own order and patterns, and these are different from those in a dyadic relationship.

The group psychotherapist must direct his empathic attention focally to the client who is talking, while he must be attentive in a peripheral way to the whole group.

Berk (1986) points out that it is a pity that studies from social psychology are barely integrated into the field of group psychotherapy. He pleads in favour of a profound knowledge of group dynamics (Berk, 1984), a proposition that I would like to underline. A phenomenon like situational leadership teaches us that the therapist in some situations needs to be more active (for instance in a crisis), or that his delegating style sometimes brings about effects other than he intended (for instance, group members sink away in a passive attitude). Sometimes groups in some phases need, and at other moments don't need, a participatory way of leading the group. The theory of group dynamics teaches us about the importance of informal leadership in influencing group processes and norms (Remmerswaal, 1996).

Of course, an experienced group therapist who relies on his own intuition and knowledge discerns these phenomena, and he knows the best way to handle them. Nevertheless, examination of the body of knowledge of group dynamics gives a more refined and differentiated view of group phenomena like leadership, norms, roles, group development, group formation, sympathy and antipathy in the group, group cohesion and so on.

Group therapists with this world of thought in their suitcases can be more efficient and competent group psychotherapists.

Thesis 5: Client-centered group psychotherapy is not individual psychotherapy in the group. It is psychotherapy in and by the group

Neither is it therapy *of* the group (Berk, 1991): it is not the group that is in therapy, but the individual clients. The group is only the medium by which therapeutic processes in individual persons can be facilitated.

I belong to the type of group therapists who look at a group through group glasses. Through many years of inter-vision, study of literature, case studies and so on, it became clear to me that a group is not just a collection or compilation of individuals, but is a separate entity, with its own undercurrent, typical interactions, norms, group identity, and so on. The group leads its own life. Agazarian and Peters (1981) conceptualise this very clearly when they write about the visible and the invisible group. Foulkes (1964) and Bion (1961) can also be found in this line of thought. In Gestalt therapy in my institute in Belgium, 'the hot-seat' procedure (in which the therapist works with one client while the rest of the group is the silent audience) is not used any more. *Beyond the Hot Seat* is the title of a book by Feder and Ronall (1980). They argue that a group is viewed as a Gestalt, as a whole that is more than the sum of his separate parts. The group is not just an audience looking at the individual psychotherapy.

I believe in the fundamental idea that it is the first task of the group therapist to use optimally the potential of the group in such a manner that the autonomous group can help its members.

In spite of all these influences, I assert that client-centered psychotherapy sometimes *is* individual therapy in the group. (I would say, not the hot seat, but rather the *soft seat*.)

A lot depends of course upon how one defines individual therapy. The presence of a group around an individual event makes the situation totally different from when it is with one therapist and one client.

Clients often come to group psychotherapy with the expectation of 'individual therapy in the group'. Very often they don't want to be working on the here-and-now, but also, or mostly, on the there-and-then. The injuries they carry in their bodies (in experiential terms), the painful or traumatic chapters in their book of life, or everyday complaints, solicit for their special attention. This does not always have to do with the interpersonal laboratory in which they have landed. They have their sufferings with them and come to group psychotherapy to work on them and to get attention, space and acknowledgement of it. Often they call for the therapist's help They rely more upon his help than upon that of the other group members. Naturally the group therapist will try to avoid this exclusive appeal by bringing in the other group members.

For me this raises a duality: the therapist delegates his power to the group, but at the same time he remains the editor-in-chief. Every one may write his article, but the way it is published is inspected by the group therapist.

In some cases we are talking about individual therapy in a group. There are sessions in which the therapist goes along with the client for some time, working on his individual problems. Especially in critical situations the group sometimes lets the therapist pull the chestnuts out of the fire.

> *This duality was noticeable in the mourning group. The group wanted to direct its own process, and yet sometimes leaned on the facilitators for further or deeper exploration when a group member asked for it. One woman was obsessed by the concrete and lugubrious details of the tragic accident; asked herself why these images kept on coming up in her. This intrapsychic exploration of this aspect of herself I would like to subsume under the category of individual therapy in the group.*

Thesis 6: The safety in the group enables all kinds of emotions and experiences to come forward

The space that psychotherapy provides, is an invitation for clients to come forward with all kinds of experiences and to participate in all sorts of emotions with other group members. One client put this richness of the group into these words: 'Group therapy is like reading several books at the same time.'

In my opinion, practice demonstrates that the warm core conditions (of phenomenologically resonating, being with the group in a positive accepting attitude, and being present as a person) only partially cover the spectrum of experiences. The core conditions that the therapist embodies are gradually adopted by (a part of) the group. This especially gives rise to the expression of feelings of vulnerability, pain, longings, grief, hurt, warmth.

My point is that the way the client-centered group therapist is present in the group increases safety for the expression of vulnerability, and at the same time is less inviting to feelings of intense aggression. It's about gradations.

The expression of these feelings occurs in group therapy, but the less provocative style of the client-centered therapist doesn't lead to these kinds of feelings in the first place.

I feel that acceptance gives rise to feelings of weakness and vulnerability, and that a well-chosen form of provocation by the therapist enables rather the strength and the power of the client.

In a recent study Missiaen and Wollants (2000) compared the tapes of Gloria by Rogers and by Perls. Gloria seems to come up with her grief and uncertainties in the presence of the gentle, mild and accepting Rogers, while in contact with a provocative Perls she seems to develop her strong (and angry) side.

Client-centered group therapies sometimes suffer from a lack of dynamics: or should I say *dynamite*? Therapy groups of therapists-in-training are extra-sensitive at this point, because they try to interact with each other in an empathic way. Empathy in groups can be very suffocating or weakening, or can elicit fusion instead of difference and autonomy.

Bolten (1995) points out that *excitement* in group therapy is essential. The therapist must take care that periods with a lack of tension (this is not the same as relaxation or relief) don't take too long. He must arrange an optimal level of tension. Bolten uses the principle *from containing to entertaining*, a pleasant way of handling the problem of excitement in groups. It doesn't mean that he must be an excellent entertainer, but — like a thermostat — he must register the group temperature and regulate it when necessary.

CONCLUSION

I feel that it is an everlasting mission for the group therapist to rely on the process of the group. A group that receives trust and confidence from its therapist will begin to develop as a trustworthy and autonomous group. On the other hand, a group therapist should not be too naive: groups have their own dynamics, and in psychotherapy sometimes the authentic presence of the therapist is a variable that gets overshadowed by another strong mechanism: transference.

Beginning group therapists should learn about group dynamics and transference before they go ahead with a group. Co-therapy with an experienced group facilitator seems an excellent learning environment to me. These two aspects (group dynamics and transference) are not given enough attention in the theory of client-centered therapy.

In my quest I also found that group psychotherapy sometimes has a very individual focus, and that the psychotherapy space (in a client-centered way) is more inviting for giving rise to vulnerability and weakness than to aggression and difference.

REFERENCES

Agazarian, Y. and R. Peters (1981), *The Visible and Invisible Group*. London: Routledge and Kegan Paul.

Berk, T. (1984), Groepsdynamische experiëntiële groepstherapie. In G. Lietaer, Ph. Van Praag, and J. C. A. G. Swildens (Eds.) *Client-centered therapie in beweging*. Leuven: Acco. pp. 521–34.

Berk, T. (1986), *Groepspsychotherapie*. Deventer: Van Loghum Slaterus.

Berk, T. (1991), Cliëntgerichte groepspsychotherapie. In H. Swildens, O. de Haas, G. Lietaer and R. Van Balen (Eds.) *Leerboek gesprekstherapie*, Amersfoort/Leuven: Acco, pp. 433–78.

Bion, W. R. (1961), *Experiences in Groups*. London: Tavistock Publications.

Bolten, M. P. (1995), Opwinding in psychotherapiegroepen. In *Handboek Groepspsychotherapie*, 7.3–7.36.

Buber, M. (1965), *The Knowledge of Man: a philosophy of the interhuman*. New York: Harper and Row.

Feder, B. and Ronall, F. (1980), *Beyond the Hot Seat*. New York: Verlag Brunner/Mazel.

Foulkes, S. H. (1964), *Therapeutic Group Analysis*. New York: International Universities Press.

Gendlin, E. (1970), A theory of personality change. In J.T. Hart, and T.M. Tomlinson (Eds.) *New Directions in Client-centered Therapy*, Boston, Houghton Mifflin, pp. 129–74.

Gendlin, E. (1973), Experiential psychotherapy. In R. Corsini (Ed.) *Current Psychotherapies*, Itasca: Peacock, pp. 317–52.

Gendlin, E. (1981), *Focusing*, New York: Bantam Books.

Lietaer, G. and Dierick, P. (1993), Cliëntgerichte groepspsychotherapie. In P. J. Jongerius and J. C. B. Eykman (Ed.) *Praktijkboek groepspsychotherapie*. Amersfoort: Academische Uitgeverij, pp. 117–30.

Lietaer, G. and Dierick, P. (1996), Client-centered group psychotherapy in dialogue with other orientations: Commonality and specificity. In R. Hutterer, G. Pawlowsky, P. Schmid and R. Stipsits (Eds.) *Client-Centered and Experiential Psychotherapy. A paradigm in motion*, Frankfurt am Main: Peter Lang.

Missiaen, C. and Wollants, G. (2000), Gloria and Carl Rogers, Fritz Perls, in het kader van experiëntiële procesbevordering. In *Tijdschrift voor Gestalttherapie. 7*(7).

Remmerswaal, J. (1996), *Handboek groepsdynamica. Een nieuwe inleiding op theorie en praktijk*. Baarn, Nelissen.

Rogers, C. R. (1970), *Carl Rogers on encounter groups*. New York: Harper and Row.

Swildens, H. (1979), 'Is er een Rogeriaanse groepstherapie?'. In *Tijdschrift voor Psychotherapie, 5*, 1–7.

Weiser. A. (1996), *The Power of Focusing*. Berkeley: Focusing Resources.

Wollants, G. and Lietaer. G. (2000), De existentiële dimensie. In *Handboek Integratieve Psychotherapie*, De Tijdstroom.

Yalom, I. D. (1985), *Theory and Practice of Group Psychotherapy* (rev. edn.) New York: Basic Books.

Marlis Pörtner
Zürich, Switzerland

Psychotherapy for People with Special Needs: A challenge for client-centered psychotherapists

For a long time psychotherapy for people with special needs has been considered impossible. Only since the 1980s has there been increasing discussion about this issue in the literature and at conferences. Yet there are still only a very few practitioners working in this field, among client-centered psychotherapists as well as in general. Perhaps the diffuse fears many people (including psychologists) have of mentally disabled persons play a part here. This is highly regrettable, because entering the world of a person with special needs can expand the psychotherapists' horizons in ways their whole therapeutic work might benefit from.

As for myself, it was by chance that I came to work in this area when, still in training as a client-centered psychotherapist, I was asked if I would do psychotherapy with a mentally disabled woman. After consulting with my training group and trainers, and despite considerable doubts — we just had learned that Rogers considered an average level of intelligence as a condition for psychotherapy — I decided to try it and soon got a second client with special needs. The experience with these two women (Pörtner, 1984, 1990) became a fundamental element of my formation as a psychotherapist and had a crucial influence on my understanding of client-centered psychotherapy. Since then I have, in addition to other clients, always some persons with mental disabilities in my practice and would not want to do without them. The insights and experiences I owe this segment of my work are essential for my therapeutic practice in general. No other clients react as sensitively, or show disapproval as naturally, as my clients with special needs when I am not completely attentive for a moment or not understanding them accurately. Particularly with them, I experienced how essential it is that as a client-centered psychotherapist I am not 'doing', but 'enabling', and that the most fundamental factor is to empathically and congruently enter the other person's world.

When I started with this work 20 years ago, it meant breaking new ground. Not only was it new for me, but also for the trainers and the supervision group who accompanied and supported me on this unknown road. It meant real encouragement when in 1981, at a Gendlin workshop in Chicago, I met Garry Prouty for the first time and realized I was not alone: there were other client-centered psychotherapists working with mentally disabled clients. Later on, I got to know Isolde Badelt's pioneering work in Heidelberg (Badelt, 1984, 1990) and, with time, that of other colleagues in different countries, such as Hans Peters in Holland (Peters, 1992, 1999). The circle slowly expanded, yet there are, scattered over different countries, still only a few client-centered psychotherapists working in this field (and the same is true for other schools).

It is time that 'psychotherapy for people with special needs' no longer remained an issue for just a few therapists, but had a broader foundation in the client-centered movement and was integrated into training programs for client-centered psychotherapists. The reasons for this are the following:

1. In this field there is a need for psychotherapy, but a lack of competent psychotherapists.
2. The Person-Centered Approach, owing to its fundamentals and its image of man, as well as in terms of its method, corresponds to what is required in this specific area.
3. Working with mentally disabled persons gives a psychotherapist fundamental insight into what client-centered psychotherapy is and what the person-centered attitude really means.
4. The work of 'pioneers' in different countries offers a solid base to build upon and is an invitation to further development.

WHY PSYCHOTHERAPY FOR PEOPLE WITH SPECIAL NEEDS?

For a long time, in psychiatry as well as in special education, behavior disorders of mentally disabled persons were attributed exclusively to organic brain defects and considered possible neither to comprehend nor to influence. Later on, it came to be understood that behavior disorders could be caused by unfavorable circumstances. Progressive educationalists became involved in getting mentally disabled people out of hospitals and tried to normalize their conditions of life. The assumption was that the organism would automatically react in a positive way to favorable circumstances. Yet, behavior disorders did not disappear just by normalizing people's conditions of life; on the contrary, they sometimes became even more apparent, because the new concepts allowed the individuality of a person with special needs to manifest itself more distinctly. It turned out that mental diseases were even more frequent among mentally disabled persons than among the average population (Gaedt, 1987; Lotz and Koch, 1994).

This is not surprising. The German psychologist Barbara Senckel (Senckel, 1998) explains very plausibly why people with special needs are 'particularly vulnerable and wounded'. The reasons she gives are 'in addition to limitations due to disabilities', traumatic experiences like 'fundamental lack of acceptance and esteem; repeated experiences of being abandoned and of separation; disparagement, neglect, isolation; heteronomy, pressure to conform, control; lack of self-determination (even where it would be possible) and lack of prospects in life' (Senckel, 1998). In the biographies of people with special needs we find again and again such experiences, and they still happen frequently in their daily life. The behavior of a person with special needs is shaped by such experiences, often in a way other people find strange and incomprehensible. They respond with no understanding or with disapproval, thus unintentionally reinforcing the unwanted behavior: a vicious circle has started that is hard to break. Social life gets difficult, the disabled person is troubled by aggressions, insecurity, tensions and diffuse feelings of guilt. The quality of life of everyone involved is considerably impaired.

There is obviously a need for psychotherapy with mentally handicapped people. The question is: how can psychotherapy cope with the specific demands of working with this population? Psychotherapists of different schools, among them some client-centered psychotherapists, have considered this question and proposed their ideas (Lotz, Koch and Stahl, 1994; Lotz, Stahl and Irblich, 1996). Interestingly enough, the specific requirements most of them describe correspond to client-centered principles. However, client-centered psychotherapists, too, need to consider what is different with these clients. They have to think about how to modify their ways of working and at the same time stay true to client-centered principles. In the following, I shall point to some specific aspects of working with mentally disabled clients and highlight in what ways the Person-Centered Approach is particularly suitable for the requirements of this field.

Requirements and difficulties

Some voices have expressed *fundamental reservations* about psychotherapy for people with special needs and claim that they should 'be accepted instead of treated' (Stahl, 1996). From a person-centered point of view, to accept a person the way she is, is not a contradiction to psychotherapy but, on the contrary, a basic condition for facilitating growth. To accept a person with special needs as she is does not imply that you do not believe her capable of further development. We have to move, so to speak, on double tracks: on the one hand accept people the way they are, not trying to change them, yet on the other hand believe them capable of taking steps of growth, be aware when those steps are in the offing and empathically support them. My formulation therefore is: we must *accept people with special needs as they are, not try to change them, but offer them conditions that make changes possible.* This, at the same time, describes a fundamental aspect of client-centered psychotherapy.

Usually with these clients *the basic condition of a voluntary decision is not granted.* Very rarely is it their own choice to come to the psychotherapist; for the most part they are induced to do so by their family or by carers (this actually is also true for most therapies with children and adolescents) who often have quite definite ideas about what the results of psychotherapy should be. Therapists must be very careful to avoid being used to carry out orders, but must remain absolutely open for the concerns of the clients themselves. Only in this way is there a chance that they will build up trust and that a therapeutic relationship may develop. It is not the point of psychotherapy to remodel a handicapped person to the desires of carers, but to facilitate their taking personal steps of growth and making their own decisions. For the therapist it is a tightrope walk as — differently from working with adults who are not disabled — he needs to *cooperate and exchange views with carers.*

Without being supported by their milieu, people with special needs are hardly able to transfer their experiences from the therapy sessions into daily life. They have little self-confidence and are quickly discouraged. Therefore it is important that carers are aware of the growth process going on, in order that they can encourage and prevent it from losing momentum. Sometimes behaviors that are perceived as irritating may be the first signs of an important step of growth. If carers are sensitized to this, they will respond more adequately. The therapist, on the other hand, sometimes learns only from the feedback of carers that positive changes have occurred or new problems are coming up with a client. Sometimes people with special needs go through a change, but don't perceive it as such: they live so much in the moment that the minute something changes, they can no longer remember how it had been before. Others may be quite aware of a change, yet not able to express or communicate it.

Another difficulty emerges from this 'living in the moment'. Many people with special needs need to talk with the therapist about their problems and conflicts the moment they occur. If there are several days between the therapy session and the crucial events, these events are no longer accessible to the client and he doesn't really know how to make good use of the therapy session. Yet if the therapist is able to refer to what happened, or to ask the right question, it might help the client to get in touch with it again. In this respect, therapists who work within an institution or community have the advantage of being in a position to arrange for a session if and when the need arises, or if the client is asking for it. A therapist in private practice, on the other hand, benefits from more distance and from not being part of any institutional structures.

An occasional exchange of views with carers is useful and necessary, yet *in any case confidentiality of the therapy session has to be maintained.* This is a subtle balance that requires sensitivity, transparency and clear differentiation from the therapist. She may, for example, help to expand the carers' comprehension by sharing *her view* of where the client's process is at the moment, without giving away anything of the content that the client has confided to her. Yet sometimes clients explicitly ask the therapist to communicate to the carers something they have expressed during the session, but feel not able to do so in daily life. In any case, it is indispensable that a person with special needs be informed about contacts between carers and the therapist, and can rely on the latter to respect the boundary between that which is open for discussion and that which is confidential.

Another reason for cooperation between psychotherapist and carers is that people with special needs have a hard time if that which is developing in psychotherapy conflicts with what is required or tolerated by the environment in which they live. Therefore the therapist should communicate with carers and facilitate their understanding for therapeutic work and for the client's growth process. Moreover, *the therapist must be empathic with carers too, take them seriously and acknowledge their frame of reference.* As mentioned before, a therapist should never carry out orders, but in some situations he might consider it useful, without taking it himself, to explain the carers' position to a client in order to help him to better cope with it.

Cooperation may benefit from the fact that the Person-Centered Approach, besides client-centered psychotherapy, offers concepts for different professional fields. These concepts provide concrete handles for carers about how to be person-centered in their daily work. They are helpful also for the therapist to recognize what is essential for a specific professional area. *Trust and Understanding* is a person-centered concept for everyday care for people with special needs, developed from my long-term experience as a supervisor and consultant of professionals working in this field (Pörtner, 1996a, 1996b, 2000). It is based on the same principles as client-centered psychotherapy, yet adapted to the conditions of everyday work in homes or institutions for people with special needs or in need of care. These conditions, as well as the tasks, are different from those of psychotherapy, but the two areas will sensibly complement each other if based on the same fundamentals, thus offering clients a *continuity* that their well-being and social life will benefit from.

Though the fundamental principles are the same, I have always pleaded for a *clear distinction between client-centered psychotherapy and the Person-Centred Approach in fields other than psychotherapy* (Pörtner and Monstein, 1985; Pörtner, 1994). Particularly where the two areas overlap — as they do here and then when working with people with special needs — it is important to discriminate. We have to know the boundary in order to be in a position to deliberately cross it if necessary. Sometimes, to defuse a critical situation, carers must respond therapeutically. On the other hand, the psychotherapist's work with a mentally disabled person at times goes along lines I would not call psychotherapy in the strict sense, but rather a therapeutic accompanying.

What is the point of psychotherapy for a person with special needs, if not to purposefully change unwanted behaviors?

For most people with special needs (as for other clients too), it is in the first place a matter of *finding another — more accepting and positive — attitude toward themselves*. Most people with special needs have a hard time accepting themselves, as they are constantly confronted with their incompetence and insufficiencies. They suffer from 'being different' and measure themselves by that what they consider 'normal'. They usually have very little self-esteem — the unrealistic over-estimation displayed by some of them is just the other side of the same coin. In this respect psychotherapy is helpful.

The following statement of an analytically oriented psychotherapist expresses exactly what is a major focus in client-centered psychotherapy: 'Thus psychotherapy often is the first experience of being taken seriously and of an accepting, not judgmental relation with another person,' (Görres, 1996). Regarding this, the specific challenge with people with special needs is that they often are verbal only in a very limited way or not at all, so that *the relation may emerge in a very subtle, pre-verbal area* of which the therapist must learn to become aware. The experience of the German psychologist Barbara Krietemeyer with a severely retarded woman (Pörtner, 1996a, 2000) is a very impressive example for this subtle and demanding level of a therapist's awareness.

To be accepted by the therapist helps clients to better accept themselves and their inadequacies. This in itself represents a change and encourages the discovering of their own hidden resources. Awareness of life improves and energies are set free that open up new perspectives and initiate further — perhaps just very small — steps of growth. What I said elsewhere about *the importance of small steps* in psychotherapy (Pörtner, 1994) is particularly true for people with special needs. They are usually so fixed on their deficiencies (as are their carers) that they are not able to acknowledge when they do take a — tiny but important — step. These small steps must be paid careful attention to — actually looked for 'with a magnifying glass', and encouraged, not only by the therapist in the therapy session, but above all in daily life by the carers, because 'each step as small as it might be, proves the capability of taking steps and has the potential for further steps' (Pörtner, 1996a, 2000).

To *establish and restore contact functions* is another crucial aspect of psychotherapy for people with special needs. These functions, defined by Prouty as 'reality-contact, affective contact and communicative contact' (Prouty, 1994), are almost always impaired with mentally handicapped persons, or not sufficiently developed. Prouty's concept of pre-therapy, based on client-centered fundamentals, offers helpful support to establish and restore contact functions. It is not limited to psychotherapy but can be helpful also in everyday situations (Prouty, 1994; Prouty, Van Werde and Pörtner, 1998; Pörtner, 1993, 1996a, 1996c, 2000).

To accept themselves more, to be more in contact with reality, with their feelings and with others inevitably has an influence on people's behaviors and opens up new possibilities. Even though we are not explicitly trying to change behaviors, changes will happen when self-esteem is improving. And it is a crucial difference whether people discover their own hidden resources and take their own steps — even though perhaps not those we would have imagined — or whether they are pushed in a specific direction. This is an essential aspect of client-centered philosophy and valuable not only for people with special needs. Taking other persons seriously, respecting their 'otherness', empathically entering their world — which at first may seem strange and incomprehensible — trying to understand their language (even though they might not be able to express themselves verbally) and accompanying them on *their* way in *their* rhythm (which may be extremely slow or extremely accelerated). All these are indispensable elements of a client-centered therapist's professional competence. To work with mentally disabled persons is a very special opportunity to acquire these elements. This is another reason for encouraging more client-centered psychotherapists to work in this field, and making psychotherapy for people with special needs an issue of training programs. The field is a challenge for client-centered psychotherapy and offers client-centered psychotherapists invaluable learning opportunities, as well as the chance to contribute to its further development. It is worth accepting the challenge, not only for the benefit of people with special needs but also for client-centered psychotherapy itself.

REFERENCES

Badelt, I. (1984). Selbsterfahrungsgruppen geistig behinderter Erwachsener. In *Geistige Behinderung, 4* (Fachzeitschrift der Bundesvereinigung Lebenshilfe).

Badelt, I. (1990). Client-centered psychotherapy with mentally handicapped adults. In G. Lietaer, J. Rombauts, R. Van Balen (Eds.) *Client-centered and Experiential Psychotherapy in the Nineties.* Leuven: Leuven University Press, pp. 671–81.

Gaedt, C. (Ed.) (1987). *Psychotherapie bei geistig Behinderten.* 2. Neuerkeröder Forum. Neuerkeröder Anstalten, Eigenverlag.

Görres, S. (1996). Ethische Fragen in der Psychotherapie mit geistig behinderten Menschen. In W. Lotz, B. Stahl and D. Irblich, D. (Eds.) *Wege zur seelischen Gesundheit für Menschen mit geistiger Behinderung — Psychotherapie und Persönlichkeitsentwicklung,* 29–39. Bern, Hans Huber.

Lietaer, G., Rombauts, J. and Van Balen, R. (Eds.) (1990). *Client-centered and Experiential Psychotherapy in the Nineties.* Leuven: Leuven, University Press.

Lotz, W. and Koch, U. (1994). Zum Vorkommen psychischer Störungen bei Personen mit geistiger Behinderung. In W. Lotz, U. Koch and B. Stahl (Eds.) *Psychotherapeutische Behandlung geistig behinderter Menschen — Bedarf, Rahmenbedingungen, Konzepte.* Bern: Hans Huber, pp. 13–39.

Lotz, W., Koch, U. and Stahl, B. (1994). (Eds.) *Psychotherapeutische Behandlung geistig behinderter Menschen — Bedarf, Rahmenbedingungen, Konzepte.* Bern: Hans Huber.

Lotz, W., Stahl, B. and Irblich, D. (Eds.) (1996). *Wege zur seelischen Gesundheit für Menschen mit geistiger Behinderung — Psychotherapie und Persönlichkeitsentwicklung.* Bern: Hans Huber.

Peters, H. (1992). *Psychotherapie bij geestelijk gehandicapten.* Amsterdam: Lisse, Swets and Zeitlinger. German edn (2001) *Psychotherapeutische Zugänge zu Menschen mit geistiger Behinderung.* Stuttgart: Klett-Cotta.

Peters, H. (1999). Pre-Therapy: a client-centered experiential approach to mentally handicapped people. In *Journal of Humanistic Psychology, 39*(4).

Pörtner, M. (1984). Gesprächstherapie mit geistig behinderten Klienten. *Brennpunkt 18,* (Bulletin der Schweiz. Gesellschaft für Gesprächspsychotherapie) and in *GwG-info 56.*

Pörtner, M. (1990). Client-centered therapy with mentally retarded persons: Catherine and Ruth. In G. Lietaer, J. Rombauts, R. Van Balen (Eds.) *Client-Centered and Experiential Psychotherapy in the Nineties,* 659–69. Leuven, University Press, pp. 659–69.

Pörtner, M. (1993). Klientenzentrierte Therapie mit geistig Behinderten und Schizophrenen — Garry Prouty's Konzept der Prä-Therapie. In *Brennpunkt 54.*

Pörtner, M. (1994). *Praxis der Gesprächspsychotherapie: Interviews mit Therapeuten.* Stuttgart: Klett-Cotta.

Pörtner, M. (1996a). *Ernstnehmen, Zutrauen, Verstehen: Personzentrierte Haltung im Umgang mit geistig behinderten und pflegebedürftigen Menschen.* Stuttgart: Klett-Cotta.

Pörtner, M. (1996b). Working with the mentally handicapped in a person-centered way: Is it possible, is it appropriate and what does it mean in practice? In R. Hutterer, G. Pawlowsky, P. F. Schmid and R. Stipsits (Eds.) *Client-centered and Experiential Psychotherapy: A paradigm in motion.* Frankfurt am Man: Peter Lang, pp. 513–27.

Pörtner, M. (1996c). Garry Prouty's Konzept der Prä-Therapie. In W. Lotz, B. Stahl and D. Irblich (Eds.) *Wege zur seelischen Gesundheit für Menschen mit geistiger Behinderung — Psychoptherapie und Persönlichkeitsentwicklung.* Bern: Hans Huber, pp. 216–26.

Pörtner, M. (2000). *Trust and Understanding: The Person-Centred Approach in everyday care for people with special needs.* Ross-on-Wye: PCCS Books.

Pörtner, M. and Monstein, P. (1985). Personzentrierte Beratung — Überlegungen zu einem Konzept. In *Brennpunkt* 22 and in *GwG-info* 60.

Prouty, G. (1994). *Theoretical Evolutions in Person-Centered/Experiential Therapy — Applications to schizophrenic and retarded psychoses,* Westport: Praeger.

Prouty, G., Van Werde, D. and Pörtner, M. (1998). *Prä-Therapie.* Stuttgart, Klett-Cotta. English edn. in preparation (2002) Ross-on-Wye: PCCS Books.

Senckel, B. (1998). *Du bist ein weiter Baum — Entwicklungschancen für geistig behinderte Menschen durch Beziehung.* München: Beck.

Stahl, B. (1996): Zum Stand der Entwicklung in der Psychotherapie mit geistig behinderten Menschen. Menschen. In W. Lotz, B. Stahl and D. Irblich (Eds.) (1996). *Wege zur seelischen Gesundheif für Menschen mit geistiger Behinderung — Psychotherapie und Persönlichkeitsentwicklung.* Bern, Hans Huber, pp.14–28.

Natalie Rogers Ph.D REAT
The Person-Centered Expressive Therapy Institute, Cotati, California

Person-Centered Expressive Arts Therapy: A path to wholeness[1]

Abstract. This chapter discusses ways of bringing nonverbal forms of self-expression into the client–counselor relationship. The Creative Connection® is an expressive arts process developed by Dr. Natalie Rogers, which interweaves movement, sound, art, writing and guided imagery, to tap into the deep wellsprings of creativity within each person. Vital to the creative process is a safe, person-centered environment of acceptance, non-judgment, freedom, and permission to play with materials. Expressive arts therapy differs from the analytic or medical model of art therapy used for diagnosis and treatment. Person-centered expressive art therapy is beneficial for both individuals and groups and has been used by many in the mental health profession. Dr. Rogers clearly states the humanistic principles involved and discusses applications of person-centered expressive therapy.

> *Creativity is like freedom: Once you taste it, you cannot live without it. It is a transformative force enhancing self-esteem and self-empowerment.* Natalie Rogers

Part of the psychotherapeutic process is to awaken the creative life-force energy. Thus, creativity and therapy overlap. What is creative is frequently therapeutic. What is therapeutic is frequently a creative process. Having integrated the creative arts into my therapeutic practice, I use the term *person-centered expressive arts therapy*. The terms *expressive therapy* or *expressive arts therapy* generally include dance, art, and music therapies, as well as journal writing, poetry, imagery, meditation, and improvisational drama. Using the expressive arts to foster emotional healing, resolve inner conflict, and awaken individual creativity is a relatively new, expanding field.

WHAT IS EXPRESSIVE ARTS THERAPY?

Art is a language. Expressive arts therapy uses various arts — movement, drawing, painting, sculpting, music, writing, sound, and improvisation — in a supportive, client-centered setting to experience and express feelings. Any art form that comes from an emotional depth provides a process of self-discovery. We express inner feelings by creating outer forms.

In the therapeutic world based on humanistic principles, the term *expressive therapy* has been reserved for nonverbal and/or metaphoric expression. Humanistic expressive arts

---

[1] This chapter is a weaving together of direct quotes from three sources: Natalie Rogers (1993), *The Creative Connection: Expressive Art as Healing,* and her chapter in *Foundations of Expressive Arts Therapy,* edited by Stephen and Ellen Levine (1988), and an article entitled, 'Counselling and creativity: an interview with Natalie Rogers,' by Tony Merry (1997).

therapy differs from the analytic or medical model of art therapy, in which art is used to diagnose, analyze and 'treat' people. Rather, we believe in the ability of individuals to find appropriate self-direction if the psychological climate is empathic, honest, and caring. Our tradition draws from many humanistic psychologists — notably, Carl Rogers, Abraham Maslow, Rollo May, Clark Moustakas, Ross Mooney, Arthur Combs, Sidney Jourard and Prescott Lecky. These pioneers defied the authoritarian medical model and created a relationship model of personal growth in which the therapist respects the client's dignity, worth, and capacity for self-direction.

To use the arts *expressively* means going into our inner realms to discover feelings and to express them through visual art, movement, sound, writing, or drama without concern about the beauty of the art, the grammar and style of the writing, or the harmonic flow of the sounds. Although interesting and sometimes dramatic products emerge, we leave the aesthetics and the craftsmanship to those who wish to pursue the arts professionally. This is an intermodal approach that emphasizes the healing process of creating art, and using the imagery for self-insight.

We use the arts to let go, to express, and to release and gain personal insight. Any feeling can be expressed nonverbally. Feelings of grief, pain, fear, anger, or the feeling of being trapped, stuck or bored can be expressed through color, form, movement, sound or poetry. Expressive art therapists are aware that involving the mind, the body, and emotions brings forth the client's intuitive, imaginative abilities as well as logical, linear thought. Since emotional states are seldom logical, the use of imagery and nonverbal modes allows the client an alternate path for self-exploration and communication.

The creative process itself is a powerful integrative force. Verbal therapy focuses on emotional disturbances and inappropriate behavior. Like verbal therapy, the expressive arts move the client into the world of emotions yet they add a further dimension, offering a way to use the free-spirited parts of oneself. Therapy may include joyful, lively learning on many levels: the sensory, kinesthetic, conceptual, emotional and mythic. Clients report that the expressive arts have helped them go beyond their problems to finding a new sense of soul or spirit and envisioning themselves taking action in the world constructively.

Using the expressive arts with clients enhances the therapeutic relationship in many ways. It helps the client:
- identify and be in touch with feelings,
- explore unconscious material,
- release energy,
- gain insight,
- solve problems and
- discover the spiritual aspects of self.

> *When the client shares her personal art she is opening a window to her soul to the therapist.* (Rogers, N., 1993)

Of tremendous importance to me is the fact that the person-centered philosophy of my father, Carl Rogers (Rogers, C. R., 1951), is the foundation on which my form of expressive arts therapy rests. I base my approach on the very deep faith in the innate capacity of each person to reach toward full potential if given the person-centered environment for growth.

Just as Carl veered away from psychoanalysis and interpretation, so, too, have I rejected analytic and interpretive forms of art and movement therapy. In terms of methodology, this means I follow the clients' leads as they discuss their art, movement, or writing.

Why are the expressive arts such an important expansion of the person-centered approach? *Simply put, we cannot integrate all aspects of self without involving all aspects of self.* We reawaken our creativity by engaging in the process of creativity.

THE CREATIVE CONNECTION®

I have coined the words, the 'Creative Connection' to describe a process in which one art form stimulates and fosters creativity in another art form, linking all of the arts to our essential nature. Using the client-centered roots of my psychological training, as well as training in movement and art therapy, I made some personal discoveries. I found that when I danced a sad or angry feeling in the presence of an empathic, non-judgmental witness my feelings and perceptions shifted dramatically. And when I drew the images after moving, the art became spontaneous, expressive, and revealing. If I followed the art with free writing, I plunged further into guarded feelings and thoughts. This is when I fully realized the empathic witness to art, movement, and journal writing was similar to the client-centered therapist. I also conceptualized the notion that using the arts in sequence evokes inner truths which are often revealed with new depth and meaning. Inner healing was taking place because of the creative connection.

USING EXPRESSIVE ARTS WITH CLIENTS

Traditionally, psychotherapy is a verbal form of therapy, and the verbal process will always be important. I realized that offering the arts as another means of expression was a departure from the way my father worked. However, that was not my major concern. I knew that my very nature was respectful of the integrity and self-direction of the client. My intent was to empathetically enter the frame of reference of the client. Yet, I had discovered (as had other colleagues) that using the arts as another language brought me even closer to the client's world. The I-thou relationship was enhanced as I listened to clients' self-exploration of their movement, image, or sound. Even more amazing was the fact that in creating the art, the client's feelings shifted.

I introduce the possibility of using the expressive arts to the client sometime during the first three sessions. I describe the client-centered philosophy and the expressive arts process. I might say something like: 'As an expressive arts therapist I have training in the use of movement and art and guided imagery to help you explore — or go on your inner journey — through symbolic, nonverbal modes. At times I will offer these methods to you. Often a healing process occurs by using this type of spontaneous, free, expression. We need not be concerned about the artistic quality of the product. However, the product can give you new information about yourself. I don't use art to diagnose you or interpret you. The art and movement processes are available to you as another avenue of self-exploration and healing.'

At this point, I ask for some reaction from the client. Some people are eager to use the materials. Others say, 'I can't draw,' or 'I'm not a creative person,' or 'I've got two left feet and can't dance.' Briefly, I reassure them that it is not a test of their creativity, or drawing or dancing ability, but a method of self-discovery. Those who are fearful usually lose that sense if they decide to take the risk and try some form of art expression.

I also assure clients that when I offer them the opportunity to express themselves nonverbally, they always have the option to say, 'No.' I might say, 'I will make suggestions and encourage you, but the decision is up to you. I will respect it.' I may hear a sigh of relief from the client. Often, however, I find that many are eager to use the expressive arts modes. It may be the therapist who feels insecure in offering them.

TRUSTING THE CLIENT'S PATH

People who observe me in a demonstration counseling session often ask, 'How did you know whether to suggest art or movement or sound with that client?' I don't *know,* in the sense that there is a right or wrong art form to offer. I use clues from the client and, most importantly, I trust the client to tell me the appropriate path. I always give a choice.

People also ask, 'At what point do you offer the opportunity to use an art process?' There are many possible entrées to choosing art as a language form. When a client is expressing strong emotion, I often ask, 'Would you like to explore that in color or movement as well?' The client may say, 'No, I need to talk some more.' That is perfectly acceptable to me. If he/she says, 'Yes, that seems like something that would help me discover more about this feeling,' I will then say, 'Would you like to draw, or move, or make sounds?' I follow the client's lead. If a client chooses visual art, I sit silently as an empathic witness. Then I ask the client to tell me what the experience was like as he/she created the piece. We look at it together and I encourage her to describe it and give it any meaning. She is allowing me to enter her world of imagery and imagination. If he wants to move or dance his picture, that furthers his journey. I constantly check: 'Does this feel right to you? Do you wish to explore more? Am I understanding you correctly? Do I get your real meaning here?'

One might ask, 'Is offering expressive art a distraction from the purpose of therapy?' I don't believe so. I tell my students, 'If you firmly hold the belief that the client has the knowledge of Self within and the ability for self-direction and you continually check to see if you are accurate in your understanding of where he/she is at the moment, you will be a good companion on that client's journey.'

THE CARL ROGERS' LEGACY

As a reader, you may be asking, 'How does your theory and counseling differ from your father's?' People who view the two videotapes where I demonstrate counseling (Rogers, N., 1988, 1997), or who witness me in person, tell me they experience my deep connection to my father's way of being. Like Carl, I usually go into an altered state of consciousness as I enter the frame of reference of the client. I try to be intuitively in tune with the feelings as well as some of the unspoken messages. I call this, 'listening to the music as well as the words'. I continually try to respond so that the client knows he or she is understood and together we adjust any misunderstandings.

Where I believe I have moved beyond Carl's work is to offer the client the arts as an additional language. I invited Carl to be on the faculty of the first three Person-Centered Expressive Therapy training programs I developed. It was a delight to have him present. He was curious about learning what we were doing and intrigued with the outcomes. I know he benefited, personally, by beginning to enjoy movement and dancing for the first time in his 84 years of life. (My mother, Helen, had already taught him some of the joys of painting.)

THE CREATIVE CONNECTION GROUP PROCESS

To involve people deeply in this creative connection process, we designed a program where group participants spend many hours each day in a sequence of art experiences that lead them into their inner realms. Each step of the way, the feelings are given artistic expression. We might start with some authentic movement, moving with eyes closed and letting the body speak. We invite participants to put sound to those movements.

After twenty minutes of turning inward yet expressing outwardly through movement, people silently express themselves in paint, pastels, clay, or collage. By now the sacred space for creativity has been created through the collective, side-by-side inner experiencing. The visual art comes out of a felt, body experience. It might be abstract colors splashed on the page with abandon, or carefully constructed collages; it doesn't matter. Each person feels safe to be free in his/her style and expression.

Next, participants write for ten minutes without stopping, censoring or being concerned about the logic of what emerges, so that they can access their free associations, or stories. The writing does not have to pertain specifically to the movement or visual art. This is a time to use a free-floating form of writing to let the subconscious emerge.

Following this sequence, there is time to share verbally. Talking about the process with an empathic listener helps one understand the experience. This can be a time to explore the meaning of the image by giving it a voice, or to experience the colors or the flow of the lines by letting them suggest movement and sound. Perhaps the writing suggests a dramatization. This spiral of activities continually peels off the layers of inhibition, dropping us into the core of our being. Finding one's center makes it possible to be open to the universal energy source, bringing vitality and a sense of oneness.

Individuals are often surprised at their capacity to paint, draw, dance, or write when they are in a stimulating, permissive, non-judgmental environment. People make such comments as, 'I started to paint a tree, but somehow it became an angel.' Or, 'I was looking for some specific images in the magazine for a collage, but somehow these other pictures jumped out at me and asked to be used.' These spontaneous events can also happen kinesthetically. One man said, 'I didn't dance, it danced me!'

THE HEALING POWER OF PERSON-CENTERED EXPRESSIVE ARTS

It is difficult to convey in words the depth and power of the expressive arts process. I hope that in sharing the following personal episode, you will vicariously experience my process of growth through movement, art, and journal writing in an environment of acceptance.

The months after my father's death were an emotional rollercoaster for me. The loss felt huge, yet there was also a sense that I had been released. I felt that his passing had opened a psychic door for me as well as having brought great sorrow. Expressive arts served me well during that time of mourning.

A friend invited me to spend a week at a cottage on Bolinas Bay. I painted one black picture after another. Every time I became bored with such dark images, I would start another painting. It, too, became moody and bleak. Although my friend is primarily an artist, her therapeutic training and ability to accept my emotional state gave me permission to be authentic.

Also, I went to a weekend workshop taught by another friend, an artist/therapist. I spent my time sculpting and painting. This time the theme was tidal waves — and again, I drew black pictures. One clay piece portrays a head peeking out of the underside of a huge wave. The details of emptying my parents' home, making decisions about my father's belongings, and responding to the hundreds of people who loved him was taking its toll. Once again, my artwork gave free reign to my feelings and so yielded a sense of relief. Being encouraged by my friend to use the art experience to release and understand my inner process was another big step. I thought I *should* be over my grief in a month, but these two women gave me permission to continue expressing my river of sadness. That year my expressive art shows my continued sense of loss as well as an opening to new horizons.

As is often true when someone feels deep suffering, there is also an opening to spiritual realms. Three months after my father's death, I flew to Switzerland to co-facilitate a training group. It was a time when I had a heightened sense of being connected to people, nature, and my dreams. I experienced synchronicities, special messages, and remarkable images. One night I found myself awakened by what seemed to be the beating of many large wings in my room. The next morning I drew the experience as best I could.

One afternoon I led our group in a movement activity called 'Melting and Growing'. The group divided into pairs, and each partner took turns observing the other dancing, 'melting', and then 'growing'. My co-facilitator and I participated in this activity together. He was witnessing me as I slowly melted from being very tall to collapsing completely on the floor. Later I wrote in my journal:

I loved the opportunity to melt, to let go completely. When I melted into the floor I felt myself totally relax. I surrendered! Instantaneously I experienced being *struck* by incredible light. Although my eyes were closed, all was radiant. Astonished, I lay quietly for a moment, then slowly started to 'grow', bringing myself to full height.

My heart had cracked open, leaving me both vulnerable and with great inner strength and light. A few days later another wave picture emerged. This time bright blue/green water was illumined with pink-gold sky.

I share these vignettes for two reasons. First, I wish to illustrate the transformative power of the expressive arts. Second, I want to point out that person-centered expressive therapy is based on very specific humanistic principles. For instance, it was extremely important that I was with people who allowed me to be in my grief and tears rather than patting me on the shoulder and telling me everything would be all right. I knew that if I had something to say, I would be heard and understood. None of my colleagues interpreted my art or gave me advice on how to grieve.

TRANSCENDING INNER POLARITIES

When I work with groups we often spend time brainstorming 'our inner polarities' and come up with long lists: love/hate, strength/weakness, close/distant, introvert/extrovert, happy/ sad, violent/peaceful, and so on. Although the opposites may appear to be 'good' or 'bad' characteristics, it is not that simple. While people in denial may need to acknowledge and accept their grief, other individuals may need to allow themselves feelings of delight or optimism.

In Jungian terms, the *shadow* is that aspect of the self that is unknown or that lives in the realm of the unconscious. The parts of the self we have rejected, denied, or repressed are frequently thought of as destructive or evil impulses. The shadow parts take emotional and physical energy to keep in check. To know, accept, express and release the dark side in not-hurtful ways is essential in preventing these powerful forces from being acted out in violent forms. Often we also relegate to the realm of the unconscious our creativity, strength, rebelliousness, sensuality, sexuality, and our willingness to love. Therefore, when we risk exploring the depths of the unconscious, we find many lost treasures. Discovering our unknown parts allows them to become allies: long-lost sub-personalities that we need in order to be complete. We become more whole, energized, compassionate people (Zweig and Abrams et al., 1990).

The expressive arts are powerful tools to help us uncover anger, fear, shame, loneliness, apathy, and the deep well of depression. I have been present while many clients or group participants have used movement and art to express their fear of death, of going insane, or of staying forever in the deep dark pit of depression. When given a voice, an image, a sound, a dance, the fears can become forces for change. When accepted for exactly what they are, they can help us on our road to recovery.

Accepting our shadow may be less difficult than embracing the light. When we talk about embracing the light, we are talking about opening to our spirituality, our ability to experience love, compassion, and all-encompassing states of consciousness. In my years as a therapist and group facilitator, I have found that people are uncomfortable acknowledging and feeling love. Readily they accept negative thoughts about themselves and others but find themselves fending off compliments, caring, and love. We tend to armor ourselves against receiving love. Being able to give and receive, whether from another person, animals, or a universal energy source, may be the prerequisite for being able to offer unconditional love.

A CASE STUDY

The following is an example of how one person felt the dramatic inner shifts in thought and feelings during a class in person-centered expressive art therapy. These intensive weekend classes are held in my large home-studio. This student, whom I shall call Maria, wrote a profoundly revealing paper about her experience. Maria is a tall, strong, attractive woman about 30 years old. She comes from a Mexican-American heritage. I have her permission to use these excerpts. Her statements are in italics to differentiate them from my descriptions and comments.

I start the second day of this class by inviting people to stand and create a sound-circle. We allow about ten minutes of free sounding, with the intention of both listening and making any sounds we wish. Some people sing, others howl, or laugh, or hum. Some people choose to be silent and just listen. Maria describes this.

> *The day began with all of us sounding in a circle. Deep sounds emerged. After some time, as the room became quiet there were different reactions to the intense sounds we had made. Some women told of suffering, wounding, wailing, and the pain of the world. Others talked of empowerment. For me it was about contacting my own inner strength and feeling grounded by the deep sounds.*

After discussing our reactions to sound, I then invited people to do a 'Wood Chopping' exercise. We again stand in a large circle, with ample room in which to move. I demonstrate what it is like to hold an imaginary axe in my hand to split an imaginary piece of wood. With great gusto, I raise my arms and with force, swing down to chop the wood. As I do so, I let out a deep 'ho' sound. I suggest that only those who would like to try this experiment do so. Others are free to watch. I also suggest that each person may choose to use this experiment with any intention they wish: they can use it to feel their strength, or to release anger, or create any other intention. Maria continues her response.

> *After awhile we stopped and there were a lot of emotions in the room.*
>
> *Some women wanted to do more of this. We formed smaller groups to continue. As I started to 'chop wood', I said the word, 'NO'. It reverberated in my whole being — my body and my spirit vibrated with it. The sound was coming from the deepest and most primal, instinctual part of my being. I had flashing images of witches burning, of men and women being abused, and of the incredible forces of nature that lie within the deepest parts of our soul. As I heard my voice, I heard generations of women crying/screaming to break from the chains of entrapment to fly into freedom.*
>
> *We were 18 women all together in the room, witnessing our power in the form of the beautiful raging beast that we carry inside. Standing there in my vulnerability, I realized it was fine to be open. This was a safe space. I could feel the immense fear of having been put down for my power — of having had to silence my voice and my truth. I felt all the fear that my voice carries. Feelings of being silenced, trembling at every attempt to speak. I felt shame. Shame in being vulnerable, shame of having been punished for my power, shame with myself for having given up on my own strength . . . As I was standing there, I realized this no longer needs to happen! It is a wound of the past, the wound that is now asking for acceptance and for being embraced, so that I can move on. I got a strong sense of a new safety space.*
>
> *As I looked around at the other women, I felt the sacredness of all of us, the beauty, the power, the creativity, the collective energies of giving birth to ourselves . . . The wounded healer creating the bridge to spirit . . . And the power of learning to speak the unspeakable.*
>
> *I went to the clay and a figure of a woman giving birth to a snake emerged. She had her mouth wide open and a scream was coming out of her. Later — as Natalie suggested — I asked her to speak to me. I wrote in my journal: 'I let go of the need to hide. I am a woman, I exist, I accept my full being wanting to explode into the universe carrying within it the scream of the rageful warrioress that will no longer sleep. She who could not see, can now see light and darkness. She who could not speak, now speaks truth. She who lied dormant is now awake.'*

The above is Maria's description after the first weekend. With so many feelings emerging she continues to digest what had happened. She writes:

> *This healing continued in the weeks that followed. I felt how important it is for us women to support each other in our growth and how difficult it can be, sometimes, to create that space for each other.*

Maria writes about the concepts she is learning from her experience:

> *I would call the work I did, 'The Voice of the Shadow'. Natalie's explicit invitation to work on the shadow was important for me as a start. Through my process I got an understanding of the Creative Connection — there is a lot of power in the combination of sounding, then movement with sounding, and later on, expressing it in clay and then finally allowing the clay piece to speak. I was amazed by the words that came out of my clay piece. It felt like something much larger than me was speaking. I just needed to let it happen.*

Maria senses how we can tap into the universal, or the collective unconscious by engaging in this creative process. She understands the power of using sound, movement, art and writing sequentially in a safe space. It allows her to experience 'something larger than herself'. She gets in touch with the pain of women over the centuries. On occasion, some participants also experience the pain of the earth as humans are mistreating it.

During the second weekend I offer to do a counseling demonstration with a volunteer from the class. Maria was the student who volunteered. The other class members are silent, supportive, witnesses to this session. First, Maria starts to talk about her sense of powerlessness. Although she had found a sense of personal empowerment in the first weekend, she then found herself losing that strength as the week went on. This can often be true — we become fearful of the new persona that is evolving. As she begins talking she uses many gestures and her body language is strikingly different from the previous weekend. She appears slumped over. I ask her if she would like to express how she feels through movement as well as with words. This is her partial description of the 45-minute counseling session with me.

> *During the weeks following the first weekend, I became deeply in touch with the part of me that collapses after every step I take into the outer world. It was important for me to start my session as a client showing how I felt through movement. It allowed me to feel the tension in my body and I could experience through bodily sensations how it felt to collapse and feel powerless, then, to move into the posture of being powerful. Back and forth, I tried each pose and noticed the shift. My insight came to me of not having been seen as a 'being of soul' in my family. In the picture that I drew after that session I had a true bodily sense that my neck was being held tight by the power of my father. I got the clear message that I needed to stay a little girl for him to stay powerful.*

In her paper, Maria next discusses the principles of counseling that she is learning.

> *I saw the three principles of the therapeutic relationship being enacted in this session. I experienced the therapist sensitively understanding my 'felt meaning'. Natalie was truly seeing and sensing what I was talking about. (She goes on at some length saying that she also experienced my congruence and positive regard.) I know the images that came forth will keep speaking to me for a long time. After the two weekends I have truly felt a coming home to my soul.*

REVIEWING MARIA'S PROCESS

In reviewing Maria's process, the random sounds made by the group, and then the strong movement and sounds she created during the wood-chopping experiment triggered profound images and the word, 'NO'. This type of expressive movement exercise allows for each individual to come up with her own sound, her own thoughts, and her own images. There is no 'goal' on the part of the facilitator other than using the kinesthetic experience to awaken any thoughts or feelings. Maria's experience was to discover her pain and her power — the pain of having been figuratively held by the throat so as not to speak her power. It is the verbal acceptance of those feelings by the facilitator that creates the safe space she speaks of. When participants feel pain or anger in these experiences, I acknowledge it verbally, giving them permission to cry or to shout. I also allow time for other participants to react and interact. All feelings are acknowledged and accepted, including any negative reactions to the experience.

In creating her clay figure, Maria releases pent-up energy as she pushes and forms the piece. She allows something to evolve from the unconscious. When she lets that archetypal figure speak to her, she discovers she no longer wants to hide. She is surprised by the message of truth the clay figure gives her. This surprise is coming from her unconscious, speaking through the figure.

As a facilitator of the group and the counselor hearing her story, I feel great empathy as she discovers the loud 'NO' voice. I let her know that I am there for her as she asks to go deeper into this feeling and imagery. The person-centered philosophy of allowing the client to lead the way is uppermost in my heart and mind. When she paints an image of a noose around her neck held by her father, I ask her if she wishes to talk about it more. I do not interpret her art. I do not suggest what it might mean to her. I follow her lead, listening empathetically, responding in the same vein. In the counseling session, when she says she feels powerless, I see and hear that as well. Although at some level I hope she will again find her inner strength, I know that I must stay with the feeling she has at the moment and let her experience it in depth. As I view her physical movements from caving in and feeling weak, to standing tall with arms outstretched, I know that I must not judge one or the other stance, but reflect back to her what she is feeling and doing. 'When you fold over and cave in, you feel powerless and helpless. When you stand with your arms outstretched you are showing me how you feel when you are confident.' To the best of my ability, I accept each moment of truth. Her art and movement are a language that speaks directly to me, helping me understand and be with her in a profound relationship. It is my heartfelt intention of being a companion on her path that strengthens our relationship.

Maria ended her paper with a long poem that I have condensed for this chapter. Poetry often emerges in the expressive arts experience. The Creative Connection process seems to stimulate this form of writing. This poem summarizes her experience.

> *I am the raging beast, the roar of the wounded warrior. I am you.*
> *I am the sound of the crashing wave into the fury of generations before and after.*
> *I am the warrior woman who reclaims her power, through the snake rejoicing in her body.*
> *I am she who claims the joy of the spirit, the power of joy, the spirit of power.*
> *I am the scream of all women, of all the lines of women before me and after me.*
> *I am the golden snake coming out of the silent womb and into the earth, dancing through*

the curves of my body, awakening the power that lies dormant.

I carry shame . . . shame in showing my self, in taking the space I rightfully reclaim.

I am the scream of despair and rage, for years of oppression of the power of the feminine.

I am the scream washed in rageful tears for all of us who have suffered abuse, torture or punishment for speaking our truth and for being powerful, for rejoicing in our instincts and passions.

I am the scream of all of us who have been caught in the web of confusion and misunderstanding about who we are.

I am the She, Thee, ME. We are women, pulling to the rhythms of the heartbeat of the earth, women washing away old wounds and karma, unleashing the chains of our imprisoned Selves.

Today we scream, YES! We are Thee. We are She.

HUMANISTIC PRINCIPLES

- Since not all psychologists agree with the principles embodied in this chapter, it is important to state them clearly.
- All people have an innate ability to be creative.
- The creative process is healing. The expressive product supplies important messages to the individual. However, it is the process of creation that is profoundly transformative.
- Personal growth and higher states of consciousness are achieved through self-awareness, self-understanding, and insight.
- Self-awareness, self-understanding, and insight are achieved by delving into our emotions. The feelings of grief, anger, pain, fear, joy, and ecstasy are the tunnel through which we must pass to get to the other side: to self-awareness, understanding, and wholeness.
- Our feelings and emotions are an energy source. That energy can be channeled into the expressive arts to be released and transformed.
- The expressive arts — including movement, art, writing, sound, music, meditation, and imagery — lead us into the unconscious. This often allows us to express previously unknown facets of ourselves, thus bringing to light new information and awareness.
- Art modes interrelate in what I call the creative connection. When we move, it affects how we write or paint. When we write or paint, it affects how we feel and think. During the creative connection process, one art form stimulates and nurtures the other, bringing us to an inner core or essence, which is our life energy.
- A connection exists between our life force — our inner core, or soul — and the essence of all beings.
- Therefore, as we journey inward to discover our essence or wholeness, we discover our relatedness to the outer world. The inner and outer become one.
- There are many discoveries to be made with this work: finding spirit, soul, the ability to laugh at oneself, new wisdom, or the knowledge that with each struggle in life there are major lessons to be learned.

APPLICATIONS OF PERSON-CENTERED EXPRESSIVE THERAPY

Although the expressive arts field is relatively new, the applications of this work are being used with success with many populations. Many of my colleagues, psychotherapists, social workers, and self-help groups find the expressive arts effective in helping people explore their feelings and change behaviors. Some people involved in Twelve-Step programs find that using expressive arts adds depth to their personal growth in each step. Alcohol treatment centers have utilized the expressive arts to give residents an opportunity to go beyond recovery to reawaken their creativity and find hopeful images for their future. It is my belief one reason people become addicted to drugs is that their creativity has been blocked. Expressive arts offer them the opportunity to reconnect with their innate ability to be creative.

With women and men who have suffered sexual abuse and have denied those experiences to awareness, expressive arts can help uncover those wounds as well as to heal them. Hospice workers and counselors assisting people with grief have found these nonverbal methods particularly rewarding. When one is mourning, often there are no words for the pain. Color and imagery are an outlet for the sorrow and anger.

Children use art freely until someone judges, grades, or misunderstands their art. Then they may stop using their creative abilities until they enter an accepting, non-judgmental environment. Play therapy has always used expressive art as a form of language for the child. Also, some corporations are beginning to use the arts to develop teamwork and look at the organizational problems and goals.

FUTURE PERSPECTIVES

It is imperative that our relationships, our families, our educational systems, our corporations, and our political leaders, stimulate, foster, and use the creative process to promote personal well-being and to bring about imaginative, enlightened collaboration for peaceful solutions to this troubled planet. The Creative Connection process — the person-centered philosophy and the expressive arts process — is one means of awakening creativity and allowing people to become authentic and empowered.

In our goal to become whole people, more fully actualized and empowered, awareness is always the first step. Without awareness, we have no choices. Personal integration is part of the natural flow of events when we use symbolic and expressive media. Once we uncover unknown aspects of self, the process includes letting these parts find their rightful places in our psyches, and we are more able to experience the ecstatic universal oneness, a sense of being connected to all life forms.

We can never expect that the peoples of the world will be of one mind — there will always be conflict and controversy — but we can expect people to respond creatively to find mutually beneficial solutions. If we are resolved, as a world community, to settle our disagreements peacefully, it can happen. We have all the technological resources and the brainpower to solve our global crises. The clash seems to be between those who want to have control over others and those who want cooperation and collaboration. The hierarchical system has not worked. For us to survive, our model must change from ladders and pyramids to circles. We need a willingness and determination to look at the potential solutions creatively, cooperatively, and without greed.

Imagine the excitement if we put as much creative energy, money, and determination into constructing a feasible future as we do in creating war. We are capable of mustering incredible amounts of goods and technology to meet a targeted goal. All we need is to use the same spirit to target a goal that will bring quality living to the earth's inhabitants.

Nothing really holds us back from solutions to our world dilemmas except the lid we have put on our creativity. Opening ourselves to the creative force within allows us to envision the possible. Envisioning the possible excites our will and determination to create it. Holding the vision is an important step in the creative process. We can be pioneers who light the candle.

REFERENCES

Allyn and Bacon Publishing (Producer). (1997). *Psychotherapy with the experts: Person-centered therapy with Dr. Natalie Rogers* [Videotape]. Needham Heights, MA: Allyn and Bacon.

Merry, T. (1997). Counselling and creativity: An interview with Natalie Rogers. *The British Journal of Guidance and Counselling, 25*(2).

Person Centered Expressive Art Therapy Institute (Producer). (1988). *The creative connection: Self-expression as a path to personal empowermen*t [Videotape]. Santa Rosa, CA: PCETI.

Rogers, C. R. (1951). *Client-centered Therapy: Its current practices, implications, and theory.* New York: Houghton Mifflin.

Rogers, N. (1993). *The Creative Connection: Expressive art as healing.* Palo Alto: Science and Behavior Books.

Zweig, C. and J. Abrams (eds.) (1990). *Meeting the Shadow: The hidden power of the dark side of human nature.* Los Angeles: J. P. Tarcher.

Bob Sikkema

Mediant Institute for Mental Health, Hengelo(O), The Netherlands

Unconditionality: Being present in an attentive way to help translate thoughts into the language of feelings

Abstract. This paper is about a long, ongoing, client-centered psychotherapy with a client diagnosed as having a Narcissistic Personality Disorder. Repeated childhood traumas were invisible during the intake and first few years of psychotherapy. An overview will be given of the development of the psychotherapy process between client and psychotherapist. Particular attention is paid to the way in which the client's own development parallels this process.

The beginning and middle phases of the therapy become visible, with theory from Client-Centered and Experiential literature. Attention is paid to the use of Focusing during the psychotherapy process. This discussion includes why Focusing was not preferable at first and then later on was used implicitly, for example, to look at body signals whose felt meaning, until then, were un-enterable for the client.

During the intake Mrs. K, who later became my client, talked about her daily life and what it was like. She reported that it all went quite well, were it not for a period of three or four months each year when she was unable to work. Research on a medical level showed that there was no physical cause for this, and she came in on the advice of her doctor.

Mrs. K was divorced, the mother of two children, and working as a teacher. Her youngest child was living with a 'time-bomb' because of a congenital heart defect. At any moment he could die but, 'If he could reach adulthood, then he would get a new heart.' His heart had stopped twice during his short life, until then. But as Mrs. K said, she 'knew that this could happen' and that she had always been with him, 'up till now', when it had.

The colleague doing the intake did not observe any emotions or feelings with Mrs. K when she spoke about this, nor when she said that she was an alcoholic. Nor did she show emotion when she talked about the medicines that did not help her, or the period when she was in a rest house to recover. Nor were any observed when she said that, except for her work and children, she had no social life and/or friendships. Because the medical examinations provided no explanation for the severe headaches that came back every year, her doctor thought that it would be good for Mrs. K to look further, and she herself thought 'that possibly something could be wrong.'

Mrs. K could not think of anything particular that might be wrong. She could not imagine that her complaints had anything to do with her failed marriage, nor with what had happened during the marriage. What did, however, make her feel 'a little bit restless' was the second time her son's heart stopped: 'It was just on the edge,' she said, meaning that he had almost died.

After the intake, the indication team for psychotherapy thought about offering Mrs. K a limited treatment of ten therapy sessions, in order to help her to structure her everyday life.

She was seen as 'cold, hard and empty', or alternatively, 'Narcissistic, without feelings'. From one moment during the intake, though, there was some reason to doubt that she was without feelings, at least as far as I was concerned. This was apparent when she mentioned her restlessness when her son's heart stopped for the second time. Mrs. K got the benefit of this doubt, and finally was offered a Client-Centered psychotherapy with me. It was suggested by colleagues that perhaps it might be possible to try and Focus with her. And the accompanying thought from those who suggested this was, perhaps through it she could learn to create some distance. In that way she could create a better overview of her everyday life, which often became too much for her. My thought was that it might provide an entrance for Mrs. K into her world of experiencing.

In a so-called 'advice session', which occurs at the same time as the first psychotherapy session, Mrs. K let me know that she wanted to try psychotherapy, and then added that, 'Something must not be all right.' She responded in a superior way to the suggestion that she pushes away feelings and experiences about situations and happenings in her life. Cynically she said, 'I keep everyone away from my door when the conversation is about myself. And otherwise, after two visits, people stay away by themselves.' She called herself (and I heard the cynicism through her words) 'a master in sending people away' from her. She said that when people asked how she is doing, after at most one sentence the conversation becomes about the other person, 'and then they will stay away or I will not open the door.' During this session, she let me know that this is the way she has always been and thus that she expects it to be like that here. My client laughs while telling me this. (And in her words I heard a warning: 'Don't come too close to me.') This is the way the first one and a half to two years of the therapy continued once a week.

During this period, my client laughed frequently, cynically and sarcastically, and criticized me continually. For example, she commented about the flowers that stood for a long time on my table and had become dried out, 'My mother would say . . .'; or about my being late a couple of minutes, twice in succession, 'It must be meant to make me angry . . .'; or about my red car, 'You always sit there so calmly in your chair, but red is the color of aggression . . .'

In this phase of the therapy, I noticed that careful empathic interventions towards my client's feeling and experiencing were quickly set aside by her in a sarcastic way, telling me that 'It is not of any importance.' Mrs. K would become tight and get severe headaches during the sessions, and would bang her head against the door before leaving my office, crying and asking me if she would ever get further. At these times she wonders if it would not be better to take medication. More than once during the sessions, feelings of uncertainty, anger, anxiety and powerlessness come up in me, and also thoughts like, 'Could they have been right in the indication team, when they were talking about Narcissism?' and 'Will my client slip away further when I listen empathically to her and reflect?' In an ongoing way, though, I become more and more familiar with what Carl Rogers calls 'the frame of reference of the client'.

During this period, Focusing inside myself on feelings that came up during the sessions helped me to make the link back to my client and to what was going on with her, including that in her that could not be said, was not allowed to be said, and which she could not then deal with. In my opinion, it was too early to suggest that my client Focus with me.

Focusing asks a certain amount of observing capacity, as well as a capacity to reflect on what is going on in the person. It is possible, by means of Focusing, to develop an observing capacity that has one's own experiencing as the object of attention. (Leijssen, 1995). In this phase of therapy, my client could not bear in any way to stand still with what was going on inside of her, let alone have someone stand still alongside her and look at it with her.

As we continued to meet, it appeared more and more that Mrs. K could hardly bear to be in the same room with me. Her defenses and her attempts to chase me away from her door, as she was used to doing successfully with other people, became tangibly insufficient. Unconditionality, mentioned by Carl Rogers (1961) as going into the frame of reference of the client in an accepting and understanding way, led (in my opinion) to a fundamental change in the therapy. In the sessions with Mrs. K up until then, I realized more and more that I was 'not allowed to touch anything'. So unconditionally staying with my client and with what presented itself, without taking hold of it and/or reshaping it, was the most helpful thing available for me to do. Pure listening, that Gendlin (1990) describes as being with complete attention with what is visible and not searching for what is not there, and which is comparable with what I do in Zen meditation (just sitting with what is there and presents itself), was very helpful to me.

In a research paper on unconditionality, Craig Matsu-Pissot (1998) writes that 'If we want to cure our segmented or compartmentalized self, we have to open ourselves to what is there. We have to approach it totally, without relying on concepts or conditions that lead to evaluation or judging.' In therapy, this 'being open to what is there', in my opinion, concerns not only the client and what he/she brings along, but encompasses also that which starts to resonate within myself as a therapist. In the psychotherapy with this client, it means that I have to be capable of containing feelings, some of which are very strong and severe, for a long time. These are feelings that she cannot bear or give words to herself, and that thus may not be verbalized yet. This appears in the following sessions.

One day, my client came in and did not want to sit down, throwing her purse in the chair and saying, 'I must be going crazy. What does my father have to do with this? He is dead for a long time already and now all of a sudden, he is there.' I did not know anything about Mrs. K's father, and felt her despair, confusion, rage, sorrow, powerlessness and helplessness. Or was it my powerlessness and helplessness as a psychotherapist with this client? Did I want to mean more to her than I could in this therapy?

Mrs. K took a seat and said, 'I do not know, I understand nothing of what is going on now.' As a psychotherapist, I did not start searching for all kinds of possibly implicit meanings. Rather, I directed my attention toward what Mrs. K herself brought in to prevent overflowing. Trying to Focus here with my client, in the sense of stimulating her to direct her attention toward and be accepting of her own body signals, or inviting her to make a space inside, would probably bring along too much confrontation with 'all that is felt implicitly' (Leijssen, 1995). In Mrs. K's life there have been so many traumatic experiences, loaded with severe emotions, where she has not been able to symbolize feelings but has instead dissociated them. So, trying to guide her to create a space and sit comfortably would probably not work out, and could lead to a psychological overflowing or even possibly to psychosis.

The friendly welcoming and accepting of what presents itself (as one does in Focusing) seemed impossible for my client, because of a fundamentally negative self-image and self-experience, which included self-destructive behavior and auto-mutilation. Mrs. K seemed to pull back from aspects of her experiences that caused pain. Therefore, it looked as if she lived her life only partially. But, at the same time it seemed that a part of her realized this partial living, and that *this* part was looking for wholeness or rediscovery (Welwood, 1990). I infer this from the fact that she always comes back, is there in a reliable way week after week, and tries to look at what presents itself within her during the sessions.

Over the next few years, Mrs. K had flashbacks during and outside of therapy. To one appointment she brought with her a girl without arms, made out of clay. The figure had eye-sockets but no eyes, a mouth without lips, no nose at all and a snake wrapped around her neck and trunk. My client pushed it into my hands with the words, 'Here, this is what love means for me.' Then she talked about everyday things, and laughed a little bit sheepishly at me. I had to save the little girl, and we did not talk about it for a long, long time.

To one of the next sessions, she brought along a writing pad and told me that she wanted to work on a diary. The closer she came to her experiencing of situations, the more she became confused and anxious. She wanted me to read what she had written, and asked me to save it. It was apparent to Mrs. K and me that there were six different handwritings. Some of the writing became smaller and smaller the closer she got to her wishes and desires, and then, all of a sudden, it became unreadable. It was about wanting to be loved and then the panic began inside of her, as I understood it. There were big scribbles that she told me that she did not understand. Something happened that she could not see or give words to. What was happening in this phase of the psychotherapy was that Mrs. K began to acknowledge her inner world, and the experiences that were there, more and more.

James Iberg (1990) describes three concepts that can help develop more the ears, eyes and, thus, the attention of a therapist in Focusing with a client on his/her experiencing world: (a) *Pregnant*, meaning that the person knows and/or acknowledges that there is something inside of her/him; (b) *Parturient*, meaning that there is something inside that is tangible, and thus there is a moving/life; and (c) *Nascent*, which means that something is being born, for example in Focusing a felt sense or felt experience. A shift takes place from (a) implicit but not functioning, toward (b) implicit functioning toward (c) explicit, as Gendlin (1996) mentions in his work.

(a), Gendlin (1996) says, concerns aspects of the experiencing process that do not function. The person has no entrance to them: he/she does not know them. In those aspects, he/she is not yet a self. Here we need someone else. In the psychotherapy with Mrs. K it was important not to respond to those aspects, because no experiential movement could come forth out of them. My client told me of some terrible experiences in her life as if they had happened to somebody else. She spoke of these events as if there were no feelings connected to them. Because of this disconnection, I decided not to reflect these events, but instead to help her become aware of and identify her bodily signals (Garry Prouty (1994) calls this making 'body reflections'). At one point during the therapy, Mrs. K pulled back her hands into the sleeves of her sweater and cried severely while doing this. I mentioned what she was doing; and my bringing her attention to this helped her to acknowledge her emotions and then connect the body signals and emotions with a meaningful situation (Leijssen, 1995). What emerged for her from these reflections were memories of her father threatening to chop off her hands with an axe if she would tell anyone he was sexually misusing her. Thus what happened is that the implicit not-functioning shifted toward implicit functioning, and then toward being expressed explicitly.

Other meaningful situations came back into Mrs. K's memory through stimulation from aspects of the actual 'here-and-now' situation between client and therapist. For example, the sitting of the therapist reminded her of the posture of her father, and thus of a time when in her presence her father grabbed the cat and suddenly pushed the animal with its tail against the burning furnace, laughing as the screaming cat ran away. Here, my client would not be helped by asking her to actively set aside this problem to help create a more positive feeling, but instead by differentiating between 'there and then' (client and father) and 'here and now' (client and therapist). And, from this moment on, she could start to experience difference in this way: that what was 'there and then' was threatening and traumatizing, and in the 'here and now' these same things would not happen here once again. Space came in the therapy room and in the relationship between client and therapist in such a way that correctional emotional experiences started to take place. This led to correction of the negative self-image and the negative self-experience. It was also the start of Mrs. K stopping the auto-mutilation and self-destructiveness.

Saying it in a different way, in this development in the therapy Mrs. K is being helped to find and give words that fit with her early childhood experiencing. These words (and/or images) help her to differentiate more between 'there and then' when she was a little girl and things were 'just done' with her, and 'here and now' where there is a safe place and nothing like that can happen to her. Within the safe space, which is literally in the therapy room, Mrs. K re-experiences the bodily felt sensations of what has been done with her as a child. She slowly begins to realize that the events/traumas, linked to what she is re-experiencing bodily now, are not being done with/to her in the 'here and now'. Her anxiety, which she expressed at first by saying, 'When it becomes safer for me here, danger is threatening, or it will be over with and I will have to leave,' becomes less.

Slowly in the therapy room a 'good place' develops, and along with it such a place inside of Mrs. K herself. She expresses this a number of times, after severe emotions and re-experiencing during the therapy session, by saying 'I do think it is good, I'm coming further with it. Some people I once in a while start to trust a little bit. Yes, I believe it can happen.' It seems that Mrs. K is developing a new sense of 'I' or 'me', there where she first was convinced of being guilty herself about that which had happened, and even about her own birth (she was an unwanted child). Mrs. K starts to develop a different relationship with the world and people surrounding her, who in former days were seen as threatening, rejecting and abandoning.

Here, the therapy takes on more a character of a new, positive parent-child relationship, where the therapist asks the question, 'What would this little child need?' In this way, Mrs. K is invited to take a step or two back out of her too-strong emotions. Here she can start to develop a broader view on the total child that she was then, instead of once again disappearing in, sinking into or getting stuck/frozen within the traumatizing experiences. Otherwise, the implicit felt-meaning, that Mrs. K was/is a child that wanted/wants to be loved and who can love, would be passed in the same kind of way by herself as has been done in former days by 'for her important others'. The possibility to turn around or change the negative self-image and self-experience would be left untouched if in the therapy Mrs. K's own wishes, desires and positive feelings were not heard, acknowledged and given words to (by the therapist as a substitute parent). With the words of Mathieu-Coughlan and Klein (1984) you could say that, 'In this micro-process the client can place her perspective from outside to inside.' (I am a child with positive longings and feelings, and it is good to not pass them myself as has been done with me.)

This changing of the self-image and self-experience in a positive direction, that takes place in this phase of the therapy, appears in many ways. Mrs K stops her abuse of alcohol, becomes more capable of intimacy and starts building up a relationship, and successfully fights to get back her job. The unconditionality that she experiences in the therapy helps her to look at her own longings and desires in a more and more non-judgmental way.

Therefore, it is necessary that unconditionality from the side of the therapist is expressed by means of giving words to those actual feelings that the client has not yet found words for inside of herself, but which are being experienced in the here-and-now. This giving words to, I agree with Gendlin (1968, 1990, 1996), helps carry the experiential process forward, which is a necessary part of change. It helps the client to start paying more attention to and to express what has been implicit (and probably frozen) until now. Therefore, listening empathically and reflecting in an accepting way from out of the frame of reference of the client is what I would call being present unconditionally.

REFERENCES

Gendlin, E. T. (1968). The experiential response. In E. Hammer (Ed.) *Use of Interpretation in Therapy.* New York: Grune and Stratton, pp. 208–27.

Gendlin, E. T. (1990). The small steps of the therapy process: How they come and how to help them come. In G. Lietaer, J. Rombauts and R. Van Balen (Eds.) *Client-centered and Experiential Psychotherapy in the Nineties,* pp. 205–24. Leuven: Leuven University Press, pp. 205–24.

Gendlin, E. T. (1996). *Focusing-oriented Psychotherapy: a manual of the experiential method.* New York: Guilford Press.

Iberg, J. R., (1990). Ms. C's Focusing and cognitive functions. In G. Lietaer, J. Rombauts and R. Van Balen (Eds.) *Client-centered and Experiential Psychotherapy in the Nineties.* Leuven: Leuven University Press, pp. 173–97.

Leijssen, M. (1995). *Gids voor gesprekstherapie.* Utrecht: De Tijdstroom.

Mathieu-Coughlan, P. and Klein, M. H. (1984). Experiential psychotherapy: Key events in client-therapist interaction. In L.N. Rice and L.S. Greenberg (Eds.) *Patterns of Change: Intensive analysis of psychotherapy processes.* New York: Guilford Press, pp. 213–48.

Matsu-Pissot, C. (1998). On the experience of being unconditionally loved. In R. Valle (Ed.) *Phenomenological Inquiry in Psychology.* New York: Plenum, pp. 321–34.

Prouty, G. (1994). *Theoretical Evolutions in Person-centered/Experiential Therapy: Applications to schizophrenic and retarded psychoses.* London: Praeger.

Rogers, C. R. (1961). *On Becoming a Person.* Boston: Houghton Mifflin.

Swildens, H., de Haas, O., Lietaer, G. and Van Balen, R. (Eds.) (1991). *Leerboek gesprekstherapie.* Amersfoort/Leuven: Acco.

William B. Stiles and Meredith J. Glick

Miami University, Ohio, USA

Client-Centered Therapy with Multi-voiced Clients:

Empathy with whom?[1]

The self has usually been considered as a more-or-less unitary entity, within client-centered theory (Rogers, 1959) as elsewhere. In contrast, some recent conceptualizations describe the self as composed of many parts. The parts emerge as their capacities and talents are called upon to deal with an ever-changing world, and they have the potential to engage one another in dialogue. The different aspects of the self have been referred to as subpersonalities (Rowan, 1990; Ross, 1999), I-positions (Hermans, Kemepen and vanLoon, 1992), parts (Schwartz, 1999), selves (Shotter, 1999), dissociated parts (Warner, 2000), and configurations of self (Mearns, 1999; Mearns and Thorne, 2000), to name just a few. We use the metaphor of *voice* to describe this internal multiplicity (Stiles, 1997, 1999a).

In this chapter, we address a specific technical point about reflections in client-centered therapy that is raised by this emerging view: How can a therapist offer respect and empathy to a client who speaks with multiple voices? To frame this issue, we describe how it emerged in our research on the assimilation model. This chapter is intended to present a tentative idea for discussion rather than a research finding.

THE ASSIMILATION MODEL

The assimilation model (Stiles, Elliott, Llewelyn, Firth-Cozens, Margison, Shapiro and Hardy, 1990) was developed as a bridge between process research and outcome research. Process research deals with small variables and time scales of minutes or seconds, for example the effectiveness of reflections in facilitating client expression. Outcome research deals with large variables and timescales of months or years, such as the decrease in clients' depression across treatment. The assimilation model seeks to bridge this gap by construing people as composed of many pieces and studying them one piece at a time. Each piece consists of the traces of an experience or of a constellation of related experiences.

In assimilation research, we identify *problematic experiences*, such as destructive relationships or the memories of traumatic incidents, and we track them across sessions, in tapes or transcripts of completed therapies (Stiles and Angus, 2001). Thus, much of our research has involved intensive qualitative study of single cases (e.g., Honos-Webb, Stiles, Greenberg and Goldman, 1998; Honos-Webb, Surko, Stiles and Greenberg, 1999; Stiles, Meshot, Anderson and Sloan, 1992; Stiles, Morrison, Haw, Harper, Shapiro and Firth-Cozens,

[1] We thank James A. Lani, Katerine Osatuke, and D'Arcy Reynolds for comments on a draft of this chapter.

1991; Stiles, Shapiro, Harper and Morrison, 1995; Varvin and Stiles, 1999). We focus on changes in a problematic experience as it moves from being feared or unwanted to being understood and integrated. Theoretically, following Piaget (1970), we say the problematic experience is assimilated into a *schema* — a way of thinking and acting that is developed or modified within the therapeutic relationship to accommodate the problematic experience.

The process of assimilation can also be formulated using the metaphor of voice to characterize problems within people (Honos-Webb and Stiles, 1998; Stiles, 1997, 1999a). The voice metaphor underlines our understanding that traces of experiences — including problematic experiences — are active agents within people. That is, the voices can speak and act. For example, the voice of a person's mother may surface in some circumstances, stating her characteristic opinions or engaging in behavior that is characteristic of the mother but not necessarily of the person. Although a person's experiences are normally assimilated and available as resources for dealing with life tasks, some voices, representing traces of traumatic or stressful life events, may be warded off or dissociated. Theoretically, in successful therapy, a problematic, unwanted, outcast voice establishes contact with the dominant community of voices within the person, negotiates an understanding and is assimilated into the community.

In the voices formulation of the assimilation model, an accurate reflection can be considered as a meaning bridge[2] between client and therapist that evolves into a meaning bridge among the client's internal voices, allowing them to communicate and engage in joint action. Meaning bridges are thus the means by which assimilation takes place. Dissociated (unassimilated) voices tend to be problems (cf. Warner, 2000, 2002 [this volume pp. 459–72]), whereas voices linked by meaning bridges can be resources — smoothly available when circumstances call for their capacities and talents.

DEBBIE'S VOICES

The voice metaphor led us to listen more carefully to expressions of different experiences in therapy tapes. We have found that it is often possible to hear different vocal qualities when internal voices express themselves, as was illustrated early in Debbie's therapy (Stiles, 1999a, 1999b).

Debbie was a 29-year-old mother of two who sought treatment at Guys Hospital in

---

[2.] Rice and Saperia (1984), first used the term meaning bridge to describe a stage in the systematic evocative unfolding of a problematic reaction point, that is, the therapeutic exploration of events in which clients reacted to some person or situation in a way that they found puzzling, unexpected, exaggerated, or unreasonable. The meaning bridge was the link that clients eventually discovered between their understanding of a problematic situation and their emotional reaction to it.

The voices formulation of the assimilation model has expanded this concept: A meaning bridge is a sign or set of signs that has the same meaning to two voices. In this conception, signs are words, sentences, gestures, actions, artifacts, and so forth, that represent or refer to something besides themselves. A sign's meaning is a person's experience of the sign. Insofar as people often have very different experiences of words, sentences, gestures, actions, artifacts, and so forth, signs often have different meanings to different people or at different times. When a sign has the same meaning to two people, for example, a therapist's accurately empathic reflection, it is considered to be a meaning bridge between them. Theoretically, internal voices that are warded off or avoided or dissociated may be described as lacking meaning bridges (Stiles, 1999a, 1999b). Any verbal or nonverbal expression that links or encompasses two or more formerly divergent voices within a person can be considered as a meaning bridge between them.

London, England, where she was seen for 16 sessions of cognitive analytic therapy (Ryle, 1997) — not client-centered therapy. Her treatment was considered successful by both Debbie and her therapist. Debbie gave consent for her tapes to be used for research and presentation. Debbie's husband of 12 years was alcoholic and had been in and out of their home for several years. He had announced during his last extended visit, 3 months previously, that he had never wanted to be with her from the beginning of their relationship. This, she said, rang true and had precipitated a severe depressive episode. She said she could not stand to see him, because it reminded her of the rejection. She had lost control and physically attacked him the last time he had shown up at her door unannounced.

In the following passage, which occurred approximately 8 minutes into the first session, Debbie was explaining that her and her husband's families had known each other since they were children and she now felt this part of her life was gone. Her narration, given in an almost childlike voice, was interrupted by a stronger, louder voice, printed here in bold type:

THERAPIST: So, you've lost more than just him.
You've lost, sort of, his brothers and sisters —
DEBBIE: Yeah, that's what I feel.
THERAPIST: who were like friends of yours, I mean.
DEBBIE: Well, his sis —
I've never,
I've never really got on well with his mum and his sister.
Because —
So that's not so much of a loss as, uh,
she's won.
She's finally got what she wanted, which was, she wanted him back —
and she wanted him away from me, basically.
That's how I feel.
Whether that's how she feels,
but that's how I fe —
y' know,
and this sort of thing's really been getting worse,
y'know.
It's getting more mad, I think.
And, um, I still keep in touch with his other brother's wife. . . .

The voice shown in bold sounded defiant and angry, in contrast to the relatively meek narrator voice. The defiant voice seemed to intrude abruptly and unexpectedly and was then interrupted in mid-word with what appeared to be a reflexive comment about the process. We hypothesized that this defiant voice was related to the problems for which Debbie had sought treatment, including the aggressive outburst against her husband on his last visit.

Over the remaining sessions, Debbie came to know the defiant voice as the 'rejecting' part of herself — a complement or shadow to Debbie's predominant experience of being rejected. This concept was introduced by the therapist as a way of naming the angry outbursts (i.e., the problematic voice). Debbie used the name *rejecting* for talking about and to this part of herself. Other voices engaged this rejecting voice in conversation, as shown in her reports (and enactments in the therapy) of internal dialogues — one part of herself speaking to another part of herself, for example:

DEBBIE: I knew that I would feel rejected after I'd said it [told husband he'd been
         irresponsible] . . .
         So I did feel like that a little bit.
         But then I thought:
         No.
         I did the right thing.
         I can't start feeling bad because I'm saying what I think's right. (from session 8)

Gradually, the defiant, rejecting voice seemed to be assimilated into the community, becoming more moderate and controlled as it did so. The assimilation was signaled by an emerging capacity for self-assertion that seemed to replace the problematic uncontrolled outbursts that had long troubled her (Stiles, 1999b). That is, the originally problematic voice became a resource.

CLIENT-CENTERED THEORY MAY NEED ADJUSTMENTS

Client-centered theory may need to make some adjustments if problematic experiences are viewed as active voices within the person, rather than as passive information to be accepted, denied, or distorted by a central executive self. Cooper (1999), Mearns (1999, Mearns and Thorne, 2000) and Warner (2000, 2002 [this volume pp. 459–72]) have already moved client-centered theory in this direction. For example, Cooper (1999) interpreted Rogers' (1959) descriptions of fluctuations in self-concept as reflecting multiple selves. He hypothesized different selves may have developed to accommodate different conditions of worth that the child encountered. For example, being a passive good girl may please one's parents, whereas being an assertive leader produces esteem from peers. Each qualitatively discrete self-concept can serve as a filter for experiences, reflecting different ways of obtaining positive regard, and yielding different constellations of behavioral, affective and cognitive acts in the world.

A multiplicity of selves demands adjustments in the practice of therapy. Among the problems is the technical point we raised earlier: How can a therapist offer respect and empathy to a client understood as consisting of multiple internal voices? Specifically, how should the therapist respond when two or more voices speak — for example, when clients express contradictory feelings or ideas?

We suggest that the therapist's attitude toward a client's multiple internal voices should be a bit like multilateral partiality in family therapy (Boszormenyi-Nagy and Spark, 1973). As respect and empathy are offered to each voice individually, conflicting internal voices can hear and come to respect each other, a crucial step on the way to developing internal meaning bridges. To implement this position, we suggest that, on hearing conflicting expressions, a therapist might better reflect one voice at a time, which we call *univocal reflection*, rather than try to encompass multiple voices in an omnibus reflection. Univocal reflection may either facilitate elaboration or stimulate an opposing response from a voice that was not reflected; either response may be productive. Trying to encompass two or more voices with one reflection, on the other hand, is likely to lead to confusion, as it's not clear which voice should respond.

Which voice should a therapist reflect first? At times, it may make sense to systematically attend to the voice that seems most alive or most vulnerable or most recent. But perhaps it doesn't much matter which voice is reflected first, so long as the therapist conveys the choice clearly and listens carefully to what follows. (a) If the reflected voice responds affirmatively, the therapist can proceed through the familiar cycle of elaboration and refinement — facilitating successive approximations until at last a meaning bridge (an accurate empathic understanding) is constructed. (b) Of course, if the client directly or indirectly indicates that the reflection is inaccurate, the therapist can acknowledge the inaccuracy and try again. (c) However, the therapist should also listen for a rejoinder by a different voice — a 'yes, but' response or an interruption that expresses a contrary opinion. Finally, (d) when a therapist-client meaning bridge is established by a fully accurate reflection, clients often explicitly confirm the understanding ('yes, exactly') and then fall silent momentarily, making room for a new voice or topic or a deeper expression (this is another way of saying that the felt sense shifts). To illustrate some of these different possibilities, we present some brief excerpts from a case of client-centered therapy in the next section.

By clarifying a feeling or provoking a disagreement, a reflection to one voice may stimulate other internal voices to speak. Regardless of which voice is reflected or which responds, accurate empathic listening can be understood as facilitating conversation and understanding among the client's internal voices as well as between client and therapist. Reflecting each voice individually creates an opportunity for further mutual exploration, clarity and synthesis.

REFLECTIONS TO MARGARET'S VOICES

To illustrate the difference between reflections directed to one versus multiple voices, we offer some examples taken from the case of Margaret, a 58-year old woman who was seen for 17 sessions of client-centered therapy in the York Depression Project (Greenberg and Watson, 1998). Leading up to the following passage, from the middle of session one, she had been describing her family situation and was discussing the burden of caring for her mother, who was in advanced stages of dementia and living in a nursing home. Margaret offered two contrasting views, representing two internal voices, and she reported an internal conversation between them. The therapist responded to just one of the voices — the one printed in italics — and the effect appeared to be facilitative. Margaret proceeded to a useful elaboration, exploring her fear of not being needed, an illustration of possibility (a) listed earlier.

MARGARET: The other day I thought — 'I just wish this was all behind me.'
I was getting ready to go over — over to see my mom, you know.
And I thought 'I just can't be bothered doing this,' you know.
Between going down to the hospital and going to see my mom, I thought, 'Is there no end to this?'
I mean, there must be something else.
But then on the other hand when I started thinking about it I thought,
'Yes, but then I wouldn't be needed.'

THERAPIST: Hm. So there's . . .

MARGARET: *Is that right?*

THERAPIST: I don't know,

> *But it seems like you came to that kind of a sense of*
> *Something about it feeling good to be needed.*

MARGARET: *Yeah.*
> *I think everyone needs to be needed you know.*
> *And I think maybe there's that little fear — with me — that,*
> *And I think that with my husband too:*
> *He doesn't need me.*
> *My children don't need me.*
> *My mother doesn't basically need me anymore.*
> *I mean, she's being looked after at the nursing home, you know.*
> *And then I thought*
> *Well, if I didn't have my mom to go see*
> *And I didn't have, you know, Aunt P. to go and see*
> *And, you know, be concerned about*
> *Or phone the hospital to see how she's doing — um*
> *Right now I wouldn't be needed.*

In the following passage, from session two, the therapist made two reflections. The first stimulated some elaboration, as in the preceding example, but the second stimulated a brief confirmation followed by a contrasting expression (in italics).

MARGARET: When [my husband] went out of town, he never had to worry about his kids.
And, like, he travelled quite a bit,
You know, when the kids were small.
THERAPIST: Yes.
So he was away [and] you had to take over.
MARGARET: He was away quite a bit, mm-hm, yeah.
So I looked after the kids.
And I feel that, you know, I gave.
THERAPIST: So somehow, 'I gave, and I gave, and I gave,
And when's it going to be my turn?'
MARGARET: Mm-hm.
THERAPIST: Yeah.
MARGARET: *And then I think: I'm wrong because I feel that.*

Despite the subsequent contradiction, the second reflection appeared accurate and seemed to facilitate the process of exploration by triggering expression by a different voice, an illustration of possibility (c) listed earlier.

In the final example, from the middle of session two, Margaret was describing her feelings about not buying a ring from her husband's aunt's estate. She had really liked the ring, and it had had some important personal meaning for her. She had decided not to buy it, however, after she perceived covert messages from her husband not to buy it. In this passage, one voice seemed to say the decision was Margaret's own — she could have made a different decision — while another voice blamed and resented her husband.

In this case, the therapist's omnibus reflection sought to encompass both voices, and, it seemed to us, Margaret's response was a transient confusion, marked by hedges, such as 'you know.' Theoretically, we suggest, the reflection did not address either voice, so neither felt understood.

MARGARET: As I say, you know, then because I've made this decision (inaudible).
I take it more on him.
Like I'm mad at him,
And I blame him for this.
And I think 'what am I doing here?' (laughs)

THERAPIST: *So you end up sort of being angry at him —*
That he sort of caused you not to keep the ring.
At the same time you wonder —
You know it was my decision —
I don't know, sort of like,
It was my decision,
And it was my problem that I didn't keep it,
Or . . .

MARGARET: Yeah, mm-hm.
This is what,
I can't make up my mind.
You know, what's right and what's wrong here, you know.

We interpret Margaret's confusion as internal competition to respond to the reflection, which attempted to express empathy with both voices at once. Such omnibus reflections are very much like what Mearns and Thorne (2000) called *zero-sum responding* (and recommended avoiding):

CLIENT: Part of me feels x . . . and part of me feels not x.
THERAPIST: So you are conflicted about how you feel?

In contrast, by facilitating elaboration, as illustrated in the first passage from Margaret's therapy, or by evoking a response from a different voice illustrated by the second, univocal reflection, we can advance the process of building meaning bridges between the separated internal voices.

CONCLUSION

Our suggestion that it's more productive to respond to voices separately rather than jointly is tentative; we certainly have not proved that this is always more productive or even that this is an all-or-nothing choice. In our work so far, we've found various intermediate sorts of strategies, and we are aware that all therapeutic interventions are — and must be — intricately responsive to the context in which they are used (Stiles, Honos-Webb and Surko, 1998).

We hope that the puzzle these examples illustrate is a clinically familiar one. We believe that the choice of which voice — or voices — to reflect confronts client-centered therapists continually. We suspect that most therapists have worked out ways to deal with such situations, at least on an intuitive and informal level. However, we suggest that both theory and practice will benefit from explicit consideration of the alternatives. For example, investigators might collect instances in which clients seem to speak with two voices within one speaking turn, divide them according to whether the therapist responds to one or both voices, and assess the productivity of the immediately subsequent process (this strategy is drawn from the events paradigm; Rice and Greenberg, 1984). More broadly, we suggest that considering people as composed of multiple parts or voices is not a purely academic exercise, but has significant consequences for the minute-by-minute practice of client-centered therapy.

REFERENCES

Boszormenyi-Nagy, I. and Spark, G. M. (1973). *Invisible Loyalties: Reciprocity in intergenerational family therapy*. Hagerstown, MD: Harper and Row.

Cooper, M. (1999). If you can't be Jekyll be Hyde: An existential-phenomenological exploration on lived-plurality. In J. Rowan and M. Copper (Eds.) *The Plural Self: Multiplicity in everyday life*. London: Sage Publications, pp. 51–70.

Greenberg, L. S. and Watson, J. (1998). Experiential therapy of depression: Differential effects of client centered relationship conditions and active experiential interventions. *Psychotherapy Research, 8*, 210–24.

Hermans, H. J. M., Kempen, H. J. G. and Van Loon, R. J. P. (1992). The dialogical self: Beyond individualism and rationalism. *American Psychologist, 47*, 23–33.

Honos-Webb, L. and Stiles, W. B. (1998). Reformulation of assimilation analysis in terms of voices. *Psychotherapy, 35*, 23–33.

Honos-Webb, L., Stiles, W. B., Greenberg, L. S. and Goldman, R. (1998). Assimilation analysis of process-experiential psychotherapy: A comparison of two cases. *Psychotherapy Research, 8*, 264–86.

Honos-Webb, L., Surko, M., Stiles, W. B. and Greenberg, L. S. (1999). Assimilation of voices in psychotherapy: The case of Jan. *Journal of Counseling Psychology, 46*, 448–60.

Mearns, D. (1999). Person-centered therapy with configurations of self. *Counselling, 10*, 125–30.

Mearns, D. and Thorne, B. (2000). *Person-centered Therapy Today: New frontiers in theory and practice*. London: Sage.

Piaget, J. (1970). Piaget's theory (G. Gellerier and J. Langer, Trans.) In P. H. Mussen (Ed.) *Carmichael's manual of child psychology* (3rd. edn., Vol. 1). New York: Wiley, , pp. 703–32.

Rice, L. N. and Greenberg, L. S. (Eds.) (1984). *Patterns of change*. New York: Guilford Press.

Rice, L. N. and Saperia, E. P. (1984). Task analysis and the resolution of problematic reactions. In L. N. Rice and L. S. Greenberg (Eds.) *Patterns of Change*. New York: Guilford Press, pp. 29–66.

Rogers, C. R. (1959). A theory of therapy, personality and interpersonal relationships as developed by the client-centered framework. In S. Koch (Ed.) *Psychology: A study of a science: Vol. III. Formulations of a person and the social context*. New York: McGraw-Hill, pp. 184–256.

Ross, C. A. (1999). Subpersonalities and multiple personalities: a dissociative continuum? In J. Rowan and M. Cooper (Eds.) *The Plural Self: Multiplicity in everyday life*. London: Sage Publications, pp. 183–97.

Rowan, J. (1990). *Subpersonalities: The people inside us*. London: Routledge.

Ryle, A. (1997). *Cognitive Analytic Therapy and Borderline Personality Disorder. The model and the method*. Chichester, UK: Wiley.

Schwartz, R. C. (1999). The internal family systems model. In J. Rowan and M. Cooper (Eds.) *The plural self: Multiplicity in everyday life*. London: Sage Publications, pp. 238–53.

Shotter, J. (1999). Life inside dialogically structured mentalities: Bakhtin's and Voloshinov's account of our mental activities as out in the world between us. In J. Rowan and M. Cooper (Eds.) *The Plural Self: Multiplicity in everyday life*. London: Sage Publications, pp. 71–92.

Stiles, W. B. (1997). Signs and voices: Joining a conversation in progress. *British Journal of Medical Psychology, 70*, 169–76.

Stiles, W. B. (1999a). Signs and voices in psychotherapy. *Psychotherapy Research, 9,* 1–21.

Stiles, W. B. (1999b). *Signs, voices, meaning bridges and shared experience: How talking helps.* Visiting Scholar Series No. 10 (ISSN 1173–9940). Palmerston North, New Zealand: School of Psychology, Massey University.

Stiles, W. B. and Angus, L. (2001). Qualitative research on clients' assimilation of problematic experiences in psychotherapy. In J. Frommer and D. L. Rennie (Eds) *Qualitative Psychotherapy Research: Methods and methodology.* Lengerich, Germany: Pabst Science Publishers, pp. 112–27.

Stiles, W. B., Elliott, R., Llewelyn, S. P., Firth-Cozens, J. A., Margison, F. R., Shapiro, D. A. and Hardy, G. (1990). Assimilation of problematic experiences by clients in psychotherapy. *Psychotherapy, 27,* 411–20.

Stiles, W. B., Honos-Webb, L. and Surko, M. (1998). Responsiveness in psychotherapy. *Clinical Psychology: Science and Practice, 5,* 439–58.

Stiles, W. B., Meshot, C. M., Anderson, T. M. and Sloan, W. W., Jr. (1992). Assimilation of problematic experiences: The case of John Jones. *Psychotherapy Research, 2,* 81–101.

Stiles, W. B., Morrison, L. A., Haw, S. K., Harper, H., Shapiro, D. A. and Firth-Cozens, J. (1991). Longitudinal study of assimilation in exploratory psychotherapy. *Psychotherapy, 28,* 195–206.

Stiles, W. B., Shapiro, D. A., Harper, H. and Morrison, L. A. (1995). Therapist contributions to psychotherapeutic assimilation: An alternative to the drug metaphor. *British Journal of Medical Psychology, 68,* 1–13.

Varvin, S. and Stiles, W. B. (1999). Emergence of severe traumatic experiences: An assimilation analysis of psychoanalytic therapy with a political refugee. *Psychotherapy Research, 9,* 381–404.

Warner, M. (2000). Person-centred therapy at the difficult edge: A developmentally-based model of fragile and dissociated process. In D. Mearns and B. Thorne (Eds.) *Person-centered Therapy Today: New frontiers in theory and practice.* London: Sage, pp 144–71.

Warner, M. (2002). Luke's Dilemmas: A client-centered/experiential model of processing with a schizophrenic thought disorder. In J. C. Watson, R. N. Goldberg and M. S. Warner, (Eds.) *Client-centered and Experiential Psychotherapy in the 21st Century: Advances in theory, research and practice.* Ross-on-Wye: PCCS Books, pp..

Nele Stinckens, Germain Lietaer and Mia Leijssen

Katholieke Universiteit Leuven, Leuven, Belgium

Working with the Inner Critic: Fighting 'the enemy' or keeping it company

INTRODUCTION

The term 'inner critic' was introduced by Gendlin in the experiential literature (Gendlin, 1981; 1996). It refers to the inner normative voice that criticizes and interrupts a person's healthy functioning. Gendlin does not pretend to have discovered a *new* phenomenon; he states that the inner critic is a universal human phenomenon that is studied in almost every therapeutic orientation, indeed in other words and from other viewpoints. In client-centered and experiential theory, this voice is considered as a process disturbance that interferes with the organismic experiencing and valuing process of the client.

Although one generally assumes that such a voice can seriously affect the therapeutic process, little systematic research has been done into the concrete manifestations of this process disturbance in psychotherapy. This lacuna was the starting point of my doctoral project (Stinckens, 2001). Inspired by the principles of the 'Events paradigm' (Rice and Greenberg, 1984), the rationale was to construct a more differentiated microtheory consisting of three components: (1) the process markers of the inner critic; (2) the microsteps of the client change process; and (3) the facilitating therapist operations. Therefore, an intensive and detailed analysis had been done of a varied sample of 75 therapy episodes in which the inner critic has been identified; these episodes were selected from the rich and well-documented archives of Rogers, the research database of the Counseling Center in Leuven (neo-client-centered/experiential episodes) and the Psychotherapy Research Center of York University, Toronto (experiential episodes). In earlier contributions (Stinckens, 1999, press; Stinckens and Leijssen, 1999), I've discussed in detail in what way the inner critic appears and unfolds in the course of therapy. In this article, I'm confining myself to the third component, the therapist approach that brings about change in the interferences of the inner critic.

In order to sketch a complete picture of the different operations that therapists make use of in client-centered and experiential therapy, I'll return to the roots of our orientation and start with the viewpoint of Carl Rogers.

ROGERS' IMPLICIT VIEW ON WORKING WITH THE INNER CRITIC

Because Rogers was a strong opponent of everything concerning technique and strategy, he didn't develop a specific microtheory in which his way of working with the inner critic was made more explicit. At the most, we find some indicators in his writings (Rogers, 1942;

1949; 1951; 1959; 1961; 1975) which specify the relational attitudes to the problem of the inner critic.

As in 1942, Rogers wrote that the therapist needs to have a warm, responsive and accepting attitude towards *everything* the client brings into therapy; the therapist needs to create an atmosphere that remains free from moral approval or disapproval. He says: 'The counselor is most effective when he aids in bringing the feeling consciously in the picture, without taking sides' (1942, p. 144). Expressing the negative feelings clears the way for the more positive, growth-enhancing impulses.

When we follow this same line of thought with respect to the inner critic, Rogers seems to assume that fully recognizing and accepting the client's critical and negative self-experiences makes them 'relax' and interfere no longer with the experiencing process. In this respect, Rogers points to a common 'therapeutic pitfall'. 'When the client is thoroughly discouraged, when he feels that he is 'no good', when his fears are overwhelming, when he hints that he has thought of suicide, when he pictures himself as completely unstable, completely dependent, entirely inadequate, unworthy of love — in short, when he is expressing any type of negative feelings toward himself, the natural tendency on the part of the inexperienced counselor is to try to convince him that he is exaggerating the situation' (1942, p. 144). According to Rogers, this reaction is very understandable but not therapeutic. The client *feels* she is worthless, even if the therapist provides evidence to the contrary. Only if the client doesn't have to prove any longer that he is worthless, can he start to discover the good things about himself. In other words, thanks to the unconditional acceptance of all the elements of the client's experience, little by little, the client will feel safe enough to explore himself more deeply and to look at those aspects of himself that were too threatening or too shameful before.

Besides that, the client will introject the accepting and understanding attitude of the therapist and come to develop more self-acceptance and self-empathy. As Rogers says: 'He'll become a more effective growth enhancer, a more effective therapist, for himself' (1975, p. 9).

TOWARDS A PROCESS-DIRECTIVE APPROACH OF THE INNER CRITIC

Since the 1980s there has been a movement in client-centered and experiential therapy from a uniform treatment to a more differential, process-directive approach (Rice and Greenberg, 1984). This implies that treatment, in addition to promoting self-acceptance and a strengthening of the self, aims at solving more *specific* problems of self-organization that emerge in therapy (Greenberg, Lietaer and Watson, 1998). Therefore, a series of different therapeutic tasks have been described, each one involving a variety of specific microprocesses.

With respect to the problem of the inner critic, different microprocesses have been worked out, all starting from the same idea: the inner critic has to be treated in an *active* way, because it doesn't tend to disappear of its own accord. As Müller says: 'The inner critic doesn't allow itself to be shut off, so it would be pointless to wait until it clears out on its own' (1995, p. 3). In the variety of process directives that have been developed recently, two important movements can be discerned.

A first group of therapists (Gendlin, 1996; McGuire, 1984a, 1984b; Müller, 1995; Harvey, 1992) emphasize the process-blocking character of the inner critic: the inner critic interferes with the organismic valuing process and undermines the inner wisdom and authority of the client. Therefore, these therapists are especially engaged with moving the critic aside (fighting 'the enemy') and changing the focus from the criticizer to the underlying criticized feelings.

A second group of therapists (Katz, 1981; Leijssen, 1995; Stone and Stone, 1993; White, 1988) also consider the inner critic as a process blockage, but they emphasize its primitive protective function. The inner critic often has the function of protecting us from a way of being or doing that is seen as too dangerous, too painful or too much for us to handle. Because of having developed its method of protecting very early in our lives, it uses methods that are very primitive (like frightening us or making us feel bad). Therefore, one cannot simply disregard it. By valuing and acknowledging the inner critic and keeping it company, it will transform from a punitive instance to a valuable ally. As Stone and Stone say: 'When the negativity of the inner critic is finally neutralized, the ideas of the inner critic become an important part of your inner support system. They are now an aspect of your objective, discerning mind. The transformed critic also helps to keep you safe. It gives you authority, objectivity and the ability to set appropriate boundaries' (1993, p. 225).

The two-chair-dialogue, an experiential technique from Gestalt therapy (Perls, Hefferline and Goodman, 1951) that is used by Greenberg, Rice and Elliott (1993) in handling conflict splits, follows fundamentally the same strategy, although the concrete process steps are slightly different. By changing from one chair to the other, thereby listening to both the critical and the experiential side, the inner critic softens and interferes no longer with the underlying feelings and needs of the client.

CLASSIFICATION OF THERAPIST OPERATIONS IN WORKING WITH THE INNER CRITIC

In order to chart in a systematic way how therapists work with the inner critic, we developed a classification system in which different therapist operations are included (cf. Scheme 1). This system is deduced from an intensive study of the existing literature, as described above, and further refined by applying it to a varied sample of concrete therapy episodes. This has been done by two different raters. One rater classified the successive therapist responses; the other rater subsequently controlled the codings of the first rater. Every single therapist response — all the therapist is saying between two client utterances — was considered as a unit for analysis and classified under the appropriate strategy *or* strategies. The way of classifying was indeed *not* mutually exclusive, which implies that one therapist response could be included under several different strategies.

On the basis of the results of this pilot study, our classification system was found to be a reliable instrument — the interrater agreement was satisfactory (kappa = 0.88). Also, it appeared to be exhaustive enough to classify all possible therapist responses.

Our classification system incorporates five main strategies (see Schema 1). The first three strategies are further divided into various therapist operations; all embody the main strategy in different ways. Concrete examples are given to illustrate the different therapist operations.

I. IDENTIFYING THE INNER CRITIC

a. Diagnosing the inner critic

The therapist alerts or exposes the client to his/her inner critic. Both the direct and the indirect expressions of the inner critic are brought to the client's notice.

For example:
- *It feels like you're never good enough.*
- *You think you're worthless.*
- *You look at yourself in a black-and-white way; there are no shades of gray.*

b. Articulating what the inner critic is saying or doing

The therapist indicates in what way the inner critic affects the client's functioning; he/she reflects how the inner critic gets the client or what kind of emotions it induces. The therapist lays his/her finger on the process-blocking character of the inner critic.

For example:
- *There seems to be a part inside of you, which always wants to blame you and make you feel guilty.*
- *Your continuous self-criticism makes you feel small and insignificant.*
- *By keeping those high expectations to yourself, you don't dare to take any risks.*

c. Intensifying the inner critic

The therapist echoes the client's inner normative voice; he/she reflects the way the client is talking to him- or herself. Often the client's words are paraphrased in a more intense, sharp or vivid way.

For example:
- *Everybody else has it pretty well made, but you are a complete disaster.*
- *I'm a real softie!*
- *You're no good for nothing.*

II. PUTTING THE INNER CRITIC AT A DISTANCE

a. Ignoring, neglecting the inner critic

The client expresses his/her inner normative voice — either explicitly or implicitly — but this isn't reflected by the therapist. Perhaps the therapist intentionally chooses to leave the inner critic aside and to follow another track. But it's also possible that the therapist neglects the inner critic because he/she doesn't notify its appearance.

b. Putting the inner critic at a distance, disidentifying the inner critic

The therapist gives a message or an instruction that helps the client to dissociate from his/her inner critic. Often the therapist tries to concretize the disidentification by asking the client to put his/her inner critic at a distance, either literally or metaphorically.

For example:
- *Could you try to place your critic in that chair?*
- *Please put all your self-judgments aside.*

c. Enfeebling the inner critic, fighting the inner critic

The therapist tries to enfeeble the client's inner critic by questioning it or fighting it more actively. The therapist points at the contradictory, incomplete and/or inaccurate character of the client's self-criticism. The therapist gives counter-arguments or brings own values and standards.

For example:

• *I think it's completely unfair to punish yourself with such an undue severity.*

• *Personally speaking, I'm not really fond of people who master their lives in a perfect way.*

d. Approaching the critic with humour: exaggerating the critical voice, making a fool of the inner critic, caricaturing the inner critic

For example:

• *Your critic should win the Nobel prize, giving you so much attention, night and day!*

• *He (= your critic) is holier than the pope.*

• *I started to worry, I didn't hear your critic for at least ten minutes.*

e. Accentuating the opposite of the inner critic, promoting self-acceptance and a strengthening of the self

For example:

• *I think you've handled this pretty well.*

• *In a way, you also feel proud of yourself . . .*

III. ATTUNING TO THE INNER CRITIC, FOLLOWING THE INNER CRITIC'S TRACK

a. Listening to the inner critic

The therapist invites the client to ventilate his/her self-criticism. The therapist allows the critic to speak.

For example:

• *If you'd give him a right to speak, what do you think he'd like to tell you?*

• *You think you've failed . . . Please tell me more about this.*

• *What are you reproaching yourself with?*

b. Inviting the client to visualize or portray the inner critic

The therapist invites the client to describe his/her inner critic. The therapist asks the client to couch his/her inner critic in a particular figure, character or metaphor. Sometimes the therapist asks the client to draw or paint his/her inner critic.

For example:

• *Can you visualize it in a sort of image or figure?*

• *How does he (= the inner critic) look like?*

• *Can you draw your critic on this sheet of paper?*

c. Exploring the genesis, the function, the meaning and the impact of the inner critic

The therapist helps the client to find out how the inner critic came into his/her life. The therapist tries to discover the inner critic's meaning and function. He/she invites the client to explore this further.

For example:

• *Maybe it's good to find out when your critic came into your life.*

• *I have the idea that your critic must have good reasons to blame you for all this.*

d. Showing respect and empathy for the inner critic

The therapist has a respectful and empathic attitude towards the client's critic. The therapist recognizes and valorizes the good intentions of the inner critic.

For example:

• *He so badly wanted to protect you.*

• *He didn't realize that he hurt you that badly.*

IV. MAKING CONTACT WITH THE ORGANISMIC LAYER OF THE SELF

a. Attuning to the underlying feelings of the inner critic

The therapist attunes to the underlying feelings of worry, anxiety and uncertainty of the inner critic. He/she explores the needs and wants of the inner critic.

For example:

• *I can imagine that your critic is really scared deep inside.*

• *How could you reassure your critic?*

• *He (= your critic) seems to be really concerned that you would be banished.*

b. Making contact with the oppressed organismic feelings

The therapist makes contact with that part of the person that has been oppressed by the inner critic. The therapist explores how it feels to be in the grasp of a criticizing and demanding part of the self. He/she invites the client to explore and unfold these oppressed feelings. Also, he/she helps the client to contain overwhelming feelings.

For example:

• *There seems to be a lot of pain underneath.*

• *You've never got any breathing space.*

• *How does your inner child feel about this?*

c. Paying attention to related feeling aspects

The therapist pays attention to feeling aspects that are not related to any of the two poles of the self. The therapist makes contact with newly evoking feelings or feelings that are connected to the client-therapist relationship. Or the therapist reflects feelings that are related to the conflict *between* the two poles of the self (being stuck, being torn . . .).

For example:

• *I have the impression that you are a bit angry with me.*

• *It seems that a new feeling is bubbling up right now . . .*

• *You're really sick of being torn between this critical part and your emotional part.*

V. INTEGRATING THE DIFFERENT ASPECTS OF THE SELF

a. Differentiating if and when the inner critic is helpful or hindering

The therapist helps the client to discover to what extent he really needs his/her inner critic. The therapist helps the client to differentiate between circumstances where he/she needs the protection of the inner critic and circumstances where the protective function of the critic is getting impeding. The therapist invites the client to explore what kind of position he/she wants to determine for the inner critic.

For example:

• *In some ways you need this critical voice, it helps you to attain things; at other times, it's a millstone around your neck.*

• *What kind of position do you want your inner critic to get?*

b. Transforming the inner critic from 'enemy' to 'ally'

The therapist helps the client to find out how his/her inner critic would be really helpful. The therapist invites the client to explore how the inner critic could be transformed into a valuable ally. He/she invites the client to look for a replacement that is more understanding, supporting and loving.

For example:

• *Can you ask him to take care of you in a more loving way?*

• *Can you imagine to replace your critic with a character that is more understanding?*

c. Bringing together the different aspects of self

The therapist tries to make an integration between the different aspects of self. He/she facilitates 'a cooperation' between the different aspects of self.

For example:

• *This critical voice and this vulnerable part are both belonging to you and you really want them to fit together.*

• *Please try to imagine how these two poles could live together in harmony.*

This classification instrument can help us to get a refined and differentiated overview of the various operations therapists use to work with the inner critic. Also, it offers the psychotherapist a broad spectrum of intervention possibilities. Besides that, it makes it possible to make comparisons between therapeutic orientations and to chart the different 'styles of working'. And last but not least, it advances our process-directiveness. In this respect, we don't give preference to any of the above strategies as such; we believe that the effectiveness of a certain strategy depends on the specific way the inner critic appears during the therapy process. Using the above strategies unthinkingly or using only a single strategy may be insufficient. For example, moving the inner critic aside is not attainable when it represents a very rigid and severe kind of self-rejection, where the critic is completely opposed to the client. Also, moving the critic aside is not effective when the critic has a protective function. Therefore, we advocate a more integrated approach that is better attuned to the specific moment-by-moment appearances of the inner critic. This will be illustrated with an 'in-depth analysis' of the client-therapist pathway in a selection of therapy episodes.

ILLUSTRATION OF THERAPIST OPERATIONS

Julia (Rogers)

Julia talks about her difficulties bringing up her children. She feels uncomfortable having to make decisions on her own and realizing that it might not have been the right decision.

C1: *I'm very indecisive, it feels like I'm not able to make a fair decision . . . But I want to learn to accept that. Be satisfied with saying that I did all that I could do. And I want to influence people around me who I sense are unkind to themselves because I feel like they did all that they could do. And they're not satisfied with it.*

T1: *You'd like them to be kind to themselves. And I guess you'd like to be kinder to yourself.*

II.a. Ignoring, neglecting the inner critic

II.e. Accentuating the opposite of the inner critic, promoting self-acceptance and a strengthening of the self

C2: *Yes. That's something I've become aware of. That you can actually be unkind to yourself. But then again, I don't want to think more highly of myself, you know. I' m wondering: 'Will this experience make me so that I can't see things like they really are? Because I think I'm more important than the person who didn't get up there?'*

T2: *'Will it make me feel superior?'*

I.c. Intensifying the inner critic, echoing the critical voice

C3: *Yes. And I worry about that. I'm concerned about that. 'Cause there's a tendency in me to think, 'Yeah, hold my shoulders up.' I want to balance that side of myself, you know. I don't really want to be perfect. I think I've gotten away from that. I just want to be acceptable to myself. A standard of excellence and not sloppy like I keep house.*

T3: *You want to be able to accept yourself. Even in your sloppy housekeeping?*

II.a. Ignoring, neglecting the inner critic

II.e. Accentuating the opposite of the inner critic, promoting self-acceptance and a strengthening of the self

C4: *Oh, I think I've probably given up on that. There's still times I'll walk by a bedroom and the bed's unmade, you know. Oh, shame on you.*

T4: *You scold yourself sometimes.*

I.b. Articulating what the inner critic is saying or doing

C5: *Yeah. 'You should've done that rather than visit with a friend. You should put your priorities somewhere else.' But I think that's the necessary part too in myself because I wouldn't accomplish anything. If I just went with the moment. I think it's the necessary part to have a scolding side. I really do.*

T5: *So you value the voice that says, 'You've really got to do this. And keep up your standards. And get those meals whether you like it or not.'*

III.d. Showing respect and empathy for the inner critic

C6: *Uhuh. I just don't want that voice in me to have too strong a hold that it makes me not* hear the parts of me that say, 'This time you spent with your friend was valuable because she needed you and that took precedence this time over your housework.'

T6: I feel like you're working toward accepting the different aspects of you: this scolding aspect, the good aspect and the tender aspect.

V.c Bringing together the different aspects of self

As appears from this therapy fragment, Rogers' theoretical view on working with the inner critic does not seem to be implemented in his real therapy practice; he is doing something other than he what says he does. Instead of fully recognizing and accepting Julia's critical and negative self-experiences, he tends to neglect them and promote her self-acceptance and a strengthening of her self. Sometimes (as in T1) this occurs by making an empathic selection in favour of the positive, growth-enhancing aspects she is expressing; at other times (as in T3), he subtly distorts Julia's words in the direction of more self-confidence. However, he doesn't stick to the strategy of moving the inner critic aside; when Julia's critic appears again, he diagnoses or echoes it (as in T2 and T4). Also, when she expresses that she thinks of her scolding side as a necessary part of herself, Rogers shows respect and empathy for it and welcomes it as a part of her personality (as in T5 and T6).

In other words, Rogers seems to attune his strategy intuitively to the specific way the inner critic turns up during the course of therapy: when the critic is 'in process' and seems to be easily given up, he chooses to leave the critic aside for the time being and focus on the awakening positive self-experiences; on the other hand, when the client seems to hold on to her critic, he changes his strategy and follows the client in her attention to the inner critic.

Ria (neo-client-centered/experiential therapist)

C1: I'm very focused on things that go wrong. I'm haunted by all kinds of mistakes that I make.

T1: Hmhm. That part inside of you that's so much focused on all things that go wrong, would you be able to visualize that or express it in a sort of image or figure?

III.b. Inviting the client to visualize or portray the inner critic

C2: (silence) An English puritan old spinster, something like that . . . who lives next door to the priest and judges the whole village . . . She herself can't do anything wrong, because she goes to church every day and she's on good terms with the priest.

T2: Could you imagine that you send that English puritan old spinster on leave or that you give her a train ticket — no return or something like that?

II.b. Putting the inner critic on a distance, disidentifying the inner critic

C3: Well, I wouldn't mind if she got lost ! (laughs)

T3: Please look how it moves you when you try to imagine this . . .

IV.b. Making contact with the oppressed feelings

C4: I think I have to be careful, because she has been the boss for a long time; she has dominated the parish inside of me for a long time . . . So you can't just give her the push. Part of the village would revolt against that, I suppose. Some people need such

> *a person . . . although most of them are really curtailed!*

T4: *In what sense can you feel that deep inside yourself you need such a person?*

III.c. Exploring the function of the inner critic

C5: *She protects me. She protects my weaknesses, she takes care that I won't be caught making mistakes. If she's lost, I'm really vulnerable, you know.*

T5: *Maybe you need another kind of protection that helps you when necessary. Can you imagine that you hand over her function to a person who's more helpful than that English puritan old spinster? Someone who's able to protect you in a wiser way?*

V.b. Transforming the inner critic from 'enemy' to 'ally'

C6: *Not really, no. I can't imagine that her function could be handed over in a right way. I get the impression that I've kept on paying her and feeding her for too long. Now that she's gone, there's nothing left, there's no one else . . . I've always had only one refuge. I don't have any idea what to do now . . . I don't want that old spinster anymore . . . if things hurt, they may hurt!*

T6: *I still feel some concern about you being completely vulnerable . . . And somehow I feel like I want to tell you that you are more than just a vulnerable being. That vulnerable side of you is one precious and important side of you, but you are more than that.*

II.e. Promoting self-acceptance and a strengthening of the self

In this therapy fragment the therapist also tries to move the critic aside, although she's doing it in her very own way; not as Rogers does, by subtly making an empathic selection in favour of the positive, growth-enhancing tendencies of the client, but by explicitly asking the client to put her critic at a distance; therefore, she dips into the imagination of the client (as in T2). In addition, she openly explores how her strategy affects the client (as in T3), whereas Rogers' sensitivity for the impact of his strategy on the client's functioning is, again, more implicit.

As in the previous therapy fragment, the therapist flexibly attunes her strategy to the way the inner critic appears during the course of therapy: she goes from moving the critic aside to exploring its function when the client expresses her concern about giving up her inner critic (as in T4). However, as appears in C5, the client chooses to drop her former protection and to admit her vulnerability. Here again, the therapist changes her former strategy: by being present in a strong and authentic way, she helps the client to contain her painful emotions and to promote her inner strength (as in T6).

CONCLUSIONS

This article clearly demonstrates that working with the inner critic is not an easy job, followed by immediate and guaranteed success; it is 'hard labour' and not a magic trick, where you pull a rabbit out of your hat and make him disappear again. In a certain sense, the two illustrations that were given are not completely representative of the real clinical practice — as they are respectively a demonstration session and a session from the end phase of a therapy. Often we are confronted with more massive and rigid types of inner critic, who are difficult to move or change. Nevertheless, I think the two illustrations clearly prove the importance of a differential process-directive approach, in which one flexibly responds to the current, moment-by-moment appearances of the inner critic, instead of holding to a single, uniform approach to this client problem.

This does not suggest a technical approach, strictly directed by protocols with no room for spontaneous, intuitive and creative responses. Working with the inner critic assumes more than applying a fixed set of strategies and operations; if anything it requires inventiveness and inspiration from the therapist to make them work. However, further research is needed to investigate what kind of responses and interventions are most appropriate, given the specific type and intensity of the inner critic. For this, a broader scope of therapy episodes has to be taken into account.

REFERENCES

Gendlin, E. T. (1981). *Focusing.* Revised edn. New York: Bantam Books.

Gendlin, E. T. (1996). *Focusing-oriented Psychotherapy: A manual of the experiential method.* New York: Guilford Press.

Greenberg, L. S., Lietaer, G. and Watson, J. C. (1998). Experiential therapy: Identity and challenges. In L. S. Greenberg, J. C. Watson, and G. Lietaer (Eds.) *Handbook of Experiential Psychotherapy.* New York: Guilford Press, pp. 451–66.

Greenberg, L. S., Rice, L. N., and Elliott, R. (1993). *Facilitation Emotional Change: The moment-by-moment process.* New York: Guilford Press.

Harvey, S. (1992). Healing from the inside out. Selfcare and the critic aspect. *The Folio. Journal for Focusing and Experiential Psychotherapy, 11,* (2), 29–34.

Katz, R. (1981). Focusing with the 'critic'. *The Folio. Journal for Focusing and Experiential Psychotherapy, 1,* (3), 16–17.

Leijssen, M. (1995). *Gids voor gesprekstherapie.* Utrecht: De Tijdstroom.

McGuire, M. (1984a). Part I of an excerpt from: 'Experiential focusing with severely depressed suicidal clients'. *The Folio. Journal for Focusing and Experiential Psychotherapy, 3,* (2), 46–59.

McGuire, M. (1984b). Part II of an excerpt from: 'Experiential focusing with severely depressed suicidal clients'. *The Folio. Journal for Focusing and Experiential Psychotherapy, 3*(3), 104–19.

Müller, D. (1995). Dealing with self-criticism: The critic within us and the criticized one. *The Folio. Journal for Focusing and Experiential Psychotherapy, 14,* 1–9.

Perls, F., Hefferline, R. and Goodman, P. (1951). *Gestalt Therapy.* New York: Dell.

Rice, L. N., and Greenberg, L. S. (1984). *Patterns of Change: Intensive analysis of psychotherapy process.* New York: Guilford Press.

Rogers, C. R. (1942). *Counseling and Psychotherapy.* Boston: Houghton Mifflin.

Rogers, C. R. (1949). The attitude and orientation of the counselor in client-centered therapy. *Journal of Consulting Psychology, 13,* 82–94.

Rogers, C. R. (1951). *Client-centered Therapy.* Boston: Houghton Mifflin.

Rogers, C. R. (1959). A theory of therapy, personality and interpersonal relationships, as developed in the client-centered framework. In S. Koch (Ed.) *Psychology: A study of a science.* New York: McGraw-Hill.

Rogers, C. R. (1961). *On Becoming a Person: A therapist's view of psychotherapy.* London: Constable.

Rogers, C. R. (1975). Empathic: An unappreciated way of being. *The Counseling Psychologist, 5,* 2–10.

Stinckens, N. (1999). *Process markers of the inner critic.* Paper at the 30th annual meeting of the Society for Psychotherapy Research, Braga, Portugal.

Stinckens, N. (2001). De innerlijke criticus in beeld gebracht: een typologie van verschijningsvormen. *Tijdschrift voor Cliëntgerichte Psychotherapie, 38*, (3).

Stinckens, N. (2001). *De innerlijke criticus in clientgericht-experiëntiële psychotherapie.* Leuven: Proefschrift K.U. Leuven.

Stinckens, N. and Leijssen, M. (1999). De innerlijke criticus in cliëntgericht-experiëntiële psychotherapie. Illustratie van een micromodel. *Tijdschrift voor Psychotherapie, 25*, (1), 5–26.

Stone, H. and Stone, S. (1993). *Embracing your inner critic: Turning self-criticism into a creative asset.* San Francisco: Harper Collins Publishers.

White, D. (1988). Taming the critic. The use of imagery with clients who procrastinate. *Journal of Mental Imagery, 12*, 125–33.

Rhonda Goldman PhD

Illinois School of Professional Psychology; Argosy University, Chicago Northwest, USA

The Empty-chair Dialogue for Unfinished Business

This chapter will describe how to use the empty-chair dialogue technique for certain types of emotional processing problems that people bring to therapy. The empty-chair dialogue is particularly helpful for work with interpersonal conflict that stems from unresolved relationships in the past. The problems people actually present in therapy, however, are not necessarily expressed as this form of conflict. Sometimes problems are expressed as general feelings of self-doubt, indecision, confusion, and feelings of depression and/or anxiety. As therapists form strong working alliances with clients, and begin to hear their subjective construal of their problems, they begin to listen for and notice certain types of emotional injuries and interpersonal conflicts that are associated with unfinished business indicating that the empty-chair technique would be ideal for addressing their problems.

The empty-chair technique can be seen as a device for bringing to awareness automated and dysfunctional emotional processes that are the source of pain or bad feelings. It provides a structure within the therapy session that allows access to deeper emotional structures that are seen as the source of problems. The technique facilitates clients' restructuring of maladaptive emotional processes to promote new, healthier emotional functioning. The empty-chair dialogue is initiated in response to specified verbal indicators, called 'markers', that suggest the presence of these types of conflict. After this, a specific set of operations is followed toward the successful resolution of the unfinished business.

This chapter will provide a brief review of the theory from which this technique arises and describe the therapeutic conditions that are necessary for the successful resolution of unresolved conflict. Then the chapter will, through case example, describe the empty-chair technique including the specific therapist operations involved in the successful working through of this type of emotional conflict.

THEORETICAL BACKGROUND

Chair work is a technique that was originally developed in the Gestalt tradition. Fritz Perls, the founder of Gestalt therapy (Perls, Hefferline and Goodman, 1951) identified different types of dysfunctional human processes that were seen as causing ongoing and long-term distress. One of them was unfinished business with a significant other from the past. This involved the use of a chair that represents an imaginary other, so that people could express unexpressed feelings and needs to the other, thereby allowing them to move forward in their lives. The technique is based on the Gestalt principles that there is a dynamic relation between figure and ground, and that significant unmet needs have not fully receded from awareness (Perls et al., 1951; Polster and Polster, 1973).

In Gestalt theory and practice, a major source of dysfunction is the disowning of healthy, growth-oriented resources and needs. The owning and reprocessing of experience to assimilate it into existing meaning structures is seen as the key to change in the Gestalt model. This is thought to occur through the process of awareness. It is through awareness of experience that people are provided options to choose what mode of functioning is best for them. To aid in this process, Gestalt therapy offers experiments of deliberate awareness, or 'techniques' designed to promote reprocessing of experience and integration into current emotional structures (Perls et al., 1951).

Since the work of Perls et al. (1951, 1969), Greenberg and colleagues (Greenberg, Rice and Elliott, 1993) have developed the Gestalt techniques that Perls (1969) and others began. Significant developments have been made on the empty-chair method for working through unfinished business with a significant other from the past (Greenberg et al., 1993; Greenberg and Malcolm, 2002). According to Greenberg et al. (1993), when specific schematic emotion memories of significant others are triggered, the person re-experiences unresolved emotional reactions. To the extent that the person does not confront embedded feelings, express unmet needs, and come to acceptance of the significant other, the 'unfinished' quality of that relation will continue to intrude, often unconsciously, on current relationships. Through chair work, clients access healthier aspects of self, such as fundamentally adaptive sadness and anger and dissociated needs that have had too little influence on their modes of acting in the world. Integration of these into existing emotion structures allows clients to navigate themselves toward their own goals (Greenberg and Paivio, 1997).

THERAPEUTIC RELATIONSHIP AND EMPATHIC ATTUNEMENT

All dialogues must be conducted within the context of a safe, trusting working alliance (Goldman and Greenberg, 1997). Therapeutic attitudes of acceptance, prizing, and empathy (Rogers, 1957) are important and continuously form the basis for the facilitation of the dialogue. These relational conditions are seen as necessary to promote trust and the clients' internalized acceptance necessary for change. The goals of the dialogues are acceptance and transformation rather than modification, control or denial. In addition, ongoing and implicit agreement on the goals of therapy and the tasks adopted to achieve those goals (Horvath and Greenberg, 1994) is seen as necessary for change to occur. Empathic attunement is key to the empty-chair process (Watson, Goldman, and Vanaerschot, 1998; Greenberg et al., 1997). Not only is empathy vital to providing clients with an optimal environment for change, it allows clients to learn what it means to be validated, nurtured and feel accepted. Acceptance and integration of experience is key to change through this process.

Another important function of empathic attunement in chair work is that it facilitates clients' awareness of emotional processing. Emotions are seen as having adaptive qualities that guide and direct people toward accessing and meeting fundamental needs and goals. When information from emotional processing is not accurately articulated and symbolized, the orienting function of the adaptive system is defeated. In the context of chair work, therapists continuously use empathic attunement and responding to help read the clients' current state and guide them through to resolution.

The operation of the empty-chair technique involves the use of therapist micro-skills that form the basis of the facilitation of the dialogue. For example, at times therapists empathically reflect the core message of their clients' communication so that clients feel understood. At other times, the therapist empathically encourages clients' exploration of their experience to find the central meaning. At other points, therapists engage in what has come to be called 'experiential teaching' (Goldman, 1991), wherein they communicate with clients about the process of the dialogue and provide an explanation of what will occur. These micro-skills are referred to throughout the explanation of the therapeutic operations of the dialogue. For a fuller explication of the therapist microskills, the reader is referred elsewhere (Greenberg et al., 1993; Elliott, Watson and Greenberg, in press).

Case example

The explanation for the working through of the empty-chair dialogue will be illustrated by a case example that will exemplify the concepts and operations. The case presented is that of Maria, who came to therapy feeling depressed, worthless, and hopeless about her life situation improving. She felt trapped in a marriage with two young children, 2 and 5, and a husband who was a compulsive gambler. She had attempted to leave the marriage on two separate occasions, but each time had returned after her husband convinced her that his behavior would change. She returned on advice from her mother who insisted that 'a good wife stand by her man', much like she had. Maria's father also had a gambling problem, and over the years, her mother had suffered with this legacy.

> At the point in therapy where we pick up with her in session 11, Maria is feeling more hopeful and less depressed than when she entered therapy. Through prior work using the two-chair process for inner conflict, she has begun to feel a great deal more self-accepting. Even though her husband was not tackling his gambling problem, she felt much less responsible for him, saying that it was his own addiction that he 'brought on himself'. She had also begun expressing feelings to him more regularly 'whether he likes it or not'. She had found a part-time job and felt much better about being 'out in the world'. Through validation and subsequent exploration of her new-sprung good feelings, regret about her past emerged. She reported feeling sad that it took her this long to feel entitled to her own feelings. She brought up her parents in this regard, saying:
>
> C: I was never able to be an individual, I don't resent them or blame them because, (sigh) I just take the perspective, what's the use, that's the way they were brought up, that they did the best they can, and it can't be changed . . .

This is a good example of a marker of unfinished business with a parent, suggesting that the empty-chair method is a worthwhile way of working through the problem. She is lodging a complaint about her parents, but at the same time feels hopeless about her feelings ever changing. Her 'understanding' position, characterized by 'they did the best they could', is stated without conviction and is fraught with resignation and detachment.

Two types of unfinished business

The empty-chair method is used for two types of unfinished business. In both types of work, the representation of the other in the chair serves a function that is integral to the resolution of the dialogue; however, the resolutions take different forms. The first type of unfinished business involves feelings over neglect or abandonment by a significant other who has been developmentally important. This type of unfinished business may emerge in the context of current relationships, but is symbolically related to past unfinished business. Examples include parents, bosses, authority figures, or current partners. The resolution involves understanding, accepting, and forgiving the other. The second form of unfinished business is with a person who has been physically, sexually, or emotionally abusive. The perpetrator can be a stranger, friend, lover, or caregiver and the person can be exposed to a single traumatic event or repeated victimization over several years by the perpetrator(s) (Paivio and Laurent, 2001). The process is somewhat different and the resolution involves holding the other accountable. While this chapter will discuss the working through of both processes, the interested reader is referred to outside sources for more specific and extensive description of how to work with trauma-related unfinished business (Paivio and Laurent, 2001; Paivio and Shimp, 1998).

Hearing the marker of unfinished business

The key features of a marker of unfinished business are: 1) the presence of lingering, unresolved feeling such as hurt and resentment; 2) the feeling(s) is related to an other who has been significant; 3) the feelings are currently experienced; 4) the feelings are not currently expressed, and there are signs of interrupted or restricted expression. When Maria stated that her parents never 'let her be an individual', she expressed current feeling toward a significant other from her past. She denied feeling resentment, and instead expressed sadness. Her affect is restricted in its expression and instead she expresses resignation and hopelessness, secondary emotions.

Markers of unfinished business are not always presented to the therapist in a clear-cut form. The expression of secondary emotions, expressed through blame or complaint about the other, is extremely common. For example, one client complained 'My mother never told me she loved me.' Another client expressed blame and bitter resignation about his father, stating 'My father and I are just not close. We never were. He always told me I would amount to nothing. I have nothing to say to him now.'

Markers of unfinished business can be expressed in direct forms as well. One client stated, 'My father always criticized and put me down. I could not stand it. At the time, I just accepted it, but now I feel very resentful.' In examples such as these, when unfinished business is directly stated, hurt and resentment may be expressed but with a constricted quality. As in this example, the other is often reproached.

Less direct examples that are important to watch for include longing or resentment when talking about ex-spouse, or tearing up when talking about a deceased parent. It is also possible for unfinished business to emerge within the context of other topics. For example, unfinished business might emerge when a client is talking about a current relationship that is particularly difficult because feelings from past relationships are being triggered and the client is in pain. An example might be: 'When he yells or slams cupboards, I get this sinking feeling and it reminds me of how my mother was when she took temper tantrums.' In this case, it is often best to put the 'current' other in the chair because this is most salient for the client and begin the dialogue. If the significant other from the past emerges in the dialogue, then the therapist makes a switch.

Markers for trauma-related unfinished business share the same components as those stated above; however, they center upon a traumatic or abusive relational experience. The relationship or trauma is also 'unfinished' in the sense that memories continue to interrupt functioning, often in the form of intrusive memories. However, in trauma-based unfinished business, a person's current life is significantly altered by the trauma, the person presents as extremely fragile, and the memories are particularly painful. Current relationships are often significantly troubled, and memories are especially unwanted. People with this type of unfinished business are often ambivalent about whether or not they want to 'return' to the source of the trauma. On the one hand, they present the issue in an attempt to rid themselves of the intrusive memories; yet on the other there is significant pain that threatens re-traumatization and/ or a fear of annihilation in the face of overwhelming pain. As a result, the empty-chair dialogue should only be suggested after a strong therapeutic relationship is secured, and when clients feel ready to face their oppressor. In trauma-related unfinished business it is especially important that clients set the pace. For example, if at first clients refuse to engage in the dialogue, the therapist should not be surprised, and validate the fear. The therapist can suggest that they may return to the unfinished business at a later date, but must communicate to the client that they control the direction of the therapy. When the idea of expressing feelings to the other is reintroduced, a graded approach to contact with the other can be followed. For example, at first it may be best not to use the chair. After that, clients may only feel comfortable with the 'chair' positioned many feet away, or placing the symbolic representation of the 'other' outside the room or in the garbage pail. Clients may also need to engage a two-chair process to resolve a split before starting the process in order to resolve their uncertainty regarding returning to the unfinished business (Elliott and Davis, 1997). In some trauma-related cases, the unfinished business dialogue is contraindicated. Specifically, when there is a risk of re-traumatization, self-mutilation behavior, suicidiality, or extreme aggressive behavior, this technique is not advised.

Again, while specific instruction for tailoring the dialogue process for trauma will be given throughout this chapter, for more detailed instruction the reader is referred elsewhere.

Finally, it is important to delineate markers of unfinished business from conflict splits that indicate that the two-chair dialogue be initiated. Conflict splits often manifest in the form of conflict between two opposing aspects of self (e.g. part of me wants to go to school, part of me wants to keep working); self-criticism (I am stupid); or self-interruption (I am afraid to express my anger). Two-chair work for conflict splits involves a separate set of operations that are beyond explanation in the current chapter. The interested reader is referred to outside sources that explain these operations in further detail (Greenberg, Rice, and Elliott, 1993; Elliott et al., in press).

EMBEDDED MARKERS

Markers of more primary unfinished business can be embedded in the context of more current unfinished business dialogues. The earlier relationship will suddenly come into focus as a the source of the unfinished business. When this occurs, the therapist must decide whether to continue to work with the 'current' other or switch to a more primary other. At that moment, the therapist must judge what is most meaningful for the client. Understanding and assessing what is most meaningful is a process-diagnostic, case-formulation skill (Goldman and Greenberg, 1997). It requires therapists to bring all of their previous knowledge of the client to bear on the decision, and decide what is most pressing, poignant, central, or meaningful. This is a hands-on judgement of what is most currently 'live' for the client, based on therapists' understandings of what has been pivotal for the client, or what they judge as the most appropriate direction. At this point, the therapist assumes an experimental attitude of 'this sounds important, let's try it and see.' This is definitely a complex, momentary judgement that, nevertheless, needs to be acted on decisively and swiftly, ensuring that the dialogue continues to flow. If the therapist decides to alter the direction of the dialogue, it is best to meta-communicate with the client about the process. This is a form of *experiential teaching*. An example is illustrated in the following interchange when the client is confronting her boss in the other chair:

C: *(enacting boss) What you have to say is not important (engaging sweeping motion of wiping away or annihilating self in other chair.) You are a nothing.*

T: *Ok, change, come back to this chair; how does that make you feel when he sweeps you away like that?*

C: *I just feel so dismissed (shoulders hunching over and beginning to cry); it reminds me of the way my mother used to talk to me.*

T: *Yeah, it really hurts, and it reminds you of how your mother used to dismiss you, just sweep you away . . . it sounds like you have feelings towards your mother about how she hurt you. Why don't we bring her in here (pointing to other chair) and you can tell her what that was like for you? How does that sound to you? Are you willing to try?*

Setting up the empty-chair dialogue

Once Maria began talking about her feelings towards her parents, the therapist validated and explored her feelings and began to move towards setting up a dialogue. At this point, one of the therapist's tasks was to determine which of her parents was to be in the other chair. When a client talks about unfinished business with both parents at the same time, there are a number of ways to set up the dialogue. One method is to ask the client whom they feel the strongest toward. Another method is to begin by putting both parents in the chair; in the working through of the dialogue, one parent will emerge as more figural than the other. The therapist proceeded as follows:

C: *Yeah I guess that is just the way my parents were, (crying) yeah, there is sadness . . .*

T: *You feel you really missed something.*

C: *Yeah, a lot of years of pent-up feelings. It is so hard for me to understand why I put so much energy into not being myself.*

T: *You sort of wonder, how come I never felt comfortable just being me?*

C: *Yeah, I just wanted to escape, or maybe I just didn't know.*

T: *Sounds like it was hard for you to be you . . . sounds like you have a lot of feelings toward your parents. When you think of being stifled, which one of your parents* comes up for you, when you feel restricted, held back?

C: *Well, my father was working, and my mother was as well, but I remember I used to*
       come home from school to take care of my brothers, and (crying) I just remember
       having an awful lot of responsibility. I was like the provider. I had to be there for
       them, and take care of the house, and make the meals.

T: *It was just expected that you would take a lot of the responsibility. Who did you feel*
       this expectation coming from the most?

C: *My mother.*

T: *Yeah, so why don't we try having you speak to your mother in the other chair and tell*
       her about your feelings about those expectations, tell her what it was like for you?
       Do you want to try that?

C: *Ok.*

In setting up a dialogue, the therapist must obtain the client's consent. This is particularly important when introducing this chair method. It is also helpful to provide *experiential teaching* at this juncture, by providing an explanation of how the dialogue will proceed in general terms. For example, the therapist might say: 'It sounds like you have a lot of anger and sadness about your mother. Perhaps we could try something that will give you an opportunity to express some of those feelings.'

Responding to problematic scenarios in the initial facilitation of the dialogue

There are various reasons clients might express hesitation over engaging in the empty-chair dialogue. First, it is seen as culturally taboo (even more in certain cultures such as African-centric, Asian or Italian cultures, for example) to 'speak back' to one's parents. Indeed, one of the ten commandments upon which the Judeo-Christian tradition is based is 'Honor thy father and mother.' People feel that expressing feelings out loud is disrespectful. Such expressions may violate what they have been taught or how they were disciplined. In this case, it is important to validate the client's concerns, explore related issues, and let the client know that it is optional to engage in the dialogue. On the other hand, the client can be reminded that the dialogue is not actually real and that the chair work provides an opportunity for expression and reprocessing, but does not necessitate action in the real world. The therapist might remind the client that it is s/he who must live with these feelings, and that it may ultimately be important to let go of them or forgive the parent. Clients are sometimes concerned about the powerful intensity of the exercise. For example, speaking about his father who had died when he was a 6-year-old boy, one client expressed: 'I have had countless conversations with him in my head. I have written to him, but just the suggestion of bringing him here, even in imagination . . . I wouldn't dream of it.' In this case, it was important for the therapist to acknowledge the power of the evocative technique and allow the client to set his own pace. Emphasizing that clients control the pace is particularly important with fragile clients. One may spend a number of sessions talking about the idea of engaging in the empty-chair and only return to it when the client feels ready.

   Clients sometimes object to participating in the dialogue, because they resigned themselves long ago to the status quo: for example, stating: 'I have said all I need to say. My parent is never going to change. I have accepted that.' In this case, the therapist may respond: 'I guess you just feel you have given up, having been so frustrated. You do have very strong feelings though, and this dialogue may help you to express some of those feelings and move forward in your life.'

Clients are sometimes confused between a current ongoing conflict with a significant other and unfinished business from the past. In this case, the therapist should make clear to the client that empty-chair dialogue is in reference to a past relationship that may indeed be fueling the current conflict. Resolution of the old conflict may help relieve the current one, but is not the same entity. If the client is having difficulty responding to the other from the past, the therapist can ask the client to speak to the other as the 'former self', such as the '6-year-old boy.'

Beginning therapists have particular difficulty with the initial introduction of the dialogue. Sometimes they hear markers, but hesitate to act on them for fear of angering or alienating clients. Some therapists worry that clients may feel that their therapist is not being empathic or will feel 'abandoned' when chair work is suggested. Often, contrary to therapist's expectations, clients do not feel abandoned. Rather, clients feel cared for, that their therapists are working *with* them on their problems. At this beginning stage, it is helpful for the therapist to provide an anxiety-reducing, reassuring comment such as, 'Many people find it helpful to express these feelings and they feel better afterwards. It seems to help them come to terms with the relationship.' Such comments prevent clients from feeling they are walking into an abyss without an end in sight. It provides a forward-looking, hopeful end to the dialogue and reassures them that the expression of painful emotion will lead them to a better place. In general, clients appreciate the opportunity to freely express their feelings, not directly to the therapist, but rather to that person with whom they have those problematic issues. It is also important for the therapist to keep in mind that clients do express extreme relief upon resolution of the dialogue. Therapists in training must remember that continued use of validation and support is essential and will reduce feelings of abandonment. On a final note, the therapist's communication of a strong sense of conviction about the utility of this method of working, and a clear and confident explanation and rationale of the process, will greatly increase the chances of the client's willingness to engage.

Without the therapist's direction, at the commencement of the dialogue, clients will often wonder about 'why' they feel this way. Therapists must resist engaging in this dialogue. While understanding advances knowledge and increases one's sense of control, it does not bring emotional clarity or alter the relationship in any significant manner in this particular context. In unfinished business, a person is stuck in a particular habitual form of negative responding, related to a disallowing of significant primary emotion and associated unmet needs that continue to affect current functioning and interpersonal relationships. With this understanding, the therapist bypasses an analytic exploration of 'why', and moves to an exploration of the complex of emotional responses that govern this form of responding. For example, in response to a client saying 'I don't know why she gets under my skin so much; there is just something about her voice and the way she is,' the therapist would reply, 'So somehow this all puzzles you. It sounds like you have some strong feelings towards her. Can you actually imagine her over there? Put her there and tell her how angry she makes you feel.' The therapist validates the query, but focuses on underlying feelings toward the other.

EVOKING THE PRESENCE OF THE SIGNIFICANT OTHER

Once Maria had agreed to participate in the dialogue, the therapist helped her actually evoke the image of her mother in the other chair:

    T: *(bringing chair to face client) Ok, can you actually see your mother over there? What is her expression?)*

    C: *Yeah, I can see her. She kind of looks disapproving.*

At the beginning of the dialogue, the therapist must ensure that the client is 'making contact' with the imagined other. Contact is a Gestalt term (Struempfel and Goldman, 2001) that means currently felt in this context. The schematic memory of the other is evoked and emotion systems are activated. If contact is not made, the dialogue is likely to lose steam and flop. Techniques designed to encourage contact at this stage include asking the client to describe what the 'other' is wearing, or to read the expression on the other's face and respond to it. For example, the therapist might say: 'What is the look on his face right now? What do you feel when you look at him?' This is an evocative set of questions that will evoke the self other construction and prompt an emotional response. When clients conjure the other, the 'other' is often symbolically performing the behavior or action that the client has recently described or to which s/he objects. If the other was described as disapproving, the imagined other may have a stern, judgmental look on his/her face. If the client has described the other as neglectful, the imagined other may be 'turning away' in the chair. For example, if the client says, 'Her head is turned away from me,' the therapist can respond, 'So she is ignoring you right now; how does that make you feel? Can you tell her what that is like for you?' Sometimes clients describe the other in one way, and the polar opposite behavior manifests in the chair. For example it is not uncommon for the client to be complaining about the negative qualities of the other, but when s/he imagines the other in the chair, positive, loving feelings emerge. The therapist should follow whatever response of the imagined other emerges, and encourage the client to respond to that action or behavior.

Clients sometimes have difficulty starting the dialogue, stating, 'Well, I am not quite sure how my parent would actually be.' This may be the result of confusion or ambivalence about engaging in the dialogue for fear of being required to express their feelings to their parent in reality. In this scenario, the therapist should emphasize that the dialogue is simply an opportunity for exploring and reprocessing the relationship for themselves, without implications for action in the real world. The client needs to be reassured that what is said in the dialogue does not have to be repeated to the parent. The therapist might respond by saying, 'If your parent were actually here, she might say something entirely different. It is your feelings that we want to explore though.'

In the beginning and throughout the dialogue, the therapist needs to focus on facilitating enactment of the other in that chair, and encouraging the exploration and expression of client's concrete, subjective experience and emotions in response. The dialogue cannot occur at an abstract, intellectual level. In general, when the dialogue does not seem to be moving forward, therapists need to evaluate whether contact is occurring and emotion systems are activated. At this crucial stage, therapists need to ensure that the client enacts the negative other. A common mistake is to allow a debate or argument to evolve where, for example, the client says, 'You weren't there' and the parent responds, 'I was,' and the dialogue stops short.

At this point, the client needs clear direction from the therapist to *be* the other and *enact* the action or behavior of the parent or other and respond to it. The purpose of enacting the negative other is to evoke the unresolved feelings for reprocessing.

Differentiating feelings toward the other

Once Maria had made contact with her imagined mother in the other chair, the therapist had her differentiate and express feelings to her mother:

> T: Uh huh, she looks disapproving; what do you feel when you see her looking disapproving?
>
> C: I feel afraid, um, afraid I am going to let her down. I didn't want to do all those things she asked.
>
> T: Tell your mother what it was like for you to have all those expectations on you, to clean the house, take care of your brothers
>
> C: You expected too much from me; you always put what you believed was right for me in my mind; you made me believe that there was no time for socializing with friends.
>
> T: Tell her what you felt?
>
> C: I felt trapped and I felt scared I would not do it right. It was awful.

At this point, the therapist is beginning to differentiate her experience of what occurred. Without proper guidance, clients will 'talk about' their experience of the other to the therapist but not directly address the other, tell stories about the other, or throw accusations at the other, describing a series of injustices committed against them. Therapists need to encourage clients to draw upon their own subjective experiences and express feelings to the other. For example, a therapist responded as follows to a client who had suffered abuse from an alcoholic parent:

> C: You were so selfish! You were never home, you just left us all alone to deal with Dad's drunken rage. And I had to be there to pick up the pieces. Literally, pick up the pieces when he started to throw things. I remember vases flying, plates, you name it.
>
> T: Yeah, that must have been really hard for you, sounds scary too ... can you tell her what that was like for you?
>
> C: Well, I hated it. I can't believe you just left me there.
>
> T: Yeah, I was so scared . . . I am angry at you for leaving me.

The client's initial response to the therapist's inquiry into the client's experience of her mother garners an externalized response. She objectifies her own experience by saying, 'I hated it,' and expresses accusatory disbelief about her mother's behavior. Her focus is outside of her own experience, and she speaks from a less powerful position than her mother. When this occurs, therapists' goals should be to empower clients by reflecting back and validating their own experience and encouraging them to speak in the first person and use 'I' language. For example, to a client who says 'I can't believe you were so mean and hurtful,' a therapist would say 'Can you say I hurt?'

Facilitating enactment of the negative other

In the beginning stages of the dialogue, the therapist must help clients to enact the 'other'. Typically, the other is cast as negative, performing the behaviors that caused difficult emotions in the client. The therapist's goal is to help the client perform, fully express and elaborate the characteristics of the other so that schematic memories can emerge. Here the therapist encourages Maria to draw upon her internal representation of her mother.

> T: *Okay, change, come over here and be your mother. What do you say in response?*
>
> C: *(as mother) I am busy. I have a lot on my plate. I don't need you bothering me. Just do what you are told (waving finger in lecturing manner). Take care of your brothers. And don't associate with those people, those friends. It is much better for you to come home after school instead of hanging out with those bad seeds.*
>
> T: *Uh huh, so as your mother, you are shutting her down, you are chastising her and dismissing her concerns. Are you aware of your hand — what does it say?*
>
> C: *(practicing hand wave again) yeah, I guess it says I am right and you are wrong and just do as you are told.*

In this sequence, the therapist facilitates the expression of the negative other. While it may feel to the therapist as if s/he is causing unnecessary pain, it is essential at this step to capture the character of the other, through enactment of their behavior or actions. The client's enactment of the negative other carries in it the client's experience of the other, that must be directly expressed from the other chair. It is common for the client to take on the tone of voice and/or physical mannerisms of the other as they experienced it. The therapist then notices and observes the mannerisms, and encourages emotional awareness and expression of them. While clients sometimes become self-conscious in response, therapists should reiterate that their intention is not to make the client uncomfortable but rather to heighten emotional awareness. The goal here is to activate the associated negative emotional processes that was originally difficult and continues to derail the client in everyday life.

Sometimes the other appears first as positive, but slowly emerges in its negative form. For example, a parent may have been benevolently controlling, or suffocating, stating: 'I just wanted the best for you.' In such cases, it may be difficult for clients to access negative feelings without feeling intense guilt. The therapist first must capture the 'quality' of the other, noticing and indeed validating the positive aspect of the parent, but also encouraging exploration of the full implications of the parent's position and behavior for the client. For example, the therapist might respond: 'I guess your mother really did want what was best for you, and on the one hand, you knew she really loved you and that was important to you, but somehow that also made it difficult for you . . . you ended up feeling stifled and suffocated and unable to say what you really wanted for fear of disappointing her.' Here, the therapist must do extra work to explore the positive and negative aspects of the parent's behavior, and allow for mixed feelings of guilt and anger or sadness. When primary emotion and experience do emerge, the therapist needs to be quick to support and encourage expression.

Differentiating meaning and encouraging expression of primary emotion

As seen above, the initial responses to the other are often global and external. Once the experience of the 'other' is sufficiently evoked, the goal of the dialogue is to move from secondary reactions into differentiating underlying meaning and encouraging the expression of primary emotional states. Both of these tasks will be elaborated in the context of the unfinished business dialogue.

Exploring meaning

To help clients explore and differentiate the meaning of their loss and experience in this significant relationship, the therapist uses both empathic attunement of presently felt, subjective experience, as well as *exploratory responses*. This is illustrated in the next piece of the dialogue with Maria.

> C: *I am not going to just do as I am told. You never listen to me (crying).*
> T: *Tell her what you missed: what you would have liked.*
> C: *I wanted to hear that you loved me. I was lonely, confused, always trying to please you, but you never expressed your love.*
> T: *Yeah, you felt so hurt; she never expressed her love, never told you how much you meant to her. Tell her.*

In the above example, the therapist helps the client articulate exactly what she missed, as well as to directly express her needs to her mother. When the client cries out plaintively to her mother 'You never listen to me!', the therapist hears an embedded need and helps her symbolize and articulate it. Differentiation of meaning generally involves elaborating clients' idiosyncratic experience in this manner, and helping clients explore their own particular pain. For example, to a client whose mother committed suicide when the client was 12, a therapist responded as follows:

> C: *There are certain times in my life when I really would have liked you to be around.*
> T: *Tell her what you wanted her around for. What you wanted. What you missed.*
> C: *I miss not being able to come home at Christmas. I miss . . .*
> T: *I miss a home.*
> C: *I miss having something to belong to . . . I have another whole family now, aunts, uncles, that I'm always trying to explain things to . . . it's impossibly complicated.*
> T: *Sounds like I miss your support in all of this.*
> C: *Yeah.*

Encouraging expression of primary sadness, anger, fear and shame

Another goal at this stage in the dialogue is to help clients differentiate secondary reactions such as hopelessness, complaint or bad feelings from primary emotion. Pure expressions of both primary sadness and anger are necessary and these two emotional states must be symbolized and expressed separately. Here, the task for therapists is to accurately assess and stay attuned to emotional states. Therapists must follow clients through emergent emotions, giving each their full expression. Therapists must be able to recognize and discern secondary emotions from primary underlying emotions. To accomplish this, therapists must (a) have knowledge of characteristics of specific emotions (Greenberg and Paivio, 1997; Greenberg, 2002); (b) have knowledge of their clients' history and emotional styles; and (c) engage in empathic attunement.

Typical secondary emotions expressed here include hopelessness, resignation, depression and anxiety. They are often expressed externally and carry a blaming tone. The therapist acknowledges and helps clients work through secondary emotions, but maintains the goal of encouraging the 'pure' expression of primary emotion. Secondary and primary emotions are often first experienced and expressed as jumbled and mixed together. For example, complaint will be fused with anger and sadness, and clients will report feeling 'sad and angry . . . kind of confused'. In cases of abuse, maladaptive fear and shame have first to be accessed, validated, and reprocessed until such as time as primary anger and sadness are accessed (Greenberg, 2002).

Clients have individual emotional styles and different modes through which they present and move through feelings. Some clients move through emotional states rather quickly. Other clients experience emotions in a more dissociated manner, having a difficult time accessing one emotional state, such as sadness, once they have fully expressed anger. Still other clients, when asked to focus on one particular feeling such as anger, quickly slide into feeling sad. Therapists must form an understanding of their clients' particular emotional styles, and help them acknowledge all emotions, with the ultimate goal of separating, differentiating and expressing sadness and anger. In Gestalt terms, the therapist engages in 'contact work' (Struempfel and Goldman, 2001), staying with the client's experience on a moment-by-moment basis until all of the client's feelings emerge and experience unfolds. An example follows below of a dialogue with an annihilating mother:

C: *(as mother) I will just sweep you away. You are a nothing. When you talk, I do not listen. What you say is stupid and worthless. Just be quiet and stay over there in the corner.*

T: *Okay, come over here (pointing to self-experiencing chair). What do you feel when she sweeps you away like that?*

C: *(shoulders hunched) I just feel frozen, like numb, kind of defeated, like what is the point?*

T: *Uh huh, hopeless. Can you stay with that feeling? What's that like inside your body? In your chest . . .*

C: *Well, it kind of feels bad. Sort of like a tight, wound-up ball . . . kind of frustrated, sad and annoyed all at once.*

T: *Uh huh, like angry and sad altogether; and what do you feel most in touch with right now?*

C: *Uh, I really feel hurt. It feels painful, like I have been punched in the gut.*

T: *Uh, so you really hurt. Tell your mother how much you hurt.*

Here we see how, by attending to and staying with the bodily felt-sense, the secondary hopelessness differentiates into more primary feelings of hurt and pain. Now the therapist needs to work with the client to fully explore her sadness and express it. Working with sadness involves the use of empathic attunement, following clients through their pain, and helping them to symbolize inchoate experience. At times, this means just being curious about the sadness, expressing caring and validation, and thereby giving permission for its full expression. Thus, therapists may find themselves saying, 'Sounds like you have a lot of pain about this, and it is very important to tell your mother about it.' At other times, and particularly with grief work, the therapists must simply provide a space, and allow room for clients to feel sad, before they even express it. For example, when the client who lost her mother at the age of 12 got in touch with her sadness, the therapist merely sat with the client, adding nods and 'yeahs', at times saying, 'Just let the tears come; there is a well of sadness there, a lot of pain.' Eventually, when the client had the opportunity to fully experience and allow her pain and tears, the therapist said, 'Tell her (mother) about the sadness.' In cases of abuse, therapists should *not* encourage clients to tell their abuser about their sadness, as the abuser is not one from whom clients want(ed) comfort. In fact, such a request may feel like a violation for a client. In such cases, it is best to have clients express sadness to a protective other, or to the therapist.

In working with anger, one needs to learn to distinguish between secondary and primary anger. Secondary rage has a blustery, empty quality to it, and serves to push the other away and/or obscure the expression of more vulnerable emotion. Its expression does not bring relief or advance movement through one's experience. Primary anger is expressed in response to violation and must be validated. Its expression is encouraged and involves an assertion of self. In unfinished business, primary anger may have been disavowed because it was unsafe to express it in the original relationship. In not being able to access primary anger, people lose access to healthy resources that can promote adaptive behavior. Thus, expression of anger and standing up to the other, by saying for example, 'It was wrong for you to hurt me like that; you were sick and I did not deserve to be treated like that' is empowering and healing.

In trauma-related unfinished business, expression of secondary rage threatens re-traumatization. In trauma work, Paivio and Laurent (2001) distinguish between generalized and chronic anger that needs focused expression to specific others for specific offenses, and constricted anger that requires intensification and expression to promote self-empowerment and self-protective behavior.

Finally, in working with emotions at this stage, therapists need to know that once primary emotions are fully and freely expressed, they move quickly. Further, anger and sadness tend to follow each other in sequence. When primary sadness is fully expressed, anger emerges and a creation of boundaries occurs. In turn, the full expression of anger allows clients to acknowledge the pain of losses and betrayal and grieve for what they missed.

Facilitating expression of unmet needs

The next stage in the dialogue involves the expression of unmet needs. These are needs that were never expressed in the original relationship because of a feeling of lack of entitlement. They are related to the satisfaction of basic interpersonal needs for attachment or separation and for self-esteem. They must be expressed as belonging to and coming from the self and with a sense of entitlement, rather than as deprivations or accusations of the other. At this stage therapists should follow clients, and encourage the expression of both emotions and needs. In addition, therapists help clients to symbolize and assert their boundaries, to say 'no' to intrusion for example, or to reassert their rights. Therapists are aware that people often disavow needs in earlier experience and that consequently, do not automatically attend to or express needs. Therapists therefore listen for needs to form and when they do, validate and encourage their expression. In response to her mother, and under the therapist's direction, Maria continues to share underlying feelings to her mother, and needs begin to emerge.

T: *Tell her what you would have liked.*

C: *To let me be an individual, who I am.*

T: *Yeah, make a demand on her.*

C: *I expected you to let me be myself. I wanted to express myself . . . to tell you what it was like for me.*

T: *Uh huh — so you wanted acceptance.*

C: *Yeah, I wanted acceptance (crying) to be told that I was loved.*

The expression of feelings and needs are highly interconnected. An exploration of feelings should be followed by a statement of related needs.

When clients do not automatically state needs, therapists should inquire into the needs and encourage clients to express them. Often the expression of unmet needs brings up deeper awareness of primary emotions.

T: *You feel so sad, so much pain, remembering not being loved, feeling so alone, so restricted. Tell her what you wanted to hear.*

C: *I wanted to hear you say that you loved me.*

T: *Tell her what it was like for you.*

C: *It was lonely and um confusing (sniff) and . . .*

T: *You felt so sad and alone. Tell her what you needed from her.*

C: *I needed you to be there to show you loved me.*

Clients do not always have full awareness of needs and have sometimes lost the ability to discern them. When clients are not aware of needs, the therapist might try a focusing exercise to increase awareness, or exploratory work to discover previously unknown needs. If clients object to stating needs, it may be beneficial to work with their objections as self-interruptions (see below). This stage may take time and only occur over multiple sessions, as clients sometimes need time to build both the self-esteem and courage necessary to both state needs and risk disappointment.

In situations where the need cannot or will not be met by the other, clients must still come to recognize their right to have needs met. This often allows the important task of *letting go of the unmet need.* At this point in the dialogue, therapists support and promote the letting go of the unfulfilled expectation(s). When letting go does not naturally flow from the expression of primary emotions, therapists may need to help clients explore and evaluate whether the unfulfilled expectation(s) can and will be met by the other, and if not, therapists should help clients explore the effects of hanging on to the expectations. In this situation, therapists can consider asking clients to express to the significant other, 'I will never give up wanting my needs met.' Finally, letting go often produces another round of grief work in which the sadness associated with mourning the loss of getting the need met from the attachment figure is worked through.

Working with interruptions to expression of primary emotion and needs

It is common for clients to run into blocks when attempting to fully express either emotions and/or needs. Either they hold back the expression and full intensity of their feelings, or they have trouble accessing or stating needs. For example, men are sometimes afraid to express rage for fear of losing control and hurting someone. Or, clients interrupt the expression of needs because they are afraid of not having them met, and of subsequent feelings of disappointment. In addition, clients interrupt the full expression of emotions and needs due to irrational albeit valid fears, such as of annihilation or loss of control.

Blocks and interruptions are often related to internalized taboos and subsequent dysfunctional beliefs and injunctions. For example, in spite of suffering years of abuse under a domineering, abusive father, an Italian Catholic client objected to telling his father of his true feelings of hatred, because 'You just don't talk back to your mother and father, let alone say you hate them.' Another client objected to telling her mother that she needed her attention, love, and affection, because at the age of 13, she decided 'I will not get what I want, and it is better not to need anyone at all.'

The beliefs that support interruptions are formed at key developmental stages and are responses to environments that did not allow for the full expression of needs. While no longer adaptive, they continue into adult life and, at an automated level, influence one's construal of the world. They are learned responses designed to cope with an unsafe environment or an internalized lack of entitlement. They are often accompanied by episodic memories that contain images of the time and location when the beliefs were formed. Whatever the source of the interruption, when they occur, therapists' goals are to heighten awareness of these maladaptive interruptive processes and help clients access and allow disavowed internal experience. To accomplish this, it is best to switch modes, and put the part of the self that is interrupting in the other chair, and ask the client to express the objections. In other words, ask the client to enact the one part of the self that holds the other back.

It is common for these injunctions to have physically expressed components. Encouraging physical expression is more likely to stimulate associated emotions and facilitate the full expression of them. Additionally, encouraging exaggeration and intensification of catastrophic expectations against emotional expression is useful in heightening awareness of the experiential impact of injunctions and blocks. For example, the therapist might say, 'Make her afraid. Tell her what might happen if she risks saying what she needs. Yeah, really scare her. How do you do that?' Awareness of tension, a sense of isolation, or powerlessness seems to increase an awareness of a desire to relieve the discomfort through expression, and propels clients to stand up for themselves. Through this exercise, clients learn how they produce their own guilt or anxiety, what they say to themselves to do so, and come to feel a greater sense of agency and control in this process. They come to realize that just as they produce these feelings, they can change them.

An example of working with an interruption follows below:

T: *What happens when you try to express your rage at your mother?*

C: *I feel like I am in a box and I cannot come out.*

T: *Okay, come over here (pointing to the other chair), be the box, and put Julie inside. What do you say as the box?*

C: *I am the box, and I have you and I will not let you out.*

T: *Okay, tell me, as the box, what is your objection to letting Julie out?*

C: *She is safe in there. I can protect her. She will not get hurt.*

T: *Okay, so tell her about how you are keeping her safe.*

C: *I am keeping you safe in there; don't come out, I am protecting you. You could get hurt if you even stick your head out a little.*

T: *Okay, now come over here and as Julie, tell your box how that feels.*

C: *Well, I feel kind of claustrophobic in here. I am squished. I would like to have a little room to breathe.*

T: *Well, she is trying to protect you. What do you say to that?*

C: *Well, I'd like to come out a little. I am not so afraid. I am a big girl. I think I can handle whatever will happen.*

T: *Okay, then can you say this to your box? Tell her what you want.*

C: *I want to come out. I want to be free.*

While such interchanges may go through a number of sequences like this one before they are resolved, when the self states a desire to express itself, the therapist should put the 'other' back into the chair, and encourage the client to express feelings to the significant other. For example,

C: *Okay, now can you put your mother back into this chair, and tell her what you felt?*

The resolution of this step is particularly important in long-standing unfinished business where the person has been resigned to the presence of unfinished business.

In trauma-related unfinished business, avoidance processes and emotional over-control are extremely common (Paivio and Laurent, 2001). Processes such as catastrophizing or guilt about experience, shutting down, going numb, and dissociation are seen as adaptive at the time of the event, but nevertheless interfering with the integration of the traumatic experience. With particularly fragile clients, it may be best to explore these processes, at least at first, through empathic responses. The successful working through of this stage will eventually allow clients to tolerate and explore avoided painful material.

Encouraging expression of shift in representation of other

Through arousal and direct expression of emotions and a strong sense of legitimacy of needs, clients begin to let go of previously salient but overly constricted perceptions, and expand their view of the other. The direction of the shift depends on the initial representation of the other and clients' experience in the relationship. In non-traumatic or abuse-related relationships, the depriving, punitive, or annihilating other becomes more positive and expresses regret. The other comes to be seen as separate and as having his/her own set of difficulties. S/he is seen as having both good and bad qualities. In abusive or trauma-related scenarios, the other becomes less bullying and dominant, and is seen as weaker and more in terms of inner failings. The other is held accountable for his or her actions and deserving of the client's negative feelings. In both instances, clients feel more empowered and worthwhile in relation to the other and entitled to their feelings. In the example below, Maria's representation of her mother as denying and demeaning becomes one of a vulnerable person without resources, and in turn Maria begins to feel compassion for her. The therapist reflects and facilitates the dialogue.

C: *I know what she was going through at the time; I know she was stuck in her own confusion because of the gambling of my father.*

T: *Can you come over here? Okay, be your Mom and tell Maria how it was for you that you could not show her love.*

> C: (as mom) I was very occupied with your father's gambling.
> T: Yeah, tell her what it was like for you.
> C: I was trying to provide for you and your brothers and I was alone and scared.
> T: You felt alone.
> C: Yeah, and I was extremely frustrated and I just didn't know what was going to happen next. I was never sure if we were going to make it.
> T: You feel sorry that you were unable to be there for her.
> C: Yeah, because I was stuck in my own little world. It was just despair; I wanted to change him, to make him see that his family was important. I was completely occupied and I didn't feel loved myself, and it was so hard for me to express those feelings to you.
> T: So you felt desperate to make your husband see what was important.
> C: Yeah and um . . . I'm sorry that I didn't allow you to do other things, to have relationships with your friends or anybody else. I needed your help at home. I had to work. I needed your help at home as much as you needed your own time and friends.

As is typical at this stage, Maria begins to articulate different aspects of her mother's life situation and state inadequacies that prevented her from meeting her daughter's needs. At this point, it is the therapist's job to recognize and support the shift in view of the other, and help the client to elaborate and consolidate the other's perspective. Ultimately this will help the person integrate the new information into their ongoing schema of self and other.

Thus, the therapist reflects and encourages the elaboration of the significant other's perspective. It is typical at this stage for the other to ask for understanding and forgiveness. However, when the other has been abusive, or traumatized the client, the other is represented as sick and dysfunctional and may accept accountability for reprehensible actions.

Resolution

Resolution means clients reach a sense that they are worthwhile, and either a) gain an increased understanding of the other, or b) hold the other accountable for the violation experienced. In non-abuse cases, the client is able to view the other with compassion and empathy, and may forgive the other. These two states will be illustrated separately below.

Allowing understanding and forgiveness

In the dialogue below, the client mourns for what was lost and allows forgiveness. The therapist promotes an empathic understanding by the client of the other and supports the offering of forgiveness. The therapist checks to see what new feelings emerge when the other asks for forgiveness. This enables the client to fully acknowledge the loss. The therapist supports and facilitates the integration of new emotional information. This further consolidates the letting go of the old relationship and allows clients to move forward in their lives.

> T: Okay, come back over here. She is saying that she thought she was protecting you from the outside world; how do you respond?
> C: I forgive her.
> T: Tell her about that.

C: *I forgive you, I guess that's the best you could do at the time. It is not what I would have wanted (crying). I know you, um, I know you love me and you care for me.*

T: *You are sad as you say this . . .*

C: *Yeah, I wanted to hear you loved me, I wanted you to say it. I was lonely and I just wanted understanding of who I was.*

T: *I felt I did not matter.*

C: *I put a part of myself aside and that was painful. I would have liked you to comfort me.*

T: *How do you feel when you say that to her?*

C: *I feel strong. I respect myself as a person.*

T: *Okay, come over here and be your mother. What do you say?*

C: *(as mother) I thought I was protecting you from falling in with the wrong crowd. I'm sorry you missed out on things that were important. I am sorry you have so much pain. You are important. You do count. It was the best I could do. It was all I knew at the time.*

T: *Okay, come back over here to the client chair.*

C: *And um yeah, I forgive her.*

T: *Tell her, I forgive you.*

C: *I forgive you (crying).*

T: *You feel sad. Tell her about it.*

C: *I missed a lot — I missed a good relationship between you and me. I would have liked you to just like me for who I was, see me as I am. I wanted acceptance, reassurance.*
        I wanted to hear that I was okay. It feels good to let it out.

T: *How do you feel towards your mother?*

C: *I forgive her, yes. I don't have anger or resentment; that was just the best she could do.*

T: *Can you tell her more about your understanding of that?*

In the above example, the client expresses what she missed, but with acceptance and a greater sense of separateness. She feels her needs were legitimate but recognizes that her mother could not provide what she needed. At this point, clients sometimes express pride in strengths and accomplishments to the other. In response, the therapist simply follows and encourages elaboration.

Holding the other accountable

In response to abuse or trauma, resolution means attributing responsibility to the other and de-blaming of the self. The client holds the other accountable for wrongs done. For example, in relation to an abusive and manipulative mother, a man says to his mother, 'As a little boy, I couldn't tell you, "Stop it. Don't do it. Keep away." But I can tell you now that I resent you for it, and I won't forgive you. I am not going to protect you any more. I'm not going to change the subject when it comes up. I'm not going to dance around you any more. I'm going to stand up for myself. I think it's time.' At this stage, the therapist supports the client in holding the other accountable for his or her actions. Clients need support of their new-found strength, and their choice to reassign blame where it belongs. In contrast to clients' previously held self-blaming positions , therapists must help clients voice that they were not to blame, but rather it is the other who initiated wrongdoing.

Regardless of whether the client resolves by holding the other accountable or through forgiveness, the end result is an experiential sense of resolution and completion with respect to the unfinished business. It is often accompanied by a sense of empowerment, optimism, and self-affirmation.

Research on the empty-chair dialogue

An analogue study (King, 1988) comparing the effects of the empty-chair dialogue and empathic reflection for unfinished business showed that, one week after an unfinished business session, the empty-chair work resulted in a greater increase in tolerance for the significant other and self-confidence in relation to the significant other. Greenberg and Foerster (1996) have shown that successful conflict resolution involves an intense expression of feelings and needs and a shift in perception of 'the other'. In an initial study relating process to outcome, Paivio and Greenberg (1995) demonstrated that in a 12-session treatment for clients with unfinished business with a significant other, those who engaged in the empty-chair dialogue with an imagined other had better psychotherapeutic outcomes than those assigned to a psycho-educational treatment. A recent study compared treatment outcome in clients who resolved unfinished business in therapy using the empty-chair method to those who did not. Resolution was defined according to three crucial resolution components: expression of an unmet need, a shift in view of the other, and resolution. Results indicated that those clients who resolved unfinished business improved significantly more on outcome indices than those clients whose therapy processes did not include these crucial performance components. Specifically, a hundred percent of resolvers were symptom-free at termination as compared to 38% of non-resolvers, while 85% of the resolvers as compared to 23% of the non-resolvers reported a clinically significant change in degree of resolution of unfinished business (Greenberg and Malcolm, 2002).

CONCLUSION

The working through of unfinished business using the empty-chair dialogue is an effective method for resolving long-standing emotional injuries that have derailed and prevented people from ongoing satisfaction and healthy relationships. The intense expression or primary feelings such as sadness and anger and associated needs, along with the acceptance and understanding of the other, is key to freeing people to move forward in their lives.

REFERENCES

Elliott, R. and Davis, K. (1998). Process-experiential therapy for Posttraumatic Stress Difficulties, In L. Greenberg, J. Watson, and G. Lietaer (Eds.) *Handbook of Experiential Therapy,* New York: Guilford Press.

Elliott, R., Watson, J., Goldman, R. and Greenberg, L. (in press). *Learning Process-Experiential Therapy*, Washington DC: APA Books.

Goldman, R. (1991). Validation of the Experiential Therapy Adherence Measure, Unpublished master's thesis, Department of Psychology, York University, UK.

Goldman, R. and Greenberg, L. S. (1997). Case formulation in process-experiential therapy, In T. Eells (Ed.) *Handbook of Case Formulation*. New York: Guilford Press.

Greenberg, L. S. (in press, 2002). *Mind in your Heart. Coaching for emotional wisdom*. Washington DC: APA Books.

Greenberg, L. S. and Foerster, F. S. (1996). Task analysis exemplified: The process of resolving unfinished business. *Journal of Consulting and Clinical Psychology, 64*, 439–46.

Greenberg, L. S. and Malcolm, W. (2002). Resolving unfinished business: Relating process to outcome, *Journal of Consulting and Clinical Psychology. 70*(2) 406–16.

Greenberg, L. S. and Paivio, S. C. (1997). *Working with Emotions*. New York: Guilford Press.

Greenberg, L.S., Rice, L. N. and Elliott, R. (1993). *Facilitating Emotional Change: The moment by moment process*. New York: Guilford Press.

Horvath, A. and Greenberg, L. S. (1994). (Eds.) *The Working Alliance: Theory research and practice*. New York: Wiley.

King, S. (1988). The differential effects of empty-chair dialogue and empathic reflection on unfinished business, Unpublished master's thesis: University of British Columbia, Vancouver Canada.

Paivio, S. C. and Greenberg, L. (1995). Resolving unfinished business: Experiential therapy using empty-chair dialogue. *Journal of Consulting and Clinical Psychology, 3*, 419–25.

Paivio, S. C. and Laurent, C. (2001). Empathy and emotion regulation: Reprocessing memories of childhood abuse, *Journal of Clinical Psychology*, 57(2), 213–26.

Paivio, S. C. and Shimp, L. (1998). Affective change process in therapy for PTSD stemming from childhood abuse. *The Journal of Psychotherapy Integration, 8*(4), 211–29.

Perls, F. (1969). *Gestalt Therapy Verbatim*. Lafayette, CA: Real People Press.

Perls, F., Hefferline, R. and Goodman, P. (1951). *Gestalt Therapy*. New York: Delta.

Polster, I. and Polster, M. (1973). *Gestalt Therapy Integrated*. New York: Bruner-Mazel.

Rogers, C. R. (1957). The necessary and sufficient conditions of therapeutic personality change, *Journal of Consulting Psychology, 21*, 95–103.

Struempfel, U. and Goldman, R. (2002). Contacting Gestalt therapy. In D. Cain and J. Seeman (Eds.) *Humanistic Psychotherapies: Handbook of research and practice*. Washington DC: APA Books.

Watson, J. C., Goldman, R. and Vanaerschot, G. (1998). Empathic: A post-modern way of being. In L. S. Greenberg, J. C. Watson, and G. Lietaer (Eds.) *Handbook of Experiential Therapy*. New York: Guilford Press.

Carla van der Moolen
Stichting GGZ Groningen, The Netherlands

Doctor, Please Make Me Well Again! On clients having severe subjective health complaints (the Somatoform Disorder)

1. INTRODUCTION

Clients with subjective health complaints or psychosomatic complaints are considered difficult to help. A crucial question is whether the origins of the complaints are somatic or psychogenic in nature. The patients are often convinced that the former is the case. It is difficult for a doctor to diagnose correctly and to motivate the client for psychotherapeutic treatment, if such is desired. The starting point for the development of our client-centered view on these matters stems from observations and examinations of the therapy process itself.

A case-study will illustrate the nature of the disorder and the guidelines for treatment. Some theoretical considerations are given, followed by the implications for clinical practice.

2. A CASE

Maria

Maria, a young woman of twenty-six years, had suffered for ten years from attacks of epilepsy. During these attacks, her consciousness would be reduced, she would become stiff as a board, she would have a few muscle spasms, and then she would fall to the ground. The average length of these attacks was three minutes, with a frequency of one to seven times a day. Afterwards she would be tired and a bit confused. Sometimes she had no attacks for a couple of days, but that was exceptional.

She was hospitalized in a centre for epilepsy to refine her medication. However, no neurological defects were found that could explain the attacks. The medication was stopped and she was referred to a mental hospital with the diagnosis 'functional attacks'.

During the intake session there, I asked her what she thought of this diagnosis. She answered: 'I still believe there must be some neurological explanation for it. But well, let it be psychological then . . . I'll just do a little therapy, and then I'll be rid of it.' She also told me that she didn't care what help she got, as long as it did the job, and as long as it did it fast.

As it appears, she tended to pass the responsibility to others. In the second session, after we had explored her history and her actual situation, she agreed with me that she had very little contact with her own emotional experience, that she was constantly busy thinking and analyzing and that she generally avoided coming into personal contact with people. She did not get involved in personal issues.

Some data form her history

Maria was the elder of two sisters. Her father was a hot-tempered man; because of a heart disease he had not worked since Maria was six years old. Her mother was very oriented towards her children and there was no aggression allowed in the family. When Maria was three years old she wanted to go to school; she did all the things in her very own way and alone.

Currently she is a university student; she has had some short-term relationships, but she wants to be free!

Diagnosis

She was diagnosed as a woman with a conversion disorder. This certainly did not look like a good indication for client-centred therapy. Nevertheless, we decided to try it.

When I asked her at the first session what she wanted to start with, she answered: 'I want to explore what I feel. I feel so little.' A striking example she gave was that she felt absolutely no tension before the session, but that she had to go to the toilet constantly and that she smoked one cigarette after another. Now she had a request for help that suited our type of therapy much better. It seems safe to assume that the way the assessment sessions had been held had contributed significantly to this.

The therapy process

In the first sessions of the therapy, Maria told me that she was angry about the insults and the headaches. She could not stand that her body had limitations. It was so usual for her to be able to do everything she wanted to do; she never felt scared, grief, anger or tired. She always presented herself with a smile. In the relationship with the therapist she kept her distance; many times she did not come and during the sessions she seemed very interested in the birds outside. She did accept some explanation about negative feelings and boundaries in general. She realized that she was not able to relax; she was always very active and she slept only a couple of hours during the night.

Her attention was directed outside, for instance at a pitiful friend and at her father who was ill. She gave them advice and she wanted the therapist to advise her. We tried to direct her attention inside, to her inner experience, at first a totally unknown activity to her.

After eleven sessions she told me that she had no insults during the last two weeks. Maybe there could be a link with therapy she assumed, but she wanted to argue and understand.

She could make some connections with the way she grew up, caring for her sick father, never being angry and protecting herself against her intrusive mother. Then the relationship with the therapist became safer for her and more intimate, but when we tried to focus she still laughed. She needed to have control over the situation: 'Let me go my own way, please!'.

She became more introspective and because of the positive regard of the therapist she could experience her own feelings a little more and was able to express them.

Her friends had also noticed this change and were reacting positively to it. She could be anxious and she no longer exposed herself to dangerous situations, like walking alone in the city by night.

Then she fell in love, but after a couple of weeks she could not stand the intimacy and she broke off the relationship, with a lot of rationalisations. In the session the therapist explored with her what this meant for her. She was able to feel her sadness about the loss and restored the relationship, feeling more able to handle her ambivalence and more intimate feelings.

She finished therapy in a personal and authentic way. The big smile was gone, her body was more relaxed and more flowing.

3. THE CLIENTS: DIAGNOSTICS

The disorder we referred to with the phrase 'subjective health complaints' up until now was called Somatoform Disorder in the DSM IV. This disorder — physical phenomena that are understood as manifestations of some psychological disorder — is classified in the following categories:
* Somatization Disorder
* Undifferentiated Somatoform Disorder
* Conversion Disorder
* Pain Disorder
* Hypochondriasis
* Body Dysmorphic Disorder
* Somatoform Disorder Not Otherwise Specified

The DSM IV classifies on the basis of phenomenological criteria and says nothing about possible etiology, even though this etiology is of crucial importance for these patients. It is often much disputed during treatment.

Alongside the disorders on Axis I of the DSM IV, these clients often suffer from some disorder on Axis II as well, a personality disorder. Especially the borderline, the histrionic and the avoidant disorders are very common.

Sometimes the physical disorder is actually there, but is interpreted in the wrong way by the client. It is therefore always important to do a thorough physical examination.

In our view it concerns clients
* with subjective health complaints
  * who think the complaint is somatic in origin
  * who ask for symptom reduction
  * who have little curiosity for, and little access to their own personal experience
  * who know few words for emotions
  * who find it difficult to differentiate between physical sensations and emotions
  * who live by external standards and criteria
* who have an unrealistic self concept
* who find it difficult to allow other people to come close to them emotionally
  * who are externally oriented towards other people.
* who evoke a feeling of powerlessness or irritation in the other.

4. SOME THEORETICAL CONSIDERATIONS

The question is how psychological and somatic processes interact. It is clear that it is not a matter of linear causality. The question is how somatic disorders arise and how they are maintained.

Research has shown that the tendency to avoid thinking about negative aspects of the self is a central aspect of this disorder. As a result of this tendency, an incomplete self-image is sustained. Coping with stress in this dysfunctional manner would then result in an organic pressure which manifests itself as a somatoform disorder (Sachse, 1995, 1997, 1998).

The stagnation can also be seen as the inability to bear the discrepancies between different aspects of the self. These clients have serious difficulties with accepting the existence of ambiguities. There exists a great discrepancy between their desired self and their actual self. There is no experiential process. Only physical signals attract attention and are misinterpreted; this goes for physical signals that are related to emotions as well. As a consequence, adequate reactions fail to occur and the clients lapse into self-destructive behaviour.

Research on human perception offers other interesting possible explanations. Subjectively perceived sensations are not only the consequence of passive registration of peripheral physiological processes. They result mainly from actively searching and selecting information, on the basis of the significance this information has for someone. Subjective experience has proven to be dependent on the attention for and the interpretation of internal and external information.

Another explanation is based upon what we know about the way people remember emotional events. What we remember consciously of emotional events is stored in the explicit or declarative memory. 'There are also aspects of emotional events we do not remember consciously. We can become emotional without knowing what triggered the emotion. This is called the implicit, emotional memory. Clients will try to find an explanation of their own for what they do not understand, a story of their own. Because of the diffuse character of pain, there is much opportunity for personal interpretation in the case of the perception of pain. This can result in what are sometimes called 'disastrous misinterpretations (Everaerd, 1999).

From the perspective of developmental psychology, we might suppose that these clients have little access to their own experience, because relevant others paid no attention to it in the past. During their development as a child, they were not 'heard'. Quite on the contrary, their parents claimed the attention of these children for themselves. The children then lost contact with their own experience and developed certain survival strategies. They became externally oriented, alert for potential dangers from outside ('What mood is mother in??'). They got out of touch with their own needs.

It remains as yet a mystery why certain clients develop this somatoform disorder and others do not.

5. CLIENT-CENTERED PSYCHOTHERAPY FOR THIS POPULATION

One of the basic principles of client-centred psychotherapy is that people can overcome process stagnation and can get in touch with their inner experience by concentrating on the felt sense. The felt sense is not a mental but a physical experience. Only the body is fully aware of how problems feel and what their essence is: 'unfolding the wisdom of the body' (Gendlin, 1978). Clients with subjective health complaints seem to make clear that there's something wrong through their body, but they do not understand this themselves because they are not in touch with their experiential process (Depestele, 1995). Their attention is drawn mainly to the complaints and to external issues. The task of the therapist is to actively help clients to focus their attention on the felt sense and on what the body expresses through the symptoms.

Complaints have an interactional significance as well. Complaining evokes irritation and a feeling of powerlessness in the other, who may be a relative, but also a doctor or a therapist!

They are often referred against their wills to the mental health service. They have the feeling they're not being taken seriously. They've often had many frustrating experiences with medical and psychological institutions. After all, they're not insane. All this is certainly not beneficial for achieving a good relationship, which should be based on mutual trust.

The Rogerian attitude is of great importance for creating such a relationship — an attitude characterized by congruence, empathy and unconditional positive regard (Rogers, 1965). The client-centered therapist looks for the person behind the complaint. He is interested in 'who the client is' instead of in 'what the patient has'.

But this Rogerian attitude is necessary but not sufficient. The question is then how this therapy can be modified in such a way as to help clients with somatoform disorders to get their stagnated process going once more. It must meet the clients where they are situated, must make a 'suitable adjustment' (Sachse, 1998).

To adapt the method to these clients, we need to know their specific characteristics first. Than we can formulate what specific therapeutic interventions are necessary for changing 'rigid' to 'process' (van der Moolen, 1998).

We will divide the treatment into four phases, based on the classification of Swildens (Swildens, 1988):

1. assessment and motivation phase
2. the symptom phase
3. the conflict phase
4. the end phase

Especially the first two phases need a more process-directive approach. The therapist can help the client to get a changing process going: that is, he can help him experience more of his inner process and suffer less from his physical complaints, by doing the following:

- He should be empathic, accepting and congruent in his relationship to the client.
- He should help the client actively to focus his attention inwards.
- He should help the client actively to link physical sensations with emotions.
- He should explore the meaning of the complaint with the client.
- He should discuss the client's interactional appeal to him with him.

We will describe these clinical guidelines in a manual.

In the third and fourth phase the treatment can return to a baseline client-centered therapy.

6. THE PROCESS

The first phase: assessment and motivation

It is important to approach the client open-mindedly during the assessment phase. The client has some rational somatic explanation and wants the doctor to cure him. Generally, he is no longer accustomed to people asking with interest about his complaints. Often, he has a long history behind him with quite a lot of struggle. His motivation for psychotherapy is often very dubious; after all, he's been sent by the doctor (van der Moolen and Eisenga, 1995). We leave the matter of somatic versus psychological origin unresolved and do not go into discussion about it. It can be very harmful to the relationship with the client if we assume prematurely that the complaints are psychogenic in nature (Speckens and van Hemert, 1997). We should not forget that the lack of an adequate somatic explanation is in no way decisive proof that the complaints are psychogenic.

At this stage, we try to arouse the client's interest in his inner experience by talking at length about his complaints and about what they mean for his relationships to others and for his life in general. We explore whether the client has access to his emotional experience and whether he is able to put his feelings into words. We check to what extent the complaint dominates the client's life and whether there are other things that are important to him besides it. In that way we can find out to what extent he identifies himself with the problem, to what extent he *is* the problem instead of *having* the problem ('that headache woman'), to what extent there is a 'healing inner relationship' (Leyssen, 1995). And we also check what the client's body evokes in us, what it is expressing to us, what it is trying to tell us. And there is a metaphorical aspect of the disorder. Finely, we try to give the client faith and hope for the future.

The symptom phase

The therapist takes the physical symptoms completely seriously and tries to find out what they mean. Much empathetic reflection and active input of the therapist are needed for this. Again the therapist accepts the hypothesis of the client. Again and again, the responsibility has to be passed back to the client. He must realize that only he, and not the therapist, can solve his problems. The therapist can be a good guide for him. As far as the physical complaints are concerned, the therapist tries to make the client look at them from a greater distance.

Manual: guidelines for the first two phases

1. The relationship with the body: physical sensations and emotions

CLIENT MARKERS
   a. The client identifies himself with the complaint.
   b. The body expresses something through the complaint.
   c. Physical sensations are not linked to emotions.
   d. Emotional reactions are held to be symptoms of an illness.
   e. The complaint is somatic in origin and just has to disappear.

THERAPEUTIC INTERVENTIONS
   a. The therapist looks to the client to see what his body evokes in him; this may be carefully shared with the client.
   b. Together with the client he creates some distance: there are also other relevant issues in the client's life.
   c. Together they are trying to find the meaning of the physical symptom.
   d. He gives some explanations and uses metaphors.

e. He suggests other possible interpretations of physical sensations.
f. He passes the responsibility for the complaint explicitly to the client.
g. He uses the first focusing movement: clearing a space

2. The relationship with oneself: self-concept and self-exploration.

CLIENT MARKERS
a. The client's self concept is unrealistic, rigid and normative.
b. Negative aspects of the self are denied.
c. The client is used to no or only very little self-exploration.
d. He thinks; he does not feel.
e. He is oriented externally, to norms and standards.
f. The client is either unable to make contact with his own inner experience, there seems to be no direct referent; or he is unable to symbolize his experience.
g. He avoids ambivalences or negative feelings.

THERAPEUTIC INTERVENTIONS
a. He checks to what extent the client can be confronted with reality, to make him recognize all aspects of the self.
b. He actively tries to direct the attention of the client inwards, to arouse his interest in his inner experience (here and now).
c. He is directing the attention of the client inwards, to the body sense of his problem, and can help the client find the words that fit.
d. He explains that people can have contradictory emotions and that both must be accepted.

3. The relationship with other people, including the therapist

CLIENT MARKERS
a. The client is externally oriented to other people, seeks their advice, wants to get rid of the complaints, provokes conflict or defies the therapist to argue with him.
b. The client keeps the therapist at an emotional distance.
c. He keeps control over his emotions.

THERAPEUTIC INTERVENTIONS
a. The therapist explicitly accepts the hypothesis of the client.
b. He tries to find a theory explaining the illness which both can agree to.
c. He does not go along with the interactional appeal of the client, but gives a reflection of the need of the client in a congruent, accepting and empathic understanding way.
d. The therapist reflects empathetically the fear of intimacy.
e. Metacommunication is used to explore the interactional appeal.

Illustrations and comments

'The complaint just has to disappear'
Anna, a 40-year-old woman, suffered from long-lasting headaches.

C1	That it will fade away in time.
T1	That it just wear out, you have to do nothing.
C2	Yes, just taking some therapy.

'Finding the meaning of the physical symptom'

Frank, a 41-year-old man, living alone, has suffered from epilepsy for more than ten years. He is always tired, sometimes dizzy and often has back-pain. There is no medical evidence.

Several times Frank cannot come to the session; he is too dizzy or too tired. During the sessions he does not like to tell the therapist about himself; he wants to discuss only external events. When the therapist invites him to say something about his private life he becomes 'dizzy' and it is hard to keep contact. The therapist reflects how hard it is for him to make some personal contact. He agrees and the therapist suggests that there could be a connection with his 'dizziness'.

'Taking the responsibility'

Maria, the young lady who suffered epileptic attacks, had met the neurologist

C3	He means that even if it is epilepsy, there's not much that can be done about it. But if something can be done, I want to know about it.
T3	But he says . . .
C4	He says it's better to concentrate on therapy. Medication doesn't make any difference.
T4	And do you agree?
C5	Yes, you create that psychological thing yourself and you don't have any influence on epilepsy whatsoever. And as the situation is now, it is coming out of my mind one hundred percent, so actually, it's me who's doing this.
T5	Yes? Is that your conclusion?
C6	Then it's me for one hundred percent who's . . .
T6	Then there's something inside of me . . . And that's a weird notion, isn't it?
C7	It's not a nice idea at all. It means that you're the source of it yourself.

'Metacommunication'

Claire, a young woman, 28 years old, is always very tired and often suffers from headaches. She has had medical examinations several times, and no somatic origin for her complaints was found. Physiotherapy did not give any relief.

In the session her body is stretched and she is looking at the therapist in a demanding way. She is rather silent and most of the times her answer is 'I don't know' or 'I don't understand.'

The therapist tries to explore what makes her so silent.

C1	I don't want to express my emotions to you.
T1	You don't want to?
C2	It is rather personal, I think . . .
T2	Personal . . . eh . . . it concerns me?
C3	Yes. (silence)
	It is not that I don't like you but . . . eh . . . I close the door.
T3	Can we find out together what is the personal thing that makes you close the door?
C4	I don't know; it is only a vague feeling, just like you can have with people. There are

people you like and people you don't like and . . .

T4   *Yes, it is not so clear, just a vague feeling.*

C5   *Yes.*

T6   *Can we maybe find out if there is something in the way we are communicating that does not feel good . . . ?*

C7   *I don't know that will be the solution.*

later on:

C8   *Eh . . . Eh . . . As if I have to do it by myself.*

T8   *By yourself, as if I leave you alone with your problems.*

C9   *You are expecting things of me and I don't know I can do that, for instance finding out or exploring something, I don't know how to do that.*

T9   *That is a very difficult thing to you, isn't it?*

C10   *Yes, very difficult.*

'Directing the attention inwards, here and now'

Peter complains about how tired he feels and how heavy. Then he can tell the therapist something about his anger.

T1   *Can we try, I know it is very hard for you, but can we try to listen to your body, to your inner world, to how it feels for you just now? You told me you felt so tired and your body so heavy . . .*

C1   *Eh . . . it becomes lighter just now.*

T2   *lighter . . . and more angry?*

C2   *Eh . . . lighter, eh . . . now I have given some words on how I think about it, it feels lighter.*

The conflict phase

In this phase, the therapist becomes less process-directive. Within a safe relationship, he can intervene in a more confronting fashion. The somatic aspect becomes less important or disappears altogether. Therapists of other schools that are symptom-oriented would consider therapy as finished at this stage. They have a different aim.

If the client is suffering from a personality disorder, it becomes a client-centered psychotherapy to treat this disorder.

When there is no Axis II disorder the client can start exploring his underlying problems; he might concentrate on his emotions or learn to focus. The self-concept is changing. New experiences can be tolerated.

The client's contact with his own experiential process, with the therapist and with relevant others becomes more open. Now and then, the initial complaint returns again, especially when the client is experiencing difficulties. Then he wants to go to the doctor again, for a new examination or pills. It is important to keep following a double track, both psychological and somatic. It is still vital for the therapist to have good co-operation with the doctors. By the way, it is important to realize that not all complaints of these clients are psychogenically determined. It wouldn't be the first time that a new somatic illness was overlooked at first.

Illustration and comments

'Changing the self-concept'

One evening, a man had been peeping in through the window at Maria's house. She claimed she had never been frightened before.

C1   *I was angry that he had frightened me. I was scared. I'm not turning into a chicken, am I?*

T1   *It seems a perfectly normal reaction to me, and nevertheless you think it's strange . . . As if you don't allow yourself to have these feelings . . .*

C2   *Yes, in a way it's losing control, you know.*

T2   *They can't frighten me. I have myself under control. But we need these feelings to react adequately . . . Not scared enough . . . It's dangerous . . .*

C3   *Yes, I think I'm like that . . .*

T3   *It seems like it, doesn't it?*

C4   *A friend said that too. Well, on the other hand, it's good that it happened. Finally, I got scared for once . . . It's one of the things I'm struggling with. I'm never scared, but that's not always a good thing. I live my life as if nothing can . . . (she laughed)*

T4   *And that's not true, is it?*

The end phase

At the end of the treatment, it is discussed how the client can cope with the pain that is still left in the future or with the restrictions the body still imposes upon him. One client formulated it as follows: 'My back was the boss back then and determined my life, but now I'm in charge and I will not allow my back to dominate me ever again.'

Sometimes, the somatic symptoms have not been discussed altogether since the symptom phase and the matter is only brought up again on parting, when client and therapist look back on what has been achieved.

7. CONCLUSION

Client-centred psychotherapy offers excellent opportunities for treating clients with subjective health complaints, or somatoform disorder. Especially at the beginning, during the diagnostic and motivation phase of the treatment, the therapist will have to intervene in a rather process-directive way, specifically to focus the client's attention on his inner experience.

Are these difficult clients? Certainly! But it is an impressive experience for the therapist to see these clients change, to observe how their bodies become less and less contorted, and more and more fluent. The relationship with these clients is detached at first, but grows richer later on. Then the real person appears, tentatively at first, with a relapse now and then, but later on more freely and more openly.

'Doctor, please make me well again.'

'Certainly, madam. I can help you to listen to the wisdom of your body.'

REFERENCES

Depestele, F. (1995). Het lichaam voor de gevoelde zin. In G. Lietaer and M. van Kalmthout (Eds.) *Praktijkboek Gesprekstherapie*. Utrecht:De Tijdstroom, pp. 109–30.

DSMIV (1994). *Diagnostic and Statistical Manual of Mental Disorders, 4th edn*. Washington DC: American Psychiatric Association.

Everaerd, W. (1999). Waarnemen en klagen. In Ph. Spinhoven, A. M. van Hemert and M. W. Hengeveld (Eds.) *Onverklaarde Lichamelijke Klachten*. Leiden:Boerhave commissie.

Gendlin, E. T. (1978). *Focusing*. New York: Everest House.

Leyssen, M. (1995). Kenmerken van een helende relatie. In G. Lietaer and M. van Kalmthout (Eds.) *Praktijkboek Gesprekstherapie*. Utrecht: De Tijdstroom, pp. 27–38.

Moolen, C. R. van der and Eisenga, R. (1995). Procesbevordering bij clienten met onbegrepen lichamelijke klachten. In G. Lietaer and M. van Kalmthout (Eds.) *Praktijkboek Gesprekstherapie*. Utrecht: De Tijdstroom, pp. 232–45.

Moolen, C. R. van der (1998). Moeilijke clienten? *Tijdschrift Clientgerichte Psychotherapie, 36*(2), 115–33.

Rogers, C. R. (1965). *Client Centered Therapy*. London: Constable.

Sachse, R. (1995). *Der psychosomatische Patient in der Praxis*. Stuttgart/Berlin/Koln:Kohlhammer.

Sachse, R. (1997). Clientgerichte psychotherapie bij psychosomatische stoornissen. *Tijdschrift Clientgerichte Psychotherapie, 35* (1), 5–33.

Sachse, R. (1998). Goal-oriented client-centered psychotherapy of psychosomatic disorders. In L. S. Greenberg, J. C. Watson and G. Lietaer (Eds.) *Handbook of Experiential Psychotherapy*. New York, London: Guilford Press, pp. 295–328.

Speckens, A. E. M. and van Hemert, A. M. (1997). Psychiatrische psychotherapie bij somatiserende patienten. *Tijdschrift voor Psychiatrie, 39*, 161–70.

Swildens, J. A. C. G. (1988). *Procesgerichte Gesprekstherapie*. Amersfoort/Leuven:Acco.

Margaret S. Warner

Illinois School of Professional Psychology, Chicago, USA

Luke's Dilemmas: A Client-Centered/Experiential model of processing with a schizophrenic thought disorder

For a number of years I have seen a client, 'Luke', who thinks about significant life experiences using very unusual categories and ideas about causation. Luke's way of processing material is prototypical of the kind of 'thought disorder' that is usually seen as a definitive characteristic of chronic schizophrenia. (Arieti, 1955; Kasanan, 1944; Karon and vandenBos, 1981). The following story that Luke recounted some years back offers a good example of the unusualness of his thought process. Luke and his family had dinner with a Roman Catholic priest who complained that Catholics, these days, were 'going to the dogs'. Luke was quite worried about this since he's Catholic and it never occurred to him that he might turn into a dog. He spent the rest of the weekend walking in the public parks scrutinizing dogs to see how they were doing. Overall, he decided that the dogs seemed pretty happy, since a lot of them seemed to have smiles on their faces. He concluded that if he turned into a dog it might not be all that bad.

Here we have very unusual ideas about what sorts of things might be identical (i.e. dogs are lapsed Catholics) and what sorts of things might transform themselves into what sorts of other things for what sorts of causal reasons (i.e. today's Catholics are going to become dogs sometime in the future). Arieti (1955) identifies this sort of thinking as 'paleologic', noting that it is 'based on a confusion between similarities and identities. A salient part or characteristic that two persons or objects have in common is enough to make them appear identical or belonging to the same category or class' (p. 85). Arieti differentiates paleologic thinking from the more traditionally logical 'Aristotelian' thought in which 'only identical subjects are identified. The subjects are immutable; Therefore only a few (and the same) deductions are possible' (p. 236).

Arieti (1955) notes that paleologic thinking tends to follow Von Domarus's principle of 'predicate thinking', in which peripheral characteristics (which would typically be in the predicate of a sentence) are enough to create a sense of identity (p. 236–8). Likewise, such thinking is often referred to as being 'concrete' (Goldstein, 1944) because of the person's apparent difficulty in separating out and shifting among various levels of abstraction relevant to a task. One manifestation of concrete thinking is a difficulty in understanding when a statement is meant metaphorically ('Catholics are going to the dogs') and when it is meant in a literal, concrete way.

Psychological researchers and theorists have focused almost exclusively on what is wrong with such 'thought-disordered' mental processes. Their focus has been on clarifying the nature of the logical deficits and on considering what sorts of neurological, developmental, familial, or existential traumas might account for the schizophrenic person's inability or unwillingness to conceptualize experience in a usual or realistic way. (Green, 1998; Arieti, 1955; Karon and vandenBos, 1981; Pao, 1979; Whitaker, 1992). Theorists from most therapeutic modalities discourage therapists from engaging directly with thought-disordered narratives for fear of reinforcing irrational or regressive tendencies in the client. When therapists do encourage schizophrenic clients to express 'irrational' thoughts, they do this primarily as a prelude to interpreting deep underlying emotional problems that they believe cause the patient to be unable to face reality (Pao, 1979; Karon and vandenBos, 1981; Whitaker, 1992).

Client-centered therapy has been unusual in this regard in encouraging therapists to connect to the experience of schizophrenic clients by applying the same core conditions of empathy, congruence and unconditional positive regard as with any clients (Rogers, 1967; Raskin, 1996). Prouty (1994) has suggested that a phase of 'Pre-Therapy' may be required when clients do not meet Rogers first core condition of being in psychological 'contact'. In spite of having done very significant work in the area of schizophrenia, however, client-centered therapists have not explicitly explored the question of how and why client-centered therapy would work in conjunction with the sort of 'thought-disordered' thinking characteristic of many schizophrenic clients.

In working with Luke, I have been struck with a positive value in his admittedly unusual ways of processing experience, that is different from that presented in most of the psychological literature. When I stay with Luke's thoughts in a very close sort of client-centered following, he tends to move through a series of very 'crazy-sounding' thoughts and often comes, in the end, to quite sensible and personally integrated conclusions. While his process isn't fast or easy, he enjoys coming to therapy, feels that therapy results in his thoughts becoming clearer, and notes that therapy allows him to have 'some little pride' in himself. While he was quite withdrawn at the beginning of therapy, after some time he began to smile and to refer to people he knows as friends. At one point he commented that when he comes to therapy, the police seem to behave better (for reasons that seemed to be a little mysterious to him . . .) He now initiates several dinners a week with family friends, goes on skiing trips, and recently asked a halfway house worker to help him go to vote in the year 2000 presidential elections.

I have become very interested in understanding how Luke's process works in comparison to that of clients who think in more normative ways. However poetic and creatively delightful Luke's thoughts are, one could easily think that such 'thought-disordered' processing would not be helpful in generating realistic understandings of himself and others. Yet, in observing Luke's process over the years, I have become convinced that his most 'thought-disordered' thoughts are often crucial to his generating a personally integrated and realistically based sense of his own feelings and preferences. I have come to see his process as impaired in some ways but not at all in others. He seems to have the same impulse and motivation to make sense of his experience as any client, but to be working with awkward tools. Luke's way of processing experience is particularly interesting to analyze in this regard, since he experiences a thought disorder without a lot of other sorts of difficulties which often co-exist with it — such as long-standing hallucinations, fixed delusions, or 'borderline' sorts of emotional reactivity.

In trying to understand Luke's style of processing experience, I have generated a model that integrates aspects of Eugene Gendlin's (1964, 1968, 1984, 1995) and Garry Prouty's (1994) models of process. (Of course, since this is a synthesis which takes elements from the work of both theorists, they themselves may not agree with all or part of my analysis.) While this model is based on the experience of a single schizophrenic client, I think that it may capture some aspects of how processing with thought disorders works for many clients. To develop this model, I will present two core concepts that I have developed in my attempts to understand Luke — 'metafacts' and 'metacauses'. I will then consider how metafacts and metacauses seem to operate in comparison to more normative styles of processing. I will give examples from a single session that show how that process works out in practice.

Luke often thinks in a way that is midway between the definiteness of facts or causes and the evocativeness of metaphors — phenomena I think of as 'metafacts' and 'metacauses'. He presents things with the definiteness that one would associate with a fact or a causal attribution (e.g. 'I never realized that Catholics became dogs.') Yet, he doesn't expect these phenomena to have the sort of stability that one would usually associate with facts or causes. An image like Catholics becoming dogs may come and go within a single session or week. And he usually doesn't seem to feel any impulse to act on the kinds of logical implications that might follow from a solid fact or cause. He doesn't think that he needs to help the 'Catholic' dogs, or to make any extended preparations for becoming a dog, for example. At the same time, core images tend to recur over periods of years and refer to the same kinds of experiential states.

To understand how processing that includes metafacts and metacauses might work, let us consider how more normative styles of processing typically work within client-centered therapy. While therapy may, of course, take many forms, the most common process involves a deep attention to and reformulation of problematic experiences. Empathy, when it is successfully communicated, results in what I would call an 'experience of recognition' (Warner, 1997). In communicating what an experience of recognition is like, a person might say 'yes, that's exactly how I feel' or 'this person understands exactly what I mean.' In that moment, a person lessens his or her sense of existential aloneness in the world, an experience that is humanly valuable in and of itself. Clients, when they feel understood by a person they believe to be genuine in caring about their well-being, are likely to feel drawn to exploring aspects of their experience that are problematic, but not yet clear to them. And, as they hold their experiences in empathic attention they tend to spontaneously reorganize their understanding of these experiences.

Several client-centered therapists have noted a spontaneous alternation in left and right hemispheric styles of processing often occurs as clients attend to and reformulate such problematic experiences. (Iberg, 1990; Warner, 1997, 2000). Rotenberg (1994) describes the distinction between left and right hemisphere processing as follows:

> . . . the basic function of the left hemisphere is a consecutive analysis of information, whether verbal or nonverbal while the function of the right hemisphere is a single-stage processing of many elements of information as an unitary whole. This makes possible rapid single-stage grasping of the essence of an object or phenomenon even before it is analyzed. (p. 488)

He notes that such right hemisphere processing allows:

> . . . a simultaneous 'capture' of an infinite number of connections and the formation, due to this capture of an integral, but ambiguous context. In such a context, the whole is not determined by its components since all specific features of the whole are determined only by the interconnection between these parts. On the contrary, any concrete element of such a context bears a determining stamp of the whole. (p. 489)

When clients attend to experiences that are troubling and not yet clear to them their experiences are often first sensed in a multifaceted way that is characteristic of right-hemispheric processing as described by Rotenberg (1994). In attending to such situations, clients often spontaneously come up with images, idiosyncratic words, or vivid descriptions of problematic scenes. These expressions seem to allow clients to hold such complex multifaceted experience in attention. Gendlin (1984) suggests that such vivid words and images serve as 'handles', much the way a handle on a suitcase allows a person to hold onto something that would otherwise be hard to grasp. And, to follow the suitcase metaphor, this holding of an ambiguous situation in attention seems to stimulate additional 'unpacking' of that which was implicit in the experience. Various related images, thoughts, feelings and memories emerge into awareness. Gendlin (1995) notes that this emerging of new experience can't be reduced to propositional logics, but is a quite different sort of process.

> A great many factors *cross* in . . . a single felt sense. Some have been separated out before, many have not. Your felt sense implicitly contains all you have heard me say, but also much that you have thought and read about these topics over the years, and your own work in all of its many relevances — and much more all *crossing* so each implicitly changes, *governs and gives relevance to* the others (p. 552?).

Gendlin notes that metaphors bring a complex crossing between the entire 'use-family' of a word or image within the language and the multifaceted aspects of a specific lived situation. An explication isn't simply a matching of logics or schemas that were already there. It is a creation of something new that 'carries forward' what was previously implicit in the lived complexity of the person's situation. The person is then able to attribute new, more articulated meaning to situations that were previously contradictory or unclear, with corresponding shifts of emotional response to those situations. In my observation of this sort of process, new formulations seem to be checked and extrapolated using the sorts of clear categories and propositional logics that are characteristic of left-hemispheric thinking as well as the felt sense of the whole characteristic of right-hemispheric thinking.

In following Luke's process over the years, I have come to the conclusion that his intuitive sensing of situations (of the sort that is characteristic of right-hemispheric processing) is often quite on-track and relevant given his overall life experience [1]. Yet, his ability to explicitly categorize situations and to use causal logics (of the sort that is characteristic of left-hemispheric processing) is severely compromised. Metafacts and metacauses serve very poorly in the formation of traditional causal logics, but they work quite powerfully as 'handles' for his intuitive sensing of his overall responses to situations.

Luke's formulations don't work well at logical propositional level, since his causal attributions are both tighter and looser than would seem realistic to an average person. Causal attributions are looser than usual in the sense that anything in a cluster of events that happened together can be seen as causing any of the other things in the cluster some time in the future. So, if a psychotic break happened in California, and his therapist takes a trip to California,

---

[1.] This is actually the opposite, I think, of what would be predicted by Rotenberg's (1994) model, which hypothesizes that schizophrenic symptoms are generated by right hemisphere disability which stimulates left-hemisphere hyperactivity in response. It would fit more easily with biological models of temporal lobe (left-hemisphere) abnormalities as presented by McCarley et al. (1993).

Luke worries that this could put her in danger of having the same thing happen to her. Causal attributions are tighter in that things that bear some resemblance to each other can be each other in some significant way. So, for example, if Luke sees someone who resembles his mother (who died some years back) on the street, that woman is experienced as *being* his mother in some significant way. In his experience, she is not exactly his real mother, but she is not entirely different either. This tightness and looseness of causal attributions makes it extraordinarily difficult for Luke to use logic to ascertain what might happen next in his life and why. This, when combined with the fact that he has no coherent sense of why he was wrestled to the ground and taken off in an ambulance at the time of his initial psychotic episodes, makes daily life feel very uncertain and potentially dangerous.

While metafacts and metacauses usually seem implausible as accounts of literal truth, they often work quite well as metaphors that serve as handles for his felt sense of the whole of his situations. For example, Luke once said that, after talking with his father, he realized that he (Luke) was 'the Boston Strangler on the sly'. As is typical, he presents this statement as if it were a factual account, and to an outsider it doesn't seem plausible as a statement of literal truth. Yet one could very plausibly say 'I was so angry at my father that I felt as if I could strangle him' — and to a person who thinks in culturally normative ways, this seems to offer a much closer sense of what Luke actually means. Yet, while these statements seem as though they would be better understood as metaphors, Luke doesn't seem to have the metaphoric distance that one would associate with metaphors. He doesn't say anything to suggest that he is making a comparison of something which is similar in some expressive, evocative way but not identical. He doesn't have an explicit or implicit 'as if' in the sentence. In speaking in metafacts and metacauses, Luke usually seems to feel quite normal to himself, and at the same time he often finds the way that others think and speak confusing and hard to follow. When people convey opinions in more ordinary logic that contradict his understanding, Luke tends withdraw from talking about the subject, capitulating without being convinced.

Metafacts and metacauses seem to be generative of process in much the way that 'handle' words and images are in more normative processing. Related situations, images, thoughts, concerns and the like emerge during most sessions, go through changes and are ultimately formulated in a more differentiated, personally integrated way. To describe how this process works, I will describe Luke's background and my style of working in somewhat more detail, and then go though excerpts of a single session.

Luke is the youngest of three sons born to a prosperous, Democratic, Irish-Catholic family. Luke met John Kennedy in his late teens, and had his picture taken with him. Given the overall similarity of his family background to that of the Kennedys, he might easily have pictured himself as having an equally successful political future. Yet in his senior year at a prestigious California university, he had a psychotic break and was hospitalized.

Several attempts at stabilization and re-integration into college life resulted in additional psychotic breaks and hospitalizations. Subsequently, Luke spent some 20 years in East coast hospitals. A change in medication to Clozaril when he was in his early forties seemed to improve his functioning somewhat. In response to this, his father brought him to live in Chicago in a half-way house. I have seen Luke for some ten years since then in twice-weekly sessions. He travels independently to come to therapy, attends regularly and is often early for sessions. Once, when his father suggested that he substitute vocational therapy for our regular sessions, Luke explained to him that we were doing important work and should not be interrupted.

In my therapy with Luke, I have been influenced by Garry Prouty's (1994) model of 'Pre-Therapy' which advocates very literal, concrete responses to clients who are 'contact-impaired' with self, world and other. I have found Prouty's overall model very helpful in guiding my attempts to respond to clients who experience psychosis, retardation, dissociation or dementia in ways that make empathic contact difficult. Luke is very much in contact with who he is, where he is, and the fact that he and I are engaging in psychotherapy. But, the unusualness of his way of processing experience and expressing himself verbally makes it very difficult for him to feel that he is in communicational contact with others.

In general, I follow a very literal, almost word-for-word style of responding to what he says. (This is, in effect, a use of one of Prouty's (1994) five kinds of contact reflections.) A word-for-word literalness of responding has seemed important in my work with Luke, because I have found that if I paraphrase or change words, he is often confused about what I mean. Occasionally, when I really think I have understood his core point or a central emotion I can say those in a non word-for-word way and he feels understood. Often, though, if I even change a word to a synonym he will say something like 'I don't know, doctor. You understand these things better than I do.'

Prouty (1994) characterizes pre-therapy responses as empathy directed at the client's expressive efforts. He differentiates this from the sort of empathy involved in client-centered therapy which he sees as having the larger aim of understanding the client's frame of reference. Unlike Prouty, I think of the concrete, word-for-word responses that I make in response to Luke as being a variant form of empathic responding, not fundamentally different in intention from the responses I make to other clients in client-centered therapy. I always attempt to understand my clients as well as I can, however minimal or rich their expressions, and I try to convey my understanding in such a way that they are able to receive (or correct) my understanding. This distinction is important to me because I do feel that I am operating within Rogers core conditions in the sessions with Luke and that they are genuine therapy rather than a precursor to some more 'real' kind of client-centered therapy.

I have found that my understanding of Luke proceeds on two levels — almost as if we lived in two different cultural worlds. I follow his exact words, and in the process come to have some understanding of what the world would look like if there were no clear distinction between facts and metaphors. At the same time, I find that I understand his point best when I consider the possibility that metafacts and metacauses capture the overall felt sense of his situation in the way that a metaphor would capture aspects of more normative experience for me. I want to emphasize, here, that I am not trying to create some more experience-distant interpretation of his meaning, but only to form an empathic sense inside myself of what he is trying to express. And, I am using Luke's own context and word-use as the source of understanding expressions that could be understood as metaphors, rather than moving to any outside interpretive frameworks that claim broad-based applicability (such as the Freudian or Jungian interpretive systems). To show the way that this works in practice, I will present selected excerpts of a session from 1995, interspersed with comments about the process as I understand it.

The session begins with Luke noting that things have been going pretty well, though with some back-and-forth over the years:

C2   *. . . I was just saying to the doctor that I've been getting back to normal as far as looking at girls and . . . Everybody's seeming very nice to me . . .*

He moves to discussing an incident he observed that morning:

C4   *. . . There are these cases, however, like the car crash today where the ambulance can be called, and you can be removed from that normal set, so to speak . . .*

T4   *Yeah, yeah, but it is kind of shocking that there are these things like that car crash today where people can be removed from everyday life. Just be taken off in an ambulance.*

C5   *Yeah that's what happened to me back in 1975 or whatever. You know I was all of a sudden at Father Pete's place out in California. Someone called the ambulance and I've been very much removed from life, except maybe a day or two with Dr. Green. And, in a way that's kind of unforgivable, I think. In some ways looking back on it all, I mean, never having any sense of pleasure or kind of getting out into the milieu in that.*

T5   *Yeah, that really has been true ever since somebody called the ambulance. You've been kind of removed from life.*

C6   *Society.*

T6   *From society.*

C7   *I'm not talking about the high fashion parties where you don't see the people that, you know, you're supposed to see. I'm talking about getting into one's own little social niche and kind of being taken away by it, which I think is basically normal behavior, as far as that goes. I mean, when you sit through a class, you don't only look at the professor, you look at the class members, girls or boys.*

Here Luke moves quite quickly to discussing an issue that is disturbing and then relates that sense of disturbance to the memory of his initial psychotic break. While some of his wording is unusual, I don't find him particularly hard to follow in this segment. He doesn't seem to feel a distinction between the kind of circumstance in which an ambulance takes someone away after a car accident and that in which an ambulance workers forcibly take a person away during a psychotic break. In my knowing of Luke, I suspect that this is literally true, that he isn't sure how, if at all, they are different. It is because of this understanding that I add the feeling word 'shocking' (one of his most common feeling words) and he does seem to feel understood by that word. He seems to be relating looking at girls to ambulances in a way that is not yet clear to me.

I have misunderstood him slightly when I paraphrased his being removed from a 'normal set' to being removed from 'life'. It is notable to me how quickly he picks up on responses that don't capture what he is trying to say. This suggests to me that he has a clear inner referent for what he is trying to express.

A few segments later he refers to:

C11   *. . . this Bobby Kennedy thing we keep talking about. There was always one thing, you know . . . when you're happy you could take a bullet in the head in Dallas or something.*

T11   *Yeah, like when you're very happy you could take a bullet in the head, like with the Bobby Kennedy thing.*

This statement is an example of what I would call a metacause. As a statement of causation, it conflates a similarity ('I am like the Kennedy brothers') with a causal logic ('Therefore, I will get shot') in a way that doesn't seem to have much predictive validity. Yet as a metaphor it works quite well. Bobby Kennedy's being shot and removed from life doesn't feel all that different from the experience of being suddenly tackled, taken away in an ambulance and removed forever from a life that had seemed to hold endless promise.

A little later he comments that:

C19   *Yeah, someone just presses the lever so to speak and there you are being very normal and sort of lively, and looking at girls and everyone's smiling and all that.*

T19   *But it's just like somebody just presses the lever and there you are. Being kind of normal and looking at girls.*

C20   *Yup, yup.*

T20   *Just being a part of things.*

C21   *Yeah, exactly. Just being a part of things.*

Here, Luke expresses the positive side of his recent feelings about life, and seems to feel very understood by my response. 'Pressing a lever' is an example of a 'metafact', in that he states it as if it were a literal fact but without expecting it to have the causal implications of a fact. Yet, in translating it into more normative language, it works quite well as a metaphor. It's as if someone turned a switch and he found himself in the middle of a normal happy existence in which it was quite ok to have feelings of sexual attraction.

Luke then brings the two sides of his experience into relation to each other:

C23   *. . . the other side, which is the ambulance going to the hospital or something . . . you just have to switch back over to the way you used to be, the way you look at girls and that someone would say to you I'm going to Las Vegas now and I've finally reached the right set.*

Here he has come to the tentative conclusion that he could just let the lever-switch happen and continue to enjoy life. But, he's not completely sure of that formulation.

C24   *But the parents for some reason seem to have a holdover, some of that too. And, they say, like when you're lying in bed and you think you have the world at your fingertips, and then someone will come in and catch you playing with yourself or something and then that's kind of the signal that maybe the parents aren't exactly right for some funny reason. Except this Bobby Kennedy thing we keep talking about in our therapy and such.*

T25   *But that's maybe a sign that you . . .*

C26   *. . . why he came out so happy in L.A. and then got this bullet in his chest and then we feel that, literally . . . we read about that.*

T26   *Yeah, yeah. And here he was coming out so happy in L.A. and then he ends up with a bullet in the chest.*

C27   *Mmmmmhmmm. And I just can't explain that doctor.*

Here Luke continues to feel into both sides of the issue using the metafacts and metacauses with (for me) increasing poignancy. As I translate this segment into my own understanding, he is saying, that maybe his parents are wrong in being so strictly judgemental about sexuality, but on the other hand the risk of getting his life cut off like Bobby Kennedy, or equivalently of being taken away in an ambulance if he does the wrong thing, feels very real to him.

He comes back to this a few segments later:

> C 37   ... *You just wonder, 'Where will it end?' On the other hand, you have a conscious mind somewhere, in the middle of all this saying, 'Be very careful after what happened to your friends, your heroes, that it doesn't happen to you.' Quite frankly, I mean most normal people looking at this tape and everything, seemingly wouldn't even think twice about things like that.*

And continuing:

> C41   *Being the jolly sort that I am, I would kind of like to get rid of all the stuff that's in there saying 'Don't do this or don't do that.' And kind of going full steam ahead, full blast with this sort of looking at girls and, you know, um Playboys and all the rest of it coming through for me. And then, kind of everything ending up happily ever after.*
>
> T41   *But in a way you'd like to get rid of all that stuff inside that says 'don't do this, don't do that.' That's when you'd like to go kind of full steam ahead.*

Here he seems to have pulled the various themes together and in the process to have differentiated the metafacts and metacauses into a personally grounded position that is expressed in a fairly normative way. The issue isn't finished, though. He continues through a series of speculations that maybe happy people don't get in trouble with the police. It's other kinds of people with 'beards and frowns' or maybe 'Puerto Ricans' that get in trouble. He talks about his mother, seeming to imply that she was happy and ended up going to heaven:

> C51   ... *My dad on the other hand just not really being sure about Luke. I mean, what do we do, doctor? I mean the lever is pressed and everything. We know that the real Luke is one of these pleasure seekers.*
>
> C53   ... *why can't I go 100% is just I suppose genetic. It's one of these unfortunate things ...*

I return to the subject of his mother:

> T56   ... *So with your mother, you figure, she's going to heaven.*
>
> C57   *I would think so. I mean, heaven in a way, has that same quality of paradise power ... I'm kind of wondering what that's all about. But maybe that's the signal that knows the answer when the lever's been pulled for Luke and then he sees all these happy people and wonders what he's doing in the insane asylum.*

'Heaven' here seems to be a metafact encompassing all of the pleasure-seeking good life, and links with having the 'lever' pulled. Luke continues with some more explicit images about taking his clothes off and running in a pool after seeing attractive girls. This may be a memory of what he did that got him in trouble during his first psychotic break at school. In the process of describing this scene, he seems to have alarmed himself, because he says:

> C62   ... *Maybe I'm going too far. Maybe I'm misreading you ... The depressing things about sirens wailing in California. Or, you know, when the devil gets out of the*

> *squad car and rolls his eyes for you and then, wants to put you in hell instead of the opposite, what do you do? It's that kind of thing that's, in a way Luke. Maybe that's the illness or maybe that's the riots. I wasn't there in '68.*

Here, very poignantly expressed, is a metafact in which the policeman who took him away is a devil; the experience of the psychotic break evil. He continues a little later:

> C66 *. . . I mean, the scars that are left from the cuffs are still there you know? . . . I mean, it's like breaking free again and then getting those beautiful blonde girls out there to look at me because someone pressed the right lever there.*

The way he is feeling freer in his life continues to be puzzling:

> C71 *. . . this whole thing about evil doesn't seem to exist any more . . . I'm not a lawyer, doctor. You'd have to ask my brother why those cuffs were put on my hands. Someone who knows more about it than I do, you know.*

This brings him back to another memory of a psychotic episode that pulls in a number of the metafacts that have structured his articulation of this issue:

> C80 *. . . this whole thing about leaving Chicago and going to the East coast and being put in a body bag and then Dad running through that fellow and hitting him in the face or something . . . I don't know whether the federal building has a little computer that knows that Luke wasn't doing well. And this kind of hero galloping off again and, towards you and that fellow for being wicked, you know. They put me in the body bag and you read about that in these novels. It's pretty unforgivable in a way.*

He describes an interaction in which he tried to cheer his nephew up so he wouldn't have to go through the sorts of things Luke had in his life. I comment:

> T87 *You're just not wanting those kinds of things to keep happening.*
> C88-90 *Yeah. Right. That's exactly where I was that day in the scheme of things. Whereas everyone else in the family, back in that day, would say yes and for some reason I say no . . . that doesn't necessarily mean that the ambulance has been called either, it's just one of these, 'Why don't they give me more cement for the puzzle' kind of things.*

> T 91: *That doesn't necessarily mean that the ambulance has been called but it did seem like that day, everybody in the family would say yes and you'd say no.*
> C92: *Yeah, that was exactly what it was like. Whereas, someone would say, well, continue to take off your clothes in the middle of the pond at school on the way to class. Something was overshadowing that. Something would say, 'No, don't do that.' What we are really looking for is how to get rid of that nonsense, I think. And, but the law would say, of course, this whole thing about adultery, but that's another world. Where I'm coming from is someone who pressed the lever and who is trying to tell you that it's ok being you and as far as I'm concerned. I'm kind of part of your universe. And then why don't those gates open up a little more for me?*

And a little later:

> C95 *. . . It's like the accident today, doctor. Those people seemed to have a little evil*

inside and all of a sudden, the skidding and all that. And, it's really, a very interesting point for me, witnessing that whole thing and then, kind of my being one of the only people who wasn't involved in a negative way. Leaving the scene and coming out clean, you know.

Evil here, still seems to be a metafact that collapses everything that goes on when things turn catastrophic, in a combination with some attribution of good and bad behavior. Yet, Luke once again takes a step of causal differentiation as he notices that even though the accident was similar in some ways to his psychotic break, it was different in that nothing bad happened to him. But still there's a lurking concern, and several more rounds of back-and-forth on the subject:

C103 *I wonder if that person out there is just fooling me? Maybe there is some evil in this world, I don't know. And something about the Catholic Church . . . for someone who is very religious, saying 'Well, you believe in the crucified Jesus' you know. Assuming that I've gone along that way all along, and then, will the door be closed again in my face as far as that's concerned? In other words, the good old days being gone, you know.*

Here he seems to take up the moral side of the metafact of evil, considering how his Catholicism might relate to his situation, without differentiating Catholic versions of evil very much from the experience of having a psychotic break. But, he returns to his sense of wanting to feel freer:

C112 *This whole thing about looking at girls . . . is kind of the way I'm willing to go. And, who cares after the lever's been pushed, you know. In some ways . . . if someone's out there who's going to frown . . . because you're in the right frame of mind, you don't even pay any attention, really.*

C115-116 *. . . I'm not a sinful person either to talk about these things . . . Maybe I'm all wrong. I don't think so . . .*

Luke returns a little bit to the possibility of having another break, but it doesn't seem to alarm him as much. He notes that it feels good talking to me about it:

C124 *. . . This whole thing about relating too is very important, doctor. We're talking about the same feel, or the same kind of thing about, hearts beating together and things, you know. I think we're coming from the same place . . . You've always been very friendly.*

Soon after this, Luke comes to a fairly integrated version of the good and bad possibilities in his situation. His way of speaking, here, is full of metafacts, but not in a way that seems hard for me to understand. In the process there is a moment both of our laughing and seeming to connect at a deep level of mutual understanding:

C127 *. . . I was really quite the man about town that day (the day of the psychotic break), and the, the evil forces caught up with me . . . I hope never to be aware of them again, quite frankly.*
T127 *Yes (both laughing). Yeah.*

> *C 128 You know. 'Turn the other cheek' is not such a bad way to do in a way, I mean, looking back on the whole thing.*
>
> *T128 Yeah. But it would be nice never to have to deal with them again.*
>
> *C129 Or to kind of slip off those x-rayed plastic cuffs a little more often these days you know.*

Still, there's one more round of Luke's wondering whether the ambulances will come to get him for talking like this:

> *C133 . . . Well, Luke, you've gone far enough, and one more sentence to Dr. Warner and it's back to . . . moving along . . . versus this whole sort of cactus-like crown that's been with me . . . all my life.*

But Luke ends by thinking that maybe he could nonverbally convey to the police that they shouldn't bother him:

> *C136 . . . So if someone is chasing me in Chicago, I can just tell them sort of physically 'Well I was born and raised here officer, and you're even . . . younger than I am, and watch your P's and Q's . . .'*

In this session, then, Luke has been able to focus on an issue that is of concern to him for a good part of a therapy hour. He identifies a daily event that is disturbing, brings to mind related traumatic events from earlier in his life that clarify why the immediate event is disturbing. He explores these events in a very vivid and immediate way. He differentiates the current event somewhat from earlier ones, and begins to consider alternate ways he could respond. He feels very understood at particular moments and allows himself to express appreciation for that. He comes to the tentative conclusion that he could allow himself to be a little freer in having sexual feelings in his current life without anything bad happening.

In my observation of Luke, he seems to use metafacts and metacauses the most when he is trying to make sense of reactions to personal situations that are not yet clear to him. For example, in this transcript cited earlier some of the strongest clusters of metafacts and metacauses come when he is trying to understand the circumstances under which he is likely to have another acute psychotic episode and weighing questions of what sorts of sexuality are acceptable for a Catholic man. In general, he talks in a normatively sensible way when he is describing events that are fairly routine to him and he will often come up with a conclusion expressed in a fairly normative way at the end of processing an issue. Since metafacts and metacauses are most involved when he is actively processing difficult issues, it seems ironic to me that psychotic expressions are so widely assumed to be ways by which a person avoids or runs away from reality.

As with client-centered work in general, this model of client-centered work with 'thought-disordered' psychotic experience doesn't depend on resolving issues of etiology. Whether the cause of psychotic experience is primarily biological (Green, 1998; Rotenberg, 1994; McCarley et al., 1993), primarily developmental/familial (Arieti, 1955; Pao, 1979; Karon and vandenBos, 1981; Whitaker, 1992) or some mixture of the two, the human impulse to communicate and to process experience remains. A client's having safe space in which to sort through thoughts, feelings and choices maximizes the person's potential for having a positive sense of self and confidence in relating to others in the world.

In listening to Luke in sessions like this over the years, I have gained a personal understanding of what life is like when a person can't process experience; just how difficult it is to live when you have difficulty figuring out what bothers you, why it bothers you and what is likely to happen next. I have gained a sense of how much having a psychotic break and being forcibly hospitalized is a traumatic experience not unlike that of being raped. And, given both of those circumstances, I am aware of how much courage it takes to stay engaged in life when you never know when people might come, assault you and take you away in an ambulance.

Psychological theorists often hypothesize that people become psychotic because they can't 'face' reality for some personal/existential reasons (Arieti, 1955; Karon and vandenBos, 1981, Pao, 1979; Whitaker, 1992). While this could be true, it seems at least as plausible to me to hypothesize that some or many people who have psychotic experiences are simply facing reality under circumstances of enormous challenge. In the same way that I wouldn't assume that someone who was paraplegic didn't want to engage in activities outside of the house, I wouldn't assume that a person who is having psychotic experiences doesn't want to engage in an active, reality-oriented life. Whatever the source of a thought disorder like that experienced by Luke, psychological interactions that allow him to find his own voice seem crucial to his having a positive sense of self and an interest in engaging in the world around him.

As is suggested by Garry Prouty's model of Pre-Therapy (1994), I have found that engaging with people's expressive efforts in whatever form they take seems to mobilize whatever processing capacities are available. The experience of communicating successfully seems to increase clients' wish to communicate and their ability to trust in their own process. Given this experience, I suspect that the common psychiatric practice of ignoring or actively discouraging expressions that sound psychotic may actually stop clients from processing experiences in ways that could allow them to gain a more integrated sense of their own reactions and preferences.

REFERENCES

Arieti, S. (1955). *Interpretation of Schizophrenia*. New York: Robert Brunner.

Gendlin, E. T. (1964). A theory of personality change. In P. Worchel and D. Byrne, (Eds.) *Personality Change*. New York: Wiley, pp. 102–48.

Gendlin, E. T. (1968). The experiential response. In E. Hammer, (Ed.) *Use of Interpretation in Therapy*.

Gendlin, E. T. (1984). The client's client: The edge of awareness. In R. F. Levant and J. M. Shlien (Eds.), *Client-Centered Therapy and the Person-Centered Approach: New directions in theory, research and practice*. New York: Praeger.

Gendlin, E. T. (1995). Crossing and dipping: Some terms for approaching the interface between natural understanding and logical formulation. *Mind and Machines, 5*, 547–60.

Goldstein, K. (1944). Methodological approach to the study of schizophrenic thought disorder. In J. S. Kasanin (Ed.) *Language and Thought in Schizophrenia*. New York: W. W. Norton.

Green, M. F. (1998). *Schizophrenia from a Neurocognitive Perspective*. Boston: Allyn and Bacon.

Iberg, J. R. (1990). Ms. C's focusing and cognitive functions. In G. Lietaer, J. Rombauts and R. Van Balen (Eds.) *Client-centered and Experiential Psychotherapy in the Nineties*. Leuven, Belgium: Leuven University Press, pp. 173–203.

Karon, B. P. and vandenBos, G. R. (1981). *Psychotherapy of Schizophrenia*. Northvale, NJ: Jason Aronson.

Kasanin, J. S. (Ed.) (1944). *Language and Thought in Schizophrenia.* New York: W. W. Norton.

McCarley, R. W., Shenton, M. E., O'Donnell, B. F. and Nestor, P. G. (1993) Uniting Kraeplin and Bleuler: The psychology of schizophrenia and the biology of temporal lobe abnormalities. *Harvard Review of Psychiatry, 1*, pp. 36–56.

Pao, P-N. (1979). *Schizophrenic Disorders: Theory and treatment from a psychodynamic point of view.* New York: International Universities Press.

Prouty, G. (1994). *Theoretical Evolutions of Person-centered/Experiential Therapy: Applications to schizophrenic and retarded psychoses.* Westport, CT: Praeger.

Raskin, N. J. (1996). Client-centered therapy with very disturbed clients. In R. Hutterer, G. Pawlowsky, P. F. Schmid, and R. Stipsits (Eds.) *Client-centered and Experiential Psychotherapy: A paradigm in motion.* Frankfurt am Main: Peter Lang, pp. 529–31.

Rogers, C. R. (Ed.) (1967). *The Therapeutic Relationship and its Impact : A study of psychotherapy with schizophrenics.* Madison, WI: University of Wisconsin Press.

Rotenberg, V. S. (1994). An integrative psychophysiological approach to brain hemisphere functions in schizophrenia. *Neuroscience and Biobehavioral Review, 18*(4), 487–95.

Warner, M. S. (1997). Does empathy cure? A theoretical consideration of empathy, processing and personal narrative. In A. C. Bohart and L. S. Greenberg, *Empathy Reconsidered: New directions in psychotherapy.* Washington, DC: American Psychological Association.

Warner, M. S. (2000). Person-centered psychotherapy at the difficult edge: A developmentally-based model of fragile and dissociated process. In D. Mearns and B. Thorne. *Person-centred Therapy Today: New frontiers in theory and practice.* London: Sage, pp. 144–71.

Whitaker, L. C. (1992). *Schizophrenic Disorders.* New York: Plenum.

Ann Lovering
ITESO University, Guadalajara, Mexico

Person-Centered and Feminist Theories: How we connect them in our work with groups of Mexican women

I would like to explain my interest in this topic and why it is a challenge to me to develop this theme. As a group facilitator, I have been working constantly with women in group situations for over twenty years. The training I received was in a master's program in Human Development in Guadalajara, Mexico, a program founded on Carl Rogers' relational model, the Person-Centered Approach. In fact, Carl was in Guadalajara for a week's work with us in 1982. The women with whom I have worked are part of a continuing education program in Human Development at the university where I teach, and the growth groups, as they are called in Spanish, form a central part of the curriculum.

In the 1980s I became gradually aware of the literature about women which was being produced in the States: Carol Gilligan at Harvard, Miller with her new psychology of women, the Wellesley College Stone Center, the Five College Center for Women's Studies in Massachusetts. In Mexico I attended a month-long summer study program on women's studies and realized that there was academic work going on all over the world in this field. I became aware of feminist theory and activist groups. Returning to my campus, we started the Center for Research and Support for Women, in 1991. This led to many different activities and study projects.

Not until recently, however, was I challenged to look at these two bodies of work: Person-Centered Approach and feminist theory, and to ask myself if and how they are compatible, and how we (three group facilitators and I) are working with them in the reality of our groups. My wish is to discover the links and perhaps the contradictions between them, and to share this with you. I selected three topics, identity, empowerment and change, through which to focus the discussion, and another theme, culture, appeared as a result of working with the first three.

The searches I made for articles in the two fields didn't reveal any which connect the two issues. Undoubtedly there are some somewhere but they weren't obvious to me. I depended on books and articles in the two fields of study for the first draft, and then consulted with my colleagues in a round-table discussion about these issues and have included their thoughts and reflections also.

TWO CONTEXTS

From the many contexts in which we have worked over the years, I have chosen two of the most recent ones. I will describe two groups, one where I am the facilitator and the other facilitated by a woman professor in Human Development. The first is a group of nine women from the middle class who have been invited to participate in a study about quality of life and economic conditions. This is not a typical growth group but rather a kind of extended focus group, during which the participants and the research-facilitators hope to learn more about their quality of life and the relation it has with their economic situation. All of these women are students in the continuing education program in Human Development at the university, which implies that they are accustomed to looking into themselves, recognizing their feelings and sharing them with other women. Many have money problems of one kind or another, and all are interested in reflecting on their quality of life. The ten weekly sessions were of 1.5 hours. During the workshop, as we called it, the participants came to know each other well and because of the norm agreed upon of confidentiality, felt free to express their feelings, which were often very strong.

One of the greatest problems these women expressed was the difficulty that their woman's role caused them in the sphere of money management and decision making in the home. This is not surprising since Mexico has a strong patriarchal tradition in decision making in the family, in the couple and in almost every other sphere of activity. One of the objectives of the workshop was to help the women to recognize that the intergenerational learning patterns, i.e. the models they learned from their mothers, if not examined critically, are most often repeated in the next generation. A further objective was to discover personal and interpersonal strengths and skills in order to better daily living. This included communication with the husband. Another objective was to better understand the difficulties the women have in changing the disagreeable or difficult aspects of the money situation and their role in it.

The second setting is a typical growth group with a group of women, both married and single mothers, who live in difficult conditions on the side of a hill on the outskirts of Guadalajara. Their homes are one- or two-room concrete-block dwellings; the family income is low, as the husbands are manual laborers and the women are homemakers. The streets are not paved and without drainage, but there are electricity and public transportation. In the beginning this was a squatter's settlement but gradually it has been legalized. There are high rates of delinquency, alcoholism and drug addiction.

The group consisted of eleven to thirteen women who brought their young children to the sessions, where they were attended separately by a teacher also in the Human Development program, who developed a program of learning games and activities. The mothers, momentarily free from maternal cares, and the two women facilitators would form a circle with their chairs and talk for the duration of an hour and a half. I refer to this group as 'typical' because of the non-structured contents. The women talked about whatever they wished, perhaps a problem with a family member, especially with the children. A characteristic of these women is their fervent desire to learn to be better mothers and to treat their children in a better way.

The role of the facilitators was to listen empathetically, to reflect sentiments and meanings, and to model communication skills, such as listening non-judgmentally and speaking in the first person. Also important was the climate of trust that built up among the women, with the solidarity that resulted.

The characteristics of the women from the two groups have much in common and the description that follows generalizes from the two groups. The women view men as potentially irresponsible people who, without their constant pressure, will not fulfill their responsibilities as providers. If a woman begins to earn her own money and becomes more self-sufficient, she experiences this situation as displacing her husband, which can cause his irresponsibility and end up in divorce or abandonment. Even though she wishes to help economically, she thinks that this activity can produce a lessening of his obligations to the family and a breakup of the family. Work, therefore, is viewed as having its dangerous aspect.

However, there are jobs which are permitted and which stabilize the status quo of the family. Especially those that the woman can do at home and that are limited to the feminine private space are recognized as acceptable. Doing handwork, cooking food for sale and taking in roomers fall into this category. Less acceptable are sales outside the home; this is permitted, but only during school and work hours, with the disadvantage that the woman 'is on the street', although at home when the other family members are there.

Women are supportive of each other with loans in times of necessity; the older generation helps the next, mothers to daughters, aunts to nieces and neighbors to neighbors. They protect each other's secrets from their husbands about the amounts they earn.

The ability to earn is ridiculed by family members, with the result that the women don't believe in their own abilities. The women fervently wish for economic independence but have few hopes that this can be achieved within the framework of the couple. Interdependence, with more flexible roles and less autocratic decisions, is practically unknown and is expressed as a utopia and not realizable. The alternative most often visualized is that of total independence through divorce, which allows more peace in the family and autonomy for the women.

In general terms, women from both middle and lower classes suffer from emotional problems that are a result of developmental and adaptive difficulties. They often seek help, but the causes of their ill-being remain unrecognized as related to social expectations and gender roles. The health system is dominated by masculine theories and guidelines, and it attempts to make the woman adapt to her unsatisfactory condition, through the use of drugs or advice.

IDENTITY

I start my discussion with identity, as the most basic core from which we move on as human beings and as male and female persons. A working definition of identity is a sense of myself, recognition of the different parts of myself, who I am with my history and my future. This can be understood in simply human terms and also in a gendered sense, as men and women.

Rogers states that the individual is formed from two sources of information: the data from internal experiencing and that from the external world. The more open the person is to this information, the better she or he will function in a unified way. This is what Rogers calls a 'whole person'. This person is moving toward a knowledge of, and harmony with, his or her innermost experience that also integrates the experience from the external environment. This is the self.

We have a self, and a potential self that develops in a caring relationship. We grow in the potential self when we develop the ability to become aware of our experiences without distortion. This leads to a different, new and expanded self-identity, which contains contradictions and polarities which come into consciousness and finally into acceptance. We become that self which we truly are. Our identity is more complete, more representative of all our aspects.

Identity, when viewed as gender identity, takes on the element of how we become girls and women, boys and men. The masculine-feminine dichotomy, with its cultural variants, establishes stereotypes that are often rigid and that condition roles and limit the personal potential because they stimulate or repress behaviors according to the gender enculturation. Since Freud the developmental theorists have presented models for this development. Freud and the psychoanalytic school speak of psychosexual stages of growth, oral, anal and genital, with the boy child separating from his mother to identify with his father in order to become a masculine person and the girl child identifying with her mother. The theories of Deutch and Horney develop and modify Freud's work, making the different stages of development such as penis envy and Oedipus complex less literal and more symbolic.

Two other schools of theory that have influenced studies in gender identity are those called social learning and cognitive development. In social learning, the child learns his or her gender roles by imitating his or her parents and repeating the conducts that receive positive responses from the parent. The parents' reactions are different for the sexes, therefore training the child in appropriate behavior for his or her sex. Also recognized as important is the influence of role models of other children of the same sex.

The cognitive development approach affirms that the child plays an active part in the gender socialization. He or she must establish a clear self-concept with includes gender identity, a sense of being male or female. This gender identity motivates the child to identify with role models, not only because of the social reinforcement, but also because of the need to be congruent with his or her self-concept. The gender identity helps the child make sense of his or her world and to understand the behavior of others.

Recent studies indicate that gender identity develops in the very early stages of life. At six months, children distinguish between masculine and feminine voices; between two and three years they recognize their own and other children's sex, establish their own gender identity and acquire stereotyped beliefs about men and women. Between five and seven years, they recognize that they will always be the same sex (gender permanence), even with the passage of time and in different circumstances, and they believe their own sex is the best one.

Some thoughts about the preceding

In the gender identity, the gender culture is embedded in the unconscious. We are not conscious of this culture because of the process of enculturation, in which we accept as usual the culture that surrounds us and is part of us. In special circumstances we are able to discern characteristics of our own culture, usually in contrast to another, such as cultures of the past or of foreign lands.

An interesting point arises with the idea of the need of the child to be congruent with his or her self-concept, which arises both in the Person-Centered Approach and in the gender theory. Rogers uses the metaphor of peeling away false layers in order to reach the real true self, which happens in an adequate climate of interpersonal relations and conscious election. Are the introjected values such as cultural stereotypes the layers that need to be removed?

In our work in women's groups, we ask ourselves if we ourselves have not recognized sufficiently the enormous importance of the prevailing culture both in ourselves and in the women participants and therefore we have not broached the subject directly and with sufficient clarity. What we realize now is that we cannot speak about the person without identifying the gender; and vice versa, we cannot separate the feminine from the person. We question if we are taking into account the culture as well as the personal internal world. We recognize that there are masculine and feminine experiences, as well as human experiences.

The Mexican woman's gender identity is oriented toward interactions with others. This has been characterized by a phrase in Spanish which has become common in gender studies: la mujer es un ser-para-el-otro (woman is a being-for-the-other). The roles she learns from childhood are to be of service to men and boys. Even at a young age, she is required to serve her brothers and to clean up after them. In the typical home, if there are no servants, the woman stays at the stove during the family meal, heating the tortillas.

Maternity is also a defining role in the woman's identity. Her social validation and her personal sense of self-worth are anchored in this function. Also, she feels totally dependent on her partner and often will remain in an unsatisfactory relationship because of her belief that she is incapable of living alone and raising her children.

EMPOWERMENT

I chose to speak of this area of personal development because it is important in both the Person-Centered Approach and in almost all feminist theories about women's development. I want to see what similarities and differences exist in the two ideas.

In his book *On Personal Power* (1977) Rogers examines the changing culture in which women have been able to develop. His work often deals with the way in which women and their world are changing, recounting the social factors which have increased the options for women, such as the social acceptance of divorce; family mobility, which puts the emphasis of marriage in the quality of the relationship between the partners; increased sexual freedom; longevity of marriage, which demands a better relationship; contraception; and women in careers. With these changes women have more options and more chance of discovering their self-worth. He credits the women's liberation movement for promoting this liberating revolution and labels it essentially person-centered.

To quote: 'if society will only create an acceptant climate for growth' women will have the capacity to develop and be creative. He continues, 'Individuals are culturally conditioned, rewarded, reinforced, for behaviors that are in fact perversions of the natural directions of the unitary actualizing tendency' (p. 247). My interpretation of these passages is that an underlying supposition is that the individual and the society (culture) are at odds with each other, and that without the restricting influence of society's norms, women (and men) would be free to be whole persons. The idea of the whole person for men and women combines the traditionally masculine and feminine traits of tenderness, lovingness, emotionality, intellectuality and achievement.

The question that was asked by feminist psychologists in the 1970s, and is still being debated, is just *how* women develop in relationships which empower or inhibit their personal power. During this decade different groups of women scholars began to challenge psychology's perception of women's development. In the traditional developmental theories, the highest stage of moral development was autonomy and women somehow just fell short of the pattern established as ideal.

In this new view, women's dependency, once viewed as a source of problems and an inferior stage of moral development, was now understood not in the dichotomy of dependence-independence, but rather within the need for connection. Being in a relationship with others, to understand others' feelings, to contribute to the other, to need the relationship are some expressions of connection. Here we have a relational theory for women's development.

In the Stone Center model of Wellesley College, the relationships a woman has are gratifying to her. Through them she develops a sense of self-worth and effectiveness at being in relationships and therefore feels good about herself. In this theory, the mother-daughter relationship, with its empathic maternal responses, helps to form the daughter's increasing ability for mutual empathy. This is called a motivational dynamic of mutual empowerment. In this relationship the girl experiences validation of her own developing empathic competence. Thus, mothers empower their daughters by allowing them to feel successful at understanding and giving support.

Some questions asked in an ongoing debate about this model (from the book by M. Roth Walsh *Women, Men and Gender: Ongoing Debates*, 1996) are: if this theory empowers women or, by glorifying women's relational skills, does it replace male chauvinism with a new model of female chauvinism? Does it reinforce separate spheres for women that put pressure on women to exhibit connection and suppress autonomy and assertiveness? Is this concern and empathy an essential female quality, or does it come from the woman's subordinate position in society?

Other feminist psychologists respond that this theory is a source of empowerment for women, affirming that we grow through relationships, and that for women connection with others is central to psychological well-being. They affirm that mutuality through mutual empathy is a central dynamic in the growth process through life for both men and women.

I have found an interesting connection between the Person-Centered Approach and the Stone Center model. The authors of this model speak of relational authenticity, which is the ongoing effort to represent oneself as fully as possible, to be real, clear and present in the relationship. It is a mutually empathic relationship that provides the energy for growth. This includes the need to be seen and understood and the need to see and understand the other as fully as possible. This would seem to relate to the basic postulates of Rogers' conditions for a growth relationship.

The woman learns to fully represent herself in a relationship, to deal with conflict within it and to recognize the impact of her actions on others. This enables her to fully represent herself in relationship. With this capacity, she is able to develop a real self that resists submersion in role stereotypes. Development in relational paths need not diminish other lines of development such as creativity, agency and initiative.

Obviously between the model and the reality there is a wide gap. Many women have not experienced this nurturing and empowering relationship with their mothers. However, in my work, I see a connection between this theory and our work in women's groups.

In my Mexican group context, I have observed that empowerment in women's groups which are facilitated by women occurs in several ways. An essential element is the creation of a climate of acceptance in which every woman is valued for herself, with her differences and similarities to the rest of the group. Each life circumstance is prized and made significant. To create this atmosphere takes time, since a usual social reaction is the rejection of difference. Empathy may be part of a woman's learning process (in the best of circumstances) but it needs to be nurtured in the group process.

A part of the empowerment process are the personal resources which emerge when a woman views her actions during her life, with all its richness and complexity. She is able to make conscious her roles and her decisions, or lack of decision, and make new decisions. She can see herself in the frame of her personal and family history, and this is often a freeing experience. She can listen to other women's experiences and alternatives, which amplifies her own choices. Thus she discovers new possibilities in herself and in her surroundings.

I want to emphasize the influence of the women facilitators. They model, woman to woman, different ways of perceiving, interpreting and acting in the group. They empathize with the participants and develop significant relationships with them, within the group context. For all involved it is a significant experience, and I propose that for those whose mother-daughter relationship was not nurturing and growth-provoking, this new female relationship is also a significant way to learn new relational skills *as a woman* and to feel self-worth.

CHANGE

When I was selecting the areas I wanted to develop, the question of change was immediately important because I view change as a result of a developing identity and increased personal power. Also, change is inevitable during the course of life.

In the 1970s, Rogers questioned the possibility of change within an oppressive society. He saw the sources of opposition as the state, tradition, status quo, the idea of one truth and that the individual should be shaped in that truth. He asked if the 'new persons' can change the culture. The new culture is depicted as one in which the tendency will be toward openness, exploration of self, and prizing individuals in spite of race and sex.

Women's developmental studies deal with the ways in which women grow in their identities and powers. Important studies have been conducted in the field of moral development, in which the voice becomes the metaphor to describe feminine identity and development. She, the woman, discovers that her voice is different from masculine voices, in the priorities she establishes in her life and in her decision-making process. In order to become true to herself, she must discover and develop her feminine voice.

How does she learn? Is the process the same for both men and women? Recent studies suggest that the road for a woman to discover her full capacity as a person of knowledge is different from a man's. She must move from a position of silence and acceptance of the male point of view (the expert viewpoint) to discover that she has an inner subjective voice, which is valid in its possibilities to guide and instruct her. This is a very significant moment in the woman's life; she becomes her own authority, her own truth and she believes with certainty that this is a source of wealth and knowledge. This moment often is accompanied by anger because of her past submission.

In our work with women, we help this new voice to begin to express itself. We see the change in the belief in self. At this point, many women discover that there is a whole world awaiting them, and they return to formal schooling to complete high school or to begin a college degree.

This developmental theory goes on to describe the next stages in the process of knowing, which lead the woman to integrate her new-found inner voice with external facts. Here she develops the ability to know objectively and subjectively, from arguments and from empathic experience. Intuition and reason combine so that she seeks what is correct, not abstractly but personally. She can express her voice not only within herself but within the family and the society.

I venture to say that this new-found ability for expression is the most significant activator of change.

The women with whom we work can be described as seeking something which often is not clear, but the need is present. They want a better quality of life, which for them means harmony and good family relations. They consider themselves responsible for the quality of family life and realize that whatever movement they make will cause repercussions in the family. They are brave women who are taking their lives and the lives of their families seriously. Often with extreme self-consciousness and even anguish, they decide to express themselves in a group setting, where they share their fears, confusions, strengths and limitations.

They are capable of manifesting attitudes of solidarity, of creating relations of trust, intimacy, warmth and support with the other women of their groups. We find that this fact runs contrary to other opinions about working with women, in which they are considered conflictive and difficult, and we suggest that a group that prizes empathy and support is a determinant factor in the relationships which develop in it.

They are dissatisfied with the traditional role that leaves them unable to value themselves, their resources, capabilities and work. This often leaves them with feelings of anger, protest and disagreement. There is distrust within the couple, and with little possibility for the women to exercise their power of decision. Often they feel trapped between their economic needs and the threat of family disintegration if they work outside the home. In many ways the traditional model does not respond to the real needs and interests of the woman, such as her own realization and her needs for dialogue, especially with her partner; nor for her need to share the power in decisions.

The women with whom we have worked want to live more authentically and be more themselves, with their ability to express their personal power. They are dissatisfied with their feeling of dependency, and visualize as the only alternative a complete rupture with their partner. Those of us who have worked with these women perceive a real lack of models in which a kind of interdependence is a viable alternative.

We have identified three positions from which the women visualize change:
• Change in the husband or partner
• Change in the situation
• Personal change

The first position is the usual starting point, in which the woman identifies her husband as the cause of the unfavorable situation. When she speaks of change, she refers to him and his need to be different. Her position is in opposition to his, and this generates a power struggle.

The second position is a kind of laissez-faire, in which change will come with the passing of time, the advancing family stages that hopefully will result in positive changes in the power relations, in the amount of money available and in fewer problems around the children. Also the woman may grow emotionally and separate herself psychologically from her husband.

The third position is a personal change, a voluntary act in order to better her quality of life. Here we see two paths, usually sequential. First she tries to better the conjugal relationship and if this is not successful, she seeks her own independence. This is usually a rupture of some kind, such as a divorce or psychological and economic separation.

When a woman develops her consciousness, it has repercussions in all the areas of her life. She becomes aware of what she wants to do and asks how she will do it. Together with this consciousness is the difficulty of changing the external situation. At the same time, the women report increased satisfaction and pleasure from their new way of being.

A significant change is in the meaning the women give to their lives. We have registered a change in the meaning of independence for the women of the different groups. Independence begins to include the possibility of deciding about one's own life without depending solely on the husband's decision or the children's needs. This changes the priority of being-for-the-other to include the possibility of a personal life.

Also significant is the meaning the woman gives to her freedom of choice, which increases through the group work. This means that she feels less predetermined in a given situation to follow the same paths she has always taken. She can find new solutions for problems which formerly seemed hopeless.

The transitional role

To change is to move along a continuum from one state to another. During this transition, there are moments of instability, doubt, anguish and delight. The woman who is in this process is modifying her internal psychic structure and her outward behavior. Although many women have lived this process, the individual woman often feels that she is in a no man's land (or a no woman's land!) that is unfamiliar and with monsters inside and outside of her. She questions if it is worth going on, especially since her changes are causing reactions in her family and husband. As one woman put it: 'I'm even afraid of myself.'

During this period, the support from other women is extremely important. In groups, women identify with each other and join forces in order not to feel so alone. They offer spiritual and practical help, feeling united in similar problems.

The women say:

Breaking my image was very hard for me . . . very! Because we always were together and many people know us.

I came to this group to see if I can learn something so as to keep struggling, fighting or to see if I can do something else. Because what I have been doing has not worked for 25 years and maybe now, maybe now . . .

I can't change my husband. And I'm not going to go on being silent . . . silent . . . silent . . .

THE SMALL GROUP CULTURE

Our educational strategy is to work in small groups of 8–15 women. We are working within a culture (ideas, beliefs, ideology, values, norms, and suppositions) that is embedded in the individual psyche of the participants and is also part of the group collective. Parts of this group culture are the academic and ideological suppositions and beliefs of the facilitators, in this case, the theories and practices of the Person-Centered Approach. In this melting-pot of experiences and beliefs, a new culture is born.

The group provides a space in which the social and personal culture of each woman is experienced, examined and decided. Here change can occur and be nourished.

We see a process that occurs through events of meaning-making. The term *event* connotes an identifiable sequence in the group process that has a beginning, middle and end. In the beginning the woman generally breaks with the tone of her discourse, with a strong expression of feeling: for example, by crying. The group reflects her feelings and tries to understand her experience. Sometimes there are expressions of support, sometimes of confrontation, sometimes offering alternative ways of viewing the situation. The participant reexamines the meaning of her experience and can identify the incongruity that produces the difficulty. At this point, she can begin to see alternatives to begin to move toward what she really is and wants. She sees her experience from a new perspective and values herself and the group for having lived this process.

When this process does not reach completion, there is no change in the meaning-making at that time.

I wish to emphasize the influence that we have seen of the woman-facilitator in a woman's group. In her verbal responses, she reinforces women's dignity, their personal power, and the value of the group construction of a path for women's growth. She and the other women mutually acknowledge their valor for living and for defending their beliefs.

The process of making new meanings is delicate. It requires an attitude of openness and searching, in order to forgo temporarily the known in order to explore the new. The group ambiance that favors this movement is acceptance and support, because the person is putting herself in a vulnerable position when she sets out on this path.

Because a woman doesn't live in isolation but rather in a social context, the new meaning must be confronted with this context. The group is the first place where she receives feedback. In his work on meaning-making, Kegan (1982, 1994) speaks of the need for confirmation from the context in order to maintain the new meaning. The woman may experience difficulty in sustaining her new understanding of herself when there is little or no supporting and reinforcing culture. We find that the need for this support varies from woman to woman.

The passage from the traditional role to the transitional one requires a favorable context. In the women's group, a new vision of the self is generally received with understanding, perhaps because the group has participated in the process. Life outside the group presents a different picture. When a woman is moving from one meaning-organization to another, there is a change of attitude and behavior, which generally causes resistance in the family. During this period of confusion, a constant review, in a climate of trust, of the meanings that are changing provides some of the necessary support in order to integrate these new meanings. Part of the support comes from the woman herself, who finds satisfaction in her new clarity and self-understanding. We, as facilitators, should recognize the need to reinforce the culture of continuity with counseling or other means in order that she integrate her discoveries with her own identity and her family and social relations.

At this time, I would like to introduce the comments and reflections of my fellow facilitators, Gabriela, Xóchitl and Pedro, who also work from the two theoretical viewpoints: gender theory and person-centered theory. The question I posed for discussion was the following: are we underestimating the force of the culture when we work with the Person-Centered Approach, and how does this promote or make difficult change?

First we debated if it is possible to speak of feminine experience without speaking of human experience. On this subject, we women felt that the group talk about the woman's experience creates strong bonds of understanding through the common experience.

We are in agreement that the changes a person experiences tend to change his or her individual ecology and a new ecology can create dissonance with the context. In the group, we create a new culture, with support for the emerging person. But sometimes the new woman emerges with such force that she breaks with her own internal culture and also with social norms. On the other hand, from having lived this experience she, in an optimum situation, learns to become acceptant of cultural differences. Armed with this knowledge, she can empathize with other's processes.

In other words, she learns to build a bridge between herself and a new culture, both inside herself and with others.

With the increasing globalization which is strongly affecting Mexico, we feel that the women (and men also) are becoming objects and not subjects of change. This means that they are not conscious of the global changes that affect their lives and when these changes cause problems, they tend to personalize and feel responsible for them. Women often feel guilty for not having the individual willpower to change. For example, with economic difficulties comes an increase in masculine violence in the home. The woman tends to feel that this is somehow her fault. On the other hand, there are now laws about family violence and perhaps she will learn that she does not have to submit to violent treatment.

I have offered this example to try to explain how the surrounding culture affects the personal and family culture and how we are questioning the ecology of change in the women. We realize that as educators we are looking for alternative methods and models, in the hope of adjusting them to the times, the twenty-first century, and the place, Mexico.

IN CONCLUSION

In conclusion, I return to my initial question of the compatibility of gender theory and the Person-Centered Approach. The gender theories that I have presented here have a humanistic framework (of which I was not conscious) and I was surprised by the value placed on the empathic relationship. As for the person-centered theory, there exists a decided limitation in the sources reviewed, since they refer solely to Rogers' work and do not take into account more recent studies. This causes an anachronistic situation, but in my opinion, even with this limitation, we can value Rogers' foresight. He was part of a patriarchal culture, but still was able to view with great objectivity the question of gender, although his experience generally was within the white Anglo-Saxon culture.

In my wanderings among the ideas, the concept of culture became strongly present and has assumed a central place. This is the area that I find has been least satisfactorily resolved in this essay. I think we need to work on including and integrating the cultural context in our work, and of course, that context in this case is Mexico at the turn of the millenium.

The small-group culture, as far as it goes, seems to be a very adequate place for change. For it to be effective, it must be long term, at least six months, and provide a new supportive culture. Here a woman can become more real, discover her voice and her authenticity. She will firmly state after this experience that it changed her life, and we believe she has found new alternatives for living more satisfactorily.

REFERENCES

Gilligan, C. (1982). *In a Different Voice*. Cambridge, MA: Harvard University Press.

Kegan, R. (1982). *The Evolving Self: Problem and process in human development*. Cambridge, MA: Harvard University Press.

Kegan, R. (1994). *In Over our Heads*. Cambridge, MA: Harvard University Press.

Rogers, C. R. (1977). *On Personal Power*. New York: Delacorte Press.

Rogers, C. R. (1961). *On Becoming a Person*. Boston: Houghton Mifflin.

Roth Walsh, M. (1976). *Women, Men and Gender: Ongoing Debates*. Yale: Yale University Press.

Kathryn A. Moon
Chicago Counseling and Psychotherapy Center, Chicago, USA

Nondirective Client-Centered Therapy with Children[1]

Abstract. This paper describes how the nondirective attitude, client-centered theory and the three attitudinal conditions inform and become evident in this therapist's psychotherapy work with children. It is asserted that the Rogerian attitudinal conditions are sufficient regardless of whether or not the client articulates and understands his or her feelings. Two of Virginia Axline's principles for child therapy are described as being somewhat in contrast with nondirective client-centered theory.

Client-centered child therapy theoretically fits, I believe, within the rubric of Carl Rogers' theory as described in his 1959 statement about therapy and personality. I think of my work with child clients as being consistent with the nondirective client-centered psychotherapy to which I aspire in my work with adults. As a therapist, my constant endeavor is to be fully attitudinally available in relationship with the client. After describing the work I do and how it relates to the theory, I shall point out some ways in which my work contrasts with Virginia Axline's (1969, 1947) seminal description of play therapy.

NONDIRECTIVE CHILD THERAPY AND THE ATTITUDINAL CONDITIONS

My choice to work nondirectively is based upon my sense of what is ethical. I do not want to waste a client's time or a client's life with my beliefs, my values or my agenda. I do not want to cultivate a false self for my client, and I do not want to lead my client in a direction that is potentially harmful to the wondrous and unique existence of that person. Rogerian theory provides me a way to work in accordance with my wish to honor the client's self-direction.

Trust in the client's innate propensity for constructive personal and social development is foremost in my thinking and basic to my working mind set. My premise is that when a person is struggling, it is helpful to have a relationship in which an in-that-moment congruent individual effectively communicates unconditional positive regard, empathic understanding and genuine availability as a participant in the relationship. Rogers' (1977, p. 8, 238–41) botanical metaphor of plants sprouting and making their way in the direction of the light

[1] This article has been greatly improved thanks to a generous amount of time and thoughtful reactions provided by Jerold Bozarth, Barbara Brodley, Susan Pildes, Bert Rice and John Shlien.

A slightly different version of this paper was published in The Person-Centered Journal, Vol. 8, No. 1–2, 2001, pp. 43–52. (Journal of the Association for the Development of the Person-Centered Approach.)

feels particularly right to me when thinking about being helpful to youngsters. If we do not trample on the sprout, if we let it have sunlight and let it have water, it will grow to be a flower, with its own inherent coloring and beauty. Rogers thought, '. . . we were all "organisms", living in an "environment" that promoted or inhibited "growth" towards the fulfillment of potential' (Merry, 1999, p. 1). I think of child therapy as a relationship that promotes rather than inhibits growth. It is a relationship in which the child client experiences acceptance from a therapist. The client then becomes more self-accepting and better able to continue to develop in the direction of self-fulfillment. I am hoping that a psychologically nurturing relationship with me, though drastically limited by time, will stimulate the inner resources and innate capacity of the child to find a way to survive and enjoy life.

Theoretically, this means that if a child, or any individual, walks anonymously into a therapy room, psychotherapy can commence if the therapist is open, available, warm, acceptant, and seeking to follow and understand. In his 1959 statement, Rogers said:

> It has been our experience to date that although the therapeutic relationship is used differently by different clients, it is not necessary nor helpful to manipulate the relationship in specific ways for specific kinds of clients. To do this damages, it seems to us, the most helpful and significant aspect of the experience, that it is a genuine relationship between two persons, each of whom is endeavoring, to the best of his ability, to be himself in the interaction. (pp. 213–14)

I believe that this is true, that the therapist does not need any historical, familial, or presenting problem information about or from a child in order to provide a helping relationship or accomplish effective therapy. With clients, I choose not to instruct, or socialize, or improve manners, or teach appropriate behavior, or dig for feelings, nor do I seek to increase the child's self-understanding.

At an international conference on play therapy there was a seminar entitled 'Play Therapy with the ADHD Child.' According to the brochure, participants would 'learn play therapy techniques to teach ADHD children "life skills" for communication, impulse control, "stop and think" behavior, and identification of feelings' (Yeager, 2000).

In contrast, client-centered theory holds that when a therapist is fairly successfully embodying the attitudinal conditions with an individual, whether the individual is narrating personal life experience or just being there in play, the relationship is therapeutic and psychological change is occurring. According to the theory, more prescribed forms of therapy with directions for scope and agenda lead to less of the client as self and person being allowed to be present in the relationship, and less of the client as self and person being accepted and understood.

Here are three vignettes from my work in elementary schools. In the school setting, the time available for each client was minimal. There was little opportunity for supplementing the child's counseling time with parent or family sessions. Each session was a brief opportunity for a therapeutic encounter with a child.

Vignette 1: Michael

A five-year-old client, Michael, was referred to me because in his kindergarten room he was noncompliant and throwing furniture. I was told by the teacher that Michael's stepfather was maybe violent, his mother was pregnant, and that Michael was erratically switched back and forth to sleep in either his mother's or his father's home. Michael did not want to come with me to counseling. But when invited to bring along any child of his choosing, he came, with his cousin who was in the same class. That day, in counseling, we played a few games. The next time he chose to come alone without his cousin. I had art supplies, games, plastic animals and family figures available for play. Michael picked up a jaws-wide-open dimetrodon dinosaur, about five inches long. He took a large-size wooden popsicle stick and crammed it snugly down the throat of the dimetrodon. Then, holding the stick, he swung, or swept the dinosaur across the table and sent the animal figures scattering across the room. He picked up as many of them as he could find, put them back on the table and swung again, and again, and again. I did not comment upon what I guessed was his underlying feeling, anger. Instead, I responded to his more manifest feeling, his apparent pleasure for what he was doing. He nodded and took several more swings before we ran out of time. After that second session, Michael always brought a friend, rotating about three different friends. He did not again bring his cousin. He never again struck out at the toys. In subsequent sessions he and his friends, who clamored to attend counseling with him, played board and card games, turning frequently to me for assistance in regulating the rules. I would do my best to clarify my understanding of their agreements and disagreements over the rules. Beginning on the day of Michael's first session with me and his cousin, there were no further reports of misconduct by Michael.

Vignette 2: Lucy

Lucy, aged five, in her first session, sat in a chair and told me about the significance of her grandfather's death in her life. Her grandfather had died when she was a baby. She explained the financial and emotional toll his death had taken upon the fabric of her life within her family, and she described the intense sadness that she carried around within herself.

Vignette 3: boys' group in an elementary school

A group of four eleven- to twelve-year-old boys, all very low academic achievers, met with me in a public elementary school. One boy was very shy. Another was frequently absent from school and seldom did any homework. The latter was over-burdened as a care-giver to his father who had lost both of his legs. I had the impression that the father watched pornography videos in the boy's presence. This group of boys spent the weekly thirty minute counseling session modeling with clay, drawing and playing cards. We spent lots of time traveling up and down three flights of stairs making cherished trips to the boys' bathroom. The boys would compare athletic shoes and argue about sports, neighborhood violence and the details of school life. At length, for many sessions, they used the clay to shape huge penises, breasts and testicles. Chatting, they would lapse into speaking Spanish and when I broke into their conversation with beginner's Spanish, they taught me how to say dirty words in their home-life language. All but the one boy who took care of his father showed improvement in school performance within the first grading period after beginning group counseling.

CHILD THERAPY LITERATURE AND THE CORE CONDITIONS

Some of the literature is perhaps misleading both about what a therapist should anticipate as outcome when working with children and about what a therapist should expect to occur in session. The literature has perhaps burdened us with unrealistic expectations concerning what the therapist is supposed to do with or to the child.

Virginia Axline's (1964, 1969) two wonderful books, *Dibs in Search of Self* and *Play Therapy*, are the play therapy Bibles. 'Implementing Rogers' profound belief in positive self-direction' (Ellinwood and Raskin, 1993, p. 260), Axline (1969) outlines eight basic principles for the therapist.

1. The therapist must develop a warm, friendly relationship with the child, in which good rapport is established as soon as possible.
2. The therapist accepts the child exactly as he is.
3. The therapist establishes a feeling of permissiveness in the relationship so that the child feels free to express his feelings completely.
4. The therapist is alert to recognize the *feelings* the child is expressing and reflects those feelings back to him in such a manner that he gains insight into his behavior.
5. The therapist maintains a deep respect for the child's ability to solve his own problems if given an opportunity to do so. The responsibility to make choices and to institute change is the child's.
6. The therapist does not attempt to direct the child's actions or conversation in any manner. The child leads the way; the therapist follows.
7. The therapist does not attempt to hurry the therapy along. It is a gradual process and is recognized as such by the therapist.
8. The therapist establishes only those limitations that are necessary to anchor the therapy to the world of reality and to make the child aware of his responsibility in the relationship.

(pp. 73–4)

I disagree with two of the above tenets, the fourth which emphasizes the reflection of feelings for gaining insight and the eighth which pertains to the setting of limits. As I describe in more detail how I think the Rogerian conditions manifest themselves in my work with younger clients, I will also attempt to address my differences with Axline.

My intention as a therapist with children is to be warmly available as a person, highly attentive to verbal and nonverbal communications from the child and as nonrestrictive as I can manage given my personal limitations and constraints. In the interest of communicating unconditional positive regard, I am friendly, respectful and open. I try to remain uninvested in obtaining positive therapeutic results.

I want to communicate the unconditionality of my regard and this is sometimes difficult for me; it connects with the question of how to remain congruent as a therapist while granting freedom of word and motion to a youngster who may be rambunctious and disinclined to converse. How do I maintain my positive regard in the face of an active child's mess and grime? As Elaine Dorfman (1951) wrote:

. . . let us consider that the therapist's acceptance of the child is an instrument by means of which the child may come to self-acceptance. What therapist can feel accepting of a child who is in the process of flattening his cranium with a mallet? (p. 258)

Axline suggested in principle 8 above that limits '. . . are necessary to anchor the therapy to the world of reality and to make the child aware of his responsibility in the relationship' (1969, p. 74). I prefer to say that limits are set in the service of the therapist. The purpose is to help the therapist maintain equanimity and positive regard towards the client. Limits are set in the service of the child only because they are necessary to the therapist in order for the therapist to remain acceptant, empathic and congruent. I consider any other purpose for limits to be didactic and contrary to the condition of unconditional positive regard.

In the *Handbook of Psychology with Children and Adolescents*, Charlotte Ellinwood and Nathaniel Raskin (1993) give some examples of limit-setting. The therapist says:

Wendy, I don't want you to draw at my desk. This table is for you.

Wendy, I think you might break the switch doing that and I want you to stop. (p. 279)

In both examples, the therapist expresses a wish for a change in client behavior based upon the therapist's feeling about the behavior. This seems to me a direct, honest and relationship-enhancing manner to address a therapist's potentially relationship-damaging feelings. In nondirective therapy, a therapist's intention when setting limits is neither to clarify for the child what the real limits of the relationship are, nor to heighten the child's awareness of his or her responsibilities in the relationship. The intention is to preserve a therapeutic capacity to embody the attitudinal conditions.

My second difference with Axline relates to the therapist's intentions when seeking to understand a client's experience. Axline (1969) wrote in principle 4: 'The therapist is alert to recognize the feelings the child is expressing and reflects those feelings back to him in such a manner that he gains insight into his behavior' (p. 73). In the interest of being empathically present, I want to be attentive to verbal and nonverbal communications from the child. I listen, watch, seek clarification and respond. When I express my understanding of what the child is intending, saying or doing, I hope that my communication of attention and interest is also communicating my unconditional positive regard. I do not consider it my role to urge a child to express the feeling or meaning that underlies a behavior or a self-expression. To press the child to do anything, is to not fully accept him or her in the present. On the other hand, I may seek clarification from a child and then, if the child is willing to clarify something for me, my fuller understanding of who the child is and what the child intends or wants leads, I hope, to the child's sense of a larger part of himself being understood and accepted by me.

Axline's guideline directs the therapist to do something for a particular purpose: to reflect a child's feelings in order to help the child gain insight. It imposes the agenda of helping the child gain self-awareness. The Rogerian hypothesis that if the therapist embodies certain attitudes the client will experience constructive change does not require that a client label his feelings or gain insight into his behavior. A therapeutic, client-centered reason for acknowledging and expressing understanding of a client's emotional expression might be to communicate to the client that the therapist is present and following along with the client's experience and accepting of the client's current feeling and expression of emotion. Barbara Temaner Brodley (1996) has written:

To the extent the therapist does *not* shift away from acceptant and empathic attitudes (and in that way distract the client with external foci such as the therapist's ideas about the client), the process of empathic following tends to facilitate the client's focus on his or her phenomenologic experiencing. (p. 28)

If as a therapist my goal is to move the client toward insight into his behavior, I am imposing my own values and agenda and increasing the likelihood that the client will experience less acceptance from me. If, as a therapist, I draw a child's attention away from play toward hearing me note feelings, I am not thoroughly accepting the person who is engrossed in playful endeavors, and, also, I am not staying empathically with the child. Prods to render the session time more socially or developmentally productive can detract from the client's self-experience, without necessarily improving the therapist's understanding of that experience. Also, these prods are not furthering the client's perception of being either understood or accepted.

In the same vein, emphasizing my wish to communicate to the child my understanding of his frame of reference can be counterproductive. I seek to understand the child's intentions in play, but sometimes, I sit quietly and try just to be with the child who is busy doing something that does not involve me. John Shlien speaks of reverberative empathy, 'relational, interactive empathy' (1997, p. 77). Elsewhere, he refers to 'the exquisite awareness of dual experience that restores consciousness of self' (1961, p. 316). This is a form of empathy a therapist and client might experience together as their relationship develops in the absence of our more routinely expected therapeutic dialog of client statement followed by an empathic understanding response by the therapist. It seems to me that children embody their feelings, and that if we can attentively and respectfully be with the child we are to some extent already being with and accepting the child's feelings. I believe that then, like a flower, the person will grow.

AN ENDEAVOR WITH NO AGENDA AND UNKNOWN OUTCOME

Axline's (1964) *Dibs: In search of self* is a compelling, novel-length case study that may have created, however innocently, inappropriate expectations in therapists who work with children. In the introduction, Leonard Carmichael wrote: 'This is the story of the emergence of a strong, healthy personality in a previously deeply disturbed child' (Axline, 1964, p. vii). In the course of his play, Dibs, who is very young, no more than six years old, used overt symbolism. For example, he buried the 'papa' soldier in the sand. Towards the end of therapy, Axline wrote that Dibs felt deeply secure, '. . . was building a sense of responsibility for his feelings . . . a concept of self as he groped through the tangled brambles of his mixed-up feelings . . .', and he was learning to control and express his feelings (p. 188). At the end of therapy she describes Dibs as '. . . a little boy who had the opportunity to state himself through his play and who had emerged a happy, capable child . . .' (p. 209).

The reader does not learn until the epilogue that Dibs scored 168 on the Stanford Binet Intelligence Test. In my experience, children's play is rarely readily obvious as a symbol for their life experiences. Dibs sets an inappropriate standard for what is likely to occur in sessions with children.

I suggest that we not push ourselves as therapists and not push the child as client to bring articulate meaning and explanation into a session or relationship when the child is not initiating such scrutiny for him or herself. It is not our role to teach clients to identify and label their feelings or to better understand themselves. Nor is it our role to impose limits to help clients deal with social realities, nor to ensure that they emerge happy and capable. To press for any such accomplishment for our client is to not accept the client. Instead, our role is to provide a unique relationship in which a child experiences unconditional positive regard from a therapist who is interested in getting to know and be with this individual young person as much as possible on the child's terms and following the child's direction and agenda.

Concerned adults often have an opinion as to what the child and therapist should do and accomplish together in order to change the child to better fit into the social demands of the culture. Regardless of the expectations of the child's care-givers, my work is not results driven. It is driven by ethical concerns and the theory that takes those concerns into account. I hope my work is helpful to the individual. I believe it is not harmful to the client. But so often, working with a child, it can feel like I don't *do* anything. There is a not-of-this-world quality to working nondirectively with children. There are moments when I think, 'Thank goodness no other adult is watching.' Sometimes I wonder, 'What am I doing? Is this work nothing?'

Fortunately, the theory seems to work. We can tell parents that therapy can effect long-term, positive change in the child. We can say so because it happens. Grades do improve, and children do become more self-controlled. But as a therapist, I do not strive for these types of results. Frequently, a child is still having difficulty in the real world, but I know from the child that he or she finds the time with me to be immensely satisfying. To me, this means that my work is constructive, even if not necessarily successful by outside standards. In my experience, child therapy outcomes most often include a belief on my part that the client has felt enhanced as a person through relationship with me and frequently include reports from parents or teachers that unwanted behaviors have abated or ceased.

Jerold Bozarth (1998) has reported that, 'The most clear research evidence is that effective psychotherapy results from the resources of the client (extra therapeutic variables) and from the person-to-person relationship of the therapist and client' (pp. 172–3). My work with children is guided by a nondirective attitude of respect and trust toward the client and not by a wish to obtain measurable results. Nonetheless, it is comforting to realize that nondirective client-centered child therapy, through its emphasis upon a relationship imbued with the therapeutic attitudes and trust in the child's resources, is consistent with 'the most clear research evidence' for 'effective psychotherapy results'. Client-centered child therapy is effective because as Bozarth (2000) says, 'The client resources for change and healing emerge from this relationship' (p. 2), and as Brodley (1999) has written, 'When clients perceive and experience these [therapeutic] attitudes, distortions diminish in the psychological expression of the actualizing tendency and the person's untapped capabilities are revealed' (p. 115).

CONCLUSION

I believe that it is *not* necessary for a therapist to urge a child client, or any client, to increase self-understanding or to help a child learn to abide by the demands of reality. According to Rogerian theory, it is necessary for the therapist to be warmly available to and acceptant of the client whom the therapist is seeking to understand. In my experience, the necessary attitudinal conditions as described in Rogers' theory statements have proven to be sufficient. In order for the therapist to provide unconditional positive regard and to be qualitatively available and understanding of the child's experience, the therapist needs to be physically and mentally comfortable. Frequently with children, in order to remain congruent, a therapist may need to communicate to the client the therapist's personally needed limits upon the situation. Even though the session time that the therapist and child share may not resemble conventional images of psychotherapy, to the extent the therapist is managing to experience empathy and acceptance of the child, therapy is occurring. The child experiences increasing self-acceptance and becomes freer to grow into an ever more mature self.

REFERENCES

Axline, V. M. (1947). *Play Therapy.* New York: Ballantine.

Axline, V. M. (1964). *Dibs: In search of self.* New York: Ballantine.

Axline, V. M. (1969). *Play Therapy* (Revised edn.). New York: Ballantine.

Bozarth, J. D. (1998). *Person-centered Therapy: A revolutionary paradigm*, Ross-on-Wye, England: PCCS Books.

Bozarth, J. D. (2000). Non-directiveness in client-centered therapy: A vexed concept. Paper presentation at the Eastern Psychological Association, Baltimore, MD., March 25.

Brodley, B. T. (1996). Empathic understanding and feelings in Client-Centered Therapy *The Person-Centered Journal, 3*(1), 22–30.

Brodley, B. T. (1999). The actualizing tendency concept in client-centered theory. *The Person-Centered Journal, 5* (2),108–20.

Dorfman, E. (1951). Play Therapy. In C. R. Rogers, *Client-Centered Therapy: Its current practice, implications, and theory.* Boston: Houghton Mifflin, (pp. 235–77).

Ellinwood, C. G. and Raskin, N. J. (1993). Client-centered/humanistic psychotherapy. In T. R. Kratochwill and R. J. Morris (Eds.), *Handbook of Psychology with Children and Adolescents.* Boston: Allyn & Bacon, (pp. 258–87).

Merry, T. (1999). On Connectedness — A humanistic biological view. Paper presented at the conference, The Quality of Presence: Exploring person-centered frontiers, Bratislava, Slovak Republic, October 6–9. Published in *Person-Centred Practice*, 8(1), 28–36.

Rogers, C. R. (1959). A theory of therapy, personality and interpersonal relationships as developed in the client-centered framework. In S. Koch (Ed.) *Psychology: A study of science: Vol. 3 Formulation of the person and the social context.* New York: McGraw Hill, (pp. 184–256).

Rogers, C. R. (1977). Carl Rogers on personal power. New York: Delacorte.

Shlien, J. M. (1961). A client-centered approach to schizophrenia: First approximation. In A. Burton (Ed.), *The Psychotherapy of the Psychoses* (pp. 285–317). New York: Basic Books.

Shlien, J. M. (1997). Empathy in psychotherapy: A vital mechanism? Yes. Therapist's conceit? All too often. By itself enough? No. In A.C. Bohart and L.S. Greenberg (Eds.) *Empathy Reconsidered: New directions in psychotherapy.* Washington, DC: American Psychological Association, (pp. 63–80).

Yeager, D. (2000). Play Therapy with the ADHD child. *17th Annual Association for Play Therapy International Conference* [Brochure]. Association for Play Therapy, Fresno, CA (Address: 2050 N. Winery Ave., Suite 101, Fresno, CA 93703)

Index

Contributors

Marijke C. L. Baljon, born in 1948, has worked since 1988 as a psychotherapist at Mental Health Care Drenthe, Assen, the Netherlands. She specialises in client-centred and group psychotherapy and teaches client-centred psychotherapy in training programs for psychiatrists, clinical psychologists and psychotherapists in Groningen and Assen. She has published several articles in Dutch about psychotherapy with psychiatric cases and the collaboration with nonverbal therapy. From 1999 – 2003 she is elected chairperson of the Dutch Association for Client-Centered Psychotherapy (VCgP).

Martina Becker, born 1971, studied psychology and education. Since 2000 she has worked as a scientific assistant at the University of Education Heidelberg. Her PhD concerns the client-centered theory of personality.

Michael Behr studied education and psychology at the Universities of Essen, Bielefeld and Bochum. Since 1984 he has worked as a therapist and later as a trainer of client-centered therapy with adults, and play-therapy with children and adolescents at the Institute for Client-centered Therapy and Counselling in Stuttgart. Since 1993 he has taught as a Professor of Educational Psychology at the University of Education Schwaebisch Gmuend, Germany. His research topics are person-centered counselling, emotion, parent-school-relationship and classroom-discipline.

Arthur C. Bohart, PhD. is a Professor of Psychology at California State University Dominguez Hills and part-time faculty at Saybrook Graduate School and Research Center. Though approaching retirement, his curmudgeonly tendencies have not mellowed with the passage of time. He is currently scared to death that adherence to a rigid, narrow view of the relationship of science to practice seriously threatens the existence of psychotherapy as most of us know it and practice it.

Jerold D. Bozarth, PhD. would have been a professional basketball player if he had been one foot taller. Instead, he wandered into an academic career in counseling and psychology working at the universities of Southern Illinois, Arkansas, Iowa, Florida, and Georgia, and published over 300 articles and book chapters and four books. He is currently Professor Emeritus of the University of Georgia. His abiding interest in client-centered therapy was learned from working with chronic psychotics. His shifting interests and hobbies have included flying, numerous sports, and a second degree black belt in Aikido. Currently, he is most involved with his grandchildren who are eleven, four, and three years old. He is a member of the Golden Pantry Coffee Club.

Barbara Temaner Brodley has been a client-centered therapist for many years and has published more than thirty articles about the approach. She received her PhD. in Human Development and Clinical Psychology from the University of Chicago and was a member of the staff of the Counseling Center founded by Carl Rogers for seven years. She has been in private practice for over thirty-five years, teaches CCT as an Associate Core Professor at the Illinois School of Professional Psychology Chicago Campus and she is Co-Director of Training at the Chicago Counseling and Psychotherapy Center.

Ton Coffeng, MD, client-centered/experiential therapist in the Netherlands (Leeuwarden), coordinates a network of Trauma/Dissociation. He published and produced videos about focusing, phasing and timing in therapy, group therapy, grief, trauma and burnout. He is trainer/supervisor of the Neth. Ass. of Client-c. Therapy, coordinator-trainer of the Focusing Institute and member of the Int. Pre-Therapy Network. He has a postgraduate program of focusing and experiential psychotherapy.

William J. Eckersell was born and grew up in the inner-mountain west of the United States where he developed a love of nature, especially mountains. He graduated from Idaho State University with a B. S. in Psychology and then attended North Dakota State University where he received a Masters degree in Counseling. He has worked as a school counselor and currently works for Madison County Juvenile Probation in the state of Idaho in the United States.

Ivan Ellingham. After meeting Professor C. H. Patterson when completing a diploma in counselling at the University of Aston in the 1970s I went to study with him at the University of Illinois gaining a PhD in counselling psychology in 1984. Whilst in the US I was introduced to the writings of Susanne Langer by another of my teachers, Michael Piechowski. The further development of person-centred theory remains an abiding interest, alongside my work as counselling psychologist in the NHS and tutor on two person-centred counselling diploma programmes. I live in rural Hertfordshire with my partner, Derryn Thomas, our two dogs and seven cats.

Ned Gaylin has been married to Rita for 43 years, they have four children and two grandchildren. He received his PhD. from the University of Chicago, committee on Human Development with a speciality in clinical child and family psychology. As professor, Ned Gaylin currently serves as director of the graduate program in Marriage and Family Therapy. He maintains an active interest in normal and abnormal development in the family context. He is also concerned with the evaluation of the process and outcome of psychotherapy, the application of client-centred theory and techniques to family therapy an the study and enhancement on creativeness.

Meredith J. Glick is a graduate student in Clinical Psychology at Miami University in Oxford, Ohio. Her research centres on the assimilation model of client change, using a qualitative method of linking process to outcome in psychotherapy.

Rhonda Goldman is a core faculty member at the Illinois School of Professional Psychology, Argosy University, Chicago Northwest. She lectures in therapy and psychopathology, and provides clinical and research supervision. She is also a staff therapist at the Family Institute at Northwestern University, where she sees individuals and couples. Her clinical interests are in depression and anxiety, grief and loss, and couples conflict and intimacy issues. She has published many articles and book chapters in the area of Emotion-focused therapies exploring topics such as case formulation, training, depression, and the relationship between emotional processing in therapy and change.

Soti Grafanaki PhD. is a full-time Assistant Professor in the faculty of Human Sciences at Saint Paul University in Ottawa, Canada. She teaches Theories of Counselling, offers training in Counselling skills and supervises students in the MA Programme of Individual Pastoral Counselling. She has been trained as an individual counsellor and is a Chartered psychologist with British Psychological Society. Her doctoral research has focused on client and counsellor experience of congruence during on-going person-centred therapy. She is currently involved in qualitative research on Spirituality and Leisure among mental health professionals.

Leslie Greenberg PhD. is Professor of Psychology at York University in Toronto, Ontario. He is the Director of the York Univ. Psychotherapy Research Clinic. He has coauthored: *Emotion in Psychotherapy* (1986); *Emotionally Focused Therapy for Couples* (1988); *Facilitating Emotional Change* (1993) and *Working with Emotions in Psychotherapy* (1997). He recently coedited *Empathy Reconsidered* (1997) and *The Handbook of Experiential Psychotherapy* (1998). Dr. Greenberg is a founding member of the Society of the Exploration of Psychotherapy Integration (SEPI), a past President of the Society for Psychotherapy Research (SPR) and is on the editorial board of a number of psychotherapy journals.

J. Wade Hannon was born and raised in a small southeast Kansas village in the United States. His bachelors (General Studies, 1975) and M.S. (Psychology, 1976) are from Pittsburg State University (Kansas, U.S.) and his Ed.D. (Counselor Education, 1983) from the University of Arkansas. He has worked as a community counselor in a variety of settings and 'teaches' in a graduate counseling program at North Dakota State University (U.S.) where he is currently an Associate Professor. He serves as President of his Union chapter at the university, co-chair of his local Green Party and is an activist in peace and social justice issues.

Sarah Hawtin is a counsellor at the University of East Anglia (UEA), UK. She has a background in the field of mental health, where she has worked in the voluntary and statutory sectors. She was previously a trainer on the UEA Person-centred Diploma in Counselling and currently works as an individual supervisor for the course

Sachiko Hayashi is a counsellor at the student counselling office of the University of Aizu, Fukushima, Japan. She obtained her MEd. in human development counselling from the Peabody College of Vanderbilt University, TN, USA in 1987. Her email address is <u>wmg08631@biglobe.ne.jp</u>.

Marion N. Hendricks PhD. is the Director of the Focusing Institute (www.focusing.org), and conducts workshops and lectures on Focusing-Oriented Psychotherapy. She conducts the Institute's two-year post-graduate training program in CCT/EXP psychotherapy in New York City. She has been in private practice for thirty years. She graduated from and received her client-centered training at the University of Chicago. She interned at the Post-Graduate Center for Mental Health in New York City, and then worked as a psychologist-trainer in the New York State Hospital system. She was a core faculty member at the Illinois School of Professional Psychology in Chicago for ten years, where she established the Experiential/Client-Centered specialization. She can be reached at <u>info@focusing.org</u>.

James R. Iberg PhD. has been in private psychotherapy practice for over 20 years in Chicago and Evanston, IL, USA. He is Associate Core Faculty at the Illinois School of Professional Psychology, and a Certifying Coordinator for the

Focusing Institute. He has taught focusing, empathic listening, and other communication skills in several countries. He conducts process-outcome studies with student and private practice therapists and their clients. He organized and directs a group of therapists serving clients outside of the third-party payer system (see Quinpro.com). Therapists in Quinpro collaborate for process-monitoring to track client process and progress, and to maintain therapist effectiveness.

Bala Jaison PhD. is a psychotherapist for individuals and couples, and Director of Focusing for Creative Living in Toronto. She has developed a unique style integrating Solution Oriented and Focusing Oriented Therapy and Interactive Focusing Therapy for couples, which she currently teaches to therapists both here and abroad. In addition to her private practice, Dr. Jaison works in the business community and the school system, translating this work into programs on conflict resolution and peacemaking. She is also the editor of The Folio, the academic journal for the International Focusing Institute

Edwin Kahn PhD. is a recently retired professor of psychology from The City University of New York. He has been a psychotherapist for over 25 years. He has written articles comparing the work of Heinz Kohut's self psychology and Robert Stolorow's intersubjectivity theory with Carl Rogers' Person-Centered Approach. He currently teaches a course on the writings of Heinz Kohut at The New York Institute for Psychoanalytic Self Psychology.

Atsushi Kara is professor at the computer communications laboratory at the University of Aizu. He obtained his PhD. in electrical engineering from Vanderbilt University, TN, USA in 1992. His email address is kara@u-aizu.ac.jp.

Dr. Kevin C. Krycka is Chair of the Psychology Department at Seattle University and a therapist in private practice. Kevin's interests include studying the effects that personal attitudes and beliefs play on physical wellbeing as well as promoting understanding of gay and lesbian issues. He conducts qualitative research and holds seminars for the public and professionals nationally and internationally. Kevin practises a form of Tibetan mediation and plays happily in his garden whenever he can.

Deborah Lambo M.A., received her Masters in Existential Phenomenological Psychology from Seattle University in 1992. She is currently a private practitioner in Monroe, Washington, and also serves as an adjunct faculty member for the Psychology Department at Seattle University.

Mia Leijssen is professor at the Katholieke Universiteit Leuven, Belgium where she teaches client-centred/experiential psychotherapy, counselling skills and professional ethics for psychologists. She is also coordinator of a three-year part-time postgraduate training programme in client-centred/experiential psychotherapy and has a practice in individual and group psychotherapy.

Germain Lietaer studied as a post-doctoral fellow with Carl Rogers at the Center for the Studies of the Person in La Jolla in 1969–1970. He is a full professor at the Catholic University of Leuven and teaches client-centred/experiential psychotherapy and process research in psychotherapy. Professor Lietaer has published widely: he is chief editor (with J. Rombauts and R. Van Balen) of *Client-Centered and Experiential Psychotherapy in the Nineties* (Leuven, Belgium: Leuven University Press) and coeditor (with L.S. Greenberg and J. Watson) of *The Handbook of Experiential Psychotherapy* (New York: Guilford Press, 1998). He is currently Chair of WAPCECP (2000–3).

Ann Lovering is the Coordinator of the Masters Program in Human Development, ITESO University, Guadalajara, Jalisco, Mexico and founder of the Center for Gender Investigation and Studies, ITESO University.

Claude Missiaen is clinical psychologist and client-centered/experiential psychotherapist. He is director of the training centre Faculteit voor Mens en Samenleving in Turnhout, Belgium and head of the Client-Centered Psychotherapy training in that institute. He is also involved in the Client-Centered Psychotherapy training of the Catholic University of Leuven. He is an individual psychotherapist and especially a group psychotherapist. Since 2000 he is a Focusing Coordinator of The Focusing Institute in New York.

Zinnia Mitchell-Williams: I am a postgraduate researcher at the Centre for Human Communication, Manchester Metropolitan University. My interest in the person-centred approach is based on a desire to democratise the research process. I am researching methods of inquiry that use individual understanding of experience rather than researcher analysis and generalisation. I am interested in collaborative inquiry, conversation and storytelling. I have found experiences of group work that is both intentionally and unintentionally person-centred to be personally developmental which inspires my research.

Kathryn Moon is a client-centered therapist in private practice in Chicago. She is passionate about the nondirective approach to therapy and unfacilitated large group meetings. Her formal education includes studies in French, library science, and clinical psychology. She is involved in training programs for the Chicago Counseling and Psychotherapy Center and is an adjunct faculty member at the Illinois School of Professional Psychology.

Marlis Pörtner was born, and lives, in Zürich, Switzerland. After having worked in different professions (playing theater, translating books) and raised two children, she graduated in Psychology and completed a postgraduate qualification in Client-Centered Psychotherapy. She has worked as a psychotherapist in private practice, for more than twenty years, with, among other clients, people with special needs. She has written several books in German, some of which have been translated in different languages. *Trust and Understanding. A Person-Centered Approach to everyday care for people with special needs* is her first book published in English. (PCCS Books, 2000).

Gillian Proctor is a clinical psychologist working in Yorkshire, UK. She uses the person-centred approach in all aspects of her work in forensic services (for clients with mental health problems who have committed, or are at risk of committing serious offences) in the National Health Service. Her particular interests are power, ethics and oppression in relation to clinical practice, mental health systems and research. She has written several articles on these subjects and her book *The Dynamics of Power in Counselling and Psychotherapy: Ethics, politics and practice* was published by PCCS Books, 2002.

Meghan Prosser was born and grew up in Nova Scotia. There she attended Acadia University where she completed a double major in history and psychology with her honours in psychology. She later moved to Toronto, Ontario to attend the Ontario Institute for Studies in Education of the University of Toronto where she completed her Masters degree in Counselling Psychology. She is currently in her second year of the doctoral program in Counselling Psychology.

Campbell Purton PhD. is Senior Counsellor at the University Counselling Service, University of East Anglia, England, and teaches on the Counselling Diploma Course at the same university. He has taught philosophy at universities in Canada and Scotland, and is at present working on a book on the relationship between person-centred and focusing-oriented psychotherapy.

Nat Raskin: I began graduate work with Carl Rogers at Ohio State University in 1940, continuing at the University of Chicago after World War II, and receiving my PhD. in 1949. I returned to New York, taught at Hunter College, New York University, and Columbia University's Teachers College, and became Director of Research Planning at the American Foundation for the Blind from 1952 to 1957. I went back to Chicago as Chief Psychologist at Children's Memorial Hospital with an appointment at Northwestern University's Medical School. I resigned from Children's in 1963 but continued at the Medical School until 1991, when I became Professor Emeritus of Psychiatry and Behavioral Sciences. I was Rogers' student, associate and friend during a span of 47 years until he died in 1987.

Natalie Rogers PhD., author of *The Creative Connection: Expressive Arts as Healing*, and *Emerging Woman: A Decade of Midlife Transitions*, and many articles, is a pioneer in expressive arts therapy, leading trainings all over the world. She trained with and was a colleague of her father, Carl Rogers, for seven summers. She worked in a psychiatric clinic, a college counseling center and as a therapist in a school for emotionally disturbed children, before going into private practice for 25 years. She founded the Person-Centered Expressive Therapy Institute, Cotati, California. She is an adjunct professor at the California Institute of Integral Studies. She was awarded the first Lifetime Achievement Award by the International Expressive Arts Therapy Association in 1998. Her website is: www.nrogers.com

Rachel Rushanski-Rosenberg has an M.A degree in counselling psychology. She has been working for the past several years as a crisis clinician in major hospitals in Toronto. She also holds the position of Regional Coordinator for the Toronto area, at the Mood Disorder Association of Ontario and Toronto.

Peter F. Schmid, Univ. Doz. HSProf. Mag. Dr. born in 1950; Associate Professor at the University of Graz, Styria and teaches at European universities. He is a person-centred psychotherapist, practical theologian and pastoral psychologist, founder of person-centred training and further training in Austria, and co-director of the Academy for Counselling and Psychotherapy of the Austrian 'Institute for Person-Centred Studies (IPS of APG)'. He is a Board Member of both the World Association (WAPCEPC) and the European Network (NEAPCEPC), and has published many books and articles about anthropology and further developments of the Person-Centered Approach.

Bob Sikkema is a client-centered psychotherapist and clinical supervisor at the Institute for Mental Health (Mediant) in Hengelo, The Netherlands, with a small private practice in addition. He has specialisations in group psychotherapy, adolescents and Borderline Personality Disorder, and trains other professionals in these areas. Bob is also certified as a Trainer and Coordinator by the Focusing Institute in New York, USA, and co-leads Focusing workshops for psychotherapists and psychotherapists-in-training in Seattle, WA, USA. He has also been sitting Zen since 1976.

William B. Stiles is Professor of Psychology at Miami University in Oxford, Ohio. He taught previously at the University of North Carolina at Chapel Hill and held visiting positions at University of Sheffield and University of Leeds (UK), University of Joensuu (Finland), and Massey University (New Zealand). He is the author of *Describing Talk: A Taxonomy of Verbal Response Modes*, Past President of the Society for Psychotherapy Research, and currently North American Editor of the journal, *Psychotherapy Research*.

Nele Stinckens PhD. Psychology, is a client-centered/experiential psychotherapist. She works at a psychotherapeutic centre for students of the Catholic University of Leuven, Belgium. Also, she gives workshops for trainees about working with the inner critic.

Gerhard Stumm PhD. born in 1950, free-lance person-centered psychotherapist in Vienna, Austria, clinical and health psychologist, trainer and training coordinator of the Arbeitsgemeinschaft Personenzentrierte Gesprächsführung, Psychotherapie und Supervision (APG)/section Forum. He has published widely on psychotherapy, including *Wörterbuch der Psychotherapie* (Dictionary of Psychotherapy) (Springer, 2000), *Die vielen Gesichter der Personzentrierten Psychotherapie* (The many faces of Person-centered psychotherapy) (Springer, 2002), *Grundbegriffe der Personzentrierten und Focusing-orientierten Psychotherapie* (Basic concepts of Person-centered and Focusing-oriented psychotherapy) (Pfeiffer bei Klett-Cotta, 2002), *Personenlexikon der Psychotherapie* (Springer, 2002)

Janet Tolan works as a counsellor and supervisor in Manchester, UK, and leads the postgraduate counselling programme at Liverpool John Moores University. She has worked in the field of counselling for over twenty years, sitting on various national and international committees, and is a Fellow of the British Association for Counselling and Psychotherapy.

Carla van der Moolen works as client-centered psychotherapist in a mental health institute in Groningen, the Netherlands. For several years she has been practising focusing and became more and more interested in what our body can tell us. Now her major interest is in working with clients who are suffering from severe and long-lasting subjective health complaints.

Martin Van Kalmthout is an associate Professor of Clinical Psychology at Nijmegen University, the Netherlands. His interest is in the foundations and history of psychotherapy and the Person-Centered Approach. He is also studying the relation between psychotherapy, science and religion or spirituality, especially in the work of Carl Rogers. He has published extensively about these topics, including the relation between psychotherapy and the human predicament. He is also in private practice as a person-centered psychotherapist.

Margaret S. Warner PhD. is a client-centered teacher and theorist who has written extensively about client-centered therapy with clients with more serious psychological disorders and on client-centered theory as it relates to other disciplines in clinical psychology and the behavioral sciences. She trained in client-centered therapy at the Chicago Counseling Center, an offshoot of Carl Rogers' original center at the University of Chicago. She has a doctorate in Behavioral Sciences from the University of Chicago, and is currently a Professor at the Illinois School of Professional Psychology.

Jeanne C. Watson PhD. (Clin. Psych.) is an associate professor in the Department of Adult Education, Community Development and Counselling Psychology, at OISE at the University of Toronto, Canada. She is coauthor of *Expressing Emotion: Myths, Realities and Therapeutic Strategies* and coeditor of the *Handbook of Experiential Psychotherapy*. In addition, Dr. Watson has written numerous articles and chapters on psychotherapy process and outcome and maintains a part-time private practice in Toronto.

Paul Wilkins: I am an academic and therapist deeply committed to the person-centred approach about which I have written papers, chapters and books. My doctoral study was concerned with what it means to be person-centred and I am currently as much interested in how to be person-centred as a researcher as I am in extending my understanding of person-centred theory and practice. I am passionate about the creativity I see as inherent in the approach and seek to apply this to all areas of my life. When I am not thinking, writing, researching or teaching I enjoy the good things the world has to offer, wild places, music, wine and food, to name but a few!